Animal Cruelty

Animal Cruelty

A Multidisciplinary Approach to Understanding

Second Edition

Edited by

Mary P. Brewster

Cassandra L. Reyes

Carolina Academic Press

Durham, North Carolina

Copyright © 2016
Carolina Academic Press, LLC
All Rights Reserved

Library of Congress Cataloging-in-Publication Data

Names: Brewster, Mary P., editor. | Reyes, Cassandra, editor.
Title: Animal cruelty : a multidisciplinary approach to understanding /
   edited by Mary P. Brewster and Cassandra L. Reyes.
Description: Second edition. | Durham, N.C. : Carolina Academic Press, [2016]
   | Includes bibliographical references and index.
Identifiers: LCCN 2015041281 | ISBN 9781611636239 (alk. paper)
Subjects: LCSH: Animal welfare--United States. | Animal welfare--Law and
   legislation--United States.
Classification: LCC HV4764 .A635 2016 | DDC 179/.3--dc23
LC record available at http://lccn.loc.gov/2015041281

Carolina Academic Press, LLC
700 Kent Street
Durham, North Carolina 27701
Telephone (919) 489-7486
Fax (919) 493-5668
www.cap-press.com

Printed in the United States of America

Contents

Foreword	xv
References	xvi
Acknowledgments	xvii

Section I · Animal Cruelty: History, Legislation, and Prevalence

Chapter 1 · Definitions of Animal Cruelty, Abuse, and Neglect
Phil Arkow and Randall Lockwood — 3

Introduction	3
Definitions of Terms	5
Perspectives on Definitions	6
Researchers	6
Government Panels	7
Public Opinion	8
Legislation, Law Enforcement, Prosecutors, and Judges	9
Forms of Animal Abuse	10
Challenges in Definitions	12
Vague, Ambiguous, and Archaic Language	12
Absence of a Universal Standard of Cruelty	13
Objectivity vs. Subjectivity	14
Establishing a Motive, Intent, or State of Mind	17
What Is an "Animal"?	18
Defenses and Exemptions	19
Conclusion	20
References	20

Chapter 2 · The History of Anti-Cruelty Laws: Concepts of Animal Welfare and Animal Rights
David Favre — 25

In the Beginnings, Just Property	25
The British Set the Stage	26
New Concerns in America	28
The Bergh Era Begins	29
Enforcement on the Streets of New York	31
The Ripple Effect	32
Development of the Concept of Animal Welfare	33
Terminology and Scope of Animal Welfare	34
Modern Animal Welfare Laws	37

A Consideration of Animal Rights	39
Appendix A: The 1867 New York Anti-Cruelty Law	42
Section 1. Penalty for Overdriving, Cruelly Treating Animals, etc.	42
Section 2. For Keeping a Place For Cock Fighting, Bull Baiting, Dog Fighting, etc.	42
Section 3. For Impounding Animals Without Giving Sufficient Food and Water	43
Section 4. In What Case Any Person May Feed, etc. Impounded Animal	43
Section 5. Penalty For Carrying Animals in a Cruel Manner	43
Section 6. License For Using Dogs Before Vehicles	43
Section 7. Penalty for Abandoning Infirm Animals in Public Place	44
Section 8. When Agent of Society May Arrest for Violations of This Act	44
Section 9. Who Shall Publish This Act, and When Shall it Be Published	44
Section 10. Proviso	44
References	44

Chapter 3 · Animal Cruelty and the Law: Prohibited Conduct
Yolanda Eisenstein

	47
Introduction	47
The Laws against Cruelty	48
Special Treatment for Companion Animals	49
The Legal Regime in Animal Protection	49
Statutory Law	49
Case Study: Three approaches to cruelty in puppy mills.	50
Case Law	51
Case Study: Upholding the Constitution and invalidating statutes.	52
Case Study: Bound to 19th-century legal precedent.	52
Who Are Companion Animals?	53
Case Study: A companion animal with fins.	53
Who Are the Victims of Animal Cruelty?	54
Case Study: Are animals victims?	54
Cruel Acts and Omissions	55
The Broad Spectrum of Abusers	56
Case Study: A limit to police immunity.	57
Who Reports and Investigates Animal Cruelty?	57
The Commitment to Enforcement and Prosecution	58
Case Study: Seizing 27,000 animals.	59
On Trial	60
The International Animal Protection Movement	61
Conclusion	62
References	62

Chapter 4 · Animal Cruelty and the Law: Permitted Conduct
Joan Schaffner

	65
Introduction	65
Animals Bred as Companions and Used in Research or Exhibition:	
The Federal Animal Welfare Act	66
Case Study: Redefining "retail pet store."	67
Case Study: Lolita's inhumane treatment under the AWA.	69
Animals Used for Food	70

Humane Methods of Slaughter	70
Case Study: Who are livestock?	71
Twenty-Eight-Hour Law	73
Laws Governing Animals on the Farm	74
Case Study: Humane or cruel?	75
Wildlife	78
Endangered Species Act	78
Marine Mammal Protection Act	79
Case Study: The MMPA and "inhumane" capture.	80
State Law	81
Private Enforcement of Animal Welfare Laws	81
Case Study: Who may seek enforcement of the law?	82
Conclusion	85
References	86

Chapter 5 · Veterinary Forensic Sciences in the Response to Animal Cruelty
Randall Lockwood and Rachel Touroo

	89
History	89
Defining Veterinary Forensic Sciences	90
Forms of Animal Cruelty	91
Recognizing and Responding to Animal Cruelty	92
Role of the Forensic Veterinarian at a Crime Scene	95
Triage	95
Evidence Handling	96
Assessment of the Scene and Its Relation to Veterinary/Medical Issues	96
The Forensic Necropsy	96
Veterinary Forensic Considerations in Different Forms of Animal Cruelty	97
Neglect	97
Institutional Neglect	97
Severe Neglect	98
Animal Hoarding	98
Intentional Abuse	99
Organized Abuse	102
Ritualized Abuse	102
Animal Sexual Assault	103
The Veterinary Professional in Court	104
Veterinary Forensics and the Response to Common Defenses	104
Trends in Veterinary Forensics	106
Future Needs	106
References	107

Chapter 6 · The Animal-Human Bond
Elizabeth B. Strand, Christina Risley-Curtiss, and Bethanie A. Poe

	113
Introduction	113
Theories of the AHB	114
The Biophilia Hypothesis	114
Anthropomorphic-Integrated-Chattel Orientation Continuum	115
Attachment Theory	116
Social Support Theory	118
Kinds of AHBs	119

CONTENTS

    Companion Animals   119
    Farm Animals   121
    Assistance Animals   122
    Wildlife   124
    Animals Used by Animal-Related Professionals   124
Violence and the AHB   126
Cultural Influences in the AHB   126
AHB and Criminal Justice: Practice Implications   129
    Assessment and Response to the AHB   129
    Preventing and Treating Violence towards Animals   130
    Animal-Assisted Interventions   131
Conclusion   133
References   133

Chapter 7 · Statistics and Measurement of Animal Cruelty
    Cassandra L. Reyes   141
Introduction   141
Overview of Animal Cruelty in the United States   141
    Pet-Abuse.com   142
        Animal Cruelty Case Trend   143
        Reporting Parties   143
        General Alleged Perpetrator Characteristics   143
        Other Aspects in Animal Cruelty Cases   144
Active Cruelty   145
    Beating   145
    Bestiality   146
    Burning: Caustic Substances   146
    Burning: Fire or Fireworks   146
    Choking, Strangulation, or Suffocation   147
    Drowning   147
    Fighting   148
    Hanging   148
    Kicking or Stomping   148
    Mutilation or Torture   149
    Poisoning   149
    Shooting   150
    Stabbing   150
    Throwing   150
    Unlawful Trapping or Hunting   151
    Vehicular   151
Passive Cruelty   151
    Neglect or Abandonment   152
    Hoarding   152
Other Forms of Animal Cruelty   153
    Theft   153
    Unlawful Trade or Smuggling   153
Strengths and Limitations of the AARDAS   154
Conclusion   155
References   155

Section II · Special Types of Animal Cruelty

Chapter 8 · Animal Cruelty for Sport and Profit
John C. Navarro, Jacqueline L. Schneider, and Egan Green — 159

- Introduction — 159
- Breeding — 159
  - Laws — 160
  - Shelters — 161
- Factory Farming — 162
  - Selective Breeding — 163
  - Confinement and Overcrowding — 164
  - Swine — 164
  - Fowl — 165
  - Mutilations — 166
- Trading in Endangered Species — 167
- Sporting Activities — 169
  - Hunting and Fishing in the U.S. — 169
    - Non-Commercial Poachers — 170
  - Canned/Captive Hunting — 170
- Blood Sports: Cock-, Dog-, and Bullfighting — 172
  - Cockfighting — 172
    - Cockfighting in Modern Times — 173
  - Policing — 174
  - Dogfighting — 175
    - Historical Accounts — 175
    - Modern Times — 176
    - Networks and Events — 176
  - Bullfighting — 178
  - Emerging Blood Sports — 178
- Cultural Festivals — 179
  - Palio Horse Race — 179
  - Jallikattu — 180
  - Running with the Bulls — 180
    - Circuses — 181
    - Regulation — 181
    - Confinement and Traveling — 182
    - Employees and Training — 182
    - Bans — 183
- Animal Tourism — 184
  - Destination Trips — 184
  - Amusement Parks — 186
- Conclusion — 188
- References — 188
  - Statutes — 197

Chapter 9 · Animal Hoarding
Arnold Arluke and Gary Patronek — 199

- Characteristics of Animal Hoarding — 199
- Causes of Animal Hoarding — 202
  - Psychological Disorder — 202

Social Enabling	205
Interventions	206
Seizing Animals	208
Medico-Legal Options	209
Conclusion	214
References	214

Chapter 10 · Animal Cruelty and Sexual Deviance
Christopher Hensley, Suzanne E. Tallichet, and Caleb E. Trentham — 217

Paraphilias	217
History of Paraphilias	218
Bestiality and Zoophilia	219
Studies of Bestiality Prevalence and Perpetrator Characteristics	221
Studies of the Dynamics Associated with Bestiality	221
Studies of the Potential Link between Bestiality and Later Interpersonal Violence	224
Theorizing about the Bestiality Link	225
Crush Videos	226
Bestiality Laws	228
Felony State Statutes	228
Misdemeanor State Statutes	229
Conclusion	229
References	230
Statutes	233

Chapter 11 · Understanding and Reducing Cruelty toward Roaming Dogs
Arnold Arluke and Kate Atema — 235

Abusing and Neglecting Stray Dogs	236
Explaining Cruelty toward Roaming Dogs	238
Dogs as Dangers	238
Dogs as Nuisances	239
Dogs as Homeless	241
Reversing Cruelty toward Roaming Dogs	242
Veterinary Interventions	242
Educational Interventions	244
References	245
Personal Communication	249

Section III · Animal Cruelty—Antecedents and Future Behavior

Chapter 12 · Animal Cruelty and Delinquency, Criminality, and Youth Violence
Nik Taylor and Tania Signal — 253

Four Main Areas of Animal-Human Research	253
Animal Abuse as Part of the Continuum of Abuse within the Family and Animal Abuse as an Indicator of Child Abuse	254
The Therapeutic Potential of Animals in Child Development and within Post-Abuse Work	255
Animal Abuse Perpetrated by Children Who Show Later Aggressive and Deviant Behavior	256
Gendered Experiences of CTA	259

CONTENTS

CTA and Generalized Deviance	260
CTA: Social and Community Considerations	262
Methodological Issues	264
Conclusion: Condoned Animal Harm	265
References	268

Chapter 13 · Family Violence and Animal Cruelty
Eleonora Gullone

	275
Family Violence and Human Aggression Defined	275
Family Violence between Humans	276
Child Abuse	276
Partner Abuse	278
Animal Cruelty Defined	280
Family and Parenting Experiences	280
Understanding Children's Cruelty toward Animals	283
The Relationship between Domestic Violence and Animal Cruelty	285
More than a Link	289
Proposed Strategies for Change	290
References	292

Chapter 14 · Animal Cruelty, Firesetting, and Homicide
Lindsey S. Davis and Louis B. Schlesinger

	301
Animal Cruelty and Firesetting: Research Findings	302
Animal Cruelty	302
Firesetting	303
Conclusion	306
Motivational Spectrum in the Classification of Homicide	307
Environmental/Sociogenic Homicides	307
Situational Homicides	308
Impulsive Homicides	308
Catathymic Homicides	308
Compulsive Homicides	309
Animal Cruelty, Firesetting, and Sexual Homicide	310
Animal Cruelty	310
The Significance of Cats	311
Case Study 1	312
Case Study 2	312
Firesetting	312
Case Study 3	313
Case Study 4	314
Discussion	315
References	316

Section IV · Theoretical Perspectives

Chapter 15 · Examining Animal Abuse through a Sociological Lens: Theoretical and Empirical Developments
Amy J. Fitzgerald, Rochelle Stevenson, and Antonio R. Verbora

	325
Introduction	325
Social Learning Theory	326

Frustration and Strain — 329
Differential Coercion — 331
Violence Graduation Hypothesis — 332
Generalization of Deviance Hypothesis — 334
Feminist Theories — 335
Masculinities — 338
(Eco)Marxism — 341
Cultural Spillover — 344
Conclusion — 346
References — 346

Chapter 16 · Psychological Theories of Animal Cruelty
Mary Lou Randour and Maya Gupta — 355
Introduction — 355
Causes and Correlates of Animal Cruelty — 356
Psychological Theories for Understanding Animal Cruelty — 357
   Instinct and Drive Theories — 357
   Social Learning Theory — 358
   Bimodal Theories of Aggression — 360
   Neurobiological Theories — 362
   Cognitive Theories — 363
      Developmental Pathways of Aggression — 364
   Attachment — 366
   Empathy Development — 368
Conclusion — 369
References — 370

Section V · Current and Controversial Topics

Chapter 17 · Animal Cruelty and Reality Television: A Critical Review
Claire Molloy — 379
Introduction — 379
Institutional Context — 380
Cultural Context — 381
Reality Television — 382
Genre Hybrids — 384
Animal Cop Shows: Voiceovers — 386
Animal Cop Shows: Titles — 387
Animal Cop Shows: Structure and Binaries — 389
Visual Evidence — 392
Conclusion — 394
References — 395

Chapter 18 · Emerging Issues and Future Directions in the Area of Animal Cruelty
Mary P. Brewster and Shannon T. Grugan — 397
Introduction — 397
   Advocacy and Activism — 397
   Research on Animal Advocates and Activists — 399
   Effectiveness of Activism — 399

Public Awareness and Mass Media	400
Changing Views of Animals and of Cruelty	402
Current Application and Future Trends in Anti-Cruelty Legislation	404
Recent Laws, Judicial Action, and Pending Legislation	404
Centralized Federal Regulation: The Way Forward?	406
Important Emerging Legislative Issues	407
The Future of Anti-Cruelty Legislation	408
Improvement in the Investigation and Prosecution of Animal Cruelty Cases	409
Increased Legitimacy as a Social Phenomenon	412
The Status of Empirical Study of Animal Violence	413
"Sui generis" study of animal cruelty	413
Agnew's (1998) Integrative Model of Animal Violence	414
The Future of Animal Cruelty Research	415
Data Collection, Maintenance, and Dissemination	416
Conclusion/Future Directions	416
References	417

Section VI · Appendix

Animal Protection Agencies and Organizations	427
Author Biographies	443
Index	451

Foreword

Wayne Pacelle,
President and CEO of The Humane Society of the United States

Animal Cruelty is a truly comprehensive look at the history of animal cruelty in the United States. There are several worthy resources devoted to cataloguing statutes and understanding the application of these codes, but there are no works as rich and multifaceted as this one. This is an anthology that should find receptive audiences among animal welfare advocates, social scientists, those within the criminal justice system, and so many others who abhor cruelty to animals and want to do something about it.

We've always had a moral intuition that cruelty to animals is wrong. In fact, the first anti-cruelty statutes in the colonies and in the states predate the first animal welfare organizations, revealing that our social instincts drove policy in the right direction even before there were groups to show us the way and remind us of the importance of an aggressive response to needless and malicious human violence toward animals. During the nineteenth century, an emerging social consensus about the problem of cruelty to animals caused a vibrant social movement devoted to the welfare of animals to coalesce, and set off a round of related lawmaking in most of the states. There was a broad acceptance of the idea that society has a general interest in cruelty, not simply because we should prevent harm to creatures capable of suffering and highly dependent on human beings, but because it was a social evil whose perpetrators might graduate to various acts of interpersonal violence against other human beings. It was already a commonplace that people who could be cruel to animals were also capable of domestic abuse, whether of wives, children, or other relatives and dependents.

This was a fine start, but as 150 years of subsequent experience have demonstrated, cruelty is a more complex phenomenon. Happily, since the revitalization of animal protection in the post-World War II period, which gained particular momentum in the mid-1950s, we have seen a steady advance in our understanding of cruelty as a social problem, and in the remedies proposed to address it. An invigorated animal protection movement has made dramatic gains in this period (Unti & Rowan, 2001).

It is possible to trace this progress by a few salient measures. The empirical evidence of cruelty to animals as a sentinel crime inextricably tied to interpersonal violence is overwhelming now, and the social science literature on this and related issues has swelled. The available typologies of cruelty have reached a level of sophistication suited to the modern era. There is a much stronger public understanding of cruelty and its implications, and there is greater concern. There is deep and pervasive evidence of how much people care for animals, and the strength of the human-animal bond (Pacelle, 2010). And finally, there is a growing scientific understanding of the emotional and cognitive capacities of animals, making acts of violence against animals all the more morally problematic.

The number of laws to protect animals has increased dramatically in recent years. Most importantly, when it comes to the basic anticruelty statutes in most states, we have seen them overhauled and fortified to include increased penalties for animal fighting, hoarding, and other cruelties. Many forms of cruelty once barely addressed are now treated as felony-level offenses, and law enforcement agents, prosecutors, and judges are treating such cases as serious crimes. While many prohibitions against dogfighting and cockfighting date back to the 19th century, many states treated this form of staged violence as a petty crime, or no crime at all. Over the last two decades, we have seen bans on cockfighting imposed in the half dozen or so states where it long remained legal. We have also seen every state adopt felony-level penalties for cruelty; in 2014, South Dakota became the 50th state to do so. Animal fighting is now a federal felony, and that too marks a tremendously significant advance in the law. More changes in the law loom, with a vigorous effort from animal advocates, law enforcement, anti-domestic violence professionals, and other key stakeholders.

Today's humane organizations and animal care and control agencies promote practical approaches to the mitigation of animal suffering, push for stronger regulatory and legislative protection, and seek to promote a better and more sophisticated understanding of cruelty within professional, public policy, and other circles. This is part of a broad effort to ensure that the principle of kindness to animals is taken seriously within every social, cultural, and political institution that might be called upon to take up the question of their treatment and status under and within our society. Contributors to this volume include a number of pioneers in the modern effort to see cruelty to animals treated as the serious problem that it is. At no time has there been more energy, more intelligence, and more initiative invested in this arena, and that's as it should be.

References

Pacelle, W. (2010). *The bond: Our kinship with animals, our call to defend them.* New York, NY: William Morrow.

Unti, B., & Rowan, A. (2001). "A Social History of Animal Protection in the Post-World War Two Period." In D. J. Salem & A. Rowan (Eds.), *State of the animals* (pp. 21–37). Washington, DC: Humane Society Press.

Acknowledgments

We would like to thank Beth Hall and the entire Carolina Academic Press family for providing the opportunity for an updated, even more comprehensive text on animal cruelty. We would like to extend our sincere gratitude to all of contributors to the book for again sharing their expertise and research findings, and to Wayne Pacelle for his willingness to write the foreword for this manuscript.

We are also grateful to our graduate assistants, Tracey Malandra and Daniel Graham, for their invaluable input on early drafts of the manuscript.

—MPB and CLR

Special thanks go to my family, Ryan, Michael, Elle, Jade, and Jet, for putting up with my absence from the dinner table on many occasions throughout this past year. Your patience, love, and support have sustained me throughout this project.

—MPB

My heartfelt thanks go to my husband, Jaime. Through his undying love and support, I have been able to continue bringing the topic of animal cruelty to the forefront. I also would like to thank our "furry kids," Honey Girl, Dylan, Diablo, and Bastet, who remind me every day of the passion I have toward fighting the victimization of nonhuman animals.

—CLR

Section I
Animal Cruelty: History, Legislation, and Prevalence

Chapter 1

Definitions of Animal Cruelty, Abuse, and Neglect

Phil Arkow and Randall Lockwood

Introduction

An ongoing, and perhaps unresolvable, challenge facing humane and law enforcement investigators, prosecutors, defense attorneys, judges, and juries is how to define such an abstract concept as animal cruelty. All human (and many non-human) societies attempt to identify actions that threaten to disrupt a stable, efficient, and harmonious group and take action against offenders. Cultural norms, laws, or other forces seek to restore balance by changing the behavior of those who transgress, or by removing them from society either temporarily or permanently. Even after two centuries of statutory language updates and case law precedents, the criminal justice system still faces a morass of conflicting legal, academic, cultural, and public perceptions in seeking to define animal cruelty.

Law and culture interact. The social norms of a particular culture give rise to the political actions that result in laws. The laws of a region (city, state, country) codify those norms and define a desired standard of behavior for all citizens. Certain elements of these laws are viewed as immutable by most people (e.g., prohibition of murder), while other provisions may change rapidly with changing social norms and sensitivities. This kind of evolution of attitudes and legal standards has been particularly true for laws addressing animal cruelty which have undergone major changes in recent decades (Favre & Tsang, 1993; Frasch, 2008).

Historically, concern about animal cruelty initially reflected human-centered concerns either about the loss of use of animals as property, or consideration of what additional harm the perpetrators of such acts might do to humans. Early writings on duties to animals did not consider the impact of cruelty toward animal victims. In *Summa Contra Gentiles*, St. Thomas Aquinas reflected this prevailing view:

> ... if any passages of Holy Writ seem to forbid us to be cruel to dumb animals, for instance to kill a bird with its young, this is ... to remove man's thoughts from being cruel to other men, and lest through being cruel to other animals one becomes cruel to human beings ... (St. Thomas Aquinas, as cited in Regan and Singer 1976, p. 59)

Some five centuries later, Immanuel Kant echoed this notion of reasons for concern about animal cruelty in his essay *Metaphysical Principles of the Doctrine of Virtue*:

> ... Our duties towards animals are merely indirect duties towards humanity. Animal nature has analogies to human nature, and by doing our duties to animals in respect of manifestations of human nature, we indirectly do our duties to humanity.... cruelty to animals is contrary to man's duty to himself, because it deadens in him the feeling of sympathy for their suffering, and thus a natural tendency that is very useful to morality in relation to other human beings is weakened. (Kant, as cited in Regan and Singer 1976, p. 125)

The idea that animal cruelty was an intrinsic, moral evil based on its impact on the animal itself is a relatively recent concept, first gaining a foothold in the late eighteenth century. This view was expressed quite clearly by Reverend Humphry Primatt in *The Duty of Mercy* (1776): "Pain is pain, whether it be inflicted on man or on beast; and the creature that suffers it, whether man or beast, being sensible of the misery of it while it lasts, suffers evil" (p. 21).

One of the most influential ideas concerning animal cruelty was buried in a footnote to *Introduction to the Principals of Morals and Legislation* by Jeremy Bentham (1789) entitled "Interests of the inferior animals improperly neglected in legislation." Bentham argued that the capacity for suffering is the vital characteristic that gives a being the right to legal consideration. The final sentence of the footnote is often used today as a foundation for those seeking to promote the cause of animals: "The question is not, Can they *reason*? nor, Can they *talk*? but *Can they suffer?*" (p. 130).

These writings stressed the contemporary concept that the definition and assessment of acts of animal cruelty must include consideration of the impact of these acts on the life, health, and well-being of the animal victim.

Despite concerns about the effects of cruelty on the animals themselves, today, as in the 18th century, animals are legally viewed as property and animal cruelty is a crime against the property owner. The status of animals as a special category of property that is capable of pain, suffering, and death, and to which we can form unique attachments, is rarely recognized in legislation or case law. However, this special status is not totally ignored. It is often what leads the courts to take animal cruelty more seriously in consideration of what the act tells us about the perpetrator and the risks he or she poses to society.

The core purpose of most Western legal systems is to achieve what the National District Attorneys Association refers to as balanced and restorative justice or BARJ (Harp, 2002). Under the BARJ model, criminal justice systems should strive to achieve three goals:

1. hold offenders accountable for their actions;
2. protect the public from those who would bring harm to people or property; and
3. restore or rehabilitate offenders who can be returned to society.

With respect to animal cruelty, the challenge is in defining acts that cannot be socially tolerated and which identify those who threaten further harm to people and property. This process must involve attempts at classification of acts of abuse and neglect and their significance in meeting these objectives.

Defining cruelty to animals (the most common legal term), animal abuse (a preferred operational term that has not yet been as widely adopted in the legislative lexicon), or neglect is a daunting challenge. Each individual has her or his own definitions of animal maltreatment, based upon personal experiences, upbringing, cultural standards, spiritual beliefs, and other variables. These definitions are organic and change based on time, experience, and situational contexts (Sinclair, Merck, & Lockwood, 2006). Individual concerns for the welfare of animals that result in reports of suspected cruelty may not meet the legal definitions of maltreatment in a specific jurisdiction, and the interpretation and enforcement of animal cruelty may vary widely from agency to agency (Arkow, 2003).

Consequently, recognizing animal cruelty, abuse, or neglect—and building a successful criminal case against it—is not always easy, particularly in a society that condones and institutionalizes such accepted practices as hunting and intensive livestock production while simultaneously revering its companion animals. If beauty is in the eye of the beholder, then its antithetical construct of cruelty is equally subjective as well. What an outraged member of the public perceives to be abusive treatment of animals may differ greatly from the bottom-line economic perspective of the animal's owner, the formal language of state statutes, an academic interpretation, and ultimately what a jury decides. In the end, the best one can say about defining cruelty is that it is like trying to define pornography: you can't define it, but you think you know it when you see it (Arkow, 2006).

Definitions of Terms

All 50 states have enacted criminal laws designed to punish individuals who commit acts of cruelty against animals. Most state anti-cruelty statutes are comprised of six elements:

1. the types of animals protected;
2. the types of acts prohibited or duties of care required;
3. the mental culpability required to meet a standard of liability;
4. the defenses to criminal liability;
5. certain activities exempted from the law; and
6. penalties for each offense.

Underlying the application of these elements are additional dimensions that can affect whether the community or the legal system will take action in response to an act. These include: the intrinsic and extrinsic value of the animal victim; the deviant nature of the act itself (e.g., its level of depravity); public and professional recognition of the victims' capacity for stress, pain, fear or suffering; and financial cost to society to address the consequences of the act.

While the concept behind these provisions may seem straightforward, the devil is in the details and the definitions underlying them can be particularly problematic. A majority of states define cruelty with such vague and ambiguous language that, unless the alleged act or omission is extreme and outrageous, it is unlikely to be perceived to violate the statute (Lacroix, 1999).

In common usage, the terms cruelty to animals, abuse, and neglect may appear interchangeable in some contexts, and more narrowly defined in others. They encompass a range of behaviors harmful to animals, from unintentional neglect to malicious killing, with tremendous differences in the underlying motivations and outcomes of these acts. Some incidents may be individualized (an owner leaving a dog without adequate food and water, a juvenile tying a firecracker to a cat) or institutionalized (abuses in puppy mills, dogfighting rings, or biomedical research enterprises). Attempting to use any one word such as "cruelty," which can describe such a broad range of behaviors and motivational states, is highly challenging at best, and runs the risk of overuse and weakened impact

(Rowan, 1999). It is difficult to arrange so many divergent acts of commission and omission along a continuum of care that is universally acceptable across a variety of cultures.

The most spectacular, egregious, and publicized cruelty cases may be rooted in psychopathological behavior or indicative of other forms of family and community violence. However, the vast majority of cases that are reported to humane law enforcement agencies represent instances of neglect, animal maltreatment that may often be unintentional due to lack of education or temporary lapses in care from an otherwise responsible owner. Some neglect may be incidental, short-term, and easily resolved through educational or social services interventions; other neglect may be long-term, large-scale, and chronic (Crook, 2000). Legislators are coming to recognize that highly-charged cruelty cases may not reflect the vast majority of animal maltreatment instances, and consequently are expanding the purview of animal welfare legislation. For example, the Hawaii legislature in 1998 noted that the existing statute identified only those acts which were the most heinous and extreme, such as beating, mutilation, poisoning, starvation, and torture. However, on a daily basis, other less overt acts such as daily neglect also resulted in the inhumane treatment of animals. Thus, the legislature agreed that pet animals deserved a minimum level of care including adequate food, water, and shelter (Hawaii State Legislature, 1998).

Perhaps the simplest and most effective definition may be one suggested in a British veterinary medical dictionary. Blood and Studdert (1999) defined cruelty as the infliction of pain or distress unnecessarily. However, even here, the authors noted that the "definition of unnecessary varies between countries and from time to time in one country. Determination of the prevailing standard of cruelty can only be decided by the courts" (p. 295). The worst cases, they noted, should be pursued under the classification of aggravated cruelty.

Black's Law Dictionary (2012) provides a somewhat more detailed definition of animal cruelty that addresses the issue of necessity. It defines it as:

> The infliction of physical pain, suffering, or death upon an animal, when not necessary for purposes of training or discipline or (in the case of death) to procure food or to release the animal from incurable suffering, but done wantonly, for mere sport, for the indulgence of a cruel and vindictive temper, or with reckless indifference to its pain.

Perspectives on Definitions

Numerous interest groups have attempted to craft specific definitions of animal maltreatment.

Researchers

Academic attempts to standardize a definition of animal maltreatment have been unsuccessful. Felthous and Kellert (1987) defined "substantial" cruelty to animals as a "pattern of deliberately, repeatedly, and unnecessarily hurting vertebrate animals in a manner likely to cause serious injury" (p. 1715).

Note the interpretational problems with such definitions: is an individual or unrepeated act of heinous physical torture that is not part of a pattern cruel? If the perpetrator is not aware of possible painful outcomes of his act, is it cruel? Should only vertebrates be afforded this protection?

Ascione (1993) said developing a widely acceptable definition of animal cruelty would be as difficult as defining interpersonal aggression. He believed that achieving consistency would prove more daunting than in the parallel child welfare field where federal definitions and specific categories of physical abuse, sexual abuse, emotional abuse, and neglect are extant. Nevertheless, he attempted to contrive a working definition of animal cruelty that captured the most common features of 50 state statutes: "Socially unacceptable behavior that intentionally causes unnecessary pain, suffering, or distress to and/or death of an animal" (Ascione, 1993, p. 228).

Parsing this working definition uncovers a range of challenging issues. "Socially unacceptable" requires subjective sensitivity to cultural variations, economic realities, and political pressures in judgments of what a community values. This definition, widely cited over the years, excludes socially approved practices related to the treatment or use of animals in veterinary practices and livestock production, animal husbandry, hunting, and laboratory research. "Behavior" is meant to include acts of omission and commission. What does Ascione (1993) mean by "unnecessary"? "Pain, suffering and distress" are described as physical conditions as distinguished from emotional or psychological suffering, the latter being more subjective, if not impossible, to verify. Although not specifically included in his definition, bestiality may be considered cruel even when proving physical harm to the animal cannot be accomplished.

As the definition was considered in a rapidly evolving corpus of literature, Ascione and Shapiro subsequently (2009) refined the original definition and called the condition animal abuse: "Nonaccidental, socially unacceptable behavior that causes pain, suffering or distress to and/or the death of an animal" (p. 570).

Note the subtle change from "cruelty" (which implies malicious intent on the part of the perpetrator) to "abuse" (which mirrors child protection systems terminology and which describes maltreatment that occurs regardless of the perpetrator's intentionality). Also note the addition of "nonaccidental," to capture new veterinary forensics terminology describing "Non-Accidental Injury" (NAI) and implying a certain measure of causality. Most importantly, note the elimination of "intentionally" from the earlier definition. Animal cruelty, abuse, and neglect cases should be able to stand on their own merits regarding the facts and evidence of the case without having to overcome a nearly impossible hurdle of proving the perpetrator's intent.

Government Panels

One of the most comprehensive attempts to address animal suffering began in 1965, when the United Kingdom government commissioned an investigation, led by Professor Roger Brambell, into the welfare of intensively farmed animals. This was driven in part, by concerns raised in the book, *Animal Machines* (Harrison, 1964). The goal of the Brambell Commission was not to offer a critique of the agricultural industry, but rather to define practices that would maximize the quality of life for animals in confinement. As a result of the Commission's initial report, the Farm Animal Welfare Advisory Committee was created to monitor the livestock production sector. In 1979, this was replaced by the Farm Animal Welfare Council, and that year, they codified what has come to be known as **the Five Freedoms:**

1. **Freedom from hunger and thirst,** by ready access to water and a diet to maintain health and vigor;
2. **Freedom from discomfort,** by providing an appropriate environment;
3. **Freedom from pain, injury, and disease,** by prevention or rapid diagnosis and treatment;
4. **Freedom to express normal behaviour,** by providing sufficient space, proper facilities, appropriate company of the animal's own kind; and
5. **Freedom from fear and distress,** by ensuring conditions and treatment, which avoid mental suffering.

The Five Freedoms have achieved worldwide recognition and are a component of national legislation, marketing, and farm assurance schemes. They have withstood much criticism and, within Great Britain, are the cornerstone of government and industry policy and the Codes of Recommendations for the Welfare of Livestock (Farm Animal Welfare Council, 2009).

Although the intent of the concept of the Five Freedoms is to set goals for promoting welfare, animal advocates have argued that these definitions can be used to help define levels of animal cruelty by noting which of these freedoms are not being met in specific circumstances. Patronek and Weiss (2011) use the concept of the Five Freedoms to illustrate how failing to meet the conditions of many of the freedoms can indicate conditions under which animal cruelty laws can be applied. They specifically apply this analysis to cases of animal hoarding in which many animals may be kept under conditions which they identify as "A life not worth living." *(See Chapter 9.)*

Similarly, Wathes (2010), a member of the Farm Animal Welfare Council, notes that the Council's most recent analysis builds on Bentham's foundations and proposes that acceptable welfare should move beyond the current test of whether the animal suffers to a new standard of whether the animal has a life worth living, from the animal's point of view.

Public Opinion

Definitions in statutes are written and negotiated by attorneys and legislators responding to public demands for change. What varying stakeholders in any jurisdiction seek to change can be highly contentious, particularly in such an emotionally charged environment as animal protection. Building a consensus depends upon achieving wide public agreement: as Abraham Lincoln said, "Public sentiment is everything. With public sentiment, nothing can fail; without it nothing can succeed" (Basler, 2001, p. 458).

But the constituents interested in issues facing animals represent a fractious element of society with highly divergent interests. Morgan (1983) first described a continuum of public attitudes toward animals ranging from radical Animal Liberation and activist Animal Rights through more centrist Animal Welfare and Animal Control to more conservative Animal Use and Animal Exploitation. Animal activists frequently define any act in which an animal is perceived to suffer as a violation of the animal's alleged inherent rights, although such rights have never been established in a legal context in a system where animals are defined as property and lacking in legal standing. Such attitudes can vary widely within and across communities as a function of economy, population demographics, education, and other variables. The criminal justice field is continually challenged by disconnects between varying professional, personal, public, and legal standards regarding alleged animal maltreatment (Arkow & Munro, 2008).

Legislation, Law Enforcement, Prosecutors, and Judges

While law enforcement, prosecutors, and jurists may take comfort in a "just the facts" approach that minimizes their need to make ethically challenging decisions, the framework for animal cruelty law is fraught with inherent ethical debates. Anti-cruelty statutes are most often found among offenses against public morals, order, and decency, with little or no recognition of the crime's effect upon the victim. Meanwhile, these laws come from a historical tradition in which animals are firmly established as property without inherent legal standing. Some constituents may prefer to resolve the problem rather than prosecute the defendant, while others seek maximum prosecution and punishment. These forces often result in a lack of clear consensus on what defines an incident worthy of prosecution.

The criminal justice system is necessarily bound by the statutes imposed by the jurisdiction and the case law underpinning each judgment. However, animal welfare laws vary inconsistently from state to state, and are continually being amended. There may be separate laws on how companion, wild, and livestock animals ought to be treated, often catering to powerful political and economic interests and cultural and religious traditions. Some incidents are considered petty offenses, while others are misdemeanors or felonies.

Despite recent advances, many state laws still incorporate the original and now antiquated anti-cruelty language first enshrined in code when these statutes were enacted over a century and a half ago. During that era, the welfare of draft horses was of prime concern and many state statutes still prohibit overdriving, overloading, and overworking as the primary targets of law enforcement interest (Donley, Patronek, & Luke, 1999).

Some of these older statutes are impossibly convoluted, such as Connecticut's 191-word sentence in § 53.247:

> **Cruelty to animals.** Any person who overdrives, drives when overloaded, overworks, tortures, deprives of necessary sustenance, mutilates or cruelly beats or kills or unjustifiably injures any animal, or who, having impounded or confined any animal, fails to give such animal proper care or neglects to cage or restrain any such animal from doing injury to itself or to another animal or fails to supply any such animal with wholesome air, food, and water, or unjustifiably administers any poisonous or noxious drug or substance to any domestic animal or unjustifiably exposes any such drug or substance, with intent that the same shall be taken by an animal, or causes it to be done, or, having charge or custody of any animal, inflicts cruelty upon it or fails to provide it with proper food, drink or protection from the weather or abandons it or carries it or causes it to be carried in a cruel manner, or fights with or baits, harasses or worries any animal for the purpose of making it perform for amusement, diversion or exhibition, shall be fined not more than one thousand dollars or imprisoned not more than one year or both.

Connecticut, like many other states, has added separate statutes covering more specific instances of cruelty, such as "maliciously and intentionally" maiming, mutilating, torturing, wounding or killing an animal, or knowingly being involved with animals fighting for amusement or gain, or intentionally injuring a working law enforcement animal.

Some statutes are remarkably simple, such as Wisconsin's § 951.02:

Mistreating animals. No person may treat any animal, whether belonging to the person or another, in a cruel manner.

States vary widely in their inclusion of specific harmful acts within the definition of cruelty. All states, with the exception of Alaska, include desertion or abandonment of animals in their cruelty codes. As of 2011, 38 states specifically include "poisoning" under cruelty. Hanging, a common presentation in cruelty cases, is specifically mentioned only in New Jersey law [N.J. Stat Ann. § 4:22-15-26]. Burning or scalding is only included in definitions used by Nebraska [Neb. Rev. Stat. § 28-1008] and Tennessee [Tenn. Code Ann. § 39-14-201 to 212], although burning of animals has often been charged as arson if the owner of the burned "property" has been identified. Drowning, another common form of cruelty, is specifically mentioned only in Arkansas state law [Ark. Code Ann. § 5-62-102 to 118].

Forms of Animal Abuse

The mistreatment of animals takes many forms and is generally codified statutorily under one catch-all term of cruelty to animals that may include acts of physical abuse, abandonment, neglect, or torture. More specialized subsets of animal harm, such as bestiality or animal fighting, are often codified in separate statutes or sections. While alleged emotional or mental abuse of animals is considered by many to be an inherent problem in animal well-being, documenting that an animal has suffered emotionally or mentally is difficult, if not impossible, especially if no other signs of abuse are present (Kurst-Swanger, 2007). Consequently, emotional abuse has not yet been included in statutory definitions within the United States.

The legal definitions of the following terms (and even the statutory definition of "animal") vary from jurisdiction to jurisdiction, and clinical descriptions and public perceptions may vary from statutory terminology. Nevertheless, the following terms are commonly used to describe the types of animal maltreatment seen in law enforcement investigations:

Animal cruelty: The most prevalent term used in animal anti-cruelty statutes, rooted in history and societies for the prevention of cruelty to animals (synonymous in the U.S. with humane societies). Cruelty implies a deliberate infliction of pain on an animal from which the abuser derives enjoyment or amusement (King, 1998).

Animal abuse: A newer and more neutral term to describe animal maltreatment, modeled after the nomenclature of the child protection system. "Abuse" describes willful failure to provide care and harmful behaviors that result in maltreatment regardless of the intent, motivation or mental condition of the perpetrator, whereas "cruelty" connotes more deliberate intention (Arkow, 2005, p. 2).

Neglect: An act, often of omission, signifying a lack of care. Neglect may often result from ignorance regarding appropriate animal husbandry or from extenuating circumstances such as poverty, family crises or substance abuse. Neglected animals endure physical injury and deprivation from careless behavior on the part of the animal's owner or caretaker, such as failure to provide adequate levels of food, water, shelter, veterinary care, grooming, or sanitation. The vast majority of cases investigated by animal protection authorities and brought to the court system involve neglect rather than physical cruelty. Of particular concern are individuals, often called collectors or hoarders, who accumulate large numbers of neglected animals (Kurst-Swanger, 2007).

Hoarding: Hoarding is animal neglect on a significant scale involving large numbers of animals. While the underlying psychosocial causes for animal hoarding behaviors are indeterminate, the crime generally means failure to provide minimal standards of nutrition, sanitation, and veterinary care, combined with a failure to act on the deteriorating conditions of the animals and the environment. Animals in hoarding situations are not only at great risk of neglectful care, but also pose public health problems in the home and surrounding community. Illinois became the first state in the U.S. to specifically define animal hoarding [§ 510 ILCS 70/2.10] in the context of a criminal act (Patronek, 2008). Hawaii's penal code [§ 711.1109.6] defines hoarding as the intentional, knowing or reckless possession of more than 15 dogs or cats, the failure to provide necessary sustenance for each one, and failure to correct conditions injurious to the health of the animals' or owner's health and well being.

Animal physical abuse: The physical abuse of animals can involve a wide range of injurious acts requiring an active engagement. Injuries may be caused by hitting, kicking, throwing, beating, shaking, poisoning, burning, scalding, suffocation, and many other actions. Institutional or commercial incidents of physical animal abuse include socially-sanctioned situations where the intention is not to harm the animal specifically, but rather to use the animal for economic benefit, often with little regard to the animal's welfare. Individual motivations for physically abusing an animal vary greatly and may manifest in inappropriate disciplinary procedures or training methods, punishment, psychopathic behavior, or assaultive behaviors meant to control or intimidate a human member of the family. Currently (as of 2012), Alaska, Arizona, Colorado, Maine, Minnesota, Nebraska, Indiana, Nevada, Tennessee, and Puerto Rico identify a special category of animal cruelty used to frighten, intimidate or coerce others or include such acts of intimidation within statutory definitions of domestic violence and elder abuse.

Non-accidental injury (NAI): A term borrowed from the British child protection field. NAI is a synonym for physical abuse, the clinical presentation of various injuries to the skeleton, soft tissues or organs of a child sustained as a result of beating or repeated mistreatment, usually by an individual responsible for its care. Munro and Thrusfield (2001a, 2001b, 2001c, 2001d) first applied this term as a synonym for physical abuse of animals.

Animal sexual abuse: Any abusive act with an animal involving the rectum, anus or genitalia; or sexual contact with animals which may or may not result in physical injury to the animal. Sometimes called interspecies sexual assault, animal sexual abuse is the preferred statutory term over the more archaic bestiality (in which sexual intercourse would have to take place) and zoophilia (a strong, erotic preference for animals), neither of which take into account the potential deleterious effects on the animal (Beetz, 2008; Beetz & Podberscek, 2005; Beirne, 1997).

Emotional abuse: Although emotional abuse, bullying, excessive teasing, intimidation, exploitation, or coercion that leads to a fragile emotional state in humans are specified in numerous criminal statutes, such terminology is currently lacking from animal cruelty laws. Persistent threatening behavior to animals or a failure to provide them with basic emotional and companionship needs is considered by some to constitute emotional abuse.

However, this has not been recognized clinically or in statutory language in the U.S., U.K. or Canada (Arkow, Boyden & Patterson-Kane, 2011).

Challenges in Definitions

Vague, Ambiguous, and Archaic Language

Throughout all state anti-cruelty statutes, animal cruelty is commonly referred to in qualified terms designed to permit investigators some flexibility and to exempt socially accepted practices. The net effect, however, is to create ambiguity that can frustrate courts. Most states, for example, define cruelty with such qualifying adjectives as *needless* mutilation (so as to exempt acceptable mutilations such as neutering a cat or docking a dog's ears), the infliction of *unnecessary* pain and suffering (to keep veterinarians from being charged with cruelty for administering inoculations), or failure to provide *proper* sustenance (so a cat owner will not be charged for putting her overweight feline on a diet). Qualifications such as these beg the question: what is "proper"? "Unnecessary"? "Needless"?

Some statutes have attempted to address this confusion with carefully crafted explanations. Missouri, for example, defines "adequate" care as "normal and prudent attention to the needs of an animal, including wholesome food, clean water, shelter, and health care as necessary to maintain good health in a specific species of animal" [§ 578.005]. Maine defines "necessary" sustenance as food "of sufficient quantity and quality to maintain all animals in good health" [§ 7-4013]. Washington goes further to define "food" as "food or feed appropriate to the species for which it is intended" [§ 16.52.011]. Michigan feels compelled to define "water" as "potable water that is suitable for the age and species of animal that is made regularly available unless otherwise directed by a licensed veterinarian" [§ 750.50].

An example of ambiguity may be found in the concept of ritual killing of animals. Many states, such as Illinois [§ 510 ILCS 75/2] require livestock to be slaughtered by a humane method, with a variety of acceptable techniques identified including the ritual Kosher slaughter, which is required by some Jews but condemned by many animal activists. However, ritual killing of animals in cult, occult, sacrificial or satanic religious practices is not similarly delineated. While a 1993 U.S. Supreme Court decision (Lukumi Babalu Aye v. City of Hialeah, 113 Ct. 2217) ruled that a municipal law prohibiting Santeria animal sacrifices was too specific in its restrictions on a specific religious organization, the court unanimously held that governments have the right to enforce more broadly-based prohibitions against cruelty. However, the case created a climate in which some prosecutors, unfamiliar with the full court decision, may be reluctant to take action against animal abuse occurring within the context of a religious practice (Sinclair, Merck, & Lockwood, 2006).

To further confound matters, many statutory definitions are rooted in archaic language highly appropriate for the 19th century, but patently outmoded for the 21st. Many states still prohibit *overdriving, overworking,* and *overloading* animals, which were significant concerns when horses were the primary form of transport, but these laws are rarely enforced today; should a humane investigator even wish to cite a farmer for improperly using his horse to pull a wagon, there are no absolute standards defining how much weight for this particular horse would constitute overloading.

Similarly, numerous states combine many offenses under the single, archaic crime of *cruelty* to animals. In recent years, several states have begun to differentiate among the various offenses comprising cruelty, recognizing that these different manifestations have differing motivations and degrees of seriousness. Penalties for offenses are now often differentiated between felony and misdemeanor categories, or by sub-categories, depending on the culpability of the offender and the intensity, duration or ultimate outcome of the act. Upgrading more serious crimes to felonies increases the gravity of the crime in the eyes of the judges and juries, and enables more law enforcement and prosecutorial resources to be brought to bear in working a case through the criminal justice system.

For example, several state statutes now define a new category of "aggravated" cruelty (e.g., Montana § 45-8-217 for a person who "purposely or knowingly kills or inflicts cruelty to an animal with the purpose of terrifying, torturing, or mutilating the animal," or inflicts cruelty on 10 or more animals). Some states, such as Illinois [§ 510 ILCS 70/3.03], consider animal "torture" a separate classification. All states consider dog fighting a separate felony offense. Many regard bestiality and inhumane transport of animals in a vehicle (e.g., Nevada § 574.190 which prohibits "inhuman" transport) as separately defined and codified offenses.

Some statutes provide elaborate and comprehensive definitions of *neglect*. For example, Indiana § 35-46-3-0.5 prohibits endangering an animal's health by failing to provide or arrange for food or drink for a dependent animal, restraining an animal for more than a brief time on a chain or tether that is too heavy or too short, failing to provide veterinary care, and leaving a dog or cat outside and exposed to excessive heat or cold.

Finding animal cruelty laws and their definitions can be a challenge. Some states (e.g., Maine) have both civil and criminal prohibitions against cruelty. Some states have separate cruelty laws for livestock and for other animals (e.g., Texas § 42.09 and 42.092, or Iowa § 717.1A and 717.B1). Some have differing provisions if the victim is a dog or cat (e.g., Maine § 17-1031 or Alabama § 13A-11-240) or a bird (e.g., Minnesota § 343.30). Relatively few states have replaced animal "cruelty" with the more objective term "abuse" (e.g., Missouri § 578.012).

Phrases such as *unnecessary suffering* or *unnecessarily kill* may be broad, but the presence of the modifier presumes that some forms of suffering (e.g., those believed to result in societal benefit) are acceptable. The ambiguity lies in determining how much suffering is acceptable, often requiring the courts to attempt to determine legislative intent (Ibrahim, 2006).

Despite the proliferation of laws and humane issues now addressed by legislation, many statutes remain ill-defined. The use of such imprecise and outdated terminology with little additional statutory guidance has left investigators, prosecutors, and the courts confused as to what acts fall within the confines of the statute. As a result, the formidable evidentiary and procedural challenges incurred in bringing a case to court are exacerbated by language-induced inconsistency and unpredictability. Redefining what constitutes cruelty is essential: before animal cruelty charges or convictions can be widely considered evidence of maltreatment, statutory language must reflect a clear and current understanding of what is meant by abusive treatment (Lacroix, 1999).

Absence of a Universal Standard of Cruelty

The child protection movement, whose origins lie in the animal protection movement (Unti, 2008), achieved significant progress following the development of medical profiles identifying child abuse and neglect (Arkow & Munro, 2008). The development of veterinary forensics as a sub-specialty, and training for veterinarians and investigators to recognize clinical symptoms of non-accidental injury, offer potential for the animal protection field to replicate the statutory objectivity of child protection. Clarification and amplification of the conditions inherent in a "battered pet" syndrome (Munro & Thrusfield, 2001a, 2001b, 2001c, 2001d) would help to distinguish accidental from non-accidental injuries in the animal and degrees of malice and intent in the perpetrator.

In the absence of such universal clinical profiles, prevailing cultural standards frequently determine what is perceived to be acceptable animal treatment. Many states for years resisted efforts to outlaw cockfighting on grounds that this was part of the cultural heritage of politically powerful Latino constituencies. California once had to enact legislation prohibiting Cambodian immigrants from humanely killing and eating their own dogs, an acceptable cultural practice in Southeast Asia but highly objectionable in the U.S. Surgically docking a Doberman pinscher's ears is considered a legitimate (albeit controversial) practice in the U.S., but is defined as illegal in the U.K.

Even animal protection officials have widely varying animal husbandry standards. For example, one of this chapter's authors (Arkow) once observed an animal shelter in Austin, Texas, that had installed an elaborate and expensive kennel heating system to respond to public criticism that the dogs might be cold when the ambient temperature occasionally dipped below 60 degrees. Meanwhile, at another shelter in Fairbanks, Alaska, officials routinely housed huskies and malamutes outdoors in unheated doghouses in sub-zero winters because it was felt to be inhumane to subject these cold-acclimated dogs to warmer indoor temperatures. To address such inconsistencies, the Association of Shelter Veterinarians issued comprehensive *Guidelines for Standards of Care in Animal Shelters* (2010) to set clear and consistent standards for meeting animals' needs. This document has been referenced in court proceedings against large scale animal hoarding situations to document how these facilities fail to meet acceptable standards of animal care in group housing conditions.

Objectivity vs. Subjectivity

Many decisions whether to pursue an investigation or a prosecution by necessity are highly subjective, based upon the evidence, availability and credibility of witnesses, the likelihood of obtaining a conviction, whether prosecution is the most appropriate response, and whether the animals' condition fits within the vague statutory definitions. To compensate for the lack of a universal definition of cruelty, there have been attempts to introduce objective, quantifiable metrics to elucidate the subjective reports of witnesses and investigators.

The equine welfare field was the first to develop standardized assessment tools to describe horse abuse (Henneke, 1995). Later, Patronek (1998) devised the Tufts Animal Care and Condition scales to assist law enforcement officials and veterinarians by quantifying objectively the adequacy or inadequacy of dog care. Similar scales to objectively describe the body condition of dogs and cats developed by Purina (available at Purina.com) are widely used in animal cruelty investigations. These scales assess body condition, weather and environmental conditions, and physical care in animals to help objectify incidents of abuse and neglect for use in cruelty prosecutions. It should be noted that the criteria in these scales focus on the consequences for the animal and are independent of human intent.

More specificity in the definitions and descriptions of cruelty would enhance prosecutions. Veterinarians seeking guidance in presenting expert witness testimony, and investigators and prosecutors leading cruelty cases, have been stymied by the absence of universally accepted standards to make informed clinical diagnoses of animal maltreatment. Munro and Thrusfield (2001a, 2001b, 2001c, 2001d) proposed a list of risk factors for abuse and neglect that could achieve mutual understanding among animal health professionals. These factors include client behaviors, such as presenting discrepant medical and care histories or clients' use of multiple animal hospitals to avoid detection; clinical conditions, such as injuries that do not match the client's explanation or multiple fractures of varying age in the same animal; and environmental concerns, such as histories of unexplained deaths or injuries to multiple animals in the household. Munro and Thrusfield (2001, a, b, c, d) noted that no one single diagnostic pointer is necessarily indicative of animal cruelty, abuse or neglect, and that there may be any number of explanations for the presenting signs.

Borrowing from these ideas, Arkow (2003) published guidelines to sensitize veterinarians to conditions that are highly suggestive of animal abuse. These include:

1. Animal welfare concerns (e.g., poor physical condition, absence of food, abandonment, collar too tight, lack of medical care, dehydration, excessive hair matting, parasitic infestation);
2. Environmental concerns (e.g., general lack of sanitation, overcrowding, presence of dead animals, inadequate ventilation or lighting, excessive numbers of animals, presence of feces or urine);
3. Human welfare concerns (e.g., owner unable to afford human or animal food; owner lives in isolation; evidence of animal fighting, bestiality, or ritualistic sacrifice);
4. Physical injuries to animal (e.g., bruising, fractures, repetitive injuries, lesions, burns or scalds, ocular injuries, internal injuries, administration of recreational drugs, poison, gunshot wounds, malnutrition, drowning, asphyxiation, untreated diseases); and
5. Sexual abuse of animals.

However, none of these or subsequent guidelines has been universally accepted or codified into standard veterinary practice or legal terminology.

Another approach to objectify vague definitions has been to propose a typology—a categorization of types of companion animal abuse based along a spectrum of maltreatment. Vermuelen and Odendaal (1993) first proposed such a typology that categorized companion animal abuse. They observed that the lack of a standardized definition of companion animal abuse leads to a wide range of definitions in usage, increases confusion, discourages reporting, and causes discrepant research findings. To comply with standards for uniformity that encourage meaningful, universal, measurable, complete and pragmatic terminologies, type of victimization was chosen to identify the different abuses. They cautioned that additional classification systems would be required in cases where multiple or secondary forms of abuse occur (see Table 1 on the next page).

Building on this foundation, Rowan (1999) proposed another typology that defined the act of maltreatment according to the perpetrator's motivations (see Table 2 on the next page). Note that in this proposed typology, the term *cruelty* is restricted to a relatively small subset of cases. In order to qualify as "cruel," the act must not involve only a deliberate act to cause harm, but also the perpetrator's desire to gain satisfaction from the infliction of pain or suffering. One would need to distinguish between motivations for power and control, curiosity, and sadism and other psychopathic behaviors to achieve an effective response that will not waste the time of law enforcement and the courts.

Table 1: Typology of Companion Animal Abuse

Physical Abuse (intentional or unintentional)	**Active Maltreatment**	Assault Burning Poisoning Shooting Mutilation Drowning Suffocation Abandonment Restriction of movement Incorrect training methods Inbreeding Trapping Abusive transportation Fireworks Bestiality
	Passive Neglect or Ignorance	Lack of food, water or shelter Lack of veterinary care Lack of sanitation General neglect
	Commercial Exploitation	Labor (draft animal) Animal fighting Overbreeding Sport Experimentation
Mental Abuse (intentional or unintentional)*	**Active Maltreatment**	Instilling fear and anxiety Isolation
	Passive Neglect	Deprivation of love and affection, lack of recreational stimuli

* Note: this typology was described for use in South Africa. The category of "mental abuse" is not specifically recognized in any anti-cruelty statutes in the United States.

Table 2: Categories of Humane Behavior and Motivation Associated with Animal Use That Sometimes Causes Distress

Term	Agent's Motivation	Animal Suffering	Societal Attitude
I. Cruel	Takes satisfaction from suffering	Always	Condemnation
II(a). Abuse	Satisfaction derived from domination or behavioral response	Usually	Condemnation
II(b). Neglect	No satisfaction derived	Usually	Condemnation
III. Use	Justified by claims to personal or societal gains	Sometimes	Approval when are attempts to minimize suffering

For the animal cruelty investigator, the absence of universally accepted definitions is a double-edged sword. On the one hand, a certain amount of discretion must be applied when evaluating the circumstances of a case and whether "cruelty" occurred. A uniform standard, for example, of acceptable ambient temperature for outdoor housing of dogs might not work equally well for a Chihuahua as for a St. Bernard; acceptable winter housing conditions for pets in San Diego might not be appropriate at Lake Tahoe. On the other hand, without highly specific definitions, a good defense attorney can argue that while animal care circumstances might not have been ideal, absent the defendant's malicious motive and intention, a case of cruelty cannot be proven.

Establishing a Motive, Intent, or State of Mind

American criminal law is predicated upon the concept of *mens rea,* or guilty state of mind. The system of crime and punishment is based upon the premise that people have the ability and free will to choose between right and wrong behaviors. In order to be considered criminal, an unlawful act or omission must be accompanied by a criminal state of mind (LaRene, 1987).

A major legalistic problem in enforcing and prosecuting anti-cruelty statutes is that it is very hard to prove the necessary *mens rea* in the case of a defendant whose actions are cruel, but also customary and acceptable (Francione, 1995).

Meanwhile, it is widely acknowledged that the overwhelming majority of cruelty cases investigated by humane authorities constitute unintentional neglect and crimes of omission, rather than deliberate, premeditated acts of physical harm, that can best be resolved through education (Humane Society of the U.S., 2004), Most cases of animal maltreatment seen in veterinary practice are the result of client ignorance and accidents rather than intention, and it has been suggested that most animal abuse occurs as isolated acts influenced heavily by opportunity, impulse, or aggravating social factors rather than by individual psychopathological behavior (Patterson-Kane & Piper, 2009).

Most state statutes have attempted to clarify this situation through the insertion of qualifying adjectives, defining cruelty solely as *intentional, willful* or *reckless* acts. The unintended consequence of this strategy, however, is to force prosecutors to prove that the alleged perpetrator intended to harm the animal, or was knowingly reckless, as opposed to merely having to prove that the abuse occurred under the perpetrator's control without regard for his or her motivations.

"Intentionally" and "willfully" are often used interchangeably and mean that the illegal act was committed consciously and with the idea of doing the act or causing the harm. The person had to have a conscious objective. It is not an essential element to the crime of cruelty to intend that the animal suffer: it can be argued that the person exercised general intent by committing acts or omissions which can foreseeably cause pain and suffering. But the party must be proven to have knowingly caused the act or omission without just cause or excuse (LaRene, 1987).

The majority of states consider *malicious harm* or *torture* to be grounds for felony-level charges of animal cruelty. Such a designation usually requires the assertion of a particular *mens rea.* New York [N.Y. Agric. & Mkts. Law § 353], Kentucky [Ky. Rev. Stat. Ann. § 525.135], and Tennessee [Tenn. Code Ann. § 39-14-202] define such acts as those "done or carried out in an especially depraved or sadistic manner." Oregon [O.R.S. § 167.322] and the US Virgin Islands [14 V.I. Code Ann. § 181] define "maliciously" as "acting with a depravity of mind and wanton disregard of life" while North Carolina [N.C. Gen. Stat. § 14.360(b)] defines it as "committed intentionally and with malice or bad motive."

Several states define *torture* in terms of its intended and ultimate effect on the victim. Illinois [510 Ill. Comp. Stat. Ann. 70/3.03] defines it as acts "motivated by an intent to increase or prolong the pain, suffering or agony of the animal." Similarly, Indiana [Ind. Code § 35-46-3-12(b),(c)] defines it as acts that "inflict upon the animal severe physical pain with a depraved or sadistic intent to cause prolonged suffering or death." Florida [Fla. Stat. Ann. § 828.12], Ohio [Ohio Rev. Code Ann. § 1717.01] and Wyoming [Wyo. Stat. Ann. § 181] all describe torture in terms of pain or suffering that is "allowed to continue when there is reasonable remedy or relief."

In general, definitions that are based more on objective documented medical evaluations of physical harm and suffering are easier to communicate to the triers of fact in a criminal case than attempts to determine the underlying mindset of a suspect. However, the nature of the injuries that are documented, such as mutilations, burning, multiple types of injuries, etc., can be used to strengthen the assertion that such harm is the result of excessive, repeated or prolonged mistreatment.

What Is an "Animal"?

Among the many definitional challenges facing investigators and prosecutors, perhaps the most unusual is the most basic: what is an *animal*? The supposedly simple task of determining which animals are protected by law is often open to question and adds to the many significant challenges in prosecuting crimes against animals (Patronek, 1997; Lockwood, 2006).

Some states provide no definition of what an animal is, leaving the definition open to the courts. Others go to great lengths to include or exclude animals subject to anti-cruelty laws. For example, Iowa denies legal protection to many species by excluding game, fur-bearing animals, fish, reptiles, and amphibians. Alaska's statutes apply to any vertebrate living creature not a human being or fish. Maryland's laws apply to "any living creature except a human being." Delaware excludes fish, crustaceans, and mollusks. Arkansas and Mississippi include "every living creature." Colorado statutes apply to "any living dumb creature." New Jersey animals are "the whole brute creation." Connecticut's definition applies to "all brute creatures and birds." Georgia excludes fish and pests "that might be exterminated or removed from a business, residence or other structure."

Wisconsin's statutes pertain to reptiles, amphibians, and warm-blooded creatures besides man. Wyoming's statutes (in the "Offenses Against Property" chapter) do not define "animal," but do define "household pet" cruelty as affecting "any privately owned dog, cat, rabbit, guinea pig, hamster, mouse, gerbil, ferret, bird, fish, reptile, amphibian, invertebrate or any other species of domesticated animal sold, transferred or retained for the purpose of being kept as a pet in or near a house."

Louisiana defines "cruel," "abandon," "proper food," "proper water," "proper shelter," and "proper veterinary care," but fails to define "animal." Likewise, Kentucky's criminal code (in the chapter for "Riot, Disorderly Conduct and Related Offenses"), and West Virginia's law (in the "Crimes Against Chastity, Morality and Decency" section), provide no definitions.

Some definitions offer intriguing statutory contradictions. In one section of its criminal code [§ 47-1-10], South Carolina defines an animal as "a living vertebrate creature except a homo sapien" but a later section [§ 47-1-40c] states, "This section does not apply to fowl." However, cockfighting was recently made a misdemeanor offense under § 16-17-650 (2010). The Texas criminal code defines an animal as "a domesticated living creature and wild living creature previously captured," unless that capture was accomplished by cruel means. These distinctions may seem trivial, but the ability to pursue a case may hinge on whether an animal alleged to have been mistreated is defined as an "animal." For example, in a celebrated Texas case a number of years ago, a jury acquitted two Baylor University students who shot and mutilated a stray cat because state law did not include feral cats as being owned and domesticated, and consequently were not covered by the statute.

However, even in the absence of appropriate definitions, prosecutions may succeed. Marquis (1996) described the case of a man who killed Victor, a 26-pound lobster, while stealing him from an aquarium in Oregon whose cruelty statute defines an animal as "any nonhuman mammal, bird, reptile, amphibian or fish." Even though crustaceans are not specifically included, prosecutors were able to obtain a conviction for theft and cruelty to animals.

Defenses and Exemptions

Bowing to political and public pressures, legislatures frequently exempt certain acts that are perceived to be justifiable based upon their potential to improve public health, safety, and often the economy. Arizona's criminal code, for example, exempts from the criminal statutes activities involving the possession, training, exhibition, or use of an animal in the otherwise lawful pursuits of hunting, ranching, farming, rodeos, shows, and security services [§ 13.2910.05]. Wyoming's law exempts rodeos and industry-accepted agricultural and livestock practices [§ 6-3-203]. South Carolina specifically exempts accepted animal husbandry practices of farm operations, the training of animals, the practice of veterinary medicine, agricultural practices, forestry, and silvicultural practices, wildlife management practices, and training dogs for hunting [§ 47-1-10].

Some exemptions seem appropriate: Kansas, like many states, exempts a person from charges of cruelty for killing in self-defense any animal found outside of the property of its owner or custodian which is injuring or posing a threat to any person, farm animal, or property [§ 21-4310]. Similarly, Georgia's statutes do not pertain to a person defending his or her person, property, livestock or poultry, or that of another, from injury or damage being caused by an animal, provided that "the method used to injure or kill such animal shall be designed to be as humane as is possible under the circumstances" [§ 16-12-4].

Other exemptions, however, appear somewhat more frivolous. Alabama § 13A-11-246 exempts a person who shoots a dog or cat with a BB gun not capable of inflicting serious injury when the dog or cat is defecating or urinating on the person's property.

It has been argued that anti-cruelty statutes, while noble in theory, are ineffective in practice because they exempt the majority of modern practices that allegedly exploit the most numerically significant number of animals. Broad exemptions for customary practices of intensive animal agriculture, bona fide laboratory experimentation, hunting, and other institutional or socially-sanctioned activities are said to weaken the intent of the laws (Ibrahim, 2006).

Conclusion

The animal welfare field has made considerable strides in recent years to enhance the ability to investigate and prosecute cases of animal maltreatment. According to the Animal Legal Defense Fund (aldf.org), as of this writing, 150 law schools in the U.S. offer curriculum courses in animal law. All 50 states have enacted statutes categorizing certain acts of animal maltreatment as felonies. Many police departments have humane law investigators, and a growing number of prosecutors' offices have created animal cruelty task forces to handle the increasing caseload and highly specialized work involved in animal cruelty cases (Benetato, Reisman, & McCobb, 2011).

Despite such notable advances, however, the field continues to be hampered by nomenclature rooted in 19th century perspectives that reflected the property status and commercial value of animals, and that required establishing that perpetrators committed cruel acts with willful or malicious intent. The definitional limitations of state statutes, coupled with a lack of training of law enforcement and veterinary professionals in documenting animal cruelty, make the prosecution of animal cruelty cases difficult, with relatively few investigated cases taken to trial and resulting in convictions (Sinclair, Merck, & Lockwood, 2006).

Effective response to animal abuse and neglect requires a community-wide, holistic approach. Greater efforts should be made to strengthen and standardize definitions of animal cruelty. The public must be better informed about what constitutes animal cruelty and how to report it. Police need to be better-trained about existing laws protecting animals and the tools for effectively processing crime scenes in which animals are both victims and evidence. Veterinarians need better training in forensics, recognition, and documentation of cruelty, and the presentation of such evidence in court. They also should have universal exemption from civil and criminal liability when providing good-faith testimony in animal cruelty cases. Prosecutors need training and assistance in building strong animal cruelty cases and making proper use of testimony from veterinarians and humane law enforcement. Finally, judges need additional training about the importance of animal cruelty as a serious and often violent crime and the appropriateness of the strong public concern that is often voiced in these cases. Fortunately, many national animal protection and law enforcement organizations have increased efforts to address all of these concerns. Such efforts will play an important role in protecting animals and people alike.

References

Arkow, P. (2006). "Old wine in a new bottle": New strategies for humane education. In A.H. Fine (Ed.), *Handbook on animal-assisted therapy: Theoretical foundations and guidelines for practice* (2nd Ed., pp. 425–452). San Diego, CA: Academic Press.

Arkow, P. (2005). Multidisciplinary prevention and interventions: Animal abuse and family violence. *Animal Anti-Cruelty League Newsletter* (Johannesburg, South Africa), 2, 1–6.

Arkow, P. (2003). *Breaking the cycles of violence: A guide to multi-disciplinary interventions. A handbook for child protection, domestic violence and animal protection agencies.* Alameda, CA: Latham Foundation.

Arkow, P., Boyden, P., & Patterson-Kane, E. (2011). *Practical guidance for the effective response by veterinarians to suspected animal cruelty, abuse and neglect.* Schaumburg, IL: American Veterinary Medical Association.

Arkow, P, & Munro, H. (2008). The veterinary profession's roles in recognizing and preventing family violence: The experiences of the human medicine field and the development of diagnostic indicators of Non-Accidental Injury. In F.R. Ascione (Ed.), *International handbook of animal abuse and cruelty: Theory, research, and application* (pp. 31–58). West Lafayette, IN: Purdue University Press.

Ascione, F.R. (1993). Children who are cruel to animals: A review of research and implications for developmental psychopathology. *Anthrozoös,* 6(4), 226–247.

Ascione, F.R., & Shapiro, K. (2009). People and animals, kindness and cruelty: Research directions and policy implications. *Journal of Social Issues,* 65(3), 569–587.

Association of Shelter Veterinarians. (2010). *Guidelines for Standards of Care in Animal Shelters.* Accessed 05/01/12 at http://sheltervet.org/associations/4853/files/Standards%20final%20bookmarks_with%20security.pdf.

Basler, R.P. (Ed.). (2001). *Abraham Lincoln: His speeches and writings.* Cambridge, MA: Da Capo Press.

Beetz, A.M. (2008). Bestiality and zoophilia: A discussion of sexual contact with animals. In F.R. Ascione, (Ed.), *International handbook of animal abuse and cruelty: Theory, research, and application* (pp. 201–220). West Lafayette, IN: Purdue University Press.

Beetz, A. M., & Podberscek, A. L. (Eds.) (2005). *Bestiality and zoophilia: Sexual relations with animals.* West Lafayette, IN: Purdue University Press.

Beirne, P. (1997). Rethinking bestiality: Towards a concept of interspecies sexual assault. *Theoretical Criminology,* 1(3), 317–340.

Benetato, M.A., Reisman, R., & McCobb, E. (2011). The veterinarian's role in animal cruelty cases. *Journal of the American Veterinary Medical Association,* 238(1), 31–34.

Bentham, J. (1789).*The principles of morals and legislation.* Reprinted in T. Regan & P. Singer (Eds.) (1976), *Animal rights and human obligations* (pp. 129–130). Princeton, NJ: Prentice Hall.

Black's Law Dictionary Free Online 2nd Ed. (2012). Accessed 05/12/2012 at http://thelawdictionary.org/cruelty-to-animals/#ixzz1mfyh4k4x.

Blood, D.C., & Studdert, V.P. (1999). *Saunders comprehensive veterinary dictionary* (2nd Ed.). London: W.B. Saunders.

Crook, A. (2000). The CVMA animal abuse position—how we got here. *Canadian Veterinary Journal,* 41, 631–633.

Donley, L., Patronek, G.J. & Luke, C. (1999). Animal abuse in Massachusetts: A summary of case reports at the MSPCA and attitudes of Massachusetts veterinarians. *Journal of Applied Animal Welfare Science,* 2(1), 59–73.

Farm Animal Welfare Council. (2009) *Farm animal welfare in Great Britain: Past, present and future.* Accessed 05/12/2012 at www.fawc.org.uk/pdf/ppfreport091012.pdf.

Favre, D., & Tsang, V. (1993). The development of anti-cruelty laws during the 1800s. *Detroit College of Law Review,* 1, 1–35.

Felthous, A. R., & Kellert, S. R.(1987). Psychosocial aspects of selecting animal species for physical abuse. *Journal of Forensic Science,* 32, 1713–1723.

Francione, G.L. (1995). *Animals, property and the law.* Philadelphia: Temple University Press.

Frasch, P.D. (2008). The impact of improved American anti-cruelty laws in the investigation, prosecution, and sentencing of abusers. In F.R. Ascione (Ed.), *International handbook of animal abuse and cruelty: Theory, research, and application* (pp. 59–86). West Lafayette, IN: Purdue University Press.

Harp, C. (2002) *Bringing balance to juvenile justice.* Alexandria, VA: American Prosecutors Research Institute.

Harrison, R. (1964). *Animal machines: The factory farming industry.* London: Vincent Stuart.

Hawaii State Legislature (1998). Senate Standing Committee Report No. 3222, Conference Committee Report No. 87.

Henneke, D. R. (1995). A condition scoring system for horses. *Equine Practitioner, 7,* 14–16.

Humane Society of the United States (2004). *Making the connection: What veterinary professionals need to know.* Washington, DC: Author [brochure].

Ibrahim, D.M. (2006). The anti-cruelty statute: A study in animal welfare. *Journal of Animal Law and Ethics, 1,* 175–203.

King, M. (1998). Red flag: Signs of animal abuse. *Veterinary Product News, 10*(1), 18–21.

Kurst-Swanger, K. (2007). Animal abuse: The link to family violence. In, N.A. Jackson (Ed.), *Encyclopedia of domestic violence,* (pp. 22–29). New York: Routledge.

Lacroix, C. A. (1999). Another weapon for combating family violence: Prevention of animal abuse. In F.R. Ascione & P. Arkow, (Eds.), *Child abuse, domestic violence, and animal abuse: Linking the circles of compassion for prevention and intervention* (pp. 62–80). West Lafayette, IN: Purdue University Press.

LaRene, S. (1987). *Handbook of animal cruelty law* (3rd Ed. Rev.) Detroit: Michigan Humane Society.

Lockwood, R. (2006). *Animal cruelty prosecution: Opportunities for early response to crime and interpersonal violence.* Alexandria, VA: American Prosecutors Research Institute.

Marquis, J. (1996). The Kittles case and its aftermath. *Animal Law, 2,* 197–201.

Morgan, K. (1983). An overview of animal-related organizations with some guidelines for recognizing patterns. *Community Animal Control, 2*(2), 18–19.

Munro, H. M. C., & Thrusfield, M. V. (2001a). Battered pets: Features that raise suspicion of non-accidental injury. *Journal of Small Animal Practice, 42,* 218–226.

Munro, H.M.C., & Thrusfield, M.V. (2001b). Battered pets: Non-accidental physical injuries found in dogs and cats. *Journal of Small Animal Practice, 42,* 279–290.

Munro, H.M.C., & Thrusfield, M.V. (2001c). Battered pets: Sexual abuse. *Journal of Small Animal Practice, 42,* 333–337.

Munro, H.M.C., & Thrusfield, M.V. (2001d). Battered pets: Munchausen Syndrome by Proxy. *Journal of Small Animal Practice, 42,* 385–389.

Patronek, G. (2008). Animal hoarding: A third dimension of animal abuse. In F.R. Ascione (Ed.), *International handbook of animal abuse and cruelty: Theory, research, and application* (pp. 221–246). West Lafayette, IN: Purdue University Press.

Patronek, G. (1998). Issues and guidelines for veterinarians in recognizing, reporting and assessing animal neglect and abuse. In, P. Olson (Ed.), *Recognizing & reporting animal abuse: A veterinarian's guide* (pp. 25–39). Englewood, CO: American Humane Association.

Patronek, G. (1997). Issues for veterinarians in recognizing and reporting animal neglect and abuse. *Society and Animals, 5*, 267–280.

Patronek, G.J. & Weiss, K.J. (2011). *Animal hoarding: A neglected problem at the intersection of psychiatry, veterinary medicine, and law.* Report on Findings from the Henderson House Interdisciplinary Workgroup, Weston, MA, July 26, 2011.

Patterson-Kane, E.G., & Piper, H. (2009). Animal abuse as a sentinel for human violence: A critique. *Journal of Social Issues, 65*(3), 589–614.

Primatt, H. (1776). *The duty of mercy.* Reprinted in R.D. Ryder (Ed.) (1992). Fontwell, United Kingdom: Centaur Press.

Regan, T., & Singer, P. (Eds.) (1976). *Animal rights and human obligations.* Princeton, NJ: Prentice-Hall.

Rowan, A. N. (1999). Cruelty and abuse to animals: A typology. In F. R. Ascione & P. Arkow (Eds.), *Child abuse, domestic violence, and animal abuse: Linking the circles of compassion for prevention and intervention* (pp. 328–334). West Lafayette, IN: Purdue University Press.

Sinclair, L., Merck, M., & Lockwood, R. (2006). *Forensic investigation of animal cruelty: A guide for veterinary and law enforcement professionals.* Washington, DC: Humane Society of the U.S.

Unti, B. (2008). Cruelty indivisible: Historical perspectives on the link between cruelty to animals and interpersonal violence. In F.R. Ascione (Ed.), *International handbook of animal abuse and cruelty: Theory, research, and application* (pp. 7–30). West Lafayette, IN: Purdue University Press.

Vermeulen, H., & Odendaal, J. S.J. (1993). Proposed typology of companion animal abuse. *Anthrozoös, 6*, 248–257.

Wathes, C. (2010, April 10). Lives worth living? *Veterinary Record*, p. 468.

Chapter 2

The History of Anti-Cruelty Laws: Concepts of Animal Welfare and Animal Rights

David Favre

Laws reflect both social awareness and social concern at the time of their adoption. When laws are enacted, a threshold of political consideration has been passed and society has new expectations about a topic. This is certainly the case with the issue of how our society considers and treats the animals that live among us. The history of the anti-cruelty laws shows a conceptual breakthrough in social thinking in the United States, beginning with the adoption of the 1867 New York cruelty law. This law, which was replicated in other states in the following decades, remains as a statement of social contract between humans and animals: we humans may use animals, but in so doing, we shall not inflict unnecessary pain and suffering. This basic contract remains the cornerstone of the law, but there has been a shift of what constitutes *unnecessary* in favor of at least some animals.

The unfolding of this story provides a full context for the exploration of the concepts of animal welfare and cruelty. Having developed the concept of animal welfare, the concept of animal rights, as a new social contract, will also be considered. This view asserts that animals deserve a more robust and visible presence in the legal system, not otherwise supported under animal welfare concepts.

In the Beginnings, Just Property

Prior to 1800 in both the United States and England, economically useful animals, such as horses or sheep, had the legal status of being property, while others, like dogs, did not exist in the eyes of the law and had no legal status. If a person possessed a dog, and a stranger harmed the dog, the possessor could do nothing about it in a court of law. If the dog was not property, then no legal action could be filed concerning the dog. The possessor had no legal rights concerning the dog. If, on the other hand, a person possessed a sheep or a horse, the animals were considered of value, were bought and sold, and therefore were considered personal property in the eyes of the law. As personal property, the possessor/owner could sue another individual for the value of his animal if the animal were harmed or killed. The human could also sue for the return of the animal if it were stolen. Additionally, the government could bring criminal charges against the human who harmed or stole the horse or sheep (but not for a dog).

One case under the Minnesota law shows the different outcomes under the law for different species. A defendant was indicted for the shooting of a dog under the criminal statute providing penalties for "[e]very person who shall wilfully and maliciously kill, maim or disfigure any horses, cattle or other beasts of another person."[1]

The court directed that the charges be dismissed, holding that no crime had been committed as a dog could not be considered a beast.

> [I]t seems to me, that all [animals] such as have, in law, no value, were not intended to be included in that general term.... The term beasts may well be intended to include asses, mules, sheep and swine and perhaps, some other domesticated animals, but it would be going quite too far to hold that dogs were intended.[2]

Thus, only animals of social/economic value, those used in the production and movement of goods, were acknowledged to exist in the eyes of the law. The quoted law above was passed not for the benefit of the animals, but for the benefit of the owner of the animal. It would not be appropriate to consider this an anti-cruelty law or a reflection of the idea of animal welfare.

While moving into the category of property was a good thing for these limited numbers of animals, as some negative human conduct might be restrained, the law really did not see these special animals any differently than the wagons they pulled. Both were simply personal property. That the horse was alive and the wagon was not alive was not particularly noticed by the law. Additionally, the rights of the human owner were not distinguished if the property in question was a wagon or a horse. The owner might take good care of both or he might not. He might chop up the wagon or the horse; the law was mute. The lawmakers, reflecting the views of their citizens, did not think it appropriate to interfere with a man's use of his property. (At this time, the law also had almost nothing to say about a man's use of his children or his slaves, where they were allowed.)

Before considering the transformation of law in the United States, it is informative to review the corresponding evolution of law in Britain.

The British Set the Stage

Notwithstanding the political independence that the United States obtained from Great Britain during the late 1700s and 1800s, there was still a considerable transfer of ideas from the intellectually mature mother country to the newly formed, and basically frontier, United States. Early articulations of concern for the moral and legal status of animals appeared in British writing.[3] Reverend Humphrey Primatt in *A Dissertation on the Duty of Mercy and Sin of Cruelty to Brute Animals,* written in 1776, pleaded for the care of animals.

> See that no brute of any kind ... whether intrusted to thy care, or coming in thy way, suffer thy neglect or abuse. Let no views of profit, no compliance with

---

1. United States v. Gideon, 1 Minn. 292, 296 (1856).
2. *Id.*
3. For a fuller discussion of the English debate about duty toward animals, see Roderick F. Nash, The Rights of Nature 16–25 (Madison Wisconsin: University of Wisconsin Press 1989); James Turner, Reckoning with the Beast: Animals, Pain and Humanity in the Victorian Mind (Baltimore: John Hopkins Press 1980).

custom, and no fear of ridicule of the world, ever tempt thee to the least act of cruelty or injustice to any creature whatsoever. But let this be your invariable rule, everywhere, and at all times, to do unto others as, in their condition, you would be done unto.[4]

Jeremy Bentham, an English barrister, was one of the few legal writers who addressed the issue of animals and the legal system. His *Introduction to the Principles of Morals and Legislation*[5] (1781) was closely studied at the time by a large number of individuals, some of whom went on to propose legislation for the protection of animals. Bentham argued that there was no reason why animals should not be accorded protection under the law. Bentham pointed out that animals, "on account of their interests having been neglected by the insensibility of the ancient jurists, stand degraded into the class of *things*."[6] Within a footnote entitled "Interests of the inferior animals improperly neglected in legislation," as noted in Chapter 1 of this text, Bentham argued that the capacity for suffering is the vital characteristic that gives a being the right to legal consideration. The final sentence of the footnote is often used today as a rallying cry for those seeking to promote the cause of animal rights. "The question is not, Can they *reason*? nor, Can they *talk*? But, *Can they suffer?*"[7]

Having made the intellectual arguments for concern about animals, the British followed up with changes to the legal system. On May 15, 1809, Lord Erskine addressed Parliament in support of the bill he had introduced for the protection of animals.[8] This may represent the first time animal protection was seriously debated by a full legislative body. In his address, Lord Erskine stated:

> They (animals) are created, indeed, for our use, but not for our abuse. Their freedom and enjoyment, when they cease to be consistent with our just dominions and enjoyment, can be no part of their natures; but whilst they are consistent I say their rights, subservient as they are, ought to be as sacred as our own ... the bill I propose to you, if it shall receive the sanction of Parliament, will not only be an honor to the country, but an era in the history of the world.[9]

The bill passed in the House of Lords, but was defeated in the House of Commons.

Some thirteen years later the battle was taken up again, this time by Richard Martin.[10] On June 10, 1822, he succeeded in obtaining passage of a law known as "Dick Martin's Act ... An Act to Prevent the Cruel and Improper Treatment of Cattle." As compromise was necessary for its passage, the law protected only animals "of another"; it was a limited first step. It was made illegal for any person to "wantonly and cruelly beat or ill-treat [any] horse, mare, gelding, mule, ass, ox, cow, heifer, steer, sheep or other cattle...." The law imposed a "fine of not more than five pounds or less than ten shillings, or imprisonment

---

4. SYDNEY H. COLEMAN, HUMANE SOCIETY LEADERS IN AMERICA 18 (Albany NY: The American Humane Society 1924) (quoting REV. HUMPHREY PRIMATT, A DISSERTATION ON THE DUTY OF MERCY AND SIN OF CRUELTY TO BRUTE ANIMALS (London 1776)).

5. JEREMY BENTHAM, AN INTRODUCTION TO THE PRINCIPLES OF MORALS AND LEGISLATION (Oxford: Clarendon Press 1781).

6. BENTHAM, *supra* note 5, at 311 (emphasis in original).

7. *Id.*

8. COLEMAN, *supra* note 4, at 20–21.

9. *Id.* at 21–22 (quoting LORD ERSKINE, ADDRESS TO PARLIAMENT (1809)). For a few more details see RICHARD D. RYDER, ANIMAL REVOLUTION 81–88 (Oxford, Basil Blackwell,1989).

10. Richard Martin was a flamboyant duelist who served in the British House of Commons for 25 years. He would go on to be a co-founder of a humane society which in time would become the present day Royal Society for the Protection of Animals. Ryder, *supra* note 9, at 84–92.

not exceeding three months."[11] From the language of the law, it is clear that the purpose of the law is to protect the listed animals from being "cruelly beat or ill-treated," rather than protecting the property interests of the owner. In the decades following the adoption of this law, an organization was formed in London that would become the Royal Society for the Protection of Animals and be an inspiration for animal advocate Henry Bergh several decades later.

New Concerns in America

Representative of the first wave of anti-cruelty laws in the United States was the New York law of 1829:

> §26 Every person who [part one] shall maliciously kill, maim or wound any horse, ox or other cattle, or any sheep, belonging to another, or [part two] shall maliciously and cruelly beat or torture any such animals, whether belonging to himself or another, shall, upon conviction, be adjudged guilty of a misdemeanor.[12]

The criminal prohibitions consist of two distinct aspects. The first part is qualified with the phrase "belonging to another" while the second is qualified "belonging to himself or another." The purpose of the first part is to provide protection for private property, while the second deals with cruelty to the animal regardless of ownership. The two parts prohibit very different actions. In the first part, the legislature has made criminal those actions which would most likely interfere with the commercial value of the animal: killing, maiming, or wounding. In the second part, the legislature has focused upon that which might be perceived as causing pain and suffering to the animal: beatings and torture.

The level of concern for the welfare of animals expressed by this legislation was modest and can be thought of as a small conceptual box. Consider this animal welfare box to have three dimensions. The first dimension is the number of species included in the protection of the statute. The second is the actions (or inactions) of the human that are made illegal. The third is the extent of the punishment that might be imposed under the criminal law. The above New York law has a very short list of species. It was not yet illegal to torture a dog or a bear. The dog is not the right species; a bear is not only not a listed species, but is not owned by a human. The legislature had not yet made the conceptual bridge that, if it is wrong to cruelly torture a cow, it should also be wrong to torture a cat or dog. The only acts made illegal are cruel beatings and torture. This is an early use of that critical word "cruel." This will be focused upon later in the chapter, but note that there is no definition of the term in this statute; it is used as a qualifier of the action "beat." A jury would have the responsibility to decide if a fact pattern was or was not a cruel beating.

The grading of the crime is a misdemeanor.[13] While the legislature decided that their concern for animals would only result in minor punishment, some additional insight on

---

11. *Id.* For a full discussion of the English law with quotes and references, see Davis v. American Soc'y for the Prevention of Cruelty to Animals, 75 N.Y. 362 (1873).

12. N.Y. Rev. stat. tit. 6, §26 (1829).

13. The gradings of crimes are divided into two categories, felonies and misdemeanors. Felonies represent the potential for a sentence of more than a year in a state prison and have consequences afterward, such as limitations on the right to vote. Misdemeanors are commonly punished by less than one year in a local jail, and usually have no long-term consequences beyond the punishment itself.

legislative attitude can be obtained from reviewing other criminal laws of that time period and the level of punishments that were set by the legislature. For instance, under a Pennsylvania statute of 1860, it was a misdemeanor, with a maximum fine of two hundred dollars, to cruelly beat a horse.[14] In the same state code, to expose and abandon one's own child under the age of seven was also a misdemeanor, but with a maximum fine of one hundred dollars.

The Bergh Era Begins

The life of Henry Bergh is set out elsewhere and will not be repeated here.[15] Bergh's impact on the legal world began in 1866. After his return from a trip to Europe, where he observed both the cruelty inflicted upon animals and the efforts of the Royal Society for the Protection of Animals on behalf of animals, he became focused upon animal cruelty issues in New York City. Because of his social and political connections, it was not difficult for him to approach the New York legislature with proposed legislation.

While not a lawyer, Henry Bergh was able to direct the drafting of legislation. He understood that the mere passage of animal welfare legislation would be insufficient. Without dedicated enforcement, the laws would never actually reach out and touch the lives of the animals about which he was concerned. Therefore, beside the drafting and passage of new criminal laws, he sought the charter of an organization which, like the Royal Society in London, would be dedicated to the implementation of the law. He asked the New York Legislature for a state-wide charter for the American Society for the Prevention of Cruelty to Animals (ASPCA), whose purpose, as set forth in its by-laws, was

> ... [t]o provide effective means for the prevention of cruelty to animals throughout the United States, to enforce all laws which are now, or may hereafter be, enacted for the protection of animals and to secure, by lawful means, the arrest and conviction of all persons violating such laws.[16]

This was granted on April 10, 1866. Henry Bergh was unanimously elected as the ASPCA's first president, a position he continued to hold until his death in 1888. In 1866, a new anti-cruelty law was also passed by the state legislature with the urging of Henry Bergh, but this was just a stepping stone to the milestone law that was passed the next year. This law of 1867 will be the focus of consideration.[17] The 1867 Act is relatively short, and is provided in Appendix A to this chapter. A summary of some of the key provisions follows.

A significant expansion of our animal welfare box is realized with this law as two of the three dimensions increased in their dimension. Section 1 defined animal as "any living creature." This marvelously sweeping statement finally eliminated the restriction that legal protection was only for animals of commercial value. One might rightly ask: did they really mean any living creature? The answer is no. While not having direct evidence of what they were thinking, it is most likely that the legislature, without much deep thought about what they were doing, was thinking mammals. The ASPCA itself, in the decades

---

14. Pa. Laws tit. IV, § 46 (1860).
15. Materials on the early events of Bergh's life are set out in COLEMAN, *supra* note 4, at 33–35; Clara Morris, *Riddle of the Nineteenth Century: Mr. Henry Bergh*, in 18 MCCLURE 414, 422 (1902).
16. AMERICAN SOCIETY FOR THE PREVENTION OF CRUELTY TO ANIMALS, 1905 ANNUAL REPORT 144 (New York, 1906).
17. N.Y. REV. STAT. §§ 375.2-.9 (1867).

afterwards, sought to use the law primarily when mammals were at issue. The most unexpected animal they brought an action about were sea turtles that were tied to the deck of a ship, on their backs, being shipped from Florida. Additionally, note that all provisions of this law applied regardless of the ownership status of the animal.

The list of illegal acts greatly expanded upon prior laws to include: overdriving, overloading, torturing, tormenting, depriving of necessary sustenance, unnecessarily or cruelly beating, and needlessly mutilating or killing. However, the punishment remained a misdemeanor. So, two of the three dimensions were significantly expanded.

This law was much more comprehensive than prior laws. Whereas prior laws were usually just one section, this law had ten sections. These additional sections went beyond the general language of the first section, and addressed specific issues. To address the ongoing problems of animals being forced to fight each other, often to their death, Section 2 of the 1867 New York Act made animal fighting illegal. While specifically identifying bull, bear, dog and cock fighting, it applied to any animal fight. The ownership and keeping of fighting animals, as well as the management of the fights themselves, was illegal. This may well have been the first state law to prohibit animal fighting. Note that for this issue it is not a jury question as to whether such an action is cruel. The legislature made the judgment itself, prohibiting all animal fighting. The jury would only have to decide if animal fighting were present, not whether it was cruel.

Also for the first time, Section 4 of this law imposed a duty to provide "sufficient quality of good and wholesome food and water" upon anyone who kept (impounded) an animal. More than likely the common sight of starving horses in the alleys of New York provided political support for the adoption of this provision. Note that this is fundamentally different from the other provisions of the law, in that it requires a human to act rather than requiring a human to not act in a particular way. As will be seen below, it will be over a century before this provision is expanded under modern duty to provide care provisions as we see today in animal welfare laws. Just as important from a practical enforcement perspective, the new law allowed any persons, even the ASPCA, to enter private premises and care for the animal's needs. This was a very practical provision which allowed immediate help to the animals regardless of whether criminal charges were later brought against the owner or keeper.

Another first for this legislation was its concern about the transportation of animals. Section 5 made it illegal to transport "any creature in a cruel or inhuman manner." Besides making the act a crime, it empowered the taking away by officials, such as ASPCA officers, any animal being transported cruelly.

Section 6 is a curious provision requiring the registration of dogs used by businesses for the pulling of loads. The registration number was to be placed on the vehicle being pulled by the dog.[18] Perhaps this was to make identification of owners easier. Large dogs were the poor man's horse at this time.

Section 7 of the 1867 Act made illegal the abandonment of any "maimed, sick, infirm or disabled creature." Under the previous law it was not at all clear what could be done with an abandoned animal. Given that there was almost no such thing as veterinarian care at this time, an abandoned animal such as a horse in an alley of New York, would simply be in pain and suffer until death came. Under this law, a magistrate, or the captain of the police, could authorize the destruction of such a creature, providing the most humane option available at the time.

---

18. *Id.* §6.

Focusing on the issue of enforcement, Mr. Bergh must have realized that the normal police forces could not be counted upon to seriously and vigorously enforce this new law. Therefore, Section 8 specifically provided that agents of the ASPCA with appointment by the sheriff had the power to arrest violators of the adopted law. This delegation of state criminal authority to a private organization was, and is, truly extraordinary. This, more than any other aspect of the 1867 Act, reflected the political power and trust that Bergh must have had within the city of New York and in the state capital. Another unusual provision was the requirement that all collected fines would be given to the ASPCA, the pragmatic Bergh again at work.[19] For the first twelve months of the society's existence, 66 convictions were secured out of 119 prosecutions, and more than $296 from criminal fines went to the operation of the society.[20] So while violations of the law remained misdemeanors, the likelihood of actual enforcement was greatly enhanced under this law.

With the threat of actual enforcement of meaningful anti-cruelty statutes came the first lobbying for an exemption from the law. Section 10 of the Act provided an exemption for "properly conducted scientific experiments or investigations," at a medical college or the University of the State of New York. Thus, one of the more heated debates about animal use of today must have been carried out over 120 years ago in the New York Legislature. Note that there is not an exception for hunting and trapping. Most likely it was not even conceivable to the legislature that anyone could suggest there was illegality in such acts; indeed, there is no sign from the annual reports of the ASPCA that they had any concern about the issue of hunting or trapping.

With this 1867 Act, an ethical concern for the plight of animals was transformed for the first time into comprehensive legislation. The focus of social concern was on the animals themselves. While it is not known who drafted the specific words used, the language was visionary in scope while addressing a number of specific, pragmatic points.

Enforcement on the Streets of New York

A law is meaningless unless it directs or controls the conduct of individuals. For this to happen the laws must be enforced. This is normally the responsibility of the police and prosecutors, but Henry Bergh realized early on that if the law were to have any meaning in the streets of New York, where the animals lived and suffered, it was up to him and his newly formed ASPCA. He had the power to arrest lawbreakers, normally reserved for the police, and was appointed a prosecutor in New York so that he could also argue for the conviction of the criminals before a judge. It is a testament to the character of Henry Bergh that this extraordinary power of the state, vested in one private individual, was apparently never abused or wrongly used. It was, however, aggressively used.

The first case for which Mr. Bergh obtained a successful prosecution under the new statute dealt with the method by which sheep and calves were transported to the "shambles" (slaughter houses). In this case, the animals had their four feet tied together and were put into carts on top of one another like so many sacks for transportation. The ASPCA brought charges, obtaining a conviction and a ten dollar fine.[21]

---

19. AMERICAN SOCIETY FOR THE PREVENTION OF CRUELTY TO ANIMALS, 1867 ANNUAL REPORT 47–54 (1867) [hereinafter REPORT 1867].
20. *Id.*, 47–54.
21. REPORT 1867, *supra* note 18, at 4, 47; *See* COLEMAN, *supra* note 4, at 42.

A landmark case which brought the ASPCA and Mr. Bergh to the attention of the general public in the first year was focused upon sea turtles.[22] As described by Sydney Coleman:

> But the general public was still apathetic and Mr. Bergh longed for some case that would turn the spotlight on the society and give it space on the front page of the newspapers. The discovery of a boatload of live turtles that had been shipped from Florida on their backs, with their flippers pierced and tied together with strings, offered this opportunity. When the captain of the vessel refused to turn the turtles over, Mr. Bergh caused his arrest, together with the members of his crew. They were taken to the Tombs, but were later acquitted of cruelty by the court.... The judge, before whom the case was tried, told Bergh to go home and mind his own business. Some of the newspapers charged him with being overzealous and many abused him roundly. A lengthy satire in the *New York Herald*, a few days later, set all New York talking. For a time, James Gordon Bennett continued to systematically ridicule Bergh and his society, but later the two men became personal friends and the *Herald* one of the staunchest supporters of the movement. The final outcome of the turtle case was to greatly increase the number of supporters and friends of the new society.[23]

During the first year, a number of different types of cruelty situations were addressed by Mr. Bergh. One of the most abusive dealt with the horses used to pull the omnibuses and street railways of the time.[24] Other topics included concern about adulterated food for horses and cattle and transportation of cattle by railroad. Bergh also fought to eliminate dog and cock fights. Bergh opened a vigorous fight against these cruelties, even instigating raids.

The Ripple Effect

The New York law would not have happened but for the energy and drive of Henry Bergh, and his actions clearly struck a responsive chord in a number of individuals around the country. Evidence of the societal readiness for animal protection laws is found in the rapid adoption of the legislation and the creation of animal protection societies around the country (indeed around the world) over the next 25 years. Bergh was the initial catalyst, but the actions in many other states required the work and support of others outside the political power and influence of Bergh. Besides the drafting of the laws, Bergh's other major contribution was the generation of publicity about the issues. Because of the force of his personality and the visible way in which he ran his campaigns against animal cruelty, he was able to generate a large volume of newspaper coverage, first in New York and then around the country.

Within a few years Massachusetts,[25] Pennsylvania,[26] Illinois,[27] New Hampshire,[28] and New Jersey[29] had adopted the same pattern of legislation as that in New York with both

---

22. Report 1867, *supra* note 18, at 5.
23. Coleman, *supra* note 4, at 42–43.
24. People v. Tinsdale, 10 Abb. Pr. (n.s.) 374 (N.Y. 1868).
25. "An Act for the More Effectual Prevention of Cruelty to Animals," Mass. Gen. L., ch. 344 (1869).
26. XXIV Pa. Stat. §§ 7770–7783 (1920).
27. "Prevention of Cruelty to Animals Act," 1869 Ill. Laws § 3.
28. 1878 N.H. Laws § 281.
29. N.J. Rev. Stat. §§ 64–82 (1873).

new criminal laws and the chartered creations of state Societies for the Prevention of Cruelty to Animals (SPCA). As of 1890, thirty-one states had some level of organized Society for the Prevention of Cruelty to Animals.[30] One exception to the pattern is Maryland, which did not adopt any statute until 1890. It then adopted a very short provision which clearly was not based on New York's statute.[31] One legally significant addition to the New York model was a clause used by a number of states which imposed a specific duty on the owner or keeper of an animal to provide it appropriate shelter or protection from the weather.[32] These statutes also tended to use slightly different terminology. While the New York statute consistently referred to "any living creature," other states would use the term "animal" and then would go on to define the term "animal" to include "all brute creatures."[33] Levels of punishment also varied between the states. While New Hampshire and Massachusetts both provided penalties of up to one year in jail and a $250 fine, Michigan provided a maximum of three months in jail and a $100 fine;[34] Illinois had no jail time and a fine of $50 to $100;[35] and Nebraska, whose law protected only domestic animals, had a fine of $5 to $50.[36] Note that the penalty decreased the further west the law traveled; perhaps this reflected a decreasing level of social concern.

Apparently, the legislation was lost on the wagon trains heading for California. In 1872, the California Legislature adopted a law similar to the 1829 New York legislation.[37] It was not until 1900 that California passed the more comprehensive legislation which had been adopted thirty years earlier in New York.[38]

Development of the Concept of Animal Welfare

Twenty years after Bergh started his efforts in New York, Judge Arnold of the Supreme Court of Mississippi provided eloquent words on how the legal system now viewed animals, especially after decades of significant change.

> This statute is for the benefit of animals, as creatures capable of feeling and suffering, and it was intended to protect them from cruelty, without reference to their being property, or to the damages which might thereby be occasioned to their owners....
>
> ... [L]aws, and the enforcement or observance of laws for the protection of dumb brutes from cruelty, are, in my judgment, among the best evidences of the justice and benevolence of men. Such statutes were not intended to interfere, and do not interfere, with the necessary discipline and government of such

---

30. AMERICAN SOCIETY FOR THE PREVENTION OF CRUELTY TO ANIMALS, 1890 ANNUAL REPORT 36. *See generally*, RYDER, *supra* note 8, 171–75 (1989).
31. 1890 MD. LAWS 198.
32. MASS. GEN. L., ch. 344, § 1 (1869).
33. New Hampshire defined animals as "all brute creatures and birds." N.H. REV. STAT. 281.31 (1878).
34. MICH. COMP. LAWS § 285.1 (1929).
35. ILL. STAT. §§ 5a.6–.7 (1869).
36. NEB. STAT. § 67d (1887).
37. CAL. PENAL CODE § 597 (1872).
38. 1900 CAL. STAT. § 154 (amending CAL. PENAL CODE § 597 (1872)).

animals, or place any unreasonable restriction on their use or the enjoyment to be derived from their possession. The common law recognized no rights in such animals, and punished no cruelty to them, except in so far as it affected the right of individuals to such property. Such statutes remedy this defect.... To disregard the rights and feelings of equals, is unjust and ungenerous, but to willfully or wantonly injure or oppress the weak and helpless is mean and cowardly. Human beings have at least some means of protecting themselves against the inhumanity of man,—that inhumanity which 'makes countless thousands mourn,'—but dumb brutes have none. Cruelty to them manifests a vicious and degraded nature, and it tends inevitably to cruelty to men. Animals whose lives are devoted to our use and pleasure, and which are capable, perhaps, of feeling as great physical pain or pleasure as ourselves, deserve, for these considerations alone, kindly treatment. The dominion of man over them, if not a moral trust, has a better significance than the development of malignant passions and cruel instincts. Often their beauty, gentleness and fidelity suggest the reflection that it may have been one of the purposes of their creation and subordination to enlarge the sympathies and expand the better feelings of our race. But, however this may be, human beings should be kind and just to dumb brutes; if for no other reason than to learn how to be kind and just to each other.[39]

This judge's statement reflects the perspective of many. There is a duty to animals beyond the status of property, and the law needs to restrain uncivilized human conduct towards animals.

Judge Shea in a trial opinion of the New York Marine Court from 1873 showed more emphasis on the latter aspect.

It is not correct to assert that the policy of this kind of legislation, especially that which has for its purpose the prevention of cruelty to brutes, is a regulation of the dominion of the private citizen over his own private property merely. It truly has its origin in the intent to save a just standard of humane feeling from being debased by pernicious effects of bad example—the human heart from being hardened by public and frequent exhibitions of cruelty to dumb creatures, committed to the care and which were created for the beneficial use of man.[40]

Terminology and Scope of Animal Welfare

Court opinions give shape and scope to the words of the legislature. They place the issues in the broader social and legal context. Judges, like legislators, usually reflect the attitudes of the times and bring their personal attitudes and beliefs with them when they make decisions. We will move from one state court opinion to another without pause because the laws are so similar in nature, and the issues so fundamental, that there is very little variation in judicial outlook around the country.

One of the functions of the court is to simply confirm the language of the legislature. The courts agreed that the language of the new statutes imposed liability without regard

---

39. *Stephens v. State*, 3 So. 458–59 (Miss. 1887).
40. *Christie v. Bergh*, 15 Abb. Pr. (n.s.) 51 (N.Y. 1873) (this case has been referred to as *The Stage Horse Cases*), available at www.animallaw.info/historical/cases/cahus/15Abbott51.htm.

to the issue of ownership; the provisions applied to one's own animals, to those owned by others, and to animals with unknown or no owners. In *State v. Bruner*,[41] where a man poured turpentine on a live goose and set it afire, the court clarified that under the statute, "a man may be guilty of cruelty to his own animal, or to an animal without any known owner, or to an animal which has in fact no owner." The court also had to clarify that the list of protected animals was, in fact, as broad as the legislature stated. In *Grise v. State*,[42] the court provided one of the first opinions which discussed the cruelty statute with a view toward assessing the types of animals to be afforded protection by the law: animal statutes "embrace all living creatures" and the "abstract rights in all animal creation … from the largest and noblest to the smallest and most insignificant."

Another function of the courts is to provide key definitions of words used in statutes, but left undefined by the legislature. An obviously important term is "cruelty." Although used frequently in every day conversation, its definition, particularly for criminal law purposes, is not so obvious. Combining the opinions of a number of cases, one useful definition of cruelty is: (1) human conduct, by act or omission; (2) which inflicts pain and suffering on a nonhuman animal; and (3) which occurs without legally acceptable justification (by legislative language or socially acceptable custom). It should be remembered that at this time there was very little understanding of the science of pain, or of suffering.

Both at common law and under the statutes adopted, the mere killing of an animal, without more, is not "cruelty." Before the killing of an animal can support a conviction under a cruelty statute, it must be found that the killing was done in a cruel manner.[43] The court in *Horton v. State*[44] held: the mere act of killing an animal, without more, is not cruelty, otherwise one could not slaughter a pig or ox for the market, and man could eat no more meat. Thus, the court held that shooting and almost instantly killing a dog was not a violation of the statute that criminalized the cruel killing of any domestic animal. The court said that the purpose of the statute was not to punish for an offense against property, but to prevent cruelty to animals. To them the word "cruelty," when taken in connection with other offenses proscribed by the statute (torturing, tormenting, mutilating, or cruelly beating), evidently meant something more than to kill. The court in *State v. Neal*[45] defined cruelty to "include every act, etc., whereby unjustifiable physical pain, suffering, or death is caused." The focus should be on the method of death. Did the method impose unnecessary pain or suffering? While it might not be cruel to use a gunshot to obtain death, burning a dog alive would certainly be judged cruel. The death can be acceptable, while the method is not.

Courts have construed "cruelty" to include beating horses;[46] burning a goose;[47] pouring acid on hooves;[48] overworking;[49] starving or depriving a horse of proper shelter;[50] freeing a captive fox in the presence of a pack of hounds and allowing the hounds to tear the fox apart;[51] and passively permitting a dog to attack or kill other dogs.[52] In most criminal

---

41. 104 N.E. 103 (Ind. 1887).
42. 37 Ark. 456 (1881).
43. *See* Horton v. State, 27 So. 468 (Ala. 1900); State v. Neal, 27 S.E. 81 (N.C. 1897).
44. 27 So. 468 (Ala. 1900).
45. 27 S.E. 81 (N.C. 1897).
46. State v. Allison, 90 N.C. 734 (1884).
47. State v. Bruner, 104 N.E. 103 (Ind. 1887).
48. Commonwealth v. Brown, 66 Pa. Super. 519 (1917).
49. State v. Browning, 50 S.E. 185 (S.C. 1905) (hiring out unfit mules).
50. Griffith v. State, 43 S.E. 251 (Ga. 1903).
51. Commonwealth v. Turner, 14 N.E. 130 (Mass. 1887).
52. Commonwealth v. Thorton, 113 Mass. 457 (1873).

cases that are brought to trial, the actions of the defendant (hitting the horse, shooting the cat, etc.) are easily proven. The more difficult question then becomes whether the actions proven in the court violate the existing standards of anti-cruelty. Was the hitting of the horse or shooting of the cat cruel and/or did it cause unnecessary pain, suffering or death? It is also the case that, generally, the courts accept that the animal experiences pain or suffering. Many cases revolve around the third part of the definition, whether or not the action is nevertheless justifiable. Under certain circumstances, cruelty and even torture, are not considered "cruelty" in the legal sense because the activity is "necessary" or "useful." For example, sport hunting, commercial trapping of wildlife, and the use of animals in scientific research are usually allowed to exist, although they clearly inflict pain and suffering.

It is generally recognized that in addition to the need to obtain food or the need for medical experimentation, there are certain other situations in which the infliction of discomfort may, as a practical matter, be accepted by the courts as "necessary." Thus, for example, it may be "necessary" to inflict pain to discipline an animal, or to train it. Discipline and training are proper and lawful ends. Therefore, the infliction of pain or suffering which can be categorized as either of these will usually be excused. In *State v. Avery*,[53] the court held that if the beating of young horses was for the purpose of training, however severe it might be, it would not be considered malicious and would be no offense under the statute. However, if the beating was aggravated by the influence of any evil motive, cruel disposition, violent passions, spirit of revenge, or reckless indifference to the sufferings, the excess pain and suffering caused would be deemed malicious and a violation of the law.

Where the defense is necessity, the defendant bears the burden of proving the necessity. Defense of one's self, or of other persons, would appear to excuse at least some degree of assault upon the offending animal, and there are a multitude of statutes and cases which justify shooting or killing animals, especially dogs, which are attacking the defendant's livestock. The court in *Hodge v. State*[54] held that a cruelty statute was not intended to deprive a man of the right to protect himself, his premises and property, against the intrusions of worthless, mischievous, or vicious animals by such means as are reasonably necessary for that purpose.

As in Henry Bergh's New York statute, sometimes a legislature provides specific exemptions. The first annual report of the ASPCA considered in some detail the pain and suffering of dogs and other animals in medical teaching facilities.[55] But for the most part, Bergh was unable to do much about this because of the specific exemption given them in Section 10 of the New York statute. This kind of blanket exemption continues in many of today's anti-cruelty statutes.

In addition to the term "cruelty," the courts have had to decide the meaning of many other terms. The words "overdrive," "override," or "overload," reflect a historical concern for those animals most closely associated with humans (beasts of burden) during a period when motorized transportation was unavailable. No standard is given to determine a violation. The number of possible variables, such as age, strength, and health of the animal, duration of load, degree of effort or weight of load, etc., make it impossible to be more precise in legislation. The riding, driving, or loading becomes cruel when more is being demanded of the animal than could reasonably be expected under all

---

53. 44 N.H. 393 (1862).
54. 79 Tenn. 528 (1883).
55. Report 1867, *supra* note 18, at 19–22.

circumstances.[56] Remember this holistic judgment will be made by a jury, not trained in the law, but by using their life experiences to provide a judgment context.

Other terms the court had to define were "torture" and "torment." Again the focus is not on the pain of the animal, but on the justification for the infliction of the pain. In *State v. Allison*,[57] the court found the defendant had unlawfully tortured or tormented a cow by beating her and twisting off her tail. Sometimes the act itself suggested no possible justification. In one court, the pouring of turpentine on a goose, and then burning it, was found to be an unjustifiable act of torture.[58] In *Commonwealth v. Brown*,[59] the defendant applied a solution of nitric and sulfuric acid to the hoofs of two horses. This was found to be a violation of the law. Note that this law requires only the general intention to do the act (pour the acid), not the specific intention to do torture. The general intention can be proven by objective witness testimony. If specific intention were required, then the prosecution would need to know what the defendant was actually thinking at the time, something very difficult to prove.

Modern Animal Welfare Laws

It is not possible to review the present status of all the different anti-cruelty laws around the United States. While the focus of this chapter is on the general criminal statutes, there are many more animal focused laws today, such as dangerous dog statutes or restrictions on exotic animals, in each state. Also, the concepts of animal welfare can be found in the federal Animal Welfare Act[60] which focuses upon animal breeding, animal fighting, and the use of animals in exhibits and scientific research. But the most important set of laws continue to be found at the state level.

A quick review of the state of Virginia's current laws will provide a sense of the present picture. First, the core language from the 1867 act can still be found in present day laws. Consider the Virginia statute (Va. § 3.2-6570(A)): "Any person who (i) overrides, overdrives, overloads, tortures, ill-treats, abandons, willfully inflicts inhumane injury or pain not connected with bona fide scientific or medical experimentation, or cruelly or unnecessarily beats, maims, mutilates, or kills any animal...." "Overrides" remains the first illegal act identified. But, with the disappearance of horses from the streets of the cities, clearly it is no longer the most import aspect of the law. Other terms from the 1867 legislation that continue to be used in the Virginia statute include "inhumane injury or pain" and "cruelly or unnecessarily beats." Our society has not changed that fundamental idea of animal welfare as articulated in the New York law. Violation of the Virginia language above, as with the 1876 law, results in just the punishment level of a misdemeanor. However, the next subpart of the section quotes many of the same words but adds the qualifier "malicious" to the language. If the actions of a defendant are malicious, then the penalty is a felony. This suggests that it is the attitude of the human and not the degree of suffering by the animal which is being punished.

---

56. *See* State v. Browning, 50 S.E. 185 (S.C. 1905) (defendant's mule with his knowledge and permission, was cruelly worked when it was unfit for labor).
57. 90 N.C. 733 (1884).
58. State v. Bruner, 104 N.E. 103 (Ind. 1887).
59. 66 Pa. Super. 519 (1917).
60. 7 U.S.C. §§ 2131–2159.

Virginia's statute redefines the term "animal" to mean "any nonhuman vertebrate species except fish." No longer does the term refer to "all of creation" or "dumb brutes." Most states that have imposed more serious punishments for violations of animal welfare laws have also become more precise about which animals are covered under the law. The strong majority of states now use vertebrates as the dividing line. Virginia is a bit unusual in excluding fish. The focus of the legislature's policy concern is that if the crime is to be a felony, there must be more certainty that the animal in question can perceive pain as we understand it and be capable of suffering as the term is generally understood. As a matter of public policy, most legislatures really are not interested in protecting insects, jelly fish, or lobsters.

While the historical language continues to exist, Virginia's laws are considerably more extensive at this point in time. The section quoted above has six parts, and there are dozens of sections that are now part of the title on animal welfare law. The definition section of the animal law article defines over 50 different words and terms, a sign of good and comprehensive drafting.

The two major areas of development in the law are the extensive expansion of the provisions against animal fighting and the requirement imposed upon an owner for the well-being of the animal in his or her care. While the 1867 law had the phrase "Any person who shall keep or use, or in any way be connected with, or interested in the management of, or shall receive money for the admission of any person to any place kept or used for the purpose of fighting or baiting any bull, bear, dog, cock, or other creature," Virginia's law is now much more precise:

§ 3.2-6571. A. No person shall knowingly:

1. Promote, prepare for, engage in, or be employed in, the fighting of animals for amusement, sport or gain;

2. Attend an exhibition of the fighting of animals;

3. Authorize or allow any person to undertake any act described in this section on any premises under his charge or control; or

4. Aid or abet any such acts.

Violations of portions of this section can result in felony convictions.

The 1867 Act which had only the phrase "deprived of necessary sustenance," created a positive duty for the owner. Again the Virginia law has expanded this duty under their present law:

§ 3.2-6503. A. Each owner shall provide for each of his companion animals:

1. Adequate feed;

2. Adequate water;

3. Adequate shelter that is properly cleaned;

4. Adequate space in the primary enclosure for the particular type of animal depending upon its age, size, species, and weight;

5. Adequate exercise;

6. Adequate care, treatment, and transportation; and

7. Veterinary care when needed to prevent suffering or disease transmission.

The provisions of this section shall also apply to every pound, animal shelter, or other releasing agency, and every foster care provider, dealer, pet shop, exhibitor, kennel, groomer, and boarding establishment. This section shall not require that animals used as food for other animals be euthanized [(e.g., live mice for feeding pet snakes)].

B. Violation of this section is a Class 4 misdemeanor.

Under the above, it is a crime to not provide one's cat with adequate exercise. While the list of obligations is very broad, note that it is limited to companion animals and that violations of the law are only misdemeanors.

The box representative of animal welfare laws today is much larger and more complex. While the newer definitions of animals appear to be narrower than the old definition, practically it is about the same as how the old law was implemented. The scope of the actions covered by the law is clearly more extensive and comprehensive than the 1867 law. The penalties are more varied. Many laws are now felony violations with jail time of two or three years. Penalties can often include forfeiture of the animal, fines in the thousands of dollars, public service and required counseling.

The social contract for animal well-being has grown in strength and supports the larger and more complex box reflected in present legislation.

A Consideration of Animal Rights

All of the above discussion of the law was accomplished without the use of the term "animal rights." This is not a surprise, as the existing law is representative of the social contract based upon a perspective of animal welfare. That is, humans have an obligation to those animals, which are used by humans, to make sure the use of the animal does not result in "unnecessary pain and suffering." Humans have a moral or ethical duty to acknowledge the welfare needs of animals. In stating this, it is not necessary to say that animals are legal entities or have legal personality.

During the development of legal protection for animals under ideas of animal welfare, domestic animals have always been considered personal property. (The other long-existing categories of property are real property and intellectual property.) Thus the law puts dogs and lizards into the same category as tables and computers. This is not a comfortable fit. Society has acknowledged the difference between tables and dogs with the adoption of anti-cruelty laws for the protection of dogs but not tables. A key concern of many who advocate animal rights is the removal of domestic animals from any status of property. The nature of the philosophical arguments seeking this change is diverse and complex.[61]

---

61. For a full discussion of the moral and legal status of animals, *see generally* ANIMAL RIGHTS (Clare Palmer ed., 2008). This book is a collection of thirty-one reprinted essays from the major authors in this area. *See also* Martha C. Nussbaum, *Animal Rights: The Need for a Theoretical Basis*, 114 Harv. L. Rev. 1506 (2001) (reviewing STEVEN M. WISE, RATTLING THE CAGE: TOWARD LEGAL RIGHTS FOR ANIMALS (2000); Gary L. Francione, *Animals—Property or Persons?*, in ANIMAL RIGHTS: CURRENT DEBATES AND NEW DIRECTIONS 108, 134 (Cass R. Sunstein & Martha C. Nussbaum eds.; Oxford, New York: Oxford Press, 2004). Professor Francione is one vocal advocate of the abolitionist perspective: "And if the treatment of animals as resources cannot be justified, then we should abolish the institutionalized exploitation of animals. We should care for domestic animals presently alive, but we should bring no more into existence.").

Many arguments resolve into the point that animals as living beings, like humans in many ways, deserve respect and status within the legal system, and that a key aspect of showing respect is their removal from the status of being personal property.[62]

If animal welfare law is represented by a three-dimensional box, then animal rights adds a fourth dimension: the categories of entities of who may assert the interests of the animals within the legal system. Consider it the dimension of time; who can move the box forward? The pure form of animal rights seeks to have the animals themselves assert their own, as yet undefined, legal rights. A number of books have been written on this topic, and this chapter can only hint at some of the complexities that are involved with the fourth dimension. This chapter is also too short to review the writers of animal rights in the realm of philosophy.

Consider the following: Roger, an eight-year-old cat owned by Mary, is shot with three arrows by Sam, a 19-year-old human male, out having some "fun." Under present legal concepts, the significant physical injury to Roger is acknowledged as harm to Mary's property. The measure of the harm is not the amount of suffering and pain endured by the cat, but the degree to which Mary's interests in the cat, primarily financial, have been harmed by the event. Financial harm is measured by determining the fair market value for property before the events in question, and then subtracting the value of the goods after the events. Roger, the cat, is not a recognized legal person and therefore cannot sue Sam for his pain and suffering. The other possible legal actor is a local prosecuting attorney of the government who may file criminal law charges against Sam for the legally recognized harm (the cruel and unjustified infliction of pain and suffering). Under existing law, the bad actor will never have to compensate the cat for the pain and suffering intentionally caused by the arrows. Concepts of animal rights would allow Roger visibility in the legal system so as to pursue the wrong inflicted by Sam, in the same way that if the victim of the onslaught of arrows were a two-year-old human, Maud. Today Maud could sue the actor Sam. Note that Maud does not have to be aware of her legal right in order to receive its benefits. Our legal system allows for the appointment of a legal guardian to assert the right of the child and could likewise do so for an animal.

It is relatively easy to conceptualize the application of animal rights concepts in the context of wild animals such as gorillas, elephants, chimpanzee and dolphins. Many of these species already are known as individuals with names and identification. The needs and interests of such animals are ascertainable in an objective way. The legal system could be structured so to allow a court to appoint an attorney to represent a particular animal, or perhaps a group of animals, when they have been harmed or are threatened with harm. This would allow the animal to be the plaintiff, for the court to consider the harm to the plaintiff animal directly and if the harm is real, to fashion a remedy to the benefit of the plaintiff animal, perhaps in the form of an injunction to stop harmful human actions. This author has suggested such a frame of reference in another article.[63] The path forward is more difficult when the animal is domestic, as in such a case there are human owners of the animals.

Before it is possible to move to more consideration of the possible legal rights of domestic animals, their personal property status needs to be considered more closely.

---

62. This author has suggested an new category of property which would acknowledge their special status. A fourth category would be designated "Living Property"; David Favre, Living Property; A New Status for Animals Within the Legal System, 93 Marquette Law Review 1021 (2010).

63. David Favre, Wildlife Jurisprudence, 25(2) Journal of Environmental Law and Litigation 459 (2010).

Historically, if something is considered property, then it is difficult to conceptualize the property as a holder of legal rights. Rather, it is conceived as the subject of legal rights. Therefore, it is often asserted that the first step in the obtaining of legal rights for animals will be the removal of their property status, and making them like wildlife, self-owned.

Intertwined with having the status of property is the reason that they are personal property, they are to be used by humans for some purpose. Indeed, before the law can find full focus on this difficult issue of property status, there has to be more full agreement on the issue of whether it is ethically permissible for humans to use animals in any circumstance. One side of the argument is that animals, as living beings on this planet, deserve equal ethical status as human and, therefore, should not be owned or used by humans. This argument would seem to require that domestic animals no longer exist in our society (e.g., no hens to lay eggs for human consumption, no horses to pull the wagon or run the races). Such a future world seems to be defined by the *negative*, animals shall *not* be property, without the *positive* vision of what *would* be acceptable. If they are not property, or a new variation of property that makes some human responsible for them, can domestic animals be a part of our daily lives? If not property, then what? This is not answered with any positive pictures by those who oppose the status of animals as property.

The other side of the discussion would point out that some uses are mutually beneficial to animals and their humans, with millions of companion animals being the primary example. Perhaps the better context for rights development would be to say that the ethical use of animals should be allowed only in the context of respectful use. This would allow the disrespectful use of an animal to give rise to a legal action, forcing the stopping of such an abuse.

Some would suggest that it is not possible to give personal property legal rights of its own. But, this is simply a failure of legal imagination. For example, a fairly recent development of law in the United States is the allowing of trusts to be created for the benefit of animals and providing for lawsuits to be filed by court appointed guardians to make sure the trustees carry out their legal duties toward the animals who are beneficiaries of the trust.[64] If Ms. Jones wishes to create a Cat Trust for her cat Zoe and fund it at $25,000, it is now permissible in many states. This makes Zoe a beneficiary of the trust having the same status as a human child for this limited purpose. If her friend Ms. Heath receives the cat and the money at Ms. Jones' death, she must use the money for the benefit of the cat. If it appears that the money is being spent on gambling trips to Las Vegas, a court action can be filed against Ms. Heath on behalf of the cat to correct this breach of duty. Thus, under existing laws, animals can have a legal personality within a narrow legal context. This is a limited legal right; the cat would have visibility in the courtroom. The needs of the cat would be the focus of concern and the outcome or remedy of the case would run directly to the cat's benefit. This is an example of how a legal right for an animal can exist.

The arguments for and against animal rights do not directly change the debate about what acts are cruel, or ought to be cruel and therefore illegal. Animal rights are about that fourth dimension of the box, about who can be a plaintiff and be allowed to file the lawsuit. In 2012, PETA filed a lawsuit in the name of several orca whales being held by Sea World, but the court rejected the argument of the lawsuit saying that the whales were not slaves under the 13th Amendment of the US Constitution and therefore there was no

---

64. Uniform Trust Code § 408.

cause of action and no standing for the whales.[65] In 2014, a series of cases were filed in New York state courts by the Nonhuman Rights Project in an attempt to establish legal personality for some privately owned chimpanzees. The vehicle for this was an assertion by the organization that chimpanzees should be considered legal "persons" under a New York statutes against the keeping of persons against their will (be seeking a writ of habeas corpus on behalf of the chimpanzees). There were hearings in three different trial courts, all of which denied the motion of the Nonhuman Rights Project. These denials were appealed to the next higher court. This level of court also has denied the plaintiff's motion. One of the court opinions directly addressed the claims of the plaintiff and rejected the concept that chimpanzee should be considered a legal person.[66] As of 2015, there has been an appeal of at least one of the cases to the highest court in New York. The organization has stated that it intends to file new law suits on this same issue, the legal status of animals, in the future.[67]

Within the world of law the concept and promotion of legal status for animals to have their own rights is just in the initial stages of development. The results of these efforts may not be known for decades.

Appendix A: The 1867 New York Anti-Cruelty Law

Section 1. Penalty for Overdriving, Cruelly Treating Animals, etc.

If any person shall overdrive, overload, torture, torment, deprive of necessary sustenance, or unnecessarily or cruelly beat, or needlessly mutilate or kill. or cause or procure to be overdrive, overloaded, tortured, tormented or deprived of necessary sustenance, or to be unnecessarily or cruelly beaten, or needlessly mutilated, or killed as aforesaid any living creature, every such offender shall, for every such offence, be guilty of a misdemeanor.

Section 2. For Keeping a Place For Cock Fighting, Bull Baiting, Dog Fighting, etc.

Any person who shall keep or use, or in any way be connected with, or interested in the management of, or shall receive money for the admission of any person to any place kept or used for the purpose of fighting or baiting any bull, bear, dog, cock, or other creature, and every person who shall encourage, aid or assist therein, or who shall permit

---

65. Tilikum ex rel. People for the Ethical Treatment of Animals, Inc. v. Sea World Parks & Entertainment, Inc. ___ F. Supp. 2d ___, 2012 WL 399214 (S.D. Cal.,2012).
66. The People of the State of New York Ex Rel. The Nonhuman Rights Project, Inc., on Behalf of Tommy, Appellant v. Lavery, Respondent, 998 N.Y.S.2d 248 (2014).
67. The website of the organization has all the legal documents about these cases posted on its site and keeps an update of its legal activities. See, http://www.nonhumanrightsproject.org/.

or suffer any place to be so kept or used, shall, upon conviction thereof, be adjudged guilty of a misdemeanor.

Section 3. For Impounding Animals Without Giving Sufficient Food and Water

Any person who shall impound, or cause to be impounded in any pound, any creature, shall supply to the same, during such confinement, a sufficient quantity of good and wholesome food and water, and in default thereof, shall, upon conviction, be adjudged guilty of a misdemeanor.

Section 4. In What Case Any Person May Feed, etc. Impounded Animal

In case any creature shall be at any time impounded as aforesaid, and shall continue to be without necessary food and water for more than twelve successive hours, it shall be lawful for any person, from time to time, and as often as it shall be necessary, to enter into and upon any pound in which any such creature shall be so confined, and to supply it with necessary food and water, so long as it shall remain so confined; such person shall not be liable to any action for such entry, and the reasonable cost of such food and water may be collected by him of the owner of such creature, and the said creature shall not be exempt from levy and sale upon execution issued at upon judgment therefor.

Section 5. Penalty For Carrying Animals in a Cruel Manner

If any person shall carry, or cause to be carried, in or upon any vehicle or otherwise, any creature, in a cruel or inhuman manner, he shall be guilty of a misdemeanor, and whenever he shall be taken into custody and therefor by any officer, such officer may take charge of such vehicle and its contents, and deposit the same in some safe place of custody; and any necessary expenses which may be incurred for taking charge of and keeping and sustaining the same, shall be a lien thereon, to be paid before the same can lawfully be recovered. Or the said expenses or any part thereof remaining unpaid, may be recovered by the person incurring the same, of the owner of said creature, in any action therefor.

Section 6. License For Using Dogs Before Vehicles

Every person who shall hereafter use any dog or dogs, for the purpose of drawing or helping to draw any cart, carriage, truck, barrow, or other vehicle, in any city or incorporated village, for business purposes, shall be required to take out a license for that purpose, from the mayor or president thereof, respectively, and shall have the number of said license and the residence of the owner distinctly painted thereon; and for each violation of this section shall forfeit and pay a fine of one dollar for the first offence, and a fine of ten dollars for each subsequent offence.

Section 7. Penalty for Abandoning Infirm Animals in Public Place

If any maimed, sick, infirm or disabled creature shall be abandoned to die, by any person, in any public place, such person shall be guilty of a misdemeanor, and it shall be lawful for any magistrate or captain of police in this state, to appoint suitable persons to destroy such creature if unfit for further use.

Section 8. When Agent of Society May Arrest for Violations of This Act

Any agent of the American Society for the Prevention of Cruelty to Animals, upon being designated thereto by the sheriff of any county in this state, may, within such county, make arrests and bring before any court or magistrate thereof, having jurisdiction, offenders found violating the provisions of this act, and all fines imposed and collected in any such county, under the provisions of this act, shall inure to said society, in aid of the benevolent objects for which it was incorporated.

Section 9. Who Shall Publish This Act, and When Shall it Be Published

This act shall take effect on the first day of May next. And the said American Society for the Prevention of Cruelty to Animals shall cause the same to be published once in each week for three weeks, in four daily papers published in New York City, or in default thereof shall forfeit the right to receive the penalties and fines as provided.

Section 10. Proviso

Nothing in this act contained shall be construed to prohibit or interfere with any properly conducted scientific experiments or investigations, which experiments shall be performed only under the authority of the faculty of some regularly incorporated medical college or university of the state of New York.

References

Bentham, J. (1781). *An introduction to the principles of morals and legislation.* Oxford: Clarendon Press.

Coleman, S. (1924). *Humane Society leaders in America.* Albany NY: The American Humane Society.

Favre, D. (2010, spring). Living property: A new status for animals within the legal system. *Marquette Law Review, 93,* 1022–1071.

Favre, D., & Tsang, V. (1993). The development of anti-cruelty laws during the 1800s. *Detroit College of Law Review, 1,* 1–35.

Nash, R. F. (1989). *The rights of nature.* Madison, WI: University of Wisconsin Press.

Palmer, C. (Ed.). (2008). *Animal rights.* Aldershot, England; Burlington, VT: Ashgate.

Ryder, R. (1989). *Animal revolution.* Oxford: Basil Blackwell.

Sapontzis, S. F. (1987). *Morals, reason, and animals,* Philadelphia: Temple University Press.

Sunstein, C. R., & Nussbaum, M. C. (Eds.). (2004). *Animal rights: Current debates and new directions.* Oxford, New York: Oxford Press.

Turner, J. (1980). *Reckoning with the beast: Animals, pain and humanity in the Victorian mind.* Baltimore, MD: John Hopkins Press.

Wise, S. (2000). *Rattling the cage: Toward legal rights for animals.* Cambridge, MA.: Perseus Books.

Wise, S. (2002). *Drawing the line: Science and the case for animal rights.* Cambridge, MA: Perseus Books.

Chapter 3

Animal Cruelty and the Law: Prohibited Conduct

Yolanda Eisenstein

Introduction

Animal law, in its most general sense, is the set of legal rules that involve or relate to animals in some way. The area is quite diverse cutting across every substantive area of the law including property, tort, contract, criminal, environmental, and administrative, and across all jurisdictions—local, state, federal, and even international. Not all laws that relate to animals are animal *protection* laws. For example, those that regulate hunting, animals used for food, and dangerous dogs are primarily about human concerns. However, there are many laws whose main purpose is animal safety and well-being. Anti-cruelty laws are just such laws and are designed specifically to protect animals from criminal abuse and neglect and, more broadly, to prevent cruelty by setting standards for their humane treatment.

As described in Chapter 2, all animals are characterized as personal property under the law. Wild animals are the property of the "common" and owned by the sovereign that has jurisdiction over the land on which the wildlife live. Thus, most wild animals in the United States are owned by the state unless they live on federal land, in which case they are owned by the federal government. Most laws governing the treatment of wildlife are part of federal and state environmental laws, with the animals treated as resources for human use and enjoyment.

The classification of animals as property is a legal constant that runs through all aspects of animal law. While a law may make it a crime to abuse one's companion animal, that law does not change the animal's property status although it would not be a crime to abuse other property, such as one's own television set. It is important to consider the property status of animals when reading through this chapter and the next. The ownership of property comes with an array of legal rights and the question arises as to whether it is an appropriate designation. All other forms of property are inanimate objects that have no feeling of pain or capacity to communicate. Animals are sentient beings who[1] can feel

---

1. I have used the word "who" in this chapter rather than "it" to refer to animals. The animals I write about are not things, but sentient beings who show emotion, feel pain, and communicate. The word "who" is a more appropriate reference and serves to promote their rightful place in society.

and suffer and thus must at least be protected from cruelty and abuse. There are stakeholders on both sides of the "property" issue and it is not likely to be decided any time in the near future.

This chapter on prohibited conduct will focus on the laws designed to protect animals from criminal abuse and to punish those who ignore the law and commit acts of cruelty. They address conduct that is prohibited because the conduct either imposes greater pain and suffering on the animal than is deemed necessary under the circumstances or that is inflicted outside the bounds of accepted human values.

The Laws against Cruelty

Anti-cruelty laws prohibit the mistreatment of certain animals. These laws are a patchwork of federal, state, and local laws, some dating back to the 1800s. While certain laws endure and maintain their relevance over time, long-standing animal laws are often inadequate, and do not reflect the current science on animal intelligence or the change over the past 200 years in public sentiment toward the animals who share our lives.

Not all anti-cruelty laws are antiquated, but they do differ, sometimes significantly, by state. All states include felony-level animal cruelty statutes, although the acts that rise to the level of a felony may vary. And a law that mandates jail time in one jurisdiction may impose only a fine in another. The level of enforcement will also vary. While most people believe that animal cruelty should be a crime punished by tough laws, that belief may not always translate into enforcement when other crimes, particularly serious ones, compete for limited human and financial resources.

People are treated differently under the anti-cruelty laws. State laws will provide exceptions and exemptions to certain individuals, groups, or businesses, or will enact separate legislation entirely.[2] If the person who commits an act of cruelty is a scientific researcher, he or she will likely be exempt from state anti-cruelty laws. Hunters and trappers will be exempted from the law if the conduct is related to the activities of hunting and trapping. For example, a person who maliciously kills a neighbor's family cat with a bow and arrow would likely violate a state's anti-cruelty law, while a hunter who kills a deer with a bow and arrow would not violate the same law, so long as the hunter complied with the state's hunting and licensing laws. Veterinarians are granted various exceptions and fall under the regulatory and disciplinary rules of their professional associations. Agricultural workers are exempted when engaged in the accepted practices of animal husbandry, regardless of whether those practices are considered illegal under the state's anti-cruelty statute.

In all states, defenses exist for anyone who commits an act of cruelty against an animal in self-defense or in the defense of others. Furthermore, in certain states, a person would not be charged with cruelty in killing a dog if the dog were attacking the owner's livestock.[3]

---

2. States may have an animal code that addresses cruelty to companion animals and a separate set of laws under the agriculture code that addresses cruelty to livestock or other animals.
3. *See, e.g.*, Ariz. Rev. Stat. §13-2910(B)(1) (2012).

Special Treatment for Companion Animals

People in the United States love their companion animals. Statistics for 2013–14 show that sixty-eight percent, or 82.5 million households own companion animals, many considered "family members" (American Pet Products Association, 2014). In 2014, owners spent $58.04 billion on food, veterinary care, grooming, boarding, and other products and services (American Pet Products Association, 2015). And there are no signs of a slowdown, with estimated expenditures for 2015 at $60.59 billion (American Pet Products Association, 2015).

Therefore, it is not surprising that companion animals are the focus of most state anti-cruelty laws. Most of the laws apply to dogs, cats, and other "companions," while other animals, such as those used for food and in scientific research, are exempted from legal protection or relegated to the federal regime. Thus, acts of cruelty deemed illegal when inflicted on the family dog may be perfectly legal when carried out on a pig or cow on a factory farm.

The Legal Regime in Animal Protection

As discussed in Chapter 2, the beginning of what is today's anti-cruelty movement started in 1866 with Henry Bergh.[4] He was greatly affected by the animal cruelty he witnessed and was responsible for the passage of New York's progressive anti-cruelty laws, as well as their enforcement and prosecution.

Those initial laws and the ones that have followed are only a part of a legal regime of reporting, investigating, enforcing, prosecuting, and punishing acts of animal cruelty. A study of anti-cruelty laws alone would be incomplete without examining the laws *plus* the processes that follow in order to use those laws to convict a person of an illegal act of cruelty.

The United States legal system is based on English law, or common law.[5] Today there is statutory law, which is legislation enacted by state and federal legislatures, and there is common law, the "body of law derived from judicial decisions, rather than from statutes or constitutions" (Garner, 2009, p. 270).

Statutory Law

As noted earlier, the anti-cruelty statutes that protect animals are found primarily in state laws and local ordinances. Factors that drive the scope and content of these laws include the state's economic and social issues, the tenor of state and local politics, the enforcement mechanisms in place, the existence and influence of any animal-based businesses and those that support them, and the citizens' attitudes about animal protection.

---

4. For a history of Henry Bergh and the American Society for the Prevention of Cruelty to Animals, see ASPCA (2012).
5. The exception is Louisiana, which bases its laws on the civil, or Roman, legal system.

Economics is a key factor and a state that is heavily dependent on agriculture or animal-related businesses will protect those industries through its laws. These groups are also likely to have a great deal of political influence with legislators. Anti-cruelty laws that are passed will often reflect the interests of the stakeholders with the most political clout. Finally, other factors may come into play, as illustrated in the example below. Three states address one problem—cruelty in puppy mills—in three different ways.

Case Study: Three approaches to cruelty in puppy mills.

Over the past several years, animal advocates have focused on acts of cruelty that affect thousands of dogs throughout the country. Large-scale commercial dog-breeding operations are in the business of churning out puppies for retail and internet sales. These are production facilities, producing live puppies rather than automotive parts or furniture. The breeders are focused on maximizing profits, too often at the expense of the dogs' welfare. The mass breeding of dogs for their puppies has resulted in the use of the term "puppy mill" to refer to these large-scale operations that have no interest in the health or quality of life of the dogs. Facilities overbreed the females, keeping them pregnant at every cycle; confine them in small wire crates stacked three to four high for their entire lives; and provide little to no veterinary medical care.

Cruelty raids conducted throughout the country have revealed horrific living conditions that exist for many of these dogs (see The Humane Society of the United States, 2015). In addition, inbreeding along with crowded, unsanitary conditions have resulted in puppies with genetic disorders and diseases being sold to an unsuspecting public, often unaware that they have contributed to a puppy mill. While breeders generally have guarantees, they usually require the purchaser to return the sick dog in order to receive another one. They rarely include reimbursement for veterinary medical care. New owners often find these guarantees unacceptable. They do not want another dog from the same breeder and know that the sick dog will likely be euthanized.

In response to the public outcry over puppy mills, the federal government has closed a loophole in the Animal Welfare Act that previously allowed internet sellers to claim "retail" status, exempting them from USDA (United States Department of Agriculture) oversight. A new rule defines retail pet store as a place of business where the seller, buyer, and animal for sale are physically present. This allows the purchaser to see the animal and talk to the seller before purchasing. Internet sellers cannot meet this requirement unless they have a physical location open to the public in addition to a website.

In addition, many states have enacted laws that heighten legal oversight of high-volume breeders and sellers. Laws may require consumer disclosures on where puppies were bred, impose penalties on breeders for violations, and establish remedies for sick puppies.

California has approached puppy mill cruelty at local and state levels, as well as retail and breeder sales.[6] State laws cover the sales of dogs by breeders and retail sellers. Breeder regulations include standards of care and housing, including a prohibition on housing dogs in crates with wire flooring. Breeders must provide purchasers with a written notice of their rights in the event that a puppy is sick or diseased. Breeders must also disclose detailed information on the puppies—description, veterinary treatment, history, and whether the puppy has any known illnesses or genetic defects. Retailers are under similar

---

6. *See* Cal.Health & Safety Code D. 105, Pt. 6, Ch. 5 Sale of Dogs and Cats for state laws regulating breeder and retail sales.

requirements and must also disclose the breeder's name and address. They must post "conspicuously" the state where the dog was bred on every dog's crate.

California cities such as Los Angeles and San Diego have gone further in an effort to stop the cruelty of puppy mills and encourage adoption by banning the retail sales of pets.[7]

The State of Missouri has the infamous distinction of being a haven for puppy mills. In 2011, the voters of Missouri collected the required signatures for a state ballot initiative, bypassing the legislature. The measure passed and Missouri citizens thought they had successfully mandated a better life for dogs in Missouri breeding facilities. However, giving in to pressure from commercial breeders and their supporters, the legislature repealed the Puppy Mill Cruelty Prevention Act, replacing it with a law that animal advocates say falls far short of the original law (Prah, 2011). Four years later, Missouri continues to top the national list of "worst puppy mills."[8]

Lastly, in 2011 the Texas legislature passed the Commercial Dog and Cat Breeders Act, which requires commercial breeders to obtain licenses, submit to inspections, and follow a new set of standards established by the Texas Department of Licensing and Regulation (TDLR).[9] The law also created an advisory board with the specific purpose of advising TDLR on proper standards of care. Despite more than 10,000 public comments and considerable support for tougher standards, TDLR issued standards that animal advocates say fly in the face of the legislative intent of the law and the will of the public. After the law was passed, opponents filed a lawsuit challenging the constitutionality of the law and have attempted to weaken or repeal it in subsequent legislative sessions. Both efforts have been unsuccessful.

These examples show how public sentiment can prevail, but lose out to economics, politics, and intermediaries, such as regulatory agencies, which may counter public sentiment and derail efforts to prevent animal cruelty.

Case Law

While judges do not actually make law as legislators do, they interpret the law through the cases that are brought before them. Judicial decisions become legal precedent, the "basis for determining later cases involving similar facts or issues" (Black's Law Dictionary, 2009, p. 1,195). It requires other judges who are in the same jurisdiction to consider, and follow, established legal precedent if the case is the same or similar. It is the legal doctrine of *stare decisis*, Latin for "to stand by things decided" (Black's Law Dictionary, 2009, p. 1,414) and is the cornerstone of our common law judicial system. Unlike statutory laws that may be passed or altered during every legislative session, precedential cases are not readily overturned or changed.

In addition to its role in establishing and preserving precedent, the court serves as a check on legislative action. A statute may unintentionally violate the Constitution and the court will overturn laws that are vague, overbroad, or violate other constitutional rights, such as freedom of speech or religion. The cases below demonstrate the commitment to upholding our constitutional rights and legal precedent.

---

7. *See* http://bestfriends.org/Resources/Jurisdictions-With-Retail-Pet-Sale-Bans for a list of cities throughout the country that have banned retail sales.

8. http://www.kctv5.com/story/25440415/missouri-kansas-top-national-list-of-worst-puppy-mills.

9. Tex. Occ. Code Ann. § 802.001—802.251 (2012).

Case Study: Upholding the Constitution and invalidating statutes.

In *U.S. v. Stevens* (2010), defendant Robert J. Stevens was convicted of violating a statute that prohibited animal cruelty depictions in crush videos (18 U.S.C. § 48). One form of crush videos caters to those with a sexual fetish for seeing animals crushed. These videos show small, and at times even larger, animals being crushed, typically by women in stiletto heels. In an effort to stop crush videos, which were openly sold via the internet, a federal law was passed making is a crime to knowingly create, sell, or possess depictions of animal cruelty with the intent to place those depictions in interstate commerce. Stevens was the first person to be prosecuted under the law, testing its validity. The U.S. Supreme Court overturned Stevens' conviction, finding the law unconstitutional on several fronts.

This case is an example of the judiciary overturning legislative action. It shows that the enactment of a statute may not be the end of the story. Irrespective of the depravity of the act of animal cruelty or the level of support for the law by the public, the court overturned a law that it found infringed on our constitutional rights. This holding freed the defendant and sent Congress back to the drawing board on drafting new legislation banning animal crush videos.

Case Study: Bound to 19th-century legal precedent.

In 1891, in *Heiligmann v. Rose*, Heiligmann had "wickedly and maliciously" poisoned Rose's three dogs. There was no question of guilt, but in determining what damages should be awarded to Rose, the Supreme Court of Texas established the "true rule in determining the value of dogs."[10] The court stated that the value was either the market value or "some special or pecuniary value to the owner, that may be ascertained by reference to the usefulness and services of the dog."[11]

The "market value" ruling in *Heiligmann* has been legal precedent for 120 years in Texas. While subsequent cases have found that inanimate objects such as heirlooms and trees have intrinsic or sentimental value, the courts have continued to rule that dogs have no sentimental value based on *Heiligmann*. Consequently, plaintiffs have never been awarded non-economic damages for the wrongful deaths of their dogs.

On November 3, 2011, in *Medlen v. Strickland* (2011, p. 576), the Court of Appeals of Fort Worth, Texas, issued a landmark decision, finding that the *Heiligmann* case never ruled out sentimental or intrinsic value. The court challenged the longstanding interpretation of *Heiligmann* in light of later Texas Supreme Court decisions that "acknowledge that the special value of 'man's best friend' should be protected" (*Medlen v. Strickland*, 2011, pp. 580–581).

In April 2013, the Supreme Court of Texas upheld the status quo, reversing the Court of Appeals decision. For now, 120 years of precedent remains in place in Texas. Much has changed since 1891, but the *Medlen* case illustrates the reluctance of the courts to overturn longstanding legal precedent, such as *Heiligmann*, even when the world has changed.

---

10. 81 Tex. at 225, 16 S.W. at 932.
11. 81 Tex. at 225, 16 S.W. at 932.

Who Are Companion Animals?

Beyond their property designation, there is no consistent definition of what constitutes a companion animal, or pet, under the law. Most of the anti-cruelty laws specifically protect these animals, but the definition, which indicates who is entitled to protection, will vary by state. Listed below are excerpts from various state statutes that show that an animal is not necessarily an animal under the law.

- "[A]ny dog, cat or other domesticated animal possessed by a person for the purposes of companionship, security, hunting, herding or providing assistance..." (Kansas)[12]
- "[A] domesticated dog or cat that is normally kept in or near the household or its owner or keeper and is dependent on a person for food, shelter and veterinary care...."(Connecticut)[13]
- "[D]omestic dogs, domestic cats, small pet birds, and other nonlivestock species...."(Colorado)[14]
- "[C]ommonly considered to be, or is considered by the owner to be, a pet. 'Companion animal' includes, but is not limited to, canines, felines, and equines."(Illinois)[15]

The states have different ideas as to the criteria to be used in determining how an animal should be defined. Kansas looks to the purpose, while Connecticut considers where animals are kept and their dependence on humans. Colorado includes all species other than livestock, and Illinois considers whether society or the owner considers the animal to be a pet.

While some of these differences seem minor, they can be significant when prosecuting animal cruelty. In the domestic violence case below, the statutory definition of companion animal was a deciding factor in a felony animal cruelty conviction.

Case Study: A companion animal with fins.

In the case of *People v. Garcia* (2006), Michael Garcia was angry with his live-in girlfriend and threw her young son Juan's fish tank into the television set and shattered it. When Juan started crying, Garcia looked at him and said, "You want to see something awesome?" and viciously stomped the goldfish, killing them. Garcia was arrested on several charges, including felony animal cruelty. He argued to the court that goldfish were not companion animals and "stomping" was not aggravated cruelty. However, the judge disagreed, in part based on New York State's legal definition of companion animal, which includes "any other domesticated animal normally maintained in or near the household...."[16] This broad statutory definition allowed the court to consider whether Juan's pet goldfish could be classified as a companion animal under the law. The court found the language of the statute and legislative intent to be clear and that Juan's goldfish were companion animals. Garcia was convicted of aggravated animal cruelty.

---

12. Kan. Stat. Ann § 47-816(c) (2012).
13. Conn. Gen. Stat. § 22-351a(a) (2012).
14. Colo. Rev. Stat. § 35-42-103(5) (2012).
15. 510 Ill. Comp. Stat. 70/2.01a (2012).
16. N.Y. Agri & Mkts. § 350(5).

Who Are the Victims of Animal Cruelty?

A victim is one harmed by a criminal act. While property, such as a car, cannot be a victim of a crime, animal abuse is one area of the law that recognizes animals as distinct from other property. An animal feels pain and suffers, or dies, from an act of cruelty. The animal's owner will be harmed by the damage to or loss of his or her "property," but the cruelty laws are specific in that they protect the animals from cruelty, including those acts that may be committed by the owner.

In most cases of animal cruelty, multiple violations, such as cruelty related to puppy mills or farm animals, generally constitute a single act of cruelty under the law. However, in the following landmark case the court held that each abused animal is an individual victim.

Case Study: Are animals victims?

In *State of Oregon v. Nix* (2014), a jury convicted the defendant of 20 counts of second-degree cruelty (neglect) of animals. At sentencing, the state asked the court to impose 20 separate sentences based on the neglect of 20 different animals. The defendant objected, arguing that animals are not victims. The trial court agreed with the defendant, sentencing him to 90 days in jail and three years of bench probation. The court then suspended the jail sentence and the state appealed.

The Court of Appeals reversed the trial court decision and the Supreme Court of Oregon affirmed. The Supreme Court agreed with the state's position that the law's intent was to protect more than a "general public interest in animal welfare;" it was to protect individual animals from suffering.

While the Oregon decision is only applicable in Oregon, the decision is significant for several reasons. It reflects a general trend to move the law closer to public attitudes regarding animal cruelty. In addition, courts look to other jurisdictions in deciding their own cases when it's a case of first impression—one the court has not previously heard.

When a crime is committed, there is a victim beyond the one injured—the public. A crime is seen as an infringement on public order and safety; society itself is a victim that is harmed. In the past, animal cruelty was seen as a victimless crime, one in which there was no impact on society. That view is no longer valid, as demonstrated throughout this book. And it is incumbent on the law to keep pace with society's concerns and current science.

Beyond the "official" victims of animal cruelty, there are others who pay an emotional price. People who witness the suffering of their neighbor's dog chained to a tree day in and day out may grow quietly insensitive and become apathetic to the suffering. Victims of domestic violence are also victims of animal abuse when their abusers take their wrath out on the family cat. Shelter workers, animal control officers, and rescue volunteers who care about animals are victims when they see repeatedly the cruelty that humans are capable of inflicting on animals.

Society is beginning to acknowledge and address these "secondary victims" of animal cruelty. States are passing "pet protection" laws that allow judges to include the family pet in protective orders along with the children. Law enforcement, social service agencies and animal welfare organizations are working together to share information in order to use animal cruelty to detect and prevent domestic violence. And shelters are looking at counseling and other ways to alleviate the stress of employees who have to care for, and then euthanize, the often large numbers of animals who are abandoned and abused.

Cruel Acts and Omissions

Various terms are used to define prohibited acts and omissions. Common terms include torture, injure, overwork, and torment.[17] These are broad terms that may include any number of actions, leaving specific interpretations and legislative intent to the courts. Beyond the legal definitions, courts will also look to the common meaning of words in their decisions. Some judges will take a narrow view, while others, a broad one. Some legislators choose to be specific with phrases such as "allows to be housed in a manner that results in chronic or repeated serious physical harm"[18] leaving less latitude to the courts.

There may be a distinction by animal, such as the Pennsylvania law that classifies killing, maiming, or disfiguring a domestic animal as a second-degree misdemeanor, but if the same acts are committed against a zoo animal in captivity it is a third-degree felony.[19] In Wyoming, animal cruelty is elevated to aggravated animal cruelty if the act is dogfighting or cockfighting.[20]

The degree of the crime, that is whether it is a misdemeanor or a felony, is determined by a number of factors. One factor is the intent, or motivation, of the abuser. In criminal law, that intent is called the *mens rea*, a Latin phrase meaning "guilty mind." The *mens rea* is characterized by words such as intentionally, negligently, knowingly, maliciously, or recklessly. The prosecutor is usually only required to prove one intent, although some states will require a combined standard, such as "knowingly and maliciously."[21]

An act committed "negligently" will be a lesser offense and most states do not include negligence in their criminal statutes.[22] Negligence is the "failure to exercise the standard of care that a reasonably prudent person would have exercised in a similar situation ... a culpable carelessness" (Garner, 2009, p. 1,056). The definition means that negligence is not typically a *criminal* act in that it is not necessarily a wrongful or unlawful state of mind. The acts or omissions simply failed to live up to the standard of the "reasonable person."[23] An omission, or failure to act, will include failure to provide food, water, care, and shelter.

Acts that are committed "knowingly" are those where the person knows and is aware that his or her conduct will cause a certain result. Intentional has the common meaning, that the actor intends that his or her acts will have a certain result. Some of the other language that may be found includes willfully, maliciously, and cruelly. Willful and malicious are sometimes used together. Willful simply means a voluntary act, one committed

---

17. *See* Wyo. Stat. Ann. § 6-3-203(c)(ii) (2012).
18. Colo. Rev. Stat. Ann. § 18-9-202(1)(a) (2012).
19. Pa. Cons. Stat. Ann. § 5511 (2012).
20. Wyo. Stat. Ann. § 6-3-201(c)(ii) (2012).
21. *See*, Kan. Stat. Ann. § 21-6412(1) (2012).
22. *See*, N.M. Stat. Ann. § 30-18-1 (2012); N.H. Rev. Stat. Ann. § 644:8 (2012). Don't confuse negligence with criminal negligence, a different standard. *See* 161 A.L.R. 10 (1964).
23. The reasonable person is a hypothetical person used in the law to exemplify the proper or standard behavior. *See* 57A Am. Jur. 2d. *Negligence* § 133 (2012). The defendant's acts will be measured against the reasonable person, who always acts prudently and carefully. *Id.*

purposefully but not maliciously. Malice is the "intent, without justification or excuse, to commit a wrongful act [with a] reckless disregard of the law or a person's legal rights" (Garner, 2009, p. 968). Cruelly is another way to describe "willfully and maliciously," but is usually specific to animal or human physical abuse. Other factors that can affect the severity of the crime and the punishment include prior convictions, the use of dangerous weapons, or threats to people.

The Broad Spectrum of Abusers

Gender statistics show that animal abusers in virtually all categories of abuse—beating, kicking, mutilation, drowning, etc.—are predominantly men (see: pet-abuse.com, 2015a). In categories such as neglect and abandonment, men and women are relatively equal in number of offenses (see: pet-abuse.com, 2015a). And in hoarding cases, women predominate (see: pet-abuse.com, 2015b). Beyond gender, animal abusers span all ages, income levels, and localities. Malevolent owners, angry neighbors, insensitive breeders, and troubled children all may commit acts of cruelty against animals. The motivation and acts of cruelty committed vary.

Owners are distinct in that they may be charged with cruelty from their omissions as well as their affirmative acts. They have a special responsibility as owners to provide proper care for their animals, such as adequate food and shelter. A failure to provide this care may result in cruelty charges. Owners also have the right to end the lives of their animals as long as they do it in a humane manner. Most owners choose to euthanize their animals to end their suffering, an act that is considered kind, not cruel. However, the euthanasia of healthy animals for trivial reasons is morally controversial and veterinarians may refuse on ethical grounds.

Angry neighbors often turn up in cases of cruelty and abuse. Poisoning, shooting, and trapping/relocating are all acts of cruelty committed by neighbors who are unhappy with their neighbors' animals. Defenses are available in some situations, where dogs are killing or threatening livestock or other property.[24]

Irresponsible breeders who operate large-scale commercial breeding facilities may be charged with cruelty when their "operations" cross the line from acceptable practices to cruelty. Their motivation is money and their crime is the cruelty of indifference, insensitivity to the suffering and quality of life of their breeding females. Hoarders are people who collect things, and animal hoarders collect animals. Although hoarders have psychological problems, most states continue to prosecute under traditional cruelty laws.[25]

The police are regularly confronted with situations involving dogs. Dogs may interfere with law enforcement's efforts to settle domestic violence disputes, make arrests, and issue warrants. When a police officer kills an owner's dog it constitutes "state action," triggering constitutional protections. The officer will usually claim, and is often granted, "qualified immunity," meaning that the officer is immune from liability because his or her actions in killing the animal were "reasonable" and therefore constitutional. However, where the killing was not reasonable, it can be a violation of the owner's rights under the

---

24. Tex. Penal Code Ann. §42.092(e)(1) (2012).
25. Hawaii is one state that has specifically addressed animal hoarding in its laws. See Haw. Rev. Stat. §711-1109.6. Retrieved from http://www.animallaw.info/statutes/stushist711_1109.htm.

Constitution, such as the Fourth Amendment prohibition of unreasonable searches and seizures. The owner may file a lawsuit, based on a provision of the Civil Rights Act of 1871, 42 U.S.C 1983, generally referred to as a "1983 lawsuit."

There are no reliable statistics on instances of police shootings of dogs, but animal advocates say it happens far too often with family pets who pose no danger. Efforts are underway in many states to mandate law enforcement training in how to deal with dogs in these situations.

Case Study: A limit to police immunity.

In *San Jose Charter of Hells Angels v. City of San Jose* (2003), the Hells Angels brought a civil rights action under 42 U.S.C. § 1983 against seven San Jose police officers and Deputy Sheriff Linderman. The Hells Angels claimed that the San Jose police violated their Fourth Amendment rights against unreasonable search and seizure when they searched the residences of two members of the group, killing three dogs. The officers argued that they were entitled to qualified immunity, which grants immunity from liability for civil damages because their conduct was reasonable and did not violate the owners' constitutional rights.

The court disagreed. In addition to finding an unreasonable execution of the search warrants in violation of the Hells Angels' Fourth Amendment rights, the court found specifically that the officers did not have qualified immunity in the shooting of the three dogs. The officers knew the dogs would be at the homes and made no provisions for dealing with them in a nonviolent manner. The judge stated that the "emotional attachment to a family's dog is not comparable to a possessory interest in furniture" (*San Jose Charter of Hells Angels v. City of San Jose*, 2003, pp. 977–978) and that the intrusion was severe. He recited past cases that should have "alerted any reasonable officer that the Fourth Amendment forbids the unnecessary [destruction of property]—i.e., when less intrusive, or less destructive, alternatives exist" (*San Jose Charter of Hells Angels v. City of San Jose*, 2003, pp. 977–978). Under the circumstances, the court summed up that a "reasonable officer would have known that the killing of the dogs ... was unlawful" (*San Jose Charter of Hells Angels v. City of San Jose*, 2003, pp. 977–978).

This case shows that qualified immunity is not absolute; it also illustrates how the property status of animals can result in an unconstitutional "taking" by the state.

Who Reports and Investigates Animal Cruelty?

Anyone can report a case of animal cruelty. Most cities allow anonymous reporting to encourage people to take action without concern of retaliation by a neighbor or family member.

The responsibility for investigating animal cruelty may be assigned to animal control officers, the county sheriff, law enforcement, or a humane society, depending on the size and legal structure of the city or county government. Rural areas and small towns do not usually have the resources to staff an animal control department and the sheriff will have the job of investigation and enforcement. In cities where animal control departments exist, staffing will be dictated by the city's budget and the officers' authority will vary.

Some officers may have the authority to immediately seize animals and others may be required to obtain a warrant.

Some cities have enlisted the services of animal welfare organizations, such as humane societies, to assist in the investigation of animal cruelty. The choice to employ humane organizations can be controversial. Opponents of this approach argue that humane societies are biased in favor of the animal; therefore, cruelty situations will not be investigated fairly. They claim that animal cruelty is a serious charge that can result in the deprivation of property and should be investigated by law enforcement or other governmental entities. Nonetheless, humane societies often play significant roles in cruelty cases regardless of whether they have authority to actually investigate and take legal action. They may house and care for animals that have been seized, they may be called on to give expert opinion as to the extent and severity of the cruelty, and they may provide veterinary services to animals who are seized. Employees are called to testify in court cases and if the animals are ultimately forfeited, it is the humane organizations that often take the animals and adopt them out to permanent homes.

Investigations do not always result in warrants, seizures, and prosecutions. Officers will have a number of options to consider based on their assessment of the situation. In less serious situations, investigators may seek to educate the person or suggest a responsible ownership class. If financial difficulties are affecting the animal's care, there are numerous humane organizations that will step in to provide food, spay/neuter, and other services to help the person care for his or her animals. Officers will also issue citations and warnings before taking more drastic steps. In serious cases of cruelty, officers will usually attempt to persuade the owner to relinquish ownership. Transferring ownership frees the investigators to immediately take possession of the animals and provide veterinary medical care. The alternative is to forcibly take the animals, either through the authority of the officers or through the issuance of a warrant from a judge.

The Commitment to Enforcement and Prosecution

A government's commitment to the enforcement of animal cruelty laws depends on a number of factors. If other crimes are not being handled satisfactorily, animal abuse may not be a priority. Cities and counties may be short-staffed and unable to devote the necessary time and effort to prosecutions. They may believe that animal cruelty is "only about animals," and therefore does not warrant the city's time or resources.

However, empirical evidence is supporting what many have believed anecdotally, that animal abuse is directly connected to human violence. And cruelty such as dogfighting is associated with other serious crimes such as gambling, drugs, and the illegal gun trade. Because of the mounting evidence of the human costs of animal cruelty, an increasing number of cities, such as Dallas, Texas, are taking a more aggressive stance against cruelty. The Dallas Animal Cruelty Unit is a specialized division of the District Attorney's Office dedicated to protecting animals from abuse. As cases of animal abuse are investigated, related instances of domestic violence and child abuse have been discovered. Convictions of animal cruelty work to prevent other related crimes.

The prosecution of animal cruelty is generally the same as the prosecution of any other criminal case. While a crime may have been committed, prosecutors must determine whether they have sufficient evidence to prove guilt. In civil cases, the burden of proof is a "preponderance of the evidence," which means there is a greater than 50 percent chance that the proposition is true. In criminal cases, the burden is much higher and requires the prosecution to prove "beyond a reasonable doubt" that the defendant is guilty. It means that no reasonable doubt exists as to the defendant's guilt.

Prosecutors are granted what is called "prosecutorial discretion" in that they may choose not to prosecute. The proper handling of the animal, witnesses, and the crime scene can make the difference as to whether the case goes forward or not. In animal cases the victim, the animal, can never say what happened. It makes the evidence even more critical to proving the case. If an animal has died, a necropsy should be performed to determine the cause of death. Mishandling the body, such as freezing, can destroy valuable evidence. A veterinarian should be on the scene to assess the situation and advise officers regarding how the animal should be handled.

One of the challenges in cruelty cases is that they may involve seizing large numbers of animals. In puppy mill raids, there may be a seizure of 500–700 dogs, with many needing veterinary medical care. The financial burden to cities in such cases can be great and may impact the decision whether or not to take action. Animal welfare organizations are often called upon to step in to assist the city in assessing the situation, seizing the animals, and providing housing and medical care. The following seizure required an extraordinary effort on the part of the city and the animal welfare organization.

Case Study: Seizing 27,000 animals.

In December 2010, the city of Arlington, Texas was involved in what was at the time the largest cruelty seizure of animals in the U.S. The defendant owned a company that imported and exported exotic animals, primarily reptiles.[26] An employee's tip to the Arlington police led to the search, which revealed a large number of dead and malnourished animals. The police seized 27,000 animals, more than 500 species, including turtles, three-toed sloths, wallabies, and tarantulas.

The police requested the assistance of the Society for the Prevention of Cruelty to Animals (SPCA) of Texas. They had been notified in advance of the raid and were at the scene when the search and seizure took place. They collected and transported the animals over a 16-hour period in freezing weather to a space at the SPCA facility that had been specifically modified to accommodate animals from the tropics. Seized animals cannot be permanently relocated until the case is complete and the defendant found guilty and divested of ownership. The care of these animals during the defendant's three-month trial involved the work of twelve animal-related agencies and experts. At the conclusion of the trial, the City of Arlington transferred ownership to the SPCA, which permanently relocated all of the animals to rescue organizations, zoos, and sanctuaries. Because of their long-time captivity, none of the animals could have survived in the wild.

The cost of caring for these animals during the prosecution was substantial and could not have been done without the help of the SPCA and other donors and organizations.

---

26. This case was tried and decided in the Arlington Municipal Court; therefore, there is no published opinion. The defendant, who was from New Zealand, left the United States. Information on the seizure can still be found on various websites, such as http://www.pet-abuse.com/cases/16137/TX/US (last visited November 18, 2015).

On Trial

If the evidence warrants moving forward with a case, the prosecuting attorney will decide whether to file felony or misdemeanor charges and start the proceedings. Of the cases that are filed, many will not go to trial as a result of a plea bargain with the defendant.

For those that do go to trial, the preparation is basically the same for animal cruelty as for any other criminal case. Defendants are entitled to jury trials, although some may choose a bench, or judge only, trial if the cruelty is particularly gruesome.

If the defendant is found guilty, a judge may have a number of options for punishment depending on the law in the jurisdiction. As in other areas of criminal law, as described in Chapter 2, there are degrees of abuse. Historically, animal cruelty has been a misdemeanor, but over the years animal advocates have pushed for stricter punishment and today every state has a felony level of animal cruelty.[27] Misdemeanors are the lesser crimes and convictions will usually impose monetary fines and/or local jail time at the discretion of the judge or jury. A felony conviction is a more serious crime and will be more likely to result in jail time. The discretionary component of a felony conviction may be the amount of jail time handed down by the court. States further categorize misdemeanors and felonies as first, second, or third degree or Class A, B, or C, with Class A being the most serious. Each state has its own classification of crimes, such as felonies and misdemeanors, with related punishments in their penal codes.

Other punishments or efforts to rehabilitate and repay society may include restitution in the form of community service. Community service to animal welfare organizations is controversial, given the nature of the crime, although some animal advocates support it. The defendant may be required to go through counseling, which can be especially important in hoarding cases. Judges also may have the discretion to prohibit the person from owning another animal as a condition of probation. Defendants may be required to reimburse the state for the money spent caring for the animals who were seized. Animal cruelty cases are complex crimes that do not necessarily fit within the current criminal justice system. Hoarding, family violence-related harm to animals, dogfighting, and neglect are all animal cruelty but are each unique, requiring different approaches by the criminal justice system. Hoarding is a psychological problem with an almost 100 percent recidivism rate. Jail time is rarely an effective punishment. Animal abuse related to family violence is usually about hurting the spouse, partner, or children and less so about the animal. Traditional punishment for animal cruelty does not get to the root of the problem. Dogfighting is usually about illegal gambling and making money. The animal abuse is a consequence of the "sport" and not the only crime. So, there may be multiple crimes under federal and state law. Neglect may occur from a lack of education or financial resources, not from an intent to harm. Criminal punishment may be less effective than teaching the proper treatment of animals and financial assistance. It is easy to see how a "one size fits all" legal approach to animal cruelty is not practical. These distinct issues are beginning to be realized and addressed by the legal system.

Fines vary, from a minimal amount, such as $500.00, to Arizona's potential fine of up to $150,000 (see also Arizona Supreme Court, 2012).[28] Enhanced punishments of ten or

---

27. States may have an animal code that addresses cruelty to companion animals and a separate set of laws under the agriculture code that addresses cruelty to livestock or other animals.
28. Ariz. Rev. Stat. Ann. § 13-801 (2012).

more years may also be handed down in some jurisdictions if dangerous weapons are used or for repeat offenders.

The International Animal Protection Movement

Historically, countries have used animal laws to protect their wildlife, and promote trade and tourism. Today, more and more countries have a more expansive view of animal protection and have passed laws that provide more comprehensive protection for all animals, including companion animals (see Wagman & Liebman, 2011). Each country has its own anti-cruelty laws that are driven by the country's culture, history, legal system, and economy (Wagman & Liebman, 2011, pp. 171–173). In China, animals, particularly companion animals, have received little to no protection. Chinese laws have been focused on wildlife conservation and economic issues. However, recent progress has been made with a draft of the first Chinese animal protection law that protects all animals (RSPCA International, 2012). The draft coincides with a growing public concern in China for the suffering of animals and interest in pet ownership, a result of increasing wealth and standards of living. Other Asian countries such as Taiwan have passed more extensive anti-cruelty laws, although dog meat is still consumed in a number of these countries.

International laws are rarely focused on companion animals. An exception is the European Union (EU) treaty, the European Convention for the Protection of Pet Animals (2012). While each EU country has its own anti-cruelty laws, the convention specifically addresses the treatment of companion animals in all countries. The treaty, drafted in 1987, is significant in that it provides broad protection to companion animals, or "pets." A pet is defined as any animal kept for "private enjoyment and companionship" [European Convention for the Protection of Pet Animals, 2012, Ch. I, Art. I(1)] and the treaty discourages the keeping of wild animals as pets, a concept that is only beginning to gain traction in the United States.

The treaty is subject to ratification and entered into force in 1992 with four ratifications—Belgium, Finland, German, and Luxembourg. Currently twenty-three countries have ratified the treaty, including Denmark, France, Greece, Italy, Sweden, and Switzerland. Notably, the United Kingdom has neither signed nor ratified the treaty.[29]

The European Convention for the Protection of Pet Animals is broad in scope and includes directives on training, surgery, killing, and breeding. It acknowledges a moral obligation to all animals and recognizes the special relationship that humans have with their pets (European Convention for the Protection of Pet Animals, 2012, Preamble). Countries enter into treaties voluntarily because they have a shared interest in an issue with other contracting countries. Nonetheless, each country is a sovereign entity and there are few avenues for international enforcement, though a country's reputation can be tarnished if it fails to live up to its obligations. One of the stated objectives of the European Convention for the Protection of Pet Animals (2012) is to set a standard and achieve "greater unity between its members" (Preamble).

---

29. A list of Council of Europe countries and signatures and ratifications of the convention can be found at http://conventions.coe.int/Treaty/Commun/print/ChercheSig.asp?NT=125&CM=8&DF=24/04/2012&CL=ENG.

Finally, the country of New Zealand is generally regarded as one of the most progressive countries in its concern for animal welfare, while at the same time being very dependent economically on animals and agriculture. The New Zealand Animal Welfare Act of 1999 is the most recent animal law and provides significant protections for animals. The law applies to owners and to "persons in charge of animals" (New Zealand Animal Welfare Act of 1999, Section 9) and requires that the "physical, health, and behavioural needs" of the animal be met in a manner that is "in accordance with good practice and scientific knowledge" (New Zealand Animal Welfare Act of 1999, Section 10). Individuals convicted of the willful ill-treatment of animals can face a penalty of $100,000 and five years in jail; corporations are subject to a $500,000 penalty (New Zealand Animal Welfare Act of 1999, Section 28). Unlike prosecutions in the United States, violations of the New Zealand Animal Welfare Act are strict liability offenses, meaning intent, or *mens rea*, is irrelevant. Whether the perpetrator committed the offense accidentally, negligently, or willfully is not relevant to the prosecution of the case. All the prosecution is required to do is prove that the person charged committed the offense (New Zealand Animal Welfare Act of 1999, Section 30). Strict liability offenses remove the burden from the prosecution to prove intent.

Conclusion

Progress has been made for companion animals in that society has become more aware of its obligations to animals and the immorality of animal cruelty. Stronger laws have been passed, but much work remains to be done in the areas of enforcement of existing laws and public education focused on the human costs of animal abuse.

For animals used for food, in scientific research, and in entertainment, the picture is not so bright. As discussed in the next chapter and elsewhere in this book, many of these animals still suffer needlessly, in part due to apathy, weak laws, and economics.

References

American Pet Products Association (2015). *Industry statistics and trends.* Retrieved from http://www.americanpetproducts.org/press_industrytrends.asp.

American Society for the Prevention of Cruelty to Animals (2012). *"Regarding Henry": A "Bergh's-eye" View of 145 years at the ASPCA.* Retrieved from http://www.aspca.org/about-us/history.aspx.

Arizona Supreme Court. (2012). *2011–2012 Criminal Code Sentencing Provisions.* Retrieved from http://azcourts.gov/portals/o/apc.prf/2011criminalguidelines.pdf.

Beirne, P. (2009). *Confronting animal abuse: Law, criminology, and human-animal relationships.* Lanham, MD: Rowman & Littlefield.

European Convention for the Protection of Pet Animals. (2015). Retrieved January 11, 2015 from http://conventions.coe.int/Treaty/en/Treaties/Html/125.htm.

Garner, B. A. (2009). *Black's law dictionary* (9th ed.). Eagan, MN: West.

Heiligmann v. Rose, 81 Tex. 222, 16 S.W. 931 (1891).

The Humane Society of the U.S. (2011a). *2011 Humane state ranking: Alabama through Missouri.* Retrieved from http://www.humanesociety.org/humane_state_ranking_2011_al_mo.pdf.

The Humane Society of the U.S. (2011b). *2011 Humane state ranking: Montana through Wyoming, Plus DC.* Retrieved from http://www.humanesociety.org/humane_state_ranking_2011_mt_my.pdf.

The Humane Society of the U.S. (2009, Mar. 16). *Oregon puppy mill raid illustrates need for statewide legislation.* Retrieved from http://www.humanesociety.org/news/press_releases/2009/03/oregon_puppy_mill_raid_shows_need_for_legislation_031609.html.

Hurdle, J. (2009). *2008 law leading to crackdown on Pennsylvania puppy mills.* Retrieved from http://www.nytimes.com/2009/08/18/us/18dogs.html.

Markel, H. (2009, Dec. 14). *Case shined first light on abuse of children.* Retrieved from http://www.nytimes.com/2009/12/15/health/15abus.html.

Medlen v. Strickland, 353 S.W.3d (Tex. 2011).

New Zealand Animal Welfare Act of 1999. (n.d.). Retrieved from http://www.legislation.govt.nz/act/public/1999/0142/latest/DLM49664.html. For more information on animal law in New Zealand see http://www.animal-law.biz.

People v. Garcia, 29 A.D. 3d 255, 812 N.Y.S.2d (2006).

Pet-Abuse.com. (2015a). *Age/Gender Graphing by Animal Abuse Type.* Retrieved from http://www.pet-abuse.com/pages/cruelty_database/statistics/age_gender_by_type.php.

Pet-Abuse.com. (2015b). *Animal hoarding aka collecting.* Retrieved from http://www.pet-abuse.com/pages/animal_cruelty/hoarding.php.

Prah, P.M. (2011, May 25). *Missouri's puppy mill politics: Dog breeders outmaneuver animal-rights movement.* Retrieved from http://seattletimes.nwsource.com/html/living/2015150141_webanimal.html.

RSPCA International. (2012) Retrieved from http://www.rspca.org.uk/ImageLocator/LocateAsset?asset=document&assetId=1232721471931&mode=prd.

San Jose Charter of Hells Angels v. City of San Jose, 402 F.3d 962 (2003).

Strickland v. Medlen, 397 S.W.3d 184 (2013).

U.S. v. Stevens, 130 S.Ct. 1577 (2010).

Wagman, B. A., & Liebman, M. (2011). *A worldview of animal law.* Durham, N.C.: Carolina Academic Press.

Chapter 4

Animal Cruelty and the Law: Permitted Conduct

Joan Schaffner

Introduction

As discussed in Chapter 3, state anti-cruelty laws are the primary laws protecting animals from abuse and neglect. However, these laws often exempt certain animals, for example wildlife and animals used for research or food. Thus these animals can be subjected to treatment that violates the anti-cruelty law provisions but are nevertheless legal. This chapter will focus on the laws that govern these animals.

The law allows for many different uses of animals—for example for research, entertainment, sport, breeding, or food—and for some of these uses the law imposes standards that govern the animals' treatment during such use in an effort to protect the animals from pain and suffering. The standards differ depending upon the specific use of the animal. Thus, the same animal, for example a rabbit, will be treated very differently under the law depending upon whether the rabbit is someone's companion,[1] bred to be a companion, used in research, exhibition or entertainment, raised for food, or lives in the wild. Of the rabbits just described, only the "companion" rabbit is protected under the state anti-cruelty laws. Every other rabbit will be subjected to a different legal regime depending upon the human use of the rabbit.

This chapter is organized around the human use of the animal and the permitted conduct under U.S. law. Since most human uses of animals may involve interstate commerce, the federal government may regulate such use under the Commerce Clause of the U.S. Constitution.[2] However, generally federal law does not preempt state regulation, and thus state law may govern the regulation of the same animals as well. This chapter will focus primarily on federal law with some mention of state law when of particular note. This chapter will discuss how the law regulates the various permissible uses and treatment of animals and explore how effective the law is in preventing cruelty, in other

---

1. Terminology shapes perceptions. Many people and the law refer to animal companions as "pets." While there is nothing particularly demeaning about the use of the term "pet"; it is less descriptive and arguably less ethically sensitive than using the term "companion" when referring to animals with whom we share companionship. Thus, this chapter will use ethically sensitive language to refer to and describe animals unless quoting the law directly.
2. *See e.g.*, 7 U.S.C. §2131 (West 2015).

words, whether the law provides for the animals' well-being or merely sanctions their abuse for human purposes.

Animals Bred as Companions and Used in Research or Exhibition: The Federal Animal Welfare Act

The law allows for animals to be used as property by humans in a variety of ways. Permissible uses of animals allegedly necessary to achieve legitimate human goals often inflict pain and suffering on the animal. Animal welfare laws define the legitimate uses of animals and set standards for their treatment in an attempt to avoid inflicting "unnecessary" pain. The World Organisation for Animal Health (OIE)[3] defines "animal welfare" to mean "how an animal is coping with the conditions in which it lives."[4]

While there are over 90 U.S. federal statutes that affect animals,[5] the leading federal statute that regulates humans' uses of animals is the Animal Welfare Act (AWA).[6] The AWA is enforced by the United States Department of Agriculture (USDA) Animal and Plant Health Inspection Service (APHIS). The AWA is designed to set humane standards for animals bred for sale as companions, used in research, exhibited to the public, or transported commercially.[7] All animals so used, however, are not covered by the law. The AWA defines "animal" to mean "any live or dead dog, cat, monkey (nonhuman primate mammal), guinea pig, hamster, rabbit, or such other warm-blooded animal."[8] Birds, rats, and mice used in research, horses not used for research, other farm animals used for food, and cold-blooded animals are excluded from protection under the AWA.

Under the AWA, animal dealers and exhibitors must be licensed and animal research facilities and transporters must be registered. "Dealer" is defined as anyone who in commerce and for compensation in excess of $500 annually buys or sells an animal, *except* a "retail pet store."[9] "Exhibitors" specifically include carnivals, circuses, and zoos but

---

3. The World Organisation for Animal Health is known by the acronym OIE for the French "Office International des Epizooties."

4. "Animal welfare means how an *animal* is coping with the conditions in which it lives. An *animal* is in a good state of *welfare* if (as indicated by scientific evidence) it is healthy, comfortable, well nourished, safe, able to express innate behaviour, and if it is not suffering from unpleasant states such as pain, fear, and distress. Good *animal welfare* requires *disease* prevention and appropriate veterinary treatment, shelter, management and nutrition, humane handling and humane *slaughter* or *killing*. Animal welfare refers to the state of the *animal*; the treatment that an *animal* receives is covered by other terms such as animal care, animal husbandry, and humane treatment." OIE, World Organisation for Animal Health, (2015). Chapter 7.1. Introduction to the recommendations for animal welfare. Terrestrial Animal Health Code. Retrieved from http://www.oie.int/index.php?id=169&L=0&htmfile=chapitre_aw_introduction.htm.

5. Chu, V. S. (2010, Feb. 1). *Brief summaries of federal animal protection statutes.* CRS 7-5700, 94-731. (noting that many "concern animals but are not necessarily animal protection statutes").

6. 7 U.S.C. §2131-2159 (West 2015); Cowan, T. (2010). *The Animal Welfare Act: Background and selected legislation.* CRS 7-5700, RS22493.

7. 7 U.S.C. §2131 (West 2015) (only animals or activities in interstate or foreign commerce or those that substantially affect such commerce are subject to these regulations).

8. *Id.* §2132(g).

9. *Id.* §2132(f).

exclude retail pet stores, livestock and other agricultural shows or fairs, rodeos, and purebred dog and cat shows.[10] Elementary and secondary schools and agricultural research institutions are *exempt* from the definition of "research facility." All general carriers including airlines, railroads, and truckers, are covered as "transporters."

Note the exemptions from both the animals covered and the entities regulated under the AWA. The animals affected by these exemptions have no legal protection and thus they may be, and often are, subject to cruel treatment. The rationale underlying these exclusions generally is based on a utilitarian balancing that the cost to protect these animals, whose intrinsic interests are not valued, is outweighed by the benefit they provide to humans. A classic example of this is the exclusion of birds, mice, and rats who[11] represent 90% (Cohen, 2006) of all animals in research labs. They are excluded from protection under the AWA because the researchers and government argued that their inclusion would require significant resources both to comply with and enforce the law. Additionally, horses,[12] when not used for research, and animals on the farm, get no protection under the AWA. The exclusion of these animals is consistent with exempting rodeos and agricultural fairs from compliance with the law. Arguably, some of these activities would be prohibited outright if the participants were forced to treat the animals humanely because the very use itself, for example by rodeos, is inhumane.

Case Study: Redefining "retail pet store."

When the AWA was first enacted, the traditional "retail pet store" was a brick-and-mortar store where customers would go to purchase animals as companions. Because these retailers sold the animals to the public in-person, the public was able to view the condition of the animals at the store providing public oversight of these establishments. Since the customers could help ensure that the animals were being treated well, the AWA exempted the "retail pet store" from regulation.

With the advent of the internet, many animal breeders are able to sell directly from their breeding facility to the general public, sight-unseen, without being regulated under the AWA because they met the definition of "retail pet store," one who sold directly to the public. As a result, over the years, APHIS began receiving numerous complaints from the public about the lack of oversight of these facilities and the resulting harm to the animals under their care. In late 2013, APHIS amended the AWA altering the definition of "retail pet store" and thus closing the loophole that allowed internet sellers of animals to bypass regulation under the AWA.[13] Now the definition expressly provides that a "retail pet store" is a place "at which the seller, buyer and the animal available for sale are physically present so that every buyer may observe the animal available for sale prior to purchasing and/or taking custody of that animal after purchase."[14] This amendment has provided greater protection for many animals bred for sale as companions.

---

10. *Id.* § 2132(h).
11. As in Chapter 3, this chapter uses the word "who" rather than "it" to refer to animals. Animals are not things, but sentient beings who show emotion, feel pain, and communicate. The word "who" is a more appropriate reference and serves to promote their rightful place in society.
12. The Horse Protection Act prohibits horses subjected to soring, the process of intentionally causing pain to a horse's front legs and hoofs to enhance his or her gait, from participating in exhibitions, sales, shows, or auctions. 15 U.S.C. §§ 1821–31 (West 2015).
13. Animal Welfare; Retail Pet Stores and Licensing Exemptions, 78 Fed. Reg. 57227 (Sept. 18, 2013).
14. *Id.* at 57228.

For those animals and entities covered under the AWA, the statute requires that the Secretary of Agriculture "promulgate standards to govern the humane handling, care, treatment, and transportation of animals ... [which] shall include minimum requirements for handling, housing, feeding, watering, sanitation, ventilation, shelter from extremes of weather and temperatures, adequate veterinary care, and separation by species."[15] Dealers and exhibitors must handle animals "in a manner that does not cause trauma ... behavioral stress, physical harm, or unnecessary discomfort"[16] and physical abuse may not be used to train, work, or handle an animal. Notably, the standards focus on the avoidance of pain and suffering rather than on providing quality care to ensure good animal welfare, a state in which the animal is physically and psychologically healthy, comfortable, well-nourished, and able to express innate behavior.

Two species are provided added protection. The AWA requires the Secretary to provide "for exercise of dogs ... and for a physical environment adequate to promote the psychological well-being of primates."[17] Interestingly, the two species granted special protections are dogs, "man's best friend," and who, in the United States, are often considered members of the family, and primates who are clearly very intelligent and emotional social beings and arguably most "human-like."[18] Of course, all animals are in need of some form of exercise and psychological stimulation but the government only provides these protections for dogs and primates.

Finally, with respect to research facilities, while the AWA states that researchers shall "ensure that animal pain and distress are minimized"[19] including the "appropriate use of anesthetic, analgesic, tranquilizing drugs, or euthanasia"[20] and "consider ... alternatives to any procedure likely to produce pain to or distress in an experimental animal,"[21] the Secretary of Agriculture has no authority to alter research protocol. Thus, if the researcher believes that it is "necessary" to inflict pain on the animals and that anesthetic will interfere with the experiment, it is lawful.

Allowing the use of any live animal in research is controversial but allowing the use of live primates, and especially Great Apes,[22] in research is highly controversial. In fact, several countries have recognized that no amount of regulation providing for the welfare of primates can justify subjecting them to invasive research and have either banned or imposed very strict limits on their use. These countries include the United Kingdom, New Zealand, the Netherlands, Sweden, Austria, Belgium, Australia, and Japan (Schrengohst, 2011). In the United States, the Great Ape Protection and Cost Savings Act was reintroduced to Congress in 2011 and would end invasive research on great apes and retire them to a suitable sanctuary.[23] The Act was never enacted. However, in June 2013,

---

15. 7 U.S.C § 2143 (a) (1)–(2)(A) (West 2015).
16. *Handling of Animals*, 9 C.F.R. § 2.131 (West 2015).
17. 7 U.S.C § 2143 (a) (2) (B) (West 2015).
18. This statement is not to suggest that other species are not intelligent, emotional, and social, only that because the great apes are humans' closest relative, humans recognize these qualities in the great apes more readily.
19. 7 U.S.C § 2143 (a)(3)(A) (West 2015).
20. *Id.* § 2143 (a)(3)(A).
21. *Id.* § 2143 (a)(3)(B).
22. Great apes include chimpanzees, bonobos, gorillas, orangutans, and gibbons. Great Ape Protection and Cost Savings Act, H.R. 1513 § 3(2), 112th Cong. (2011).
23. Great Ape Protection and Cost Savings Act, H.R. 1513, 112th Cong. (2011), S. 810, 112th Cong. (2011).

the National Institutes of Health announced that it would significantly reduce the number of chimpanzees it used for research and retire to a sanctuary most of the chimpanzees it then currently owned (National Institutes of Health, 2013).

In February 2015, a CNN investigation determined that of the 310 chimpanzees to be retired only six had left the research facilities while dozens had died waiting for their release. The delay, in part, was due to the selection of the 50 chimpanzees who would remain for research. On November 19, 2015, NIH announced it would retire all of its chimpanzees to Chimp Haven in Louisiana, the nation's only federally-approved chimp sanctuary.[24]

Enforcement of the AWA is important to ensure that the regulated entities are in fact meeting the standards set to protect the animals. The Secretary, through APHIS, is given broad discretion "to make such investigations or inspections *as he deems necessary*"[25] to determine if a covered entity has violated any regulation. If a violation is found, the Secretary "*may*" suspend or revoke a license,[26] assess a civil penalty "of not more than $10,000,"[27] issue a cease and desist order,[28] or file criminal prosecution against the violator for knowing violations of the statute.[29] Note that the Secretary has unfettered discretion in determining whether to investigate and what, if any, sanction to impose if violations are found. Humane organizations (American Society for the Prevention of Cruelty to Animals (ASPCA), 2003) and the Government Accountability Office (GAO) (2010) have reported that the Secretary has failed to adequately enforce the AWA, allowing the inhumane treatment of animals by covered entities.

Case Study: Lolita's inhumane treatment under the AWA.

Lolita is an orca whale who has spent 45 years in captivity for public display at the Miami Seaquarium. Lolita was captured off the coast of Washington state in 1970, ripped from her mother and pod at the age of four. The captors bombed the pod trying to separate the calves from the adults, resulting in the drowning death of four calves and one adult. Although Lolita made it out alive, she now lives alone with no orca companionship since Hugo, her tank mate, died in 1980 after repeatedly ramming his head into the walls of the tank.[30] Miami Seaquarium has been licensed under the AWA for decades although the conditions under which they maintain Lolita fail to meet AWA standards. First, although Lolita's tank is to have a minimum horizontal dimension of at least 48 feet, it is only 35 feet. Second, although she is to be housed in a tank that is protected from direct sunlight, she is exposed to the mid-day Florida sun, when it is the hottest. Third, although she is to have appropriate social interaction with animals of the same or a biologically-related species, Lolita lives with white-sided dolphins who, arguably, are not sufficiently biologically related to Lolita to provide proper social interaction for her.[31]

---

24. Cohen, E. & Bonifield, J. (2015, Nov. 9). NIH promises to retire all research chimps. *CNN*. Retrieved from http://www.cnn.com/2015/11/19/health/nih-chimpanzee-research-announcment/index.html?eref=rss_topstories.
25. 7 U.S.C § 2146(a) (West 2015) (emphasis added).
26. *Id.* § 2149(a) (emphasis added).
27. *Id.* § 2149 (b).
28. *Id.* § 2149 (b).
29. *Id.* § 2149 (d).
30. PETA, et al. 2013, Jan 23. Before the Secretary of Commerce. Petition to Include the Orcinus Orca known as Lolita in the ESA Listing of the Southern Resident Killer Whales. Retrieved from http://www.nmfs.noaa.gov/pr/pdfs/petitions/killerwhale_lolita.pdf.
31. Animal Legal Defense Fund, et al. v. USDA, Case3:12-cv-04407-SC, Complaint for Declaratory and Injunctive Relief (N.D. Cal. Aug. 22, 2012).

In August 2012, advocates filed a complaint against the USDA challenging their renewal of Miami Seaquarium's AWA license in light of these violations. The USDA did not dispute the violations but rather supported their renewal of the license under their regulations stating that violation of AWA standards is not grounds for denying the renewal of an AWA license and the court agreed! The court first found that Congress did not speak to the specific issue of "whether the AWA requires that a licensee demonstrate compliance with the statute prior to renewal."[32] Thus, if the USDA's regulations governing renewal procedure is "based on a permissible construction of the statute"[33] it must be upheld. The court then found the regulations met this requirement. The court noted that the statute does not require a renewal of an issued license and only allows for cessation of a license in an enforcement proceeding. Thus, since the USDA "ensures compliance with the AWA (1) prior to issuing a license, and (2) through enforcement proceedings, it does not, and need not, ensure the same (or require demonstration of the same) prior to renewals."[34] Moreover, the USDA "has discretion with respect to how and when non-research licensees are subject to compliance inspections."[35] The result is that animal advocates have no recourse to help Lolita and she is destined to remain in inhumane conditions that fail to meet the minimal standards of the AWA until the USDA decides to enforce their own standards against Miami Seaquarium.

In February 2015, Lolita was given one final glimpse of hope. In 2005, the SRKW Distinct Population Segment of orca whales (to which Lolita had belonged) was listed as endangered[36] but because Lolita was in captivity in 2005, she was exempted from the listing. Ten years later the exclusion for captive orcas was removed and Lolita was included in the SRKW listing as endangered.[37] In July 2015, advocates filed a lawsuit against Seaquarium for violation of the ESA and seeking Lolita's retirement to a sea pen in her native waters arguing that her captivity in circumstances that violate AWA regulations constitute "harassment" which violates the "take" provision under the ESA.[38] The case is proceeding.

Animals Used for Food

Humane Methods of Slaughter

Animals used for food are excluded from protection under most state anti-cruelty laws and the federal AWA. Two federal statutes govern animals used for food during their transport and slaughter but neither addresses their treatment while on the farm. Congress has chosen to preempt the field in the area of transport and slaughter and thus the federal

---

32. Animal Legal Defense Fund, et al. v. USDA, et al., Case 1:13-cv-20076 JAL, Order Granting Defendants' Motion to Dismiss or in the Alternative for Summary Judgment, 9 (D.E. 68) (S.D. Fl. Mar. 25, 2014).
33. Chevron, USA, Inc. v. Natural Resources Defense Council, Inc., 467 U.S. 837, 843 (1984).
34. Animal Legal Defense Fund, et al. v. USDA, et al., Case 1:13-cv-20076 JAL, Order Granting Defendants' Motion to Dismiss or in the Alternative for Summary Judgment, 15 (D.E. 68) (S.D. Fl. Mar. 25, 2014).
35. *Id.* at 16.
36. 50 C.F.R. §224.101; 70 Fed. Reg. 69903 (Nov. 18, 2005).
37. 80 Fed. Reg. 7380 (Feb. 10, 2015).
38. Complaint for Declaratory and Injunctive Relief, PETA, et al. v. Miami Seaquarium, et al., Civ No. 1:15-cv-22692-XXXX (S.D. Fla., July 20, 2015).

law sets not only a floor but a ceiling on the protection that may be afforded animals in these contexts. In other words, states may not set more protective standards for animals during transport or slaughter.[39]

The Humane Methods of Slaughter Act (HMSA) defines slaughter to be "humane" if livestock is rendered insensible to pain by a rapid and effective means "before being shackled, hoisted, thrown, cast or cut"[40] or if slaughtered in accordance with religious ritual requirements whereby "the animal suffers loss of consciousness by anemia of the brain caused by the simultaneous and instantaneous severance of the carotid arteries with a sharp instrument."[41] The law is enforced by the Food Safety and Inspection Service of the Department of Agriculture (FSIS) pursuant to the Federal Meat Inspection Act (FMIA) incorporating the HMSA standards.[42]

Case Study: Who are livestock?

Notably, poultry, who represent 95–98% of all animals slaughtered for food,[43] are *excluded* from protection under the HMSA because they are not included within the term "livestock." The HMSA covers "cattle, calves, horses, mules, sheep, swine, and other livestock."[44] The Secretary of the USDA interprets the term "livestock" to exclude birds. That interpretation was challenged in court by poultry slaughterhouse workers[45] arguing that such interpretation is inconsistent with the language and purpose of the statute and the intent of the legislature.[46] The court, in an exhaustive exercise in statutory interpretation, upheld the Secretary's interpretation.

First, the court noted that the term "livestock" was ambiguous and dictionaries differed as to whether it encompassed all animals "kept or raised on a farm" or impliedly limited such animals to "quadrupeds" only.[47] Second, a review of the legislative debate showed that some members of Congress intended that birds be included while others did not. Moreover, there is a separate statute that governs poultry, although it does not provide for humane slaughter, suggesting birds were not intended for coverage under the HMSA.[48] Turning then to the traditional canon of construction that the ambiguous term must be interpreted in light of the other enumerated terms, the court held that since the enumerated animals were all quadrupeds, and goats, also quadrupeds, were not enumerated, the term "other livestock" should be limited to quadrupeds only.[49] Alternatively, one could argue

---

39. National Meat Assoc. v. Harris, 132 S. Ct. 965 (2012) (finding the FMIA expressly exempted California law prohibiting sale of federally inspected meat of "nonambulatory" animals for human consumption and requiring immediate euthanization of nonambulatory animals).
40. 7 U.S.C. § 1902 (a) (West 2015).
41. *Id.* § 1902 (b).
42. 21 U.S.C. §§ 603(b), 610(b) (West 2015); U.S. Department of Agriculture (USDA), Food Safety & Inspection Service (FSIS) (2012). *Fact sheet: Production and inspection.* Retrieved from http://www.fsis.usda.gov/wps/portal/fsis/topics/food-safety-education/get-answers/food-safety-fact-sheets/production-and-inspection/key-facts-humane-slaughter/key-facts-humane-slaughter.
43. HSUS. (2015, June 25). Farm Animal Statistics: Slaughter Totals. Retrieved at http://www.humanesociety.org/news/resources/research/stats_slaughter_totals.html?referrer=https://www.google.com/.
44. 7 U.S.C. § 1902 (West 2015).
45. Note the plaintiffs are poultry workers challenging the law for their own interests, not on behalf of the birds.
46. Levine v. Connor, 540 F. Supp. 2d 1113 (N.D. Cal. 2008), *vacated and remanded*, Levine v. Vilsack, 587 F.3d 986 (9th Cir. 2009).
47. *Id.* at 1115–16.
48. *Id.* at 1117–18.
49. *Id.* at 1120–21.

that if goats were the only other "livestock" left off the list that Congress would have just listed goats rather than use the much broader term, "livestock." Finally, in response to the poultry workers' argument that exempting 98% of all slaughtered animals from the HMSA is inconsistent with the overall intent of the statute of providing for humane slaughter, the court stated that had Congress intended to cover such a large portion of slaughtered animals, they would have expressly included poultry in the list of enumerated animals.[50] On appeal, this case was reversed and remanded for lack of standing. The appellate court found that the poultry workers were not proper plaintiffs to file this suit as their alleged injuries were not redressable through the lawsuit.[51]

This case exemplifies the Secretary's narrow reading of laws designed to protect animals and the court's literal approach to the interpretation of the statute and reluctance to invalidate the Secretary's findings. Note that, like the AWA, the HMSA exempts from protection over 95% of the animals affected. This is quite disturbing and suggests that perhaps Congress' purpose in enacting these laws is to mislead the public into believing the animals are treated humanely when, in fact, over 95% of them are not.

Americans find especially cruel the slaughter of horses for human consumption often because many Americans consider horses to be "companions" rather than animals used for food. However, the slaughter of horses in fact inflicts greater cruelty than the slaughter of other animals because it is very difficult to slaughter horses in compliance with the HMSA. The reason is that horses are flight animals and, instinctively, when afraid, they panic and try to escape. The chutes used by most slaughterhouses are built for cattle, thus the stalls are too wide, and the captive-bolt stun gun method used for cattle is ill-suited for horses. The result is that horses will thrash their heads in the stalls making it difficult to effectively stun them before slaughter.

In 2005, Congress effectively ended the slaughter of horses on American soil by defunding USDA inspections at horse slaughterhouses (Public Law 109-97, 2006). However, tens of thousands of horses were still transported for slaughter to Mexico and Canada where the HMSA does not apply. This arguably results in a greater infliction of cruelty by adding a long and often uncomfortable transport preceding the inhumane slaughter.[52] In December 2011, Congress reinstituted funding for USDA inspections of horse slaughter facilities in the U.S. In January 2014, before plants were able to reopen, President Obama signed a budget measure withholding money required for federal inspections. In an effort to permanently end horse slaughter in the United States, members of Congress introduced the Safeguard American Food Exports (SAFE) Act that would prohibit both the slaughter of horses for human consumption and the export of live horses for the same purpose.[53]

The USDA's Food Safety and Inspection Service has been criticized by the GAO for inadequate enforcement of the humane slaughter provisions citing no comprehensive en-

---

50. *Id.* at 1116 n.4.
51. Levine v. Vilsack, 587 F.3d 986, 997 (9th Cir. 2009); *see infra*, Private Enforcement of Animal Welfare Laws, for a discussion of standing.
52. Arguably, even if slaughterhouses in the United States did not have the proper equipment for horses, they are at least subject to the HMSA, while slaughterhouses in Mexico and Canada are obviously not. Sulzberger, A. G. (Oct. 23, 2011). Slaughter of horses goes on: Just not in U.S. *N.Y. Times.* Retrieved from http://www.nytimes.com/2011/10/24/us/Horse-Slaughter-Stopped-in-United-States-Moves-Across-Borders.html?pagewanted=all.
53. SAFE Act, S. 541; H.R. 1094 (Mar. 12, 2013). The bill died in Congress. Retrieved from https://www.govtrack.us/congress/bills/113/s541 (last visited Nov. 20, 2015).

forcement strategy and inadequate training of inspectors.[54] The failure of government to properly enforce the humane slaughter law is due to inadequate funding and lack of incentive. Arguably this may change as scientists study the effect of these practices on human workers in factory farms and slaughterhouses. Researchers have recently begun to study the correlation between acts of slaughtering animals and increased crime rates in surrounding communities. One study from 2009 found that "slaughterhouse employment is a significant predictor of both arrest and report rate scales ... [and] has significant effects on arrests for rape and arrests for sex offenses" (Fitzgerald, Kalof, & Dietz, 2009, p. 16). This study is an important first step to understanding the link between institutionalized cruelty and violence against humans. Like the way that studies linking traditional animal cruelty with human violence affected the enforcement and sanctions afforded under state anti-cruelty laws, such research may justify a dramatic shift away from the currently socially accepted institutionalized cruelty against animals slaughtered for food.

Twenty-Eight-Hour Law

The Twenty-Eight-Hour Law prohibits transporting any animal (including those used for food) for more than twenty-eight consecutive hours (or thirty-six consecutive hours at the request of the owner) without being unloaded for five hours for rest, food, and water.[55] This law is enforced by the U.S. Attorney General who may impose a civil fine of between $100 and $500 for each knowing and willful violation.[56] The law was enacted in 1906 and, despite the tremendous changes in transportation methods, the standards have remained the same. Moreover, the law is rarely, if ever, enforced.[57]

In comparison, the European Union sets terms for journey times depending on the type of animal and imposes greater restrictions on the transporters. For example, cattle, sheep, and goats may only travel for fourteen consecutive hours, followed by one hour's rest to enable the animals to drink, followed by a further fourteen hours of travel. This may be repeated provided the cattle, sheep, and goats are "unloaded, fed, watered and rested for at least 24 hours at an approved control post."[58] These laws are significantly more protective of the animals than the Twenty-Eight-Hour Law.

---

54. GAO (2010, Feb.). *Humane methods of slaughter act: Actions are needed to strengthen enforcement.* GAO-10-203.

55. 49 U.S.C. § 80502 (a) (West 2015).

56. *Id.* § 80502 (d).

57. Animal Welfare Institute, (2010, August). Legal Protections for Farm Animals During Transport. Retrieved from https://awionline.org/sites/default/files/uploads/legacy-uploads/documents/FA-LegalProtectionsDuringTransport-081910-1282577406-document-23621.pdf. ("Lacking a mechanism under the auspices of either the USDA or the Department of Justice for monitoring truck transport, for all intents and purposes, there is no federal transport law in the United States.")

58. The entire provision states: "unweaned animals, i.e., animals still drinking milk (nine hours of travel, followed by one hour's rest to enable the animals to drink, followed by a further nine hours of travel), pigs (24 hours of travel, provided there is continuous access to water), horses (24 hours of travel, with access to water every eight hours), cattle, sheep and goats (14 hours of travel, followed by one hour's rest to enable the animals to drink, followed by a further 14 hours of travel). The above sequences may be repeated provided the animals are unloaded, fed, watered and rested for at least 24 hours at an approved control post." Europa (2004). *Animal welfare during transport.* Retrieved from http://europa.eu/legislation_summaries/food_safety/animal_welfare/f83007_en.htm (summarizing Council Reg. (EC) No 1/2005 of 22 December 2004 on the protection of animals during transport and related operations and amending Directives 64/432/EEC and 93/119/EC and Regulation (EC) No 1255/97).

Laws Governing Animals on the Farm

As discussed, at the federal level only 5% of all animals used for food have any legal protection and such protection is afforded only when being transported and at the moment of death. As such, intensive farming practices that include over-crowding of livestock and poultry; housing gestating sows and veal calves in tiny crates and chickens in battery cages with insufficient space to turn around or perform natural behaviors; and docking pig tails, dehorning cattle, and trimming poultry beaks with no anesthesia; although arguably "cruel," are legal in most states. In recent years a few states have enacted laws through voter initiative ballot measures to prohibit some of the worst abuses, including California's 2008 Proposition 2 that requires that "veal calves, pregnant pigs and egg-laying hens be given enough space to lie down, stand up, fully extend their limbs, and turn around freely" by 2015 with "misdemeanor penalties of up to $1500 and/or 180 days in jail" for violations.[59] The law not only requires that California egg producers comply but bans the sale of all eggs laid by hens who are kept in cages that fail to meet the requirements. In 2014, six states filed suit challenging the California law as imposing a substantial burden on interstate commerce and thus violating the Commerce Clause of the U.S. Constitution. The case was dismissed for lack of standing.[60]

In 2009, voters in Ohio elected for an alternative approach to provide more humane conditions for animals on the farm. The voters, backed by the agricultural community, elected to create an Ohio Livestock Care Standards Board of 13 members representing veterinarians, farmers, experts in food safety, and consumer groups tasked with setting animal welfare standards for animals on the farm. In adopting rules, the following factors are among those considered by the Board: "best management practices for the care and well-being of livestock, food safety, prevention of disease, protection of local, affordable, food supplies for consumers, and generally accepted veterinary medical and livestock practices."[61]

Arguably, California's approach is superior to Ohio's for reducing cruelty against animals on the farm. California expressly sought to "prohibit the cruel confinement of farm animals"[62] and set specific parameters for accomplishing that goal. In contrast, Ohio created a Board with members drawn primarily from the agricultural community to establish standards "governing the care and well-being of livestock."[63] There is no assurance that the goal of prohibiting cruel treatment of animals will be accomplished. In fact, it is probable that the standards established will merely replicate so-called "standard agricultural practices," many of which are cruel. The Ohio Livestock Care Standards enacted in 2011 demonstrate this. For example, the standards provide for a minimum of 67 square inches per hen layer, the same standard that exists under conventional battery cage systems.[64] Thus, the standard failed to improve the lives of egg-laying hens. The following case study presents a real-life example of the issues that arise in trying to protect animals' interests when the agency that is tasked with setting animal welfare standards has the primary mission to promote the interests of the industry that uses and abuses the animals.

---

59. Cowan, T. (2010, Sept. 13). *Humane treatment of farm animals: Overview and issues.* CRS 7-5700, RS21978 (p. 1).
60. Missouri, et al. v. Harris, et al., 58 F. Supp. 3d 1059 (E.D. Cal. Oct. 2, 2014).
61. OH Rev. Code § 904.03 (West 2015).
62. California Proposition 2, Prevention of Farm Animal Cruelty Act, Sec. 2. Purpose (2008). Retrieved from https://www.animallaw.info/statute/ca-initiatives-proposition-2-farm-cruelty.
63. OH Rev. Code § 904.03(A) (West 2015).
64. Ohio Livestock Care Standards § 901:12-9-03(F) (2011).

Case Study: Humane or cruel?

In 1996, the New Jersey Legislature added a new section to the state's cruelty statute that directed the New Jersey Department of Agriculture (Agency), within six months of its enactment, to develop standards for the humane treatment of livestock. Further, the law directed that any treatment of livestock in accordance with such standards would be presumed not to constitute animal cruelty.[65]

In 2005, *nine years later*, the Agency adopted regulations to establish "humane" standards for livestock. The regulations defined "humane" as "marked by compassion, sympathy, and consideration for the welfare of animals"[66] and "animal welfare" as "a state or condition of physical and psychological harmony between the animal and its surroundings characterized by an absence of deprivation, aversive stimulation, over stimulation or any other imposed condition that adversely affects health and productivity of the animal."[67] Although "animal welfare" focused on the absence of deprivation, the regulations also defined "well-being" as "good health and welfare."[68] However, the Agency chose specifically to establish only "the minimum level of care that can be considered humane"[69] in consideration of the agency's overarching mission to "preserve our farms, fight for our farmers, and ensure that our agricultural industry is profitable and strong, innovative and poised for a bright future."[70] Most notably, the regulations provided a safe harbor for all "routine husbandry practices," many of which are not "humane," and expressly allowed for a variety of inhumane practices including: tail docking,[71] castration, dehorning,[72] and debeaking[73] animals without anesthesia so long as the practices are performed by "knowledgeable individuals in a sanitary manner in a way to minimize pain," and the confinement of calves and pigs in veal and sow gestation crates[74] (the very practices targeted by California Prop 2).

A number of organizations, including the New Jersey Society for the Prevention of Cruelty to Animals (New Jersey SPCA), and concerned citizens filed suit against the Agency asking the court to invalidate the regulations as arbitrary, unreasonable, and inconsistent with the legislative mandate to create "humane" standards.[75] The trial court, noting the highly deferential review standard of agency actions, held that the regulations were not arbitrary, unreasonable, or in derogation of the statutory mandate and thus were valid. The plaintiffs appealed and the New Jersey Supreme Court struck several of the provisions as inconsistent with the statutory mandate to establish "humane" standards.

---

65. N.J. Soc'y for the Prevention of Cruelty to Animals v. N.J. Dep't of Ag., 196 N.J. 366 (N.J. 2008).
66. N.J.A.C. 2:8-1.2(a) (West 2015).
67. Id.
68. Id.
69. *N.J. Soc'y for the Prevention of Cruelty to Animals*, 196 N.J. at 375.
70. Id.
71. A "procedure that involves 'the amputation of the lower portion of a dairy cow's tail.' Lawrence J. Hutchinson, *Tail Docking for Cattle* (1997)." Id. at 403.
72. A procedure that involves removing the horns from, or preventing the growth of the horns of, an animal as by cauterization. *The Free Dictionary*. Retrieved from http://www.thefreedictionary.com/dehorn.
73. A procedure that involves removing the "tip of the upper mandible" of a bird, such as a chicken. *Merriam-Webster Dictionary*. Retrieved from http://www.merriam-webster.com/dictionary/debeak.
74. *N.J. Soc'y for the Prevention of Cruelty to Animals*, 196 N.J. at 378.
75. N.J. Soc'y for the Prevention of Cruelty to Animals v. N.J. Dep't of Ag., 2007 WL 486764 (N.J. Super. A.D.).

The New Jersey Supreme Court set the focus for its decision as follows:

> The dispute before this Court has nothing to do with anyone's love for animals, or with the way in which any of us treats our pets; rather, it requires a balancing of the interests of people and organizations who would zealously safeguard the well-being of all animals, including those born and bred for eventual slaughter, with the equally significant interests of those who make their living in animal husbandry and who contribute, through their effort, to our food supply.[76]

The Court first addressed the provision that defined all "routine husbandry practices" as "humane." The Court noted that the legislature sought to exempt only "humane" practices from prosecution as compared to other states that exempt "routine, common, or accepted practices" from their cruelty statute and that to interpret "humane" as "routine" would "abuse the interpretative process and ... frustrate the announced will of the people."[77] Next, the Court struck "tail docking" from the regulations finding a "consensus among scientists that tail docking is without any apparent health, welfare, or human health justification, ... causes acute pain, and interferes with the ability of the affected animals to perform natural behaviors, including slicking their tails to chase away flies in the summer."[78] The Court stated that the Agency failed to adhere to the Legislative mandate that the Agency "permit only those practices that it finds to be humane (as opposed to not inhumane)" and held the regulation allowing tail docking arbitrary and capricious.[79]

Note the court observed the difference between defining a practice as "humane" as compared to "not inhumane." The varied treatment of animals by humans falls along a broad spectrum of conduct. At one extreme are our beloved family companions who many people pamper and treat quite well. At the opposite extreme is the heinous torture of animals that is clearly inhumane and cruel. Arguably, "humane" treatment, "marked by compassion" would be easily distinguished from "inhumane" or cruel treatment.

The third set of so-called "humane" provisions allowed for a variety of mutilations, such as castration and debeaking so long as performed by "knowledgeable individuals in a sanitary manner in a way to minimize pain."[80] These mutilations are necessary only because the animals are so intensively confined that they climb upon and peck one another and can become aggressive and cannibalistic. However, the Court refused to opine on the controversial debate over whether intensive confinement of animals is itself appropriate stating it was not addressed in the statute.[81] Nevertheless, the Court did find that because the regulation is so vague, it provides no objective criteria and is entirely "circular in its logic, for it bases the definition of humane solely on the identity of the person performing the task, while creating the definition of that identity by using an undefined category of individuals of no discernible skill or experience."[82] Thus, the Court found these regulations failed to set a standard to ensure that the practices are humane or enforceable and were invalid.

Finally, the Court turned to the intensive confinement of calves and pigs in crates so small that they prohibit the animals from moving freely or even turning around,

---

76. *N.J. Soc'y for the Prevention of Cruelty to Animals*, 196 N.J. at 371. Note that the court found "equally significant" humans' interest in profits to animals' interest in welfare and life.
77. *Id.* at 396–403.
78. *Id.* at 403–04.
79. *Id.* at 405.
80. N.J.A.C. 2:8-2:6(f) (West 2015).
81. *N.J. Soc'y for the Prevention of Cruelty to Animals*, 196 N.J. at 406–07.
82. *Id.* at 411.

causing significant distress in the animals. The Court held that although controversial, the Agency must account for the "interests of the farmers whose livelihood depends on such techniques and whose existence would be threatened were they to be banned"[83] and thus the determination to allow such confinement was within the Agency's expertise and discretion.

In closing, the Court emphasized that by striking the provisions of the regulations, the Court was not banning the practices. These practices merely are not exempt from the anti-cruelty statute and thus may be found cruel if challenged by the enforcing authority with the burden of proving the practice cruel on the enforcer.[84] Interestingly the New Jersey SPCA, one of the plaintiffs in this case, enforces the New Jersey anti-cruelty laws.

This case exemplifies the difficulty with institutional uses of animals for profit and the struggles of animal protection lawyers to seek even the most minimal standards of care for the animals' treatment. First, the agency that is tasked to protect the animals is the same agency whose mission is to promote the regulated industry. As a result, the agency has little incentive to impose regulations that would dramatically change the industry's production methods or reduce their profits. Second, the same agency typically enforces the regulations and often does not adequately oversee implementation or enforcement of the laws. In this case, the New Jersey Department of Agriculture is the agency tasked with enforcing the so-called "humane" laws while the New Jersey SPCA is tasked with enforcing the anti-cruelty laws. Thus the New Jersey SPCA has no authority to police the "humane" regulations. Third, judicial review of agency findings is highly deferential. A court may invalidate the agency's regulations only if it finds that they are arbitrary, unreasonable, or contrary to the legislative mandate. Moreover, the challenger has the burden of proof. As a result, judges often will rubber stamp agency action, as the trial judge did in this case. Fourth, on appeal the court struck the most egregious aspects of the regulations; however, the effect is that they are not deemed "humane" under the law. The practices are not banned; they merely are not exempt from coverage under the anti-cruelty law. Given the practical problems of enforcement, they likely remain in wide practice throughout the state. Finally, private oversight is difficult and expensive, if not impossible. As we will see, it is difficult to find persons who have the ability to file suit, especially at the federal level. Moreover, since much of the abuse takes place behind closed doors, discovering, documenting, and proving the abuse is very difficult. In fact, some states have enacted laws, typically called "ag-gag" laws, that prohibit the making of unauthorized videos and sound recordings, or the taking of unauthorized photographs by activists, journalists, and even employees of the company.[85] Ag-gag laws are designed to censor efforts by animal advocates who are working to raise public awareness of the horrific plight of animals on farms, to hold those who inflict cruelty on these animals accountable, and to improve farmed animal welfare. Thus, instead of prosecuting persons who inflict animal cruelty these states are prosecuting those investigating animal cruelty! Plaintiffs, representing animal rights, works' rights, and environmental groups, filed two lawsuits challenging the constitutionality of Utah's and Idaho's ag-gag laws respectively as violations of free speech and equal protection rights, and as preempted under the federal whistleblower provisions of the False Claims Act. In August 2015, federal district Judge Winmill held

---

83. *Id.* at 415.
84. *Id.* at 417–18.
85. *See e.g.*, Iowa, H.F. 596 (2011), Utah, H.B. 187 (2012). Seven states now have ag-gag laws— Kansas, Missouri, Montana, North Dakota, Idaho, Iowa, and Utah. ASPCA, Ag-Gag Legislation by State. Retrieved from https://www.aspca.org/animal-protection/public-policy/ag-gag-legislation-state. (last visited Nov. 20, 2015).

Idaho's ag-gag law unconstitutional in violation of the first and fourteenth amendments.[86] As of December 2015, the Utah case is proceeding.

Wildlife

Endangered Species Act

The Convention on International Trade in Endangered Species of Wild Fauna and Flora (CITES)[87] is an international agreement among countries designed to ensure that international trade in wild animals and plants does not threaten their survival. It was entered in force in 1975 and now boasts 175 Parties—countries agreed to be bound by the Convention. All import and export of species covered under CITES by Parties must be authorized through a licensing system.[88] The United States was an original Party to CITES and implemented CITES through enactment of the Endangered Species Act (ESA).

The ESA authorizes the Secretary of the Interior (or Commerce for marine mammals) to promulgate lists of species who are endangered, "in danger of extinction throughout all or a portion of its significant range"[89] or threatened, "likely to become endangered within the foreseeable future,"[90] and to designate critical habitat for them.[91] Congress in enacting the ESA declared that animal species had become extinct as a "consequence of economic growth and development untempered by adequate concern and conservation" and that such species are of "aesthetic, ecological, educational, historical, recreational, and scientific value to the Nation and its people."[92] Note that the rationale behind the ESA is to protect human interests in preserving ecological diversity rather than to protect animals from cruelty.

To protect endangered species from extinction, the ESA prohibits importing, exporting, selling, purchasing, or taking any member of an endangered species.[93] The ESA defines "take" to mean "harass, harm, pursue, hunt, shoot, wound, kill, trap, capture, or collect, or to attempt to engage in any such conduct."[94] The Secretary may issue permits authorizing a take to "enhance the propagation or survival of the affected species"[95] or when "incidental to, and not the purpose of, carrying out an otherwise lawful activity."[96] Such protections generally extend to endangered species held in captivity.[97] The Secretary of the Interior or Commerce may assess civil penalties that range from $500 to $25,000,[98] as well as criminal penalties not to exceed $50,000 or imprisonment for not more than one year

---

86. Animal Legal Defense Fund v. Otter, 2015 WL 4623943 (D. Idaho, Aug. 3, 2015).
87. CITES web site (http://www.cites.org/).
88. CITES (2012). *What is CITES*. Retrieved from http://www.cites.org/eng/disc/what.php.
89. 16 U.S.C. § 1532(6) (West 2015).
90. *Id.* § 1532(20).
91. *Id.* § 1533.
92. *Id.* § 1531(a).
93. *Id.* § 1538(a).
94. *Id.* § 1532(19).
95. *Id.* § 1539(a)(1)(A).
96. *Id.* § 1539(a)(1)(B).
97. *Id.* § 1538(b)(1).
98. *Id.* § 1540(a).

for violation of the statute.[99] In addition, and unlike the other federal statutes discussed, the ESA allows private citizens to file suit to enforce certain provisions of the statute.[100] Congress provided for such private attorney general enforcement of the ESA in order to encourage and enhance enforcement of its provisions because they feared that regulators "may work out 'agreements' [with the regulated entities] that are not necessarily true to the spirit of the environmental law in question."[101]

Marine Mammal Protection Act

Wildlife not designated as endangered or threatened generally have few protections although Congress has provided for some protection for certain animals such as migratory birds,[102] bald and golden eagles,[103] and marine mammals.[104] The Marine Mammal Protection Act (MMPA) has received greater publicity in recent years since the tragic death of a Sea World trainer at the jaws of Tilikum, the largest orca held in captivity. The event demonstrated the horrific effects of captivity on these magnificent, social, and intelligent creatures after decades of confinement solely for human pleasure. Nevertheless, the MMPA allows permits to take wild marine mammals for public display.

Congress enacted the MMPA in 1972, soon after the horrific capture of Lolita (discussed earlier). Congress acknowledged that

> ... man's impact upon marine mammals has ranged from ... malign neglect to virtual genocide. These animals, including whales, porpoises, seals, sea otters, polar bears, manatees, and others, have only rarely benefitted [sic] from our interest; they have been shot, blown up, clubbed to death, run down by boats, poisoned, and exposed to a multitude of indignities, all in the interests of profit or recreation, with little or no consideration of the potential impact of these activities on the animal populations involved.[105]

The MMPA sets limits on the take of marine mammals and allows permits for takes only when consistent with the purpose of the MMPA—to maintain the optimum sustainable population of marine mammal species and population stocks in order to maintain the health and stability of the marine ecosystem. Congress directed the Secretary of Commerce via the National Oceanic and Atmospheric Administration's (NOAA), National Marine Fisheries Service (NMFS) for cetaceans and seals, and the Secretary of the Interior, for all other marine mammals, to implement and enforce the MMPA.

The MMPA allows permits for "scientific research, public display, or enhancing the survival or recovery of a marine mammal species of stock."[106] Generally wildlife laws

---

99. *Id.* § 1540(b).
100. *Id.* § 1540(g). Citizens may not enforce the permit provisions of the ESA. Am. Soc'y for the Prevention of Cruelty to Animals v. Ringling Bros. & Barnum & Bailey Circus, 502 F. Supp. 2d 103, 111–12 (D.C.C. 2001).
101. Beverage, E. (2010). Arise under the big top: Seeking legal protection for circus elephants after ASPCA v. Ringling Brothers. *Vanderbilt Journal of Entertainment & Technology Law 43*, 155–84 (citing Wald, P.M. (1992). The role of the judiciary in environmental protection. *Boston College Environmental Affairs Law Review 19*, 519–46).
102. Migratory Bird Treaty Act, 16 U.S.C. §§ 703–712 (West 2015).
103. Bald and Golden Eagle Protection Act, 16 U.S.C. §§ 668–668(d) (West 2015).
104. Marine Mammal Protection Act, 16 U.S.C. §§ 1361–1407 (West 2015).
105. House Report (Merchant Marine and Fisheries Committee) No. 92-707, Marine Mammal Protection Act of 1972, 1972 U.S.C.C.A.N. 4144, 92nd Cong. 2nd Sess. 1972.
106. 16 U.S.C. §§ 1371(a)(1); 1374(c).

do not focus on the welfare of the animals but permits for public display under the MMPA are subject to certain limitations that arguably are designed to protect the welfare of the marine mammal during capture. Specifically, no permit may issue for public display if the marine mammal was "(1) pregnant at the time of taking; (2) nursing at the time of taking, or less than eight months old, whichever occurs later; ... or (4) taken in a manner deemed *inhumane* by the Secretary."[107] Additionally, the applicant for a public display permit must show they offer a program of education or conservation based on professionally recognized standards, have a license to exhibit under the Animal Welfare Act (AWA), and maintain facilities open to the public on a regularly scheduled basis.[108]

Case Study: The MMPA and "inhumane" capture.

In 2012, in the wake of the tragedy at Sea World when Tilikum killed his trainer, the Georgia Aquarium submitted a permit request to NMFS to import eighteen wild-caught beluga whales from Russia for public display. This request sparked a tremendous response from animal advocates as it was the first request in some 20 years for the import of wild-caught marine mammals for public display, a highly controversial use of these intelligent and social wild animals. NMFS received over 9,000 public comments, most in opposition to the permit request on several grounds including that the proposed capture and transport of the animals was inhumane. NMFS ultimately denied the permit, the first time in the history of the MMPA that a permit request for public display was denied.[109]

While this was a victory for marine mammal advocates,[110] the reasoning of NMFS for denying the permit was the effect of the take on the wild population, not concern for the welfare of the individual animals.[111] NMFS rejected the arguments that their capture was, or their transport would be, inhumane. The reasoning lies in how the MMPA defines "humane." While most animal biologists recognize that the term "humane" identifies an objective standard that is either met or is not, the MMPA does not. Instead the MMPA defines "[h]umane in the context of taking a marine mammal [as] that method of taking which involves the least possible degree of pain and suffering practicable to the mammal involved."[112] Thus the take will occur no matter how objectively "inhumane" the capture technique may be, so long as the technique used is the "best" available. That standard sets no objective standard at all. Although no video of the captures was supplied, the petitioner described the process as similar to the capture of research captures of belugas in Alaska several years before. NMFS found no violation, stating, "Although some may argue that capture techniques are per se inhumane, the captures were accomplished in a

---

107. *Id.* § 1372 (b) (emphasis added).

108. *Id.* § 1374(c).

109. The Georgia Aquarium filed suit challenging the denial of the permit as arbitrary and capricious and in September 2015 the case was dismissed. Georgia Aquarium v. Penny Pritzker, et al., Order, Civil Action No 1:13-cv-03241-AT (N.D. Ga., Sept. 28, 2015), available at http://www.nmfs.noaa.gov/pr/permits/ga_court_decision_092815.pdf.

110. Sadly the eighteen beluga whales had been captured over the course of six years and were being held in a dolphinarium in Russia. Their fate is that they are likely to be held in captivity somewhere, even if not in the United States. Thus, the case was hardly a victory for them.

111. Many comments raised the more general concern that whales should not be on public display at all because there is no humane way of holding these animals in captivity. NMFS summarily dismissed these comments stating that the statute provides for permits for public display and the AWA provides standards to ensure the animals' welfare. Lolita's captivity demonstrates that the AWA often fails to protect marine mammals on display.

112. 16 U.S.C. § 1362(4) (West 2015).

manner with as minimal a degree of pain and suffering to the animals involved as possible, consistent with the statutory definition of humane" (Payne, 2013, p. 12).

Regarding transport, transporting the belugas from Russia to Atlanta, Georgia would have required simultaneous flights of approximately thirty hours in duration through Liege, Belgium to Atlanta, Georgia, USA. NMFS noted that the legal standard demands that the transport "not present any unnecessary risks to the health and welfare of the marine mammals."[113] Thus NMFS determined that so long as the proposed method of transport was the best available option, it would be deemed "humane." Under such an analysis, there is no per se inhumane methods of capture or transport, even if the best available methods impose great pain and suffering upon the animals.

State Law

Wildlife protection from cruelty at the state level is quite minimal. Many states either exempt the hunting and trapping of wildlife or exempt all wildlife from their anti-cruelty laws, leaving the state's game laws as the only law governing these animals. The game laws generally set hunting periods for a variety of wildlife species and may impose limits on the kill without any provisions to protect the animals from cruelty. However, in recent years, some states have banned certain cruel hunting and trapping methods. Such methods include leg-hold traps, comprised of two jaws powered by high strength springs that slam shut on an animal's paw causing injury and severe pain, but not death (Clermont, 2004), and bear baiting, placing materials out to attract a bear and then shooting the bear from a blind spot.[114] Bowhunting, although illegal in the United Kingdom and in several other European countries, is legal in most states even though a report on bowhunting summarizing twenty-four studies across the United States concluded that bow hunting is inhumane and wasteful. The report stated:

> The possibility of a deer being impaled by a broadhead arrow and then dying instantaneously is extremely slight. Wounding and crippling losses are inevitable. Every one of these studies has concluded that for every deer legally killed by bowhunters, at least one or more is struck by a broadhead arrow, wounded, and not recovered. The studies indicate an average bowhunting wounding rate of 54%, with the shots per kill averaging 14. (Animal Rights Coalition, n.d., p. 1)

In general, animals in the wild have very little protection from cruelty.

Private Enforcement of Animal Welfare Laws

A statute or regulation can provide for the protection for certain animals, but if the provision is not enforced it is meaningless. The under-enforcement of laws designed to protect animals is a serious problem in the United States resulting from inadequate funding

---

113. *Id.* at 14.
114. *E.g.*, RCW 77.15.245 (West 2015). Bear baiting is legal in 11 states: Alaska, Arkansas, Idaho, Maine, Michigan, Minnesota, New Hampshire, Oklahoma, Utah, Wisconsin, and Wyoming. Humane Society of the United States. (HSUS). *Bear Baiting Laws and Legislation.* Retrieved from http://www.humanesociety.org/issues/bear_hunting/facts/bear-baiting-fact-sheet.html?referrer=https://www.google.com/ (last visited Nov. 21, 2015).

and lack of incentive. Moreover, private citizens often are unable to access the courts to seek their enforcement.

The doctrine of "standing" must be met to file suit in federal court. Animals do not have "standing" thus a private (human) citizen or organization must file suit to enforce the law. Federal standing has both a constitutional requirement and a "prudential" statutory requirement.[115] Article III of the U.S. Constitution grants courts the authority to hear "cases or controversies." This means that any person filing suit must establish that he/she has suffered injury to a "legally cognizable interest" that is (1) concrete and particularized, (2) actual or imminent, (3) fairly traceable to the defendant's actions, and (4) redressable by the relief requested.[116] Note, since animals do not have standing, the human plaintiffs must show injury to themselves, not to the animals. Legally cognizable interests include aesthetic, environmental, and economic interests as they are "important ingredients of the quality of life in our society."[117] Plaintiffs seeking to enforce animal welfare laws generally allege injury to their aesthetic interests because of agency action that fails to properly protect endangered species from extinction or animals from abuse.

Prudential standing, that which allows a party to sue under a given statute, requires that the plaintiff fall within the "zone of interests" to be protected under a statute that itself provides for a private right of action.[118] Although the AWA does not grant citizens a private cause of action, the Administrative Procedures Act (APA) provides that a "person suffering legal wrong because of any agency action, or adversely affected ... by agency action within the meaning of the relevant statute, is entitled to judicial review thereof."[119] Animal advocates have used the APA as the procedural hook to challenge agency actions implementing the AWA. Nevertheless, it is very difficult to find a "person" who falls within the "zone of interests" of the AWA, since arguably the AWA was intended to protect animals, who are not recognized for purposes of standing, not humans. However, the ESA grants standing to "any person" and thus advocates are able to enforce it so long as they meet the constitutional standing requirements. The following case provides a unique and interesting view into the current animal welfare legal regime in the United States and the ability of private citizens to enforce the law in an attempt to protect animals from cruelty.

Case Study: Who may seek enforcement of the law?

In recent years the use of exotic animals, such as elephants and tigers, in travelling circuses has come under scrutiny. In July 2000, plaintiffs filed suit to protect endangered Asian elephants from abuse by Feld Entertainment, owners of Ringling Brothers circus. On December 30, 2009, after almost ten years of litigation and six weeks of trial, the federal district court judge issued his opinion finding that plaintiffs failed to establish standing under the Constitution and, without reaching the merits of the case, found for Ringling Brothers.[120]

Thomas Rider worked as a "handler" tending the elephant barns for Ringling.[121] He witnessed Ringling employees beat the elephants with sharp bull hooks, chain them for

---

115. Lujan v. Defenders of Wildlife, 504 U.S. 555, 559 (1992).
116. *Id.* at 560–61.
117. Sierra Club v. Morton, 405 U.S. 727, 734 (1972).
118. Bennett v. Spear, 520 U.S. 154, 162–64 (1997).
119. 5 U.S.C. §702 (West 2015).
120. Am. Soc'y for the Prevention of Cruelty to Animals v. Feld Entertainment, 677 F. Supp. 2d 55 (D.D.C. 2009).
121. Am. Soc'y for the Prevention of Cruelty to Animals v. Ringling Bros. Barnum & Bailey Circus, 317 F.3d 334, 335 (D.C. Cir. 2003).

long periods of time, and forcibly remove baby elephants from their mothers before they were ready to be weaned. These actions caused the animals pain and suffering exemplified by the lesions and rope burns on the elephants and their stereotypic behavior.[122]

Ringling is licensed under the AWA as an exhibitor and thus subject to AWA regulations detailing the proper handling of animals under their care. This treatment of the elephants, if proven, clearly violates the requirements that "physical abuse shall not be used to train, work or otherwise handle animals," that "handling of all animals shall be done ... in a manner that does not cause trauma ... behavioral stress, physical harm, or unnecessary discomfort," and that "young or immature animals shall not be exposed to rough or excessive public handling."[123] In fact, USDA investigators routinely documented these and other violations of the AWA by Ringling but failed to impose serious fines and thus the abusive treatment continued (American Society for the Prevention of Cruelty to Animals (ASPCA), 2003).

After two years, Rider left Ringling because of this mistreatment and joined with several animal welfare organizations to enjoin Ringling from abusing the elephants. The most obvious legal channel would be to file suit to compel enforcement of the AWA. Unfortunately, this channel was not available because agency enforcement decisions are presumptively unreviewable by courts[124] and the plaintiffs lacked prudential standing to enforce the AWA directly.

However, the Asian elephants are listed as endangered under the ESA. Under the ESA, no one may "take" a member of an endangered species unless they have a permit and such permits are only granted to promote the propagation or survival of the species.[125] Moreover, the permits require that wildlife "be maintained under humane and healthful conditions"[126] and in accordance with all applicable laws, including the AWA. Ringling had a permit for twenty-one of the twenty-eight elephants under their care. Thus, the plaintiffs filed suit under the ESA to enforce the permit requirements for the twenty-one elephants subject to the permit, and for violation of the "take" provision for the seven elephants not subject to the permit. The court ultimately held that the plaintiffs lacked standing to enforce both.

For the twenty-one elephants held subject to the permit, the court held that, although the ESA allows for citizen enforcement of violations of the ESA under section 11(g), only sections 11(a), (b), and (e) specifically reference permits. As such, the court found the statute contemplates only government enforcement of issued permits.[127]

For the remaining seven elephants, the trial judge held that plaintiffs lacked constitutional standing to file suit to enforce the "take" provision and dismissed the case.[128] Plaintiffs appealed this decision to the U.S. Court of Appeals for the District of Columbia. In 2003, the appeals court held that based on the allegations of the complaint, if proven at trial,

---

122. *Id.*
123. 9 C.F.R. § 2.131(a),(b) (West 2015).
124. To rebut the presumption the statute must provide guidelines for agency enforcement discretion and the agency must consciously and expressly adopt a policy that abdicates its statutory responsibilities. Heckler v. Cheney, 470 U.S. 821, 831–32 (1985). Because the AWA grants the Secretary broad discretion, the presumption is virtually impossible to overcome. Animal Legal Defense Fund v. Glickman, 943 F. Supp. 44, 63 (D.D.C 1996), *rev'd*, 204 F. 3d 229 (D.C. Cir. 2000).
125. 16 U.S.C. § 1539(a)(1)(A) (West 2015).
126. 50 C.F.R. § 13.41 (West 2015).
127. Am. Soc'y for the Prevention of Cruelty to Animals v. Ringling Bros. Barnum & Bailey Circus, 502 F. Supp. 2d 103, 112 (D.D.C. 2007).
128. *Am. Soc'y for the Prevention of Cruelty to Animals*, 317 F. 3d at 336 (district court held that Rider's "exposure to the mistreatment of the elephants in the past did not cause him any present injury or threaten to cause any injury in the near future").

Tom Rider would have standing to sue as he met each element of constitutional standing. First, the court explained that if the animals continued to be mistreated by Ringling, Rider would suffer both aesthetic and emotional injury. As a matter of first impression, the court held that "emotional attachment to a particular animal ... could form the predicate of a claim of injury."[129] Second, the injury was sufficiently concrete, particularized, and imminent because, although Rider no longer worked for Ringling, Rider alleged that he would attend the circus and see the effects of the mistreatment. Finally, Ringling's mistreatment of the elephants is the source of Rider's injuries and if Rider won the case and Ringling was enjoined from mistreating the elephants, his injuries would be redressed.[130] This was a huge victory for animal advocates because the court recognized that not only aesthetic injury but emotional injury based on an emotional attachment to the animal was cognizable under the standing doctrine.

Unfortunately, after years of litigation and six weeks of trial, the plaintiffs ultimately lost the case on standing grounds. Although the plaintiffs introduced extensive evidence of Ringling's use of bull hooks and chains to train and work the elephants, as well as expert testimony on the emotional and physical injury it caused the elephants, the trial court, upheld on appeal, ultimately found that "Rider failed to prove that he had a 'personal and emotional attachment' to the seven elephants with whom he worked sufficient to establish injury in fact."[131] *The primary lesson of this case is that private enforcement of animal protection laws is extremely limited, even when abuse is proven.*

Ironically, exactly one month after the D.C. Circuit released its decision the USDA reached a settlement agreement in which Feld Entertainment paid a civil penalty of $250,000 for alleged violations of the AWA, the largest ever assessed against an exhibitor (USDA, 2011). Of course, for a company that in 2004 made $800 Million in revenue, it is a miniscule cost of doing business (Feld Entertainment Inc., 2004). That same month, November 2011, U.S. Representative Jim Moran of Virginia introduced a bill to amend to the AWA that would "restrict the use of exotic and non-domesticated animals in traveling circuses and exhibitions."[132] A few months later, in March 2012, the United Kingdom Department for Environment Food and Rural Affairs announced that legislation would be introduced to ban all wild animals in traveling circuses. The U.K. Animal Welfare Minister Lord Taylor said, "There is no place in today's society for wild animals being used for our entertainment in travelling circuses. Wild animals deserve our respect" (Department for Environment, Food and Rural Affairs (DEFRA), 2012, np). Until the ban takes effect, any circus that uses a performing wild animal must "be licensed, meet strict welfare standards, prepare and follow plans for caring for every animal and have a retirement plan for each animal."[133] In March 2015, the bill banning the use of wild animals in

---

129. *Id.* at 337.
130. *Id.* at 337–38.
131. Am. Soc'y for the Prevention of Cruelty to Animals v. Feld Entertainment, 659 F.3d 13, 20 (D.C. Cir. 2011) (quoting Am. Soc'y for the Prevention of Cruelty to Animals v. Feld Entertainment, 677 F. Supp. 2d 55, 89 (D.C.C. 2009)). Regarding the standing of the organizational plaintiffs, the court held they lacked "informational standing" because the "take" provision of the ESA under which they filed suit does not require disclosure of information. Finally, if injury to the organizational plaintiffs' advocacy and educational work may be cognizable, they failed to prove that Ringling's unlawful practices harm their efforts by creating the public impression that such conduct is humane even because Ringling conceals such conduct from the public. *Id.* at 27–28.
132. Traveling Exotic Animal Protection Act, H.R. 3359, 112th Cong. (2011). The bill died in Committee and was reintroduced in 2014 as H.R. 4525 but was not enacted.
133. *Id.*

travelling circuses was blocked for the twelfth and final time despite having the support of 90% of the British public.[134] Although these legislative efforts ultimately failed, they support animal advocates' claims that no regulations can provide for the proper welfare of wild animals forced to travel chained or in cages for many hours. Moreover, subjecting these animals to such conditions for mere human entertainment is unjustified and thus must be banned. In March 2015, in the face of public pressure and the increasing local bans on the use of bull hooks, Ringling Brothers announced that it would phase out all elephant acts by 2018.[135]

Conclusion

The laws protecting animals from cruelty and providing for their welfare are often illogical and inconsistent. The very same act of abuse directed toward the same animal, for example a pig, may be prosecuted as a felony, if the pig is a companion to a human, and yet be codified as "humane," if the pig is used for food. The pig feels the same pain and suffers regardless of where or with whom he or she lives. The law follows societal attitudes and until society respects the intrinsic interests of animals, independent of the owners' use of the animal, this paradox will remain in the law.

As societal attitudes change and humans recognize the true nature of nonhuman animals, legal protections for animals will follow. For example, in April 2012, India banned the use of all live animals in dissection and other experiments in research and educational institutions although exempting new molecular research from the ban (Baliga, 2012). One year later, India banned all dolphinaria in their country finding that

> ... cetaceans ... are highly intelligent and sensitive, and various scientists who have researched dolphin behavior have suggested that the unusually high intelligence as compared to other animals means that dolphin[s] should be seen as 'non-human persons' and as such should have their own specific rights and [it] is morally unacceptable to keep them captive for entertainment purposes.[136]

As we have discussed, countries are beginning to prohibit wild animals from traveling circuses and animal fighting has been widely banned. As a society, we must decide whether the serious harm inflicted on other sentient beings to satisfy human interests is ever justified. Moreover, even if some uses may be considered important enough to justify the use, can the law effectively regulate and enforce standards to adequately protect the animals?

One federal law not discussed in this chapter is the U.S. Constitution, the legal document that establishes fundamental principles and protections for all in this country. The reason it is absent from this chapter is because animals are absent from the U.S. Constitution; it only recognizes "people."

---

134. Bawden, T. (2015, Mar. 6). Ban on wild animals in circus blocked by Tory backbenchers. *Independent*. Retrieved from http://www.independent.co.uk/news/uk/home-news/ban-on-wild-animals-in-circus-blocked-by-tory-backbenchers-10092779.html.

135. Perez-Pena, R. (2015, Mar. 5). Elephants to Retire from Ringling Brother Stage. *N.Y. Times*. Retrieved from http://www.nytimes.com/2015/03/06/us/ringling-brothers-circus-dropping-elephants-from-act.html?_r=0.

136. Government of India, Ministry of Environment & Forests, Central Zoo Authority. (2013, May 17). Circular, Policy on establishment of dolphinarium, F. No. 20-1/2010-CZA(M).

In contrast, for over 100 years Switzerland has granted

> ... constitutional protection to the 'dignity of creature,' explicitly according esteem to all non-human living beings, namely animals, at the highest legal level. The principle encompasses all legal aspects of human/animal interrelations and is supposed to restrict in particular the kind of treatment of animals that, although not necessarily associated with pain, suffering or damage, nevertheless affects other animal interests that must be respected by humans. Central features in this regard are the protection of animals from humiliation, from excessive instrumentalisation, and from intervention in their appearance. (Bolliger, 2007, np)

In 2002, Article 20a of the German Constitution, was amended to include "and the animals" and now states: "The state, aware of its responsibility for present and future generations, shall protect the natural resources of life and the animals within the framework of the constitutional order through the legislature and, in accordance with the law and principles of justice, the executive and judiciary."

In 2008, the European Union ratified the Lisbon Treaty, the "equivalent" of a constitutional text that states:

> In formulating and implementing the Union's agriculture, fisheries, transport, internal market, research and technological development and space policies, the Union and the Member States *shall, since animals are sentient beings, pay full regard to the welfare requirements of animals*, while respecting the legislative or administrative provisions and customs of the Member States relating in particular to religious rites, cultural traditions and regional heritage.

The explicit recognition of animals as sentient beings and the requirement that their welfare be regarded when formulating and implementing public policy is a monumental step towards greater legal protections for animals' inherent interests. Sometime in the not too distant future, Americans also may formally recognize animals as sentient beings and provide them fundamental protections in the highest law of our land, the U.S. Constitution.

References

American Society for the Prevention of Cruelty to Animals (ASPCA) (2003). *Government sanctioned abuse: How the United States Department of Agriculture allows Ringling Brothers Circus to systematically mistreat elephants*. Retrieved from http:// www.awionline.org/sites/default/files/uploads/documents/GovSantcionedAbuse-FullReport-2003.pdf.

Animal Rights Coalition (n.d.). *Report on bowhunting*. Retrieved from http://www.animalrightscoalition.com/doc/bowhunting_report.pdf.

Baliga, L. (2012, Apr. 17). Govt bans use of live animals for education, research. *The Times of India*. Retrieved from http://articles.timesofindia.indiatimes.com/2012-04-17/india/31355109_1_cpcsea-control-and-supervision-cruelty.

Bolliger, G. (2007). *Summary: Animal welfare in constitutions*. Retrieved from http://www.tierimrecht.org/de/PDF_Files_gesammelt/Abstract_Bruessel_TIR_Papier.pdf.

Clermont, E. (2004). 2003 legislative review, *Animal Law 10*, 363–95.

Cohen, H. (2006). The Animal Welfare Act. *Journal Animal Law 2*, 13–24.

Department for Environment, Food and Rural Affairs (DEFRA) (2012). *Circuses to be banned from using performing wild animals.* Retrieved from http://www.defra.gov.uk/news/2012/03/01/circus-wild-animal-ban/.

Feld Entertainment Inc. (2004). *The Washington Post.* Retrieved from http://www.washingtonpost.com/wp-srv/business/post200/2004/FELD.html.

Fitzgerald, A. J., Kalof, L., & Dietz, T. (2009, June). Slaughterhouses and increased crime rates: An empirical analysis of the spillover from the "jungle" into the surrounding community. *Organization & Environment 22(2),* 158–84.

Government Accountability Office, (GAO) (2010, Sept.). *USDA's oversight of dealers of random source dogs and cats would benefit from additional management information and analysis.* GAO-10-945.

National Institutes of Health. (2013, June 26). *NIH to reduce significantly the use of chimpanzees in research.* Retrieved from http://www.nih.gov/news/health/jun2013/od-26.htm.

Payne, M. P. (2013, Aug. 5). Report on the Application for a Public Display Permit (File No. 17324): Recommendation for Denial, Memorandum to Donna S. Weiting, Director, Office of Protected Resources, NMFS, 12.

Public Law 109-97 (2006). *Agriculture, Rural Development, Food and Drug Administration, and Related Agencies Appropriations Act.* Retrieved from http://www.gpo.gov/fdsys/pkg/PLAW-109publ97/pdf/PLAW-109publ97.pdf.

Schrengohst, K. (2011). Animal law—Cultivating compassionate law: Unlocking the laboratory door and shining light on the inadequacies & contradictions of the Animal Welfare Act. *Western New England Law Review, 33,* 855–900.

Sullivan, M., (2007). The Animal Welfare Act—What's that?. *New York State Bar Journal 79-Aug,* 17–23. USDA (Nov. 28, 2011).

USDA (2011, Nov. 28). *USDA and Feld Entertainment, Inc. reach settlement agreement.* Retrieved from http://www.usda.gov/wps/portal/usda/usdahome?contentid=2011/11/0494.xml&contentidonly=true.

Chapter 5

Veterinary Forensic Sciences in the Response to Animal Cruelty

Randall Lockwood and Rachel Touroo

History

Today we recognize that the response to and prevention of animal abuse and neglect cannot be effective without the involvement of veterinary professionals. That has not always been appreciated. The growth of organized animal protection efforts in America in the 19th century and the development of veterinary medicine as a formal, science-based field occurred in parallel. Therefore, the role of veterinarians in addressing animal cruelty has evolved along with animal protection. Prior to the formation of the American Veterinary Medical Association (AVMA) in 1863 and the American Society for the Prevention of Cruelty to Animals (ASPCA) in 1866, both fields were represented by an assortment of people with a common interest in animals, without formal training and no central focus on effective actions to promote animal welfare or address animal cruelty.

The welfare of working horses was a major concern of ASPCA's founder, Henry Bergh. Much of the care and treatment of horses at the time was in the hands of farriers, self-styled "horse doctors" and quacks (Lane & Zawistowski, 2008). In 1867, the ASPCA introduced horse ambulances and hired veterinary surgeons to provide care for the ambulance horses as well as the animals they aided. Bergh was concerned with the lack of standards for veterinarians and called for legislation in New York to address this. Cornell University opened in 1868 as the first statutory college in New York and incorporated instruction in veterinary medicine from the outset. Dr. James Law, a renowned graduate of the Edinburgh Veterinary College in Scotland, was hired to oversee veterinary training. Cornell set higher requirements for a veterinary degree than any other institution in North America. By 1871, it required four years of study for a Bachelor of Veterinary Science (BVS) degree and an additional two years for a Doctor of Veterinary Medicine (DVM), a degree previously unavailable from any institution in the United States. This eventually lead to the founding of the New York State College of Veterinary Medicine in 1894 (Cornell University College of Veterinary Medicine, 2015). Bergh met frequently with another leading veterinarian, Dr. Alexandre Liautard, a founder of the Veterinary College in New York City in 1875 and one of the first officers of the AVMA who also championed improvements in veterinary education to improve the welfare of animals.

Bergh also recognized the importance of working with law enforcement agencies, as well as veterinarians, in combating animal cruelty. (See Chapter 2.) The original patrons of the ASPCA included the Police Board President (the equivalent of the current Police Commissioner) and the District Attorney for New York County. Bergh also succeeded in being appointed to the bar and being given authority to act as an assistant district attorney to help prosecute the cases that came under the ASPCA's authority as the enforcement agency for New York state's animal cruelty statutes that had been passed shortly after the establishment of the ASPCA.

This blending of resources and goals of veterinary medicine, law enforcement, and animal protection continues today and is best reflected in the emerging discipline of veterinary forensic science, defined here as "the application of a broad spectrum of sciences, including veterinary medicine, to answer questions of interest to a court of law."

Defining Veterinary Forensic Sciences

The broader term "forensic medicine" is used to encompass all aspects of forensic work of a medical nature. In the past, this term was often used interchangeably with "forensic pathology." Forensic pathology, however, refers to the branch of forensic medicine which deals with death investigations. Nowadays, the term "clinical forensic medicine" is applied to the branch of forensic medicine involving the living.

In some ways, the role of the forensic veterinarian can be compared to that of a human medical examiner. The duties of a forensic veterinarian, however, are often broader, including the triage, examination and treatment of live victims, necropsy of deceased victims, evidence identification, documentation, preservation, assessment of the scene and its effects on the victims, and expert witness testimony. Unlike human forensic cases, most animal abuse investigations typically have not had access to supporting forensic specialists until recent years. Without such expertise, vital evidence may go undetected, may not be properly preserved, processed or analyzed, or may not withstand scrutiny in court.

We will review the qualities that describe the practice of veterinary forensic science and give examples of the many ways in which this new field is enhancing the investigation, prosecution, and prevention of animal cruelty. It is a field still in the process of being defined. At this point there is only a single degree-granting program in Veterinary Forensic Sciences, begun in 2014 at the University of Florida, but a growing number of veterinary schools are adding electives or other forensic trainings to supplement traditional veterinary instruction. It is a discipline now recognized by the American Academy of Forensic Sciences and is represented by a nascent professional organization—the International Veterinary Forensic Sciences Association, started in 2008.

Several pioneering publications introduced many of the key concepts of the application of veterinary sciences to legal cases (Byard & Boardman, 2011; Cooper, 1998; Green, 1979, 1980; Munro, 1996; Munro & Thrusfield, 2001a, 2001b, 2001c, 2001d; Stroud, 1998) but there was no compilation of this information in a comprehensive way until the last decade with the publication of a handful of textbooks devoted to the subject (Cooper & Cooper, 2007, 2013; Merck, 2007, 2013; Miller & Zawistowski, 2013; Munro & Munro; 2008; Sinclair, Merck, & Lockwood, 2006).

The practice of veterinary forensic medicine expands the core skill set of practitioners to include activities that allow veterinary facts and opinions to serve the purpose of the law. We consider a forensic veterinarian to be a veterinarian with additional knowledge, training and experience to include:

- Applying veterinary medical knowledge to answer questions of interest to the law;
- Basic understanding of the local, state, and federal laws that may apply to cases of animal abuse or neglect;
- A thorough understanding of animal welfare concerns, especially animal pain, suffering and distress;
- Knowledge of forensic science and medicine;
- Experience with treating victims of animal abuse;
- Experience testifying in court and authoring forensic reports;
- Acting as a "teacher" to clearly convey what has or has not happened to an animal based in science and fact, in order to assist the judge and/or jury in understanding the evidence;
- Acting as an advocate for the truth, putting the pieces of the puzzle of an animal cruelty case together in the most logical and reasonable fashion;
- Interacting with other forensic professions—toxicology, pathology, DNA, ballistics, behavior, etc. to become familiar with the contributing advances that these fields can make to veterinary forensic medicine; and
- Educating veterinarians on recognizing potential indicators of animal cruelty and the need to report such suspicions to the appropriate authorities.

Animal victims cannot speak, but careful study of their medical condition and behavior as well as other evidence can create a narrative of what they have experienced. The forensic veterinarian plays a role analogous to that of a medical examiner explaining the death of a human and providing a voice for the voiceless in a court of law or other forum.

Forms of Animal Cruelty

As noted elsewhere in this volume (see Chapter 1), animal cruelty is defined in many different ways and exists in many forms. The most common cases seen by forensic veterinarians include:

- Simple neglect—failure to provide appropriate food, water, shelter or veterinary care;
- Institutional neglect—including "puppy mills," inadequate shelters or rescue groups, farms, exhibitors;
- Severe neglect—including starvation, animals in left hot or cold vehicles, embedded collars;
- Animal hoarding—the keeping of many animals in substandard conditions in connection with possible mental disorders;
- Intentional abuse—including burns, blunt force trauma, sharp force trauma, strangulation, gunshot, poisoning;
- Organized abuse—including "bloodsports" such as dogfighting and cockfighting;
- Ritualized abuse—animal cruelty in the context of "occult" or other religious rituals; and

- Animal sexual assault.

There are certain protocols and procedures that will be part of the response of forensic veterinarians in *any* case of suspected animal abuse or neglect. In addition, there are special considerations unique to each form of cruelty, which will be discussed later. In all cases, the appropriate response begins with recognizing that animal cruelty has or may have occurred and taking suitable action.

Recognizing and Responding to Animal Cruelty

Many authors have noted the importance of having veterinarians recognize and report animal cruelty (Arkow, 1999; Arkow, Boyden, & Patterson-Kane, 2011; Arkow & Munro, 2008; Landau, 1999; Miller & Zawistowski, 2005; Robertson, 2009; Veterinary Council of New Zealand, 2013; Yoffe-Sharp & Loar, 2009). Much of this has been motivated by the growing appreciation of the connections between animal cruelty and interpersonal violence reviewed in this volume and elsewhere (Ascione, 2008; Ascione & Lockwood, 2001; Linzey, 2009; Lockwood, 2014; Lockwood & Ascione, 1998; Merz-Perez & Heide, 2004).

Currently, 15 states have laws that *require* veterinarians to report animal cruelty: Alabama, Arizona, California, Colorado, Illinois, Kansas, Maine, Minnesota, Nebraska, North Dakota, Oklahoma, Oregon, Pennsylvania, West Virginia, and Wisconsin. In addition, 34 states have laws that provide immunity from civil liability for veterinarians who report in good faith (AVMA, 2015). There continue to be obstacles to the effective involvement of veterinarians in responding to such cases. Veterinarians are not traditionally trained to identify features that raise the index of suspicion of animal abuse or to recognize signs consistent with or highly suggestive of abuse. Additionally, veterinarians often fall into the trap of thinking that owners who care enough about their animals to provide veterinary care are unlikely to abuse their animals; however, this is simply not the case. The largest barriers to diagnosing abuse are a lack of training on indicators of abuse and the existence of emotional blocks in the minds of professionals. These can be so powerful that they prevent the diagnosis from even being considered in quite obvious cases. The most important step in diagnosing animal abuse is to force oneself to think of it in the first place as a potential differential diagnosis.

Veterinarians may become involved with an animal cruelty case in several ways. They may witness suspected abuse in animals presented in their own practice and may be mandated or otherwise motivated to report it to appropriate authorities. They may become involved in a suspected case at the request of local humane, animal control or law enforcement agencies. This can be the most effective route since it can provide the opportunity to be present when animals are first encountered and assess the environment in which they have been maintained. In other cases, the veterinarian may be called in after the fact to assess living or deceased animals or to comment on evidence or medical histories provided by law enforcement, serving as an expert witness.

The role of the veterinarian in such cases can include:

- Documenting the physical condition of all animals associated with an abuse case and documenting changes in their condition in response to care and treatment;
- Commenting on reasonably prudent actions and standards of care that could have been taken to prevent disease, injury or death including basic vaccinations and other preventative care;

- In the case of deceased animals, determining the cause of death, sequence of injuries and estimating the timing of antemortem or postmortem wounds;
- Offering expert opinion to distinguish between death and injury resulting from human versus non-human causes (e.g., predation) or intentional vs. accidental injury;
- Identifying and preserving physical evidence that may link the injuries to a particular suspect (e.g., projectiles, ligatures, trace evidence);
- Offering opinions regarding the speed of unconsciousness or death, and degree of pain or suffering to evaluate whether the death or killing was humane.

The primary distinction between conventional veterinary procedures (e.g., examination, treatment, necropsy) and *forensic* or medicolegal veterinary procedures is that forensic efforts require that the practitioner be aware that *every* action taken or omitted may be open to the intense scrutiny of the court (McEwan, 2012). Every step must be carefully documented and all evidence must be handled and preserved in a manner that carefully limits access to the evidence and tracks the chain of custody of such evidence. A veterinary forensic medical examination can be defined as a detailed exam done in order to methodically document physical findings and facilitate the collection of evidence from the patient's body.

Oregon's mandatory veterinary reporting law (2003) is the most specific *statutory* description of the kind of evidence and information that should be gathered in cases of suspected animal cruelty (Miller, 2006, p. A6). It notes:

Oregon 686.455 Duty to report aggravated animal abuse.

(1) A veterinarian who has reasonable cause to believe that an animal with which the veterinarian has come in contact has suffered aggravated animal abuse, or that any person with whom the veterinarian has come in contact has committed aggravated animal abuse, shall immediately report the suspected aggravated animal abuse in the manner prescribed in subsection (2) of this section.

(2) A report of suspected aggravated animal abuse required under subsection (1) of this section shall be made to a law enforcement agency, either orally or in writing, and shall include, if known:

(a) The name and description of each animal involved;

(b) The address and telephone number of the owner or other person responsible for the care of the animal;

(c) The nature and extent of the suspected aggravated animal abuse;

(d) Any evidence of previous aggravated animal abuse;

(e) Any explanation given for the suspected aggravated animal abuse; and

(f) Any other information that the person making the report believes may be helpful in establishing the cause of the suspected aggravated animal abuse or the identity of the person causing the aggravated animal abuse. [2003 c.275 §3]

Guidelines from the Colorado Veterinary Medical Association (2007, p. 5) go into even greater detail in recommending steps veterinarians should take when animal cruelty is known or suspected. They note that the following information should be collected and included in reports that go to law enforcement:

Signalment
- Date and time of exam
- Animal's name, species, gender and reproductive status, age, color, identification or unusual markings, tattoos, microchip, etc.
- Name of owner, contact information, how long the owner has had the animal
- All veterinary staff members involved with exam

Verbal Account of Injury
- Reason for bringing in the animal and chief complaint (by client)
- Documentation of what the client tells you when explaining the animal's condition including relationship, behavior, conduct concerning the animal's injury, any changes/inconsistencies of the account, age of suspected abuser (adult, child, etc.)
- Timeliness of seeking veterinary care

Photography
- Take "before and after" pictures, and full body shots as well as close-ups. Document that all photos came from the same animal.
- Take full body shots and close-ups.
- Video recording could be used to document an animal's gait or other behavior, if applicable.

Physical Findings
- Perform a complete physical exam noting any abnormalities, injuries
- Note if these are new or old injuries. A wound diagram using a silhouette drawing for that species may be helpful.

Guidelines from the American Veterinary Medical Association (Arkow et al., 2011) offer additional suggestions that apply to proper handling of animal evidence that might be part of any criminal investigation or other legal procedure. In addition to the procedures outlined above, they note that attending veterinary professionals should prioritize the collection of evidence. An item of evidence is anything that can prove or disprove a fact in contention. Evidence most likely to be destroyed by time, other people, or environmental conditions should be collected first. In addition, all staff handling the animals should avoid cross contamination of evidence and utilize sterile procedures, as necessary.

They further note that the physical examination of the animal should not just focus on the chief complaint or obvious abnormalities or overlook the unremarkable. If a parameter is normal, that should be stated. The record should include necessary diagnostics such as a complete blood count (CBC), chemistry panel, fecal, urinalysis and whole body radiographs. The animal and everything associated with it could be evidence and must be preserved and documented, and its integrity maintained. Standard procedure involves a secure evidence storage area and the keeping of an evidence log with details of each item. An evidence receipt should accompany every item of evidence in order to document chain of custody.

Photography is an important aspect of proper evidence documentation. Forensic photography is utilized to:
- Identify the victim;
- Show the condition of evidence or injuries at the time of discovery or examination;
- Record and document injuries and evidence that cannot be preserved or left unaltered;

- Allow for later review of the evidence (Sharma, 2003);
- Document injuries or conditions and record what they looked like before and after medical intervention;
- Illustrate and supplement a written medical report;
- Demonstrate the absence or presence of alleged injury or findings; and
- Present in a court of law, the items of evidence as they were found, thereby validating the testimony being presented.

In addition to careful record keeping and preservation of chain of custody, veterinary forensic medicine also often involves the application of forensic methods and techniques that are not part of the conventional veterinary clinical toolkit. As we will see, the documentation of suspected cruelty cases may involve use of techniques such as alternative light sources, DNA analysis, toxicology, ballistics, entomology, blood spatter analysis, grave excavation, applied animal behavior, and other forensic methods.

Role of the Forensic Veterinarian at a Crime Scene

Forensic veterinarians can have the greatest impact on the investigation of an animal cruelty case if they are involved in the planning of the operation and are present at the scene when action is taken. Their role will include triage of live victims, assisting law enforcement with evidence identification, documentation, and preservation including assessment of the scene and its effects on the victims.

Triage

Triage is the rapid sorting of animals on scene for examination and treatment priority based on medical condition. Animals are triaged at two different points on scene. The first is a "critical triage," conducted during initial walk through on scene in order to identify red-coded (critical) animals. This is followed by an "intake triage," conducted prior to or during the removal of animals from the scene in order to identify yellow- and green-coded animals. Red-coded animals include animals that are recumbent or unresponsive, actively hemorrhaging, reluctant to move, vocalizing in apparent pain, actively seizuring, have open fractures, or are in respiratory distress.

Red-coded animals will require immediate medical attention, provided either at an onsite mobile clinic or a nearby veterinary clinic. Yellow-coded animals include animals that have swollen limb(s) or face, non-weight-bearing lameness, significant abdominal distension, draining wounds, eyes closed/reluctant to open, corneal perforation, or are dehydrated. Yellow-coded animals will also require veterinary attention and examination prior to being transported off scene, such accommodations need to be anticipated and planned out prior to being on scene. Green-coded animals are animals that are bright, alert, and responsive. They may have minor medical conditions such as diarrhea or vomiting for which treatment can wait until after transportation off scene. Care should be taken so that transient evidence, such as mild dehydration, is documented on scene.

When possible, it is desirable to have two veterinarians on scene, with one functioning as a forensic vet and the other functioning as a "treating" vet. This treatment veterinarian will allow for the forensic vet to concentrate on the collection of evidence on scene, while they focus on patient care.

Evidence Handling

On scene, the veterinarian may need to assist law enforcement with the identification of evidence and identifying its potential value and the proper preservation of evidence. The types of evidence that a veterinarian may assist law enforcement in identifying and examining could include:

- Situational evidence—Elements of the scene that may or may not change. For example, lighting conditions, weather conditions, smells, ammonia levels, sounds and temperature
- Physical evidence—Any tangible object that can establish that a crime has been committed, or can provide a link between a crime and its victim or a crime and a suspect

The forensic veterinarian may need to assist law enforcement in ensuring that some evidence is properly preserved. If a deceased animal is found on site, it typically will not be examined at the scene. The veterinarian must ensure that any physical evidence that is thought to be present on the body is properly preserved by handling the body as little as possible, placing paper bags on all four feet and securing them in place with rubber bands, and wrapping the body in a clean sheet prior to placing it in a body bag (Di Maio & Dana, 1998).

Assessment of the Scene and Its Relation to Veterinary/Medical Issues

A veterinarian cannot fully interpret exam findings without crime scene information. This is why it is ideal to have him/her present at the scene. If this is not possible, it is essential to have good photographic and/or video documentation of the conditions available for review and animal examinations should occur as soon as is possible. The animal is just one piece of the puzzle that needs to be considered. For example, the veterinarian may observe dehydration due to poor water quality, interdigital dermatitis, or bacterial conjunctivitis due to dirty and wet living conditions. Depending on the ambient temperature, hypothermia may be observed due to the inability to remain dry without the provision of adequate shelter. Scene photographs may also show safety issues such as exposed metal or broken glass or the presence of possible pesticides, toxins, or poisonous plants which may guide the veterinarian in the workup of the animal.

The Forensic Necropsy

General considerations for live animal examinations in suspected cruelty cases are outlined above. In cases in which animals are deceased, a primary role of the forensic veterinarian will be to complete a forensic necropsy. The goals will be to first determine the cause of death, the event that initiated the chain of events that led to the death. The primary cause of death is often identified by the statement "if it weren't for X, this animal would still be alive," where X is the first, earliest injury or disease in the sequence of events that culminated in death. *Causes* of death are in contrast to the *mechanism(s)* of death, the altered physiology and/or biochemistry set into motion by the cause of death. Mechanisms of death are nonspecific and include the common pathophysiologic events and pathways that precede termination of brain, heart, and/or lung function (e.g., septicemia, organ failure) (Gerdin & McDonough, 2013). If an animal has been euthanized due to suffering or non-survivable injuries, it is important to note that the cause of death is the rationale for euthanasia (e.g., spinal injuries, extensive burns). Some defense attorneys attempt to assert that the veterinarian who performed humane euthanasia, rather than his or her client, was the person responsible for death of the animal; therefore, it is important to make this distinction.

The necropsy report will also usually attempt to clarify the *manner of death*, either natural (disease, age), accidental, non-accidental (which implies an intentional act), euthanasia, or undetermined. However, there is currently no universally accepted standard for classifying the manner of death in animals as we have established in human forensic pathology. The manner of death explains how the cause of death came about. In many cases, it will be desirable to offer estimates of postmortem interval or time since death. This may be based on physical or physiological measures or entomological evidence based on the life stages of insects found in association with the body. In order to determine the cause and manner of death, the veterinarian will need to consider the crime scene findings, any available history, as well as the necropsy findings.

Veterinary Forensic Considerations in Different Forms of Animal Cruelty

Many of the forensic procedures applied in animal cruelty cases are universal to crime scenes involving human or animal victims. However, the development of a specialized field of veterinary forensics has been necessitated by the fact that many crimes against animals such as dogfighting, cockfighting, illegal hunting, and ritualistic sacrifice have little or no counterpart in human forensic pathology (Gerdin & McDonough, 2013). We will provide an overview of some of the specific veterinary forensic concerns related to several forms of cruelty. This is not intended to serve as a complete guide to investigations. Detailed discussion of these kinds of cases is provided in the texts mentioned previously.

Neglect

The majority of animal cruelty cases investigated by animal care and control and humane law enforcement involve "simple neglect" in the form of failure to provide adequate food, water, shelter, sanitation, or veterinary care which has not resulted in death or prolonged suffering. Such cases usually result in citations or, at most, misdemeanor charges. However, the investigation of these cases still requires good documentation of the living conditions of the animal(s), their overall health and body condition, the quality and quantity of food, availability of potable water, and sanitation of the primary enclosure. In addition, notation should be made of signs of pica (ingestion of non-edible items) and the course of weight gain and general recovery when given adequate food and water.

Institutional Neglect

Larger scale neglect cases may involve "puppy mills" or other breeders, pet shops, substandard animal shelters or rescue groups, animal exhibitors and livestock operations.

Since these cases may involve a larger number of animals or a longer history of neglect, they are more likely to result in criminal charges. In addition to the information collected in the simple neglect cases described above, forensic veterinarians should also review any available records of past and current veterinary treatments, any drugs found on site (and whether they have been dispensed), and quality, quantity and appropriateness of food found at the scene. In addition, large scale operations may have resulted in the death and disposal of animals. The investigation should include a search for deceased animals—either buried or concealed on the premises (e.g., in freezers). It can also be helpful to review financial records to see if expenditures for food and veterinary care are reasonable for the number and type of animals on the scene.

Severe Neglect

Severe neglect cases involve serious injury, suffering or death that may be prosecuted as felony or high-level misdemeanor crimes. This can include cases of starvation/malnutrition, untreated injuries that might necessitate amputation, heavy matting that interferes with normal urination and defecation, overgrown or ingrown hooves and nails, or ingrown collars or chains. In cases of poor body condition, the forensic veterinarian will often be called upon to rule out causes unrelated to cruelty, such as underlying disease processes that are being treated. In some cases, death from starvation may be documented through necropsy and analysis of bone marrow fat. The percentage of bone marrow fat may be quantified for recently deceased (< 24 hours) horses, cattle, dogs, pigs, cervids, and sheep by submitting an entire intact femur for analysis to a diagnostic laboratory. This test might also be useful in bovine and equine cases with a postmortem interval (PMI) of 30 to 60 days, but the test has not been validated for other species with PMIs greater than 24 hours (Gerdin & McDonough, 2013).

Cases in which animals have been subjected to extremes of temperature (e.g., left in a hot or extremely cold vehicle) have also been prosecuted, particularly if such neglect has resulted in death. In such instances, veterinary testimony about the pathological changes associated with such stresses help document the cause and mechanism of death (Bruchim, Loeb, Saragust, & Aroch, 2009; Drobatz & Macintire, 1996). This may be supplemented with evidence from the scene, such as evidence of attempted escape.

Animal Hoarding

A special form of severe neglect is animal hoarding, the keeping of large numbers of animals in extreme unsanitary conditions. This has received increasing attention from the veterinary, animal protection, law enforcement and mental health communities (Arluke & Patronek, 2013; Berry, Patronek, & Lockwood, 2005; Frost, 2000; Frost, Patronek, & Rosenfield, 2011; Patronek, 1999). It potentially affects hundreds of thousands of animals each year. Veterinary forensics can play an important role in describing the effects of such treatment on the animals involved. This analysis can play an important part in supporting legal actions (i.e., prosecution for animal cruelty) or documenting the need for social service and/or mental health intervention for the people responsible.

Animal hoarding cases can differ from other neglect cases in several ways that necessitate special veterinary forensic considerations. By definition, hoarding cases involve large numbers of animals, often several hundred. Although such cases primarily involve dogs and/or cats, a wide variety of domestic and wild species have been encountered in such cases, necessitating special veterinary knowledge and attention to concerns about potential zoonotic diseases. Hoarders usually lack insight into the severity of problems many of their animals may have developed—or they may have employed their own ineffective remedies to treat serious illnesses. Attending veterinarians should be alert to the need to document ailments that have been untreated or improperly treated.

Hoarders may have animals acquired at different times or have special "companions" within the population. The presence of healthy animals amidst many sick ones should be noted since it helps convey the fact that the person involved knew how to care for animals but *intentionally* chose to deny care to some.

In addition to the conventional documentation needed in neglect cases, forensic veterinarians examining victims of hoarding should also be aware of and document conditions common in hoarding. Animals that spend time in environments with large accumulations of urine and feces commonly show urine scalds on extremities and may show general bleaching of the fur. High levels of ammonia can create or exacerbate upper respiratory ailments. Competition for food can result in cannibalization of other animals, particular newborn or stillborn animals. Evidence of such problems should be collected and documented.

Intentional Abuse

Cases of intentional abuse are among the most important cruelty cases to require the careful attention of a forensic veterinarian for several reasons. First, such cases usually have the potential for the most serious criminal penalties, often at the felony level, thus defendants in such cases usually seek strong legal defense. In addition, intentional abuse is a form of cruelty most strongly associated with the potential for interpersonal violence, particularly domestic violence and child abuse. Third, such cases are often of high public and media concern and the responsiveness and effectiveness of law enforcement, animal care and control and veterinary professionals involved in the case will be closely scrutinized.

Intentional or "non-accidental" injuries (NAIs) include a variety of presentations described below. Munro (1996, 1998) and Arkow et.al. (2011) describe some general principles that should raise the "index of suspicion" that an injury or ailment may be the result of intentional actions or willful neglect of needed treatment. Such indicators include:

- The client presents an inconsistent history (the story doesn't fit the injuries);
- The client presents a discrepant history (the history changes). The client may offer different histories to various staff members, or various family members may present different histories;
- Types of injuries. Some of the more common physical injuries that might raise an index of suspicion include old injuries evident on examination, ultrasound or x-ray. Rib injuries (fractures) in particular should raise suspicion;
- A history of repetitive injury; and/or
- A history of unexplained injuries or deaths in other animals in the household.

A given case may involve more than one form of injury. We will briefly review some of the specific forensic concerns associated with common forms of NAI.

Blunt force trauma

Blunt force trauma can be the result of falls, being hit by a vehicle, or other accidental injuries. However, such injuries from direct beatings, being thrown against a wall or floor, or stomping or crushing are frequently seen in association with interpersonal violence where harm or threats of harm to a pet are part of the dynamic of the exercise of power and control by an abuser (Ascione, 2008a; Gupta, 2008). Animal victims of blunt force trauma should undergo full-body radiographs in order to possibly identify fractures at multiple stages of healing. Certain patterns of injuries may raise additional suspicions, such as injuries that might reflect the dimensions of the instrument used to inflict injury (e.g., boot tip, hammer, rod). In the case of live animals, bruising may not be apparent even if a wound area is shaved to reveal the skin. In the case of deceased animals, the extent and pattern of blunt force trauma may not be revealed until the skin is reflected to show damage to the underlying tissues.

Sharp force trauma

Sharp force injuries include incised wounds from knives, axes, or other implements, as well as bite wounds, which usually also involve blunt force trauma. In addition to standard information collected in all suspected cruelty cases, the forensic veterinary examination of sharp force trauma should include description of the anatomical location of the injury, the shape and depth of the wound and description of the tissue characteristics and underlying structure. In some cases it may be possible to match these wound characteristics to the type of instrument that may have been used.

One of the most common cases presented for forensic analysis is the mutilation of small animals, usually cats, where it is suspected that the injuries were inflicted by a person. In the majority of cases, such injuries are ultimately attributed to the actions of predators (dogs, coyotes, foxes) whose bites can produce clean injuries that may appear to untrained observers to have been caused by a knife. Several characteristics help identify such trauma as having been caused by predation. First, wound edges are usually not as smooth as described, skin has often been torn rather than cut. Second, hairs around the wound show no signs of clean cuts. When blades are used to inflict injury, a portion of the overlying hair is usually cleanly cut. Finally, predator-related deaths usually show signs of bite wounds with associated saliva, which may be revealed by use of alternate light sources and which can be swabbed for DNA that can reveal the species of animal involved or even the specific individual, if reference samples are available.

In blunt or sharp force trauma cases where there is a human suspect, it is possible that the animal victim may have scratched or bitten the suspect while being restrained or attacked and may have some DNA evidence from the suspect, particularly embedded in claws. The forensic veterinarian should coordinate with other investigators to see if efforts should be made to gather such evidence.

Projectile injuries

Veterinary forensic analysis of animals that have received projectile injuries from bullets, pellets, BBs, arrows, darts, or other projectiles should include full body radiographs. In some cases, not all injuries will be externally visible or the animal may have received repeated injuries over time. Any projectiles recovered from the animal should be carefully handled to avoid disturbing other potential evidence such as fingerprints, DNA, or other markings. Efforts should be made to distinguish between entry and exit wounds, path through the body and, if possible, determine the orientation of the animal with respect to the shooter. This may prove significant in deciding whether an animal was approaching or fleeing at the time it was shot.

In the case of deceased victims, the veterinarian may be asked to provide opinions regarding the time between injury and death, how far the animal may have traveled, the sequence of injuries, and the overall "humaneness" of the killing (Sinclair et al., 2006).

Strangulation

Strangulation and hanging are not uncommon animal cruelty presentations and, like blunt force trauma, are frequently associated with intimate partner violence. In addition to a complete forensic necropsy, careful attention should be paid to any external items or lesions possibly created by such an item used to bind, tie, or hang the animal. Ligatures often contain traces of DNA from a suspect and tape used to bind an animal may have both DNA and fingerprint evidence. All such evidence should be carefully handled and packaged. In cases of hanging, one goal of the investigation may be to determine whether the hanging was a direct cause of death or occurred post-mortem following an unrelated cause (e.g., hit by car) or intentional killing by some other means followed by display of the animal to frighten or intimidate a person.

Drowning

Diagnosis of drowning as a cause of death is difficult. It is often a diagnosis by exclusion—no other cause of death is evident and other circumstances support an interpretation of drowning. As with blunt and sharp force trauma, there may be other evidence associated with restraint and struggle and possible injuries to the perpetrator.

Burning

Burns to animals may take the form of thermal injuries (scalding or direct heat/fire) or chemical burns from caustic substances such as lye. As with other forms of injuries, serious burns may be accidental or intentional. Careful documentation of the nature of the injuries (location, pattern, depth) may help distinguish between intentional harm (e.g., pouring or throwing hot or toxic liquid on animal) versus spills. Cases in which animals have been deliberately set on fire are particularly significant given the close connection between firesetting, animal cruelty, and a high risk of perpetrating interpersonal violence (Becker, Stuewig, Herrera, & McCloskey, 2004; Heath, Hardesty, & Goldfine, 1984). The pattern of injuries should be carefully documented and photographed. In the case of chemical burns, injury sites should be swabbed to collect samples for further analysis. If an accelerant (e.g., gasoline, kerosene, lighter fluid) were used in connection with burning of an animal, samples should be collected of fur and any other material contaminated by the accelerant. These samples should be stored in an airtight metal container for later analysis. Veterinary testimony regarding the pain and suffering associated with burn injuries could be particularly important at trial.

Poisoning

The ASPCA's National Animal Poison Control Center handles nearly 200,000 calls per year. Intentional exposures comprise less than 1% of all exposures of animals to potentially toxic agents, and malicious poisonings account for less than 0.5% of all poisonings reported (Hansen, Murphy, Khan, & Allen, 2001). Most cases involve ingestion of human prescription drugs or exposure to household pesticides, fertilizers, or other chemicals. When the Center is called to consult on a case, the following information is considered essential for diagnosis (Miller & Zawistowski, 2005):

- A thorough, detailed history including the presence of any toxins or poisonous plants in the immediate or surrounding environment;
- The use of any pesticides, fertilizers or chemicals by the owner, neighbors or local authorities;

- A list of both veterinary and human medications that the animal may have had access to or been given, such as Tylenol, in case the poisoning was accidental; and
- A history of the animal's diet, including snacks, in case a nutritional deficiency has been confused with a poisoning.

In suspected cruelty cases, the forensic veterinarian may be asked to:
- Identify the toxin and possible route of delivery based on medical symptoms;
- Estimate the time of exposure based on the progression of symptoms;
- Help identify possible evidence based on items in stomach contents or vomitus;
- Help exclude possible natural or accidental exposures such as snake or insect bites, toxic plants; and
- Provide testimony as to amount of pain and suffering induced by any intentional exposure to toxins.

Domestic animals can ingest many potentially harmful things, voluntarily or through human maliciousness. The forensic veterinarian can play a key role in trying provide an accurate account of what and animal was exposed to, what consequences it caused, and how it may have been prevented.

Organized Abuse

Many veterinary forensic investigations focus on animal victims of organized abuse, most commonly in the form of the illegal "blood sports" of dogfighting and cockfighting. Detailed discussion of the role of veterinarians in these investigations is provided elsewhere (Lockwood, 2011; 2013). Such investigations usually involve documenting the separate crimes of animal cruelty and animal fighting. Since animal fighting punishments can carry federal and state felony penalties, these charges may take precedence over general animal cruelty charges.

Dogfighting prosecutions are usually based on the preponderance of circumstantial evidence such as the presence of dogfighting paraphernalia and training equipment as well as medical supplies specific to the training and treatment of fighting dogs. Another key form of evidence is the documentation of injuries found in the animals that have been seized. The pattern of injuries on the animals' bodies as well as the presence of wounds in various stages of healing can be strongly indicative of a history of fighting rather than the result of a single "yard accident" fight between two dogs. In addition, veterinarians should note other medical conditions consistent with dogfighting such as filing of teeth or unprofessional ear cropping or tail docking. These actions may result in additional charges of cruelty or unlicensed practice of veterinary medicine. Forensic veterinarians should familiarize themselves with the range of drugs and supplements commonly encountered in dogfight operations and be prepared to discuss how they may be used and which are restricted or otherwise regulated.

Ritualized Abuse

Forensic veterinarians may be asked to examine deceased animals that have allegedly been used in ritualistic sacrifice. Such cases are rare and tend to involve cats or small animals killed by "self-styled" occult practitioners or other animals associated with the practice of certain forms of "cultural spiritualism" such as Santeria, Palo Mayombe or Voodoo (Sinclair et al., 2006). In many cases, animals or animal parts have been discovered in public places. As noted above, an important first step in such investigations is to consider the possibility that the remains are the results of predator activity. If there is clear evidence of human involvement, care should be taken to preserve any evidence that might be found in association with the animal. Certain rituals involve placing coins or notes on or in the animal and, in some cases, potentially toxic substances such as mercury may have been involved.

It is often assumed that animal sacrifice cannot be prosecuted as animal cruelty since it is protected by First Amendment religious freedoms. However, such protection does not offer a defense from charges of animal cruelty (Perdue & Lockwood, 2013). The role of the forensic veterinarian in such cases may be to comment on the speed and humaneness of the manner of killing involved—particularly in the case of larger mammals such as sheep or goats. Many animal sacrifice rituals involve chickens or doves. In such cases, veterinarians may also be asked to comment on the humaneness of the method of killing or on possible risks to other livestock posed by avian diseases in unregulated populations kept or sold for sacrifice.

Animal Sexual Assault

"Animal sexual assault" is the term more accurately used to describe what had earlier been referred to in laws as "bestiality." This represents a rethinking of both the underlying motivations and impact on the animal victim. Beirne (1997) makes this argument very clearly, noting that sexual abuse of animals parallels that of sexual abuse of women and children and is also problematic because (1) human-animal sexual contact is almost always coercive; (2) such practice often causes pain or death for the animal, and (3) animals are unable to consent or to communicate about their abuse. Likewise, Ascione (1993) notes that bestiality may be considered cruel even in cases when physical harm to an animal does not occur, drawing a parallel to cases of adult sexual activity with a child where consent is presumed to be impossible. As with other forms of animal cruelty, there has been increased attention to animal sexual assault in part because of evidence of connections to the potential for interpersonal violence (Beetz, 2005; Fleming, Jory, & Burton, 2002; Hensley, Tallichet, & Dutkiewicz, 2010). This has increased the likelihood that suspected cases of animal sexual assault will be reported and prosecuted.

With few exceptions, veterinarians have been slow to recognize occurrences of animal sexual assault and receive little or no training on how to address such cases (Munro, 2006; Munro & Thrusfield, 2001c). Detailed discussion of appropriate veterinary examination of animal victims of sexual assault is provided elsewhere (Bradley & Rasile, 2014; Merck, 2013, Sinclair et al., 2006). Evidence of any form of injury should be noted, particularly traumatic injury to the anus, rectum, or vulvar/vaginal area. This should include inspection of the entire animal with a UV light source, such as a Woods lamp, which may cause semen stains to fluoresce. In addition, if there is any evidence to suggest that there has been sexual contact between the animal and the abuser or with a human victim of the abuser, care should be taken to collect human or animal semen, seminal fluid, vaginal fluids, epithelial cells, pubic hairs, and any other existing evidence. A standard human Sexual Assault Evidence Kit (often referred to as a "rape kit") can be useful in processing evidence from animal victims as well. It is possible that the animal bit or scratched the perpetrator. The teeth, gums, and lips should be swabbed for possible DNA testing and scrapings of the nails saved. As with other forms of abuse that may involve violent restraint, full body radiographs should be taken to document possible underlying injuries, such as those that might be produced in restraining the animal victim. Animal sexual assault is rarely prosecuted in the absence of harm to the animal, so detailed veterinary testimony can be essential to moving such cases forward.

The Veterinary Professional in Court

One of the most important roles for a forensic veterinarian is to testify in court to help tell the story of an animal that may have suffered or died. This is a role that few veterinarians receive any formal training in as part of their veterinary education. As a result, they may be hesitant to become involved. Veterinarians are the logical and natural advocates for animals in society. However, in a court of law, the veterinarian's duty is to the court. The lawyer is the advocate for the animal, while veterinarians are the advocate for the truth, which should be their opinion. It can place them in an unfamiliar adversarial relationship with the opposition, one which can call their competence and training into question as a common defense tactic. However, good preparation and communication with prosecutors can make the process easier. Veterinarians also benefit from the fact that they are among the most trusted of all professionals and are almost universally admired by jurors; thus, their testimony is given great weight and defense attempts to undermine their efforts can easily backfire.

It is important to remember that the responsibility to "prove" a case does not lie on the veterinarian alone. His or her role is part of a multidisciplinary approach in which veterinary evidence is only part of the case. Ultimately, the judge or jury is the trier of fact and the veterinarian should simply present the facts of the case and his or her interpretation or conclusion drawn from such facts to assist the court in a resolution of the case.

Veterinary Forensics and the Response to Common Defenses

As the potential for serious consequences for conviction for animal cruelty has increased, defense attorneys have increased their efforts to vigorously challenge the prosecution of these cases and raise some measure of doubt about their client's guilt. Often veterinary forensic evidence serves as one of the most significant factors in overcoming such challenges. Good animal cruelty case preparation requires anticipating possible defenses even if they seem illogical, inconsistent, or far-fetched. Phillips and Lockwood (2013) review some of the most common defenses.

The animal had an accident.

The defendant may claim the animal was hit by a car, fell off of a high level (bookshelf, stairs, etc.) and broke its leg, or inadvertently got into some poison. As noted earlier, there is a wealth of information to aid veterinarians and others to distinguish between accidental and non-accidental injury, with well-established guidelines on situations that should raise suspicions of abuse (Phillips & Lockwood, 2013).

Someone else did it!

Forensic evidence specifically linking the defendant or his/her property (e.g., tools or weapons) or residence to the animal victim (e.g., fur, blood, feces, DNA) can help counter this defense. In general, DNA samples should be collected and stored from most animal victims for potential future reference to other evidence (Phillips & Lockwood, 2013).

It was a "mercy killing."

This defense is common in states where the law allows the "humane" killing of one's own animals. In some states the killing must also be "justified" (e.g., animal was sick, aged or had attacked someone). However, the methods used (e.g., drowning, blunt force trauma, multiple gunshot, poisoning, suffocation) may fall outside of the definition of a given state statute and the euthanasia guidelines of the American Veterinary Medical Association (AVMA, 2013), and thus can be challenged as being an inhumane killing, particularly if there is veterinary or other evidence that the animal was not killed quickly and painlessly. It should not be assumed that a practice that has been tolerated in the past (e.g., drowning unwanted young animals) meets contemporary societal and veterinary standards for humane killing (Phillips & Lockwood, 2013).

It was self-defense.

This is sometimes seen in cases involving the killing of an animal that allegedly was involved in an attack. In some cases the age, size and temperament of the animal may contradict this defense (as in the killing of a small cat by a large person). In a shooting situation, veterinarians may be asked to review forensic or ballistics evidence of where the animal was shot to demonstrate whether the animal was acting aggressively or retreating. If the defendant went back into his/her home to retrieve a gun, then that evidence will work against this defense (Phillips & Lockwood, 2013).

The animal is a "picky eater."

This defense may be offered to explain the poor body condition of animals involved. It is important for a veterinary exam to rule out medical problems that might result in failure to maintain weight. The feeding habits of the animal after being seized should be documented closely. Humane agencies often make a video recording of the first time a seized animal is offered food or water to document its response. In addition, data from weekly weighing that show a consistent weight gain with proper access to food can defeat such claims (Phillips & Lockwood, 2013).

The animal was recently rescued and was received in bad condition.

Refuting this defense may require other evidence regarding how long an animal has been in the defendant's care. Evidence that an animal has been at the facility for some time may include testimony from concerned staff or volunteers, testimony from individuals or organizations who may have originally surrendered the animal, or physical evidence such as the accumulation of feces in an unclean cage (Phillips & Lockwood, 2013).

The defendant claims to be an animal hospice provider and says animals are dying from other causes.

Some rescue hoarders will claim that the animals in their care were already diagnosed with a fatal disease and they simply allowed the animals to live out their lives in their care. There are established veterinary medical standards for animal hospice care.[1] The difference between a hoarder and a true hospice caregiver is that the hospice caregiver does not deny veterinary care or food, and they provide a clean and safe environment for the animal. For the animals, it is important to obtain prior documentation of the claimed "fatal" disease. If no documentation can be provided, an examination of the surviving or deceased animal(s) may determine whether the animal(s) truly had a fatal disease (Phillips & Lockwood, 2013).

---

1. See International Association of Animal Hospice and Palliative Care, http://www.iaahpc.org.

Trends in Veterinary Forensics

The growth of veterinary forensic sciences in addressing animal cruelty is not simply a fad building on popular interest in forensics and "CSI-type" stories. It has become an essential tool in the investigation and prosecution of an increasing number of cases. McEwen (2012) reviewed 1,706 medicolegal cases submitted to the Animal Health Laboratory of the University of Guelph, Ontario, Canada between 1998 and 2010. Criminal cases are the only medicolegal case category that consistently increased over the 12-year period. Based on pathology reports for the 271 criminal cases, 117 (43.1%) were consistent with neglect, 79 (29.2%) were compatible with non-accidental injury (NAI), including two cases of sexual abuse, 13 (4.80%) were poisoning, 29 (10.7%) were deemed to be due to natural disease, and 31 (11.43%) were inconclusive. Of the 79 cases of NAI, the majority (52%) were solely blunt force trauma, which on occasion was accompanied by sharp force injury, gun-shot, or asphyxia.

The field has also seen the growth of specialty animal forensic laboratories including the Veterinary Genetics Laboratory at the University of California, Davis and major expansion of the Fish and Wildlife Service's Forensic Laboratory in Ashland, Oregon. Most of the efforts of this laboratory involve identifying species that may be the victim of illegal hunting or trafficking and assisting in legal cases involving wildlife by determining the cause of death and assessing factors that contribute to an environment that may be unhealthy or lethal to protected species (Stroud, 1998). As with veterinary forensics in general, the field of wildlife forensics has seen a recent growth in textbooks devoted to the subject (Cooper & Cooper, 2013; Huffman & Wallace, 2011; Linacre & Tobe, 2013).

Future Needs

There have been significant improvements in the recognition, reporting, prosecution and prevention of animal abuse and neglect in the last decade, and the involvement of veterinarians and forensic scientists has helped produce and sustain these changes. Future progress will benefit from additional advances in various ways.

Improved tracking of animal cruelty cases

Animal cruelty is defined differently in every state and the responsibility for responding to cruelty is often delegated to a variety of different agencies and organizations, including police, sheriff's departments, health departments, animal care and control, humane societies, and SPCAs. This has made the accurate tabulation of such crimes extremely difficult since no centralized reporting mechanism exists. This in turn hampers attempts to assess the effectiveness of responses to these crimes.

Thanks to efforts led by the National Sheriffs Association and the International Association of Chiefs of Police, a proposal to include animal cruelty in the Federal Bureau of Investigation's (FBI) Uniform Crime Reports (UCR) was approved in June of 2014. The measure, part of a wholesale redesign and redevelopment of the UCR, would add Animal Cruelty as a Group A offense. It would expand Data Element 12 (Type Criminal Activity/Gang Information) to include four categories of animal crimes: simple/gross neglect; intentional abuse and torture; organized abuse; and animal sexual abuse. Definitions of these crimes would include torturing, tormenting, mutilating, maiming, poisoning, abandoning, and failing to provide shelter, food, water, and veterinary care. Transporting or confining an animal in a manner likely to cause injury or death, causing animals to fight with one another, and inflicting repeated or excessive pain and suffering would also be included. Significant obstacles remain in implementing these changes, as each state has its own laws and definitions and many states do not participate in the system. However, it is significant that the U.S. Department of Justice now recognizes cruelty to animals as a matter worthy of law enforcement concern. Hopefully, this will inspire state and local law enforcement agencies to initiate better tracking systems for animal cruelty, abuse, neglect, and fighting in order to provide valuable information to assist communities in allocating animal care and control resources and training.

Incorporation of animal cruelty reporting and veterinary forensics into veterinary curricula

Although the University of Florida, Gainesville is currently the only school offering a degree program in veterinary forensics sciences, several schools currently offer electives in the subject or incorporate coverage of the field into shelter medicine programs. It is hoped that this trend will follow that seen with the addition of animal law programs to over 150 law schools in the last decade (Animal Legal Defense Fund, 2015).

Incorporation of animal cruelty investigation into the core of law enforcement training

Growing recognition of the connection between animal cruelty and other serious crimes has attracted the attention of many law enforcement agencies, but inclusion of training on animal cruelty laws, cruelty investigations and the capabilities of veterinary forensic sciences into police academies or state-mandated Police Officer Standards and Training (POST) is still in its infancy. In the past, law enforcement response to intimate partner violence was similarly dependent upon the level of concern about the issue shown by local law enforcement leadership, but societal pressures have resulted in it becoming a core part of all contemporary police training and response. Similar realization of the importance of effective response to animal cruelty will hopefully follow a similar course.

Society's response to animal abuse and neglect has become truly interdisciplinary, as evidenced by the diversity of professional viewpoints represented in this volume. It is exciting to add the field of forensic sciences and the specialized discipline of veterinary forensics to the broad base of expertise united in efforts to address violence and cruelty in all its forms.

References

American Veterinary Medical Association. (2013). *AVMA guidelines for the euthanasia of animals*. Schaumburg, Illinois: American Veterinary Medical Association.

American Veterinary Medical Association. (2015). Abuse Reporting Requirements by State. https://www.avma.org/KB/Resources/Reference/AnimalWelfare/Pages/Abuse-Reporting-requirements-by-State.aspx, accessed 11/9/2015.

Animal Legal Defense Fund. (2015). Animal law courses. Retrieved from http://aldf.org/animal-law-courses/.

Arkow, P. (1999). Initiating an animal abuse reporting policy at a veterinary teaching hospital. In F. R. Ascione & P. Arkow (Eds.), *Child abuse, domestic violence, and animal abuse: Linking the circles of compassion for prevention and intervention* (pp. 257–259). West Lafayette, IN: Purdue University Press.

Arkow, P., & Munro, H. (2008). The veterinary profession's roles in recognizing and preventing family violence: The experiences of the human medicine field and the development of diagnostic indicators of Non-Accidental Injury. In F. R. Ascione (Ed.), *International handbook of animal abuse and cruelty: Theory, research, and application* (pp. 31–58). West Lafayette, IN: Purdue University Press.

Arkow, P., Boyden, P., & Patterson-Kane, E. (2011). *Practical guidance for the effective response by veterinarians to suspected animal cruelty, abuse and neglect.* Schaumburg, IL: American Veterinary Medical Association.

Arluke, A., & Patronek, G. (2013). Animal hoarding. In, M. P. Brewster & C. L. Reyes, (Eds.), *Animal cruelty: A multidisciplinary approach to understanding* (pp. 197–214). Durham, N.C.: Carolina Academic Press.

Ascione, F. R. (1993). Children who are cruel to animals: A review of research and implications for developmental psychology. *Anthrozoös, 6:* 226–247.

Ascione, F. R. (Ed.). (2008). *International handbook of animal abuse and cruelty: Theory, research, and application.* West Lafayette, IN: Purdue University Press.

Ascione, F. R. (2008a). Animal/pet abuse. In C. Renzetti & J. Edleson (Eds.). *Encyclopedia of interpersonal violence.* Thousand Oaks, CA: Sage.

Ascione, F. R., & Lockwood, R. (2001). Cruelty to animals: Changing psychological, social, and legislative perspectives. In D. J. Salem & A. N. Rowan (Eds.). *The State of the Animals 2001* (pp. 39–54). Washington, DC: Humane Society of the U.S.

Becker, K., Stuewig, J., Herrera, V., & McCloskey, L. (2004). A study of firesetting and animal cruelty in children: Family influences and adolescent outcomes. *Journal of the American Academy of Child and Adolescent Psychiatry, 43*(7), 905–912.

Beetz, A. M. (2005). Bestiality and zoophilia: Associations with violence and sex offending. In, A.M. Beetz. & A.L. Podberscek (Eds.). *Bestiality and zoophilia: Sexual relations with animals* (pp. 46–70). West Lafayette, IN: Purdue University Press.

Berry, C., Patronek, G., & Lockwood, R. (2005). Long-term outcomes in animal hoarding cases. *Animal Law Review, 11,* 167–194.

Bradley N., & Rasile, K. (2014, April). Recognition and management of animal sexual abuse. *Clinician's Brief,* 73–75.

Bruchim, Y., Loeb, E. Saragust, J., & Aroch, I. (2009) Pathological findings in dogs with fatal heatstroke. *Journal of Comparative Pathology, 140,* 97–104.

Byard, R. W., & Boardman, W. (2011). The potential role of forensic pathologists in veterinary forensic medicine. *Forensic Science, Medicine and Pathology, 7,* 231–232.

Colorado Veterinary Medical Association (2007). *Mandatory Reporting of Cruelty to Animals and Animal Fighting.* Retrieved January 18, 2015 from www.colovma.org/resource/resmgr/imported/Animal%20Cruelty%20Issue%20Brief.pdf.

Cooper. J. E. (1998). What is forensic veterinary medicine? Its relevance to the modern exotic animal practice. *Journal of Exotic Pet Medicine, 7*(4),161–165.

Cooper, J. E. & Cooper, M. (2007). *Introduction to veterinary and comparative forensic medicine.* Ames, IA: Wiley-Blackwell.

Cooper, J. E. & Cooper, M. (2013). *Wildlife forensic investigation: Principles and practice.* Ames, IA: Wiley-Blackwell.

Cornell University College of Veterinary Medicine. (2015). History and archives. Retrieved February 12, 2015 from http://vet.cornell.edu/about/history.cfm.

Di Maio, V. J. M. & Dana, S. E. (1998). *Forensic Pathology*. Georgetown, TX: Landes Bioscience.

Drobatz, K. J., & Macintire, D. K. (1996). Heat-induced illness in dogs: 42 cases (1976–1993). *Journal of the American Veterinary Medical Association, 209*,1894–1899.

Fleming, W. M., Jory, B., & Burton, D.L. (2002). Characteristics of juvenile offenders admitting to sexual activity with nonhuman animals. *Society & Animals, 10*(1), 31–45.

Frost, R. (2000). People who hoard animals. *Psychiatric Times, 1*(4), 25–29.

Frost, R., Patronek, G., & Rosenfield, E. (2011). Comparison of object and animal hoarding. *Depression and Anxiety, 28*, 885–891.

Gerdin, J. A., & McDonough, S. P. (2013). Forensic pathology of companion animal abuse and neglect. *Veterinary Pathology Online, 50*(6), 994–1006.

Green, P. D. (1979). Protocols in medicolegal veterinary medicine I. Identification of cases and preparation for court. *Canadian Veterinary Journal, 20*, 8–12.

Green, P. D. (1980). Protocols in medicolegal veterinary medicine II. Cases involving death due to gunshot and arrow wounds. *Canadian Veterinary Journal, 21*, 343–346.

Gupta, M. (2008). Functional links between intimate partner violence and animal abuse: Personality features and representations of aggression. *Society & Animals,* 16,3, 223–242.

Hansen, S. R., Murphy, L. A.; Khan, S. A., & and Allen, C. (2001). An overview of malicious animal poisonings. *North American Congress of Clinical Toxicology*. October 4–9, 2001. Montreal, Quebec, Canada.

Heath, G. A., Hardesty, V. A., & Goldfine, P.E. (1984). Firesetting, enuresis, and animal cruelty. *Journal of Child and Adolescent Psychotherapy 1*, 97–100.

Hensley, C., Tallichet, S. E., & Dutkiewicz, E. L. (2010). Childhood bestiality: A potential precursor to adult interpersonal violence. *Journal of Interpersonal Violence, 25*(3), 557–567.

Huffman, J. E., & Wallace. J.R. (2011) *Wildlife forensics: Methods and applications*. Ames, IA: Wiley-Blackwell.

Landau, R. (1999). The veterinarian's role in recognizing and reporting abuse. In F.R. Ascione & P. Arkow (Eds.), *Child abuse, domestic violence, and animal abuse: Linking the circles of compassion for prevention and intervention* (pp. 241–249). West Lafayette, IN: Purdue University Press.

Lane, M. S., & Zawistowski, S. L. (2008). *Heritage of care: The American Society for the Prevention of Cruelty to Animals*. Westport, CT: Praeger.

Linacre, A., & Tobe, S. (2013). *Wildlife DNA analysis: Applications in forensic science*. Ames, IA: Wiley-Blackwell.

Linzey, A. (Ed.). (2009). *The link between animal abuse and human violence*. Eastbourne, East Sussex, UK: Sussex Academic Press.

Lockwood, R., & Ascione, F. (Eds.) (1998). *Animal cruelty and interpersonal violence: Readings in research and application*. West Lafayette, IN: Purdue University Press.

Lockwood, R. (2011). *Dogfighting toolkit for law enforcement: Addressing dogfighting in your community*. Washington, D.C.: Community Oriented Policing Services, U.S. Department of Justice.

Lockwood, R. (2013). Animal fighting, in L. Miller & S. Zawistowski (Eds). *Shelter medicine for veterinarians and staff* (2nd ed.) (pp. 441–452). Ames, IA: Blackwell.

Lockwood, R. (2014). *Cruelty to animals and interpersonal violence: An update.* Training key #689. Arlington, VA: International Association of Chiefs of Police.

McEwen, B. J. (2012). Trends in domestic animal medico-legal pathology cases submitted to a veterinary diagnostic laboratory 1998–2010. *Journal of Forensic Science, 57*(5), 1231–1233.

Merck, M. (2013). *Veterinary forensics: Animal cruelty investigations.* 2nd ed. Ames, IA: Wiley-Blackwell.

Merck, M. (2007). *Veterinary forensics: Animal cruelty investigations.* Ames, IA: Wiley-Blackwell.

Merz-Perez, L., & Heide, K. M. (2004). *Animal cruelty: Pathway to violence against people.* Walnut Creek, CA: AltaMira Press.

Miller, L. (2006). *The recognition and documentation of animal abuse.* Salem, OR: Oregon Veterinary Medical Association.

Miller, L., & Zawistowski, S. (2005). A call for veterinary forensics: The preparation and interpretation of physical evidence for cruelty investigation and prosecution. In P. Olson (Ed.), *Recognizing and reporting animal abuse: A veterinarian's guide* (pp. 63–67). Englewood, CO: American Humane Association.

Miller, L., & Zawistowski, S. (Eds.) (2013): *Shelter medicine for veterinarians and staff.* (2nd ed.). Ames, IA: Blackwell.

Munro, H. M. C. (1996). Battered pets. *Irish Veterinary Journal, 49,* 712–713.

Munro, H.M.C. (2006). Animal sexual abuse: A veterinary taboo? *The Veterinary Journal, 172*(2), 195–197.

Munro, H. M. C., & Thrusfield, M. V. (2001a). 'Battered pets': Features that raise suspicion of non-accidental injury. *Journal of Small Animal Practice, 42,* 218–226.

Munro, H. M. C., & Thrusfield, M. V. (2001b). 'Battered pets': Non-accidental physical injuries found in dogs and cats. *Journal of Small Animal Practice, 42,* 279–290.

Munro, H. M. C., & Thrusfield, M. V. (2001c). 'Battered pets': Sexual abuse. *Journal of Small Animal Practice, 42,* 333–337.

Munro, H. M. C., & Thrusfield, M. V. (2001d). 'Battered pets': Munchausen Syndrome by Proxy (factitious illness by proxy). *Journal of Small Animal Practice, 42,* 385–389.

Munro, R., & Munro, H. M. C. (2008). *Animal abuse and unlawful killing: Forensic veterinary pathology.* Philadelphia: Elsevier/Saunders.

Patronek, G. (1999). Hoarding of animals: An under-recognized public health problem in a difficult to study population. *Public Health Reports, 114,* 82–87.

Perdue, A., & Lockwood, R. (2014). *Animal cruelty and freedom of speech: When worlds collide. U.S. v. Stevens and other challenges on public policy and animal protection.* W. Lafayette, IN: Purdue University Press.

Phillips, A., & Lockwood, R. (2013). *Investigating & prosecuting animal abuse: A guidebook on safer communities, safer families & being an effective voice for animal victims.* Alexandria, VA: National District Attorneys Association.

Robertson, I. (2009). A legal duty to report suspected animal abuse—are veterinarians ready? In A. Linzey (Ed.), *The link between animal abuse and human violence* (pp. 263–272). Eastbourne, East Sussex, UK: Sussex Academic Press.

Sharma, B. R. (2003). Clinical forensic medicine—management of crime victims from trauma to trial. *Journal of Clinical Forensic Medicine*, 10(4), 267–273.

Sinclair, L., Merck, M., & Lockwood, R. (2006). *Forensic investigation of animal cruelty: A guide for veterinary and law enforcement professionals.* Washington, DC: Humane Society of the U.S.

Stroud, R. K. (1998). Wildlife forensics and the veterinary practitioner. *Journal of Exotic Pet Medicine.* 7(4),182–192.

Veterinary Council of New Zealand. (2013). *Guidance for veterinarians dealing with cases of suspected or actual animal abuse and family violence.* Retrieved from http://nationallinkcoalition.org.

Yoffe-Sharp, B. L., & Loar, L. M. (2009). The veterinarian's responsibility to recognize and report animal abuse. *Journal of the American Veterinary Medical Association*, 234(6), 732–737.

Chapter 6

The Animal-Human Bond

Elizabeth B. Strand, Christina Risley-Curtiss, and Bethanie A. Poe

Introduction

"I just don't want to be the bad guy no more ... I *don't* want to be the bad guy no more and the puppies showed me that I don't have to be. It is all right to be a person, it is all right to express myself, it is all right to want to help someone."

—Michael Jenkins
Prison Inmate, Orange County Prison New York
("BBC NEWS | Americas | Prisoners raise puppies in jail," n.d.)

In the Puppies Behind Bars (PBB) program, incarcerated inmates are given a chance for rehabilitation instead of simple "warehousing," through raising puppies to be service animals. The trained dogs end up serving the justice department through bomb detection, and serving the needs of physically and mentally wounded veterans coming back from war, as well as serving the needs of people who are blind, deaf, or have other disabilities. In the program, puppies live with prisoners 24 hours a day, seven days a week. These prisoners are responsible for socializing these dogs to become good working companions for the human beings who need them (Cheakalos, 2004). Prison-based animal programs (PAPs) are increasing and highlight how attention to the animal-human bond is being recognized and included in the field of criminal justice in practical ways (Furst, 2006).

The animal-human bond (AHB) is a broad concept, however, with the PBB program being just one example of a mechanism through which people bond with animals. For many of us, animals are considered companions, best friends, and family members. Animals even meet human needs emotionally and socially by providing unconditional love, being part of daily activities and routines, and being a witness to and sharing important life experiences (Toray, 2004). Additionally, animals and people are connected through working animal relationships such as those with guide dogs and police dogs, as well as through attention to wildlife like watching bird feeders in the yard or going to visit animals at the zoo. People are bonded to many types of animals besides just traditional companion animals like cats and dogs. People are also connected to animals as a food source, and sadly, bonds with animals can even be violent in families where aggressive and abusive behavior occurs.

Therefore, what has traditionally been referred to as the AHB is now being expanded to all types of animal-human relationships. The term "bond" has traditionally put focus on the positive side of animal-human relationships, but as our awareness and study of animal-human relationships increases and more attention is being given to the breadth of our relationships with them, the AHB is more often referred to as "animal-human relationships" or "interactions." These terms are more inclusive and include both positive and negative animal-human interactions. The study of animal-human relationships encompasses a wide variety of disciplines, including social work, biology, psychology, sociology, anthropology, medicine and economics, each with its own focus, methodologies, and vocabularies making it difficult to contextualize the multidisciplinary scope of the field (Hosey & Melfi, 2014).

With attention to this breadth of the AHB, this chapter reviews four main areas: 1) theories that help explain how and why people bond with animals, 2) the different types of AHBs that can occur, 3) what is known about cultural influences and animals, and 4) the criminal justice implications of the AHB.

Theories of the AHB

While there are many theories that explain aspects of the AHB, we will briefly discuss the biophilia hypothesis, the anthropomorphic-chattel continuum, attachment theory, and social support theory. Also, given there are other chapters dedicated to the issue of theories of violence to animals in this volume, we will focus here more on the general theories that describe these relationships.

The Biophilia Hypothesis

"It should come as no great surprise to find that *Homo sapiens* at least still feels an innate preference for the natural environment that cradled us" (Wilson, 2001, p. 241). Developed by evolutionary biologist E. O. Wilson, the biophilia hypothesis posits that human beings are genetically predisposed to paying attention to nature. Hunting and locating food through paying attention to the natural world meant survivability to early humans (Beck & Katcher, 2003). This means that, from an evolutionary perspective, attending to the natural world was not simply a pleasurable activity, like walking in the park or enjoying the birds singing, but rather a habit that was directly related to one's ability to maintain life (Kellert & Wilson, 1993). Frumkin (2001) defines the domains within the biophilia hypothesis to be animals, plants, landscapes, and wilderness experiences. Given the fact that animals are a main focus point in people's experience of nature, this theory has been used to describe the AHB.

Gullone (2000) notes that the biophilia hypothesis is exhibited in three main ways. From an animal-related human experience (ARHE) perspective, *adaptive approach behaviors* are when a situation is deemed to be safe and secure because animals in the environment are calm and engaging in normal behaviors. For instance, someone afraid of flying may request permission to bring his or her companion dog on an aircraft and feel safe as long as the dog looks calm and relaxed. This experience gives the message that one can "approach" a situation safely. *Avoidance behaviors*, alternatively, are when animals show signs of stress or are fleeing, giving the message that a situation is unsafe and must be avoided. For example, horses or cattle that are disturbed may alert a person that potential danger is near. Therefore, from an evolutionary perspective, paying attention to animals helps humans make life and death decisions. Moreover, Gullone (2000) describes a third category of survival behaviors called *restoration and stress recovery*. This explains how the presence of animals can help a person overcome challenging circumstances, such as the benefits of service animals for war veterans or even birds for prison inmates (Furst, 2006). Even people suffering from dementia benefit from the presence of animals. Using a pretest-posttest design, Edwards, Beck, and Lim (2014) found that Alzheimer's patients in a nursing facility improved on scales of uncooperative, irrational, sleep, and inappropriate behaviors after the addition of a fish tank. When individuals are in environments lacking contact with nature, the biophilia hypothesis may suggest that absence of contact with the natural world thwarts appropriate development leading to problems with mental health, violence, and substance abuse (Besthorn, 2002; Frumkin, 2001; Gullone, 2000). Indeed, keeping animals as pets may be one way human beings seek to satisfy this need to have nature around on a consistent basis (Beck, 2014). However, because the theory of biophilia is so broad, covering animals, plants, and the environment, as well as all of the human genetic code, it is difficult to research and understand precisely the factors that underlie the AHB (Joye, 2011).

Anthropomorphic-Integrated-Chattel Orientation Continuum

Myna Milani, DVM has written extensively on the AHB in veterinary medical practice (Milani, 1991, 1995, 2011) and has identified a continuum of the way people themselves relate to animals. The continuum goes from an anthropomorphized view of animals to a view that considers animals as chattel.

In the anthropomorphized view, people see their animals as having human qualities. Milani (1995) acknowledges that, to a certain extent, we have no choice but to anthropomorphize animals because the only perspective we can ultimately take is our own—that of the human being. The benefits of anthropomorphizing animals are that through this type of connection, people express care and concern and have deep emotional connections with animals. However, there are limitations to this view as well, such as when animals are so anthropomorphized that they are no longer treated as animals, but as human beings, causing the animals' needs to go unseen and unmet. This may occur when, instead of giving an animal prescribed medications, the person gives his own medication because he believes it will work for his dog just as it works for him. It can also manifest in a deep and unhealthy emotional dependency on an animal that prevents the animal from living a life natural to its species, such as in animal hoarding situations (Nathanson, 2009). This can also be true when a person uses an animal to get human attention. An extreme example is when a person intentionally harms an animal in order to get attention from the veterinarian as in Munchausen syndrome by proxy (Milani, 2006; Munro & Thrusfield, 2001b).

On the other end of the continuum is the chattel orientation that is characterized by emotional detachment from an animal, seeing them more like machines to be utilized than as beings with whom one can emotionally connect. This may be the case in situations where animals serve a utilitarian purpose such as food animals or animals that are for show. In these relationships, the animal is utilized by people as tools for income, entertainment, and perhaps, work. On the positive side of a chattel orientation is the willingness of the person who is responsible for decisions regarding the animal to accept scientific and health-related recommendations without placing irrelevant or excessive emotional content into decision-making. Additionally, sometimes having a chattel orientation can be protective for the emotions of a person who may be in a situation such as caring for large numbers of unwanted animals that must be euthanized (Baran et al. 2009; Chur-Hansen, 2010). On the negative side of the chattel orientation is the possibility of a person using an animal as a tool to harm another human being as in domestic and family violence situations (Faver & Strand, 2007). Moreover, separating oneself emotionally from animals, which is required in the chattel orientation, may result in abusive behaviors in the food animal industry (Porcher, 2010).

Milani (1995) writes, "people who maintain an integrated approach relate to animals neither as people [nor] as objects, but rather as separate, animate beings who become incomprehensible beyond a certain limit" (pp. 25–26). Because the human experience of the animal is incomprehensible at a certain point, it becomes necessary for the human to set limits that may seem arbitrary to others but meaningful to them. These relationships can be emotional and connected, but may also come to an end because the person in the relationship makes decisions based on his/her needs, instead of the needs of an animal, which are deemed "incomprehensible." This is a difficult area to define because the point at which a person makes a decision about an animal varies according to his or her own culture, previous experience with animals, and available resources, not from seeing the animal as either human (anthropomorphized) or inanimate (chattel).

Attachment Theory

Similar to the biophilic idea that attention to animals is an evolutionary instinct is the concept of attachment theory for humans developed by a 20th century British psychiatrist and psychoanalyst, John Bowlby. Attachment theory holds that proximity-seeking of the infant to the caregiver (attachment figure) is an evolutionary survival tool to ensure protection and eventual growth of the infant into adulthood. Bowlby's perspectives on attachment were significantly influenced by research in the field of ethology—namely the imprinting instincts of goslings studied by Konrad Lorenz and his collaboration with many other well-known ethologists such as Robert Hinde and Harry Harlow (Horst, LeRoy, & Veer, 2008). Of particular influence to Bowlby was Harlow's research with rhesus monkeys demonstrating that "contact comfort" (in a clinical laboratory setting) was more important to the infant rhesus monkey, than food. Given the ethological influences that contributed to attachment theory, it is logical that researchers would look to the attachment model as a theoretical explanation for how animals and humans bond.

There are four behaviors that are inherent in the development of an attachment relationship: 1) *proximity maintenance* with the attachment figure, 2) experiencing the attachment figure as a *safe haven* from discomfort and stress, 3) using the attachment figure as a *secure base* from which exploration and risk-taking can occur, and 4) experiencing *separation distress* when not with the attachment figure (Zilcha-Mano, Mikulincer, & Shaver, 2011). Mary Ainsworth and Silvia Bell (1970) contributed "attachment styles" to the theory, using a test called "The Strange Situation." Ainsworth observed the behaviors of young children (12 to 18 months) interacting with their attachment figure through periods of separation and re-unification. She differentiated between *secure attachments* and *insecure attachments*. Ainsworth identified two types of insecure attachments: resistant/ambivalent and avoidant. Later Main, Kaplan, and Cassidy (1985) added the disorganized insecure attachment style.

Recent research has supported the relevance of attachment theory to describe the AHB. Peacock, Chur-Hansen, and Winefield (2012) explored the mental health implications of the AHB using attachment theory. Zilcha-Mano et al. (2011) developed an assessment tool, the "Pet Attachment Questionnaire" (PAQ) to explore the animal-human relationship in terms of anxious and avoidant attachments. Additionally, Palmer and Custance (2008) utilized attachment theory to demonstrate the animal-human attachment through the application of a modified version of Ainsworth's Strange Situation test.

Peacock et al. (2012) measured the AHB by assessing proximity maintenance with the animal, the owner's experience of emotional reciprocity in the relationship, and level of commitment to the animal (i.e., whether the animal would be relinquished if it posed health threats to the owner). The researchers found that level of attachment was a significant predictor of somatoform (physical) symptoms, depression, and anxiety for the owners. However, the researchers found that level of human social support was not a moderating factor between level of animal-human attachment and psychological distress. In other words, if there was poor social support, people reported poor psychological wellbeing regardless of attachment to their pets. This finding was in opposition to some earlier studies indicating that the presence of animals was associated with better psychological well-being (Garrity, Stallones, Marx, & Johnson, 1989).

Zilcha-Mano et al. (2011) explored attachment and animal-human relationships, through the development and administration of the PAQ, as well as animal-human attachment and mental health, attachment styles in human relationships, and human experiences of animal loss. The PAQ assesses the insecure attachment styles of anxious attachment and avoidant attachment. Findings of the study indicate that attachment insecurities in animal-human relationships *match* more than they *compensate* for attachment insecurities in human-human relationships. In other words, anxious animal-human attachments were associated with being sensitive and insecure in human relationships and avoidant animal-human attachments were related with being more solitary in human-human relationships. The researchers also found that anxious animal-human attachments were related to psychological distress.

It seems as if attachment behaviors in the AHB are reciprocal across species. For instance, Palmer and Custance (2008) randomly assigned 38 dog owner pairs into one of two conditions modeled after the Ainsworth's Strange Situation Test: Condition 1 allowed the dog and owner to enter the new setting together first and Condition 2 placed the dog with a stranger in the new setting first. Findings indicated that the owner did serve as a *secure base* for the dog as evidenced by the dog exploring its surroundings more in the presence of the owner and less when the dog was with a stranger or alone. Although the dogs were willing to engage the stranger in both conditions (unlike with human infants) those dogs who met the stranger with the owner present more quickly engaged the stranger. Independent play was also depressed in dogs when they were with the stranger only or alone. Therefore, there is evidence that supports that owners can serve as a secure base in canine-human connections.

Scholars have indicated that the application of attachment theory to animal-human relationships is perhaps weak because, a) many of the instruments used do not actually adhere to the attachment theory itself (Collis & McNicholas, 1998; Crawford, Worsham, & Swinehart, 2006), and b) more research indicates that social support theory may be a more appropriate representation of the animal-human relationship (Collis & McNicholas, 1998). However, there has been progress in the measures used to explore attachment theory to understand the animal-human connection (Palmer & Custance, 2008; Zilcha-Mano et al., 2011), as well as applying both social support theory and attachment theory to this relationship (Peacock et al., 2012).

Social Support Theory

Sidney Cobb, a seminal leader in the field of social support theory held that there are three main ways social support occurs: "1) information leading the subject to believe that he is cared for and loved, 2) information leading the subject to believe that he is esteemed and valued, and 3) information leading the subject to believe that he belongs to a network of communication and mutual obligation" (Cobb, 1976, p. 300). As the theory developed, additional factors were added to these three including: tangible/practical/instrumental support and the opportunity to provide nurturance (Collis & McNicholas, 1998). Moreover, the way in which social support is most effective has also been explored (Lakey & Orehek, 2011; McConnell, Brown, Shoda, Stayton, & Martin, 2011).

Social support generally is understood to operate in two ways: direct effects and buffering effects. Direct effects mean that the presence of social support is life-enhancing even when things are calm. Buffering effects mean that social support helps buffer the negative health and well-being consequences that may occur when things are stressful. People who live in communities that have a great deal of mutual aid and enjoy a lot of support may be experiencing the direct effects described in social support theory, whereas those people who have been in a tornado and are surrounded by a church or other community reinforcements may be experiencing the buffering effects described in social support theory. Moreover, there is a difference between perceived social support (how a recipient feels about his or her level of social support) and enacted social support (concrete resources or intervention for the recipient), with perceived social support sometimes being experienced as more helpful than enacted social support (Lakey & Orehek, 2011).

Lakey and Orehek (2011) argue that relational support (providing and receiving emotional, behavioral, and cognitive regulation through human-to-human contact) and quasi-relational support (interacting with or just thinking about animals, special activities, objects, or ideas, and symbolic people such as revered religious leaders) are important factors in how social support functions. The more people share the same preferences in communication style and quasi-relational support, the more beneficial are the emotional, behavioral, and cognitive regulation. This theory may explain why animals are sometimes called social lubricants (Messent, 1985). According to this model, the presence of an animal may become a shared quasi-relational focus between people, making their connection feel more supportive. The ways animals "lubricate" social connections between people has been observed with children (Friedmann et al., 1983), people receiving some form of medical treatment (Wesley, Minatrea, & Watson, 2009), and people with disabilities (Eddy, Hart, & Boltz, 1988).

McConnell, Brown, Shoda, Stayton, and Martin (2011) conducted three studies to explore how animals provide social support for people. The findings of their first two studies suggested that people who reported that their animals provided them with good social support had better well-being than non-animal owners. They also found that animals provide a *complementary* as opposed to a *compensatory* form of social support. In other words, people who felt more supported by their animals also felt more supported by the people in their lives. People low on human social support did not compensate with higher levels of social support from their animals. These two studies provide evidence for the main effects method of social support theory. McConnell and colleagues' third study explored whether social support offered by companion animals served as a buffer for stress. The researchers placed people into groups where they wrote about a humiliating story and then either, a) wrote about their animals, b) wrote about a best friend, or c) drew a map of campus. Findings suggested that those who wrote about both their animals and their friends after the humiliating story reported significantly higher levels of social support than those individuals who drew a map after the humiliating story. These findings support a buffering hypothesis for social support provided by animals as well as suggest that the quasi-relationships offered by remembering important people and animals has an effect of perception of social fulfillment.

In another stress-buffering social support study, Duvall Antonacopoulos and Pychyl (2010) conducted an on-line survey of 132 cat and dog owners to explore levels of human social support, attachment to companion animals, depression, and loneliness. They found that for those individuals living alone, level of attachment to a companion animal had no effect on levels of depression or loneliness. However, dog owners with high human social support were significantly less lonely than non-companion animal owners with high levels of human social support. For owners with high attachment to companion animals and low human social support, depression and loneliness were also significantly higher than for owners with low levels of attachment to their animals. Therefore, in this study, support was again found for the *complementary* more than *compensatory* hypothesis of animals as social supports.

Thus far, attention has been given to general theories that may describe the AHB including biophilia, the anthropomorphic-chattel continuum, attachment theory, and social support theory. Additionally, findings from the research studies shared thus far indicate how the AHB benefits people as well as mimics human-to-human bonds. Some evidence has also pointed to increased levels of depression and loneliness for people highly attached to companion animals.

Sadly, there is also a negative side to the AHB that includes violence to animals, and the co-occurrence of violence to animals with other forms of interpersonal violence. While the theories and research that underlie these negative relationships are discussed at length in other chapters, it is appropriate to acknowledge that being part of the family can make animals victims of violence as well. Attention to some of the research in this area will be briefly covered later in this chapter as well as some of the innovative ways in which animals are being integrated into programs to rehabilitate individuals who have exhibited aggressive and anti-social behaviors as well as depression and substance abuse.

Attention will now turn to some of the different types of relationships people have with animals. The following section will cover companion animals, assistance animals, farm animals, wildlife, and AHBs among animal-related professionals such as animal control and police officers, research laboratory, and animal shelter workers.

Kinds of AHBs

Much of the attention in the previously cited studies has focused on companion animals, such as dogs and cats (Peacock et al., 2012), and sometimes horses or small reptiles (McConnell et al., 2011), however the breadth of AHBs is far greater than these relationships. In fact, the AHB occurs within subcultures according to species and/or function.

Companion Animals

The human–companion-animal bond has been shown to serve a familial function for many, with these animals often being described as children or at least "members of the family" (Cohen, 2002; Risley-Curtiss et al., 2006; Risley-Curtiss, Holley, & Kodiene,

2011). Even though most laws categorize animals as property, very few people consider their companion animals as such (American Veterinary Medicine Association, 2007), but rather close friends or family who both give and receive care and nurturance (Cohen, 2002). The research attention given to the companion AHB has had varying foci and varying results. Some findings suggest that pet ownership is beneficial and associated with emotional and physical health and well-being (McConnell et al., 2011). For instance Sugawara et al. (2012) explored the biological and psychological benefits of a familiar companion dog on healthy owners using heart rate variability, brain activity, and a measure of psychological stress. Measures were completed in two conditions: one while in the presence of a companion dog and one without the dog. Results showed responses in regions of the brain associated with relaxed states when the dog was present. Findings also showed significant decreases in participants' subjective experience of stress, although there were no differences between conditions in heart rate variability.

On the other hand, some research suggests that companion animal ownership is not associated with these things (Winefield, Black, & Chur-Hansen, 2008), and that intense relationships with animals can sometimes be associated with negative mental health and personality characteristics (Zilcha-Mano et al., 2011). For instance, Miltiades and Shearer (2011) conducted a study of older adults living in a rural environment to explore attachment to companion animals and depression. Results indicated that older adults who were more attached to their companion animals had higher levels of depression than did those older adults who had lower levels of attachment to their companion animal. However, being able to meet the needs of the companion animal and having a social network were associated with lower levels of depression.

For those individuals who fall into the category of being seriously and persistently mentally ill (SPMI), however, there seem to be some reliable benefits of having a companion animal. For instance, Wisdom, Saedi, and Green (2009) found that 57% (101 of 177) of individuals diagnosed with schizophrenia, schizoaffective disorder, bipolar disorder, or affective psychosis who were living in the community owned companion animals. Through both quantitative and qualitative methods, the researchers discovered that animal owners: a) were more likely to be diagnosed with bipolar disorder or affective psychosis than a schizophrenia-related disorder, b) were more likely to have a co-occurring addiction, c) were more likely to live with another person than by themselves, and d) were less likely to have been hospitalized. Almost 75% reported that their animal companions were "very important to them" and 67% of non-animal owners wished that they had an animal but could not due to residential restriction and other reasons. Wisdom et al. (2009) also found four qualitative themes about how animals helped participants heal from mental illness. Participants reported that their animals: 1) provided them with empathy and non-judgmentally "sensed" their emotions, 2) helped them stay connected to something outside the isolation of mental illness and gain social support with other people, 3) filled the role of family members who were either absent or with whom the relationship was strained, and 4) provided them with a sense of self-worth and self-efficacy in their care of the companion animal.

Likewise, Zimolag and Krupa (2009) also studied animal ownership among people with SPMI living in the community through the help of around the clock mental health and case management support teams. Surveys were sent to 60 program participants (20 animal owners and 40 non-animal owners). Findings indicated that more women than men owned animals, and animal owners had higher Global Assessment of Functioning (GAF) scores than non-animal owners. Animal owners also had higher levels of perceived meaningful activities as well as social and psychological integration into the community. As found in Wisdom et al. (2009), people with schizophrenia were less likely to own pets and 68% of non-pet owners wished to own a pet but did not because of cost and housing policies. Participants reported that the main reason they owned an animal was the companionship offered and having someone to love.

Another element of the AHB manifests in the grief many people feel when their animals become ill and die, or if they have to be separated from their animal companions due to illness or even deployment at wartime. This form of grief can be considered a disenfranchised grief; that is, not everyone immediately understands the intensity of feelings that arise for people who are deeply attached to their animal companions. There are books that have been written about the topic (Allen, 2007), emotional and clinical support for people in animal-related bereavement such as The University of Tennessee's Veterinary Social Work Program (for more information, see www.vet.utk.edu/socialwork), and increasing attention to the experience in the scholarly world (Packman, Field, Carmack, & Ronen, 2011; Toray, 2004).

For instance, Packman, Field, Carmack, and Ronen (2011) conducted a survey of 33 individuals whose dog or cat had died within the past year and measured psychosocial adjustment to the loss using the Continuing Bonds (CB) theory. This theory posits that people maintain continuing bonds with others who have died and that this process is healthy in grieving the loss. Findings suggested that death of a companion animal is experienced similarly to human loss and that attachment to the animal continues after death just as it occurs in human loss. Some people report that the loss of their companion animal has even been more difficult than the loss of other important people in their lives (Weisman, 1990). Factors associated with more intense animal-related grief include strength of the AHB (Planchon, Templer, Stokes, & Keller, 2002), and whether the owner is socially isolated (living with one other person or less) (Planchon & Templer, 1996) and/or experiencing co-occurring social stressors (Gosse & Barnes, 1994).

Farm Animals

One of the most varied types of human-animal relationships is that between human beings and animals raised for food and fiber. The domestication of wild animals by humans began thousands of years ago and would change the future for both. For the animals, it meant the selective breeding over time of animals that were morphologically and temperamentally different. Bred to be less dangerous and easy to handle, domestic breeds are more docile and generally have finer bone structure including shortened skulls, and therefore smaller brains, as well as smaller teeth than their wild counterparts. By cultivating domestic plants and animals, people were able to have consistent food source in one location meaning people no longer had to lead a nomadic existence to survive. The population increased, agriculture became the norm, and eventually urban societies developed (Magee, MacHugh, & Edwards, 2014). Today, 661 out of every 1,000 households have livestock animals according to the AVMA 2012 *U.S. Pet Ownership & Demographics Sourcebook*.

In contemporary society, farmers must balance the seemingly contradictory needs of animal welfare against being able to make money in a market that demands inexpensive food. Much of the literature on livestock refers to "production animals" and "animal husbandry", and "human-animal interactions." These terms are often utilized by animal activists in their campaigns against industrialized farming to emphasize that the animals are seen as commodities (Croney, 2014). However, AHBs occur between farm animals and people. Although the function of that bond *may* fall more on the chattel side of the spectrum as described by Milani (1995), the evidence of the relationship is clear, ranging from the everyday interactions between a farmer and his or her herd (Porcher & Schmitt,

2012) to the relationship between the abattoir worker and the animals "going to market" (Coleman, McGregor, Hemsworth, Boyce, & Dowling, 2003).

For example, Porcher, Cousson-Gélie, and Dantzer (2004) explored farmers' affective relationships with their animals and found four relevant factors: 1) the status farmers gave to the animals, 2) the status farmers gave to the farming profession, 3) self-perception of behavior toward the animals personally as well other farmers' behavior toward their animals, and 4) how the affective bond was demonstrated with the animal. They found two orthogonal dimensions: Friendship and Power relationships with animals. Friendship was associated with emotional difficulty at time of slaughter and preferring the company of animals over the company of people. Power was associated with increased distance from animals such as thinking it ridiculous to talk with animals or show feelings at work. Women seemed to be higher on the Friendship factor than were men, and the older the stock person the higher the scores were in Power, indicating greater emotional distance. Findings also suggested that the more animals on the farm, the higher the scores were on the Power dimension.

Zasloff (2010), through surveys exploring relationships between people and their goats, donkeys, and chickens, also found strong bonds on the farm. For goat owners, 55.4% of respondents considered all their goats "pets," 9.8% considered none of their goats "pets," and 34.7% reported that some in the herd were considered "pets" and some were not. Respondents indicated various reasons for owning goats such as for a hobby activity, for milk and cheese production, for participation in 4-H activities, for clearing brush around the property, and for meat. Individuals who had goats for their meat reported challenging experiences at times of slaughter. Many would limit time spent with their meat goats and if names were given, the names were more food-oriented such as "Taco" or "Burger Boy." Zasloff also found that more and more people are having "backyard chickens" that serve both as pets and as working animals. These chickens provide eggs for their owners and many respondents indicated that they would continue to care for the chickens beyond their egg-laying years. These backyard chickens are serving the roles as pets more and more as evidenced by some owners even putting diapers on their chickens and playing them classical music. Of the donkey owners surveyed, 89% had donkeys for human companionship, but also reported some working functions such as breeding, guarding livestock, carrying packs, and participating in sporting events (Zasloff, 2010). The quality of the human-animal relationship can vary greatly across and within farms with some animals experiencing gentle, consistent care while others receive infrequent or rough handling. Overall, having a positive AHB would be beneficial for all of the creatures involved. For the animals, in addition to receiving adequate care, having a positive experiences with people reduces fear and stress responses such as bolting or trying to escape which can lead to injury, illness and death. For the farmers, having positive associations with the farm animals means that they are going to be more likely to enjoy their work in addition to reaping the economic and public health benefits of having more healthy and productive animals (Waiblinger et al., 2006)

Assistance Animals

Given the strong bonds that people often develop with animals, animals have the potential to help people in many ways. One such way is as an assistance animal. Assistance animals can be defined in three ways: 1) companion animals or "pets" who provide benefits to their owners (see McConnell et al., 2011; Wisdom et al., 2009), 2) animal-assisted therapy (AAT) or animal-assisted activity (AAA) animals that participate in animal-assisted interventions (AAI) with special populations such as the elderly, disabled children, or people with cancer, and 3) service animals which are typically dogs (but not always) specially trained to provide care for people who have a mental or physical disability. Attention has been given to animal companions in the AHB, and later in this chapter attention will be given to AAI for therapeutic benefits, and so attention now will be given to the bond between service animals and people.

Service animals differ from companion animals in that they are considered to be "working animals." They have targeted responsibilities that they are specially trained to provide. They also differ from companion animals in that service animals have civil rights protection in the United States under the Americans with Disabilities Act of 1990 (ADA) meaning they must be accommodated by businesses and places to which the general public has access. Service animals also differ from AAI animals because many AAI animals are companion animals that have been behaviorally and medically screened and deemed good candidates for AAI. This usually means they are healthy, are well-behaved, and appear to enjoy affectionate interactions with specific populations such as the elderly or children. AAI also occurs with animals in farm or marine settings (Breitenbach, Stumpft, Fersen, & Ebert, 2009; Pedersen, Martinsen, Berget, & Braastad, 2012).

Service dogs, alternatively, are traditionally trained from an early age to provide a *service* for an individual with a disability, or they can be owned by an occupational therapy service that has one or two handlers who oversee their care (Wenthold & Savage, 2007). They can be paired with people who are blind or deaf, people with physical disabilities, or people with emotional or mental disabilities. Instruments to help appropriately match people with service dogs have been developed (Zapf & Rough, 2002) and the ethical issues of maintaining proper animal welfare for these animals is important and has received attention (Wenthold & Savage, 2007).

People who benefit from relationships with service animals report strong attachment to their helpers. Kwong and Bartholomew (2011) conducted a qualitative study, interviewing 25 individuals who lost an assistance dog to retirement or death. Using an attachment theory framework, they explored the presence for "*secure base,*" "*safe haven,*" and "*separation anxiety*" in the human-service dog bond. They also explored the "role of caregiving" and "grief experiences" present in these relationships. They found evidence for both *safe haven* and *secure base* for the humans in the human-service dog attachment experience. Caregiving was also an intense emotional experience for the human being as was the loss of the service dog.

People report that service animals help them to be more connected to others and the world around them as well. For instance, Solomon (2010), in an ethnographic study of service dogs with children and families affected by autism, found that "child-dog interactions afford an experience of emotional connection between an autistic child and family members, as well as between the child and the dogs" (p. 161). This is also true for veterans with combat-related disabilities and post-traumatic stress who were paired with service dogs. The National Education for Assistance Dog Services' (NEADS) Canines for Combat Veterans and the Trauma Alert Dog Program provide these services for veterans. NEADS is a leader in the field of service dog training for people with sight and hearing disabilities and developed the Prison PUP Program to help in the socialization and training of their canines (Foreman & Crosson, 2012). Anecdotal evidence to date suggests that the use of service dogs for veterans results in improved emotional regulation and engagement, and decreased startle response, as well as pain medication use, and that the presence of these service dogs has had beneficial effects for the families as well as the staff who are caring for the veterans (Yount, Olmert, & Lee, 2012).

Wildlife

The National Survey of Fishing, Hunting, and Wildlife-Associated Recreation reported that in 2011, 90.1 million people in the United States engaged in wildlife associated recreation—including hunting and fishing (37.4 million) and wildlife watching (71.8 million). For the wildlife watchers, 68.6 million watch wildlife around their home, 22.5 million take special trips away from home to watch wildlife, and 19.3 million do both (U.S. Fish and Wildlife Service, 2011). In the 2011 Conference Proceedings for the World Association of Zoos and Aquariums, it was reported that 700 million people visit zoos worldwide each year (Penning, 2011).

Though the AHB with wildlife can be both biophilic (pleasant) as well as biophobic (fearful or unpleasant) (Gullone, 2000), clearly humans have a natural interest in wildlife. Bird feeding in backyards, family trips to the zoo, and natural fears of spiders, snakes, or sharks, as well as the annoyances of mice in the house, raccoons in the garbage, or even bears in the backyard (Harker & Bates, 2007) all point to the ways people pay attention to wildlife.

Researchers in the AHB field have also explored this connection. For instance, Smith, Ham, and Weiler (2011) conducted a qualitative study with 18 individuals about their "profound" experiences interacting with wildlife. They found that these experiences were pleasurable and incited a desire for more connections with wildlife, as well as an impulse to help wildlife. Bjerke and Ostdahl (2004) in an exploration of how urban adult residents felt about wildlife found that small birds, squirrels, butterflies, and hedgehogs were well-liked animals, and that rats, mosquitoes, and mice were the least-liked animals. In this study, gender also affected positive attitudes towards wild animals with females liking animals such as cats, crows, seagulls, and grasshoppers, and men preferring birds of prey, bumblebees, bats, beetles, and snails (Bjerke & Ostdahl, 2004). There is also evidence that having a companion animal is associated with more positive attitudes towards wild animals unless the companion animal owner had had a problem with a wild animal, like an opossum in the house.

Researchers have also explored AHBs at the zoo, both for visitors and for zookeepers. For instance, Sakagami and Ohta (2010) found that zoo visitors' blood pressure and quality of life scores were lower and better after a zoo visit than before. Phillips and Peck (2007) explored how the personalities of zookeepers and tigers affected the zookeeper-tiger bond. They found that zookeepers who had a higher propensity for anger gave fewer "pats" to the tigers, and that conscientious and more neurotic zookeepers interacted with the tigers less. Findings also suggested that the tigers' personalities did not greatly influence the zookeeper-tiger interactions (Phillips & Peck, 2007).

Animals Used by Animal-Related Professionals

Like zookeeper-tiger bonds, many other animal-related professionals also experience bonds with the animals in their care. These animal-related professionals may include animal control officers, police officers affiliated with canine units or mounted horsemen, veterinary professionals, people who work with animals in research laboratories, and animal shelter workers to name only a few. Very often, people who "love animals" pursue employment where they can work with animals. These types of jobs may require dealing with animals that are sick, abused, unwanted, or used in research settings. It also may mean watching an animal, in the line of duty, come into harm's way (Hart, Zasloff,

Bryson, & Christensen, 2000; Sanders, 2006). For many animal-related professionals, the affection felt for animals naturally results in the development of bonds with the animals with whom they interact and for whom they care (Arluke, 1999; Black, Winefield, & Chur-Hansen, 2011; Chur-Hansen, 2010; Frommer & Arluke, 1999). These professionals often suffer from what is referred to as 'compassion fatigue' and may need help to maintain their professionalism and resiliency.

In the criminal justice system, the AHB within professional services occurs for animal control officers and police officers. Animal control officers can feel a great deal of stress addressing animal-related conflicts between neighbors, enforcing animal cruelty laws, and witnessing the warehousing of animals caught in animal cruelty legal cases. These experiences take an emotional toll on these professionals (Leinberger, 2009). Innovative programs like Maricopa County Sheriff's Office's Animal Safe House Program (for more information, see http://mcso.org/MASH) can help. MASH is a no-kill shelter that was created to house the 'evidence' of animal crimes—the abused and neglected animals.

Police officers can experience ambivalence about the bonds with their working animals, seeing them as "tools" for conducting their work as well as sentient beings whom they love (Sanders, 2006). Of the 265 police officer canine teams surveyed by Hart et al. (2000), 75% indicated that their dogs were important members of the family who helped the police officer with stress and maintaining good health. One-third reported that the dogs had even saved their lives. Where the dogs slept was indicative of attachment to the dogs with those officers who let their dogs sleep inside (38%) being more likely to express that they loved their dogs than those whose dogs slept outside. The bond between police and their canine officers can also been seen how the dogs are honored in death. Police dogs have been buried with full police honors after being killed in the line of duty (Kuruvilla, 2014) and K9 monuments have been erected across the country.

It has been confirmed that professionals who care for animals used for research also experience AHBs (Arluke, 1999; Chang & Hart, 2002; Rohlf & Bennett, 2005; Russow, 2002). The animals under these professionals' care can even show preference for a particular human caregiver as well (Chang & Hart, 2002). Research veterinary technicians may feel uneasy and conflicted between the bond they feel with the research animals and the scientific manipulations they must perform for the research protocol (Arluke, 1999). Caregivers of research animals report being rewarded when they actively enrich the lives of the research animals under their care (Chang & Hart, 2002) and also grieve when the animals die (Chang & Hart, 2002; Rohlf & Bennett, 2005). Because of these emotional experiences, attention has been given to the ethical implications of AHBs in laboratory settings (Herzog, 2002; Russow, 2002) and placing an emphasis more on supporting an "ethic of care" than a "utilitarian" relationship in the laboratory environment (Russow, 2002). To accomplish this, Herzog recommends ensuring direct care providers have a "voice" on the Institutional Animal Care and Use Committee (IACUC) (Herzog, 2002).

The problem of companion animal over-population and unwanted and homeless animals is a very difficult one (Kass, New, Scarlett, & Salman, 2001). People who feel a strong affinity towards animals generally and unwanted animals in particular, very often engage in efforts to care for and rescue these animals (Neumann, 2010). The sickness and death of these animals can be very difficult for these animal-related professionals and volunteers (Baran et al., 2009).

Violence and the AHB

Although hard to understand, there is a dark side to the AHB that results in violence to animals. One commonly accepted definition of animal abuse is: "socially unacceptable behavior that intentionally causes unnecessary pain, suffering, or distress to and/or death of an animal" (Ascione, 1993, p. 28). This unnecessary violence to animals can occur in the form of "bruises, fractures, ... burns and scalds, stab and incised wounds, poisoning, asphyxiation, ... drowning, sexual abuse and injuries specifically caused by firearms" (Munro & Thrusfield, 2001a, p. 279). Violence to animals can also come in the form of neglect such as in animal hoarding situations (Patronek, 1999), as well as animal fighting (Humane Society of the United States, 2003)

For over 30 years, there has been increasing scholarly attention to the link between violence to animals and violence to people (Flynn, 2001). The presence of violence to animals has been associated with bullying, (Gullone & Robertson, 2008) family violence situations (Ascione et al., 2007), and life histories of incarcerated felons (Merz-Perez et al., 2001).Violence towards animals can occur for pleasure and entertainment such as in blood sports, better known as animal fighting. While animal fighting may occur on a small scale, such as between gang members meeting on the street corner, there is also an entire black market industry for breeding fighting animals, training instruments, and spectator events. The pride a person takes in their fighting animals is deep and there are strong social networks that center around animal fighting. These social networks are male-dominated and include criminal behaviors like illegal gambling, drug and weapon offenses, and animal theft (Kalof & Taylor, 2007). Violence to animals, however, can also be associated with neglect instead of active harm, such as in cases of animal hoarding. Animal hoarding is the excessive collection of, and retention of, animals far beyond an individual's capacity to humanely house and care for them. Scholarly attention has begun to focus on the motivations for animal hoarding behavior; for instance, Steketee et al. (2011) found that the animal hoarders had more childhood stressful life events, anthropomorphized animals more, and demonstrated more negative attachment style. Moreover, some people have sexual impulses towards, and therefore engage in, sexual acts with animals (Hensley, Tallichet, & Dutkiewucz, 2010; Zequi et al., 2012)—a practice termed as zoophilia or bestiality.

Thorough attention to the theoretical concepts and research findings on the link between violence towards animals and people is paid in later chapters in this volume (e.g., family violence, see Chapter 13; animal hoarding, see Chapter 9; blood sports, see Chapter 8; bestiality, see chapter 10). Here, it is simply important to note that some people's attachment histories and own pathology influence the negative bonds they establish with animals, in both active and passive forms of cruelty.

Cultural Influences in the AHB

Attention will now turn to the ways in which cultural influences affect the AHB. Since the criminal justice system touches the lives of people from a wide variety of cultural, racial, and ethnic backgrounds, putting effort toward understanding how these backgrounds might affect the AHB is important. Unfortunately, there is relatively little research that examines how culture, ethnicity, or race may impact the AHB. Most of what research there is examines differences between racial/ethnic groups, with a smaller number of studies looking at within-group attitudes, beliefs, and practices. For example, Marx, Stallones, Garrity, and Johnson (1988) examined demographics of companion animal ownership among US. adults aged 21–64 and found that Whites were statistically more likely than were people of color to have such animals. There was, however, no exploration of this finding. In a study that yielded more information regarding differences between racial and ethnic groups, Siegel (1995) interviewed 877 urban non-Latina/o White, Latina/o, African American, Asian, and "other" adolescents between the ages of 12 and 17. She found distinct racial/ethnic differences in companion animal ownership and attachment. African Americans were least likely to have companion animals in their homes while Whites were most likely to, followed by Latino/as and Asians. White youth also rated their companion animals as significantly more important to them than did Latina/o youth, while African American and Asian youth reported intermediate levels of attachment but were not significantly different from any of the other groups. Having sole responsibility for the care of one's companion animal was also related to race/ethnicity with African American youth most likely to have sole responsibility, followed by Latina/o, White, and Asian youth.

Brown (2011) examined racial variations in attachment to companion animals among 76 African American and 57 White veterinary students. Among her findings were that more White students had companion animals (100% versus 86%); they had a larger number of such animals, and were more likely to sleep with their animals than were African American students (70% versus 53%). Additionally, Whites had significantly higher scores on an animal attachment scale than did African Americans. There were differences in responses to attachment statements such as "no family is complete without a pet," and to questions about taking animals to visit friends and relatives. Brown concluded that how attachment to animals is shown may vary from culture to culture. She also noted that differences in housing, socio-economic factors, and urban-rural background may help in explaining the differences she found.

Schoenfeld-Tacher, Kogan, and Wright (2010) interviewed 419 Hispanics and non-Hispanics with companion animals, who presented at three veterinarian clinics and found that the majority considered companionship as a major benefit of having their animals. Differences in sterilization rates were found, but no differences were found in how Hispanics and non-Hispanics viewed their companion animals. They did, however, challenge the validity of the animal attachment instrument (Lexington Attachment to Pets Scale) being used for Hispanic populations. Risley-Curtiss et al. (2006), in their study of women of color and their relationships with companion animals, also questioned the validity of such scales based on their findings that what "family" means when people say they consider their animals to be family may differ based on race/ethnicity as well as other factors.

Risley-Curtiss, Holley, and Wolf (2006) examined the relationship of race/ethnicity to companion animal beliefs and practices in a random sample telephone survey of 587 adults in a southwestern metropolitan area. They found that Whites and Indigenous people were most likely to have companion animals and that Asians were least likely; Latina/os were less likely to have cats (for a similar finding, see Schoenfeld-Tacher et al., 2010) and birds than other animals, and were also less likely than other groups to have their animals sterilized. Asians were most likely to agree that "Animals do not feel pain." Almost 97% of those with companion animals agreed with the statement that "My pet is a member of my family."

More recently, Risley-Curtiss, Holley, and Kodiene (2011) found in a qualitative study of 12 men (including nine men of color) and their relationships with animals that the majority of men in the sample engaged in physical activities such as playing, walking, or running with their pets. However, the four men who did not talk about play were either Indigenous or immigrants, suggesting the influence of ethnic and national cultures on men's interactions with animals. Additionally, all four immigrants and two of the three Indigenous men raised the issue of cultural differences in the treatment of animals. This reflects one of the effects of living as a person of color in a majority white culture—that "outsiders" might be better able to identify characteristics of the "insider" culture. Two Indigenous men who raised the topic of animals as a source of food described the cultural traditions related to killing animals for food. Recognizing the contrast between their own cultures and that of the dominant U.S. culture, some men came to consider their own culture's treatment of animals as better than that of the larger U.S culture, while others changed the way they treated animals as they learned what one of the participants called the "cultural rules" of the U.S. The authors concluded that the men's relationships were influenced—though not determined—by individual perceptions and experiences, family perceptions and experiences, perceptions and experiences of peers at the intersection of ethnicity, national origin, social class, urban/suburban/rural setting, and U.S. white, middle class culture.

In a study of within-group similarities and differences, Johnson and Meadows (2002) examined 24 dog-owning Latina/os over age 50 with regard to their relationships with their dogs and whether attachment to a dog was related to self-perceived health and functional ability. The majority of participants viewed their dogs as equals (54%) and as members of their family (79%). Sixty-seven percent stated that their dog was the reason they got up in the morning and 62% stated that their dog comforted them. Although the study results did not support any relationship between animal companion relationship and a participant's health or functional ability, the authors concluded that for these Latino/as, dogs were as important as they have been reported to be among Whites and that dogs are considered, among these elderly Latina/os, to be valued members of their families.

In addition, Faver and Cavazos (2008) surveyed Latina/o university students and found that of the 69.2% (of 208) who had companion animals, most had dogs, and 92% of the dog and cat guardians regarded their companion animals as family. Over 80% stated that they received companionship and unconditional love as benefits of animal guardianship and 86% of those with dogs also specified protection as a benefit. In the first study of the co-occurrence of animal abuse and domestic violence specifying Hispanic participants, Faver and Cavazos (2007) also found that animal abuse is a component of domestic violence in Hispanic families similar to non-Hispanic families. Finally, Vaughn et al. (2011) reported on what appears to be the first national assessment of the prevalence of animal cruelty in the U.S. and included race/ethnicity in their analysis. They found animal cruelty to be more common among males, those born in the U.S., and African-Americans, and less likely among Latina/os; however, it is unclear why certain racial/ethnic categories were grouped together (e.g., Indian/Alaskan/Asian).

As evidenced above, there has been some research on ethnic/racial populations and the AHB. In particular, the research on Hispanics and Latina/os seems to be increasing, though not the research on African or Asian Americans nor on Indigenous populations. Nonetheless, two major national AHB surveys periodically done by American Pet Products Manufacturers Association and the American Veterinary Medical Association have begun to include ethnicity/race in their demographics. Unfortunately, there continues to be relatively little attention in the broad professional literature to the impact of ethnic/racial culture on the AHB in the U.S. (Risley-Curtiss, Holley & Wolf, 2006; Schoenfeld-Tacher et al., 2010).

In discussing the relevance of culture to the link between animal abuse and family violence, Kaufman (1999) noted that "rarely has animal protection in general, and the violence link specifically, been discussed in the context of a multicultural society" (p. 260). The non-professional *Best Friends* magazine in 2004 published a planned series of articles on the lack of people of color in the animal welfare field. The first report was on African Americans and was anecdotal, but it made an important observation regarding the lack of people of color in animal welfare work: "[W]hite people often believe that minority communities simply don't care about animals..." (Richard, 2004, p.14). This attitude is implied throughout the AHB literature by treating all those with companion animals as one and by the apparent lack of interest in studying populations of color (Kaufman, 1999).

This lack of attention to race or ethnicity applies across virtually all areas of AHB research, including the animal abuse and interpersonal violence research, other areas of research on the AHB as well as the research on AAI. This translates into a lack of knowledge to apply to practice; for example, how might the race/ethnicity of clients influence their reception to and the effectiveness of AAI?

More research is needed on the influence of racial or ethnic culture on the AHB in order to better understand how it functions, how it impacts those touched by the criminal justice system, and how it might be utilized in AAI programs. For example, just as the meaning of *"family"* may vary for different racial/ethnic groups, so too may the meaning of attachment to companion animals. Psychometric qualities should also be considered as current animal attachment scales require norming for populations of color, or new measures are created for evaluating animal-related programs. Research also needs to examine differences in the therapeutic effects of AAI across different ethnic/racial groups. Given the research that suggests the benefits of animal companionship, can companion animals provide emotional, psychological, physical, and spiritual support for racial/ethnic groups facing adverse circumstances, such as racism, family violence, abuse, and/or incarceration?

We do know from completed studies that companion animals have meaning for people of color and that culture, among other factors, influences the AHB. Most people of color see their companion animals as family, and receive comfort, companionship, and a sense of safety from them.

AHB and Criminal Justice: Practice Implications

There are three main implications of the AHB within the criminal justice system. The first is in the thorough assessment and response to AHBs that exist for those touched by or entering the system. The second is the legal response and psychological treatment of perpetrators of animal cruelty. The third is the utilization of AAI for rehabilitation and prevention.

Assessment and Response to the AHB

A thorough psychosocial assessment for people touched by or entering into the criminal justice system must include questions about animals. This not only gives important information about violence to animals in people's lives, but also about attachments that people may have to animals that affect treatment planning and interventions. For instance, many victims of domestic violence will delay leaving an abusive situation because of concern for the safety of their animals (Strand & Faver, 2005). Thus, when a victim of domestic violence is seeking services, such as an order of protection, asking about animals is essential in finding out about any barriers that may prevent seeking safety. Moreover, victims of domestic violence, especially those without children, worry and grieve over their animals when they have to leave them behind (Strand & Faver, 2005). This grief and worry may also be true for people who must leave animals behind when they are incarcerated. Risley-Curtiss, this chapter's co-author, supervised social work students working with female inmates caring for the cats and dogs at the MCSO MASH unit. Anecdotally, the students related stories from some of the inmates about how much they worried about the animals they had to leave behind when they entered jail. The grief people feel over the loss of attachments to animals is a real form of loss (Packman et al., 2011), and this may affect how children and adults cope with losing animals they have cared for in AAI such as Humans and Animal Learning Together (for more information, see www.vet.utk.edu/halt) or Puppies Behind Bars (for more information, see www.puppiesbehindbars.com). Finally, a thorough psychosocial assessment may also show that a person has committed violence to animals, which may affect what type of treatment or legal response is needed.

Preventing and Treating Violence towards Animals

Given the co-occurrence of violence to animals and violence to people, it is beneficial that, as of March 2014, all 50 states have felony-level laws to convict animal cruelty (Animal Legal Defense Fund, 2014), 32 states have mandated counseling for people convicted of animal cruelty, and eight states allow victims of domestic violence to include their companion animals on orders of protection (National Link Coalition, 2015)). Additionally, 14 states now have cross-reporting laws which mandate or at least encourage animal and human welfare government professionals to report to the other when evidence of violence to animals or people is occurring (National Link Coalition, 2015).

Although there is some progress in the ways in which violence to animals is detected and addressed, much work still needs to be done in how it is treated. In a survey of 174 therapists about their experiences with violence to animals in their counseling practices, Schaefer, Hays, and Steiner (2007) found that 87% of respondents agree that violence to animals is a mental health issue. Sixty-seven percent of the mental health professionals indicated that they inquire about the safety of animals with clients, and 49% indicated that they would be supportive of a voluntary reporting law, but only 29% said that they would support a mandatory reporting law of violence toward animals. Most respondents cited the reason against mandatory reporting was concern about breaking client confidentiality. Unfortunately, while recognizing animal abuse, therapists too often do not intervene in it directly (Signal, Ghea, Taylor, & Acutt, 2013). Currently, the only known cohesive treatment protocols for addressing animal cruelty are the AniCare Model for Adults and Children developed by The Institute for Animals and Society (see http://www.animalsandsociety.org) and the Children and Animals Together Assessment and Diversion Program (CAT) (see http://ssw.asu.edu/research/animal-human-bond) developed, implemented and currently directed by this chapter's co-author, Dr. Risley-Curtiss. CAT was actually started to help a juvenile probation officer who was looking for a diversion program for two young boys who had killed a kitten.

In animal hoarding situations, it has become increasingly clear that intervention must be interdisciplinary in nature. The professionals who must come together to intervene in such situations are law enforcement, public health professionals, animal welfare professionals, psychological services, and the legal system, as well as public housing and human medical professionals. Without a comprehensive intervention such as this, it has been estimated that there will be a 100% recidivism rate (Patronek, 1999). If the only interventions include removing animals and animal cruelty convictions, which may or may not carry jail time, perpetrators will again begin their hoarding behavior in another location given that the underlying problems contributing to the behavior have not been resolved (Patronek, 1999).

Humane education programs could also be utilized to detect the presence of violence to animals among school-aged children and their families, as well as increase empathy these children have toward both animals and people (Arbour, Signal, & Taylor, 2009; Ascione, 1997; Faver, 2010). Currently, humane education programs are not utilized on a broad basis in schools even though more and more attention has been given toward anti-bullying programs (Faver, 2010). There has been a call for human services to take the lead in integrating humane education programs as a prevention effort to reduce aggressive behavior among children and increase empathy (Faver, 2010). Given the evidence that violence to animals and childhood bullying behavior can co-occur (Gullone & Robertson, 2008; Henry & Sanders, 2007), it seems fitting that humane education should be incorporated into anti-bullying programs utilized in school systems today. Even though not widespread, there are a few examples where anti-bullying and animal-assisted humane education programs are paired that are demonstrating positive results (Sprinkle, 2008).

Animal-Assisted Interventions

Integrating AAI into the criminal justice system may serve both preventative and rehabilitative functions. The same humane education programs mentioned above that incorporate animals as a form of teaching empathy and promoting self-esteem, as well as reducing anti-social youth behaviors such as bullying and aggression (Dupper, 2013), can serve both functions. Results from a study of one such program, Healing Species, indicate that empathy increased, and out-of-school suspensions due to violent behavior decreased, as did aggressive behaviors for the 4th, 5th, and 6th graders who participated in the program. Healing Species incorporates animal shelter dogs as "teachers" in each of the 12 sessions in the curriculum. Another program that incorporates animals as topics for teaching humane attitudes and reducing bullying and violence is Mutt-i-grees® (see http://education.muttigrees.org/) which now has 900 programs in 28 states (Peters, 2011). This program does not consistently include animals in the curriculum, but does allow visits to the animal shelter as service learning or visits from a "therapy dog" to enhance its sessions.

While few diversion programs exist for juveniles or adults who abuse animals, there are many animal-related intervention programs in both juvenile and adult correctional facilities. Examples in juvenile facilities include Project Pooch—an animal-centered correctional vocational program (see www.pooch.org) and Project Second Chance in Michigan and New Mexico.

AAI is increasingly happening for incarcerated adults through animal-related programs. For instance, South Carolina has at least three programs, among them one in which female inmates foster greyhounds until adoption (see www.gpa-sc.com/Prison%20Foster%20Program.htm) and another that rehabilitates racehorses (see www.trfsc.org/about-us). North Carolina has at least 17 correctional sites for their program called "A New Leash on Life" in which their state prisons partner with animal welfare agencies of all sorts to train dogs to assist them in getting adopted (see www.doc.state.nc.us/dop/program/leash.htm). Furst (2006), in a national survey of adult Prison Based Animal Programs (PAPs), found that animal visitation programs, wildlife rehabilitation programs, livestock care programs, pet adoption programs, service animal socialization programs, vocational programs, community service programs, and multimodal programs were represented in 36 states. Males were more likely to participate in such programs, and the most commonly used animal was the dog. Community service programs that help animals become more adoptable or actually adopted by inmates were the most common types of programs. Ninety-eight percent of wardens reported that they thought the programs were beneficial, noting such positive results for the prisoners as sense of responsibility, anger management, patience, empathy, self-esteem, communication skills, and self-control. Organizational benefits were also cited and included humanizing the facility and calming the inmates. Moreover, many programs offer vocational certificates such as grooming, animal care assistant, and farm animal management. It is important to note, however, that there has been some concern that utilizing animals in such facilities may cause harm to the animals. Given that so many incarcerated felons have a history of animal abuse (Merz-Perez et al., 2001), this seems like a valid concern. To address this, 71.8% of programs have a pre-participation interview and assessment process to determine whether an inmate is appropriate for the program. This pre-assessment may include review of the inmate's psychological evaluation, administration of standardized measures, and review of disciplinary history. Some program administrators make decisions about participation in PAPs based on the nature of the crime, excluding those convicted of such offenses as animal abuse, sexual perpetration, and child abuse, while some program administrators do not exclude any inmates from participating (Furst, 2006). Moreover, Hennessy, Morris, and Linden (2006), through an intervention-control group design, found that shelter dogs who participated in a prison-based socialization program were better behaved at post-test than were those dogs who remained in the shelter. Evaluation for the well-being of other animals utilized in PAPs is warranted.

People who are involved with the criminal justice system very often have mental health and substance abuse problems as well. Therefore, the efficacy of AAI for adults with mental health and substance abuse problems is also salient in developing rehabilitative programs for people touched by the criminal justice system. There is some evidence to support the potential benefits of AAI for these issues. For instance, Pedersen, Martinsen, Berget, and Braastad (2012) investigated the application of an AAI utilizing farm animals with a population of individuals who had been diagnosed with major depression. Participants were randomly assigned into intervention (n=16) and wait-list control (n=13) groups; those in the intervention group went to work alongside dairy farmers twice a week for 12 weeks for up to 3 hours at a time. Intervention group participants were able to choose to engage in physical contact with the cows, feeding, taking care of calves, mucking stalls, milking, and grooming activities. Researchers administered the Beck Depression Inventory (BDI), the State-Trait Anxiety Inventory-State Subscale, and the Generalized Self-Efficacy Scale. Results indicated that participants in the intervention had significant reductions in depression and significant improvement in self-efficacy at the end of the intervention, and that these gains were maintained at a 6-month follow-up. Qualitative results suggest that not only did the animals have a calming and positive influence on participants, but the collegial relationship with the farmer was also beneficial. Given that 14% of Prison-based Animal Programs (PAPs) (Furst, 2006) are livestock programs, further research is warranted to explore the mental health benefits of such programs.

In many prisons, group counseling is a form of rehabilitation. The integration of an animal in these groups may have positive effects on group cohesion. For instance, Wesley, Minatrea, and Watson (2009), in an experimental study utilizing a therapy dog for in-patient substance abuse group counseling, found that the members of the group with a dog reported more positive feelings about the group than did the control group members without a dog.

Conclusion

This chapter has provided evidence to show that the AHB is real, broad, complex, and powerful. Whether it involves a cat or a bird, whether it occurs in a home environment or in an institutional setting, attention to the AHB provides insights into human functioning as well as support and therapy for people in need. Incorporating the AHB into the criminal justice system can occur in a multitude of ways, and the results of such integration must be meticulously studied to ensure that people as well as animals are supported in the chance to live a good life.

References

Ainsworth, M. D., & Bell, S. M. (1970). Attachment, exploration, and separation: Illustrated by the behavior of one-year-olds in a strange situation. *Child Development*, *41*(1), 49–67. doi:http://dx.doi.org/10.2307/1127388.

Allen, M. A. (2007). *Coping with Sorrow on the Loss of Your Pet* (20 Anv Exp.). Dog Ear Publishing, LLC.

American Veterinary Medicine Association. (2007). *U.S. Pet Ownership & Demographics Sourcebook 2007* (1st ed.). Amer Veterinary Medical Assn.

Animal Legal Defense Fund (2011, January). Animal fighting case study: Michael Vick. Retrieved on March 25, 2015 from http://aldf.org/resources/laws-cases/animal-fighting-case-study-michael-vick.

Animal Legal Defense Fund (2014, March 14). All 50 states now have felony animal cruelty.

Arbour, R., Signal, T., & Taylor, N. (2009). Teaching Kindness: The Promise of Humane Education. *Society & Animals*, *17*, 136–148.

Arkow, P. (2011, July). The Link Letter. *The National Link Coalition*. Retrieved from http://www.nationallinkcoalition.org.

Arluke, A. (1999). Uneasiness among laboratory technicians. *Occupational medicine (Philadelphia, Pa.)*, *14*(2), 305–316.

Ascione, F. (1997). Humane education research: Evaluating efforts to encourage children's kindness and caring toward animals. *Genetic Social and General Psychology Monographs*, *123*, 55–57.

Ascione, F. (1993). Children who are cruel to animals—A review of the research and implications for developmental psychopathology. *Anthrozoos*, *6*, 226–247.

Baran, B., Allen, J., Rogelberg, S., Spitzmuller, C., DiGiacomo, N., Webb, J., Carter, N., et al. (2009). Euthanasia-related strain and coping strategies in animal shelter employees. *JAVMA—Journal of the American Veterinary Medical Association*, 83–88.

BBC NEWS | Americas | Prisoners raise puppies in jail. (n.d.). Retrieved May 11, 2012, from http://news.bbc.co.uk/2/hi/americas/8280726.stm.

Beck, A. M. (2014). The biology of the human–animal bond. *Animal Frontiers, 4*(3), 32–36.doi:10.2527/af.2014-0019. https://www.animalsciencepublications.org/publications/af/pdfs/4/3/32.

Beck, A., & Katcher, A. (2003). Future directions in human-animal bond research. *American Behavioral Scientist, 47*, 79–93.

Besthorn, F. H. (2002). Natural environment and the practice of psychotherapy. *Annals of the American Psychotherapy Assn, 5*(5), 19–20.

Bjerke, T., & Ostdahl, T. (2004). Animal-related attitudes and activities in an urban population. *Anthrozoos: A Multidisciplinary Journal of The Interactions of People & Animals, 17*(2), 109–129.

Black, A. F., Winefield, H. R., & Chur-Hansen, A. (2011). Occupational Stress in Veterinary Nurses: Roles of the Work Environment and Own Companion Animal. *Anthrozoos: A Multidisciplinary Journal of The Interactions of People & Animals, 24*, 191–202. doi:10.2752/175303711X12998632257503.

Breitenbach, E., Stumpft, E., Fersen, L., & Ebert, H. (2009). Dolphin-Assisted Therapy: Changes in Interaction and Communication between Children with Severe Disabilities and Their Caregivers. *Anthrozoos, 22*, 277–289.

Brown, S. E. (2011). Theoretical Concepts from Self Psychology Applied to Animal Hoarding. *Society & Animals, 19*, 175–193. doi:10.1163/156853011x563006.

Chang, F. T., & Hart, L. A. (2002). Human-animal bonds in the laboratory: how animal behavior affects the perspectives of caregivers. *ILAR JOURNAL, 43*(1), 10–18.

Cheakalos, C. (2004). New leash on life. *Smithsonian, 35*(5), 62–68.

Chur-Hansen, A. (2010). Grief and bereavement issues and the loss of a companion animal: People living with a companion animal, owners of livestock, and animal support workers. *Clinical Psychologist, 14*(1), 14–21. doi:10.1080/13284201003662800.

Cobb, S. (1976). Presidential Address—1976. Social support as a moderator of life stress. *Psychosomatic Medicine, 38*(5), 300–314.

Cohen, S. P. (2002). Can pets function as family members? *Western Journal of Nursing Research, 24*(6), 621–638. doi:10.1177/019394502320555386.

Coleman, G., McGregor, M., Hemsworth, P., Boyce, J., & Dowling, S. (2003). The relationship between beliefs, attitudes and observed behaviours of abattoir personnel in the pig industry. *Applied Animal Behaviour Science, 82*, 189–200.

Collis, G. M., & McNicholas, J. (1998). A theoretical basis for health benefits of pet ownership: Attachment versus psychological support. *Companion animals in human health.* (pp. 105–122). Thousand Oaks, CA, US: Sage Publications, Inc, Thousand Oaks, CA. Retrieved from http://proxy.lib.utk.edu:90/login?url=http://search.proquest.com/docview/619171382?accountid=14766.

Crawford, E. K., Worsham, N. L., & Swinehart, E. R. (2006). Benefits derived from companion animals, and the use of the term "attachment." *Anthrozoös, 19*(2), 98–112. doi:10.2752/089279306785593757.

Croney, C. (2014). Bonding with commodities: Social constructions and implications of human–animal relationships in contemporary livestock production. *Animal Frontiers, 4*(3), 59–64. doi:10.2527/af.2014-0023. https://www.animalsciencepublications.org/publications/af/pdfs/4/3/59.

Dupper, D. R. (2013). *School Bullying: New Perspectives on a Growing Problem.* New York: Oxford University Press.

Duvall Antonacopoulos, N. M., & Pychyl, T. A. (2010). An examination of the potential role of pet ownership, human social support and pet attachment in the psychological health of individuals living alone. *Anthrozoos: A Multidisciplinary Journal of The Interactions of People & Animals*, *23*(1), 37–54.

Eddy, J., Hart, L. A., & Boltz, R. P. (1988). The effects of service dogs on social acknowledgments of people in wheelchairs. *Journal of Psychology: Interdisciplinary and Applied*, *122*(1), 39–45.

Faver, C. (2010). School-based humane education as a strategy to prevent violence: Review and recommendations. *Children and Youth Services Review*, *32*, 365–370.

Faver, C.A., & Cavazos, A. M. (2007). Animal abuse and domestic violence: A view from the border. *Journal of Emotional Abuse*, *7*(3), 59–81.

Faver, C.A., & Cavazos, A. M. (2008). Love, safety, and companionship: The human-animal bond and Latino families. *Journal of Family Social Work*, *11*(3), 254–271.

Faver, Catherine A., & Strand, E. B. (2007). Fear, guilt, and grief: Harm to pets and the emotional abuse of women. *Journal of Emotional Abuse*, *7*(1), 51–70. doi:10.1300/J135v07n01_04.

Flynn, C. P. (2000). Battered women and their animal companions: Symbolic interaction between human and nonhuman animals. *Society & Animals: Journal of Human-Animal Studies*, *8*(2), 99–127. doi:10.1163/156853000511032.

Flynn, C. P. (2001). Acknowledging the "Zoological connection": A sociological analysis of animal cruelty. *Society & Animals: Journal of Human-Animal Studies*, *9*(1), 71–87. doi:10.1163/156853001300109008.

Foreman, K., & Crosson, M. D. (2012). Canines for Combat Veterans: The National Education for Assistance Dog Services. *The United States Military Medical Journal*, Canine Assisted Therapy in Military Medicine, April–June, 63–64.

Friedmann, E., Katcher, A., Thomas, S., Lynch, J., & Messent, P. (1983). Social-interaction and blood-pressure—influence of animal companions. *Journal Of Nervous And Mental Disease*, *171*(8), 461–465. doi:10.1097/00005053-198308000-00002.

Frommer, S. S., & Arluke, A. (1999). Loving them to death: Blame-displacing strategies of animal shelter workers and surrenderers. *Society and Animals*, *7*(1), 1–16.

Frumkin, H. (2001). Beyond toxicity: human health and the natural environment. *American Journal of Preventive Medicine*, *20*(3), 234–240.

Furst, G. (2006). Prison-Based Animal Programs: A National Survey. *The Prison Journal*, *86*(4), 407–430. doi:10.1177/0032885506293242.

Garrity, T. F., Stallones, L., Marx, M. B., & Johnson, T. P. (1989). Pet ownership and attachment as supportive factors in the health of the elderly. *Anthrozoös*, *3*(1), 35–44. doi:10.2752/089279390787057829.

Gosse, G. H., & Barnes, M. J. (1994). Human grief resulting from the death of a pet. *Anthrozoös*, *7*(2), 103–112. doi:10.2752/089279394787001970.

Gullone, E. (2000). The biophilia hypothesis and life in the 21st century: Increasing mental health or increasing pathology? *Journal of Happiness Studies*, *1*(3), 293–322.

Gullone, E., & Robertson, N. (2008). The relationship between bullying and animal abuse behaviors in adolescents: The importance of witnessing animal abuse. *Journal of Applied Developmental Psychology*, *29*, 371–379.

Harker, D., & Bates, D. C. (2007). The black bear hunt in New Jersey: A constructionist analysis of an intractable conflict. *Society and animals*, *15*(4), 329–352.

Hart, L. A., Zasloff, R. L., Bryson, S., & Christensen, S. L. (2000). The role of police dogs as companions and working partners. *Psychological reports*, *86*(1), 190–202.

Hennessy, M. B., Morris, A., & Linden, F. (2006). Evaluation of the effects of a socialization program in a prison on behavior and pituitary–adrenal hormone levels of shelter dogs. *Applied Animal Behaviour Science*, *99*(1), 157–171.

Henry, B., & Sanders, C. (2007). Bullying and animal abuse: Is there a connection? *Society & Animals*, *15*, 107–126.

Hensley, C., Tallichet, S. E., & Dutkiewicz, E. L. (2010). Childhood Bestiality A Potential Precursor to Adult Interpersonal Violence. *Journal of Interpersonal Violence*, *25*(3), 557–567. http://doi.org/10.1177/0886260509360988.

Herzog, H. (2002). Ethical aspects of relationships between humans and research animals. *ILAR Journal*, *43*(1), 27–32.

Horst, F. C. P., LeRoy, H. A., & Veer, R. (2008). "When Strangers Meet": John Bowlby and Harry Harlow on Attachment Behavior. *Integrative Psychological and Behavioral Science*, *42*(4), 370–388. doi:10.1007/s12124-008-9079-2.

Hosey, G., & Melfi, V. (2014). Human-animal interactions, relationships, and bonds: A review and analysis of the literature. *International Journal of Comparative Psychology*, *27*(1), 117–142. http://escholarship.org/uc/item/6955n8kd.

Humane Society of the United States. (2003). *2003 Animal Cruelty Report*.

Johnson, R. A., & Meadows, R. L. (2002). Older Latinos, Pets, and Health. *Western Journal of Nursing Research*, *24*(6), 609–620. doi:10.1177/019394502320555377.

Joye, Y. (2011). Biophilia in Animal-Assisted Interventions—Fad or Fact? *Anthrozoos: A Multidisciplinary Journal of The Interactions of People & Animals*, *24*(1), 5–15. doi:10.2752/175303711X12923300467249.

Kass, P. H., New, Jr., J. C., Scarlett, J. M., & Salman, M. D. (2001). Understanding animal companion surplus in the United States: Relinquishment of nonadoptables to animal shelters for euthanasia. *Journal of Applied Animal Welfare Science*, *4*(4), 237–248.

Kaufman, M. E. (1999). The relevance of cultural competence to the link between violence to animals and people. In F. R. Ascione & P. Arkow (Eds.) Child abuse, domestic violence, and animal abuse (pp. 260–270). West Lafayette, IN: Purdue University Press.

Kellert, S. R., & Wilson, E. O. (1993). *The Biophilia Hypothesis*. Washington, D.C.: Island Press.

Kuruvilla, C (2014, August 28). Kye the K-9 police dog is buried with full honors; cops investigate handler who shot animal's killer. *New York Daily News*. Retrieved from: http://www.nydailynews.com/news/national/kye-k-9-police-dog-laid-rest-full-honors-article-1.1920699 on June 10, 2015.

Kwong, M., & Bartholomew, K. (2011). "Not just a dog": An attachment perspective on relationships with assistance dogs. *Attachment & Human Development*, *13*(5), 421–436. doi:10.1080/14616734.2011.584410.

Lakey, B., & Orehek, E. (2011). Relational regulation theory: A new approach to explain the link between perceived social support and mental health. *Psychological Review*, *118*(3), 482–495. doi:10.1037/a0023477.

Leinberger Jr, R. C. (2009). *The Emotional Impact of the Animal Control Profession*. Thesis, University of Richmond School of Continuing Studies.

Magee, D. A., MacHugh, D. E., & Edwards, C. J. (2014). Interrogation of modern and ancient genomes reveals the complex domestic history of cattle. *Animal Frontiers*, *4*(3), 7–22. doi:10.2527/af.2014-0017. https://www.animalsciencepublications.org/publications/af/pdfs/4/3/7.

Main, M., Kaplan, N., & Cassidy, J. (1985). Security in infancy, childhood, and adulthood: A move to the level of representation. *Monographs of the Society for Research in Child Development*, 66–104.

Marx, M. B., Stallones, L., Garrity, T. F., & Johnson, T. P. (1988). Demographics of pet ownership among U.S. adults 21 to 64 years of age. *Anthrozoos: A Multidisciplinary Journal of The Interactions of People & Animals*, *2*(1), 33–37.

McConnell, A. R., Brown, C. M., Shoda, T. M., Stayton, L. E., & Martin, C. E. (2011). Friends with benefits: On the positive consequences of pet ownership. *Journal of Personality and Social Psychology*, *101*(6), 1239–1252. doi:10.1037/a0024506.

Merz-Perez, L., Heide, K., & Silverman,, I. (2001). Childhood Cruelty to Animals and Subsequent Violence against Humans. *International Journal of Offender Therapy and Comparative Criminology*, *45*(5), 556–573. doi:10.1177/0306624X01455003.

Messent, P. (1985). Pets as social facilitators. *Veterinary Clinics of North America—Small Animal Practice*, *15*(2), 387–393.

Milani, M. (1991). Considering the human/animal bond. *Journal of the American Veterinary Medical Association*, *198*(10), 1706–1707.

Milani, M. (1995). *The Art of Veterinary Practice: A Guide to Client Communication*. University of Pennsylvania Press.

Milani, M. (2006). Problematic client-animal relationships: Munchausen by proxy. *The Canadian veterinary journal. La revue vétérinaire canadienne*, *47*(12), 1161–1164.

Milani, M. (2011). The art of private veterinary practice: intellectual communication. *The Canadian Veterinary Journal. La Revue Vétérinaire Canadienne*, *52*(8), 897–898.

Miltiades, H., & Shearer, J. (2011). Attachment to Pet Dogs and Depression in Rural Older Adults. *Anthrozoos: A Multidisciplinary Journal of The Interactions of People & Animals*, *24*(2), 147–154. doi:10.2752/175303711X12998632257585.

Munro, H. M. C., & Thrusfield, M. V. (2001a). 'Battered pets': Non-accidental physical injuries found in dogs and cats. *Journal of Small Animal Practice*, *42*(6), 279–290.

Munro, H. M., & Thrusfield, M. V. (2001b). "Battered pets": Munchausen syndrome by proxy (factitious illness by proxy). *The Journal of Small Animal Practice*, *42*(8), 385–389.

Nathanson, J. N. (2009). Animal hoarding: Slipping into the darkness of comorbid animal and self-neglect. *Journal of Elder Abuse & Neglect*, *21*(4), 307–324. doi:10.1080/08946560903004839.

National Link Coalition (2015, March). The Link Letter, 8(3), p.7.

National Link Coalition (2015, March 8). Pets in protection orders by state. Retrieved on March 21, 2015 from www.nationallinkcoalition.org.

Neumann, S. L. (2010). Animal welfare volunteers: Who are they and why do they do what they do? *Anthrozoos: A Multidisciplinary Journal of The Interactions of People & Animals*, *23*(4), 351–364. doi:10.2752/175303710X12750451259372.

Packman, W., Field, N. P., Carmack, B. J., & Ronen, R. (2011). Continuing bonds and psychosocial adjustment in pet loss. *Journal of Loss and Trauma, 16*, 341–357. doi:10.1080/15325024.2011.572046.

Palmer, R., & Custance, D. (2008). A counterbalanced version of Ainsworth's strange situation procedure reveals secure-base effects in dog-human relationships. *Applied Animal Behaviour Science, 109*(2–4), 306–319. doi:10.1016/j.applanim.2007.04.002.

Patronek, G. J. (1999). Hoarding of animals: An under-recognized public health problem in a difficult-to-study population. *Public Health Reports, 114*, 81–87. doi:10.1093/phr/114.1.81.

Patronek, G. J. (2006). Animal hoarding: Its roots and recognition. *Veterinary Medicine, 101*, 520.

Patronek, G. J., & Nathanson, J. N. (2009). A theoretical perspective to inform assessment and treatment strategies for animal hoarders. *Clinical Psychology Review, 29*, 274–281. doi:10.1016/j.cpr.2009.01.006.

Peacock, J., Chur-Hansen, A., & Winefield, H. (2012). Mental health implications of human attachment to companion animals. *Journal of Clinical Psychology*.

Pedersen, I., Martinsen, E. W., Berget, B., & Braastad, B. O. (2012). Farm animal-assisted intervention for people with clinical depression: a randomized controlled trial. *Anthrozoos: A Multidisciplinary Journal of The Interactions of People & Animals, 25*(2), 149–160. doi:10.2752/175303712X13316289505260.

Penning, M. (2011). Welcome address by the WAZA President (pp. 9–10). Presented at the 2011 Annual World Association of Zoos and Aquariums Conference in Prague.

Peters, S. (2011, September 9). Dogs help schools lick bullies. *USATODAY.COM*. Retrieved June 10, 2012, from http://yourlife.usatoday.com/parenting-family/story/2011-09-28/Dogs-help-schools-lick-bullies/50592574/1.

Phillips, C., & Peck, D. (2007). The effects of personality of keepers and tigers (Panthera tigris tigris) on their behaviour in an interactive zoo exhibit. *Applied Animal Behaviour Science, 106*(4), 244–258.

Planchon, L. A., Templer, D. I., Stokes, S., & Keller, J. (2002). Death of a companion cat or dog and human bereavement: Psychosocial variables. *Society and Animals, 10*(1), 93–105.

Planchon, L. A., & Templer, D. I. (1996). The correlates of grief after death of pet. *Anthrozoös, 9*(2–3), 107–113. doi:10.2752/089279396787001491.

Porcher, J., Cousson-Gélie, F., & Dantzer, R. (2004). Affective components of the human-animal relationship in animal husbandry: Development and validation of a questionnaire 1. *Psychological reports, 95*(1), 275–290.

Porcher, J. (2010). The relationship between workers and animals in the pork industry: a shared suffering. *Journal of Agricultural and Environmental Ethics, 24*(1), 3–17. doi:10.1007/s10806-010-9232-z.

Porcher, J., & Schmitt, T. (2012). Dairy cows: Workers in the shadows? *Society & Animals: Journal of Human-Animal Studies, 20*(1), 39–60. doi:10.1163/156853012X614350.

Risley-Curtiss, C, Holley, L., & Wolf, S. (2006). The animal-human bond and ethnic diversity. *Social Work, 51*, 257–268. doi:http://dx.doi.org/10.1093/sw/51.3.257.

Risley-Curtiss, C., Holley, L. C., Cruickshank, T., Porcelli, J., Rhoads, C., Bacchus, D. N. A., Nyakoe, S., et al. (2006). "She was family": Women of color and animal-human connections. *Affilia, 21*(4), 433–447. doi:10.1177/0886109906292314.

Risley-Curtiss, Christina, Holley, L. C., & Kodiene, S. (2011). "They're there for you": Men's relationships with companion animals. *Families in Society, 92*(4), 412–418.

Rohlf, V., & Bennett, P. (2005). Perpetration-induced traumatic stress in persons who euthanize nonhuman animals in surgeries, animal shelters, and laboratories. *Society and Animals, 13*(3), 201–220.

Russow, L. M. (2002). Ethical implications of the human-animal bond in the laboratory. *Ilar Journal, 43*(1), 33–37.

Sakagami, T., & Ohta, M. (2010). The effect of visiting zoos on human health and quality of life. *Animal Science Journal, 81*(1), 129–134.

Sanders, C. R. (2006). "The dog you deserve": Ambivalence in the K-9 officer/patrol dog relationship. *Journal of Contemporary Ethnography, 35*(2), 148–172. doi:10.1177/0891241605283456.

Schaefer, K., Hays, K., & Steiner, R. (2007). Animal abuse issues in therapy: A survey of therapists' attitudes. *Professional Psychology—Research and Practice, 38*, 530–537.

Schoenfeld-Tacher, R., Kogan, L. R., & Wright, M. L. (2010). Comparison of strength of the human-animal bond between Hispanic and non-Hispanic owners of pet dogs and cats. *Journal of the American Veterinary Medical Association, 236*(5), 529–534.

Siegel, J. M. (1995). Pet ownership and the importance of pets among adolescents. *Anthrozoos: A Multidisciplinary Journal of The Interactions of People & Animals, 8*(4), 217–223.

Signal, T., Ghea,V., Taylor, N., & Acutt, D.(2103). When do psychologists pay attention to children harming animals? *Human-Animal Interaction Bulletin, 2*, 82–97.

Smith, L. D. G., Ham, S. H., & Weiler, B. V. (2011). The impacts of profound wildlife experiences. *Anthrozoos: A Multidisciplinary Journal of The Interactions of People & Animals, 24*(1), 51–64. doi:10.2752/175303711X12923300467366.

Solomon, O. (2010). What a dog can do: Children with autism and therapy dogs in social interaction. *Ethos, 38*, 143–166. doi:http://dx.doi.org/10.1111/j.1548-1352.2010.01085.x.

Sprinkle, J. E. (2008). Animals, empathy, and violence: Can animals be used to convey principles of prosocial behavior to children? *Youth Violence and Juvenile Justice, 6*(1), 47–58. doi:10.1177/1541204007305525.

Steketee, G., Gibson, A., Frost, R. O., Alabiso, J., Arluke, A., & Patronek, G. (2011). Characteristics and antecedents of people who hoard animals: An exploratory comparative interview study. *Review of General Psychology, 15*, 114–124. doi:10.1037/a0023484.

Strand, E. B., & Faver, C. A. (2005). Battered women's concern for their pets: A closer look. *Journal of Family Social Work, 9*(4), 39–58. doi:10.1300/J039v09n04_04.

Sugawara, A., Masud, M. M., Yokoyama, A., Mizutani, W., Watanuki, S., Yanai, K., Itoh, M., et al. (2012). Effects of presence of a familiar pet dog on regional cerebral activity in healthy volunteers: A positron emission tomography study. *Anthrozoos: A Multidisciplinary Journal of The Interactions of People & Animals, 25*(1), 25–34. doi:10.2752/175303712X13240472427311.

Toray, T. (2004). The human-animal bond and loss: Providing support for grieving clients. *Journal of Mental Health Counseling, 26*(3), 244–259. doi:http://dx.doi.org/10.17744/mehc.26.3.udj040fw2gj75lqp.

U.S. Fish and Wildlife Service. (2011). *2011 National Survey of Fishing, Hunting, and Wildlife-Associated Recreation.*

Vaughn, M. G., Fu, Q., Beaver, K. M., DeLisi, M., Perron, B. E., & Howard, M. O. (2011). Effects of childhood adversity on bullying and cruelty to animals in the United States: Findings from a national sample. *Journal of Interpersonal Violence, 26*(17), 3509–3525. doi:10.1177/0886260511403763.

Waiblinger, S., Boivin, X., Pedersen, V., Tosi, M. V., Janczak, A. M., Visser, E. K., & Jones, R. B. (2006). Assessing the human–animal relationship in farmed species: a critical review. *Applied Animal Behaviour Science, 101*(3), 185–242.

Weisman, A. D. (1990). Bereavement and companion animals. *Omega: Journal of Death and Dying, 22*(4), 241–248. doi:10.2190/C54Y-UGMH-QGR4-CWTL.

Wenthold, N., & Savage, T. A. (2007). Ethical issues with service animals. *Topics in Stroke Rehabilitation, 14*(2), 68–74. doi:10.1310/tsr1402-68.

Wesley, M. C., Minatrea, N. B., & Watson, J. C. (2009). Animal-assisted therapy in the treatment of substance dependence. *Anthrozoos: A Multidisciplinary Journal of The Interactions of People & Animals, 22*, 137–148. doi:10.2752/175303709X434167.

Wilson, E. O. (2001). Nature matters. *American Journal of Preventive Medicine, 20*(3), 241–242. doi:10.1016/S0749-3797(00)00318-4.

Winefield, H. R., Black, A., & Chur-Hansen, A. (2008). Health effects of ownership of and attachment to companion animals in an older population. *International Journal of Behavioral Medicine, 15*(4), 303–310. doi:10.1080/10705500802365532.

Wisdom, J., Saedi, G., & Green, C. (2009). Another breed of "service" animals: STARS Study findings about pet ownership and recovery from serious mental illness. *American Journal of Orthopsychiatry, 79*, 430–436.

Yount, R. A., Olmert, M. D., & Lee, M. R. (2012). Service dog training program for the treatment of posttraumatic stress in service members. *The United States Army Medical Department Journal—Canine Assisted Therapy in Military Medicine*, April–June, 63–69.

Zapf, S. A., & Rough, R. B. (2002). The development of an instrument to match individuals with disabilities and service animals. *Disability & Rehabilitation, 24*(1–3), 47–58.

Zasloff, L. (2010, May). *Chickens and donkeys and goats—Oh my! Exploring relationships with other kinds of pets.* Presented at the University of Tennessee Veterinary Social Work Summit.

Zequi, S. de C., Guimarães, G. C., da Fonseca, F. P., Ferreira, U., de Matheus, W. E., Reis, L. O., ... Lopes, A. (2012). Sex with Animals (SWA): Behavioral Characteristics and Possible Association with Penile Cancer. A Multicenter Study. *The Journal of Sexual Medicine, 9*(7), 1860–1867. http://doi.org/10.1111/j.1743-6109.2011.02512.x.

Zilcha-Mano, S., Mikulincer, M., & Shaver, P. (2011). An attachment perspective on human-pet relationships: Conceptualization and assessment of pet attachment orientations. *Journal of Research in Personality, 45*, 345–357. doi:10.5014/ajot.63.2.126.

Zimolag, U., & Krupa, T. (2009). Pet ownership as a meaningful community occupation for people with serious mental illness. *American Journal of Occupational Therapy, 63*, 126–137.

Chapter 7

Statistics and Measurement of Animal Cruelty

Cassandra L. Reyes

Introduction

The primary focus of the chapters in this text is on animal cruelty through both prohibited and permitted human conduct. Previous chapters have defined many kinds of animal cruelty (see Chapters 1, 3, 4, and 5). To provide the foundation for further in-depth discussion about different types of animal cruelty (e.g., profit-related, sports-related, other active cruelty, hoarding), its prevalence will be presented in this chapter through available statistical data. First, an overview of animal cruelty in the United States will be provided. Next, active cruelty offenses will be discussed, followed by passive cruelty acts, and finally other forms of animal cruelty. The data on the categories under each form of cruelty will include the number of known incidents, the types of animal victims, the characteristics of the known perpetrators, and the states in which the highest percentages of these known acts have occurred.

Overview of Animal Cruelty in the United States

On March 14, 2014, South Dakota's Governor Dennis Daugaard signed a new law to set felony penalties for malicious acts of animal cruelty, which marked the first time that animal cruelty became a felony in all 50 states in the United States (Beller, 2014; Berry, 2014; Cronin, 2014; Twining, 2014). However, gathering data to measure the prevalence of animal cruelty in this country can be a daunting task. Although many local jurisdictions throughout the country keep records of the number of cruelty cases that are processed through their criminal justice systems, it is difficult to find this information on a state or national level.

Recently, Lynn Addington and Mary Lou Randour (2012) sought to understand the state-level collection of animal cruelty data. Of the representatives for 50 states contacted for their study, 28 agreed to participate. Eighteen of those states reported that they amassed data on animal cruelty crimes, with the majority receiving the information through their

Incident-Based Reporting Systems (Addington & Randour, 2012). Yet, even though many states collected identifiable statistics on animal cruelty cases within their jurisdictions, at the time the article was written, it did not appear that any had analyzed these data. However, local law enforcement agencies can voluntarily report case information to the FBI, which could provide a means for evaluating the data on the national level.

At the time of their study, Addington and Randour (2012) wrote that although the Federal Bureau of Investigation (FBI) acknowledged the advantages of accumulating information on animal cruelty offenses, it did not collect distinguishable data on such cases under either the Uniform Crime Reports (UCR) summary system or the National Incident Based Reporting System (NIBRS). Instead, these acts were captured under Part II "All Other Offenses" in the UCR and Group B 90Z "All Other Offenses" under NIBRS (Addington & Randour, 2012). The apparent anonymity of offense information made it a challenge to assess the prevalence of animal cruelty across the country.

As mentioned in Chapter 5 of this text, the FBI recently upgraded animal cruelty to a Class A Felony in September of 2014 (Bernier, 2014; Brinkerhoff, 2014; Halpern & Blasher, 2015; Kirby, 2014; Lautner, 2015; Manning, 2014; Pacelle, 2014). Although changes will be made to the FBI's NIBRS to include animal cruelty in 2015, and the data collection will begin in 2016, the data will not be available to the public until 2017 (Bernier, 2014). However, according to Gerbasi (2004), Pet-Abuse.com is a current source for available animal cruelty case data.

Pet-Abuse.com

Run by a non-profit organization, Pet-Abuse.com (2015) is a Website that is dedicated to offering nationwide statistics on known animal cruelty cases. Launched in January 2002, the Animal Abuse Registry Database Administration System (AARDAS) project includes information on the prevalence of animal cruelty cases, the kinds of animals being abused, the characteristics of the alleged and convicted perpetrators of these offenses, and the locations in which these offenses occur. These data have been collected through police records, court documents, and the media since the year 2000. According to the ticker on the Website, there are 19,448 searchable cases that have accumulated since the Website began in 2001 (Pet-abuse.com, 2015). Of the 17,267 accessible types of U.S. animal abuse classifications that are provided in the AARDAS, approximately one-third (5,586) of the cases are for neglect or abandonment, 2,145 (12%) are for hoarding, 1,955 (11%) are for shooting, 1,506 (nearly 9%) are for fighting, and 1,209 (7%) are for beating (Pet-abuse.com, 2015). Further discussion on the categories of cruel acts will be provided later in this chapter. With regard to the non-human victims in the listed 20,656 cases on the "Most common animals in animal cruelty cases" table, the most common type of animal in the overall number of cruelty cases was the non-pit bull dog (8,485), which equated to 41%[1] of all cases. Cats (3,381) accounted for 16% of the cases and were the second-most common animal victim. The 2,464 pit bull dogs (12%) were the third most common animal victim. Horses were involved in 8% of the cases (1,641). Chickens (779) were victims in nearly 4% of the cases whereas pet birds (384) comprised 1.8% of the cases. Other common animal victims encompassed 377 cows (1.8%), 373 pet rabbits (1.8%), and 354 goats, which represented 1.7% of all cases (Pet-abuse.com, 2015). As

---

1. Please note that most of the percentages throughout this chapter are rounded up or down to the nearest whole number.

mentioned earlier, within the discussion of the categories of offenses, the most common types of animal victims in each one will be presented.

Animal Cruelty Case Trend

Over the 13 years that the AARDAS has been available, there has been a documented trend within the collected data on known animal cruelty cases. These data date back to 2000, when there were 485 known cases recorded in the AARDAS (Pet-abuse.com, 2015). The number of cases increased each year and peaked during the year of 2006 with 2,714 cases (Pet-abuse.com, 2015). The number of recorded cases then decreased yearly until 2009, when there were 1,019 reported that year. The yearly number of cases rose again and peaked in 2011 with 1,666 cases reported that year (Pet-abuse.com, 2015). Interestingly, there were only 82 cases documented in 2014. At the time of this writing (June 2015), no statistics are available through the AARDAS for the number of animal abuse cases thus far in 2015. Given the apparent escalation in the number of recorded animal cruelty cases in 2006, it would seem that this type of behavior is becoming more frequent in the United States. However, an increase in the number of cases does not necessarily indicate a rise in the commission of the acts themselves. As will be discussed in Chapter 17 of this text, the media has played a major role in the public's awareness of animal cruelty, which may result in an increase in the number of reported cases that may have been ignored or not recognized previously. As in other types of crime, an offense is not known until it is reported. Thus, it is important to understand who is reporting these cases to law enforcement, humane law enforcement, and other animal protection agencies.

Reporting Parties

As mentioned earlier, Pet-Abuse.com (2015) acquires its statistics from a variety of sources. Since 2007, Pet-Abuse.com has provided data on those who initially report the cruelty, when said information is available. Among the most common types of reporting parties are neighbors, who accounted for 36% of the cases (Pet-abuse.com, 2015). Owners of the animals being abused comprised another 14% of the reporting parties. As with many other types of offenses, people who are unknown to law enforcement may report crimes. In regard to the animal cruelty cases in the AARDAS, 10.5% of the reporting parties were unknown (Pet-abuse.com, 2015). Police were involved in 9% of the cases which, according to Pet-Abuse.com, often implies that the officer was at the location for another reason and discovered the alleged cruelty. Like some other crimes, some people may wish to remain anonymous for various reasons. Seven percent of the animal cruelty cases in the AARDAS have been reported by anonymous sources (Pet-abuse.com, 2015). In addition, the category of "Other" encompassed 11% of the reporting parties. Finally, not surprisingly, the alleged abusers accounted for only 0.2% of the people who reported these offenses (Pet-abuse.com, 2015). Perhaps these individuals are not reporting these cases in order to avoid prosecution or they may not be aware that their actions are considered cruel due to mental illness or ignorance of the law. In addition, it is possible that the alleged perpetrators believe that their behavior is justified. As a result, some general characteristics of these alleged perpetrators will be presented next.

General Alleged Perpetrator Characteristics

As with other types of crimes, there is some information available about the characteristics of the known alleged abusers in animal cruelty cases (see Chapters 8, 9, 10, 12, 15, and 16 in this text). Overall, in the accumulated animal cruelty cases found in the AARDAS where the gender of the alleged perpetrator was known (14,300), males accounted for 75% of the cases[2] (Pet-abuse.com, 2015). Additionally, within this group of known perpetrators where both the offenders' gender and age range were known, the divergence between the genders becomes visible. Of the 10,784 known male abusers, 2,222 (21%) were between the ages of 31 and 40 (Pet-abuse.com, 2015). In regard to the 3,516 known female abusers, 859 (24%) were aged 41 to 50 at the time of the offense. Not only was there a difference between the genders with respect to their ages, the types of acts most commonly committed vary, which will be addressed later in this chapter. In addition to the gender and age range of the alleged or convicted offenders, there are other aspects about the known animal cruelty cases available. These elements follow next.

Other Aspects in Animal Cruelty Cases

As discussed in Chapters 6 and 13, the relationship between the animal and the alleged offender is another factor in animal cruelty cases. According to the AARDAS, the animals' caregivers were the alleged abusers in 63% of 9,738 cases involving 248,933 animals (Pet-abuse.com, 2015). Of these cases, approximately 29.5% of the animals died. With regard to the cases in which the owner was not the alleged abuser, approximately 47% of the animals died (Pet-abuse.com, 2015). Given these statistics, it is possible that the mortality of the animals in these cases could have been affected by the animal-human bond that was reviewed in Chapter 6.

As discussed in Chapter 6, 10, 13, and 14 in this text, an offender's use of drugs and/or alcohol may be related to the commission of animal cruelty. In the information regarding the 10 most common abuse classifications in the 659 known cases in the AARDAS where drugs or alcohol was an issue, nearly 15% were fighting cases (Pet-abuse.com, 2015). Twelve percent of the cases involved neglect or abandonment; in approximately 10% of the cases, the animals have been beaten; in a little over 7% of the cases, the perpetrators shot the animals; and in almost 7% of the cases, the animals were stabbed (Pet-abuse.com, 2015). Of the remaining types of abuse classifications provided, throwing, mutilation or torture, kicking or stomping, hoarding, and the use of a vehicle accounted for approximately 5%, 5%, 4%, 3.5%, and 3%, respectively, of the cases (Pet-abuse.com, 2015).

Retaliation (which is also addressed in Chapters 3, 12, and 14 of this text) is another aspect of the known animal cruelty cases presented through the AARDAS. The data provided on retaliation are in reference to cases in which a cat or dog was off-leash or otherwise unconfined (Pet-abuse.com, 2015). In these 287 cases, the alleged perpetrators indicated to be retaliating against the animals' bad behavior (Pet-abuse.com, 2015), not in retaliation for the actions of another human. Animals were shot in 73% of these cases, beaten in 10% of these cases, and poisoned in 6% of these cases (Pet-abuse.com, 2015). The other types of abuse included stabbing (4%), mutilation or torture (4%), vehicular (2%), and kicking or stomping (1%). As these were cases where the animals were roaming free, the final section in this overview is in regard to animals who were either tethered or otherwise bound or tied-up at the time the abuse occurred.

According to Pet-Abuse.com (2015), there have been 971 known cases where a dog has been tethered at the time of the abuse and 240 cases where an animal was intentionally bound or tied. Of the cases where a dog was tethered, 61.5% suffered neglect or abandonment, 18% were involved in fighting, nearly 7% were victims of hoarding, 3% were

---

2. Please note that the data available on the perpetrators' gender in the AARDAS are presented only as male and female.

shot, and 2% were beaten (Pet-abuse.com, 2015). Fifty-four percent of the dogs who were tethered in those cases were non-pit bull dogs. With regard to the cases where the animals were intentionally bound or tied, only the situations in which the animal had its limbs, muzzle, etc. intentionally bound are included in the AARDAS (Pet-abuse.com, 2015). Of these cases, 22.5% of the animals were mutilated or tortured, 16% were neglected or abandoned, and 10% were beaten (Pet-abuse.com, 2015). In addition, 6% were choked, strangled, or suffocated; 6% were hit by a vehicle, and 5% were shot (Pet-abuse.com, 2015).

This section of the chapter has provided an overview of the extent of the recorded animal cruelty cases in the AARDAS. In the next section, the focus will shift to information on individual offense categories of active and passive cruelty (many of these offenses have been described in Chapters 1 and 5 of this text). For each type of offense discussed, statistics on the animal who was most commonly victimized, data on known perpetrator characteristics, and the state location in which the most acts occurred during 2013 (the most recent yearly report available on Pet-Abuse.com) will be given. These offenses will be discussed under three categories: active cruelty, passive cruelty, and other forms of animal cruelty. The review of these categories begins with active cruelty.

Active Cruelty

Active cruelty includes acts of commission. This type of cruelty usually implies intent, where the perpetrator intentionally and deliberately causes harm to an animal (Pet-abuse.com, 2015). According to the American Society for the Prevention of Cruelty to Animals (ASPCA), "intentional cruelty occurs when an individual purposely inflicts physical harm or injury on animal…" (ASPCA, 2012). As described in Chapters 1 and 5 of this text, some examples of these physical acts are beating, bestiality, burning, fighting, kicking, poisoning, shooting, suffocation, throwing, and trapping. As also discussed in Chapters 1 and 5, this kind of behavior is sometimes called Non-Accidental Injury (NAI). This section will provide information on a variety of offenses that are considered active cruelty. These offenses are listed alphabetically; the order does not imply a ranking in terms of prevalence or incidence. The first offense to be addressed is beating.

Beating

The beating of animals can be found in domestic violence situations and in other circumstances (See Chapters 1, 2, 10, and 13 of this text for further information). Currently, there are 1,445 beating cases found in the AARDAS (Pet-abuse.com, 2015). As in the overall animal cruelty statistics, the non-pit bull dog was the most common animal victim of beating. There were 753 cases in which this type of dog was beaten, representing 52% of the total cases in this category (Pet-abuse.com, 2015). There also were 263 beating cases involving cats, which portray 18% of the cases; 12% (172) of the cases were comprised of pit bull dogs; and 57 (4%) cases include wild birds who have been beaten (Pet-abuse.com, 2015). In addition, 3% (41) of the cases concerned horses, 18 cases (1.2%) were comprised of pigs, and 13 cases (.9%) each of cows and raccoons (Pet-abuse.com, 2015). Of the 1,193 known abusers in the beating cases currently in the AARDAS, 94% are male (Pet-abuse.com). Additionally, in the cases where the gender and age range of the perpetrator were known, both males and females between the ages of 31 and 40 were more likely than any other given age range to have beaten an animal (Pet-abuse.com, 2015). Finally pertaining to the states that have the highest percentages of the nine known beating cases during 2013, 22.22% of the cases were in Florida, Illinois, and Connecticut each; and 11.1% were in Louisiana, Massachusetts, and New York (Pet-abuse.com, 2015).

Bestiality

The second category of active cruelty offenses is bestiality, which has been defined as having sexual contact with a non-human animal (see Chapters 1 and 5 of this text). According to Pet-Abuse.com (2015), as in the overall animal cruelty and beating statistics, of the 212 known bestiality cases, the most common animal who was a victim of bestiality was the non-pit bull dog (116 cases), representing 55% of the cases. At the time of this writing, 17% (36) of the bestiality cases involved horses, 16 cases (7.5%) concerned pit bull dogs, and 10 cases (5%) pertained to sheep (Pet-abuse.com, 2015). Of the 275 known abusers in the bestiality cases currently in the AARDAS, 88% are male (Pet-abuse.com, 2015). Additionally, in the cases where the gender and age range of the perpetrator were known, similar to the beating cases, both males and females between the ages of 31 and 40 (in their respective genders) were more likely than any other given age range to have engaged in bestiality with an animal (Pet-abuse.com, 2015). Finally, in regards to which states have the highest percentages of the two known bestiality cases during 2013, Illinois and California each had one of the known bestiality cases (Pet-abuse.com, 2015). The offense of bestiality will be more thoroughly addressed in Chapter 10 of this text.

Burning: Caustic Substances

There are two categories of burning offenses listed within AARDAS, burning with caustic substances and burning with fire or fireworks (see also Chapter 5 of this text). Burning with caustic substances will be addressed first. According to the AARDAS (Pet-abuse.com, 2015), as in the overall animal cruelty, beating, and bestiality statistics, the non-pit bull dog (75 cases) was the most common animal who was a victim of being burned with a caustic substance and accounts for 55% of the cases. Currently, out of the 137 burning with caustic substances cases, there also were 27 (20%) cases involving cats, 12 cases (9%) concerning pit bull dogs, and five cases (4%) where horses have been burned with caustic substances (Pet-abuse.com, 2015). Of the 49 known abusers in the burning with caustic substance cases presently in the AARDAS, 73% are male (Pet-abuse.com, 2015). Additionally, in the cases where the perpetrators' gender and age range were known, males aged 31 to 40 and females between the ages of 21 and 25 were more likely than any other available age range to have burned an animal with a caustic substance (Pet-abuse.com, 2015). Finally, Illinois, Pennsylvania, Washington, and California each had one of the four known burning with caustic substance cases during 2013 (Pet-abuse.com, 2015).

Burning: Fire or Fireworks

Burning with fire or fireworks is the second form of burning and was mentioned in Chapter 1 of this text. According to the AARDAS, the most common animal who was the victim of the 458 burning with fire or fireworks cases was the cat (Pet-abuse.com, 2015). The cat was a victim in 172 cases, which signifies 38% of the known cases (Pet-abuse.com, 2015). Presently, there also are 165 (36%) burning with fire or firework cases involving non-pit bull dogs, and 57 (12%) cases comprising of pit bull dogs (Pet-abuse.com, 2015). In addition, horses and opossums were each the victims of burning with fire or fireworks in eight cases, each of which equates to 17% of the cases (Pet-abuse.com, 2015). Of the 349 known abusers in the burning with fire or fireworks cases currently in the AARDAS, 90% were male (Pet-abuse.com, 2015). Additionally, in the cases where the gender and age range of the perpetrator were known, males between the ages of 15 and 17 and females aged 31 to 40 were more likely than any other given age group to use fire or fireworks to burn animals (Pet-abuse.com, 2015). Of the six known burning with fire or fireworks cases during 2013, one each was reported to have occurred within the borders of Illinois, New Jersey, New York, Ohio, South Carolina, and Florida (Pet-abuse.com, 2015).

Choking, Strangulation, or Suffocation

Choking, strangulation, and suffocation share this offense category, which was introduced in Chapters 1 and 5 of this text. According to Pet-Abuse.com (2015), there were 338 cases of choking, strangulation, and suffocation in the AARDAS. As in the overall animal cruelty and other offense statistics, the non-pit bull dog was the animal victim in 55% (187 cases) of these cases (Pet-abuse.com, 2015). At present, there also were 84 choking, strangulation, or suffocation cases (25%) involving cats; 22 cases (6.5%) in which pit bull dogs were victimized; wild birds were the victim in eight cases (2%); and pet rabbits were the victim in seven of the known cases (2%) (Pet-abuse.com, 2015). Of the 180 known abusers in the choking, strangulation, or suffocation cases currently in the AARDAS, 85% are male (Pet-abuse.com, 2015). Additionally, in the cases where the gender and age of the perpetrator were known, males aged 31 to 40 and females between the ages of 41 to 50 were more likely than any other given age group to have choked, strangled, or suffocated an animal (Pet-abuse.com, 2015). There were no known choking, strangulation, or suffocation cases listed by state in 2013. However, in the 26 known choking, strangulation, or suffocation cases during 2010 (the latest known year), 19.2% of the cases occurred in California and 11.5% were in Florida (Pet-abuse.com, 2015). In addition, Georgia, New York, Massachusetts, Colorado, and Ohio each had 7.9% of the cases (Pet-abuse.com, 2015).

Drowning

Drowning cases are the next form of active cruelty to be presented (see also Chapter 5 of this text). This type of cruelty is sometimes the fate of the breeding females in puppy mills who are no longer of use to the mill's owner (T. Loller, personal communication, March 26, 2010). More information about puppy mills can be found in Chapters 1, 3, 5, and 8 of this text. In addition, Michael Vick was convicted of drowning dogs at the Bad Newz Kennels (FindLaw, 2007).[3] In the 162 drowning cases reported in the AARDAS, as in the burning with fire and fireworks cases, cats (70 cases) were the most common animal victim (43%) (Pet-abuse.com, 2015). At the time of this writing, there also are 66 (41%) drowning cases involving non-pit bull dogs and 13 cases (8%) involving pit bull dogs (Pet-abuse.com, 2015). Of the 100 known abusers in the drowning cases presently in the AARDAS, 80% are male (Pet-abuse.com, 2015). Additionally, when the gender and age range of the perpetrator were known, aged 18 to 20 and 41 to 50 (there were an

---

3. In addition, Michael Vick's case is further examined in Chapter 8 in this text.

equal number of cases in each group), and females aged 41 to 50 were more likely than any other given age range to have drowned an animal (Pet-abuse.com, 2015). There were no known drowning cases listed by state in 2013. However, in the last reported year, 2010, there were 12 known drowning cases. New Jersey, California, and Florida each had 16.7% of the cases (Pet-abuse.com, 2015). In addition, New York, North Carolina, Oregon, Michigan, Tennessee, and Montana each had 8.3% of the cases within their borders (Pet-abuse.com, 2015). The offense of drowning is also discussed in Chapters 1, 3, 5, 6, and 10 in this text.

Fighting

Animal fighting (see also Chapter 5 in this text) has become a familiar issue in the media due to events such as Michael Vick's case in 2007, which will be addressed in greater depth in Chapter 8 in this text. According to the AARDAS, the most common animal who was a victim of the 1,660 fighting cases was the pit bull dog (999 cases), which represented 60% of the known cases (Pet-abuse.com, 2015). As of June 16, 2015, there had also been 487 fighting cases (29%) involving chickens, 111 cases (6.6%) encompassing non-pit bull dogs, 17 cases (1%) entailing pigs, and 14 cases (.8%) where cats were incorporated into fighting (Pet-abuse.com, 2015). Of the 2,718 known abusers in the fighting cases, 94% were male (Pet-abuse.com, 2015). Additionally, in the cases where the gender and age of the perpetrator were known, both males and females between the ages of 31 and 40 were more likely than any other given age group to have participated in animal fighting (Pet-abuse.com, 2015). Finally, there were eight known fighting cases during 2013 (Pet-abuse.com, 2015). Of these cases, there were two cases each in Mississippi and North Carolina; and one case each in Florida, New York, South Carolina, and California (Pet-abuse.com, 2015).

Hanging

Hanging statistics are the next category of offense (see also Chapter 5 of this text). In addition to drowning, Michael Vick was also convicted of hanging dogs at the Bad Newz Kennels (FindLaw, 2007). According to Pet-Abuse.com (2015), out of the 169 hanging cases currently available in the AARDAS, as in several other types of animal cruelty cases, the non-pit bull dog (86 cases) has been a victim in 51% of the cases and was the most common animal in these cases. In addition, presently there also were 42 hanging cases (25%) involving cats and 29 (17%) cases where pit bull dogs have been hung (Pet-abuse.com, 2015). Of the 74 known abusers in the hanging cases presently listed in the AARDAS, 85% are male (Pet-abuse.com, 2015). Additionally, when the gender and age range of the perpetrators were known, males who were equally represented in three age groups (18 to 20, 26 to 30, and 41 to 50) and females who were in the 26 to 30 age range were more likely than any other given age range to have hung an animal (Pet-abuse.com, 2015). Finally, the only known hanging case with a state designation in 2013 occurred in Iowa (Pet-abuse.com, 2015).

Kicking or Stomping

Kicking or stomping is another form of active cruelty that was previously mentioned in Chapters 1 and 5 of this text. According to the AARDAS, of the 393 known kicking or stomping cases, non-pit bull dogs (203 cases) were the most common animal (52%) who was a victim of the cases listed (Pet-abuse.com, 2015). Additionally, there has also been 84 (21%) kicking or stomping cases involving cats, and 35 cases (9%) including pit bull dogs (Pet-abuse.com, 2015). In addition, 13 cases (3%) of kicking or stomping entailed pets that were rodents or other small mammals; 11 cases (3%) were comprised of wild birds; pet birds, horses, and chickens were each victims in six cases (1.5%); and reptiles and other wildlife were victimized in five cases (1%) each (Pet-abuse.com, 2015). Of the 263 known abusers listed for the kicking or stomping cases currently in the AARDAS, 89% are male (Pet-abuse.com, 2015). Furthermore, when the gender and age of the perpetrator were known in these cases, males between the ages of 21 to 25 and 31 to 40 (equally) and females aged 31 to 40 were more likely than any other given age range to have kicked or stomped an animal (Pet-abuse.com, 2015). Finally, the only known kicking/stomping case with a listed state in 2013 occurred in Illinois (Pet-abuse.com, 2015).

Mutilation or Torture

According to Pet-Abuse.com (2015), the category of mutilation or torture encompasses deeds of excessive brutality and deliberate actions. Torture is also discussed in Chapter 1 of this text. Similar to other forms of animal cruelty that were previously enumerated, of the 1,206 known mutilation or torture cases in the AARDAS, the non-pit bull dog was the most common animal victim. It was involved in 35% (428) of the cases (Pet-abuse.com, 2015). In addition, cats were victimized in 334 of the cases (28%), pit bull dogs were mutilated or tortured in 122 (10%) of the cases, and horses fell victim in 53 (4%) of the cases (Pet-abuse.com, 2015). Additionally, there were 29 cases (2%) involving goats, 28 cases (2%) comprising of cows and chickens each, and 27 cases (2%) regarding wild birds (Pet-abuse.com, 2015). Of the 678 known abusers in the mutilation or torture cases currently in the AARDAS, 86% are male (Pet-abuse.com, 2015). Additionally, when the gender and age range of the perpetrator were taken into consideration, males aged 18 to 20 and females between the ages of 31 and 40 were more likely than any other provided age group to have mutilated or tortured an animal (Pet-abuse.com, 2015). Finally, of the six known mutilation or torture cases during 2013, one case each happened in Georgia, Illinois, New York, Rhode Island, Washington, and Connecticut (Pet-abuse.com, 2015).

Poisoning

Poisoning cases will now be addressed, which also was mentioned in Chapters 1 and 5 of this text. The AARDAS currently lists a total of 366 poisoning cases (Pet-abuse.com, 2015). As with many other types of animal cruelty, the non-pit bull dog has been the victim in 64% (236 cases) of the known poisoning cases, again making it the most common type of animal in this type of cruelty (Pet-abuse.com, 2015). Also, cats have been poisoned in 60 cases (16%) and wild birds were the focus in 12 (3%) of the cases (Pet-abuse.com, 2015). Additionally, 10 cases (3%) consisted of pet marine mammals; other wildlife and pit bull dogs have been poisoned in eight cases (2%) each (Pet-abuse.com, 2015). Of the 120 known abusers in the poisoning cases presently in the AARDAS, 76% are male (Pet-abuse.com, 2015). In addition, males between the ages of 41 and 50 and females between the ages of 51 and 60 were more likely to have poisoned an animal than any other age group for each gender (Pet-abuse.com, 2015). Finally, during 2013, Iowa and California each had one of the two known poisoning cases (Pet-abuse.com, 2015).

Shooting

Shooting is the next offense category and was mentioned earlier in this chapter in regard to retaliation against an animal. Shooting also was listed in Chapters 1 and 5 of this text. Presently, there are 2,087 shooting cases in the AARDAS (Pet-abuse.com, 2015). As with the majority of the other offenses that were previously detailed in this chapter, the most common animal to be shot was the non-pit bull dog, which has accounted for 1,185 cases (57%) (Pet-abuse.com, 2015). There also were 365 shooting cases (17%) involving cats, 143 cases (7%) entailing pit bull dogs, and 97 cases (5%) where horses were shot (Pet-abuse.com, 2015). In addition, there were 67 cases (3%) including wild birds and 59 cases (3%) comprising of cows (Pet-abuse.com, 2015). Of the 1,024 known abusers in the shooting cases currently in the AARDAS, 95% are males (Pet-abuse.com, 2015). Additionally, when the gender and age range of the perpetrator were taken into consideration, both males and females between the ages of 41 and 50 were more likely than any other given age group to have shot an animal (Pet-abuse.com, 2015). Finally, of the 19 known shooting cases during 2013, there were three each in New York and Pennsylvania; two in Idaho; and one each in South Carolina, Maine, Connecticut, Virginia, Florida, Washington, Oklahoma, Oregon, Indiana, Louisiana, and California (Pet-abuse.com, 2015).

Stabbing

The next offense type to be presented is stabbing (see also Chapter 5 of this text). According to Pet-Abuse.com (2015), as in many other offense categories, the non-pit bull dog was the most common animal victim (263 cases) of the known 514 stabbing cases, which represented 51% of these cases (Pet-abuse.com, 2015). Also, there were 84 cases (16%) involving pit bull dogs, 55 cases (11%) consisting of cats, 22 cases (4%) of horses, and 20 cases (4%) where pigs were stabbed (Pet-abuse.com, 2015). Of the 382 known abusers in the stabbing cases currently in the AARDAS, 93% are male (Pet-abuse.com, 2015). Additionally, males aged 21 to 25 and females between the ages of 41 and 50 were more likely than any other given age group to have stabbed an animal (Pet-abuse.com, 2015). Finally, out of the five known stabbing cases during 2013, two cases were in New York; and there was one case each in Georgia, Illinois, and Massachusetts (Pet-abuse.com, 2015).

Throwing

The act of throwing an animal, which was mentioned in Chapters 1 and 5 of this text, is discussed next. According to Pet-Abuse.com (2015), as demonstrated in various other offense categories previously listed, of the 553 known throwing cases in the AARDAS, the non-pit bull dog was the most common animal victim (Pet-abuse.com, 2015). The 279 cases in which the non-pit bull dog was thrown represented 50% of all the cases available (Pet-abuse.com, 2015). There also were 183 throwing cases (33%) involving cats and 52 cases (9%) including pit bull dogs (Pet-abuse.com, 2015). Also, pet rabbits, and pet rodents and other small mammals were victims in 10 throwing cases (2%) each and seven cases (1%) where reptiles were thrown (Pet-abuse.com, 2015). Of the 369 known abusers in the throwing cases currently in the AARDAS, 88% are male (Pet-abuse.com, 2015). Additionally, like the cases of theft (to be discussed later), in cases where the perpetrators' gender and age were known, both males and females between the ages of 21 and 25 were more likely than any other age range to have thrown an animal (Pet-abuse.com, 2015). Finally, of the two known throwing cases during 2013, one case each occurred in New York and Florida (Pet-abuse.com, 2015).

Unlawful Trapping or Hunting

Unlawful trapping and hunting is the next offense category to be addressed. Unlike the other offenses enumerated in this chapter, the most common animal who was a victim of the 166 unlawful trapping or hunting cases was the deer (46 cases), which was 28% of all of the known cases listed (Pet-abuse.com, 2015). At present, there also are 42 unlawful trapping or hunting cases (25%) involving other wildlife, 26 cases (16%) comprising of wild birds, and 12 cases (7%) where reptiles were unlawfully trapped or hunted (Pet-abuse.com, 2015). Of the 167 known abusers in the unlawful trapping or hunting cases currently in the AARDAS, 96% are male (Pet-abuse.com, 2015). Additionally, of the known gender and age ranges of the perpetrators listed, males aged 31 to 40 and females between the ages of 41 and 50 were more likely than any other given age group to have unlawfully trapped or hunted an animal (Pet-abuse.com, 2015). Finally, there were no known choking, strangulation, or suffocation cases listed by state in 2013. However, of the six known unlawful trapping or hunting cases during 2010 (the latest year available), 33.3% of the cases were in Connecticut (Pet-abuse.com, 2015). The remaining cases (16.7% each) were in Wisconsin, Ohio, Oregon, and South Dakota (Pet-abuse.com, 2015). Unlawful trapping and hunting will be discussed further in Chapter 8.

Vehicular

The final offense to be presented under active cruelty is vehicular, which is the intentional striking of an animal with a motor vehicle (see also Chapter 5). According to Pet-Abuse.com (2015), as with the majority of the offense categories discussed in this chapter, the non-pit bull dog was the most common animal victimized in vehicular cases (Pet-abuse.com, 2015). Of the 357 vehicular cases in the AARDAS, the non-pit bull dog was the victim in 201 cases, which accounts for 56% of the cases (Pet-abuse.com, 2015). Presently, there also are 35 vehicular cases (10%) involving horses, 31 cases (9%) comprising of cats, 29 cases (8%) entailing wild birds, and 24 cases (7%) where pit bull dogs were hit by vehicles (Pet-abuse.com, 2015). Of the 243 known abusers in the vehicular cases currently in the AARDAS, 91% are male (Pet-abuse.com, 2015). Additionally, both males and females between the ages of 41 and 50 were more likely than any other listed age group to have hit an animal intentionally with a vehicle (Pet-abuse.com, 2015). Finally, the only known vehicular case with a listed state in 2013 occurred in California (Pet-abuse.com, 2015).

Passive Cruelty

As stated in Chapter 5 in this text, passive cruelty encompasses acts of omission. For example, when an animal is neglected, it often suffers from issues such as starvation, dehydration, inadequate shelter, or lack of proper veterinary care. Hoarding (see Chapter

10 in this text for a more thorough discussion on hoarding) is another form of passive cruelty to be presented in this section. As with the types of active cruelty offenses, the statistics on the types of animals who were commonly abused, characteristics of the alleged perpetrator, and state ranking in the year 2010 (as stated earlier, the most recent yearly report available), will be provided for each of these forms of passive cruelty. Because neglect is often a component of hoarding, it will be discussed first.

Neglect or Abandonment

According to Pet-Abuse.com (2015), as in several types of active cruelty offense statistics, the most common animal who was a victim of neglect or abandonment cases was the non-pit bull dog (3,379 cases), which represented 43% of the 7,783 cases listed in the AARDAS (Pet-abuse.com, 2015). At the time of this writing, there also are 1,114 neglected or abandonment cases (14%) involving horses, 1,022 cases (13%) comprising of pit bull dogs, and 689 cases (9%) where cats were neglected or abandoned (Pet-abuse.com, 2015). In addition, there were 201 cases (2.5%) entailing cows, 179 cases (2%) encompassing goats, 148 cases (2%) regarding pet rabbits, 150 cases (2%) including chickens, and 101 cases (1%) where pigs were neglected or abandoned (Pet-abuse.com, 2015). Of the 3,983 known abusers in the neglect or abandonment cases presently in the AARDAS, 59% are male (Pet-abuse.com, 2015). Additionally, when the gender and age of the perpetrator were known, both males and females between the ages of 41 and 50 were more likely than any other presented age group to have neglected or abandoned an animal (Pet-abuse.com, 2015). Finally, of the 61 known neglect or abandonment cases during 2013, 13 cases occurred in New York; five were in Kentucky; four in each West Virginia and Ohio; three in Texas; and two each in Michigan, Iowa, Connecticut, North Carolina, Virginia, Maryland, Washington, Indiana, and Pennsylvania (Pet-Abuse.com, 2015). In addition, there was one case of neglect or abandonment in each of the following states: Rhode Island, Arkansas, Minnesota, Kansas, South Carolina, Mississippi, Florida, Missouri, Georgia, Oregon, Nebraska, Arizona, and New Mexico (Pet-Abuse.com, 2015). The passive cruelty acts of neglect and abandonment were further highlighted throughout several chapters in this text (see Chapters 1, 5, 9, 12, 13, 15, 16, 17).

Hoarding

The final passive cruelty act to be discussed in this chapter is hoarding, which is animal neglect involving large numbers of animals (see Chapters 1, 3, 5, 6, and 9). According to Pet-Abuse.com (2015), as in the many of the other offense statistics, the most common animal who was a victim of the 4,184 known hoarding cases was the non-pit bull dog (1,342 cases), which accounted for 32% of these cases. At present, there also are 1,248 hoarding cases (30%) involving cats, 231 cases (5.5%) entailing horses, and 224 cases (5%) where pet birds were hoarded (Pet-abuse.com, 2015). In addition, there were 181 cases (4%) consisting each of pet rodents/other small mammals and pet rabbits, 108 cases (2.5%) including chickens, 107 cases (2.5%) of reptiles, and 103 cases (2%) regarding goats who were victims of hoarding (Pet-abuse.com, 2015). Of the 1,901 known abusers in the hoarding cases currently in the AARDAS, unlike every other offense category listed in this chapter, the majority of the perpetrators (65%) is female (Pet-abuse.com, 2015). Additionally, when the gender and age of the perpetrator was taken into consideration, both males and females between the ages of 51 and 60 were more likely than any other given age group (in their respective gender categories) to have hoarded animals (Pet-abuse.com, 2015). Finally, of the 13 known hoarding cases during 2013, there were two each in the states of Georgia, Pennsylvania, New Mexico, and Florida (Pet-abuse.com, 2015). There were also one known case each in Oklahoma, Minnesota, South Carolina, Mississippi, and New York (Pet-abuse.com, 2015).

Other Forms of Animal Cruelty

The preceding sections detailed the known prevalence of active and passive acts of cruelty. However, there are two kinds of cruelty, theft and unlawful trade or smuggling, which do not truly belong under those groupings. As a result, they are listed as other forms of animal cruelty. Theft will be discussed first followed by unlawful trade or smuggling.

Theft

Theft is the first type of offense to be addressed in this section. According to Pet-Abuse.com (2015), as was the case for the majority of the offenses within this chapter, the non-pit bull dog was the most common animal victim of the 310 known theft cases available in the AARDAS (Pet-abuse.com, 2015). The non-pit bull dog was the victim in 53% (164 cases) of the theft cases (Pet-abuse.com, 2015). At present, there also are 62 cases (20%) involving pit bull dogs, 23 cases (7%) entailing cats, and 17 cases (5.5%) where horses have been stolen (Pet-abuse.com, 2015). Of the 109 known abusers in the theft cases currently in the AARDAS, 77% are male (Pet-abuse.com, 2015). Additionally, both males and females between the ages of 21 and 25 were more likely than any other given age group to have stolen an animal (Pet-abuse.com, 2015). Finally, the only known kicking/stomping case with a listed state in 2013 occurred in Louisiana (Pet-abuse.com, 2015).

Unlawful Trade or Smuggling

The final offense category to be discussed in this chapter is unlawful trade or smuggling, which is addressed in greater detail in other chapters (see Chapters 3 and 8 in this text). According to the AARDAS, as in other offense statistics, the most common animal who was a victim of the 248 known unlawful trade or smuggling cases was the non-pit bull dog (89 cases), which represented 36% of those cases (Pet-abuse.com, 2015). There also were 43 unlawful trade or smuggling cases (17%) entailing reptiles, 38 cases (15%) involving captive exotics, and 17 cases (7%) comprising of horses (Pet-abuse.com, 2015). Also, other wildlife and cats were unlawfully traded or smuggled in eight cases (3%) each (Pet-abuse.com, 2015). Of the 186 known abusers in the unlawful trade or smuggling cases currently in the AARDAS, as with all but one of the offenses (i.e., hoarding) in this chapter, 80% are male (Pet-abuse.com, 2015). In addition, males between the ages of 31 and 40 and females aged 51 to 60 were more likely than any other given age group to have unlawfully traded or smuggled an animal (Pet-abuse.com, 2015). Finally, there were no known unlawfully traded or smuggled cases listed by state in 2013. However, were three known unlawful trade or smuggling cases during 2010 (the latest year available), one each in Mississippi, New Hampshire, and Wisconsin (Pet-abuse.com, 2015).

Strengths and Limitations of the AARDAS

As mentioned earlier, the Animal Abuse Registry Database Administration System (AARDAS) has been available through Pet-Abuse.com (2015) since January 2002. This is the only known database that provides real-time data on the known animal cruelty cases in the United States. In addition, the information is collected through various means allowing AARDAS to be more credible in regard to its data. One of the goals of Pet-Abuse.com is to provide animal welfare and protection organizations (i.e., the Humane Society of the United States, ASPCA) with statistics that can be utilized in making comparisons and in the dissemination of information to the general public (Pet-abuse.com, 2015). Although the AARDAS supplies a plethora of material regarding animal cruelty throughout the United States, there are a couple of limitations found within.

The main limitation of the AARDAS is the inconsistency of the data. Upon review of the data and graphs provided through the AARDAS, which can be generated in real-time, the numbers of known animal abuse cases, for example, have been found to be different in various locations on the Website. For instance, the information (as of June 16, 2015) under the title of "Animal Abuse Crime Database," stated that there were 19,448 cases in the Pet-Abuse.com (2015) animal abuse database. However, when the number of cases included in the "Most common animals in animal cruelty cases" graph was calculated, there were 20,656 cases in total, plus the "Number of Animal Abuse Cases in the U.S. by the Year" listed 16,062 cases and the pie chart entitled "U.S. Animal Abuse Classifications" showed 17,267 total cases (Pet-abuse.com, 2015). Another example would be in regard to the number of known perpetrators. On June 16, 2015, the "Age Graph for Animal Abusers" graph indicated that there were 14,350 abusers total. Finally, there were a number of tables and charts that had the same statistics on August 8, 2012, and June 16, 2015, (i.e., most common animals in burning—caustic substance, theft, unlawful trapping/hunting cases; abuser age/gender mapping for burning—caustic substance, theft, unlawful trade/smuggling, unlawful trapping/hunting cases). The second limitation with the AARDAS is innate to basically any form of data collection, the "dark figure of crime." As with other types of offenses, it is likely that a number of animal cruelty cases go unreported. This could be from a lack of knowledge about what constitutes an act of animal cruelty, fear of retaliation from the perpetrator if the offense were reported, denial that the act was committed, etc. As with other crimes, if the act is not reported or otherwise known to law enforcement, no action can be taken. Because the AARDAS receives its data from the police, courts, and the media, these agents cannot have information on unreported animal cruelty, thus resulting in missing data. However, despite these two limitations, as mentioned previously, the AARDAS is the only current known source of animal cruelty statistics on a national level within the United States. Although the FBI's statistics on animal cruelty throughout the U.S. will be available to the public in 2017, it will share the same limitations with the AARDAS with regard to reporting. It is possible that once these data are available through NIBRS, the information can be compared for a more reliable overview of the prevalence of animal cruelty in the U.S. Despite its limitations, the AARDAS provides a good foundation of data for animal advocacy and protection, research, legislative efforts, and public awareness of a problem where the victims have no voice of their own.

Conclusion

This chapter has provided a statistical foundation for numerous types of active and passive cruelty that were addressed throughout this text. In the majority of the provided kinds of offenses, the non-pit bull dog was the most common animal victim. In addition, in all but one of the offenses listed, males were the alleged perpetrator in the majority of these acts. As discussed elsewhere, females were more likely to be involved in cases of passive cruelty such as neglect and hoarding than they were in the active forms of animal cruelty. As other sources of state, nation, and perhaps world-wide animal cruelty data become accessible, it will become easier to truly assess the prevalence of this behavior in society. However, this chapter has presented a glimpse of known animal cruelty cases in the United States.

References

Addington, L. A., & Randour, M. L. (2012, Spring). *Animal cruelty crime statistics: Findings from a survey of state uniform crime reporting programs.* Retrieved from http://awionline.org/sites/default/files/products/ca-12fbireportfinal040312_0.pdf.

American Society for the Prevention of Cruelty to Animals. (2012). *Cruelty glossary.* Retrieved on August 10, 2012, from http://www.aspca.org/fight-animal-cruelty/cruelty-glossary.aspx.

Beller, K. (2014, March 29). Animal abuse is felony in all 50 states. *Liberty voice: Boldly inclusive.* Retrieved June 16, 2015, from http://guardianlv.com/2014/-3/animal-abuse-a-felony-in-all-50-states/.

Bernier, L. (2014). The FBI just made animal cruelty a top-tier felony and the reason isn't what you think. *Barkpost.com.* Retrieved June 16, 2015, from http://barkpost.com/animal-cruelty-felony/.

Berry, C. (2014, March 14). All 50 states now have felony cruelty provisions! *Animal Legal Defense Fund.* Retrieved June 16, 2015, from http://aldf.org/blog/50-states-now-have-felony-animal-cruelty-provisions/.

Brinkerhoff, N. (2014, October 16). FBI upgrades animal cruelty to Class A Felony. Retrieved June 16, 2015, http://allgov.com/news/controversies/fbi-upgrades-animal-cruelty-to-class-a-felony-141016?news=854546.

Cronin, M. (2014, March 14). All 50 U.S. states now have felony charge for animal cruelty. *The dodo.com.* Retrieved June 16, 2015, from https://www.thedodo.com/all-50-us-states-now-have-felo-465803412.html.

FindLaw. (2007). *Michael Vick's dogfighting plea agreement.* Retrieved on August 12, 2012, from http://news.findlaw.com/hdocs/docs/sports/usvick82407plea.html.

Gerbasi, K. C. (2004). Gender and nonhuman animal cruelty convictions: Data from Pet-Abuse.com. *Society and Animals, 12*(4), 359–365.

Halpern, M., & Blasher, A. (2015, January 1). Animal cruelty category added to NIBRS. *FBI Podcast*. Retrieved June 16, 2015, from https://www.fbi.gov/news/podcasts/thisweek/animal-cruelty-category-added-to-nibrs.mp3/view.

Kirby, D. (2014, October 16). This is how the FBI will crack animal cruelty cases. *The dodo.com*. Retrieved June 16, 2015, from https//www.thedodo.com/this-is-how-the-fbi-will-crack-767883698.html.

Lautner, J. (2015, April 7). FBI upgrades animal cruelty to a felony. *Pussington post: The online cat newspaper*. Retrieved June 16, 2015, from http://pussingtonpost.com/fbi-upgrades-animal-cruelty-to-a-felony/.

Manning, S. (2014, October 1). FBI makes animal cruelty a top-tier felony to help track abuse. *The huffington post.com*. Retrieved June 16, 2015, from http://huffingtonpost.com/2014/10/01/fbi-animal-cruelty-felony_n_5913364.html.

Pacelle, W. (2014, September 17). Big news: FBI to start tracking animal cruelty cases. *A humane nation: Wayne Pacelle's blog*. Retrieved June 16, 2015, from http//blog.humanesociety.org/wayne/2014/09/animal-cruelty-uniform-crime-report.html.

Pet-Abuse.com. (2015). *Cruelty database*. Retrieved on June 16, 2015, from http://www.pet-abuse.com.

Twining, S. (2014, March 14). South Dakota lawmakers enact stronger animal cruelty penalties. Retrieved from June 16, 2015, from http://www.humanesociety.org/news/news_briefs/2014/03/south-dakota-lawmakers-enact-stronger-animal-cruelty-penalties-031414.html.

Section II
Special Types of Animal Cruelty

Chapter 8

Animal Cruelty for Sport and Profit

John C. Navarro, Jacqueline L. Schneider, and Egan Green

Introduction

This section of this text focuses on specific types of animal cruelty. This chapter addresses various types of animal cruelty that are committed for profit and sport, and even entertainment. Although some types of cruelty may be committed purely for sport, purely for profit, or purely for entertainment, these three motives are not always mutually exclusive. For example, some people may consider the illegal pursuit and successful capture of an animal to be sport, and also be willing to sell the animal or its parts, thereby fulfilling both sport and profit motivations. Similarly, blood sports may be motivated by financial gain, but also by the desire to participate in the "sport." Animal abuse may be incorporated into cultural festivals to provide entertainment value, but may also be motivated by financial gain. This chapter encompasses animal cruelty that is related to sport, profit, and entertainment and includes offenses related to breeding, factory farming, trading in endangered species, poaching, blood sports, and cultural festivals.

Breeding

The beginnings of puppy mills are rooted from post-WWII endeavors for farmers to overcome the crop failures in the American Midwest. The U.S. Department of Agriculture (USDA) deemed puppies to be a cash crop. Unfortunately, these farmers were not experienced in rearing dogs. Farmers allowed any of the dogs to breed and then housed them in chicken coops, neglecting their socialization and veterinary needs (Reuben, 2002; "What is a puppy mill," n.d.; Woolf, 2014). Dogs raised in puppy mills succumb to diseases, illnesses, and congenital and heredity conditions and defects. Though not an exhaustive list, these include heart/kidney disease, musculoskeletal diseases, respiratory disorders, pneumonia, mange, and deafness (Prah, 2011; "What is a puppy mill," n.d.).

While some of these farmers may have been familiar with breeding cattle and swine, none understood the intricacies of responsibly breeding canines. What resulted was a generation of poorly bred animals that had numerous health and social problems. Profits were the primary purpose rather than trustworthy breeding. Irresponsible breeding practices continued until the U.S. Animal Welfare Act (AWA) of 1971 was adopted, thus providing to the USDA regulatory powers over these types of breeding facilities and activities.

According to Woolf (2014), a puppy mill today is a commercial enterprise whereby animal breeders produce litters continuously in order to make a profit. Typically, these breeders pay little attention to animal placements, and as previously mentioned, animal health or socialization. Further, most puppy mill breeders have no scientific knowledge or education in animal husbandry, which is an agricultural science that focuses on responsible animal breeding and the care of livestock. Puppy mill owners are, by definition, not worried about the science behind the puppy, but rather they are only concerned about the profit the puppy brings.

Conditions in puppy mills are generally substandard and deplorable. The former governor of Iowa, Chester Culver became interested in the issue, stating that dogs from puppy mills are sold "with little to no regard for the dog's health, genetic history, or future welfare" ("Iowa Gov. Culver signs bill to combat puppy mills," 2010, para. 6). Some problems that have been documented include the following: inbreeding, overcrowded cages, minimal veterinary care, and poor quality of food (Reuben, 2002).

The Pet Industry Joint Advisory Council (PIJAC) "estimates that pet stores sell 300,000 to 400,000 puppies every year" (Reuben, 2002, para. 5), but figures are much higher from Humane Society of the United States (HSUS)—believing that stores sell approximately 500,000 per year. Female dogs, known as brood bitches, face a different type of abuse. They are pressured to reproduce with almost no recovery between litters, and after a few years, when physically exhausted, they are often killed (Reuben, 2002; "What is a puppy mill," n.d.). The major protection agencies, the American Society for the Prevention of Cruelty to Animals (ASPCA), HSUS, and Companion Animal Protection Society, estimate that 9 of 10 puppies sold at pet shops originate from puppy mills (Reuben, 2002).

The requirements to operate a puppy-producing facility include having a minimum amount of space for each dog, shelter from inclement weather, a feeding and veterinary care program, fresh water every 24 hours, proper drainage of the kennel, and appropriate sanitary procedures to assure cleanliness (Woolf, 2014). Unfortunately, most of these requirements are not met. An additional obstacle is that only large-scale, commercial facilities that breed or broker animals for resale are required to be licensed and inspected by the USDA ("Puppy mills," 2015). Since they are considered wholesale operations, they come under a higher degree of scrutiny; whereas a private citizen, who breeds dogs for extra income, does not have to worry about USDA regulation or inspection.

Every state in the U.S. has implemented anti-cruelty laws that protect dogs in puppy mills; however, they vary and are rarely enforced. Iowa, Oklahoma, and Missouri are the top three puppy-producing states in the U.S ("Iowa Gov. Culver signs bill to combat puppy mills," 2010; "What is a puppy mill," n.d.). Many operations are located in rural regions of the country (Prah, 2011; Reuben, 2002) and are frequent violators of the standards set by the AWA. In reality, rarely are they fined or have license suspensions ("Puppy mills," 2015).

Laws

In early 2010, then-Governor of Iowa, Chester Culver signed a bill that allowed the state more control over his state's puppy mills. State officials can now inspect puppy mills that sell to pet stores, when originally they could only investigate facilities that sold directly to the public via online or classified ads. In the previous year, 10 states proposed laws that would protect dogs and consumers from puppy mills ("Iowa Gov. Culver signs bill to combat puppy mills," 2010); be that as it may, additional steps need to take place in order to ensure that practices either stop or are improved.

Missouri's largest puppy mill distributor in the U.S.—responsible for 30% of the country's 10,000 puppy mill operations—put enough pressure on Governor Jay Nixon (D-MO) to repeal the Puppy Mill Cruelty Prevention Act in 2011 (Prah, 2011). In spite of the fact that Missouri's puppy mills have been repeatedly found in violation of AWA and USDA regulations (Reuben, 2002), Nixon saw his decision as a compromise between what breeders and animal rights activists demanded. The law increases fees for a license to operate a dog facility from US$500 to $2,500. Although more humane changes will not be implemented immediately, breeding operations have up to five years to follow the new law. Such change will require the breeder to provide the dog more space, access to exercise, and no new enclosures with wire-strand flooring (Prah, 2011).

The 2008 Puppy Uniform Protection Act was sponsored by Reps. Sam Farr (D-CA), Jim Gerlach (R-PA), Lois Capps (D-CA), former representative Terry Everett (R-AL) and then-senator Rick Santorum (R-NY), and Senator Richard Durbin (D-IL). It was written to address the commercial sale of animals directly to the public via the Internet and direct sales; however the act was never signed into legislation. Not giving up, Senator Durbin solicited support from Senator David Vitter (R-LA) and Sam Farr and reintroduced a new version of the 2008 act. The 2010 Puppy Uniform Protection and Safety Act again would require any breeder selling more than 50 dogs a year to be licensed and subject to inspection. Further, this version required dogs to be released from their cages for exercise each day. This piece of legislation again was not signed into law. However, Pennsylvania passed a puppy-mill law that doubles the floor space for each dog, mandates the removal of wire flooring in cages, and requires two veterinary exams per year (Prah, 2011). In 2013, the Puppy Uniform Protection Act (2013–2014) was again introduced in the House of Representatives, although has not yet made any advancement since its proposal.

So-called lemon laws that protected consumers against bad car purchases now exist in many states and now apply to those who have unknowingly bought puppies from mills. These laws mandate that buyers be reimbursed for veterinary bills amassed from their sick puppies. Arizona's puppy lemon law states that the pet dealer must give the following information if known: the date of the animal's birth, state in which the animal was born, date the dealer received the animal, any veterinary treatment the animal has received, veterinarian's statement of the animal, and information if the animal is suffering from any sort of medical condition (Reuben, 2002). Hopefully, these laws will assist in more humane production of pets—although more research is needed in order to monitor the lemon laws' impact.

Shelters

Shelters are responsible for the care of the animals whenever there is a large seizure of dogs from a puppy mill, and typically half will be euthanized (Reuben, 2002). Unfortunately, the cost and removal process is overwhelming for local shelters. Derango (2012) expressed concerns about HSUS' practices of dropping off animals at local humane shelters and without offering any financial support for the local shelter. Actions like these surfaced after Hurricane Katrina when HSUS would kindly rescue abandoned animals and then drop them at a local shelter that was already overwhelmed by normal business before Katrina ever made landfall.

Factory Farming

As societies' populations expand, a paradox emerges. More people have to be fed, but agricultural land is lost to residential and business developments that will house and employ the expanding population. Farmers are tasked with providing food in order to feed the world's people and in order to achieve this goal, new farming methods have to be designed and implemented. In the Western world, agrarian societies have largely disappeared, as have the majority of family farms. In recent years, farming has moved to large-scale operations so that food production could indeed meet world demand.

Industrial animal agriculture, more commonly referred to as factory farming, produces the vast majority of meat for consumption in the U.S.: 99.9% of chickens; 97% of laying hens; 99% of turkeys; 95% of pigs; and 78% of cattle (Safran-Foer, 2010; Zacharias, 2011). In addition to the goal of producing food for human consumption, factory farming also seeks to maximize profits. When profit maximization is the primary goal, some believe that inhumane methods can be utilized, such as, extremely confined spaces, overcrowding, and mutilations (D'Silva, 2006).

There have been improvements in agricultural practices so that many constituents' needs are met. For example, the nutritional value of various crops has increased due to advancements in horticultural science, thus farmers are able to meet global demands for nutritious food. Animal rights and welfare groups have called for more humane treatment of species that provide meat-based protein. Agricultural industries and governments have worked together to improve the living conditions of those animals, as well as those involved in their slaughter. When combined, profit margins have remained healthy for most industrial farms so they are able to recapitalize profits to further aid advances in agricultural sciences and industry. Advancements are somewhat related to nutrition and management, but most improvements in selective breeding have helped the industry meet its production expectations.

The care and condition of farm livestock remain firmly at the forefront of animal rights and welfare activists, who have always held that animals have emotional capabilities, as well as the ability to feel pain (see Singer, 1990). At the same time, many animal activists hold the belief that farmers, especially factory farmers have little or no concern about animal welfare, which is not the case with the vast majority of farmers in the U.S. Opponents of the perspective that animals have emotional capabilities believe that society is anthropomorphizing animals—meaning that humans are transferring human characteristics, including the ability to feel pain, to their animal counterparts. Regardless, the Treaty of Amsterdam has recognized that animals have the ability to feel pain (D'Silva, 2008). Research has shown that people who believe that animals have lower mental capacities feel more comfortable eating animal products ("Denying mental qualities to animals in order to eat them," 2011).

Factory farming is not without its problems. Some farms and their practices are harmful not only to animals, but also to the environment. Research shows that factory farms "cause soil contamination, loss of biodiversity, greenhouse gas emissions, and land, energy and water wastage" (Zacharias, 2011, para. 3). In addition, these animals contain "hormones, antibiotics, pesticides and dioxins" (para. 4) received through injections and/or through their diet, which have been associated with serious human health conditions, such as cancer, heart, and other degenerative diseases. Though this is not an exhaustive list, there are many welfare problems within factory farms, which include overcrowding, unnatural social groupings, confinement, barren environments, mutilations, selective breeding, and feed restriction/inappropriate diet (Pickett, 2003).

According to animal rights activists, optimal farming conditions are compromised when farmers try to achieve their role of feeding the world. This, however, is open to debate. Farmers who raise pigs in gestation crates are able to monitor each animal's health, food intake, and veterinary needs, in addition to safeguarding the animals from eating their young, fighting, and committing similar destructive behavior. Animal rights activists, on the other hand, argue that these stalls are too small for the pigs' free movement and too restrictive for "social" interaction and/or play, and that the animals become bored and depressed. Activists would prefer that the animals roam freely. Interestingly, each group actually wants the same end result—well-kept and cared-for animals. Farmers know that sick, malnourished, or stressed animals will not yield profits, in addition to knowing that if they continually present these types of animals at the slaughterhouse, the farmers' reputations will be jeopardized, significantly reducing the likelihood of their animals being purchased in the future.

The farmers' response to these issues is simple—farmers justify their treatment of animals by arguing that the pigs are generally bred in-house and raised from piglets, the restrictive stalls are all they know, so they cannot miss what they have not experienced. Moreover, caring for free-roaming pigs is dangerous to humans as they can seriously hurt, maim, or kill a farmer if he or she is pinned down or trampled. Further, there is no practical way to monitor closely the animal for disease or illness, thus increasing mortality rates among livestock.

Selective Breeding

Going back to the axiom that farmers are tasked with producing quality food in order to feed the world, science can help them become more efficient in completing this objective. For example, through selective breeding, farmers can breed cows whose meat has more protein per ounce than those whose meat is less nutritious. Genetics and genetic engineering play significant roles in improving agricultural animal-based yields.

Selective breeding is defined as the intentional breeding of animals as a way to produce desirable characteristics and to eliminate less desirable ones (Derango, 2012). Most reputable factory farms practice selective breeding practices in order to maximize their animals' marketable traits. According to animal activists, this is done in order to yield results that are beneficial for the company's profits, but according to farmers, this practice is needed to produce the highest quality meat and/or plants for human consumption.

According to animal activists, the process of selective breeding comes at a cost of negatively affecting the animals' skeletal and cardiovascular systems (D'Silva, 2006; Pickett, 2003). According to D'Silva (2006, p. 54), the time taken for a broiler chicken to reach a weight of 2 kg declined from 57 to 37 days between 1972 and 1999, and that bodyweight gain per day has increased from 34 to 53 g, a 54% increase.

This rapid body growth has contributed to lameness in these chickens, such as skeletal abnormalities caused by rapid growth, thus making a chicken unable to support itself with its own legs. It is estimated that 27% of chickens suffer from this man-made affliction

(Hickman, 2008). The pace of their growth has been increased, but their maturity rate has not changed, which affects their behavioral patterns (D'Silva, 2006; Pickett, 2003).

Cows have similar experiences in factory farms. Cattle farms, according to animal activists, are so focused on their own financial goals that they neglect the well-being of the animal. An HSUS report (2009) discovered that, "from 1987 to 2007, the number of dairy operations declined by 69% and the number of cows decreased by 11%, while the average number of cows per facility increased by 183%" (p. 1). Increases in milk production per cow were also recorded. Further, their research showed that a U.S. dairy cow produced 20,267 pounds of milk in 2007, more than double the per-cow milk yield in 1967 and 47% more than the per-cow milk yield in 1987. The goal in increasing the milk yields versus the concern for the health and welfare of the cow has contributed to cows succumbing to mastitis, which is a painful inflammation of the udder ("An HSUS report," 2009; D'Silva, 2006; Pickett, 2003). Inbreeding is also associated with mastitis ("An HSUS report," 2009).

Confinement and Overcrowding

As is the case with chickens, lameness—physical disorder that affects gait—is another serious affliction associated with current U.S. dairy industry practices ("An HSUS report," 2009). In 2006, 14% of U.S. cows suffered from this affliction, but in Wisconsin and Minnesota, the two states that lead the nation in dairy production, 24.6% of herds experienced lameness. Factors such as concrete flooring, which is also associated with hoof lesions, and insufficient physical exercise, have increased the possibility of lameness. A majority of U.S. dairy operations keep their cows indoors in small spaces that suppress movement. Poor flooring and bedding increases the cows' stress because they cannot lie down or rest. Cows prefer soft surfaces versus the concrete or gravel commonly found in indoor facilities ("An HSUS report," 2009).

As previously mentioned, mastitis is one of the most prevalently reported health problems among dairy cows. Approximately 16.5% of cow deaths in the U.S. dairy industry are due to mastitis. A pathogenic bacterium claims a substantial number of these cases, which is related not only to inbreeding, but also to the small amount of space given and lack of cleanliness of the allotted space. Increased space and hygiene can decrease mastitis cases in cows ("An HSUS report," 2009).

Conditions under which male calves are raised for white veal production have come under scrutiny for decades. These young calves are kept in veal crates, and fed a low-iron reconstituted milk powder once or twice a day (D'Silva, 2006; "An HSUS report," 2009). This meal plan keeps the male calf just above an anemic state—ensuring that its meat will remain extremely pale rather than either pink or red. It is not uncommon for these animals to lick any rusted, metal object in order to obtain more iron. Veal calves gain incredible amounts of weight in relatively short amounts of time. Because of their weight and their limited mobility, when the calves are removed from their crates for slaughter, they can barely walk (D'Silva, 2006; Pickett, 2003).

Swine

Sow stalls, also known as gestation crates, and veal creates have been banned in the U.K. (Pickett, 2003; Safran-Foer, 2010). While the European Union (E.U.) has banned the use of crates that do not permit the calf to turn around, North American nations have not yet restricted their use (D'Silva, 2006). Derango (2012) states that these gestation crates give farmers the ability to individualize and adequately care for their animals and prevent sows from fighting (and thereby injuring each other). However, these pigs, which are bred to be meatier and heavier, develop leg sores from the concrete floors (D'Silva, 2006). The lack of movement also results in other undesirable conditions, like physical discomfort, elevated stress levels, and reduced muscle and bone strength and cardiovascular wellness (Pickett, 2003).

Fowl

Chickens are another type of livestock that have been known to live in extremely crowded conditions. Pickett (2003) reveals that male chicks are killed because they offer no economic value for meat, while the hens are kept in battery cages with four or more birds (D'Silva, 2006; "McDonald's cruelty," n.d.). The small space that hens are allowed disrupts their instincts of pecking for food on the ground or dust-bathing, a process through which chickens clean themselves of parasites by digging into dirt and flipping dust onto their feathers and bodies. Overcrowding results in birds pecking each other—oftentimes causing serious injury. In order to prevent this from occurring, chickens are de-beaked immediately after being born. Because the beak is rich with blood vessels and nerve endings, the birds experience immediate pain when the beak is cut off. In 2011, this practice was banned in the U.K., along with forced feeding. In the U.S., this practice is still utilized (Pickett, 2003).

Furthermore, due to the lack of exercise within their battery cages, 35% of hens die from bone fragility-associated illnesses, also known as cage layer osteoporosis. The limited space in these battery cages also does not permit a suitable nest site. Many researchers have agreed that without a nest site, hens become extremely frustrated and display odd behaviors (D'Silva, 2006), such as cannibalism and feather pecking (Pickett, 2003). Thus, lack of care for these hens also includes not replacing old sawdust with new leading to burns on their legs from walking through each other's urination (Hickman, 2008). Finally, one to four percent of birds die from sudden-death syndrome—a syndrome only related to living in factory farms (Safran-Foer, 2010). Fortunately, the E.U., California, Michigan, Whole Foods, Subway restaurant, and a few other organizations refuse to buy eggs from distributors that operate with battery cages ("McDonald's cruelty," n.d.).

Even though a few organizations refuse to buy from distributors of factory farms that cruelly treat their hens and chickens, there still is no federal law that protects birds at every stage of life—the hatchery, the factory farm, the slaughterhouse ("McDonald's cruelty," n.d.). Unfortunately, the cruelty that chickens face is due to customers requesting cheaper prices. Organic chickens that experience free-ranges and less cruelty are three times more expensive than typical chickens (Hickman, 2011). It is important for the public to understand what free-range means as there may be a misconception that chickens are able to roam around without restriction for the entire 24 hours.

The definition of free-range for poultry according to the USDA is "five minutes of daily open-air access" (Deneen, n.d., para. 2). Further, the door of a coop or stall can be opened for five minutes "and if the animal(s) did not see the open door or choose not to leave ... it could still qualify as 'free range'" (Deneen, n.d., para. 2). Unfortunately, there is a lack of supervision to ensure this procedure is conducted.

Furthermore, there are varying definitions of free-range. With the E.U. trying to enforce the cage ban, there is a major concern that 12 countries have not complied with the ban's requirements, which was originally slated on January 1, 2012 (Driver, 2014). Currently, Switzerland is leading the E.U. with 82% of their eggs coming from free-range environments, although they have had a cage ban for some time (Deneen, n.d.). Cases such as that of Keith Owen, 44, of Worcestershire in England may have instigated the E.U. cage ban. Owen owned Heart of England Eggs Unlimited that claimed to raise free-range or organic eggs, but he was actually mislabeling his product and therefore abusing public trust. This impacted the largest supermarkets in the U.K. such as Morrison's, Sainsbury's, and Tesco, all of which were victims of Owen's scam. The stores purchased a dozen organic eggs at 90 pence (US$ 1.38) and 70 pence for free-range (US$ 1.07) while Owen bought them for 35 pence (US$ .54). Owen was forced to relinquish his £3 million (US$ 3,708,990) or face up to six-and-a-half years in prison (Pidd, 2010).

Consumers, who desire to purchase free-range eggs, can buy their eggs at farmers markets or ask supermarkets or food companies how their animals are raised (Deneen, n.d.). In order to ensure that supermarkets are receiving properly labeled free-range eggs, they can, with the correct equipment, differentiate a free-range and a cage-egg with a ultra-violet light. When an egg is laid, it is wet and picks up the marks on the surface. In the case of Keith Owen, investigators used the light, which showed whether the marks were from wires, turf, or straw (Pidd, 2010).

In late 2011, Mercy for Animals exposed Sparboe Egg Farms' animal cruelty in Colorado, Iowa, and Minnesota ("McDonald's cruelty," n.d.; York, 2011). Hidden video camera footage revealed:

> ... rotten hens, decomposed beyond recognition as birds, left in cages with hens still laying eggs for human consumptions; a worker tormenting a bird by swinging her around in the air while her legs were caught in a grabbing device; live chicks thrown into plastic bags to be suffocated." ("McDonald's cruelty," n.d., para. 2)

Sparboe Egg Farms' largest client, McDonald's, came under fire when Sparboe's cruelty was released to the media. McDonald's soon dropped Sparboe as their egg supplier ("McDonald's cruelty," n.d.; York, 2011). Sparboe was then cited for five violations—some including inadequate rodent/fly prevention. If the violations are not corrected, additional violations could be added.

Another case of bird cruelty occurred at a Butterball turkey farm located in North Carolina, which was raided after Mercy for Animals revealed to authorities their video footage of turkeys being abused. Butterball is the U.S.'s largest producer of turkeys, owning 20% of the nation's total turkey manufacturing (Jenkins, 2011; Phillips, 2012; "Police investigates Butterball cruelty cover-up," 2012). The company, in their defense, responded with a statement claiming that they have a " ... 'zero tolerance policy for any mistreatment of [their] birds or the failure to immediately report mistreatment of [their] birds by any associates'" (Jenkins, 2011, para. 6). It was later discovered that this particular Butterball facility was aware of Mercy for Animals reporting their cruelty to turkeys, and attempted to conceal their cruel farming practices. Authorities were also notified that a member of the North Carolina Department of Agriculture was complicit in the farm's attempt to cover-up the cruel practices ("Police investigates Butterball cruelty cover-up," 2012).

Mutilations

Pigs have a tendency to bite each other's tails off, which leads to inflammation and infections. In order to prevent this, tails are cut off during infancy—without anesthesia.

Pigs that are in an open range do not display this type of biting behavior, due to a more stimulated environment with toys and bedding material (D'Silva, 2006). Derango (2012) refutes this claim by saying that keeping animals in a free-range environment will not give farmers the opportunity to protect their animals from attacks and that pigs in open ranges often do engage in fights that result in worse injuries.

Cows undergo a practice called tail-docking, which is accomplished by placing a rubber ring around the tail, allowing the appendage to atrophy and eventually detach. It is also accomplished by removing it with a sharp instrument. Arguments made for tail-docking included "improved udder and milk hygiene and cleaner milking parlors and holding areas" ("An HSUS report," 2009, p. 6). However, tails are instrumental to a cow's well-being. The tail is a form of defense against fly bites and without it, cows suffer from numerous bites that can result in infestation and infection. In 2001, a USDA survey discovered that 50.5% of U.S. dairy operations perform tail-docking ("An HSUS report," 2009).

Trading in Endangered Species

Schneider (2008, 2012) explains that the illegal trafficking in endangered species has been devoid of attention by the criminological community far too long. Activities, such as poaching protected species and transporting their body parts across national borders, are jeopardizing the survival of some of the most important species on the planet. Many of these animals are apex predators, who help reduce the number of lower order animals, thus ensuring the proper environmental and ecological balance. Hunting, killing, dissecting, transporting, and selling endangered species has been the subject matter of conservation agencies for decades. However, criminality is not the domain for biologists, conservationists, zoologists, and ecologists. These scientists simply do not have the expertise to disrupt, reduce, or eliminate illegal markets, especially when markets transcend global boundaries. Criminologists, if they continue to ignore the subject of trafficking in endangered species, will be complicit in the extinction of various protected species.

There are varying estimates of the monetary size of the illegal market in wild animals and animal parts. The market grew large enough to attract attention in the 1980s although the market had been present for decades prior to that (Amidon, 1968). A consensus of sources agrees that the international illegal wildlife market is growing in terms of scope and profitability. The illegal trade has quickly becoming one of the most profitable crimes of modern times. Currently, the profits generated from the illicit trade are said to be second only to the illegal international drug trade (Zimmerman, 2003). There are, however, conflicting accounts of just how much profit is generated.

Farnsworth (1980) estimated that the U.S. illegal animal and animal parts market alone is worth approximately US$175 million. The U.S. Fish and Wildlife Service estimated the U.S. market to be US$200 million in 1991 (Poten, 1991). By 1993, the U.S Fish and Wildlife Service updated the estimate to between US$250 million and US$985 million (Davis, 1993). An estimate for the worldwide trade, which was calculated on the declared import values, was US$159 billion; whereas a figure offered by the United Kingdom's Scotland Yard estimates the profits from illegal activity as being US$5 billion (Schneider, 2012). Because the attention paid to these crimes is relatively new, it is extremely difficult to know how much money is generated from the illegal trading in endangered flora and fauna. By 2007, Interpol (as cited in Cadman, 2007) estimated it to be US$12 billion American dollars. More recent estimates put the maximum figure at between US$23 billion (Nelleman, Henriksen, Raxter, Ash, & Mrema, 2014) and US$33 billion (Wyler & Sheikh, 2013).

The illicit trade in endangered species involves several steps. First, a consumer must exist who is interested in owning either the animal itself or merely a specific piece harvested from that animal. Second, the protected animals must be hunted and killed. Locals who have extensive knowledge of breeding grounds, habitats, and locales where desired species live are typically those responsible for hunting and killing. Third, once the animal is obtained, it must be prepared for shipment in its entirety or dissected into smaller parts. These animals are normally worth more when individual parts, teeth, tails, skins, organs, are sold rather than the entire carcass. Once the demanded parts are assembled, they must be shipped to various locations throughout the world, which is the fourth step in the process. Shipping can take place through a variety of steps—depending on the location of the final destination. Finally, the desired goods must make their way to the consumer. It is critical to understand that demand is the driving force behind the illegal trafficking. If there were no demand, the various protected species would be safe from poachers. It is important to note that the animals being hunted, killed, and traded are not the only animal victims in this crime. Other non-protected animals are used to conceal the endangered byproducts. For example, illegal products are surgically implanted in the bodies of live or dead animals for concealment purposes (Schneider, 2008, 2012).

Much of the illegal market's demand comes from the Far East (Liddick, 2011; Schneider, 2012; The White House, 2014; Wyler and Sheikh, 2013). Traditional Asian medicines utilize parts of various terrestrial and marine species in their ingredients. This school of medicine believes that by ingesting parts of animals, the user takes on characteristics such as sexual vitality that are attributed to the animals (Ellis, 2005). Therefore, a segment of the illegal market seeks voracious animal parts like tiger bones and bear gall bladders for use in these remedies. The belief is that the more ferocious the animal, the more those characteristics will be transferred to the person ingesting dried, ground tiger penis, tiger bone tea, or bear gall bladders. Wildlife traffickers do not ignore the remaining animal parts. A market exists for the other animal parts as novelties, conversation pieces, and decorations. Items such as Walrus penis bones, referred to as oosiks, are on the illegal market along with animal skins, skulls, and claws (Neme, 2009; Poten, 1991).

This same market has contributed to the rapid decline of elephant and rhinoceros populations in Asia and Africa (Traffic, 2011). Elephants are hunted for their ivory tusks. The illegal ivory market consists of intricate, decorative carvings, as well as raw ivory. Rhinoceros populations have come under great poaching pressure due to a developing market for their horns. Users in the Far East believe that ground rhino horn has medicinal properties that are capable of healing a number of ailments including cancer. Traditional Chinese medicine has long prescribed ground rhino horn for a number of ailments, but the recent belief that it cures cancer has contributed to increased poaching of the animal (WWF, n.d.). Rhino horn is made of keratin, a protein that humans naturally create in the form of hair and fingernails, therefore there is no evidence that rhino horn actually offers medicinal benefits.

Notably, Japan has engaged in the hunting and killing of whales under the guise that such activities were for the purposes of scientific research. For this reason, the International Whaling Commission (IWC) has allowed Japan to continue to kill whales—in the Southern Ocean—even though a global ban was instituted in 1986 toward commercial whaling. Since the establishment of the ban, Japan has killed over 14,000 whales (McCurry, 2013). In 2013, Australia, together with New Zealand pursued to reveal the true intentions of Japan's commercial whaling practices. They were successful in their efforts in that the International Court of Justice (ICJ) decided in March 2014 that Japan's scientific research claims for the commercial hunting of whales were invalid, thus resulted in the termination of the Japanese whaling program JARPA II (International Court of Justice, 2014). Since ICJ's ruling, Japan responded with a revised whaling program, Newrep-A, in order to continue their commercial hunting of whales for scientific purposes. Even though Japan stipulated a lesser number of whales to be killed, the IWC rejected their revised whaling program as Japan did not successfully establish a scientific justification for the killing of whales (McCurry, 2015). As of 2014, Norway and Iceland are the only remaining countries that commercially hunt whales, although Greenpeace presumed that Norway's whaling industry will wither due to a lack of demand (France-Presse, 2014).

The law of supply and demand dictates that when there are fewer products for a market, the price increases. As an animal species becomes less common, the animal and/or its parts become more valuable to the black market. Therefore, species are stressed more as their numbers decrease from commercial poaching. Furthermore, because trophy-sized animals are most sought in the black market, the population genetics suffer, resulting in a genetically inferior population of animals in the wild (Poten, 1991). Additionally, because illegal market consumers seek the purest animals, there has been an increase in animal poaching in national parks in the U.S. (Davis, 1993; Lukas, 1999; Milstein, 1989; Poten, 1991). One study concluded that rangers in two-thirds of the U.S. national parks believed poaching in their parks was a major problem. This percentage was higher than other crimes in those parks such as violent crime and drug-related offenses (Lukas, 1999).

Sporting Activities

Humans have pursued animals for food or trophy for centuries. The earliest cave paintings show large animals being surrounded by men with tools thus telling anthropologists that once men figured out how to use tools, their source of nutrition could be expanded. In modern societies, hunters still provide food for their sustenance through the harvesting of various fauna. Hunts also exist for the thrill of the kill. It is this type of hunting that draws criticism amongst animal rights activists. However, perhaps the single most offensive activities to animal welfare enthusiasts are blood sports like cock-, dog-, and bullfighting. These topics are discussed in the following section.

Hunting and Fishing in the U.S.

Hunting for fauna has, at times, been a controversial subject with the U.S. public. Ethical questions surround the need for hunting in modern times. In previous eras, citizenry were largely dependent on hunting in order to have game meat for food. However, the expansion of the international economy has led to increased farm production of all kinds of food including meat ("The Environmental Food Crisis," n.d.). The increase in food availability, government programs that provide food for indigent citizens, public support, and concerns about the manner in which wild animals are killed have created ethical concerns about the need for, and therefore, legality of hunting in the U.S. (Dickson, 2009).

Despite these concerns, recent trends indicate that public support for hunting is high though fewer Americans are hunting than in previous generations (Duda & Jones, 2008; Duda, Jones, & Criscione, 2010). The increase in acceptance may be attributable to successful wildlife management practices that have led to large increases in the populations of white-tailed deer and geese. Public support seems to be related to the acceptance of wildlife management policies established by state governments and a willingness to allow people to hunt game for food specifically. Support drops drastically when the purpose of hunting is to collect a trophy or for sport (Moyer, 2011).

Whether it has been the need to hunt for sustenance or because of a society's acceptance of hunting, history has demonstrated that there is a need to protect animals from over-exploitation resulting from hunting. Wildlife management practices help determine the amount of control and the forms of control necessary to maintain viable populations of wildlife. Public opinion also influences wildlife management practices, particularly the control of predators.

To understand crimes revolving around hunting and fishing behaviors, some definitions are necessary. Poaching has had a number of definitions over the centuries. Commonly used definitions account for the illegal taking of natural resources (Young, van Manen, & Thatcher, 2011). This definition includes the illegal taking of wildlife, plant or animal. The taking of fauna includes killing animals or capturing them while they are still alive. This definition includes the illegal trapping of wild animals, as well as catching and keeping fish illegally. The taking of flora refers to the illegal harvesting of plants or trees. For example, some national parks have to combat the illegal harvesting of American ginseng plants within their parks (Young et al., 2011). However, because the focus on the current discussion is animal poaching, the discussion will revolve around animal poachers—people who intentionally engage in the illegal taking of wild fauna.

Non-Commercial Poachers

Muth and Bowe (1998) note the non-commercial motivations for illegally killing game animals. These reasons include household consumption, recreation, trophy acquisition, property protection, and "poaching as a traditional right" (p. 9). Thrill killing is another explanation that appears in the literature (Amidon, 1968; Forsyth & Marckese, 1993; Muth & Bowe, 1998) which refers to hunters illegally killing game to experience the psychological excitement of killing an animal and using their skills to successfully evade detection or capture by the authorities. It is worth noting that there is little evidence to suggest that many people illegally harvest game as a means of subsistence (Muth & Bowe, 1998; Scialfa, 1992).

Canned/Captive Hunting

Private hunting preserves have become more common since the 1990s (Buck, 2002; Diez, Gilsdorf, & Werge, 2002; Kluger, August, Billips, Liston, & Liston, 2002). At these types of ranches, land owners build high fences around large tracts of land. They purchase exotic, often non-indigenous wildlife, and then sell the rights to kill these animals for profit. The prices that customers pay vary according to the size of the animal or its antlers, but prices are typically run into the thousands. However, many hunters condemn the unsportsmanlike nature of this type of hunting. Even the Boone and Crockett Club (2012), a pro-hunting organization, which scores big game kills and provides prestige to successful trophy hunters, condemns the practices that take place on private hunting ranches and will not recognize successful hunters from these situations in their records. The club states:

[t]he Boone and Crockett Club is opposed to canned shoots because they create an artificial relationship between predator and prey. The Club upholds the moral principle that hunting is justified under the conditions of Fair Chase because of the value of the predator-prey relationship. Consistent with this position, the Club will not include in The Records of North American Big Game any animal taken in a canned shoot (Boone and Crockett Club, 2012, para. 2).

It only takes a peripheral understanding of hunting-ranch practices to understand why these unethical practices are not accepted widely. A number of academic and journalistic sources document unethical hunting practices. For example, Kluger et al. (2002) noted that many of the animals available to hunting customers at these ranches are raised from infancy by the ranch workers. This tames them to human presence as the workers feed and pet them. When a customer pays for the privilege to kill an animal, the ranch workers summon the animal or several animals with feed buckets. In other instances, predatory animals have been declawed so as to insure that the customers are not at any actual risk when pursuing typically dangerous animals. This makes the animals virtually defenseless and completely removes any semblance to an actual hunting experience.

To further reduce danger and similarities to authentic hunting experiences, quarry are drugged before being hunted (The HSUS, 2011; Williams, 2010) or simply shot while they are still in their cages ("Canned hunting," 2013; International Institute for Animal Law, n.d.; Kluger et al., 2002). Williams (2010) notes that animals are sometimes tethered to stakes to prevent their escape before they are killed. In one example from a Montana hunting ranch, a customer sat in a truck to shoot an elk. He shot it through the lung, which mortally wounded the animal, but the elk did not die immediately. The customer refused to fire a final killing shot thereby causing the animal to die a slow, painful death for 20 minutes (Herring, 1997).

Some ranches have websites where pictures of the animals available to be killed are advertised (Williams, 2010). Customers will then pay to kill a specific animal before even arriving at the ranch. The ranches often cover thousands of acres of land, so the ranch laborers must be able to provide the ill-fated animals when the customers arrive. This is sometimes accomplished by placing customers in tree stands over baited areas where the captive animals frequently visit. Technological advances such as insertion of microchip transponders in animals are now used. This allows the ranch employees to always know the location of any animal that a customer may choose to kill.

These practices contribute to debate about how wildlife management agencies should address the issue of allowing hunting ranches to legally operate. If the animals were in the wild instead of on private property, these practices would be illegal in most jurisdictions in the U.S. The animals are not subject to many of the hunting regulations that states apply to free-range animals because the ranch owners are purchasing the animals that are originating from sources other than their states' indigenous animal populations. Some laws apply to the protection of these animals, but enforcement is difficult on fenced property so many violations may go undetected. For example, animals protected by the Endangered Species Act are available as prey at some hunting ranches (The HSUS, 2011).

Further obfuscating the issue, owners who maintain hunting ranches try to avoid law enforcement jurisdiction by lobbying to have their industry regulated by state agricultural departments rather than wildlife law enforcement agencies (Diez et al., 2002). This becomes problematic because aside from the damage done to the game that are captive inside these fences, wildlife management experts have concerns about issues that may impact free-range wildlife outside of hunting preserve boundaries. Specifically, the greatest concern is the spread of new diseases to animals outside the fences. For example, chronic waste disease is the cervid equivalent to "mad cow disease" that causes deer to deteriorate physically. It has begun spreading among deer in North America causing state wildlife management agencies to take further precautions to protect free-range species. Wildlife managers have reason to believe that "mad cow disease" originated from captive animal populations (Diez et al., 2002; Poten, 1991; Williams, 2010).

The unethical practices lead law-abiding traditional hunters to reject captive hunting as bearing little resemblance to hunting animals in the wild. They also note that it violates the ethical maxim of fair chase by which legal traditional hunters abide. They fear their legal form of hunting will be confused with these practices and they will be considered in a similar vein by members of the general public who know little about the differences in their approaches to hunting.

Blood Sports: Cock-, Dog-, and Bullfighting

Animal blood sports, specifically cock-, dog-, and bullfighting have a long history of social acceptance in many societies inside and outside of North America, but, in more recent decades have generally fallen out of favor with the mainstream U.S. public. Because of the stigma attached to these sports, these practices devolve into secret networks ranging from highly organized international fighting rings to spontaneous street dogfights between the pets of human rivals. To understand the challenges that U.S. police and prosecutors face when dealing with these crimes, it is necessary to understand the background of the participants as well as the deviance.

Cockfighting

This sport, where gamecocks fight to the death, has been extremely popular on a global scale for centuries. This was certainly the case in Colonial America. In fact, it is said that President Abraham Lincoln's nickname, "Honest Abe," was due to his honesty in judging cockfights (Morrow, 1995). In the U.S., fights had no fixed locations, but combatants and locations were advertised in local papers. Conversely, in London, there were specifically constructed fight arenas for fighting birds. Fans of the sport included the wealthiest and most respected people of society, as well as those belonging to the "less desirable" classes. Gambling, most times illegal, occurs simultaneously with the fight itself. Landlords of pubs where fights often took place received payments for allowing the fight to take place on the premise, which provided support for the practice to continue (Crews, n.d.).

Existing literature demonstrates a long history of social acceptance of cockfighting from as far back as 528 BCE in Asia Minor (Hawley, 1993) into the Middle Ages in England. However, social acceptance of it began to decline and it was eventually criminalized in England in 1835 (Middleton, 2003). Cockfighting in the U.S. initially took root in the rural South (Hawley, 1982). Maunula (2007) proposes that it is the South's oldest game, and that the peak of cockfighting in England coincided with the establishment and subsequent growth of southern colonies in the New World. Cockfighting was entrenched with the developing southern culture as slaves were imported to establish the plantation economy. It exemplified the southern culture's emphasis on honor and bravery and seems to have been a bonding experience for males that ignored racial and economic boundaries (Maunula, 2007).

The social acceptance was generally limited to the South as demonstrated by the criminalization of cockfighting in Massachusetts and Pennsylvania prior to the Civil War, yet the southern states kept it legal well into the twentieth century (Maunula, 2007). States gradually strengthened the penalties for involvement in cockfighting, including training, transporting, and attending the events. The penalties were slowly increased, but in some areas this progress was slow as the cockfighters felt enough legitimacy in their actions to hire lobbyists and form political action committees to work in favor of their actions. They won enough legal legitimacy for their sport to occasionally stave off the increasing illegality of cockfighting. For example, they were successful enough in 1987 to have cockfighting legally removed from the threat of enforcement for animal cruelty laws (Hawley, 1993, 1989), and some cockfighters claimed to have had legislators firmly entrenched on their side of the debate. Nevertheless, the growing criminalization of the blood sport continued as penalties increased, and its statutory classification increased from misdemeanors to felonies in some states (Hawley, 1993). Louisiana became the last state to make it illegal in 2008 (Maunula, 2007). Yet despite this criminalization, it remains a popular, though clandestine, blood sport in some southern communities.

This history is helpful for modern participants in cockfighting. They refer to biblical justifications for their sport, refer to the history of its social acceptance, and even note its popularity among significant figures in American history (Hawley, 1993). This also serves to neutralize the illegality of the actions. The cockfighters and trainers, referred to as cockers, note the evolution from a socially acceptable behavior to one that is condemned by members of social classes who have enough social power to label the behavior of others as deviant.

Cockfighting in Modern Times

Modern cockfights occur in pits surrounded by spectators, gamblers, trainers, and owners. Two roosters that are matched by size are placed in the pit to fight (Darden & Worden, 1996). However, there are variations in fight specifics. For example, the cocks sometimes fight with no implements, but they are often equipped with small knife-like blades or pointed spurs that expedite bleeding and death. Roosters fight for several rounds until they are either exhausted or one is killed. When the cocks are exhausted, they are dragged to a secondary pit when a winner is decided by one of them rising to peck at the other thereby demonstrating relentless gameness (Darden & Worden, 1996).

There is a strict, unwritten code of conduct at cockfighting events. It regulates gambling, admission, and behavior (Muanula, 2003). For example, fighting among humans at cockfights is not tolerated and gamblers or spectators who begin or participate in physical confrontations are ejected (Hawley, 1993). Further, the cockfighting events attract small-time capitalists who sell trinkets as well as fighting roosters and cockfighting training aids and spurs (Darden & Worden, 1996). The unwritten rules of this sport require the ironic situation where the groups of people involved in the deviant activity are required to demonstrate trustworthiness and honesty among the participants.

Publications and websites dedicated to cockfighting provide much of the information about schedules and fight results. They also serve to glorify champion roosters and their careers. This leads to the irony of many cockers demonstrating great affection for their roosters, while pitting them in fights to the death with other roosters. Successful trainers and owners are promoted more frequently, and use their roosters in high profile fights that result in bigger purses. This serves to provide some sense of legitimacy to the sport.

Despite the growing illegality of the sport, it retains a following in many communities. This following is almost exclusively male, but cuts across other social boundaries such as race and economic status. The long history of gambling associated with the sport allows traditional barriers to be overlooked while focus is placed exclusively on the gameness of the roosters. Tournament formats allow not only wealthier participation, but also poorer participants to enter roosters. The poorer participants merely enter fewer roosters into the tournament because they have fewer resources to prepare a large group of cocks. Racial boundaries are also overlooked as cockfights include African-Americans, Asians, Hispanics, and Whites. The long, slow decline of cockfighting legality led to decreased participation, but some participants believe that the increasing participation from Hispanic groups has revitalized the sport. This growing involvement, specifically from Hispanics, seems to have increased attendance at cockfighting events and injected new commercial opportunities into the cockfighting subculture (Maunula, 2007).

Support for cockfighting revolves largely around the exemplification of machismo, courage, and honor that participants believe cockfighting demonstrates. They believe cockfighting has historically provided examples of manliness for humans to follow. This ranged from providing examples of how to be a good husband to models for courage and tenacity (Hamill, 2009; Middleton, 2003). The roosters' willingness to fight to the death is thought to provide a metaphor for male preparation for life challenges, and therefore, involvement in the sport builds character. In some southern states, some high school coaches use cockfights to rouse their players to greater efforts. They even extend the derogatory terms of the sport, such as "dunghill roosters," which refers to roosters who do not have the inclination to fight, to student athletes who may not be inclined to put maximum effort into their competitions. In fact, the fighting spirit of a rooster is often viewed as an indicator of the personality of its owner (Hawley, 1993).

The focus on honor in the face of adversity leads some participants to indoctrinate young males into the sport. Men often bring their children to the cockfighting events to teach them the espoused honorable personality characteristics taught by the fights (Hawley, 1993; Maunula, 2007). The boys are told to follow the rooster's lead in protecting family, turf, and honor (Hawley, 1993). Novice cockers are mentored into the sport by more experienced participants once they have been properly accepted into a cockfighting circle. This is considered quite an honor, particularly if the mentor has raised and trained successful fighting roosters over a long period of time (Darden & Worden, 1996; Hawley, 1993). This indoctrination helps insure the continuation of cockfighting. It also serves to demonstrate a hierarchy of cockers ranging from professionals to amateurs who are not given respect until they have proven their worth through their roosters' capabilities.

Policing

In the areas where cockfighting occurs, it has been common for the police to be tolerant of the activity (Hawley, 1993; Maunula, 2007). Sheriff elections sometimes include tacit understandings that local cockfighting circles will remain unmolested if a candidate is elected (Maunula, 2007). Hawley (1993) reported two decades ago that local police agencies allow cockfights, as long as they do not lead to problems, like other crimes or rowdy visitors from outside the community causing problems to the local citizens. (This law enforcement perspective may have changed in recent years.) In an earlier work, Hawley (1982) notes a lack of crime problems surrounding cockfighting, and Maunula (2007) found participants who note that other than the gambling, cockfighting is free of criminal activities. However, Darden and Worden (1996) note the presence of some minor forms of deviance such as drug dealing, money laundering, and illegal weapons offenses. Nevertheless, these offenses are not the serious, violent types of offenses, and the unspoken code of the events apparently would not permit crimes that would disturb community peace to the point that it would force local law enforcement to intervene. One prosecutor admitted that his office was preoccupied by violent crimes and crack cocaine offenses, and therefore set priorities such that cockfighting are largely overlooked (Hawley, 1993).

It is also clear that cockfighting circles are extremely secretive and selective of membership. The acceptance requires demonstrations of trustworthiness and confidentiality to screen out unwelcome intruders (Maunula, 2007). This serves to keep out animal rights activists, as well as law enforcement agents who will intervene negatively. The secretive subculture makes prosecution more difficult as witness cooperation is paramount for this type of prosecution. Witnesses are rarely willing to assist investigators, and they would be subject to punishment from the participants. The challenges of prosecuting cockfighting cases are shared with other blood sports. These include long histories, former social acceptance, and development in rural areas.

Today the practice of cockfighting is banned in all 50 states and the District of Columbia, but it is still widely practiced in other countries, including Mexico, France, Belgium, Spain, Haiti, Italy, and Malaysia (ASPCA, n.d.). Clandestine operations can result in either a misdemeanor or a felony arrest/conviction, depending on the circumstances of the fight and the participants. However, cockfighting provides an opportunity to earn significant money to not only the birds' owners, but also to those who wager on their fights. Without stronger enforcement of existing legislation, this blood sport will continue.

Dogfighting

In 2007, Michael Vick, a U.S. football star, was arrested for his involvement in a large-scale dogfighting ring. He was later convicted of these crimes at both the state and federal levels, and subsequently served time for his involvement. His criminal activities shone considerable light on a form of deviance and criminality that historically drew little attention. The crimes for which Vick was convicted incited an incredible amount of public outrage, which led to several states to revise their dogfighting statues, including stiffer penalties and/or felony classification (Ortiz, 2009).

Historical Accounts

Dogfighting is considered a legitimate sport by those involved in training, organizing, watching, and betting on the fights. The history of dogfighting supports this notion to a degree, but society's evolving sense of decency no longer tolerates it. Dogfighting, and its associated illegal gambling, has a lengthy history that can be traced back to Roman times. The Romans pitted their dogs against those of the English. The ferocity of England's fighting dogs spread through Europe (Villavincencio, 2007). In the 12th century, an ancillary sport to emerge from dog-on-dog fights was that of baiting, whereby dogs are pitted against other chained animals, such as bears, badgers, or bulls. With regard to bulls, dogfighting in England derived from the 12th-century practice of bull baiting in which dogs were made to attack bulls as a way to tenderize the meat that was to be procured from the bull (Ortiz, 2009). These types of sports were favored by the upper classes, aristocracy, and medieval gentry (Evans, Gauthier, & Forsyth, 1998; Gibson, 2005). After hundreds of years of this sport, British Parliament banned all baiting sports as a result of the concerns over animal cruelty (Villavincencio, 2007).

The Industrial Revolution led to large-scale migrations of citizens to urban areas, which shifted the practice of bull baiting to one in which dogs fought each other. This is because less space was necessary and artificial light allowed the fights to be conducted at night. However, social acceptance of dogfighting decreased, and it was criminalized in 1835 in the U.K. with the Cruelty to Animals Act (Ortiz, 2009).

Modern Times

The English blood sport practices were brought to the New World by immigrants, and the American Pit Bull Terrier was developed for its tenacity and fighting skill. Just as societal standards had developed in England, American states began outlawing dogfighting by the late 1800s (Gibson, 2005; Ortiz, 2009). Despite this, it remained popular in some circles, particularly male subcultures in the Deep South (Evans et al., 1998). Therefore, it moved to clandestine locations and developed into a criminal subculture. This sport is not only cruel, but it also offers participants an opportunity to place bets on the fighters. This form of gambling is illegal, and it helps to perpetuate the continuation of the illegal fighting (Villavincencio, 2007).

The state-level criminalization continued and dogfighting eventually became illegal in all fifty states (Evans et al., 1998; Gibson, 2005). Federal legislation did not address it until the AWA was amended in 1976 to forbid animal fighting. Congress again addressed animal fighting in the midst of public outrage about the Michael Vick case with the Animal Fighting Prohibition Enforcement Act of 2007. This Act made violation of its animal fighting prohibitions a felony with a possible incarceration penalty of three years (Ortiz, 2009, Searle, 2008). While the vast majority of countries worldwide have banned this blood sport, Japan does not have a national ban, but, many prefectures have banned the practice (Villavincencio, 2007).

No matter its legal status, organized dogfights continue to take place. The HSUS estimates that there are 40,000 dogfight participants in the U.S. alone (see Gibson, 2005). The sport is a clandestine one so as not to alert authorities. As previously mentioned, this particular blood sport was brought back into the limelight in 2007 by the conviction of American National Football League (NFL) quarterback, Michael Vick (Prah, 2011). Ironically, after his release from prison, Vick formed what some called an unnatural alliance in the form of a relationship with HSUS as their spokesperson.

Networks and Events

Types of dogfighting events range from an organized circuit to small-scale to amateur operations; with a new type of dogfighting event that has become more common, the unplanned street fight. The major events operate as part of a network of national and international dogfighting rings (Gibson, 2005; Ortiz, 2009; Searle, 2008). These organized events are typically planned for months and only selected spectators and participants are informed. In modern times, this information is transmitted via the Internet as are the locations of the events. Yet even this information is vague; the precise fighting locations remain secretive until shortly before the scheduled fight so as to avoid the attention of law enforcement (Gibson, 2005; Ortiz, 2009). Even then, the participants will sometimes meet at a location where they hand over their cell phones and keys and are bussed to the fight location (Ortiz, 2009).

Once the matches are prepared, they are surprisingly organized with specific rules and expectations for behavior. Participants, handlers, spectators, and referees are expected to abide by a rulebook written in the 1950s entitled *Cajun Rules*, which dictates the exact rules for conducting an organized dogfight (Ortiz, 2009).

The expectation of conformity to a set of rules is odd because of the high number of criminals and other criminal events that take place at the fights (Ortiz, 2009, Searle, 2008). The list of crimes that accompany dogfighting events includes human violence, theft, gambling, gang participation, prostitution, drug intoxication, and drug dealing (Gibson, 2005; Ortiz, 2009). Gibson (2005) states, "[o]rganized dog fights are staged by leaders of the drug trade as forums to distribute narcotics" (p. 7). Additionally, the fighting dogs are used as guard dogs for drug trafficking operations. The deviants will even have their dogs' vocal cords severed so they will not bark before attacking intruders. Yet, despite all the accompanying criminal activity, the biggest payoff for organized dogfighting is the money from the illegal gambling which is often in the tens of thousands of dollars (Ortiz, 2009), but sometimes reaches the hundreds of thousands of dollars (Gibson, 2005).

Amateurs and dogfighting hobbyists get involved in less organized dogfighting events (Gibson, 2005). They tend to work within a local network and repeatedly use specific dogfighting locations. These types of fights were once considered largely a rural phenomenon (Evans et al., 1998), but now appear to occur in urban areas as well. Gambling obviously takes place at this level of dogfighting as well, but not being part of a national or international circuit of dogfighters, thus the purses are smaller.

The newest evolution of the dogfighting culture is appearing in urban communities. Gangs use fighting dogs to settle disputes, intimidate witnesses and other community members, earn street credibility, overcome boredom, and win gambling proceeds (Ortiz, 2009). This group of dogfighters appears to be the most violent type (Gibson, 2005). The more ferocious their dogs, the more prestige the gang members receive. The dogfights are much more loosely organized than the professional dogfighting circuit, and tend to stay in specific locations. Additionally, some dogfights among this group of dogfighters are rather spontaneous. As potential rivals see or confront each other, they will use their dogs to defend their masculinity and an unplanned dogfight will occur (Searle, 2008). The newest type of street fight involving dogs is called "trunking" (Ortiz, 2009). This type of dogfight involves throwing two canines into the trunk of a vehicle and making bets on which dog will still be alive when the trunk is opened. Participants then drive the car around for a while before returning to the betting location to open the trunk and see which dog survived. Similarly, urban dogfights are sometimes arranged in such a way that multiple dogs will be locked in an abandoned building with a small package of dog food. They are left there until one dog kills the other dogs or survives by keeping the other dogs from eating until they starve (Ortiz, 2009).

The largest dogfighting raid to date occurred in Missouri in late 2009, resulting in 26 arrests and 500 dogs rescued from eight states. This was the result of an 18-month investigation involving the Federal Bureau of Investigation (FBI), USDA, U.S. Marshals, U.S. Attorney General, and Missouri State Highway Patrol. Hundreds of volunteers from 22 organizations throughout the U.S. cared for the dogs rescued ("Humane Society of Missouri," 2009). Unfortunately, the future of rescued dogs is somewhat bleak. Due to their violent training and aggressive skills, these dogs are not likely to be placed in caring homes so they can lead normal lives; many are euthanized.

Bullfighting

Bullfighting can be traced back to ancient times and has taken many forms; however, the practice that is more familiar today—a lavishly dressed matador taunting an angry bull with a cape—can roughly be traced back to the 1700s when Francisco Romero of Ronda, Spain brought the estoque (sword) and the muleta (the cape) into the ring ("Bullfighting history," 2012). Typically, three matadors kill up to six bulls in an afternoon of fighting. Fighting bulls are preferred over domesticated bulls, which have to be trained to charge. Training can include starvation and torture in order for the bull to become aggressive. The fight is divided into several parts. The first part of the encounter is with the matador who engages with the bull in a series of graceful and daring maneuvers. The cruelty really begins in the second part where the picadors on horseback enter the ring. It is at this stage that picadors attack the animal with lances all while the banderilleros, who work on foot, attack with barbed sticks. The best location for the attack is at the animal's shoulders. The matador hides his sword under his cape and begins the last part of their fight—the kill—which is accomplished by passing the sword's blade in the small space between the bull's shoulder blades. The animal endures a long, painful, and torturous death—all to the jeers of thousands of spectators while its dying body is dragged around the arena.

In 2012, the first bullfighting ban was enacted in the Catalonia region on the mainland of Spain. The Canary Islands banned bullfighting in 1991 ("Bullfighting in Barcelona ends with Catalonia ban," 2011; Worden, 2011). Lawmakers' decisions were influenced when attendance to these staged fights had dropped significantly, as well as the 180,000 people who had signed a petition in support of the Catalonia ban. Nearly 250,000 bulls are killed annually during the duels between pairs of matadors and bulls in front of spectators (L. E., 2011). Lawmakers in Spain have now listed bullfighting as "an artistic discipline and cultural product" (Worden, 2011) in order to protect other regions from future bullfighting bans. Bullfighters and supporters of bullfighting are stating that the sport is a symbol of Spanish cultural heritage (L .E., 2011; Worden, 2011). A poll conducted by Spain's highest circulated daily newspaper, *El Pais*, discovered that only 40% of Spaniards enjoyed bullfighting (Worden, 2011), thus indicating a decline in enthusiasm and spectator participation.

Emerging Blood Sports

One of the newest blood sports that appears to be increasing is hog-dog fighting, also known as hog-dog rodeos and hog dogging (Ring, 2004). It has been in practice for a number of years, but has not drawn much public attention; therefore there is no research on this deviance and little is known about it. This much is known: fighting dogs, typically pit bull terriers, are sicced on wild boars in closed pens. Hogs that refuse to fight or try to defend themselves are shocked with a cattle prod. To even the odds, the boar's tusks are sometimes removed. Dogs rip hogs' ears and snouts and typically pin the hogs to the ground in short order. The dogs' jaws are pried apart and the pig is allowed to survive and heal long enough to be the victim of another dog's attack at another public spectacle.

This blood sport shares characteristics with the other blood sports discussed in that the events tend to take place in rural, southern states. Ring (2004) states that this sport derives from hog hunting. This is often done with dogs chasing feral hogs, which rural residents consider nuisance animals.

Though this sport has remained largely unknown to the general public, hog-dog fighting exhibitions have begun drawing law enforcement and media attention. Publicized arrests have been made in South Carolina, Alabama (Ring, 2004), and Florida (Robert, 2006). Laws specifically addressing this practice are rare so animal cruelty laws have been used to limit this blood sport. Bills that would specifically outlaw hog-dogging have begun being introduced in state legislatures (Ring, 2004). With growing public knowledge of this sport, lawmakers are attempting to limit its spread before it becomes as firmly entrenched in some subcultures as cock-, dog-, and bullfighting has done already.

Cultural Festivals

Cultural festivals provide humans a great deal of enjoyment. As previously mentioned, bullfighting, a blood sport that pits man against beast, has been an important cultural, and thrilling sporting event in Spain, Mexico, and other Latin countries for hundreds of years. There are other cultural festivals that are oftentimes the highlight of local residents' annual activities. The most popular of these have drawn visitors from all around the globe. Foreigners attend the festivals in order to experience a new culture, and a country's ceremonial and/or ritualistic way of celebrating their heritage. Some of the world's most popular are described here.

Palio Horse Race

In 1581, the first Palio horse race was run in Siena, Italy. The city was divided into 17 distinct neighborhoods (contrade) in 1729, as they remain today. Each contrada has its own colors and emblems, signifying entrance into various sections of the city, but more importantly, signifying allegiance and heritage for a person's entire life. The race is run twice a year; the race, Palio of Provenzano, held on July 2, is in honor of the Madonna of Provenzano. And on August 16, the race of Palio of the Assumption honors the Virgin Mary's Assumption. On the day of the race, a large parade takes place throughout the city, in which nearly 600 citizens wear historical costumes, to celebrate the coming of the race. This event typically brings in 30,000 to 40,000 people a day, many of whom are foreigners. Like auto racing's Le Mans' Grand Prix, the Palio is run on city streets that have been covered in clay. It is an extremely dangerous run for horses and riders. Horses have to navigate through ancient and extremely narrow streets all at the speed of a gallop. This, of course, results in horses running into walls and other horses. At high speeds, horses (and riders) can foster extremely serious injury and even death. The danger to and injury sustained to the animals has resulted in the race's scrutiny ("The Palio in Siena," n.d.).

In 2011, Italy's tourism minister, due to fears of animal cruelty, stopped the race from being nominated for United Nations Educational, Scientific and Cultural Organization (UNESCO) World Heritage status (Squires, 2011). This caused public outcry from the city's residents, as well as from other politicians. Had the race reached UNESCO World Heritage status, it would have been listed as one of the most treasured cultural events globally. Italy has progressed in preventing animal abuse by banning the Palio horse race. Unfortunately, the race has been responsible for 49 or 50 horse deaths, either during the race or through post-race euthanasia since 1970 ("Italian festivals sanctioned for animal cruelty," 2011; Squires, 2011). Animal welfare activists were pleased with the removal of the race from consideration; however if horses are afforded better protection, it could be submitted for consideration for status in the years to come.

Jallikattu

Another popular animal event is called Jallikattu—the sport of "taming the bull," which is annually held as part of the Pongal festival in Tamil Nadu, India (Suroor, 2012b). During the event, young men try to literally tame an undomesticated bull. Men use any means necessary to achieve their goal, including beating, snapping, twisting, and breaking the bull's tail. Additionally, they jump on the bulls, wrestle them, rub chili powder in their eyes, and give them alcohol (Suroor, 2012a). An Irish animal rights group, Animal Rights Action Network (ARAN) is calling for a boycott to this cruel event. In India, there is a ban on the use of bulls as performance animals (Suroor, 2012c), but in spite of that ban, the Madras High Court gave their approval for the sport to continue in Tamil Nadu (Suroor, 2012a). PETA has also called for the cessation of the practice, as well as for the government to enforce its own laws prohibiting the use of these animals in performances (Suroor, 2012b). In May 2014, Jallikattu bull fights were subsequently banned by the Indian Supreme Court (*Animal Welfare Board of India v. A. Nagaraja & Ors.*, 2014).

Running with the Bulls

A similar race is the world-wide known event during the Fiesta de San Fermin in Spain known as the running with the bulls—Pamplona (Bils & Gregory, 1995; "Clean start to Pamplona's running of the bulls," 2011; Etxaburu, 2007; Govan, 2009; "Pamplona 'bull runner' killed," 2009). The festival originates from the 16th century (Etxaburu, 2007). Ernest Hemingway popularized the event with his 1926 novel, *The Sun Also Rises* (Etxaburu, 2007; Goodman, 2009; Govan, 2009; Webb, 2009). This event, which is held between July 7 and 14, triples the population of the village of Pamplona of 190,000 with visitors, tourists, and adrenaline junkies (Bils & Gregory, 1995; Goodman, 2009). Pamplona is comprised of eight total runs with each run consisting of six bulls and six steers to guide them through an 850-meter [930 yards] course that usually takes 2.5 minutes to reach the bull ring where they are set to die in a bullfight ("Clean start to Pamplona's running of the bulls," 2011; Goodman, 2009; "Man gored at Pamplona bull run," 2008). Another purpose for the steers is that they act as herding dogs—without them the bulls would desist charging after 100 meters [109 yards]. ("Clean start to Pamplona's running of the bulls," 2011).

Since record keeping began in 1924 to 2015, there have been 15 reported human deaths due to trampling or goring. The latest fatality occurred in 2009 (Goodman, 2009; Govan, 2009; "Pamplona 'bull runner' killed," 2009) when Daniel Jimeno Romero, 27, of Spain was hit by a bull's horn, puncturing his lung and giving him another severe wound at the neck (Goodman, 2009; Govan, 2009; "Pamplona 'bull runner' killed," 2009; Webb, 2009). Prior to Romero's death, Fermin Etxberri, 63, was trampled to death in 2003 (Govan, 2009). In 1995, the first and only American, Matthew Peter Tassio, 22, of Glen Ellyn, Illinois was gored to death (Bils & Gregory, 1995; Goodman, 2009; Govan, 2009; "Pamplona 'bull runner' killed," 2009). This University of Illinois engineer graduate received grave wounds to his liver and had his primary abdominal artery severed (Bils & Gregory, 1995).

Pamplona-like events have also occurred in Illinois amongst other states. The American version of running with the bulls began as early as 1998, but such events were intermittent. It was not until two lawyers established their company the Great Bull Run that a consistent schedule of running with the bulls events was formed (Bearak, 2013). Their first official event began in 2012 in the state of Virginia with 12,000 attendees ("The Great Bull Run comes to Florida," 2014) and 4,000 participants that engaged in the Great Bull Run (Bearak,

2013). In 2013, a 10 city schedule would host Great Bull Runs in the states of California, Florida, Illinois, Minnesota, Pennsylvania, and Texas (Martin & Felberbaum, 2013). Later in 2014, a Great Bull Run was cancelled in Los Angeles, California as a permit would not be granted due to public safety standard violations (Franzetta & Backus, 2014). Great Bull Run organizers argued that the American version of the running of the bulls is safer than the Pamplona version. The U.S. running of the bulls events do not kill the bulls afterwards, maintain less harsh terrain onto the bulls' hooves as they run on grass courses (Eltagouri, 2014), and safe zones are found along the course (Martin & Felberbaum, 2013). As of 2015, only Chicago, Illinois was set for a Great Bull Run ("About," 2015), which has since been canceled, with ticket prices that ranged from US$69 to $89 ("Tickets," 2015).

Circuses

Circuses consist of wild animals, such as elephants, tigers, bears, and horses, performing unnatural acts that include riding bicycles or jumping through rings of fire. These tricks are taught by using electric prods, bull-hooks (also known as ankuses), and sometimes pitchforks ("Abuse of Britain's last circus elephant caught on camera," 2011; "Circuses," n.d.; Nelson, 2011; "Ringling Bros. and Barnum & Bailey Circus," 2011). An ankus is a "tool" that is roughly three feet in length with a sharp metal end that has a point and hook combination (Nelson, 2011). While the point is used for pushing an animal, the hook, usually inserted in the mouth or at the top of the ear, is for pulling. Either end is sharp enough to pierce elephant hide, which is approximately one inch (2.54 cm) thick. The AWA does not outlaw the use of this type of equipment, and this lack of legislation and regulation has allowed circus organizations to bypass humane treatment of these wild animals used in their performances, and employ untrained workers to take care of these animals (see Chapter 4). This has led to many incidents of workers, wild animals, or audience members to be placed in danger and be injured or killed, and in some countries enacted laws that have banned circuses.

Regulation

The AWA, passed in 1966, is the only federal legal protection around that protects circus animals. Congress expanded the AWA in 1970 by having the USDA maintain the "humane standards for treatment of warm-blooded animals by researchers, breeders, and exhibitors—including circuses" (Nelson, 2011, para. 26). The USDA enforces the AWA standards (Woolf, 2014), though many would argue about its lenient "standards for the handling, care, treatment, and transport of wild animals in circuses" (Preiss, 2009, para. 5). Facilities that do not comply with AWA standards primarily receive warnings, and are rarely federally prosecuted and/or lose their animals (Preiss, 2009; "Puppy mills," 2015). Moira and Bobby Roberts of Bobby Roberts Super Circus may be the first circus owners to be prosecuted under the AWA violations of 2006. Undercover video footage showed an Asian elephant named Annie being abused by its caretaker with a pitchfork, as well as being kicked in the body and face. The Roberts' stated they were not aware of this incident and were horrified by the news ("Abuse of Britain's last circus elephant caught on camera," 2011; Ellicott, 2011). It is, however, their responsibility, as owners, to ensure that all their wards—animals or humans—are provided with adequate care.

Even though many of the atrocities are illegal as defined in various laws, enforcement and prosecution remain elusive. The lack of any apparent or consistent legal punishment may be a result of the transient nature of circuses, which makes for difficult monitoring, investigation, and prosecution. For any animals deemed to be considered endangered and therefore protected, such as elephants and tigers, the expansion the Endangered Species Act was passed in 1973 by Congress disallowing "harm or harassment of listed animals," thus providing an extra level of protection (Nelson, 2011).

Confinement and Traveling

"Ringling Bros. and Barnum & Bailey Circus boasts that its three units travel more than 25,000 miles as the circus tours the country for 11 months" ("Circuses," n.d., para. 6). During their travels, circuses animals can be kept in trailers for days—an area in which the animals travel, urinate, defecate, and sleep. In addition, these cramped quarters restrict movement, and endure varying weather without constant care via food and water ("Abuse of Britain's last circus elephant caught on camera," 2011; "Circuses," n.d.; Preiss, 2009; "Ringling Bros. and Barnum & Bailey Circus," 2011). The USDA has established guidelines for transporting cattle and swine (see "Cattle and swine trucking guide for exporters," n.d.; see also Chapter 4 in this text). Interestingly, USDA guidelines state clearly that cattle cannot be transported for more than 40 hours without a period of rest in which the animals are fed and watered. Further, these guidelines stipulate that animals that have been in transit for more than 24 hours should be rested for between eight and 12 hours ("Cattle and swine trucking guide for exporters," n.d.). The animals are removed from their transportation trailers and given the opportunity to eat, drink, and walk. However, specificity is lacking with regard to animals used for exhibition, including entertainment purposes like circuses. U.S. Title 7 (Agriculture), Chapter 54 (Transportation, sale and handling of certain animals) only stipulates that animals must be afforded "humane handling, care, treatment, and transportation" (7 U.S.C. 54 § 2143). The code makes reference to providing these animals humane conditions; however, the law makes no mention of transportation time limits or periods for resting, feeding, and watering animals used for exhibition purposes—many of which can be animals carrying protected statuses like the elephants and tigers.

The Liebel Family Circus has been fined almost US$3,000 for violating the standards set by the AWA. Such violations include not providing veterinary care to an elephant named, Nosey, for her overgrown footpads and chronic skin ailment, which are associated with being confined in these trailers for days on end. These violations are identified as serious considering that "foot ailments are the leading cause of death in captive elephants" (O'Connor, 2012, para. 2). Tuberculosis is also another serious ailment among elephants, and accounts for "12% of captive Asian elephants in the U.S., including many at Ringling" (Ringling Bros. and Barnum & Bailey Circus, 2011, para. 4).

As noted in Chapter 4, Feld Entertainment, which owns Ringling Bros., had agreed to pay US$270,000 for violations against the AWA, which is the largest civil penalty issued against them by the USDA in the AWA's history (Messenger, 2011; Nelson, 2011). Such violations included forcing their sick elephants to work and feeding their big cats meat with feces (Messenger, 2011). Ringling Bros. also paid another major fine of US$20,000 to the USDA due to their failure to give veterinary care to a dying baby elephant (Nelson, 2011; Ringling Bros. and Barnum & Bailey Circus, 2011). Because of their violations, any employee who has contact with animals after March 31, 2012 must undergo training within 30 days of being hired (Lo, 2011).

Employees and Training

Regardless of these fines and violations against the AWA standards, Ringling Bros. and Barnum & Bailey Circus have continued to operate and allegedly abuse their animals.

Many previous Ringling employees have said that elephants are routinely abused with bull-hooks, along with baby elephants being put through violent training procedures. These include baby elephants being tied and wrestled to the ground by employees, gouged with bull-hooks, and shocked with electric prods in order to train them. Elephants have been shown to be emotive creatures—grieving the loss of one of their family members. If they are able to grieve for a death, one wonders if they are able to do so for those abused. Ringling Bros. and Barnum & Bailey's other alleged violations include "a camel with bloody wounds ... endangering tigers who were nearly baked alive in a boxcar because of poor maintenance of their enclosures, [and] failure to test elephants for tuberculosis" (Ringling Bros. and Barnum & Bailey Circus, 2011, para. 4). The employees contracted by circuses rarely have experience caring for these animals, which has resulted in abusive training methods and employees, members of the public, and animals being injured or killed ("Circuses," n.d.; Nelson, 2011; Preiss, 2009; "Ringling Bros. and Barnum & Bailey Circus," 2011).

Bans

In February 2011, Bolivia became the first country in the world to ban all animals in circuses, including domesticated animals like dogs ("Bolivia bans all circus animals," 2009; "Greece bans animal circuses," 2015). Bolivia is amongst other countries that Animals Defenders International (ADI) has made aware of the impoverished conditions circus animals are kept in and the abuses they experience. Peru became the next country to ban the use of animals in circuses (Tyler, 2011) South American countries are seen as advocates that lead the cause for banning circuses that use wild animals in their performances ("Greece bans animal circuses," 2015; Tyler, 2011). Most recently, Mexico has joined nine other countries that have enforced a national ban of the use of animals in circuses, which became effective as of July 2015 (Hay, 2015).

The ADI was also successful in assisting Greece in recognizing the cruelty faced by animals in circuses. Greece is the first country in Europe to ban animal circuses, followed by Bosnia, with Austria and Croatia banning wild animal acts. In addition, other European countries, Portugal and Denmark, are slowly increasing their control on wild animals in circuses ("Greece bans animal circuses," 2015). Moreover, the ADI has influenced the U.K. to consider completely banning wild animals to be used in British circuses, for which 50 British lawmakers unanimously voted in 2011. Events such as the Annie incident in the Bobby Roberts Super Circus have inspired these events to occur (Seltzer, 2011).

Public pressure may put an end to circuses and/or their use of animals in their performances. Violations and fines alone cannot put a circus out of business, as indicative of amount of fines and violations amassed by Ringling Bros and Barnum & Bailey's alone. In 2001, Kenny Darnell, owner of Paulo's Circus, was experiencing record low attendance rates. Inspired by other circuses, Darnell added wild animals to his performances to boost his attendance rates. Unfortunately (or fortunately—depending on perspective), the public protested the use of animals in Darnell's circus, and, in time, he dropped the animal acts. Darnell later stated that the animals are a huge hassle that brought in extra cost and worry, and preferred human acts because they do not require the attention and care that animals do (Jeory, 2012). In March 2015, an historic announcement took the headlines worldwide. Ringling Brothers Circus declared that after 145 years of using elephants as part of their show, their Asian elephants would be retired to conservation centers in 2018 (Bittel, 2015).

Animal Tourism

Eco-tourism is a relatively recent innovation whereby humans travel to remote locations with the aim of interacting with some of the most fascinating flora and fauna on earth, many of which are endangered and thus protected. These activities are created under the guise that the tourist activities bring much-needed income to areas of economic deprivation while satisfying the travelers' curiosity. In fact, eco-tourism, while incredibly profitable, can sometimes be detrimental to the very species humans want and need to observe. A long-standing version of eco-tourism is amusement parks that focus on animal performance for the delight of spectators.

Destination Trips

Animal-related tourism can contribute to animal cruelty by participating in events that exploit animals, and place risk toward animals as well as humans. These events include such activities as hiking into the mountains of Rwanda and Uganda in order to see the endangered eastern lowland and Bwindi gorillas ("Mountain gorillas of Uganda," n.d.), diving with various species of shark, riding elephants in India and Thailand, or swimming with dolphins programs, thus debilitating protection efforts worldwide ("Animal friendly tourism," n.d.).

Due to their close genetic-make up and their lack of human interaction, gorillas are susceptible to various human diseases. Eco-tours bring humans and gorillas together in extremely close proximity, thus putting the animals at risk of serious illness or even death from something as simple as the human common cold. While no doubt profitable, these tours offer little or no protection to the endangered species.[1] Tourists tend not to think about the effect their presence in the forests have on the delicate eco-system.

Shark dives, with and without cages are becoming a very popular destination for scuba divers. Dives are offered literally around the globe, with a variety of available types of dives dependent on what species of sharks migrate and swim nearby. No waters are exempt. For example, the once extremely restricted waters of the Galapagos Islands, a UNESCO World Heritage site, even offers not only tourist shark dives, but also shark fishing. The delicate balance in the eco-system is affected once the divers enter the water. The price for cruising and diving the Islands is over US$4,200 per person, and varies by tour company. Diving in open waters carries with it risk on behalf of the diver and the sharks, but at least the sharks have the ability to swim away.

Dives with whale sharks are slightly different. Whale sharks are the largest species of fish in the oceans—reaching nearly 30 feet [9 meters] (Schneider, 2012), with the largest known whale shark reaching 40 feet in length (12 meters) ("Whale shark," n.d.). While divers can come across whale sharks in open water, typically, eco-dives are done in large nets where the whale sharks are confined, and therefore not free to leave the vicinity of

---

1. Geographic Expeditions offer tours to in Uganda and Rwanda to see the mountain and Bwindi gorillas. For a ten-day tour, the cost per person is approximately US$11,685, which includes land costs, gorilla permits, and internal airfare. While other companies offer similar trips, this is merely one example. On their website, there are health precautions for American to take before travelling in Africa; however no such warnings are offered about necessary precautions for the gorillas' health and wellbeing.

divers. Studies have not been conducted on the long-term effects of restricting the swimming space of these giant marine animals.

Wild elephants have been domesticated for use in the forestry/farming and tourism and industries in Thailand. While revered in Thai culture, these animals have endured cruel conditions and abuse for many decades. There are several potentials for abuse of the elephants in Thailand. The first and most obvious is the killing of elephants for the poaching of their ivory, skin, and even hair (Schneider, 2012). Second, these animals are used in forestry and agriculture practices, road construction, and the commercialization of forest reserves where tourists receive rides from the animals (Lohanan, 2002). The use of elephants in the logging industry has been outlawed for some time in Thailand; however, mahouts[2] still use their elephants illegally in order to haul logs in the forest. Oftentimes, the mahouts give their charges highly addictive drugs, especially amphetamines, to force their elephants to work longer, harder, and more quickly. The combination of overwork and drug use always ends poorly for the elephants, with many dying as a result of either the drugs or through work accidents, such as falling off cliffs (Schneider, 2012; Tian, 2012). Many times, illegal operations work the elephants until they literally drop dead from exhaustion. Third, elephants are also used in festivals, and mahouts often will tranquilize the elephants for greater ease of control. Typically, this is not done under the care of veterinarians, thus subjecting the elephants to potential overdose (Cheeran, Panicker, Kaimal, & Girdas, 2002). Fourth, there are approximately 1,000 elephants specifically used in the Thailand tourism industry. Although these animals are primarily used to transport visitors on eco-tours into forest areas; they are also used in elephant shows for the tourists to enjoy (Lohanan, 2002). In order for these unsuspecting tourists to have stories to tell upon return home, these animals are deprived of adequate food, water, and living conditions, which typically are unclean and unsanitary. Captive, domesticated, and/or zoo elephants are subject to other forms of abuse. Living conditions in zoos vary by country and even within a given country—largely due to varying zookeeper expertise and knowledge, funding sources, and available space. Even in zoos with the best intentions, keeping these extremely large animals in confined spaces creates undue stress and anxiety for the elephants. Some elephants have been known to attack their charges after long periods of confinement—even with the best care provided by staff, animal behaviorists, and veterinarians.

Vietnam is another country that has utilized its natural beauty to attract tourists. As a result, the country's animals are exploited for their financial gain with tours and excursions. Animals affected include dogs, monkeys, goats, and bears—all of which are "trained" to perform unusual and bizarre tricks. For example, black bears cycle on tiny bicycles with chains around their neck, muzzles on their mouths, and fez hats on their heads (Probert, 2011). This is hardly the manner in which these magnificent animals were meant to live. Other countries such as Greece and Turkey capture bears as cubs and pierce their lips, nose, or palate in order to attach a chain or rope so that their "trainers" can force them to dance—again a practice neither innate nor dignified ("Compassionate traveler," n.d.).

Another popular tourist destination is Santorini, a Greek Island, where tourists are given the option of donkey taxis. These donkeys usually work from 9:00 a.m. to 7:00 p.m., with minimal rest, shelter, and water provided ("Petition to stop the abuse of donkey taxis in Santorini," n.d.). Jordan and Egypt have been facing criticism for their mistreatment of donkeys acting as taxis, but the practice continues. Donkey handlers are locals who

---

2. A mahout is the elephant's keeper and one who drives the animal.

live in extreme poverty. They barter with tourists for prices. Because of the high demand and need for the donkeys to be available to tourists with money, the handlers tend to neglect to feed the donkeys and oftentimes place a load that is too heavy for them to handle (Ballinger, 2009).

Nepal is yet another country that exploits animals for tourism purposes. Wild parrots are illegally trapped and subsequently have their wings and tail feathers clipped to prevent flight (i.e., their means of escape). There are high death rates among these parrots due to the cruelty they experience and the unnatural existence in which they are forced to live. Snake charmers are another fascinating tourist attraction that necessitates the mutilation of snakes. Those snakes utilized by snake charmers endure a number of cruel actions, which include having their teeth pulled without painkillers, having their venom ducts pierced with hot needles, and having their mouths sewn shut with only a small gap for food and fluids ("Animal friendly tourism in Nepal," n.d.). The tourists who watch in amazement are in awe by the snake charmers' tricks, but live in the bliss of ignorance as they do not have to ponder the cruel sacrifices made by the snakes themselves.

British Columbia is an extremely popular tourist destination where animals are called upon to participate in the tourism industry. In colder seasons, tourists turn to dog sledding as a source of travel, excitement, and amusement. While visitors may never be skilled enough for a run in the Iditarod, they can live out their fantasies with a journey arranged by the local sledding company. Like those who swim with dolphins or ride elephants, the participants remain uninformed of the dogs' living conditions, health care, and/or their fate when business takes a downward trend. For example, in early 2011, a man was ordered to kill 100 of 300 sled dogs owned by a sled dog tour company in Whistler, British Colombia, due to the decline in tourism after the 2010 Winter Olympics in Vancouver ("100 healthy sled dogs slaughtered in Whistler, B.C.," 2011; Lin, 2011). A search to place the unneeded dogs in new homes failed, and as a result, the employee shot, stabbed, and buried these sled dogs in a massive gravesite over a three-day period ("100 healthy sled dogs slaughtered in Whistler, B.C.," 2011). The news of the slaughter was most likely kept relatively quiet so as to not risk of upsetting the next season's potential tourists.

Amusement Parks

The plight of dolphins and porpoises has been highlighted through the award-winning film *The Cove*.[3] *The Cove* is a film that depicts the gruesome practice of herding wild dolphins[4] into a hidden cove in Taiji, Japan, where commercial buyers choose the dolphins for use in their aquariums. Those not chosen are immediately slaughtered rather than being returned to open waters. The rationale for the slaughter remains unclear. According to Kageyama (2010), Japanese government officials have come under great scrutiny since the release of the film, but continue to defend the practice at Taiji as tradition. Further, the government allows approximately 20,000 catches each year. They see the slaughter no differently than raising livestock for slaughter. However, in an unusual turn, fishermen in Taiji started turning some of the dolphins loose, which was thought to happen as a result of growing international pressure to stop drives like that in Taiji, Japan. Aqua parks

---

3. *The Cove*, directed by Louie Psihoyos, produced by Fisher Stevens and Paula DuPré Pesmen, has won 47 international film awards, including the Academy Award for best documentary; Sundance Film Festival; and best documentary at the Toronto Film Festival, just to name a few.

4. This is also known as driving-fishing.

and aquariums outside the U.S. fuel the demand for wild dolphins. Markets, both legal and illegal,[5] are driven by the economic law of supply and demand. In this instance, the number of dolphins sought by the various aquariums worldwide will dictate how many dolphins and porpoises are caught, traded, and slaughtered each year. Until the nature of that market changes or international laws change to protect these marine species, the drive-fishing and killings are likely to continue.

Attractions like swimming with dolphins have been available to tourists worldwide, who desire the thrill to interact with these animals in their own environment. Whether available through dolphin drive-fishing or not, these dolphins are taken from their natural habitat of open oceans where they enjoy an active lifestyle of swimming up to 50 miles a day to be placed in cramped quarters (by their standards) where they are forced to swim continuously and unnaturally in circles. Unfortunately, 53% of these dolphins end up dying within three months of their capture due to various reasons, which include suffering from sunburn due to shallow water swimming, chlorine poisoning, and intestinal disease. The popularity of these programs has led to the establishment of many more in the U.S., Mexico, Latin America, and the Caribbean ("Plight of the captive dolphins," n.d.). Another marine attraction includes whale watching, which has recently experienced rapid growth with 10 million people participating, each year—resulting in the industry's profit of US$1.25 billion dollars ("Whale watching," n.d.). The tourists who partake in these types of events unwittingly contribute to the abuse, confinement, and neglect of the animals, which at times can lead to the animals' death ("Plight of the captive dolphins," n.d.; Tian, 2012).

Following the success of *The Cove*, major controversy arose about the treatment of orcas after the release of the critically acclaimed film *Blackfish*. Focus was placed on the commercial exploitation of orcas held in captivity. Specifically, the film documented the life story of a male orca named Tilikum, who has been involved in the death of three people while in captivity (Gallagher, 2013). The first human death occurred at a facility called Sealand, which resulted in Tilikum's transfer to SeaWorld Orlando. At SeaWorld Orlando another death took place that involved a drunk man that climbed into Tilikum's water tank during the night and found the next morning (Brower, 2013). But, the most notable of these three deaths was SeaWorld Orlando's trainer Dawn Brancheau in 2010 (Gallagher, 2013). Tilikum's aggressive behavior was largely attributed to his early capture off the coast of Iceland at two years of age, coupled with the abuse he experienced by female orcas during captivity. *Blackfish* questioned how Tilikum was allowed to continue to engage with humans following each death. Even more troubling, Tilikum has contributed a great amount of sperm while held captive, in which half of the orcas at SeaWorld were birthed from Tilikum's sperm (Brower, 2013). SeaWorld has questioned the validity of the claims demonstrated in the film. The company mentioned how the film misrepresented their purpose (Gallagher, 2013), and discussed the lack of focus on their conservation and research efforts (Ahmed, 2013). They also argued that the death of Brancheau was merely horseplay gone wrong (Brower, 2013). The backlash against SeaWorld has been enormous. Bands have canceled tours at SeaWorld (Ahmed, 2013), a 26-year relationship with Southwest Airlines was severed (Stout, 2014), a five percent drop in annual attendance occurred, and the bad publicity extended to affect Busch Gardens' revenue and attendance (Trigaux, 2014).

---

5. It should be noted here, that at the time of writing, dolphins and porpoises are not endangered species that are afforded international protections. Therefore, the drive-fishing that takes place in Taiji, Japan, while extremely distasteful and disturbing, is legal.

Like Tilikum, the star of the *Free Willy* trilogy series, Keiko was also captured off the coast of Iceland at a young age. The success of the films resulted in the creation of paraphernalia that was then sold to the general public (Brower, 2013). After the release of the first film interest by the public was generated once it was discovered that Keiko was maintained in unsuitable living conditions. As a result, millions of dollars were invested toward the rehabilitation of Keiko in order to reintroduce him into the wild. Once released into the wild, Keiko joined other orcas to the Norwegian coast where he befriended the community members. Soon after, Keiko beached himself and died in 2003 ("History," 2015).

The exploitation of wildlife animals as tourist attractions has led to habitat loss. It has already led to the extinction of the white-handed gibbon on Thailand's largest island, Phuket. Females were frequently captured and/or killed and have led to a genetic viability problem, where the gibbons are becoming monogamous and mates for life (Waters, 2011). Tourists need to be aware and prepare themselves with the knowledge of the abuses of animals that are used for tourist purposes.

Conclusion

Animals and humans have played important, and at times critical, roles in each other's lives. The parameters for our interaction have changed significantly over the centuries. In today's western society, societal expectations mandate that humans treat their animals — be they domesticated or wild — with care and compassion. This chapter has addressed animal cruelty that occurs when humans have used animals for the purposes of sport, profit, and entertainment, three motivations that are often inextricably linked. Offenses related to breeding, factory farming, trading in endangered species, poaching, blood sports, and cultural festivals are among the types of crimes often motivated by sport, entertainment and/or profit. Although these activities are garnering increased criticism among animal rights advocates and the general public, these types of offenses are likely to persist until societal views of animals and their treatment have overwhelmingly moved towards a more appropriate and humane perspective. As the public demands change, animals will receive a new standard of care and protection.

References

100 healthy sled dogs slaughtered in Whistler, B.C. (2011, January 31). *CTV News*. Retrieved from http://www.ctv.ca/CTVNews/Canada/20110131/bc-sled-dogs-killed-110131/.

About. (2015). Retrieved from http://www.thegreatbullrun.com/about/.

Abuse of Britain's last circus elephant caught on camera. (2011, March 26). Retrieved from http://www.telegraph.co.uk/news/uknews/law-and-order/8408914/Abuse-of-Britains-last-circus-elephant-caught-on-camera.html.

Ahmed, S. (2013, December 9). Heart cancels SeaWorld show amid 'Blackfish' controversy. *CNN.com*. Retrieved from http://www.cnn.com/2013/12/08/showbiz/seaworld-heart-blackfish/.

Amidon, P. (1968). *New York Deer Hunters: A comparison of deer law violators and non-violators*. Unpublished master's thesis. State University of New York at Syracuse.

An HSUS report: The welfare of cows in the dairy industry. (2009). *The Humane Society of the United States.* Retrieved from http://www.humanesociety.org/assets/pdfs/farm/hsus-the-welfare-of-cows-in-the-dairy-industry.pdf.

Animal friendly tourism in Nepal. (n.d.). Retrieved from http://www.responsibletravel.com/copy/animal-friendly-tourism-in-nepal.

Animal friendly tourism. (n.d.). Retrieved from http://www.wspa-international.org/helping/animalfriendlyliving/travel.aspx.

Animal Welfare Board of India v. A. Nagaraja & Ors. (2014). C. A. 5387 of 2014.

ASPCA. (n.d.). Dogfighting and cockfighting. *Animal Watch.* Retrieved from http://www.aspca.org/ASPCAKids/Real-Issues/dog-fighting-and-cockfighting.aspx.

Ballinger, L. (2009, May 1). Give the donkeys a rest! Plea to visitors over tourist site cruelty. *Mail Online.* Retrieved from http://www.dailymail.co.uk/news/article-1176270/Give-donkeys-rest-Plea-visitors-tourist-site-cruelty.html.

Bearak, B. (2013, November 14). For thrill seekers, a bull run with a different hook. *The New York Times.* Retrieved from http://www.nytimes.com/2013/11/17/sports/for-thrill-seekers-a-bull-run-with-a-different-hook.html?_r=0.

Bils, J., & Gregory, T. (1995, July 14). *Chicago Tribune.* Retrieved from http://articles.chicagotribune.com/1995-07-14/news/9507140148_1_san-fermin-pamplona-bulls.

Bittel, J. (2015, March 5). Ringling Bros. to retire its circus elephants. *National Geographic News.* Retrieved from http://news.nationalgeographic.com/news/2015/03/150305-ringling-bros-retires-asian-elephants-barnum-bailey/.

Bolivia bans all circus animals. (2009, July 31). *The Guardian.* Retrieved from http://www.guardian.co.uk/world/2009/jul/31/bolivia-bans-circus-animals.

Boone and Crockett Club (2012, June 13). Canned shoot statement. Retrieved from www.boone-crockett.org/about/positions-CannedShoots.asp?area=about&ID=6B455080&se=1&te=1.

Brower, K. (2013, August 4). Opinion: SeaWorld vs. the whale that killed its trainer. *National Geographic.* Retrieved from http://news.nationalgeographic.com/news/2013/08/130803-blackfish-orca-killer-whale-keiko-tilikum-sea-world/.

Buck, J. M. (2002, April, 3–7). *Status and management implications of captive cervid farming in the northeast.* Paper presented at Transactions of the Sixty-Seventh North American Wildlife and Natural Resource Conference. Dallas, TX.

Bullfighting history. (2012). Retrieved from http://www.spanish-fiestas.com/culture/bullfighting-history/.

Bullfighting in Barcelona ends with Catalonia ban. (2011, September 25). *BBC News Europe.* Retrieved from http://www.bbc.co.uk/news/world-europe-15050706.

Cadman, M. (2007). *Consuming wild life: The illegal exploitation of wild animals in South Africa, Zimbabwe and Zambia. A preliminary report.* Prepared for Animal Rights Africa and Xwe African Wild Life. Retrieved from http://www.nacsa.co.za/Downloads/ Consuming_Wild_Life_290307_final.pdf.

Canned hunting. (2013, April 3). Retrieved from http://bigcatrescue.org/abuse-issues/issues/canned-hunting.

Cheeran, J. V., Panicker, K. C., Kaimal, R. K., & Giridas, P. B. (2002). Tranquillization and translocation of captive bulls. *Food and Agriculture Organization of the United*

Nations, Giants on our hands: Proceedings of the international workshop of the domesticated Asian elephant. Retrieved from http://www.fao.org/docrep/005/ad031e/ad031e0o.htm.

Circuses. (n.d.). Retrieved from http://www.peta.org/issues/animals-in-entertainment/circuses/.

Clean start to Pamplona's running of the bulls. (2011, July 7). *The Independent.* Retrieved from http://www.independent.co.uk/news/world/europe/clean-start-to-pamplonas-running-of-the-bulls-2308316.html.

Compassionate traveler. (n.d.). Retrieved from http://www.worldanimalprotection.us.org/take-action/be-compassionate-traveler.

Crews, E. (n.d.). Once popular and socially acceptable: Cockfighting. *The Colonial Williamsburg Foundation.* Retrieved from http://www.history.org/foundation/journal/autumn08/rooster.cfm.

D'Silva, J. (2006). Adverse impact of industrial animal agriculture on the health and welfare of farmed animals. *Integrative Zoology, 1,* 53–58. doi: 10.1111/j.1749-4877.2006.00013.x.

D'Silva, J. (2008). The impact of livestock farming: Solutions for animals, people and the planet. *Compassion in world farming.* Retrieved from http://www.ciwf.org.uk/includes/documents/cm_docs/2008/i/impact_of_livestock_farming.pdf.

Darden, D. K., & Worden, S. K. (1996). Marketing deviance: The selling of cockfighting. *Society & Animals, 4,* 211–231. doi: 10.1163/156853096X00160.

Davis, H. H. (1993, December 19). Plunder from the fields. *The Denver Post.* 16A, 20a.

Deneen, S. (n.d.). Free range foods: Animal welfare for livestock. *The Daily Green.* Retrieved June 18, 2015 from http://preview.www.thedailygreen.com/living-green/definitions/Free-Range-Foods.

Denying mental qualities to animals in order to eat them. (2011, November 27). Retrieved from http://www.sciguru.com/newsitem/11437/Denying-mental-qualities-animals-order-eat-them.

Derango, R. "Agriculture 109." Illinois State University. Normal, Illinois. 20 February 2012.

Dickson, B. (2009). The ethics of recreational hunting. In B. Dickson, J. Hutton, & W. M. Adams (Eds.), *Recreational hunting, conservation and rural livelihoods: Science and practice* (pp. 59–72). Hoboken, NJ: Blackwell Publishing Ltd.

Diez, J. R., Gilsdorf, M., and Werge, R. (2002). *The federal role in regulating alternative livestock operations.* Paper presented at the Transactions of the Sixty-Seventh North American Wildlife and Natural Resources Conference. Dallas, TX.

Driver, A. (2014, April 23). Record egg prices seen on back of battery cage ban. *LA Times.* Retrieved from http://www.latimes.com/opinion/editorials/la-ed-hens-eggs-california-proposition2-ab1437-20141226-story.html.

Duda, M. D., Jones, M. F., & Criscione, A. (2010). *The Sportsman's voice: Hunting and fishing in America.* State College, PA: Venture Publishing.

Duda, M. D. & Jones, M. (2008). *Public opinion on and attitudes toward hunting.* Paper presented at Transactions of the Seventy-Third North American Wildlife and Natural Resource Conference. Phoenix, Arizona.

Ellicott, C. (2011, November 11). Circus boss and his wife are charged with animal cruelty after secret footage revealed elephant being beaten. *Mail Online.* Retrieved from http://www.dailymail.co.uk/news/article-2059862/Anne-elephant-Circus-boss-Bobby-Roberts-wife-Moira-charged-animal-cruelty.html.

Ellis, R. (2005). *Tiger bone & rhino horn: The destruction of wildlife for traditional Chinese medicine.* London: Island Press.

Eltagouri, M. (2014, July 11). Cicero re-creates Pamplona bull stampede. *Chicago Tribune.* Retrieved from http://www.chicagotribune.com/news/local/breaking/chi-cicero-recreates-pamplona-bull-stampede-20140711-story.html.

Etxaburu, J. (2007, July 9). 7 crushed in Pamplona bull run. *USATODAY.com.* Retrieved from http://www.usatoday.com/news/world/2007-07-08-bulls-spain_N.htm?csp=34.

Evans, R., Gauthier, D. K., & Forsyth, C. J. (1998). Dogfighting: Symbolic expression and validity of masculinity. *Sex Roles, 39,* 825–838.

Farnsworth, C. L. (1980). *A descriptive analysis of the extent of commercial poaching in the United States* (Unpublished doctoral dissertation). Sam Houston State University, Huntsville, TX.

Forsyth, C. J., & Marckese, T. A. (1993). Thrills and skills: A sociological analysis of poaching. *Deviant Behavior, 14,* 157–172.

France-Presse, A. (2014, August 25). Norway whale catch reaches highest number since 1993. *The Guardian.* Retrieved from http://www.theguardian.com/world/2014/aug/25/norway-whale-catch.

Franzetta, L., & Backus, M. (2014, July 31). Canceled: Dangerous and illegal California Great Bull Run. *Animal Legal Defense Fund.* Retrieved from http://aldf.org/press-room/press-releases/canceled-dangerous-and-illegal-california-great-bull-run/.

Gallagher, P. (2013, July 26). Cruelty of the aquarium exposed in killer whale documentary 'Blackfish'. *The Independent.* Retrieved from http://www.independent.co.uk/environment/nature/cruelty-of-the-aquarium-exposed-in-killer-whale-documentary-blackfish-8733758.html.

Gibson, H. (2005). Detailed discussion of dog fighting. *Animal Legal & Historical Center.* Retrieved from http://www.animallaw.info/articles/ddusdogfighting.htm#s1.

Goodman, A. (2009, July 10). Man killed in Pamplona's running of the bulls. *CNN.com.* Retrieved from http://www.cnn.com/2009/WORLD/europe/07/10/spain.pamplona.bulls.death/index.html.

Govan, F. (2009, July 10). Man gored to death by bull in Pamplona run. *The Telegraph.* Retrieved from http://www.telegraph.co.uk/news/worldnews/europe/spain/5793950/Man-gored-to-death-by-bull-in-Pamplona-run.html.

Greece bans animal circuses. (2015, April 17). Retrieved from http://www.ad-international.org/animals_in_entertainment/go.php?id=2528&ssi=10.

Hamill, T. A. (2009). Cockfighting as cultural allegory in early modern England. *Journal of Medieval and Early Modern Studies, 39,* 375–406.

Hawley, F. (1982). *Organized cockfighting: A deviant recreational subculture* (Unpublished doctoral dissertation). Florida State University, Tallahassee, FL.

Hawley, F. (1989). Cockfight in the cotton: A moral crusade in microcosm. *Contemporary Crises, 13,* 129–144.

Hawley, F. (1993). The moral and conceptual universe of cockfighters: Symbolism and rationalization. *Society & Animals, 1,* 159–168.

Hay, M. (2015, April 1). Where will all the freed Mexican circus animals go? *Good Magazine.* Retrieved from http://magazine.good.is/articles/mexican-circus-animals-freed.

Herring, H. (1997, November 10). On a Montana ranch, big game and big problems. *High Country News.* Retrieved from https://www.hcn.org/issues/118/3765.

Hickman, M. (2011, September 18). The true cost of cheap chicken. *The Independent.* Retrieved from http://www.independent.co.uk/news/uk/home-news/the-true-cost-of-cheap-chicken-768062.html.

History. (2015). Retrieved from http://keiko.com/history.html.

Humane Society of Missouri confirms: Guilty pleas entered in federal court to charges from largest dog fighting raid and rescue in U.S. history. (2009, September 14). Retrieved from http://member.hsmo.org/site/PageServer?pagename=Federal_dog_fighting_case_press_release_9_14.

International Court of Justice. (2014). Whaling in the Antarctic (Australia v. Japan: New Zealand intervening) [Press release]. Retrieved from http://www.icj-cij.org/docket/files/148/18162.pdf.

International Institute for Animal Law. (n.d.). *Canned hunts.* Retrieved from http://www.animallaw.com/Model-Law-Canned-Hunts.cfm.

Iowa Gov. Culver signs bill to combat puppy mills. (2010, March 9). Retrieved from http://www.humanesociety.org/news/press_releases/2010/03/iowa_puppy_mill_bill_signed_030910.html.

Italian festivals sanctioned for animal cruelty. (2011, August 10). Retrieved from http://dawn.com/2011/08/10/italian-festivals-sanctioned-for-animal-cruelty/.

Jenkins, C. (2011, December 30). Butterball turkey facility raided for abuse of birds. *The Raw Story.* Retrieved from http://www.rawstory.com/rs/2011/12/30/butterball-turkey-facility-raided-for-abuse-of-birds/.

Jeory, T. (2012, February 5). Circus drops animal acts after public stay away. *Express.co.uk.* Retrieved from http://www.express.co.uk/posts/view/300137.

Kageyama, Y. (2010). 'The Cove' in Taiji, Japan persists with dolphin hunt. *Huffington Post.* Retrieved from http://www.huffingtonpost.com/2010/10/12/the-cove-in-taiji-japan-p_n_759155.html.

Kluger, J., August, M., Billups, M., Liston, A., & Liston, B. (2002). Hunting made easy: Shooting captive animals to mount their heads on a wall is a booming sport. Should Congress step in? *CNN.* Retrieved from http://www.cnn.com/ALLPOLITICS/time/2002/03/11/hunting.html.

L. E. (2011, August 30). Bullfighting isn't culture, it's cruelty. *Care2 Causes.* Retrieved from http://www.care2.com/causes/bullfighting-isnt-culture-its-cruelty.html.

Liddick, D. R. (2011). *Crimes against nature: Illegal industries and the global environment.* Santa Barbara, CA: Praeger.

Lin, D. (2011, February 2). 100 sled dogs killed in Canada after tourism slump. *About.com.* Retrieved from http://animalrights.about.com/od/animalsinentertainment/a/100-Sled-Dogs-Killed-In-Canada-After-Tourism-Slump.htm.

Lo, S. (2011, December 31). New rules for Feld Entertainment, Inc.: Pay and comply. *Animal Blawg.* Retrieved from http://animalblawg.wordpress.com/2011/12/31/new-rules-for-feld-entertainment-inc-pay-and-comply/.

Lohanan, R. (2002). The elephant situation in Thailand and a plea for co-operation. *Food and Agriculture Organization of the United Nations, Giants on our Hands. Proceedings of the International Workshop on the Domesticated Asian Elephant.* Retrieved from http://www.fao.org/docrep/005/ad031e/ad031e0r.htm.

Lukas, L. (1999). *National park service law enforcement: To conserve and protect.* Incline Village, NV: Copperhouse Publishing Company.

Man gored at Pamplona bull run. (2011, July 8). Retrieved from http://www.guardian.co.uk/world/2011/jul/08/man-gored-pamplona-bull-run.

Martin, J., & Felberbaum, M. (2013, August 3). Inspired by Pamplona, Great Bull Run coming to US. *The Seattle Times.* Retrieved from http://www.seattletimes.com/nation-world/inspired-by-pamplona-great-bull-run-coming-to-us/.

Maunula, M. (2007). Of chickens and men: Cockfighting and equality in the South. *Southern Cultures, 13,* 76–85.

McCurry, J. (2013, June 28). License revoke? Australia takes Japan to court to stop whale hunts. *The Christian Science Monitor.* Retrieved from http://www.csmonitor.com/World/Asia-Pacific/2013/0628/License-revoked-Australia-takes-Japan-to-court-to-stop-whaling-hunts.

McCurry, J. (2015, April, 13). Experts reject Japan's new whaling plan. *The Guardian.* Retrieved from http://www.theguardian.com/environment/2015/apr/14/experts-reject-japans-new-whaling-plan.

McDonald's cruelty: The rotten truth about egg mcmuffins. (n.d.). Retrieved from http://www.mcdonaldscruelty.com/.

Messenger, S. (2011, November 28). Ringling Bros. fined for animal-welfare violations. *TreeHugger.* Retrieved from http://www.treehugger.com/corporate-responsibility/ringling-bros-gets-hefty-fine-animal-welfare-violations.html.

Middleton, I. M. (2003). Cockfighting in Yorkshire during the early eighteenth century. *Northern History, XL,* 129–146.

Milstein, M. (1989, May/June). The quiet kill. *National Parks, 1989,* 19–25.

Morrow, L. (1995). History they don't teach you: A tradition of cockfighting. *White River Valley Historical Quarterly, 35.* Retrieved from http://thelibrary.org/lochist/periodicals/wrv/v35/n2/f95d.htm.

Moyer, B. (2011, January 2). Support for hunting, fishing remains strong even as participation wanes. *Pittsburgh Post-Gazette.* Retrieved from http://www.post-gazette.com/pg/11002/1114966-358.stm.

Mountain gorillas of Uganda. (n.d.). *Geographic Expeditions Inc.* Retrieved from http://www.geoex.com/adventure-travel/uganda/bwindi-gorilla-safari.asp.

Muth, R. M., & Bowe Jr., J. F. (1998). Illegal harvest of renewable natural resources in North America: Toward a typology of the motivations for poaching. *Society & Natural Resources, 11,* 9–24. doi: 10.1080/08941929809381058.

Nellemann, C., Henriksen, R. Raxter, P., Ash, N., & Mrema, E. (Eds). (2014). The environmental crime crisis—Threats to sustainable development from illegal exploitation and trade in wildlife and forest resources. United Nations Environmental Programme. Retrieved June 18, 2015, 2015 from http://www.unep.org/unea/docs/rracrimecrisis.pdf.

Neme, L.A. (2009). *Animal investigators.* New York: Scribner.

Nelson, D. (2011, Nov/Dec). The cruelest show on Earth. *Mother Jones.* Retrieved from http://motherjones.com/environment/2011/10/ringling-bros-elephant-abuse.

O'Connor, J. (2012, January 18). Circus smacked with nearly 3 dozen charges. *People for the Ethical Treatment of Animals.* Retrieved from http://www.peta.org/b/thepetafiles/archive/ 2012/01/18/circus-smacked-with-almost-three-dozen-charges.aspx.

Ortiz, F. (2009). *Making the dogman heel: Recommendation for improving the effectiveness of dogfighting laws.* Retrieved from http://works.bepress.com/cgi/viewcontent.cgi?article= 1000&context=francesca_ortiz.

Pamplona "bull runner" killed. (2009, July 10). *National Geographic.com.* Retrieved from http://news.nationalgeographic.com/news/2009/07/090710-bullrun-death-video-ap.html.

Petition to stop the abuse of donkey taxis in Santorini. (n.d.). Retrieved from http://drupal.thedonkeysanctuary.org.uk/campaign/santorini.

Phillips, T. (2012, January 2). Butterball's animal abuse comes to light. *Global Animal.* Retrieved from http://www.globalanimal.org/2012/01/02/butterballs-turkey-abuse-comes-to-light-video/62232/.

Pickett, H. (2003). Industrial animal agriculture. *Compassion in World Farming Trust.* Retrieved from http://www.ciwf.org.uk/includes/documents/cm_docs/2008/i/industrial_animal_farming_booklet.pdf.

Pidd, H. (2010, March 11). United Kingdom: Egg boss jailed for 'free range' fraud. *The Guardian.* Retrieved from http://forests.org/shared/reader/welcome.aspx?linkid=154738&keybold=food%20AND%20%20fraud.

Plight of the captive dolphins. (n.d.). Retrieved from http://www.wspa-international.org/helping/animalfriendlyliving/captivedolphins.aspx.

Police investigates Butterball cruelty cover-up. (2012, January 11). Retrieved from http://vegan.com/blog/2012/01/11/police-investigate-butterball-cruelty-coverup/.

Poten, C. J. (1991, September). A shameful harvest: America's illegal wildlife trade. *National Geographic,* 106–132.

Prah, M. P. (2011, May 11). Missouri's puppy mill politics: Dog breeders outmaneuver animal-rights movement. *The Seattle Times.* Retrieved from http://www.seattletimes.com/lifestyle/missouris-puppy-mill-politics-dog-breeders-outmaneuver-animal-rights-movement/.

Preiss, B. (2009, October 2). Circuses. *The Humane Society of the United States.* Retrieved from http://www.humanesociety.org/issues/circuses_entertainment/facts/circus_facts.html.

Probert, L. (2011, April 12). Vietnam tourism boosted by animal cruelty. *World Tourism and Aviation News.* Retrieved from http://www.travel-news.co.uk/2456/2011/12/vietnam-tourism-boosted-by-animal-cruelty/.

Puppy mills: Frequently asked questions. (2015, January 16). Retrieved from http://www.humanesociety.org/issues/puppy_mills/qa/puppy_mill_FAQs.html.

Puppy Uniform Protection and Safety Act, H.R. 847, 113 Cong. (2013–2014).

Reuben, N. (2002). What is a puppy mill? Retrieved June 18, 2015 from http://www.petfinder.com/how-to-help-pets/animal-cruelty-puppy-mills.html.

Ring, D. (2004, December 2). Hog-dog fights: Blood "sport" packaged as family entertainment. Retrieved from http://www.humanesociety.org/issues/hogdog_fighting/facts/hog-dog_bloodsport.html.

Ringling Bros. and Barnum & Bailey Circus. (2011, September 27). Retrieved from http://www.mediapeta.com/peta/PDF/RinglingFactsheet.pdf.

Robert, J. (2006, February 27). Dog vs. hog fighting club broken up. *Associated Press*. Retrieved from http://www.cbsnews.com/stories/2006/01/27/national/main1245804.shtml.

Safran-Foer, J. (2010, February 22). The truth about factory farming. *The Guardian*. Retrieved from http://www.guardian.co.uk/environment/2010/feb/22/jonathan-safran-foer-factory-farming.

Schneider, J. L. (2008). Reducing the illicit trade in endangered wildlife: The market reduction approach. *Journal of Contemporary Criminal Justice, 24*, 274.

Schneider, J. L. (2012). *Sold into extinction: The global trade in endangered species*. Santa Barbara, CA: Praeger/ABC-CLIO.

Scialfa, M. A. (1992). *An ethnographic analysis of poachers and poaching in northern Idaho and eastern Washington* (Unpublished master's thesis). University of Idaho, Moscow, ID.

Searle, A. M. (2008). *Release the dogs: Creating a social remedy to the dog fighting epidemic*. Retrieved from http://works.bepress.com/amanda_searle/4.

Seltzer, S. (2011, June 24). Breaking news: UK unanimously votes for circus ban. *Care2 Causes*. Retrieved from http://www.care2.com/causes/breaking-news-uk-unanimously-votes-for-circus-ban.html.

Singer, P. (1990). *Animal Liberation* (2nd ed.). New York: Random House.

Smith, K. (2014, September 6). Descartes' life and works. *The Stanford Encyclopedia of Philosophy*. Retrieved from http://plato.stanford.edu/entries/descartes-works/.

Squires, N. (2011). Palio horse race banned from heritage status because of cruelty claims. *The Telegraph*. Retrieved from http://www.telegraph.co.uk/news/worldnews/europe/italy/8441233/Palio-horse-race-banned-from-heritage-status-because-of-cruelty-claims.html.

Stout, D. M. (2014, August 1). So long, Shamu: Southwest SeaWorld end times. *Time.com*. Retrieved from http://time.com/3069051/so-long-shamu-southwest-seaworld-end-ties/.

Suroor, H. (2012a, January 16). Bullish about Jallijattu. *The Hindu*. Retrieved from http://www.thehindu.com/news/states/tamil-nadu/article2805789.ece.

Suroor, H. (2012b, January 24). Jallikattu: Irish group calls for tourism boycott. *The Hindu*. Retrieved from http://www.thehindu.com/news/international/jallikattu-irish-group-calls-for-tourism-boycott/article2828878.ece.

Suroor, H. (2012c, January 26). Jallikattu is a black mark on India's reputation, says PETA. *The Hindu*. Retrieved from http://www.thehindu.com/news/national/jallikattu-is-a-black-mark-on-indias-reputation-says-peta/article2832288.ece.

The Environmental Food Crisis. (n.d.). Retrieved from http://www.grida.no/publications/rr/food-crisis/page/3562.aspx.

The Great Bull Run comes to Florida. (2014, February 21). *PR Newswire*. Retrieved from http://www.bizjournals.com/prnewswire/press_releases/2014/02/21/MN69052.

The Humane Society of the United States. (2011, June 21). *New undercover investigation reveals tame and drugged animals shot for trophies at captive hunts*. Retrieved from http://www.humanesociety.org/news/press_releases/2011/06/captive_hunt_undercover_investigation_animal_planet_062111.html.

The Palio in Siena. (n.d.). Retrieved from http://www.discovertuscany.com/siena/palio-siena.html.

Tian, B. (2012, February 11). To entertain tourists, elephants in Thailand face cruelty. *UPIU.* Retrieved from http://next.upi.com/archive/2012/02/11/Giants-in-danger/2621328999087/.

Tickets. (2015). Retrieved from http://thegreatbullrun.com/#rev_slider_5_3.

Traffic. (2011, December 29). 2011: "Annus horribilis" for African elephants, says TRAFFIC. Retrieved from http://www.traffic.org/home/2011/12/29/2011-annus-horribilis-for-african-elephants-says-traffic.html.

Trigaux, R. (2014, November 17). As SeaWorld suffers 'Blackfish' impact, Busch Gardens suffers, too. *Tampa Bay Times.* Retrieved from http://www.tampabay.com/news/business/tourism/as-seaworld-suffers-blackfish-impact-busch-gardens-suffers-too/2206864.

Tyler, S. (2011, July 29). Peru bans wild animals in circuses after ADI investigation. *PlanetSave.* Retrieved from http://planetsave.com/2011/07/29/peru-bans-wild-animals-in-circuses-after-adi-investigation-video/.

Villavincencio, M. (2007, July 16). A history of dogfighting. *NPR.* Retrieved from http://www.npr.org/templates/story/story.php?storyId=12108421.

Waters, S. (2011, June 11). Wildlife tourism in Thailand: Cruel and exploitative? *The Scavenger.* Retrieved from http://www.thescavenger.net/animals/wildlife-tourism-in-thailand-cruel-and-exploitative-735.html.

Webb, J. (2009, July 10). Bull kills man during Spain's annual Pamplona run. *Reuters.com.* Retrieved from http://www.reuters.com/assets/print?aid=USTRE5691BZ20090710.

Whale shark: Rhinocodon typus. (n.d.). Retrieved from http://animals.nationalgeographic.com/animals/fish/whale-shark/.

Whale watching: A humane alternative. (n.d.). *World Society for the Protection of Animals.* Retrieved from http://www.wspa-international.org/helping/animalfriendlyliving/whalewatching.aspx.

What is a puppy mill. (n.d.). Retrieved from https://www.aspca.org/fight-cruelty/field-investigations-and-response-team/puppy-mills.

Williams, T. (2010, November–December). Real hunters don't shoot pets. *Audubon Magazine.* Retrieved from http://archive.audubonmagazine.org/incite/incite1011.html.

Woolf, B. N. (2014). Just what is a puppy mill? *Dog Owners Guide.* Retrieved from http://www.canismajor.com/dog/puppymil.html.

Worden, T. (2011, July 31). Bullfighting saved from the sword as Spain rules it is an artistic discipline. *The Guardian.* Retrieved from http://www.guardian.co.uk/world/2011/jul/31/bullfighting-saved-spain-artistic-discipline.

WWF (n.d.) *Rhinos.* Retrieved from http://www.worldwildlife.org/species/rhino.

Wyler, L. S., & Sheikh, P. A. (2013). *International illegal trade in wildlife: Threats and U.S. policy.* Washington D.C.: Congressional Research Service.

Young, J. A., van Manen F. T., & Thatcher, C. A. (2011). Geographic profiling to assess the risk of rare plant poaching in natural areas. *Environmental management, 48,* 577–587.

York, E. (2011, November 18). McDonald's drops egg supplier over animal cruelty report. *Chicago Tribune.* Retrieved from http://articles.chicagotribune.com/2011-11-18/news/chi-mcdonalds-drops-egg-supplier-over-animal-cruelty-report-20111118_1_egg-farmers-animal-welfare-egg-supplier.

Zacharias, N. (2011, October 19). It's time to end factory farming. *Huffington Post.* Retrieved from http://www.huffingtonpost.com/nil-zacharias/its-time-to-end-factory-f_b_1018840.html.

Zimmerman, M. A. (2003). The black market for wildlife: Combating transnational organized crime in illegal wildlife trade. *Vanderbilt Journal of Transnational Law, 36,* 1657–1689.

Statutes

7 U.S.C. 54 § 2143

Chapter 9

Animal Hoarding

Arnold Arluke and Gary Patronek

For much of the twentieth century, unconventional ownership of large numbers of animals was considered to be an eccentricity. As part of American folklore, neighborhood "cat ladies" were largely tolerated, although not understood, for their excesses. Considered "strange" or "odd," their amassing of animals, although not fully revealed to outsiders, was typically ignored and not seen as an expression of a serious problem for people or animals. If not called "crazy cat ladies," these cases were less stereotypically called "animal collectors," albeit still an imprecise term in need of revision as we see below.

Beginning with Patronek's definition of animal hoarding (1999), members of the Hoarding of Animals Research Consortium (HARC) have built a considerable research base about this behavior. Patronek (1999) and HARC (2002) were the first to note the considerable similarity between the hoarding of objects and the hoarding of animals. In the intervening years, members of HARC have published numerous papers further refining this concept (http://vet.tufts.edu/hoarding/), and recently a major review comparing features of object hoarding and animal hoarding (Frost, Patronek, & Rosenfield, 2011).

We have also learned a great deal about animal hoarding cases in recent years because humane organizations have been more willing to intervene to stop hoarding and remove animals from harm, generating anecdotal, but useful, reports about how best to manage these cases. Finally, through increasing media coverage of hoarding on the cable networks *Animal Planet* and the *Discovery Channel*, these formerly hidden deviances have been brought out into the open for the general public to see and understand beyond the outdated stereotypes and myths that have surrounded this practice for years.

Characteristics of Animal Hoarding

Although once considered rare, epidemiological estimates suggest that animal hoarding commonly occurs in many American communities (Patronek, 1999), a finding paralleled by ethnographic studies of hoarding in other cultures (Svanberg & Arluke, in press). A survey of health officers in Massachusetts who were queried about reported cases of all types of hoarding (object and animal) estimated the five-year prevalence rate of 26.3 per 100,000 population, or 5.3 per 100,000 per year (Frost, Steketee, & Williams, 2000). The authors reported that animals were hoarded in roughly a third of these cases, which suggest about 1.75 cases per 100,000 per year that involved animals. The authors also indicated that methodological problems likely resulted in underreporting during the first three years of the study. Nevertheless, this figure, if extrapolated to the entire U.S. population, would indicate a minimum of 5,100 reported cases per year. Presuming an average of 50 animals per case, it would not be unreasonable to suggest that nearly a quarter million animals are subjected to this form of abuse each year. Moreover, this rate of 1.75 cases is very underreported because the data are just from health officers who responded; not all health officers who were sent surveys responded. The basic point is that animal hoarding is common and the number of cases appears to climb each year. How much of this is due to increased reporting and how much is attributable to increased incidence is unknown, but given the severity of so many of these cases, it seems unlikely that they were previously unrecognized and that the apparent increase is solely due to increased reporting.

Hoarders keep a variety of animals. Cats and dogs are the most commonly hoarded species, but wildlife, dangerous exotic animals, and farm animals have been involved, even in urban situations. One study of 71 animal hoarders (HARC, 2002) found that approximately 82% of the cases involved cats, 55% dogs, 17% birds, 6% reptiles, 11% small mammals, 6% horses, and 6% cattle, sheep, or goats.

Animal hoarders come from varied backgrounds, contrary to the stereotype of the neighborhood "cat lady" who is pictured as an older, single female, living alone. As with many stereotypes, however, there is an element of truth to this image. In one study (Worth & Beck, 1981), 70% of the sample were unmarried women who had cats, while in another study (Patronek, 1999) 76% of the sample were women, 46% were over 60 years of age, most were single, divorced, or widowed, and cats were most commonly involved. In another study (HARC, 2002), 83% were women, with a median age of 55 years, and nearly three-quarters of the sample were single, widowed, or divorced. Finally, a searchable online database containing thousands of cases of various sorts of animal abuse also support this gender imbalance (Pet-abuse.com). (See Chapter 6 for more about this database.)

However, it is not uncommon for hoarders to be living with dependents—children, the disabled, the elderly—as well as husbands, wives, girlfriends, and boyfriends. One such example is Barbara Erickson, a hoarder of over 500 dogs[1] who lived with a dependent-husband, who she claimed had Alzheimer's disease. In reality, this behavior cuts across all demographic and socioeconomic boundaries. As most hoarders are very secretive, many can lead a double life with a successful professional career; hoarding behavior has been discovered among doctors, nurses, public officials, college professors, and veterinarians, as well as among a broad spectrum of socioeconomically disadvantaged individuals (HARC, 2002).

There also is not one type of animal hoarder (Patronek, Loar, & Nathanson, 2006). Although not full-fledged hoarders according to the original law enforcement definition of animal hoarding (Patronek, 1999), some people with many animals may be headed in that direction. This original definition was based on hoarding cases that came to the attention of law enforcers because they were extremely severe. But this behavior exists on a spectrum in terms of time and severity. Many people may be hoarders but do not yet fit this law enforcement definition. These *incipient* hoarders try to meet minimum standards of animal care as proscribed by law, and are likely to be aware of problems that develop.

---

1. This chapter draws heavily from Arluke and Killeen's (2009) detailed case study of the Erickson hoarding case because it is the most in-depth study of an animal hoarder to date.

However, their ability to provide proper animal care deteriorates, unless their situations change markedly.

A second type of hoarder, the *breeder-hoarder*, at first breeds animals for show or sale, but the animals are not kept in the home and human living conditions are good compared to other types of hoarders. Eventually, it becomes increasingly difficult to provide proper care, but despite deteriorating conditions, the breeder hoarders continue to breed because they have little insight into the animals' condition and their ability to care for them.

The *overwhelmed caregiver* minimizes rather than denies animal care problems that result from economic, social, medical, or domestic changes, such as loss of job or health, but cannot remedy these problems. Despite their strong attachment to animals, the overwhelmed caregivers' compromised situations gradually lead to a deterioration of animal care. Although socially isolated, they are less secretive and more cooperative with authorities than are most hoarders.

The fourth type of hoarder, *the rescuer*, has a missionary zeal to save all animals. Not that socially isolated, rescuers may be part of a network of enablers whose offers of animals are never declined. They also actively seek to acquire animals because they believe that only they can provide adequate care and because they oppose euthanasia. Indeed, this behavior can plague organizations as well as individuals. It was recently suggested that as many as one-quarter of cases now may involve some sort of formal quasi-rescue effort or institutional situation (Manning, 2011).

Finally, the *exploiter* hoarder is the most challenging type to manage. Considered to be sociopaths and/or to have severe personality disorders, exploiter hoarders lack of empathy for people or animals means that they are indifferent to the harm they cause them. Somewhat charismatic and articulate, they present an appearance that suggests competence to the public, officials, and the media.

Although there are different types of animal hoarders, their animals share a similar fate. Those responding to these cases often discover large numbers of animals, sometimes in the hundreds, suffering from malnutrition, various diseases, and untreated physical impairments because they have not received food, water, appropriate shelter, and veterinary care. Furthermore, these cases transcend similar situations of individual animal neglect because of the multiplicative consequences of collective neglect—a situation where the whole indeed becomes much worse than the sum of its parts. Severe crowding compounds whatever suffering is already present through increased noise, aggressive interactions between animals, restriction of movement, and the inability to escape to a safe, clean, quiet location. It also greatly enhances spread of disease and compounds the difficulty of recognizing medical conditions requiring veterinary care.

In some animal-hoarding situations, other family members, like minor children, dependent elderly persons, or disabled adults, are present and are also victims of this behavior. Serious unmet human health needs are commonly observed, and the conditions often meet the criteria for adult self-neglect, child neglect, or elder abuse (Nathanson, 2009).

For most hoarders, living spaces are often compromised to the extent that they no longer serve the function for which they were intended. Appliances and basic utilities (heat, plumbing, and electricity) are frequently inoperative. Household functioning is often so impaired that both food preparation and maintaining basic sanitation are impossible. From a community health perspective, the clutter can pose a fire hazard. In some cases, fireplaces and kerosene heaters are used for heat. Rodent and insect infestations, as well as odors, can create a neighborhood nuisance. These are important public health aspects of animal hoarding that go largely unrecognized and which may provide avenues for intervention, such as the health risk from elevated ammonia resulting from an accumulation of animal urine (Castrodale et al., 2010).

Causes of Animal Hoarding

Understanding why people hoard animals is complex and any explanation must be tentative. It is complex because it is likely that a number of different psychological, social, and even cultural factors are behind the emergence and recognition of this behavior. It is tentative because the current state of research knowledge about animal hoarding is somewhat limited and still evolving; social science explanations of this behavior are relatively recent, replacing the antiquated, but still expressed, view that it is mere eccentricity or uncontrolled, excessive "love" for animals.

Psychological Disorder

Hoarding was recognized as a specific psychological disorder in the fifth version (2013) of the American Psychiatric Association's *Diagnostic and Statistic Manual* (*DSM-5*) used by mental health workers to diagnose various disorders. Although animal hoarding is mentioned under the DSM-5 hoarding disorder (HD), its clinical place remains unclear (Mataix-Cols, 2014) because the DSM-5 criteria for HD are based on object hoarding. DSM-5 describes animal hoarding as an associated feature defined by "the accumulation of a large number of animals and a failure to provide minimal standards of nutrition, sanitation, and veterinary care and to act on the deteriorating condition of the animals (including disease, starvation, or death) and the environment (e.g., severe overcrowding, extremely unsanitary conditions)" (American Psychiatric Association, 2013, p. 249).

The similarities between animal hoarding and object hoarding have been noted (Frost, Patronek, & Rosenfield, 2011). Indeed, the primary difference between the two is that animal hoarding is likely to be more severe. Object hoarding is known to be associated with multiple psychological co-morbidities, and it is likely that animal hoarding is also a complex disorder from a diagnostic perspective. And elements of numerous known disorders have been previously reported among animal hoarders with each model having some diagnostic validity. These different approaches to understanding animal hoarders should not be viewed as competing with each other but rather as overlapping theories that can share some of the same psychological explanations for this complex behavior.

For example, the delusional aspects of animal hoarding have been noted (HARC, 2000). Like people who hoard inanimate objects (Frost, 2000), animal hoarders lack insight into the problematic nature of their behavior. Most have a persistent and powerful belief that they are providing proper animal care, despite obvious and overwhelming contradictory evidence. And most are equally unable to grasp the extent to which their home environments have become unfit for any living creature, sometimes to the point of needing to be torn down. Further suggestion of delusional disorder in hoarders is evidenced by their paranoia about officials and their belief that they have a special ability to communicate with animals. The delusional model easily fits what we know about Barbara Erickson's adult life (Arluke & Killeen, 2009). She claimed to speak with Federal Bureau of Investigation (FBI) agents, to have graduated with five degrees, and to be a lawyer and a veterinarian. When it came to her animals, she repeatedly turned down offers of help, including taking some of the dogs and relieving her responsibility, because help was not needed and the dogs' condition was fine. As Celeste Killeen observes, Barbara not only failed to see that her home and animals were deteriorating, she could not see how these conditions adversely affected her husband's and her own health.

When animal hoarding was first recognized as a problem for the animal welfare community, it was noted that parallels with addiction seemed to fit the thinking and behavior of many hoarders (Lockwood, 1994). As with substance abusers, hoarders are preoccupied with animals, are in denial over their problems, have many excuses for their situation, are socially isolated, claim to be persecuted, and neglect themselves and their surroundings. Other evidence consistent with the addictions model is the similarity of hoarders with people suffering from impulse control problems, such as compulsive shopping (Frost, 1998) and compulsive gambling (Meagher, Frost, & Riskind, 1999). Some hoarders report to compulsively collect strays and shelter animals. Flores (2004) has noted how addictions can be viewed as rooted in attachment problems, a concept which seems to help weave some of these seemingly disparate features together and overcome some of the issues associated with applying overly simplistic diagnostic labels to a complex problem.

Refining what has been learned, Nathanson and Patronek (2011) and Patronek and Nathanson (2011) have woven these disparate models and approaches together, and rather than applying diagnostic labels to animal hoarders, have suggested that the problem would be better understood by focusing on the thoughts and actions exhibited by hoarders (see Figure 1). From this perspective, animal hoarders often manifest axis II traits such as suspiciousness, mistrust, fear of abandonment leading to unstable and intense interpersonal relationships, feelings of emptiness, difficulty with anger, and occasional paranoia. Those having these traits often come from families where they had a history of unresolved grief due to tragic, untimely deaths or losses and emotional or physical abuse (Cassidy & Mohr, 2001; Lyons-Ruth, Dutra, Schuder, & Bianchi, 2006). This is consistent with what has been observed in other forms of addictive behavior (Flores, 2004). Absence of nurturing relationships in childhood cause these people to have a deep sense of aloneness in adulthood that can never be filled. This leads them to seek a "perfect love" to repair their wounded self and make them feel worthy, only to be constantly disappointed, given the nature of human relationships.

Animals may provide this perfect, unconditional love, as reported by Worth and Beck (1981). However, just as their own need to be loved was not met by their parents, so too do they neglect the needs of animals dependent on them. As some animals die from lack of care, the hoarder's sense of unworthiness is confirmed, as is their fear of being abandoned, in this case by the dying animals. Nathanson (2009) has suggested that a primary feature of animal hoarding may be less about love than about animals providing a conflict-free relationship to the hoarder, and that features such as control and constancy may be more appropriate ways to characterize the relationship than "love."

In this way, animal hoarding can be viewed as one manifestation of pathological altruism, or the compulsion to devote as much time as possible to giving rather than receiving care (Nathanson & Patronek, 2011). Adult compulsive care-giving has its roots in traumatic losses that leave children feeling like they need care and help which parents fail to provide. As these children reach adulthood, they have learned to reverse parenting roles but have lost the ability to express needs or ask for care. They are always trying to help others when deep inside they want care and help. Although it can be argued that hoarders are notorious for not providing care, they adopt a care-giving role by claiming

Figure 1: Working model of how animal hoarding develops.

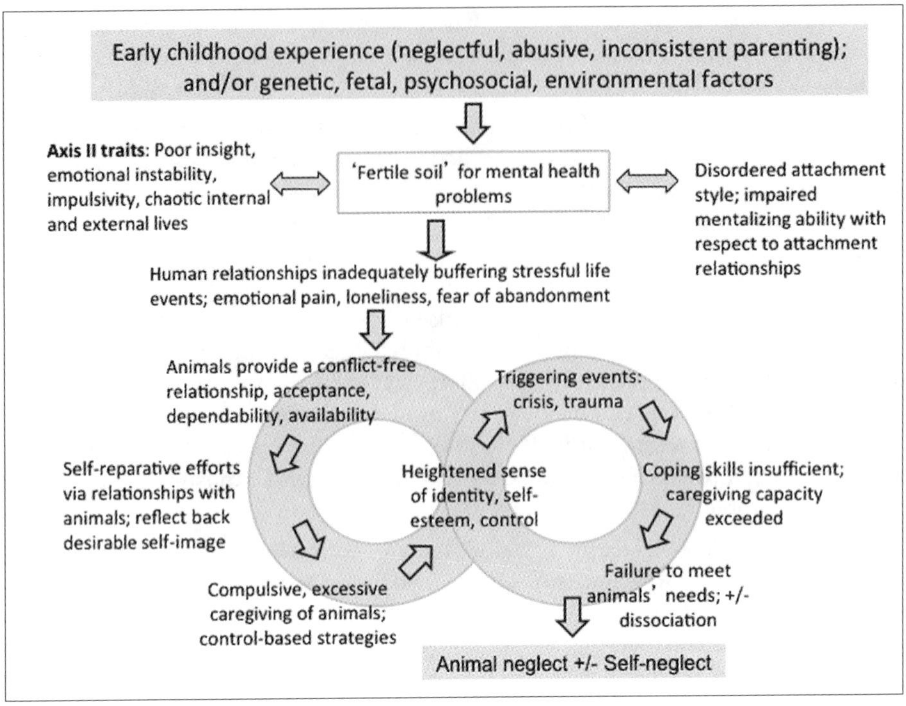

```
Early childhood experience (neglectful, abusive, inconsistent parenting);
and/or genetic, fetal, psychosocial, environmental factors
                              ⇩
Axis II traits: Poor insight,      'Fertile soil' for mental health      Disordered attachment
emotional instability,        ⇔        problems              ⇔          style; impaired
impulsivity, chaotic internal                                            mentalizing ability with
and external lives                                                       respect to attachment
                                       ⇩                                 relationships
            Human relationships inadequately buffering stressful life
            events; emotional pain, loneliness, fear of abandonment
                                       ⇩
            Animals provide a conflict-free      Triggering events:
            relationship, acceptance,            crisis, trauma
            dependability, availability

   Self-reparative efforts          Heightened sense          Coping skills insufficient;
   via relationships with           of identity, self-        caregiving capacity
   animals; reflect back            esteem, control           exceeded
   desirable self-image

                  Compulsive, excessive               Failure to meet
                  caregiving of animals;              animals' needs; +/-
                  control-based strategies            dissociation

                       Animal neglect +/- Self-neglect
```

Adapted from Nathanson and Patronek (2011) by permission of Oxford University Press, Inc.[2]

to rescue and save many animals from certain death (Patronek & Nathanson, 2009). Results by Steketee et al. (2011) support this model of hoarding animals.

As a case in point, Barbara Erickson (Arluke & Killeen, 2009) appears to have experienced little if any consistent parental affection, or "love," during her childhood due to significant losses and abuse. To Killeen, these emotional traumas played out in Barbara's adult life as a "search for love" that could never be satisfied. Presumably, she displaced the need for these unfulfilled emotions into perpetual accumulation of dogs as both a source and object of love. Her reluctance to surrender their animals—even to responsible parties who promised to care for them—reflected how seriously and dearly she played the parental role with her animals. This role is also suggested by her emotionality when considering the loss of any one of her many dogs, and by the fact that she allegedly lost her own baby and had been unsuccessfully searching for it throughout her life. Indeed, Barbara often referred to her dogs as her "children." Seeing the dogs this way meant that they could serve as objects of care and sources of nurturance, allowing her to simultaneously play parent and child roles.

Of course, caution must be exercised when applying these labels or approaches to anyone until individual hoarders are thoroughly examined and more is known about the psychological causes of this behavior. With this caution in mind, a number of these

---

2. *Pathological Altruism* edited by Barbara Oakley, Ariel Knafo, Guruprasad Madhavan & David Wilson (2011) Ch. 8 'Animal Hoarding' by Jane N. Nathanson & Gary J. Patronek pp. 107–115 Figure 8.1 from p. 108 (adapted).

disorders have roots in a chaotic, if not traumatic, childhood characterized by loss of significant others and abuse. Most hoarders, too, have psychological and social histories beginning in childhood that are chaotic and traumatic. Preliminary research (HARC, 2002) suggests that hoarders grew up in households with inconsistent parenting, in which animals may have been the only stable feature. The vast majority reports feelings of insecurity and disruptive and experiences in early life, including frequent relocations, parental separation and divorce, and isolation from peers. For example, Barbara Erickson was reportedly (Arluke & Killian, 2009) raped as a child by her grandfather and father, only to have one of her dogs intervene to stop one rape and another dog to comfort her after those terrifying moments. Barbara also experienced difficult losses as an adolescent, including being abandoned by her mother and losing her baby after her father allegedly killed it.

Although those who directly deal with animal hoarders are often convinced that some mental disorder is present, and that some such psychological approach is warranted, it seems unreasonable to lump together all these cases. While some animal hoarders are no doubt plagued by very really pathologies, others may not be. The latter subgroup of cases may represent an entirely different ilk of animal hoarding where the problem is due to social breakdown or highly compromised living situations that result from personal, familial, neighborhood, or community social problems.

Social Enabling

Those seeking to explain animal hoarding have taken a psychological approach to the problem that views it as a mental disorder emanating solely from within the individual. While we must continue to explore the psychological roots of animal hoarding, interpersonal and cultural factors must also be considered if our goal is to produce a more complete understanding of the nature and origin of this behavior. Family, friends, neighbors, the wider community, and society at large must be factored into our analysis of why and how hoarding starts and continues. By taking a broader and more complex view of the problem, interventions can address the contextual roots of the problem rather than only focusing on the individual's underlying mental disorder.

For example, some cases of animal hoarding are likely a product of, or at least facilitated by, a dysfunctional society rather than being due solely to the acts of disturbed individuals. If the finger of blame is to be pointed, in such instances, it must be shared with the larger society. In many parts of America, abandoned and stray animals remain a big problem, in part due to irresponsible breeding of pets that produces millions of unwanted animals. Euthanasia practiced by open-admission shelters becomes a way to manage this overpopulation problem, since not all of these unwanted animals could be adopted or kept indefinitely in their cages.

Animal hoarders, and whatever family and emotional support systems they have, become an expedient and injurious dysfunctional system that responds to this societal problem. People in the community, knowing the hoarder's reputation for apparently wanting so many animals, may drop off unwanted pets at the hoarder's home, thereby feeding her ever-growing collection. In this way, the neighborhood "cat lady" or "dog lady" serves as a convenient, impromptu shelter where there will be no guilt imparted by staff members for dropping off unwanted animals (Frommer & Arluke, 1999) and no risk of euthanasia. According to Barbara Erickson (Arluke & Killeen, 2009), she played this role in her community when people anonymously left animals at her door rather than abandoning them or taking them to a shelter.

Animal hoarding also can be perpetuated—indeed even started—through social support that provides animals to hoarders as well as food, veterinary care, and other essentials for them. One type of support comes from networks of like-minded or sympathetic people. Friends who identify with the hoarder's feelings and approach to animals may deliberately acquire unwanted animals from various sources, such as veterinary offices or shelters, and to prevent their euthanasia, give them to the hoarder. In the Erickson case (Arluke & Killeen, 2009), after Barbara's dogs were seized in one intervention, her friends tried to get her animals from the shelter by claiming that they were their own, presumably to return them to her.

Another type of support comes from misguided people who inadvertently enable hoarders to amass many animals. They can sometimes "pass" as normal appearing people and conceal their private world with animals. One such hoarder, who masked herself as a legitimate breeder, was protected by friends in her community who did not understand the depth of her psychological problem or the way she treated her dogs (Stola Education Group, 2006). She did not allow anyone to visit her home and was charming at public dog events.

Finally, there is an interpersonal component to animal hoarding when other people know about the problem but choose to ignore, if not tolerate, it. Neighbors, friends, and relatives can be aware that hoarding is taking place, but do nothing to intervene or even report it to authorities. Understandably, it is difficult to take such action for fear of alienating personal relationships with the hoarder and for lack of hard evidence to provide authorities. Nevertheless, such inaction allows hoarding to continue unchallenged.

Interventions

Keeping large numbers of animals in inappropriate, inadequate, and over-crowded conditions that cause starvation, disease, behavioral problems, or death seriously challenges relatives, friends, neighbors, and community agencies that want to help hoarders and their animals. However, the complex nature of hoarding cases makes them difficult to investigate and to resolve. The jurisdiction for these cases crosses many state and local agencies and departments, including mental health, police, humane law enforcement, zoning, sanitation, fish and wildlife, child welfare, animal control, public health, building safety, aging, and social services. So it is the rule rather than the exception that they are procedurally cumbersome, time consuming, and costly to resolve. Although common sense suggests that the accumulation of large numbers of animals in homes can have important public health implications, including placing neighborhoods at risk due to unsanitary living conditions, facilitating the spread of zoonotic diseases, and endangering the health of vulnerable household members, particularly children or dependent elderly, the potential for these consequences in animal hoarding cases is not widely appreciated by government agencies.

The absence of joint agreements between agencies over their missions and roles in these cases may create more conflict than cooperation. And to date, most communities have not discovered how to bring together available resources, expertise, and authorities to achieve comprehensive solutions. Arluke and Killeen's (2009) description of the community's handling of the Erickson case is more the exception than the rule. In this case, veterinarians, shelters, police, volunteers, and journalists worked together rather seamlessly when they intervened in this case without any formal agreements between county and state agencies. They accomplished this by focusing on the problem and how to solve it, rather than on their own jurisdictional issues. This is exemplified in the Idaho Humane Society's offering resources to a case in Oregon, and in the Second Chance Shelter in Fruitland, Idaho, which worked closely with an Oregon Sheriff's office prior to the rescue by reporting the problem and organizing the rescue, then offering to house and care for over 500 dogs.

Difficult issues of personal freedom, lifestyle choice, mental competency, and private property rights also confound intervening in these cases. For one, to protect people's civil rights, most laws restrict agencies from intervening unless others are being harmed. Options for intervention are also limited because few hoarders seem to meet the criteria for mental incompetence or immediate danger to self or others. Indeed, hoarders are rarely evaluated, which is the first step before declaring danger. One of the questions that may be raised in the future is whether the concept of dangerousness should be applied to animals, and whether a fuller appreciation of the consequences of their actions for people and animals by mental health authorities would lead to improved recognition of the scope of dangerousness often present.

Cases typically come to the attention of authorities because of complaints from neighbors. The primary problems reported about hoarders are unsanitary conditions, "strong," "obnoxious" odors or "stench," and occasionally nuisance problems such as "barking loudly." Neglect is seldom the initial complaint because animals are usually concealed inside hoarders' homes, as occurred in the Erickson case (Arluke & Killeen, 2009). There, neighbors complained to the Oregon Health Department about smells coming from the farm, leading to an investigation, an order to remove the waste, and a threatened 500-dollar fine that was dropped after the Ericksons removed the waste. Sanitary conditions often deteriorate to the extent that public health authorities condemn dwellings as unfit for human habitation. By the time these situations have deteriorated to the point at which they cannot be ignored, expenses for veterinary care and housing of animals, litigation, and cleanup or demolition of premises can run into the tens of thousands of dollars. Unfortunately, because of ill health, contagious diseases, and the large numbers involved, euthanasia is often the only option for many of the animals rescued from such situations.

Initial attempts to follow up complaints are usually unsuccessful. Often described as "uncomfortable around people," or as "quiet and somewhat reclusive," hoarders sometimes board up windows, erect tall fences, rarely appear outside, and do not answer phone calls or doorbells, making them notorious for their fortress mentality and hostility toward and suspicion of outsiders. Arluke and Killeen (2009) point out that the Ericksons had a sign posted on the door proclaiming, "This is Private Property. Stay to Hell Out!" If approached, outsiders are almost always turned away before they get into the hoarder's home. The Ericksons also never allowed anyone inside their home; Barbara would intercept potential visitors before they got to the front door. On more than one occasion, she suffered health problems requiring an ambulance, but instead of inviting paramedics into the house to treat her, she met them at the street. This isolation makes it difficult, if not impossible, for neighbors to know much about hoarders or their animals. Law enforcement authorities are eventually called to the scene, typically discovering many suffering or dead animals that are taken away from angry or grieving owners who potentially face charges of cruelty and possible conviction and sentencing.

Seizing Animals

Because of the severity of animal suffering and need for expediency, a common scenario is for the hoarder's animals to be removed for their own protection through use of a search warrant, with the hoarder subsequently prosecuted under state anti-cruelty laws. (Unless relinquishment can be negotiated, the animals must be held as evidence until the case is concluded). However, seizing animals in hoarding cases is a complicated, expensive, labor intensive, and emotionally upsetting process. The entire financial cost of managing these cases, including the seizure itself, can easily run into the tens of thousands of dollars to cover expenses from veterinary care, animal sheltering, staff salaries at different agencies, and legal fees.

Seizing animals typically requires the coordination of many agencies and organizations, let alone friends and family. The last and largest "rescue" of the Ericksons' dogs required coordination among humane societies in Idaho and Oregon, some of which lacked sufficient funds to pay for all the animal care and staff salaries required in such cases, local veterinarians and animal shelters, law enforcement officials, firefighters, reporters, and volunteers (Arluke & Killeen, 2009). Within the past five years, national animal protection organizations such as the American Society for the Prevention to Cruelty to Animals (ASPCA) and the Humane Society of the United States, among others, have come together to coordinate disaster-type responses to the big cases, bringing in teams of people to set up temporary shelters and veterinary teams to evaluate the animals. Some of the big animal-related charitable foundations sponsored by the pet industry provide tractor-trailers full of supplies to help rescuers' efforts.

The field of veterinary forensics has also come of age with the establishment of the International Veterinary Forensics Sciences Association, and is increasingly playing a role when intervention occurs to collect and present the evidence needed to obtain a criminal conviction. As a sign of this rapid growth, the University of Florida School of Veterinary Medicine recently held a well-attended two-day training session for responding to big cases. And many more resources and networking for the animals are now an option, allowing many more animals to be rehabilitated and rehomed instead of being euthanized.

Emotional costs are high as people venture into disturbingly chaotic homes, deal with hoarders who can be extremely sad or very angry, see animals that are dead, emaciated, very sick, and often living in cramped, inhumane conditions, and end up euthanizing some. Those who intervene often find the experience of carrying out the "rescue" (less often called a "seizure" or even "raid") to be very dramatic and disturbing as they try to help animals or people put in danger by hoarders. A law enforcement presence is usually necessary to manage hoarders and take aggressive steps needed on behalf of animal victims who need to be "taken away" with some urgency. Steps may also be taken to monitor and manage the distress and sadness of hoarders who feel as though their "children" will be taken from them. There have been at least three news reports of people who were being investigated and committed suicide. One woman lit a charcoal grill in her bedroom and died of carbon monoxide poisoning along with her pets.

A study of hoarding cases reported in the news (Arluke et al., 2002) found that rescuers often paint each case as the "worst" or "most horrifying" incident, describing animal neglect in superlative terms. One news article cites a humane official who said, "'You can't imagine people accumulating that sort of filth and garbage.... Frazier said that it was the most foul scene he had encountered in his six years on the job.'" Another official maintained that a different case involved the "largest number of neglected animals ever seen."

Humane society staff and volunteers tirelessly work to clean, feed, and water the many seized animals. Sometimes, however, many seized animals are so sick, they must be euthanized. For example, when shelter workers seized more than 500 dogs kept by the Ericksons in Midvale, Oregon, over 100 had to be euthanized because they were too ill to be rehabilitated (Arluke & Killeen, 2009). Many of the dogs that were adopted had such entrenched behavioral problems they were returned to local shelters within weeks of the rescue.

Hoarders predictably protest and resist rescues, claiming unlawful and unnecessary seizure of their "children." One is described in a news article as "so belligerent the police were called to help," at which point the hoarder wrestled with police, who sprayed him with pepper spray and finally arrested him. Others have histories of being uncooperative or hostile. It is common for news reports to describe repeated attempts, sometimes spanning years, to take animals away from hoarders who resist these efforts by authorities (Arluke et al., 2002). In one case, an article features the headline, "Notorious Cat Hoarder Jailed" and details the exploits of a "wily and elusive foe." Another article notes that "as is true of most animal hoarders, Becker had a track record," listing her history of being deceptive and difficult with authorities as she chronically acquired animals.

Rescuers also will be confounded by hoarders' paradoxical accounts of their own behavior, sometimes professing great love for animals. Indeed, Arluke and Killeen's (2009) take on Barbara Erickson is that she saw herself as one with a "limitless need to love" that was turned on dogs. Certainly, the thought of losing her dogs seriously disturbed Barbara Erickson and made her cry. It is not clear, however, whether this "love" is a genuine motivation or a dishonest way to appear socially acceptable, if not praiseworthy. Others may claim to be pet rescuers or "no-kill" shelters attempting to help unwanted pets, and some may be professional or hobby animal breeders. All too frequently, these excuses may be used as effective ploys for the media or as defenses in court (Vaca-Guzman & Arluke, 2005). Despite these claims of professionalism and good intentions, hoarders are usually oblivious to the extreme suffering, obvious to the casual observer, of their animals.

Medico-Legal Options

Every state has statutes that mandate that caretakers provide animals with sufficient food and water, a sanitary environment, and necessary veterinary care in case of illness or injury. Therefore, technically speaking, hoarding violates animal cruelty statutes in every state, making hoarders criminal under the law. It is, however, important to recognize that animal cruelty statutes were written with the goal of identifying criminal neglect and punishing offenders, not to ensure optimal or even adequate care for animals. A more recent concept for assessing quality of life across the entire range of potential situations where groups of animals may be kept is to consider the Five Freedoms (Figure 2). This concept stems from an effort in 1965 in the United Kingdom to establish relevant and appropriate measures of welfare for agricultural animals. More recently this concept was applied to the care of populations of companion animals (Newbury et al., 2010).

Those who investigate hoarding cases perhaps should be mindful of these considerations, including freedom from hunger, thirst, discomfort, pain, injury, disease, fear, and distress, and freedom to express normal behavior, when trying to establish the presence of suffering and deteriorating animal care. Attitudes towards proper treatment of animals are evolving, and while in the past, cruelty was typically prosecuted under a fairly narrow range of criteria (e.g., frank starvation or failure to provide required veterinary care for relief of suffering), it is clear from this diagram that care begins to deteriorate and animals suffer a myriad of detrimental effects to their well-being long before this is typically recognized.

Figure 2: Relationship of presence of the Five Freedoms for animal welfare to quality of life for animals.

Quality of life	From hunger, thirst	From pain, injury, disease	From fear and distress	From discomfort	To express normal behavior	Quality of caregiving and results:
High	Yes	Yes	Yes	Yes	Yes	**Competent Care** — Animal welfare safeguarded
Good	Yes	Yes	Yes	+/-	+/-	
Borderline	Yes	+/-	+/-	+/-	No	**Borderline Care** — Animals at risk
Ideal intervention threshold: evaluate competency to provide care						
Poor	+/-	+/-	No	No	No	**Incompetent Care** — Animal suffering present
A life not worth living	No	No	No	No	No	

Cruelty typically prosecuted

Hoarding cases are often initially investigated and handled by representatives of the local animal shelter, humane society, or other animal protection group. In cases where an animal protection organization does not have jurisdiction, local police officers or municipal animal control officers may be the initial agents to investigate a case.

In some jurisdictions, violations of animal cruelty statutes may be summary offenses prosecuted by local humane agents or animal control officers in front of a magistrate, whereas in others, they may be misdemeanors, or in some cases, felonies, requiring prosecution by the district attorney's office. Penalties in the event of a guilty finding can range from a nominal fine to forfeiture of the animals and jail time (Arluke & Luke, 1997). Some state statutes provide for the recovery of the costs of boarding and medical care for animals in cruelty cases.

Although their actions are clearly a violation of animal cruelty laws in every state, hoarders can be difficult to successfully prosecute. Cases involving many animals are often prosecuted as a single case because the expedience of judges discourages multiple counts of cruelty. And in some jurisdictions, cruelty law focuses on the abuser's intent to harm and torture a comparatively small number of animals rather than the suffering of many. Hence, hoarders are legally viewed as chronically neglecting, rather than purposely abusing, a single animal. The absence of intent, then, can make it difficult for law enforcement to prosecute to the fullest in some jurisdictions, even though hoarders deliberately acquire and keep animals they cannot care for properly. Indeed, the recent attempt by many states to impose more serious penalties on abusers by classifying the intentional harm of animals as a felony crime may have unintentionally sidelined equally egregious cases of neglect with enormous suffering seen in hoarding cases (Patronek et al., 2006).

Portraying the plight of animals as mere neglect seems to diminish the seriousness of their mistreatment, downgrading it from more serious abuse. Hoarding outcomes can be more disturbing than incidents of deliberate cruelty toward or torture of individual animals. Often, the former affects many animals kept for months or even years under conditions of horrendous deprivation and suffering (Lockwood & Cassidy, 1988). Without apparent intent, hoarders cause an enormous amount of suffering and death, far surpassing the number of animals harmed or the duration of their suffering found in the vast majority of intentional animal abuse cases. They ignore basic animal care, failing to properly feed and water, if at all, their animals, and to treat veterinary problems that exist or develop. Consequently, these animals can suffer severe emaciation, have serious health and behavioral problems, or even die as a result of their neglect. Those rescuing the Ericksons' dogs in the 2003 case found many of those alive to be starved and dehydrated to the point of immobility (Arluke & Killeen, 2009). Those that could be rescued had many health problems such as roundworm, Demodectic mange, Cheyletiella mites, coccidiosis, Giardia, open sores, and old bodily injuries.[3]

In this vein, one article (Colin, 2002, p.2), entitled "Loving Animals to Death," describes animal hoarders as "keeping a light foot in the serial killer camp: Like serial killers they are pathetic but obsessively thorough and are motivated by a perversion of something that could maybe almost make sense." Further on, the article contains an interview with a California resident. He stated: "I think that [hoarders] believe they are loving those animals ... but animal cruelty is just as bad as cruelty to children" (Colin, 2002, pp. 2–3). Some have noted the irony in the hoarders' belief that there is no fate worse than death, given that their treatment of animals creates a condition that is worse than death—a living death— or a life of suffering. Because of the scale and degree of suffering in these cases, the term passive cruelty may be more fitting than neglect (Vaca-Guzman & Arluke, 2005).

The role played by animals in criminal proceedings also encumbers prosecution. Because seized animals are treated as evidence, they must be held in shelters until cases are completed. In complicated cases, protective custody can last for years. According to one study (Berry, 2005), to avoid re-victimizing animals through such extended stays, humane agents may negotiate dropping charges and restricting future ownership of animals in return for immediate custody.

In the past, news reports of hoarding cases suggested that cruelty charges actually being filed were uncommon (Arluke et al., 2002). When charges were filed, they tended to be

---

3. However, not all their animals were that badly neglected; a number of outdoor dogs appeared healthy and had food and shelter, although they were lethargic, filthy, and needy for attention.

for other problems like child endangerment or assault and battery of an investigating police officer. Guilty verdicts or no contest pleas were rare. If any sentence were passed, hoarders were ordered to give up animals, not get any more either temporarily or permanently, and/or stop breeding them. Occasionally, they were modestly fined or made to reimburse shelters for the cost of food and veterinary care. Jail time was rarely imposed except for contempt of court, fraud, and violation of probation.

National groups are trying to change this situation. The Animal Legal Defense Fund (ALDF) has made a major effort to provide resources for prosecutors on their website. Also, the Association of Prosecuting Attorneys has created a subsection on animal abuse that is developing strategies for effectively prosecuting these cases (Sylvester & Baranyk, 2011a, 2011b). These strategies include, but are not limited to, using the financial aspects of these cases to provide leverage as a crime (e.g., failure to pay taxes, misuse of funds, fraud).

There are many reasons for this prior leniency in court, although hoarders think it is stern to impose any limit on their animal ownership. Certainly, hoarding—despite the numbers of animals involved and the extent of their suffering—will be overshadowed in court by the many serious crimes against humans that officials see, and hoarding is classified under the law as neglect rather than abuse, calling forth more sympathetic than punitive responses. In addition, the prevailing view of hoarders as eccentric, if not mentally ill, makes criminalization seem inappropriate.

Arluke and Killeen (2009) note that the first time Barbara Erickson appeared in court for animal neglect, charges were dropped against her after she agreed to stop selling dogs, spay and neuter her animals, and allow a veterinarian to make unannounced visits. However, after the final rescue of 552 dogs, the Ericksons were charged with felony criminal mischief (for destruction of their rental house), 134 counts of misdemeanor animal abuse (the euthanized dogs), and 418 counts of misdemeanor animal neglect (the survivors). Barbara was jailed for several weeks, ordered to pay $15,000 in restitution and obtain psychological counseling, sentenced to 60 months supervised probation, and limited to no more than two dogs.

Although there are many challenges in prosecuting animal hoarders, prosecution has an important role to play in how hoarding cases can be approached in the future. Taking a criminal justice approach to these cases may help encourage prosecutors, judges, police, and legislators take them more seriously than they have in the past. Also, a therapeutically-oriented intervention or negotiation may not work with certain types of hoarders who are very irrational and uncooperative. Aggressive prosecution may be the only effective way to deal with hoarders who must be stringently monitored and strictly sanctioned to prevent recidivism. As noted by Patronek et al. (2006), the "broken windows approach" to crime (Wilson & Kelling, 1982) may apply to cases of hoarding as well; in other words, the progression to major offenses can be prevented by aggressively intervening when there are early warning signs of social breakdown, whether they are small crimes in the neighborhood or the first stages of animal hoarding. However, current laws make this type of proactive approach difficult (Patronek & Weiss, 2012).

Some states mandate psychological counseling of offenders, whereas others make it an option for the court. Although over 30 states have legislation for evaluation or treatment, no one knows exactly what this involves. However, at least as reflected in press reports of judges' actions, courts have not always viewed hoarders as seriously disturbed (Arluke et al., 2002). Judges in these news stories rarely suggest or require counseling. Indeed, even when they allude to possible mental health problems in hoarders, they may not order or recommend therapy. In one such case, the judge simply commented, "I think it's clear you are fixated on animals. In your obsession, you really are misguided." This reticence to recommend psychological help is surprising for three reasons. First, a number of hoarders' behaviors seemed symptomatic of serious psychological disorder based on how badly they neglected their animals, homes, and themselves. Second, sometimes hoarders' own attorneys cited their clients' histories with mental illness, suggesting chronic and serious problems. And third, sometimes investigators specifically asked judges to approach hoarders as irrational or disturbed individuals.

Even with court-ordered counseling, there can be several problems implementing it. Hoarders in general are very resistant to treatment and few clinicians are trained to work with object hoarders let alone animal hoarders, so they are hesitant to take on hoarders as patients. If hoarders are on fixed incomes or are unemployed, they will not have funds. Even if they have health insurance, they may only qualify for a limited number of visits to mental health providers and reimbursement rates to these providers can be low. If providers are seen on a fee-for-service basis, it is likely that hoarders will pay them slowly or not all, given their resistance to treatment. Monitoring required counseling, when it comes to matters such as attendance and responsiveness to a counselor's recommendations, will fall in the hands of a probation officer who, in all likelihood, will already be overwhelmed with a very large caseload. Regardless, the probation system is not designed for long-term monitoring of chronic offenders.

Occasionally, there may be prohibitions on future pet ownership, or limitations imposed on the number of animals, along with a requirement of periodic monitoring of the situation by authorities. Supervised probation has been recommended over court probation as a better way to ensure compliance. Prohibitions against future pet ownership are effective only to the extent that monitoring is practical.

Some communities attempt to either prevent or remedy hoarding situations by passing ordinances that limit the number of pets a person can own. There were no laws in Oregon that restricted the number of dogs the Ericksons could have, although some states do have such regulations in place. There are no data to indicate whether these measures are effective, but what is known is that they are wildly unpopular and difficult to enforce, and likely to be opposed by a broad coalition of pet fanciers, breeders, rescue groups, and animal protection organizations. This is a harsh and probably ineffective remedy that needlessly penalizes responsible pet owners.

The worst situations may be avoided through regulations that stipulate housing densities, sanitation requirements, and veterinary care, and which provide for regular inspections of licensed facilities. For example, Colorado has developed licensing requirements and comprehensive standards for the operation of an animal shelter or pet rescue organization. Such criteria also could help the media and the public, as well as the courts, distinguish between legitimate sheltering efforts and hoarding. Because of the Erickson case discussed throughout this chapter, Oregon's Malheur County enacted a law requiring a shelter license for anyone with 10 or more pets. The license allows for periodic inspections inside the home by officials who could then report neglect or abuse.

Managing these cases is complicated by the fact that hoarders not only have a high recidivism rate, often continuing their behavior after seizures leave them without animals, but also sometimes move to different towns or states where they are unknown and under the radar of local humane and law enforcement authorities. In a typical example, two 50-year-old women and their 73-year-old mother were discovered living with 82 live, and 108 dead, cats. They fled from the investigation, rented a new apartment nearby, and had seven cats and a dog two days later. A hoarder can escape enforcement, even when monitoring is practical, by moving to a new jurisdiction, often only across town or county lines. Indeed, Barbara Erickson abandoned many dogs at her prior rental house in Midvale, Idaho, when moving to another home in Council, Idaho, although she returned to feed them after her eviction (Arluke & Killeen, 2009). After a complaint was filed against Erickson for 50 dogs kept in her Council, Idaho, home she moved to Oregon.

Conclusion

We are learning a lot more about mental health issues involved in animal hoarding. With increased knowledge and understanding of this behavior, mental health professionals will be better prepared to intervene in these cases. Further enhancing the effectiveness of these interventions are new efforts to engage in interdisciplinary cooperation to bring together a broad array of resources and expertise to resolve these cases in a humane and timely fashion. Because the DSM-5 recognizes hoarding as a specific disorder, there should be increased involvement by mental health professionals and researchers in the care and study of this complex disorder. Engagement of forensic psychologists and psychiatrists could also be a consequence of this designation.

At the same time, advances are underway that will increase the efficacy of interventions by law enforcement and criminal justice authorities in animal hoarding cases. Professional and advocacy organizations like the National District Attorneys Association and the Animal Legal Defense Fund in combination with veterinary forensics are accelerating our ability to successfully prosecute crimes like hoarding once they have occurred. Despite such progress, intervention could be even more effective were it possible to intervene in hoarding cases before they become so severe that a prosecutable crime has occurred and victims have suffered. At present, humane law enforcement officers are limited in their options to preventively help animals when hoarding behavior is recognized but the situation has not deteriorated sufficiently that successful prosecution is yet likely. Input and collaboration between mental health authorities, members of the criminal justice system, animal advocates, and legislators will be required to bring animal cruelty laws developed in the nineteenth century into alignment with twenty-first-century crimes against animals.

References

American Psychiatric Association. (2013). *Diagnostic and statistical manual of mental disorders.* Arlington, VA: American Psychiatric Publishing.

Arluke, A. (2004). *Brute force: Animal police and the challenge of cruelty.* Lafayette, IN: Purdue University Press.

Arluke, A., Frost, R., Steketee, G., Patronek, G., Luke, C., Messner, E., ... Papazian, M. (2002). Press reports of animal hoarding. *Society & Animals, 10,* 113–135.

Arluke, A., & Killeen, C. (2009). *Inside animal hoarding: The case of Barbara Erickson and her 552 dogs.* Lafayette, IN: Purdue University Press.

Arluke, A., & Luke, C. (1997). Physical cruelty toward animals in Massachusetts, 1975–1996. *Society & Animals, 5,*195–204.

Berry, C. (2005). Long-term outcomes in animal cases, *Animal Law, 11*, 167–194.

Cassidy J., & Mohr J. (2001). Unsolvable fear, trauma, psychopathology: Theory, research, and clinical considerations related to disorganized attachment across the lifespan. *Clinical Psychology: Science and Practice, 8*, 275–298.

Castrodale, L., Bellay, Y., Brown, C., Cantor, F., Gibbins, J., Headrick, M., … Yu, D. (2010). General public health considerations for responding to animal hoarding cases. *Journal of Environmental Health, 72*, 14–18.

Colin, C. (2002). Loving animals to death. [Electronic version]. Salon.com. Retrieved June 6, 2002 from http://www.salon.com/people/feature/2002/03/08/hoarders/index.html.

Flores, P. (2004). Addiction as an attachment disorder. Jason Aronson: Lanham, MD.

Franklin, A. (1999). *Animals and modern cultures: A sociology of human-animal relations in modernity.* Thousand Oaks, CA: Sage.

Frommer, S., & Arluke, A. (1999). Loving them to death: The blame-displacing strategies of animal shelter workers and surrenderers. *Society & Animals, 7*, 1–16.

Frost, R. (1998). Hoarding, compulsive buying and reasons for saving. *Behavioral Research and Therapy, 36*, 657–664.

Frost, R. (2000). People who hoard animals. *Psychiatric Times, 17(4)*, 25–29.

Frost, R., Hartl, T., Christian, R., & Williams, N. (1995). The value of possessions in compulsive hoarding: Patterns of use and attachment. *Behavioral Research and Therapy, 33*, 897–902.

Frost, R., Patronek, G., & Rosenfield, E. (2011). Comparison of object and animal hoarding. *Depression and Anxiety, 28*, 885–891.

HARC. (2002). Health implications of animal hoarding. *Health and Social Work, 27*, 125–131.

Lockwood, R. (1994). The psychology of animal collectors. *American Animal Hospital Association Trends Magazine, 9*, 18–21.

Lockwood, R., & Cassidy, B. (1988). Killing with kindness? *The Humane Society News,* Summer, 1–5.

Lyons-Ruth K., Dutra, L., Schuder, M., & Bianchi, I. (2006). From infant attachment disorganization to adult dissociation: Relational adaptations or traumatic experiences? *Psychiatric Clinics of North America, 29*, 63–86.

Manning S. (2011). When animal rescuers become animal hoarders. Retrieved January 26, 2011 from http://www.msnbc.msn.com/id/38978396/ns/health-pet_health/t/when-animal-rescuers-become-animal-hoarders/#.T5Rxcu2xHaQ.

Mataix-Cols D. (2014). Clinical practice. Hoarding disorder. New England Journal of Medicine, *370,* 2023–30.

Meagher, E., Frost, R., & Riskind, J. (1999). Compulsive lottery, scratch ticket, and keno gambling: Its relation to OCD, hoarding, impulsivity, and the urge to buy. Paper presented at the annual meeting of the Association for the Advancement of Behavior Therapy, Toronto, November.

Nathanson, J. (2009). Animal hoarding: Slipping into the darkness of comorbid animal and self-neglect. *Journal of Elder Abuse, 21,* 307–324.

Nathanson, J., & Patronek, G. (2011). Animal hoarding: How the semblance of a benevolent mission becomes actualized as egoism and cruelty. In B. Oakley, A. Knafo, G. Madhavan, & D. Wilson (Eds.), *Pathological Altruism,* (pp.107–115). New York, NY: Oxford University Press.

Newbury, S., Blinn, M. K., Bushby, P.A., Cox, C. B., Dinnage, J. D., Griffin, B.... Spindel, M. (2010). *Guidelines for standards of care in animal shelters.* Association of Shelter Veterinarians.

Patronek, G. (1999). Hoarding of animals: An under-recognized public health problem in a difficult to study population. *Public Health Reports, 114,* 82–87.

Patronek, G. (2001). The problem of animal hoarding. *Municipal Lawyer, 42,* 6–19.

Patronek, G., Loar, L., & Nathanson, J. (Eds.) (2006). *Animal hoarding: Structuring interdisciplinary responses to help people, animals and communities at risk.* Hoarding of Animals Research Consortium.

Patronek, G., & Nathanson, J. (2009). A theoretical perspective to inform assessment and treatment strategies for animal hoarders. *Clinical Psychology Review, 29,* 274–281.

Patronek G., & Weiss K. (2012). Animal hoarding: a Neglected Problem at the intersection of psychiatry, veterinary medicine, and law. Findings from the Henderson House Workgroup. Poster 117–64; American Psychology Law Conference, San Juan, March 17, 2012. Retrieved from: http://www.tufts.edu/vet/hoarding/index.html.

Steketee, G., Gibson, A., Frost, R., Alabiso, J., Arluke, A., & Patronek, G. (2011). Characteristics and antecedents of people who hoard animals: An exploratory comparative interview study. *Review of General Psychology, 15,* 114–124.

Stola Education Group. (2006). Animal hoarding: A hidden danger in the sport of purebred breeding? *IG Times, Spring.*

Sylvester, S., & Baranyk, C. (2011a). When animal hoarding is warehousing for profit/part 1. *Tales of Justice, 1*(2), 1–3. National Center for Prosecution of Animal Abuse.

Sylvester, S., & Baranyk, C. (2011b). When animal hoarding is warehousing for profit/part 2. *Tales of Justice, 1*(3), 1–4. National Center for Prosecution of Animal Abuse.

Svanberg, I. & Arluke, A. (in press). The Swan Lady: Images of heroism and hoarding in Swedish media reports. *Society & Animals.*

Vaca-Guzman, M., & Arluke, A. (2005). Normalizing passive cruelty: The excuses and justifications of animal hoarders. *Anthrozoos, 18,* 338–357.

Wilson, J., & Kelling, G. (1982). Broken windows: The police and neighborhood safety.*The Atlantic Monthly, March,* 29–38.

Worth, C., & Beck, A. (1981). Multiple ownership of animals in New York City. *Transactions and Studies of the College of Physicians of Philadelphia, 3,* 280–300.

Chapter 10

Animal Cruelty and Sexual Deviance

Christopher Hensley, Suzanne E. Tallichet, and Caleb E. Trentham

Paraphilias

The term paraphilia literally means abnormal love. According to a relatively recent edition of the *Diagnostic and Statistical Manual of Mental Disorders* (DSM), a paraphilia is a sexual deviation marked by fantasies, feelings, and behaviors that are necessary for sexual arousal (American Psychiatric Association, 2000). The essential features of a paraphilia involve "recurrent, intense sexually arousing fantasies, urges, or behaviors" that occur over a period of at least six months (American Psychiatric Association, 1994, p. 523). These fantasies and behaviors typically involve non-human objects, the suffering or humiliation of oneself or one's partner, or children or other nonconsenting persons. In addition, paraphilias cause significant damage to social, occupational, and other forms of normal functioning (American Psychiatric Association, 2000). According to the DSM-5, a paraphilia "denotes any intense or persistent sexual interest other than sexual interest in genital stimulation or preparatory fondling with phenotypically normal, physically mature, consenting human partners" (American Psychiatric Association, 2013, p. 685).

Paraphilic behaviors often hinge on other components, including deviant sexual fantasies, facilitators (drugs, alcohol, and/or pornography), and compulsive masturbation (Hickey, 2010). Deviant sexual fantasies serve to influence and motivate deviant sexual or violent behaviors. Facilitators lower inhibitions, allowing for people to fantasize about or actually engage in aberrant sexual behaviors. Compulsive masturbation, often in conjunction with pornography, serves to reinforce deviant sexual fantasies, as well as deviant sexual behaviors (Hickey, 2010).

Paraphilias exist on a continuum that ranges from mild to moderate to severe, and have the potential to become more extreme over time (Hickey, 2010). What distinguishes those people who have a mild paraphilia from those who suffer from a severe paraphilia is that the former can sexually function without the deviant sexual fantasies, facilitators, and compulsive masturbation that the latter often requires. The behavior is considered severely paraphilic when the individual completely depends on the aberrant fantasy for sexual stimulation and gratification (Hickey, 2010).

The most recent DSM-5 adds terminology that distinguishes between those who engage in paraphilias and those who have a paraphiliac disorder, defining a paraphilic disorder as "a paraphilia that is currently causing distress or impairment to the individual or a paraphilia whose satisfaction has entailed personal harm, or risk of harm, to others" (American Psychiatric Association, 2013, pp. 685–686). This allows for a clear distinction between a healthy person with a non-normative sexual behavior who requires no psychiatric intervention and a person with a psychopathological non-normative sexual behavior who needs such intervention (American Psychiatric Association, 2013).

History of Paraphilias

Prior to the publication of the DSM-I, paraphilias were classified as cases of psychopathic personality with pathologic sexuality. The DSM-I included sexual deviation as a personality disorder of a sociopathic subtype. The major sexual deviations discussed in the DSM-I included fetishism, homosexuality, pedophilia, sexual sadism (including rape), and transvestism (American Psychiatric Association, 1952).

The DSM-II continued to use the term sexual deviation to describe what would later be termed a paraphilia. These sexual deviations, however, were no longer seen as being attributed to personality disorders, but rather were listed alongside personality disorders in a category described as "personality disorders and certain other nonpsychotic disorders." Such sexual deviations included exhibitionism, fetishism, homosexuality, masochism, pedophilia, sadism, transvestism, voyeurism, and other sexual deviations. However, no examples of sexual deviation were provided for the "other" category (American Psychiatric Association, 1962).

In 1980, the term, paraphilia, was introduced in the DSM-III as a subset of a new category described as "psychosexual disorders." The paraphilias listed included atypical paraphilia, exhibitionism, fetishism, pedophilia, sexual masochism, sexual sadism, transvestism, voyeurism, and zoophilia. Homosexuality was removed from that edition of the DSM-III (American Psychiatric Association, 1980). Seven years later, the DSM-III-R renamed psychosexual disorders to sexual disorders and atypical paraphilia to paraphilia NOS (not otherwise specified). In addition, frotteurism was added to the list of main paraphilias and transvestism was renamed to transvestic fetishism. Zoophilia was relegated to the paraphilia NOS category along with coprophilia, klismaphilia, necrophilia, partialism, telephone scatologia, and urophilia (American Psychiatric Association, 1987).

The DSM-IV retained the sexual disorders classification, but added a broader category titled, "sexual and gender identity disorders" for paraphilias. It also kept the same paraphilias and the same paraphilia NOS list as the DSM-III-R (American Psychiatric Association, 1994). The DSM-IV-TR provided clinical criteria for only certain paraphilias, including exhibitionism, fetishism, frotteurism, pedophilia, sexual masochism, sexual sadism, transvestic fetishism, and voyeurism. The paraphilia NOS category included coprophilia, emetophilia, klismaphilia, necrophilia, partialism, telephone scatologia, urophilia, and zoophilia (American Psychiatric Association, 2000). The DSM-5 also outlines clinical criteria for only certain paraphilic disorders, including voyeuristic disorder, exhibitionistic disorder, frotteuristic disorder, sexual masochism disorder, sexual sadism disorder, pedophilic disorder, fetishistic disorder, and transvestic disorder. Examples of the "other specified paraphilic disorders" include, but are not limited to, "recurrent and intense sexual arousal involving telephone scatologia, necrophilia, zoophilia, coprophilia, klismaphilia, urophilia" (American Psychiatric Association, 2013, p. 705).

Bestiality and Zoophilia

One of the least occurring paraphilias is zoophilia. As previously mentioned, zoophilia was not introduced to the DSM until 1980 with the publication of the DSM-III. The diagnostic criterion for someone suffering from zoophilia was described with the following language: "the act or fantasy of engaging in sexual activity with animals is repeatedly preferred or the exclusive method of achieving sexual excitement" (American Psychiatric Association, 1980, p. 270). All of the subsequent editions of the DSM placed zoophilia under the paraphilia NOS category, with the exception of the current DSM-5 which describes it as an "other specified paraphilic disorder." In addition, anyone who is diagnosed with zoophilia under the DSM must be accompanied by distress or interference with normal functioning (American Psychiatric Association, 2013).

Sexual contact between humans and animals in academic literature has been described using a number of terms, including zoophilia, zoophilism, bestiality, zooerasty, and zoorasty (Aggrawal, 2011). Zoophilia and zoophilism are typically synonymous terms used to describe someone who is both emotionally and sexually attracted to animals. Zoophiles (or zoos) claim to have developed a deep emotional attachment to the animals with which they have sexual contact, often regarding these animals as their lovers. In other words, they feel they truly love the animal (Aggrawal, 2011). Zooerasty and zoorasty are terms that are very similar to bestiality with one notable exception. The zooerast may enjoy sex with an animal even when other normal sexual outlets are available (Aggrawal, 2011). Regardless of the presence of other normal sexual outlets, people who engage in bestiality are most certainly using animals for their own sexual gratification and whether their claim that an emotional bond exists between them and the animal is irrelevant to defining any form of bestiality as anything less than animal abuse.

Aggrawal (2011) identified ten separate classes of zoophiles. Class I zoosexuals include "human-animal role-players." They do not have actual sex with animals; rather, they dress their intimate partners in the likeness of certain animals (i.e., dogs, pandas, foxes, etc). Such would include members of the "furry fandom." Class II zoosexuals include romantic zoophiles. They keep animals as pets but do not have intimate contact. However, they do achieve some type of mental arousal (i.e., psychosexually stimulated) from having the animal in their proximity. Class III zoosexuals are referred to as zoophilic fantasizers. This group, again, does not have sexual relations with the animals, but rather may masturbate in the presence of their animals. Zoophilic voyeurs and zoophilic exhibitionists are included in this class. Class IV zoosexuals are described as tactile zoophiles. They receive sexual gratification from touching, stroking, or fondling an animal or their genitalia (i.e., frotteurism). Although they receive sexual arousal from the animals, they do not engage in penetration. Class V zoosexuals are also known as fetishistic zoophiles, using animal parts, in particular fur, for sexual aids. In fact, there is a documented case of a woman who used a deer tongue as a masturbatory tool. Aggrawal believed that individuals in Classes I — V could be treated with behavior modification.

According to Aggrawal (2011), Class VI zoosexuals are characterized as sadistic bestials. This group uses torture (i.e., zoosadism) to receive sexual gratification; however, they do not engage in sexual intercourse with the animals. Class VII zoosexuals comprise opportunistic zoosexuals. They are able to engage in normal sexual relations with people; however, if the opportunity presents itself, they will have sexual relations with animals. They do not develop emotional attachments with animals. Class VIII zoosexuals are referred to as regular zoosexuals. They prefer sex with animals over humans, but can engage in sexual activity with both. Unlike Class VII, they can develop an emotional bond with the animals and sex is a part of the relationship. Class IX zoosexuals are identified as homicidal bestials. People in this class must kill animals to have sex with them (i.e., necrozoophiles). They have the ability to have sexual relations with people but prefer dead animals. Serial killers Jeffrey Dahmer and Henry Lee Lucas would have been included in this category (Hickey 2010). Class X zoosexuals comprise exclusive zoosexuals who only engage in sexual activity with animals to the exclusion of all humans. Aggrawal (2011) argued that those individuals in Classes VI—X must be treated more rigorously and medicated.

Zoophiles may argue that because their preferred sexual animal intimacy is exclusive to adult animals and includes an emotional attachment, it is their alternate sexual orientation that is largely misunderstood and is, therefore, either unacceptable or invisible to most members of society. They believe that their behavior constitutes a sexual preference rather than a form of sexual deviance. Similarly, some researchers may regard bestiality as simply sexual contact between humans and animals or the physical contact humans have with an animal that results in their own sexual arousal (Beetz, 2002, 2004; Miletski, 2002). Such incidents of sexual intimacy include bodily contact, human genital contact with an animal's mouth, masturbation of the animal, and interspecies coitus (Peretti & Rowan, 1982). However, the majority of researchers, such as Ascione (1999), view bestiality as a legitimate form of animal abuse. Furthering this approach, Beirne (1997) has proposed replacing the term "bestiality," referring to it as "interspecies sexual assault." Along with animal advocates, these researchers posit that similar to pedophilia, there is an interspecies imbalance of power that makes sexual contact with an animal coercive and that animals are neither able to consent to nor report such an episode (Beirne, 1997). In addition, sexual activity with an animal often causes pain and sometimes death to that animal.

Using mostly case studies and surveys, the research investigating bestiality has been developing over the past several decades. Generally, the early studies focused on the prevalence of bestiality and identified bestialics' demographic characteristics (Hunt, 1974; Kinsey, Pomeroy, & Martin, 1948; Kinsey, Pomeroy, Martin, & Gebhard, 1953). Subsequent studies have examined the dynamics of bestiality itself, including perpetrators' abuse histories, family dynamics, motives for bestiality, and the types of animals involved (Alvarez & Freinhar, 1991; Hunt, 1974; Kinsey et al., 1948; Miletski, 2001; Peretti & Rowan, 1982; Sandnabba, Santtila, Nordling, Beetz, & Alison, 2002; Weigand, Schmidt, & Kleiber, 1999). Many of the most recent studies investigate bestiality as sexual deviance in its relationship with other forms of deviance among institutionalized and non-institutionalized respondents and among juveniles and adults. Specifically, these studies have examined bestiality within the context of animal cruelty and interpersonal violence (Duffield, Hassiotis, & Vizard, 1998; Fleming, Jory, & Burton, 2002; Flynn, 1999; Hensley, Tallichet, & Dutkiewicz, 2010; Hensley, Tallichet, & Singer, 2006; Merz-Perez & Heide, 2004; Merz-Perez, Heide, & Silverman, 2001; Ressler, Burgess, Hartman, Douglas, & McCormack, 1986).

Studies of Bestiality Prevalence and Perpetrator Characteristics

In perhaps the earliest study on bestiality, Kinsey et al. (1948) estimated that 8% of the 5,300 White adult American males in their sample had engaged in sexual contact with animals and further suggested that these practices were confined largely to "farm boys" because prevalence rates were much higher among rural males than among their urban counterparts. Specifically, they found that over 40% of adolescent males raised on farms had engaged in bestiality with one-third having started by the age of nine. The most common animals included calves, sheep, donkeys, large fowl (i.e., ducks and geese), dogs, and cats. Males were more likely to engage in vaginal intercourse with the animals and allow the animals to orally stimulate them. In their study of 5,792 women, Kinsey et al. (1953) found that 5% reported having sexual contact with an animal. Females in the study reported more involvement with household pets who performed oral sex on them. Twenty-one years later, Hunt (1974) found that only 4.9% of 932 adult men and 1.9% of 1,044 adult women reported having engaged in bestiality. Moreover, Miletski (1999, 2002) found that among 82 bestialic males and 11 bestialic females in her study, only about one-fourth had lived on farms.

Regarding educational levels, Kinsey et al. (1948) found that although frequencies of contact were higher among rural males with lower educational levels, rural males with a college education had a 26% prevalence rate of bestiality compared with a 14% prevalence rate among those who had only completed grade school. More recently, Miletski (1999, 2002) also reported that almost half of the men and 45% of the women in her sample who had sexual contact with animals had at least a college education or better. Similarly, Beetz (2002) reported that among the 113 bestialic males in her study, 70% had at least some college education or beyond. However, Flynn (1999) found very low prevalence rates for bestiality among his sample of 267 college students. Specifically, only 2.4% of men and 1.1% of women undergraduate students reported having sexual contact with an animal.

Based on the current literature, it can be assumed that individuals who engage in bestiality began at an early age, have little formal education, and are predominantly from rural areas. Nonetheless, it should be noted that most of the samples in the foregoing studies regarding the prevalence and demographic characteristics of bestialics were non-random and that farm and rural populations have declined dramatically since the Kinsey studies of the late 1940s and 1950s. Indeed, Beirne (2001) has declared that "no valid generalizations can be made about the prevalence of bestiality from the data of Kinsey and colleagues" due to the non-random nature of his sampling and his aggressive interviewing style (p. 47). While later studies attempted to fill the void regarding the age, residence, and educational levels of those who engaged in bestiality, relatively little is still known about the prevalence of bestiality and more studies need to be conducted to profile bestialics.

Studies of the Dynamics Associated with Bestiality

Studies examining the dynamics of human/animal sexual contact suggest that bestialic participants may demonstrate a failure to relate to members of their own species. In their case study of an indiscriminate animal and human sex offender since age 15, Wilcox, Foss, and Donathy (2005) found that even in his mid-40s, "Mr. Z" demonstrated cognitive impairment and ungainly social presentation. He admitted to feeling awkward around his potential human sex partners and on occasion had become enraged when rejected by them. Based on interviews, the authors declared him to be socially marginalized, pointing out that at the time of the study he was often ostracized or "scapegoated" by other members of his treatment group.

Using structured interviews, Peretti and Rowan (1982) investigated the motives of 27 men and 24 women who said they had engaged in habitual acts of bestiality. Men reported that sexual expression was the primary reason for engaging in bestiality (93%), followed by sexual fantasy (81%). Men also indicated that having sex with an animal allowed them to bypass the negotiation process for sex with human partners (74%) or that they could avoid having any human interaction whatsoever (63%). Moreover, the men said that financial reasons contributed to their engagement in bestiality (59%) and that emotional involvement with the animal played an important role (26%). A majority of the women in the study cited emotional involvement as a reason for engaging in bestiality (88%). Almost as many reported doing so because it did not require human interaction (77%). Not having to negotiate for sex was the reason that over half of the women preferred having sexual contact (58%) followed by desire for sexual expressiveness (46%), sexual fantasy (38%), and financial reasons (21%). Although there were some noteworthy differences between men and women's motivations for engaging in bestiality, foregoing interaction and/or negotiation with other humans were predominant motives for both sexes.

Miletski (1999) found, in a study of 82 bestialic men and 11 bestialic women, that 76% of males and 45% of females reported having sexual fantasies with animals. In addition, the motives that men provided for having sex with an animal included: a sexual attraction to the animal (91%); love and affection for the animal (74%); the animals being accepting and easy to please (67%); no human partners available (12%); and too shy to have sex with humans (7%). Females reported the following reasons for having sex with the animals: a sexual attraction (100%), love and affection (67%), and because the animal wanted it (67%). The majority of the sample preferred sexual activity with the dogs (87% of the males and 100% of the females) and/or horses (81% of the males and 73% of the females). Interestingly, 8% of the male subjects wanted to stop having sex with animals while none of the females did.

Other recent studies also demonstrate that among both juvenile and adult populations, bestiality may be associated with psychological disorders that include aggressive tendencies and behaviors toward humans. Duffield, Hassiotis, and Vizard (1998) found that seven out of 70 youths in their sample who were sent to a psychiatric center for juvenile sexual offenders had engaged in bestiality. These youthful interspecies sex offenders showed a disproportionately higher rate of mental disorders compared with the rest of the sample and were also more likely to have been neglected or abused in their homes. Moreover, their bestiality was almost never an isolated paraphilia. Indeed, many of them planned, targeted, and created situations for abusing both animal and human victims alike. As a result of their findings, these investigators argued that bestiality in the sexual history of a juvenile offender was a warning sign that other sexual paraphilias may be present and that such as individual may be at greater risk for sexually abusing another person in the future.

In their study of 381 youthful offenders from three Midwestern juvenile institutions, Fleming, Jory, and Burton (2002) administered questionnaires inquiring about juvenile offenders' exposure to sexual abuse and childhood trauma, their level of sexual aggression, and the offenders' family dynamics. Among their sample, 42.3% reported committing sexual offenses only against humans, while 6.3% reported previous sexual contact with an animal. Moreover, 23 of the 24 individuals who reported previous acts of bestiality also reported committing sexual offenses against humans. The 24 juveniles in the bestiality group were further questioned in detail about the nature of their reported sexual acts with animals. Among them, 16.7% reported having placed their mouth on the genitals of an animal, 58.3% reported having rubbed their genitals against an animal, 41.7% reported having committed penile penetration, 25% reported having penetrated an animal with a finger, and 8.3% reported having inserted an object into an animal's genitalia.

Further analysis of the study participants' family dynamics showed that members of both the bestiality group and the sex offender group reported a higher incidence of negative family communication than did non-sexual offenders, with individuals in the bestiality group indicating significantly less positive family communication than did individuals from the sex offender group. Both bestiality and sex offender group members also reported significantly lower levels of family attachment and family adaptability than the non-sexual offender group. Significant differences in positive family environment were also found between each group, with the bestiality group suffering from the most negative family environment followed by the sex offender group, with the non-sexual offender group indicating the most positive family environment (Fleming et al., 2002). Specifically, as one might expect, members of both the bestiality and sex offender groups suffered from significantly more emotional neglect, and more emotional, physical, and sexual abuse than the non-sexual offender group. Bestiality group members were found to have suffered significantly more emotional neglect and emotional abuse than did the sex offender group, but not more physical or sexual abuse. Finally, the authors found that members of the bestiality group reported significantly higher rates of victimization and offending than did members of either the sex offender or the non-sexual offender groups.

Other researchers have examined the fantasies along with the behaviors of bestialics, and in some cases have found that bestiality may be associated with acts of sadomasochism. In their study of bestiality, Alvarez and Freinhar (1991) surveyed 20 staff members, 20 medical in-patients, and 20 psychiatric in-patients at a single psychiatric institution. From their results, they developed an index indicating overall respondents' fantasies and experiences with bestiality. The scores on this index were significantly higher for male psychiatric patients than for male medical in-patients or male psychiatric staff members. The psychiatric patients were significantly more likely than both medical in-patients and psychiatric staff to have engaged in bestiality or to have fantasized about sexual contact with an animal.

Miletski (1999) found that among the 82 bestialic men in her non-random sample, 17% reported having sadomasochist fantasies and one-quarter said that they had either forced someone or been forced by someone to perform a sex act that either they or their partner did not want to do. In a later study of bestialic men, Sandnabba et al. (2002) collected data from questionnaires sent to members of two sadomasochistic clubs. They found that 12 of the 186 respondents (6.4%) reported having had sexual contact with an animal during the past year. After further investigation using a matched-groups design due to the small sample size, the authors found that the men's engagement in bestiality most often followed the onset of sadomasochistic sexual practices. Moreover, the bestiality group was significantly more likely to engage in sexual experimentation than were their control groups.

Finally, studies examining the potential bestialics have for committing further violence have found that they have the highest crossover rate for deviant sexual offending (Abel,

Becker, Cunningham-Rathner, & Rouleau, 1987; Abel & Rouleau, 1990). More specifically, Abel and his colleagues have declared that individuals convicted of sexual offenses with animals were discovered to be the most indiscriminate and deviant of sexual offenders and that they showed the greatest degree of crossover, meaning that they moved from one type of offending to another, such as abusing animals to abusing humans. This finding has been tempered by Wilcox et al. (2005) who suggest that the risk of crossover may be lower among some bestialics than others. However, they warn that having sexual contact with an animal is not necessarily performed as a substitute for sexual contact with or the sexual assault of another human and that some bestialics may be equally likely to offend against an animal as they would a human.

Studies of the Potential Link between Bestiality and Later Interpersonal Violence

Ultimately, then, it is possible that bestiality may also be a potentially significant predictor of interpersonal violence. One of the first studies to recognize and explore this potential relationship was conducted by Ressler et al. (1986). They compared the characteristics of 12 sexual killers who had been sexually abused during childhood with 16 sexual killers who had not and found that the sexually abused killers reported higher rates of animal cruelty in general, as well as higher rates of bestiality in particular. In their landmark study investigating the relationship between childhood animal abuse and interpersonal violence, Merz-Perez and Heide (2004) and Merz-Perez et al. (2001) discovered the commission of bestiality among members of their inmate sample of violent and nonviolent incarcerated offenders. Using structured interviews with 45 violent and 45 nonviolent inmates to examine the specific acts of animal cruelty, the researchers found three violent offenders (6.6%) reported having engaged in bestiality while no nonviolent offenders reported having engaged in any such behavior. Two of these cases involved pet animals while the third involved a farm animal. In the latter case, this violent subject was a repeat sex offender who had been convicted as an adolescent incarcerated in a reformatory for sodomizing a pig (Merz-Perez & Heide, 2004).

In the first investigation of the association between abusers' demographic characteristics along with self-reported bestiality and later interpersonal violence, Hensley et al. (2006) surveyed a sample of 261 inmates housed in one maximum- and two medium-security Southern correctional facilities. Specifically, they examined demographic characteristics (race, education level, and residence while growing up), being convicted of a personal crime, the number of personal crimes for which the respondent had been convicted, and how those factors affected acts of bestiality. Of the 261 inmates, 16 (16.3%) indicated that they had engaged in bestiality. There were no significant racial or residential differences between the 16 bestialics and the overall sample. Of those in the bestiality group, about one-third (31.3%) had less than an eighth-grade education relative to only 9.2% of the sample. Moreover, an additional 31.3% of inmates in the bestiality group had completed high school compared to 39.6% of the overall sample. They also found that three-quarters of the bestiality group had been convicted of a personal crime compared with 47.9% of the non-bestialic sample. Finally, 31.4% of the bestialic group had been convicted of more than three personal crimes compared to only 5.4% of the rest of the sample. All three of these relative differences between bestialics and non-bestialics in the sample regarding formal education, conviction of a personal crime and its frequency were statistically significant. In the same study, the researchers also found that inmates with less education and those who had been convicted of committing crimes against people on one or more occasions were more likely to have had sex with animals during their childhood or adolescence than were those in the overall sample.

Four years later, Hensley et al. (2010) sought to replicate their previous study by surveying 180 inmates at a medium- and maximum-security prison in another Southern state. Their investigation also examined whether inmates who had engaged in childhood bestiality differed from those who had not in terms of race, childhood residence, education, commission of a personal crime, and the number of personal crimes committed. Similar to their earlier findings, there were no significant differences between the study sample and inmates who had engaged in bestiality with regard to race or residence while growing up. However, in this study, there were also no significant differences in the educational level between bestialics and the sample inmates. At the same time, as Hensley et al. found in their 2006 study, there were significant differences between the sample and inmates who had engaged in bestiality regarding their commission of a personal crime and the frequency with which they did so. In other words, inmates who had engaged in youthful bestiality were more likely to commit adult interpersonal crimes on two or more occasions as compared to non-bestialics in the sample (Hensley et al., 2010).

Theorizing about the Bestiality Link

The study of animal abuse, including bestiality, as a potential harbinger of later interpersonal violence provides us with an opportunity to develop a more conceptual understanding of this phenomenon. Previous studies about animal cruelty, including the sexual abuse of animals, have supported social learning theory and, in particular, two relatively opposing explanations: the graduation (or progression) hypothesis and the generalized deviance hypothesis. Studies of bestiality per se have also supported the sexually polymorphous theory.

Bestiality is one of several different forms of animal cruelty. As Beetz (2005) has noted, the data have shown that bestiality is found most often among violent offenders, sex offenders, and the sexually abused. At this point in the research on the link between animal cruelty (including bestiality) and interpersonal violence, researchers are divided over the specification of the time-ordered sequence of animal abuse and interpersonal violence. On the one hand, the graduation hypothesis posits that individuals who begin abusing animals during their youth move on or "graduate" to committing violent acts against humans. The studies by Hensley et al. (2006, 2010) demonstrated that inmates who reported having committed bestiality as youths were more likely to have been convicted of or to have committed personal crimes as adults.

On the other the hand, according to the generalized deviance hypothesis, there is no specific time order to the sequence of violence committed against animals and people by deviant individuals such that personal crimes are no more likely to follow the abuse of animals than the reverse. A few studies have supported this hypothesis, such as the study by Arluke, Levin, Luke and Ascione (1999) that compared the criminal records of 153 animal abusers with a matched control group of 153 nonabusers. Although animal abusers were five times more likely to have been convicted of violent crimes than were nonabusers, generally there was no specific order to their crimes against animals relative to humans.

None of the studies that supported the generalized deviance hypothesis have investigated the sexual abuse of animals, with the exception of an Australian study by Alys, Wilson, Clarke, and Toman (2009). Their study compared 20 incarcerated male sexual homicide offenders, 20 male sex offenders from an outpatient treatment program, and 20 male college students. While the results actually supported both hypotheses, of importance here is that the sexual murderers reported significantly more sexual abuse of animals than either the sex offenders or the controls. Moreover, none of the sex offenders reported having abused animals as youths, while almost all of the sexual homicide offenders did.

As Flynn (2011) has noted, the youthful commission of animal abuse may not be a determinative risk factor for later adult interpersonal violence, but nor should it be disregarded. The findings from the foregoing studies suggest that perhaps when animal cruelty is refined in terms of the form it takes, then that risk may become more determinative. Bestiality as a form of animal abuse or, as Beirne (1997) has declared, as "interspecies sexual assault" is significant in the present discussion since the studies that have been conducted linking youthful bestiality and adult interpersonal violence also support the sexually polymorphous theory discussed by Merz-Perez and Heide (2004).

According to Merz-Perez and Heide (2004), the sexual abuse of animals (and humans for that matter) provides the perpetrator with a psychological and/or physiological "release" because, for them, sex and aggression have been learned together. Infantile sexuality can assume a number of different forms. In certain individuals, "perverse sexual activities" are violent ones that fall outside the parameters of acceptable behavioral norms. These activities, including bestiality, occur when "sexuality and aggression have become developmentally fused, and the two are mutually inclusive in the psyche of the offender" (Merz-Perez & Heide 2004, p. 66). These sex acts are acts of violence during which animals, like humans, are reduced to the status of objects to be manipulated, exploited, and controlled. It could be speculated that as children, these now adult perpetrators were exposed to adults engaging in violent sexual behaviors in the home or elsewhere. Clearly, the foregoing studies represent only a starting point for future research in this area because much is still unknown about those individuals who have had sexual encounters with animals and their propensity for interpersonal aggression.

Crush Videos

Research on the topic of animal crushing, however, is quite limited. Though laws and legislation have been enacted in Washington since the late 1990s, criminal justice scholars have yet to give the topic of crushing the attention it deserves. Even with the lack of academic research, internet sites such as peta.com and stopcrush.org are informative in educating the public and preventing the spread of animal crushing videos. As these incidents of animal cruelty begin to increase worldwide, there will be a need for further research in order to understand what causes this behavior and whether it could possibly lead to interpersonal violence.

Crush videos graphically depict the beating, burning, cutting, stabbing, skinning, and killing of small animals (The Mary T. and Frank L. Hoffman Family Foundation, 2008). These films serve as sexual gratification for those who can only be aroused by the torturing of animals. Crush films can be broken down into two categories, soft crush and hard crush (Humane Society of the United States, 2010). The most common form of crushing is soft crush; this is the torture of invertebrates, such as worms and spiders. Less common, but more horrific is the practice of hard crush. Hard crush is the act of inflicting pain on larger animals such as cats and dogs. Though the animals differ from film to film, most crushing films show females from the legs down physically dominating and brutally destroying small creatures with high-heeled shoes (The Mary T. and Frank L. Hoffman Family Foundation, 2008). The women in these films make anywhere from $25 to $1,000 per video, while viewers pay anywhere between $80 for 1 clip to $200 for 3 clips (Ahyong, 2011). To date, this viral commodity has proven to be as difficult to regulate as it is profitable (Humane Society of the United States, 2010).

Hard crush videos begin with a woman "teasing" the viewer by pinning the animal down with her stiletto heel and slashing its eyes and stomach with their other heel in a clear and torturous display of dominance over the animal (Brady, 2007). After the initial "teasing" is complete, the torturer takes the animal's life by crushing it between their stilettoes, buttocks, or breasts. With most individuals, this fetish usually begins with an interest in soft crush. Once viewers are no longer sexually aroused by watching the crushing of insects, they move on to larger animals such as frogs and mice. It is believed to be that once the viewer's sexual gratification runs its course with small insects and small animals, they begin to explore larger game which customarily consists of cats and dogs (Brady, 2007). Once known as a repulsive but rare fetish, the development of the internet and streaming video has allowed for crushing films to reach a larger and wider audience. Moreover, because these videos can be uploaded anonymously and perpetrators' faces are hidden from view, the detection and prosecution of those who produce and participate in them is almost impossible.

Even so, there are laws that ban crush films. In 1999, the first statute was enacted making it illegal to possess, create, and sell a depiction of animal cruelty (18 USC § 48). However, in 2008, the United States Court of Appeals for the Third Circuit ruled that the ban on the sale and procession of such films was a violation of the Constitution under the 1st Amendment (*United States v. Stevens*, 2008). Due to the vagueness of the legislation that was enacted in 1999, the United States Supreme Court affirmed the decision made by the United States Court of Appeals for the Third Circuit (Liptak, 2010). In its creation, the initial legislation did not differentiate between animal cruelty and the art of hunting. It was not until President Barack Obama signed the Animal Crush Video Prohibition Act of 2010 that clarity was given to the previous law by making it illegal to create, sell, distribute, advertise, market, or exchange crush films (Animal Crush Video Prohibition Act of 2010, 2010).

In July 2012, Ashley Nicole Richards and Brent Wayne Justice from Houston, Texas were arrested for making, producing, and distributing crush videos. They were the first defendants to be charged under the 2010 federal statute. Ms. Richards used weapons including meat cleavers, knives, and high heels to torture and crush dogs and cats. Both defendants were charged with five counts of animal cruelty under the 2010 statute, which carried a maximum of 45 years in prison. In addition, prosecutors added two counts of obscenity independent of the crush statute. However, in April 2013, a U.S. District Court Judge threw out the crush video charges on First Amendment grounds and that animal crush videos were not obscene (Malisow, 2013). He argued that the Animal Crush Video Prohibition Act of 2010 was unconstitutional and too broad. On May 29, 2014, however, Ms. Richards pled guilty to three counts of animal cruelty and was sentenced to 10 years in prison while Mr. Justice remained in jail (ABC13, 2014).

On June 13, 2014, the U.S. Court of Appeals for the Fifth Circuit ruled that the 2010 law was constitutional because it prohibits obscenity not protected by the First Amendment and that Congress has an interest in preventing the violence depicted in those videos (Dunn, 2014). The Court reversed and remanded the case from the U.S. District Court in the Southern District of Texas, reinstating the charges against Ms. Richards and Mr. Justice.

Bestiality Laws

Currently, the federal government does not provide any criminal statutes against bestiality, with the exception of the Uniform Code of Military Justice (UCMJ). Interestingly, immediately prior to the passage of the National Defense Authorization Act for Fiscal Year 2012, Article 125 of the UCMJ was almost repealed (National Defense Authorization Act for Fiscal Year 2012, 2011). The language banning sodomy and bestiality was dropped from the original bill, only to be added after criticism from the People for the Ethical Treatment of Animals (PETA) and the Family Research Council, a conservative group (Morgenstern, 2011). In December 2013, a provision of the National Defense Authorization Act of 2014 repealed the ban on consensual sodomy found in Article 125 and added a provision that specifically bans bestiality (National Defense Authorization Act for Fiscal Year 2014, 2013).

Article 125 of the UCMJ states that any person who engages in "unnatural carnal copulation with an animal is guilty of bestiality and shall be punished as a court-martial may direct" (10 USC § 925—Art 125). However, 39 states have criminal laws which make sexual activity between a human and an animal either a felony or misdemeanor (Wisch, 2014).

Felony State Statutes

Of the 39 states that make bestiality a crime, 18 states provide felony penalties for violating bestiality statutes. Those states are: Arizona, Delaware, Georgia, Idaho, Illinois, Indiana, Massachusetts, Michigan, Mississippi, Montana, North Carolina, Oklahoma, Rhode Island, South Carolina, South Dakota, Tennessee, Virginia, and Washington.

In Arizona, engaging in any sexual contact with a dead or live animal is punishable as a Class 6 felony, the same felony classification as used in South Dakota and Virginia (AZ ST § 13-1411; SD ST § 22-22-42; VA ST § 18.2-361). People convicted under Arizona law may also be required to undergo a psychological assessment and pay for their own counseling. In addition, if the animal was taken to an animal shelter, the person convicted of bestiality may have to reimburse the animal shelter (AZ ST § 13-1411). These same stipulations are also found in the Illinois, Tennessee, and Washington statutes on bestiality. All three of these states also require that people convicted of sex crimes against an animal relinquish any animals that currently reside in their residence and may prevent them from having animals in the future (IL ST CH 720 § 5/12-35; TN ST § 39-14-214; WA ST 16.52.205).

In Delaware, "a person is guilty of bestiality when the person intentionally engages in any sexual act involving sexual contact, penetration or intercourse with the genitalia of an animal or intentionally causes another person to engage in any such sexual act with an animal for purposes of sexual gratification." It is considered a class D felony in Delaware (DE ST TI 11 § 775) and Indiana (IN ST 35-46-3-14).

The Georgia bestiality statute states that "a person commits the offense of bestiality when he performs or submits to any sexual act with an animal involving the sex organs of the one and the mouth, anus, penis, or vagina of the other" (GA ST § 16-6-6). Anyone convicted of bestiality in Georgia has committed a felony punishable by no less than one year and no more than five years in prison. Anyone who violates the buggery statute in South Carolina faces a maximum of five years in prison or a fine of not less than $500 or both (SC ST § 16-15-120). However, in Idaho, the minimum sentence for committing bestiality is no less than five years in prison (ID ST § 18-6605) and in Rhode Island the minimum is seven years with a maximum of 20 years (RI ST § 11-10-1) .

In Mississippi, Montana, and Oklahoma, the maximum number of years for violating the state's crime against nature law is 10 years (MS ST § 97-29-59; MCA 45-8-218; OK ST T. 21 § 886). However, the Michigan statute sets a maximum of 15 years but further states that, "if such person was at the time of the said offense a sexually delinquent person, [the crime] may be punishable by imprisonment in the state prison for an indeterminate term, the minimum of which shall be 1 day and the maximum of which shall be life" (M.C.L.A. 750.158). The Massachusetts bestiality law states that "whoever commits the abominable and detestable crime against nature, either with mankind or with a beast, shall be punished by imprisonment in the state prison for not more than twenty years" (MA ST 272 § 34).

Misdemeanor State Statutes

Twenty-one states also provide misdemeanor penalties for violating bestiality statutes. Those states are: Alabama, Alaska, Arkansas, California, Colorado, Connecticut, Florida, Iowa, Kansas, Louisiana, Maine, Maryland, Minnesota, Missouri, Nebraska, New York, North Dakota, Oregon, Pennsylvania, Utah, and Wisconsin. In most of these states that allow for misdemeanor punishment for bestiality, the statutes are sparsely worded (Wisch, 2014). However, in Iowa, a person convicted of bestiality is guilty of an aggravated misdemeanor and must submit to a psychological evaluation and treatment at that person's expense (IA ST § 717C.1). According to the Minnesota statute, "Whoever carnally knows a dead body or an animal or bird is guilty of bestiality, which is a misdemeanor. If knowingly done in the presence of another, the person may be sentenced to imprisonment for not more than one year or to payment of a fine of not more than $3,000 or both" (MN ST 609.294). In Missouri, a person who commits unlawful sex with an animal once is guilty of a misdemeanor. However, if that person has already been convicted of that crime, it is a Class D felony (MO ST 566.111). Currently, although the following 11 states may have animal abuse statutes in effect, they have yet to criminalize bestiality specifically: Hawaii, Kentucky, Nevada, New Hampshire, New Jersey, New Mexico, Ohio, Texas, Vermont, West Virginia, and Wyoming.

Conclusion

Significant changes are needed in our criminal statutes forbidding the sexual abuse of animals. In particular, we need legislation that provides preventative measures, such as humane education in public schools, along with increased and improved rehabilitation facilities and treatment programs aimed at both juvenile and adult sex offenders. Legislation needs to keep pace with current technologies to effectively address current developments, such as the dramatic rise in the popularity of crush videos. We need to encourage and foster greater public awareness about the sexual abuse of animals and to encourage animal advocacy toward creating a more compassionate society that improves the lives of both humans and animals.

To the extent that bestiality is linked to other forms of violence perpetrated against humans, the paucity of research begs the question as to how that connection develops and unfolds. Thus, more studies need to be done using both incarcerated and general populations, examining the extent to which crimes against animals are related to those committed against humans and, ultimately, how the erosion of empathy for any and all sentient beings occurs. Methodologically, future studies using a multi-method approach may provide the empirical support required to examine this complex relationship between bestiality and human violence. At that point, both practitioners and policy-makers can more accurately identify potential warning signs in order to stem further animal abuse and violent human crime.

References

ABC13. (2014). Houston woman sentenced for animal cruelty over 'crush videos. Retrieved from http://abc13.com/pets/woman-sentenced-for-animal-cruelty-over-crushvideos/83489/.

Abel, G. G., Becker, J., Cunningham-Rathner, J., & Rouleau, J. L. (1987). Self-reported sex crimes of 561 non-incarcerated paraphilias. *Journal of Interpersonal Violence, 2,* 3–25.

Abel, G. G., & Rouleau, J. L. (1990). The nature and extent of sexual assault. In W. L. Marshall, D. R. Laws, & H. E. Barbaree (Eds.), *Handbook of sexual assault: Issues, theories, and treatment of the offender* (pp. 9–12). New York: Plenum Press.

Aggrawal, A. (2011). A new classification of zoophilia. *Journal of Forensic and Legal Medicine, 18,* 73–78.

Ahyong, V. (2011). Crush fetish video making couple to be charged for animal cruelty. Retrieved from http://www.environmentphilippines.com/2011/07/news-crush-fetish-video-making-couple.html.

Alvarez, W. A., & Freinhar, J. P. (1991). A prevalence study of bestiality (zoophilia) in psychiatric patients, medial in-patients, and psychiatric staff. *International Journal of Psychosomantics, 38,* 1–4.

Alys, L., Wilson, J. C., Clarke, J., & Toman, P. (2009). Developmental animal cruelty and its correlates in sexual homicide offenders and sex offenders. In A. Linzey (Ed.), *The link between animal abuse and human violence* (pp. 145–162). Eastbourne: Sussex Academic Press.

American Psychiatric Association. (1952). *Diagnostic and statistical manual of mental disorders* (1st ed.). Washington, DC: Author.

American Psychiatric Association. (1962). *Diagnostic and statistical manual of mental disorders* (2nd ed.). Washington, DC: Author.

American Psychiatric Association. (1980). *Diagnostic and statistical manual of mental disorders* (3rd ed.). Washington, DC: Author.

American Psychiatric Association. (1987). *Diagnostic and statistical manual of mental disorders* (3rd rev. ed.). Washington, DC: Author.

American Psychiatric Association. (1994). *Diagnostic and statistical manual of mental disorders* (4th ed.). Washington, DC: Author.

American Psychiatric Association. (2000). *Diagnostic and statistical manual of mental disorders* (4th ed., text revision). Washington, DC: Author.

American Psychiatric Association (2013). *Diagnostic and statistical manual of mental disorders* (5th ed.). Washington, DC: Author.

Animal Crush Video Prohibition Act of 2010, H.R.5566, 111th Congress, 1st Session. (2010).

Arluke, A., Levin, J., Luke, C., & Ascione, F. R. (1999). The relationship to animal abuse to violence and other forms of antisocial behavior. *Journal of Interpersonal Violence, 14*(9), 963–975.

Ascione, F. R. (1999). The abuse of animals and human interpersonal violence. In F. R. Ascione & P. Arkow (Eds.), *Child abuse, domestic violence, and animal abuse: Linking the circles of compassion for prevention and intervention* (pp. 50–61). West Lafayette, IN: Purdue University Press.

Beetz, A. M. (2002). *Love, violence, and sexuality in relationships between humans and animals*. Aachem, Germany: Shaker Verlag.

Beetz, A. M. (2004). Bestiality and zoophilia: A scarcely investigated phenomenon between crime, paraphilia, and love. *Journal of Forensic Psychology Practice, 4*(2), 1–36.

Beetz, A. M. (2005). Bestiality and zoophilia: Associations with violence and sex offending. In A. M. Beetz & A. L. Podberscek (Eds.), *Bestiality and zoophilia: Sexual relations with animals* (p. 46–70). West Lafayette, IN: Purdue University Press.

Beirne, P. (1997). Rethinking bestiality: Towards a concept of interspecies sexual assault. *Theoretical Criminology, 1*(3), 317–340.

Beirne, P. (2001). Peter Singer's 'heavy petting' and the politics of animal sexual assault. *Critical Criminology, 10*, 43–55.

Brady, L. (2007). Crush videos: Animal torture and murder as a fetish. Retrieved from http://voices.yahoo.com/crush-videos-animal-torture-murder-as-fetish-324553.html?cat=17.

Duffield, G., Hassiotis, A., & Vizard, E. (1998). Zoophilia in young sexual abusers. *The Journal of Forensic Psychiatry, 9*(2), 294–304.

Dunn, L. (2014). Fifth circuit rules that animal crush video law prohibits obscenity and Congress has significant interest in preventing animal cruelty. Retrieved from http://aldf.org/blog/fifth-circuit-rules-that-animal-crush-video-law-prohibits-obscenity-and-congress-has-significant-interest-in-preventing-animal-cruelty/.

Fleming, W. M., Jory, B., & Burton, D. L. (2002). Characteristics of juvenile offenders admitting to sexual activity with nonhuman animals. *Society & Animals, 10*(1), 31–45.

Flynn, C. P. (1999). Animal abuse in childhood and later support for interpersonal violence in families. *Society & Animals, 7*(2), 161–172.

Flynn, C. P. (2011). Examining the links between animal abuse and human violence. *Crime Law and Social Change, 55*, 453–468.

Hensley, C., Tallichet, S. E., & Dutkiewicz, E. L. (2010). Childhood bestiality: A potential precursor to adult interpersonal violence. *Journal of Interpersonal Violence, 25*(3), 557–567.

Hensley, C., Tallichet, S. E., & Singer, S. D. (2006). Exploring the possible link between childhood and adolescent bestiality and interpersonal violence. *Journal of Interpersonal Violence, 21*(7), 910–923.

Hickey, E. W. (2010). *Serial murderers and their victims* (5th ed.). Belmont, CA: Wadsworth Cengage Learning.

Humane Society of the United States. (2010). Animal crush videos: Senate committee testimony. Retrieved from http://www.humanesociety.org/news/resources/animal_crush_video_senate.html.

Hunt, M. (1974). *Sexual behavior in the 1970s*. Chicago: Playboy Press.

Kinsey, A. C., Pomeroy, B., & Martin, C. E. (1948). *Sexual behavior in the human male*. Philadelphia, PA: W. B. Saunders.

Kinsey, A. C., Pomeroy, W. B., Martin, C. E. & Gebhard, P. H. (1953). *Sexual behavior in the human female*. Philadelphia: W. B. Saunders.

Liptak, A. (2010). Justices reject ban on videos of animal cruelty. *New York Times*. Retrieved from http://www.nytimes.com/2010/04/21/us/21scotus.html?ref=dogfighting.

The Mary T. and Frank L. Hoffman Family Foundation (2008). About crush. Retrieved from http://www.stopcrush.org/?page_id=2.

Malisow, C. (2013). Open season: Do laws against animal crushing videos violate free speech? Retrieved from http://www.houstonpress.com/2013-05-16/news/ashley-nicole-richards/full/.

Merz-Perez, L., Heide, K. M., & Silverman, I. J. (2001). Childhood cruelty to animals and subsequent violence against humans. *International Journal of Offender Therapy and Comparative Criminology, 45*(5), 556–573.

Merz-Perez, L., & Heide, K. M. (2004). *Animal cruelty: Pathway to violence against people*. Lanham, MD: Rowman & Littlefield Publishers, Inc.

Miletski, H. (1999). *Bestiality—zoophilia: An exploratory study*. San Francisco: The Institute for the Advanced Study of Human Sexuality.

Miletski, H. (2000). Bestiality/zoophilia: An exploratory study. *Scandinavian Journal of Sexology, 3*, 149–150.

Miletski, H. (2001). Zoophilia—implications for therapy. *Journal of Sex Education and Therapy, 26*, 85–89.

Miletski, H. (2002). *Understanding bestiality and zoophilia*. Bethesda, MD: East-West Publishing, LLC.

Morgenstern, M. (2011). Sodomy and bestiality bans will stay in military law books. *The Blaze*. Retrieved from http://www.theblaze.com/stories/sodomy-bestiality-bans-will-stay-in-military-law-books/.

National Defense Authorization Act for Fiscal Year 2012, H1540CR.HSE, 112th Congress, 1st Session. (2011).

National Defense Authorization Act for Fiscal Year 2014, H3304CR.HSE, 113th Congress, 1st Session. (2013).

Peretti, P. O., & Rowan, M. (1982). Variables associated with male and female chronic zoophilia. *Social Behavior and Personality, 10*(1), 83–87.

Ressler, R. K., Burgess, A. W., Hartman, C. R., Douglas, J. E., & McCormack, A. (1986). Murderers who rape and mutilate. *Journal of Interpersonal Violence, 1*, 273–287.

Sandnabba, N. K., Santtila, P., Nordling, N., Beetz, A. M., & Alison, L. (2002). Characteristics of a sample of sadomasochistically-oriented males with recent experience of sexual contact with animals. *Deviant Behavior, 23*, 511–529.

United States Court of Appeals for the Third Circuit. (2008). *United States of America v. Robert J. Stevens*. Retrieved from http://randazza.wordpress.com/2008/07/20/united-states-v-stevens-protecting-animals-is-not-a-reason-to-amputate-part-of-the-first-amendment/.

Wiegand, P., Schmidt, V., & Kleiber, M. (1999). German shepherd dog is suspected of sexually abusing a child. *International Journal of Legal Medicine, 112,* 324–325.

Wilcox, D. T., Foss, C. M., & Donathy, M. L. (2005). A case study of a male sex offender with zoosexual interests and behaviours. *Journal of Sexual Aggression, 11*(3), 305–317.

Wisch, R. F. (2014). Overview of state bestiality laws. Retrieved from http://www.animallaw.info/topic/table-state-animal-sexual-assault-laws.

Statutes

10 USC § 925—Art. 125. Forcible sodomy; bestiality.

18 USC § 48—Animal Crush Videos

AZ ST § 13-1411

DE ST TI 11 § 775

GA ST § 16-6-6

ID ST § 18-6605

IA ST § 717C.1

IL ST CH 720 § 5/12-35

IN ST 35-46-3-14

MA ST 272 § 34

MCA 45-8-218

M.C.L.A. 750.158

MN ST 609.294

MO ST 566.111

MS ST § 97-29-59

OK ST T. 21 § 886

RI ST § 11-10-1

SC ST § 16-15-120

SD ST § 22-22-42

TN ST § 39-14-214

VA ST § 18.2-361

WA ST 16.52.205

Chapter 11

Understanding and Reducing Cruelty toward Roaming Dogs

Arnold Arluke and Kate Atema

Research on animal cruelty typically focuses on the victim's species (Vermeulen & Odendaal, 1993) or how it was abused (Arluke & Luke, 1997). While useful as a general way of categorizing cruelty, doing so overlooks significantly different expressions of cruelty in terms of the magnitude of harm suffered by victims and corresponding efforts to combat it. For example, mass animal cruelty, or the intentional abuse or neglect of large numbers of animals of the same species or breed that is not sanctioned by law, is rarely studied. And when scholars do examine mass cruelty, it is usually directed toward a relatively small number of animals over a short period of time, such as the "great" French cat massacre in the 1730s (Darnton, 1984) and the American sparrow "war" in the 1870s (Fine & Christoforides, 1991), as opposed to long-term indiscriminate abuse and neglect of scores of animals.

Of course, some scholars argue that large-scale industrial animal production and slaughter constitute mass cruelty almost by definition (Nibert, 2013), although saying so conflates legally sanctioned handling and use of animals with political views of such treatment. Nevertheless, even when state-sanctioned, the way that animals are treated and killed can sometimes violate legal or everyday definitions of animal cruelty held by external organizations, subgroups of natives, expatriates, or tourists.

This chapter examines one often uncounted or unacknowledged form of mass cruelty—that toward roaming dogs[1] on a global scale. Despite attempts by various animal welfare organizations to call attention to the mass abuse and neglect of roaming dogs, this form of cruelty has escaped the attention of researchers, and when studied at all, the focus has been on the ecology of stray dogs (Beck, 1973) and the effectiveness of veterinary interventions to reduce their population size or the incidence of diseases like rabies. Roaming dogs may occupy a liminal zone between domestic pets and wild animals. In terms of numbers, they are more at risk of abuse or neglect than are domestic dogs in Western societies (Flynn, 2008) and, compared to confined pets, "strays" are much less likely to be protected by anti-cruelty laws in countries that have such protection (Phillips, 2013). The result, especially in some less developed nations, is for the observer to see roaming dogs with protruding rib cages suggesting starvation, severe and extensive skin diseases, physical injuries, and disabilities, although certainly not all appear this way (Morters, 2014).

---

1. Rather than referring to these dogs as "stray" or "street," we prefer the term "roaming" because the former implies they are truly homeless, without any human interest in or responsibility for them. Anecdotal and survey data suggest otherwise for many of these populations of animals.

To explore the nature of cruelty toward roaming dogs as well as its sources and possible remedies, this chapter draws from 45 interviews with program managers who provide humane interventions for dogs, residents of towns with large roaming dog populations, and experts from public health, sociology, community mental health and development, human-animal studies, evaluation research, and applied ethnography, along with an extensive review of the literatures from these diverse fields.

Abusing and Neglecting Stray Dogs

Attitudes toward roaming dogs vary widely and fall on a continuum from abuse and neglect to tolerance and even kindness when comparing one community to another, or even within communities that are divided in their view of these animals. At the former extreme, strong dislike of roaming dogs, and a view of them as objects to be avoided or destroyed, can be normative—built into a local culture's beliefs and widely accepted by most citizens as expected behavior. For example, in The Bahamas, roaming dogs seen as nuisances are routinely stoned or even poisoned (Fielding, Mather, & Isaacs., 2005), in Samoa, 26% of those surveyed said that they believed that "harming or killing of dogs was good for Samoan society" (Farnworth, Blaszak, Hiby, & Waran, 2012), and on Navajo Native American reservations, some residents deliberately try to run over roaming dogs on the roads, in part due to livestock predation (Spicer, 2014), but also because these dogs are seen as pests to be eliminated by any means, much how some communities in Australia viewed Cane toads and crushed them with their cars (Lewis, 1989).

As a normative form of mass cruelty, harming roaming dogs can be state-sanctioned and expressed in different ways. For example, government-sanctioned rough handling or harming of dogs can occur when adults in official positions, such as municipal dogcatchers, forcibly capture struggling dogs with steel tongs or nets (Rowan, 2013), perceived by some residents as "cruel treatment" (Lee, 2013). Although netting was thought to be more humane than using steel tongs or wire nooses, their use left a lot to be desired because nets became covered in urine and feces, so people did not want to touch the dogs, and some kicked the dogs instead (Rowan, 2013). In Jamshedpur, India, one expert claims that if municipalities do anything in response to complaints about specific roaming dogs, it is usually to poison them (Less, 2014b). Dogs targeted for this mistreatment exhibit protracted suffering in full view of passersby, including children, who see poisoned dogs writhe in pain, convulse as the strychnine paralyzes their muscles, and finally suffocate to death (Hiby, 2010). In some Eastern European countries, the public may complain to local authorities about dog nuisances to no avail, but when a dog attack or fear of rabies is sensationalized in the media, it can spark government sanctioned culling of dogs through a number of means from euthanasia to poisoning or shooting (Lee, 2014b). Mass shooting of dogs has also been documented as a nuisance-dog management measure in Northern Canada (Hannah, 2014), Israel (Court, 2001), and Bosnia where, for instance, children in primary school can at one moment feed and play with dogs in the school garden and in the next moment watch hunters kill these dogs (Bojicic, 2014). Unfortunately the bounty system can create its own "economy" where those paid to shoot dogs come to expect routine work, until the budget is exhausted for that year, which leads to more dogs being harmed. As Hannah (2014) recalls, a Canadian public safety officer said to her,

> 'Yeah, the dog shooters are pissed because they haven't had any work.' So his concern was 'I have to provide work for these dog killers.' So it can create its own

economy that then the community tries to fill. You constantly hear stories of dog killers taking dogs off chains because they get paid to kill them, luring dogs off private property so they can get paid to kill them.

But support for these acts also comes from the passage of laws that legally define dogs as unwanted pests that should be destroyed. In Romania (Occupy for Animals, 2014), the recently passed "eradication program," also known as the "slaughter law," legalized the mass culling of dogs seen by many citizens there as a blight in need of elimination.

While not explicitly state-sanctioned, such broad governmental and cultural support for harming roaming dogs unofficially encourages citizen vigilantes to take matters into their own hands by poisoning or shooting specific dogs that have allegedly attacked and bitten residents. In Jamshedpur, India, if a dog is biting people in a neighborhood, local residents will band together to kill the dog. Lee (2014b) cites a case where a dog was beaten almost to death after biting three people and a case where a pet dog was poisoned because he allegedly bit someone.

Social conflict over roaming dogs can become an emotional flash point in the community involving politicians, animal welfare advocates and their opponents, bureaucrats, city administrators and everyday citizens who bitterly take one side of this issue, often with dogs being killed as a result of these heated and polarized exchanges (Plant, 2013). Ethnographic and journalistic reports from Europe, Asia, and the Caribbean describe situations where the tension over roaming dogs approximates the moral panics reported in highly publicized killings of other animals, like cats (Bulc, 2002) or wolves (Arluke & Bogdan, 2010). These emotionally-laden actions often occur when people are motivated by fear of widely exaggerated or non-existent threats (Goode & Ben-Yehuda, 2010). For example, in some Northern Canadian communities, panics ensue when people, especially children, are purportedly "mauled" to death by "packs" of dogs (CTV News, 2014), after which residents "just go shoot everything" (Hannah, 2014). Fearful residents of the affected towns then feel an urgent need to eradicate dogs, whatever the method and regardless of the efficacy of their approach. Scores of dogs may be shot and killed even if they are not dangerous to residents, while others die slow and torturous deaths from severe wounds, such as the media profiled dog "Trooper" (CBC News, 2013). Regarding a similar panic over an alleged mauling to death of a child in Romania, "they've never had so much media hysteria from morning until night" (Plant, 2013). Panic over roaming dogs, long after alleged attacks on humans, can evolve over time into culturally-normalized culling where an "open season" on killing dogs is legitimized and sanctioned by municipalities who provide bounties for these animals, producing locally-recognized jobs as dog cullers and ritualizing these killings as yearly or seasonal community events (Hannah, 2014).

The cultural trickling down of cruelty toward roaming dogs also leads to everyday roughness and abuse. More conventional animal abuse occurs when adolescents or others physically harm dogs by kicking, stoning, driving over, throwing, or burning them. About a third of the respondents studied in Samoa (Farnworth et al., 2012) said that over their lifetimes they were "aware" of people who harmed or killed dogs, most commonly because the dogs were too aggressive or sick, or considered to be a nuisance. In Australia, Aboriginal children have been observed to pick up puppies by one leg and kick them as footballs (Allen, 2014). And in The Bahamas, some people allegedly can be seen capturing and using roaming dogs as live bait to train fighting pit bulls (Fielding, 2014).

Some cruelty toward roaming dogs manifests as indifference or neglect rather than deliberate harm. The failure of owners to be responsible for street dogs rather than letting them roam freely puts these dogs at risk of frequent loss and trauma associated with roaming on city streets that can be heavily trafficked. For example, in Taiwan more than one-third of dog-owners studied report having lost a dog or had one escape because a significant number of dog owners either keep their dogs outside their homes or allow them to wander off and become lost (Hsu, Severinghaus, & Serpell, 2003). In addition, the longer dogs are allowed to wander the streets, the more likely they are to become lost, injured, or killed by traffic, poison, or another dog, or be abused, caught by animal control authorities, or mistakenly "rescued" by concerned tourists who think the dogs are truly unowned (Spicer, 2014). For example, one Chilean respondent noted the "harsh visual impact" of seeing dogs "that have been hit by cars. We have lots of dogs that we see hit and no one does anything, so they just die there. Some dogs have illnesses like tumors and it's obvious they are suffering."

Of course, perceptions of cruelty will depend on the perspective of those who observe roaming dogs. Long-time residents can grow accustomed to seeing underfed, sick, and injured dogs and over time become hardened as a defense mechanism which might make them increasingly incapable of or uninterested in recognizing or doing anything about the plight of roaming dogs. However, this sight will often disturb others, whether local or outside the community, who subscribe to different animal welfare standards. Tourists, in particular, can become emotionally upset when seeing roaming dogs that appear to be in wretched and unacceptable condition because they are underfed, have missing eyes and limbs or are otherwise physically disabled, and suffer from unsightly skin conditions. For example, in Oaxaca, Mexico, about half the tourists were concerned about dog welfare (Ruiz-Izaguiree & Ellers, 2012) and in The Bahamas, over 80% "felt sorry" for street animals perceived as in "not good" condition and almost half said they "felt sad" (Grennan & Fielding, 2008). And in another study, 34% of 1,200 tourists when asked about their experience seeing roaming dogs at different destinations gave "upset" as the first answer (Webster, 2013).

Explaining Cruelty toward Roaming Dogs

The perception that roaming dogs are dangerous or dirty nuisances can justify their abuse while their status as homeless can result in neglect.

Dogs as Dangers

Reports suggest that dog bites can make residents feel unsafe or insecure because they fear attacks, mauling, disease transmission, or even death, despite the fact that the vast majority of roaming dogs are friendly or submissive to humans and pose no threat (Majumder, Chatterjee & Bhadra, 2014). For example, in Guatemala, over 80% of respondents claimed their families were scared of dogs because of physical risks and possible disease transmission (Lunney, Jones, Stiles, & Toews, 2011). Bites or threats of attack allegedly occur, with some frequency, in communities with roaming dogs. For example, in Guatemala 17% of residents studied reported at least one dog bite in the prior two years (Lunney et al., 2011); in India, some towns estimate as many as 20,000 non-fatal dog bites a year; in Cambodia, 28% of respondents recalled having been bitten within the prior five years (Lunney et al., 2012); in The Bahamas, about a third of residents said that they had been physically threatened by dogs in the last five years (Fielding, 2007);

and in American Samoa, dog bites are the most frequently reported injury (Vargo, DePasquale, & Vargo, 2012).

Fear over being bitten or mauled is even greater when there is concern about rabies transmission (Bhanganada, Wilde, Sakolsataydom, & Pairoj, 1993; Kasempimolporn, Jitapunkul, & Sitprija, 1993; Leney & Remfry, 2000; Savvides, 2013a; Srinivasan, 2013; Srinivasan & Nagaraj, 2007), especially when there is an outbreak as opposed to having a long-standing rabies concern (Cleaveland, 2014; Morters, 2014), or when neighbors or relatives die from rabies or have to seek treatment for it (Bardosh, Sambo, Sikana, Hampson, & Welburn, 2014); conversely, rabies vaccination has been shown to mitigate this fear (Cleaveland, Kaare, Knobel, & Laurenson, 2006). Fear of a rabies outbreak can swell into collective panic over roaming dogs, leading to violent and deadly attacks by many residents against large numbers of dogs whether or not they are rabid. For example, a 2008 deadly epidemic of rabies in Bali sent local residents to the hospital and placed a death warrant on the heads of the remaining canine population. Daily they were shot, beaten, and poisoned indiscriminately (nomadajourneys.com, 2013). And in 2010, panic continued in Bali as the human rabies death toll mounted to 65 from the prior two years, leading to the formation of a 25-man team that indiscriminately killed dogs with strychnine darts (Maynard, 2010).

When considered to be dangerous, roaming dogs can threaten people and inhibit their walking, biking, and jogging (Kneckerman, et al., 2009; Seeley, 2010), in turn justifying the harsh treatment or destruction of these dogs. For example, in Sri Lanka, roaming and sometimes domestic dogs have been reported to deter pedestrians, especially children, the elderly, and the weak (Dayaratne, 2011). In small villages in Calgary, Canada, elders sometimes do not leave their homes because they fear street dogs (Kutz, 2014). Among the Australian Aboriginals, children may fear roaming dogs, especially when in packs, to the point where children walk in groups to protect themselves from threatening dogs (Allen, 2014). In an Arizona community, packs of up to 15 Chihuahuas allegedly have chased children, fearing that they will be bitten, as they walked to school (ABC news, 2014). Indeed, studies report that urban children in general fear roaming dogs (Nikitina-Den Besten, 2008), even in the absence of rabies concern.

Adults, in general, also report fearing roaming dogs. In a distressed section of Houston, roaming dogs were viewed as an environmental threat to public safety that reduced walkability in that area of the city (Solitaire, Andress, Lewis, Crossley, & Crossley, 2012), as in Sparks, Texas, where 81% of sampled residents claimed that dogs sometimes prevented them from walking outdoors (Poss & Bader, 2007). There are also anecdotal reports of people being warned not to walk down certain streets in cities populated with roaming dogs, such as Bangkok, Thailand (Savvides, 2013b) or on the streets of Native American reservations where fear of bites makes people feel like they cannot go out and do certain things or as paraphrased by one anthropologist, "Gee I'd like to walk down that certain trail or that certain place, but I can't because of the bites" (Spicer, 2014).

Dogs as Nuisances

Nuisance and irritation caused by roaming dogs can also lead to their victimization by local residents and governments. Large and uncontrolled roaming dog populations contribute to residents' perceptions of their cities as disorderly, messy, and decaying due to continuous or episodic barking, especially at night, harassment and stalking of pedestrians and bikers, messiness from spreading rubbish, knocking over trash bins, and scavenging for food, causing road accidents, fouling public places with feces, unsightliness and, as noted above, disease transmission and biting (Lee, 2014a; Leney & Remfry, 2000; Srinivasan, 2013). For example, in Samoa, almost 80% of respondents cited street dogs as a nuisance (Farnworth et al., 2012) and in The Bahamas, there is substantial residential irritation with barking especially at night, with it being the most commonly reported nuisance out of a list of 29 human and animal annoyances (Fielding, 2008b), followed closely by dogs roaming on property and spilled garbage by roaming dogs (Fielding, 1999). And dog-related nuisances can be exacerbated when unwelcomed roaming dogs bring these problems inside homes, dirtying houses and bothering residents.

Friction often develops between neighbors over the disorder and mess allegedly caused by roaming dogs, leading to the poisoning or other harm of a neighbor's dog. For example, "rez dogs" on some Native American reservations can contribute to tension between neighbors when people resent someone's dog for causing trouble, defecating in their yards, or attacking their dogs (Spicer, 2014). There are also anecdotal reports of neighbors disagreeing over whether roaming dogs should be fed. In India (Lee, 2014b) and in Thailand (Savvides, 2014) residents who dislike the presence of roaming dogs will blame neighbors or others who feed them for their continued presence and the problems they allegedly cause on streets or in markets, while in Bosnia (Bojicic, 2014), individuals who try to feed roaming dogs may stop doing it openly after being harshly criticized by neighbors who dislike these dogs and do not want them around. Bojicic (2014) cites a case of an elderly woman with several puppies who concealed her affection and caring for these dogs to avoid criticism from neighbors.

> She had a little stick. She was guiding these little puppies like she has sheep, but she was so gently touching them. She couldn't properly touch the dogs because someone might see her and shout at her 'What are you doing?' It's so frustrating for me because I saw her smiling in secret because she was feeding them and she loved them.

And among the First Nation communities of Canada, people who try to bathe their dogs or even let them inside their homes are allegedly publicly ridiculed with comments like "Why would you bother? What are you doing? That's gross. That's dirty. How could you do that?" (Hannah, 2014).

Concern over losing tourist business because of roaming dog nuisances can also lead to their mistreatment through inhumane lethal methods of control (Meltzer & Rupprecht, 1998). For example, in Bali, the local government tried to remove roaming dogs so tourists could enjoy its magnificent beaches without the distressing experience of seeing sick and injured dogs who might beg and follow them (Loeffler, 2014). In Samoa, concern about losing tourist trade prompted a Parliament member to propose to kill stray dogs and export them as dog meat (Samoa Observer, 2013). And recently in Sochi, Russian officials justified the mass extermination of roaming dogs by claiming that they compromised the safety of certain Olympic events and to ensure that tourists would not be bothered or bitten by these "pests" (Luciew, 2014; Vasilyeva, 2014).

Those who see roaming dogs as nuisances, let alone dangers, will often be disinterested in them or treat them roughly, which can create a self-fulfilling prophecy by making dogs less sociable, more scared, and, therefore, more threatening. In other words, the resulting unruly, if not aggressive, behavior of dogs reinforces whatever aversion or hatred already exists toward them, in turn preventing people from seeing dogs as capable of acting in friendly and solicitous ways and justifying their disregard and mistreatment (Lee, 2014b). These untoward instances become "anti-teaching moments" where instead of people learning empathy, they become numb to hurting dogs with impunity because no one owns them, they are in plentiful supply, and adult authority figures, such as teachers, who stand by do not use the moment to teach alternative ways of interacting with dogs (Fielding, 2014). It is unsurprising, therefore, that in more tolerant communities there are, reportedly, friendlier dogs, while in less tolerant communities, unfriendly ones are more common. For example, on the Samoan Islands (American and Independent) people throw rocks at packs of dogs and as a consequence the dogs remain unsocialized and appear to be aggressive, which justifies in residents' minds the practice of abusing them (Clifford, 2013).

Dogs as Homeless

In some locations, individuals or families may be attached to dogs and consider them as their own, but interact differently with them than is the norm in most North American or Western European contexts. Despite (or even because of) their connection to dogs, many of these residents allow their dogs to roam the streets, where they can be injured, abused, or killed (Bojicic, 2014, Fielding, 2014, Hsu et al., 2003, Ortolani, Vernooij, & Coppinger, 2009). It may also be the norm to allow pet dogs to go without basic veterinary care, or even proper food, water, and shelter.

One major barrier to providing adequate guardianship is poverty (Omemo, 2011). For example, in parts of Kenya, dog keeping is common but residents cannot meet the basic needs of these animals (Kitala et al., 2001), forcing owners to allow their dogs to forage for food since they cannot be properly fed at home (Patronek, Beck, & Glickman, 1997). And in Dominica (Alie, Witkind, Fielding, Maldonado, & Galindo, 2007) many of what are called "passive" owners cannot afford to take their pets for veterinary care when they think they are sick, let alone for preventive care that almost no one can afford or consider. Poverty also prevents people with loose canine affiliations from reclaiming their missing dogs from animal control. As observed in Mexico (de la Torre, 2014), most people cannot afford to pay animal control fines, have no way of getting to distant animal control offices, and cannot use public transportation or taxis since dogs are not permitted inside these vehicles.

Local beliefs can further erode responsible pet ownership in these communities. In some cultures dogs are seen as able to fend for themselves, such as the Australian Aboriginals who see dogs as direct descents of the wild dingo (Allen, 2014). Allen (2014) notes,

> They still see the dogs as an independent thing like dingoes—still a mate, a companion, but able to look after themselves. So the dog is more like a buddy that can feed itself and you know that that's not necessarily the case.

This belief justifies the practice of letting them freely roam during the daytime, since it is assumed they can find enough food on their own. In other cultures, there can be deeply held beliefs about the independence and freedom of dogs that also justify the practice of allowing them to roam, as is common in some Mexican communities (de la Torre, 2014).

Gender also influences whether local residents take responsibility for dogs considered theirs. With gender, interest in and responsibility for dogs can vary within one family. In some countries, it is common that one person—often a male in the family—might feel some connection to a dog, while others in the family do not because of the gendered nature of human-dog relationships in these societies (Al-Fayez, Awadalla, Templer, & Arikawa, 2003; Hsu et al., 2003; Knobel et al., 2008; Morris, 1998), such as in The Bahamas (Fielding, 2014) or Samoa (Farnworth et al., 2012) where almost three quarters of dog owners are male. Women in undeveloped or developing nations may have more negative views of dogs (Serpell, 2014) because they and their children face disproportionate danger from roaming dogs (Boyd et al., 2004; Georges & Adesiyun, 2008; Reece & Chawla, 2006). And gender expectations of dogs can make owners resistant to cooperating with humane interventions, as happens among Romanian men who disagree with the idea of neutering male dogs (Cocia & Rusu, 2010) or Mexicans who believe that male dogs should not be neutered (de la Torre, 2014), although some studies provide contrary findings (Blackshaw & Day, 1994; Fielding, Samuels, & Mather, 2002).

Reversing Cruelty toward Roaming Dogs

In communities with significant roaming dog populations, effective humane interventions usually seek to improve the welfare and/or the guardianship of roaming dogs, In turn these interventions may change how residents in targeted communities regard and interact with dogs, reducing their abuse and neglect over time. Although these interventions take a variety of forms, we first focus on veterinary interventions impacting dogs themselves, such as sterilization, vaccination, and preventive care to select animals, that are only one aspect of a comprehensive community plan to effectively manage dogs.

Veterinary Interventions

Prior to veterinary interventions, residents may perceive roaming dogs as "ugly" because they have skin conditions including mange and ringworm, are malnourished and often coated in a layer of solid filth, are semi-furred, semi-naked, dusty and dirty with skin like cracked cement, while others constantly scratch from fleas and worms, limp around on burned paw pads, or have hip fractures, dislocations and other mobility problems (Savvides, 2013b). Effective veterinary intervention programs are presumed to positively change human-dog relationships by making dogs more appealing as co-interactants, since they are healthier looking, less aggressive, and no longer thought of as disease-carrying, and because they can live longer and perhaps provide more time for humans with whom they interact to develop stronger bonds with them (Rowan, 2013). Among owned dogs, these improvements in the appearance and behavior of dogs may give them higher status or greater social value, and for unowned dogs, a healthier appearance may make them appear less threatening, so they will less likely be targeted for abuse. After providing these veterinary interventions, humane workers in these communities anecdotally report residents being more "positive" about having roaming dogs in their neighborhoods (Subasinghe, 2014).

For example, sterilization can affect the appearance of dogs, since dogs may appear healthier without the stress of pregnancy and lactation that can cause them to be more susceptible to a wide variety of maladies, including skin problems (Rowan, 2013). Experts report that residents are more likely to touch, interact with, and perhaps even establish relationships with dogs that live longer on the streets and that look healthier because they are well-fed and do not have mange. Dog behavior may also change as methods of capture, like steel tongs, wire nooses, and even netting, are replaced by gentle methods that do not stress dogs and confer respect for individual animals, who then show increased willingness to be friendly around humans (Lee, 2014a). Additionally, it is hoped that willingness to touch and bring dogs into homes might increase as topical anti-parasite methods are more widely used by residents who keep their dogs outside because they do not want to bring fleas and ticks inside (Rowan, 2013).

Studies have documented these positive changes in dogs and their potential to shift human attitudes. Veterinary interventions can lengthen the lives of street dogs; neutered roaming dogs in The Bahamas had a higher average age than intact dogs (Plumridge, Fielding, & Bizzell, 2007), allowing for deeper human-animal bonds to form since dogs survive longer and perhaps become less aggressive and healthier. In Colombo, Sri Lanka, sterilized and vaccinated dogs increased their body mass with some becoming quite obese (ICAM, 2014), due to increased feeding by people who perceived these dogs as "safe" (Obeyesekere, 2014). That such interventions can foster more positive perceptions of roaming dogs, and presumably more humane interaction with them, is also supported by research in Sri Lanka where conducting a mass rabies vaccination program improved non-dog owners' perception of roaming dogs, such that respondents reported to "like" them more (Sankey, Hasler, & Hiby, 2012). There are similar anecdotal reports with roaming dogs among the Australian Aboriginals (Allan, 2014; Archinal, 2014).

Veterinary interventions will also likely decrease residents' perception of roaming dogs as nuisances. Some dog-related irritants can be addressed through interventions by reducing the number of sick or injured dogs on the street, which reduces the volume or magnitude of the perceived nuisance. For example, sterilization of roaming dogs should lessen the most common complaints about dogs. Dogs are often particularly noisy during mating behavior, when males are fighting over females in heat; sterilizing dogs curbs some of these mating behaviors and should significantly decrease the level of barking and howling over time.

Veterinary interventions may also increase residents' sense of safety and security in communities with roaming dogs, potentially reducing their abuse or destruction. While vaccinating against rabies should allay the public's fear of dog bites (Cleaveland et al., 2006), sterilizing dogs should reduce the number of dog bites by decreasing the maternal protective behavior of street dogs, since many bites involve females protecting their pups. For example, in Jaipur, India (Reece, Chawia, & Hiby, 2013), a roaming dog sterilization program lead to a significant decline in the number of animal bites after 2003. The Jaipur program reduced the number of dog bites treated in emergency hospital rooms from 700 per 100,000 to 200 per 100,000 in the past 15 years, compared to 100 per 100,000 in the United States (Rowan, 2013). In Ahmedabad, India, the number of dog bites was lower and more stable during a sterilization project in 2006, but when the project stopped after 2006, the number of dog bites increased and the seasonal fluctuations were greater (Lee, 2014b). That such interventions can reduce residents' fear of dogs was very apparent when one program in Sri Lanka stopped its anti-rabies vaccination after five years; when they stopped vaccinating, a lot of people came to them, allegedly saying, "Please come and vaccinate the dogs on my street. For the last five years we had no fear of them being on the street because we knew they were vaccinated and sterilized" (Subasinghe, 2014). Without a vaccination program, these residents are thinking of "removing" the dogs in their community (Subasinghe, 2014).

Some interventions may reduce neglect of unowned dogs by allowing residents to take on increased responsibility for roaming dogs that might lead to greater tolerance if not attachment to them. For example, rather than releasing roaming dogs into the community after sterilization, vaccination, and rabies control, one program in Colombo, Sri Lanka, releases the dogs to a community caretaker who takes responsibility for the animal for a few days until it is better (Obeyesekere, 2014). Anecdotal evidence suggests that people asked to care for dogs after veterinary interventions may become more attached to particular roaming dogs and more inclined to seek veterinary care if it is available.

Veterinary interventions might also reduce the neglect of owned dogs. For example, among First Nations people in Canada, residents "reached out" more to veterinarians when their dogs become sick or injured after such services were made available and staff members reinforced residents' compassion, caring, and pride for their dogs by "validating" these feelings when visiting the veterinarian (Hannah, 2014). Hannah claims, "it's really important we validate those people. 'Oh my God, your dog looks great. Oh my God it's so great to see him. Have you had any issues?' And people shine when you remember their dog and you remember them, you can see there is pride" (Hannah, 2014). And among the Australian Aboriginals, residents were more inclined to bring dogs in need of medical treatment to visiting veterinarians after interventions in the community improved the appearance of these animals (Allen, 2014). Also, when free or low-cost veterinary services are provided, veterinary staff can educate owners about what constitutes responsible pet ownership through deliberate teaching or unintentional role modeling.

Educational Interventions

Educational interventions can also challenge taken-for-granted ways of thinking about and acting toward roaming dogs. Anecdotal reports illustrate how role modeling can help people to interact kindlier and gentler with dogs seen as "scary" or unfriendly. For example, in India, Bhutan, and the Philippines, several humane programs that primarily vaccinate sterilize dogs are also designed to give street dogs a much better life by improving the community's tolerance of them through hands-on education (Lee, 2013, 2014a). These interventions engage local residents by allowing them to watch what staff members do and copy how they interact with dogs. A dog handling specialist walks the streets of designated areas to interact with every dog encountered to show residents how they should behave with dogs and to gain the animals' trust and cooperation so they can be more easily caught for sterilization or vaccination. The handler and team members greet, call, feed, pet, and talk to street dogs to assess their friendliness and sociability. Residents not only see these behaviors for the first time—like gentle touching of a dog—but also see for the first time that dogs respond in friendly ways to such gestures by nuzzling, licking, tail wagging, and moving closer to the person, as the dog becomes more responsive to the handler.

A different kind of educational intervention—the introduction and diffusion of new ideas or ways to behave—happens at the level of organizations interacting with their surrounding communities, such that the mere presence of a humane organization in a community can influence how local residents think about and treat roaming dogs in more tolerant and caring ways. Individuals who were reluctant to care for these dogs for fear of criticism or because they had no interest in caring for them might be more inclined to do so in a supportive atmosphere created by these organizations. For example, in Sri Lanka, humane organizations can increase residents' concern for roaming dogs by serving as a "lifeline" (Obeyesekere, 2014). Obeyesekere reports that after their programs become known and accepted by residents in a community, people will ask a program officer to help a sick or injured dog on the street out of concern for its welfare even though the dog is unowned. In her words, "Even if they can't afford it, they'll ask 'Can someone pay for it? I'll bring the dog to you.' There is more concern and looking after of street dogs, probably because we got involved there" (Obeyesekere, 2014). Anecdotal reports such as these suggest that humane organizational involvement in the community can create a halo or positive chilling effect by letting residents know that veterinary care can be provided to dogs in need and that reporting such dogs to humane organizations is an acceptable way to act.

As we have seen, neglect of and cruelty toward roaming dogs can assume a wide variety of forms, but nearly all are related to the perception of the dog as a nuisance or problem. If humane means address these problems, community members often shift their perceptions of the dogs as outcast groups, in turn reducing outright cruelty and actively seeking positive solutions. However, attempts to change the perception of dogs will not likely produce normative change when outsiders to the community initiate these interventions. When humane interventions can be driven and maintained by locals, systematic cruelty to animals and its normative support may, over time, be reduced permanently.

References

ABC news. (2014). Retrieved from http://abcnews.go.com/blogs/headlines/2014/02/chihuahuas-rampage-in-arizona/. February 18th.

Al-Fayez, G., Awadalla, A., Templer, D., & Arikawa, H. (2003). Companion animal attitude and its family pattern in Kuwait. *Society & Animals, 11*, 17–28.

Alie, K., Witkind, D., Fielding, W., Maldonado, J., & Galindo, F. (2007). Attitudes toward dogs and other "pets" in Roseau, Dominica. *Anthrozoos 20*, 143–154.

Arluke, A., & Bogdan, R. (2010). *Beauty and the beast.* Syracuse: Syracuse University Press.

Arluke, A., & Luke, C. (1997). Physical cruelty toward animals in Massachusetts, 1975–1996. *Society & Animals, 5*, 195–204.

Bardosh, K., Sambo, M., Sikana, L., Hampson, K., & Welburn, S. (2014). Eliminating rabies in Tanzania? Local understandings and responses to mass dog vaccination in Kilmbero and Ulanga districts. *PLOS Neglected Tropical Diseases, 8*, e2935.

Beck, A. (1973). *The ecology of stray dogs: A study of free-ranging urban animals.* West Lafayette, IN: Purdue University Press.

Bhanganada, K., Wilde, H., Sakolsataydorn, P., & Pairoj, O. (1993). Dog bite injuries at a Bangkok teaching hospital. *Acta Tropica, 55*, 249–255.

Blackshaw, J., & Day, C. (1994). Attitudes of dog owners to neutering pets: Demographic data and effects of owner attitudes. *Australian Veterinary Journal, 71*, 113–116.

Boyd, C. M., Fotheringham, B., Litchfield, C., McBryde, I., Metzer, J. C., Scanlon, P., Somers, R., & Winefield, A. (2004). Fear of dogs in a community sample: Effects of age, gender, and prior experience of canine aggression. *Anthrozöos, 17*, 146–166.

Bulc, G. (2002). Kill the cat killers: Moral panic and juvenile crime in Slovenia. *Journal of Communication Inquiry, 26*, 300–325.

CBC News. (2013). "Rescue groups call for ban on First Nation dog culls." Retrieved April 1, 2013 from http://www.cbc.ca/news/canada/manitoba/rescue-groups-call-for-ban-on-first-nation-dog-culls-1.1326064cdc.gov/healthy/pets/.

Cleaveland, S., Kaare, M., Knobel, D., & Laurenson, M. (2006). Canine vaccination-providing broader benefits for disease control. *Veterinary Microbiology, 117*, 43–50.

Clifford, E. (2013). Animal balance 2013 report. Retrieved from https://www.google.com/webhp?hl=en&tab=mw&gws_rd=ssl#hl=en&q=animalbalance.net%2Fcore-programs.

Cocia, R., & Rusu, A. (2010). Attitudes of Romanian pet caretakers towards sterilization of their animals: Gender conflict over male, but not female, companion animals. *Anthrozoos, 23*, 185–191.

Court, D. (2001). Unity and conflict in an Israeli village. *Contemporary Jewry, 22*, 1–17.

CTVnews. (2014). Stray dog solution sought after Manitoba girl fatally mauled. Retrieved April 18, 2014, from http://www.ctvnews.ca/canada/stray-dog-solution-sought-after-manitoba-girl-fatally-mauled-1.1781791.

Darnton. R. (1984). *The great cat massacre and other episodes in French cultural history.* New York: Vintage Books.

Dayaratne, R. (2011). Towards transforming Colombo to a "walkable" city: Policies and strategies. *Built-Environment Sri Lanka, 9/10(1–2)*, 2–13.

Farnworth, M., Blaszak, K., Hiby, E., & Waran, N. (2012). Incidence of dog bites and public attitudes toward dog care and management in Samoa. *Animal Welfare, 20*, 477–486.

Fielding, W. (1999). Perceptions of owned and unowned animals: A case study from New Providence. *Bahamas Journal of Science, 6*, 17–22.

Fielding, W. (2007). Knowledge of the welfare of nonhuman animals and prevalence of dog care practices in New Providence, The Bahamas. *Journal of Applied Animal Welfare Science, 10*, 153–168.

Fielding, W. (2008a). Attitudes and actions of pet caregivers in New Providence, the Bahamas, in the context of those of their American counterparts. *Anthrozoos, 21*, 351–361.

Fielding, W. (2008b). Dogs: A continuing and common neighborhood nuisance of New Providence, the Bahamas. *Society & Animals, 16*, 61–73.

Fielding, W., & Mather, J. (2000). Stray dogs in an island community: A case study from New Providence, the Bahamas. *Journal of Applied Animal Welfare Science, 3*, 305–319.

Fielding, W., Mather, J., & Isaacs, M. (2005). *Potcakes: Dog ownership in New Providence, The Bahamas.* West Lafayette: IN: Purdue University Press.

Fielding, W., Samuels, D., & Mather, J. (2002). Attitudes and actions of WestIndian dog owners towards neutering their animals: A gender issue? *Anthrozöos 15*, 206–226.

Fine, G. A., & Christoforides, L. (1991). Dirty birds, filthy immigrants, and the English sparrow war: Metaphorical linkage in constructing social problems. *Symbolic Interaction, 14*, 375–393.

Flynn, C. (2008). A sociological analysis of animal abuse. In Ascione, F. (Ed.) *The international handbook of animal abuse and cruelty: Theory, research, and application*, (pp. 155–174). West Lafayette, IN: Purdue University Press.

Georges, K., & Adesiyun, A. (2008). An investigation into the prevalence of dog bites to primary school children in Trinidad. *BMC Public Health, 8*, 85.

Goode, E., & Ben-Yehuda, N..(2010). *Moral panics: The social construction of deviance.* Chichester, West Sussex: Wiley-Blackwell.

Grennan, E., & Fielding, W. (2008, April). Tourists' reactions to non-human animals: Implications for tourist-animal research in the Caribbean. Report to the Pegasus Foundation. Concord, New Hampshire. Retrieved from http://www.hsi.org/assets/pdfs/2008_caribbean_animalwelfare_conference/caribbean_tourism_survey_report.pdf.

Hiby, E. (2010, March 11). Bali dog cull appeal [video file]. YouTube. Retrieved from https://www.youtube.com/watch?v=8hH0ra5pdw4.

Hsu, Y., Severinghaus, L., & Serpell, J. (2003). Dog keeping in Taiwan: Its contributions to the problem of free-roaming dogs. *Journal of Applied Animal Welfare Science, 6*, 1–23.

ICAM. (2014, January). Coalition indicators project. Unpublished draft report.

Kasempimolporn, S., Jitapunkul, S., & Sitprija, V. (2008). Moving towards the elimination of rabies in Thailand. *Journal of the Medical Association of Thailand, 91,* 433–437.

Kitala, P., McDermott, J., Kyule, M., Gathuma, J., Perry, B., & A. Wandeler. (2001). Dog ecology and demography information to support the planning of rabies control in Machakos District, Kenya. *Acta Tropica, 78,* 217–230.

Kneckerman, K., Lovasi, G., Davies, S., Purciel, M., Quinn, J., Feder, E., & Rundle, A. (2009). Disparities in urban neighborhood conditions: Evidence from GIS measures and field observation in New York City. *Journal of Public Health Policy, 30,* 264–285.

Knobel, D., Laurenson, K.M., Kazwala, R.R., Boden, L.I., & Cleaveland, S. (2008). A cross-sectional study of factors associated with dog ownership in Tanzania, *BMC Veterinary Research, 4,* 5.

Lee, J. (2013, July 31). Jamshedpur communities dog population & rabies management project. Unpublished report to Humane Society International.

Leney, J., & Remfry, J. (2000). Dog population management. In Macpherson, C., Meslin, F., & Wandeler, A. (Eds.) *Dogs, zoonoses and public health,* (pp. 299–332). New York: CABI Publishing.

Lewis, S. (1989). *Cane toads: An unnatural history.* New York: Dolphin/Doubleday.

Luciew, J. (2014). Death comes for stray dogs of Sochi: Dark side of Winter Olympics 2014, Retrieved June 15, 2015, from http://www.pennlive.com/olympics/index.ssf/2014/02/ death_comes_for_the_stray_dogs.html.

Lunney, M, Fevre, S., Stiles, E., Ly, S., San, S., & Vong, S. (2012). Knowledge, attitudes and practices of rabies prevention and dog bite injuries in urban and peri-urban provinces in Cambodia, 2009. *International Health, 4,* 4–9.

Lunney, M., Jones, A., Stiles, E., & Toews, D. (2011). Assessing human-dog conflicts in Todos Santos, Guatemala: Bite incidences and public perception. *Preventive Veterinary Medicine, 102,* 315–320.

Majumder, S., Chatterjee, A. & Bhadra, A. (2014). A dog's day with humans—Time activity budget of free-ranging dogs in India. *Current Science, 106,* 874-878.

Maynard, R. (2010, July 4). Bali targets stray dogs as 65 people die from rabies *The Independent.* Retrieved from http://www.independent.co.uk/news/world/australasia/bali-targets-stray-dogs-as-65-people-die-from-rabies-2017906.html.

Meltzer, M., & Rupprecht, C. (1998). A review of the economics of the prevention and control of rabies: Part 2: Rabies in dogs, livestock and wildlife. *PharmacoEconomics, 14,* 481–498.

Morris, B. (1998). *The power of animals: An ethnography.* Oxford: Berg.

Nibert, D. (2013). *Animal oppression and human violence: Domesecration, capitalism, and global conflict.* New York: Columbia University Press.

Nikitina-Den Besten, O. (2008). Cars, dogs and mean people: Environmental fears and dislikes of children in Berlin and Paris. In K. Adelhof, B. Glock, J. Lossau, & M. Schulz (Eds.). *Urban trends in Berlin and Amsterdam,* (pp. 116–125). Berliner Geographische Arbeiten, Nomada Journeys. (2013). Retrieved June 15, 2015, from nomada journeys.com.

Occupy for Animals. (2014). *The invisible rape of Europe. The psychological, financial, political, human, and legal aspects of the Romanian stray animals eradication program.* Retrieved from http://theinvisiblerapeofeurope.weebly.com/about.html.

Omemo, P. (2011). Responsible dog ownership options. Unpublished report presented at the FAO/WSPA/ICT meeting on dog population management, Banna, Italy, March 14–19.

Ortolani, A., Vernooij, H., & Coppinger, R. (2009). Ethiopian village dogs: Behavioural responses to a stranger's approach. *Applied Animal Behaviour Science, 119,* 210–218.

Patronek, G., Beck, A., & Glickman, L. (1997). Dynamics of dog and cat population in a community. *Journal of the American Veterinary Medical Association, 210,* 637–642.

Phillips, C. (2013). Introduction. In *Animal abuse: Helping animals and people* (pp. xv–xvi) Wallingford, Oxfordshire, U.K.: CABI Publishing.

Plumridge, S., Fielding, W., & Bizzell, P. (2007). A description of the clients (humans and animals) of a "free" neutering programme in New Providence, the Bahamas. Unpublished report submitted to Proud Paws.

Poss, J., & Bader, J. (2007). Attitudes toward companion animals among Hispanic residents of a Texas border community. *Journal of Applied Animal Welfare Science, 10,* 243–253.

Reece, J., & Chawla, S. (2006). Control of rabies in Jaipur, India, by the sterilization and vaccination of neighbourhood dogs. *Veterinary Record, 159,* 379–383.

Reece, J., Chawia, S., & Hiby, H. (2013). Decline in human dog-bite cases during a street dog sterilization programme in Jaipur, India. *Veterinary Record, 172*(18), 473.

Ruiz-Izaguiree, E. & Eilers, C. (2012). Perceptions of village dogs by villagers and tourists in the coastal region of rural Oaxaca, Mexico. *Anthrozoos, 25,* 75–91.

Samoa Observer. (2013, June 12). Stray dogs costing tourism millions. Retrieved from http:// samoaobserver.ws/home/headlines/5351-stray-dogs-costing-tourism-millions.

Sankey, C., Hasler, B., & Hiby, E. (2012, September 5). Change in public perception of roaming dogs in Colombo City. Paper presented at 1st International Conference on Dog Population Management. York, England.

Savvides, N. (2013a). Living with dogs: Alternative animal practices in Bangkok, Thailand. *Animal Studies Journal, 2,* 28–50.

Savvides, N. (2013b). Speaking for dogs: The role of dog biographies in improving canine welfare in Bangkok, Thailand. In DeMello, M. (Ed.) *Speaking for animals: Animal autobiographical writing,* (pp. 231–244). New York: Routledge.

Seeley, E. (2010). Comparing walkability of ethnically diverse, Low-income neighborhoods of Sacramento, California. (Dissertation). University of California, Davis.

Serpell, J. (2011). Human-dog relationships worldwide. Unpublished report presented at the FAO/WSPA/ICT dog population management meeting, Banna, Italy, March 14–19.

Solitare, L., Andress, L., Lewis, C. A., Crossley, D., & Crossley, J. B. (2012). A health impact assessment of transit-oriented development at the Quitman light rail station in Houston, Texas.Retrieved from http://www.pewtrusts.org/~/media/Assets/2012/06/6/HoustonTODHIAFinalReport.Pdf.

Srinivasan, K. (2013). The biopolitics of animal being and welfare: Dog control and care in the UK and India. *Transactions of the Institute of British Geographers, 38,* 106–119.

Srinivasan, K., & Nagaraj, V. (2007). Deconstructing the human gaze: Stray dogs, indifferent governance and prejudiced reactions. *Economic and Political Weekly, 42,* 1085–1086.

Vargo, D., DePasquale, J., & Vargo, A. (2012). Incidence of dog bite injuries in American Samoa and their impact on society. *Hawai'I Journal of Medicine & Public Health, 71,* 6–12.

Vasilyeva, N. (2014). Sochi city hall orders killing of stray dogs. *Huffington Post.* Retrieved February 3, 2014, from http://www.huffingtonpost.com/2014/02/03/sochi-stray-dogs-killing-city-hall-olympics_n_4717305.html?utm_hp_ref=tw.

Vermeulen, H., & Odendaal, J. (1993). Proposed typology of companion animal abuse. *Anthrozoos, 6,* 248–257.

Webster, D. (2013). The economic impact of stray cats and dogs at tourist destinations on the tourism industry. CANDi International. Retrieved from http://www.candiinternational.org/newsevents/229-the-economic-impact-of-stray-cats-and-dogs-at-tourist-destinations-on-the-tourism-industry.

Personal Communication

Allen, J. (2014). Telephone interview with first author. February 6th.

Archinal, M. (2014).Telephone interview with first author. January 28th.

Bojicic, E. (2014). Face-to-face interview with first author. February, 28th.

Cleaveland, S. (2014). Telephone interview with first author. June, 26.

de la Torre, J. (2014). Telephone interview with first author. February 4, 2014.

Fielding, W. (2014). Telephone interview with first author. January 10.

Hannah, J. (2014). Telephone interview with first author. April 25.

Kutz, S. (2014). Telephone interview with first author. April 3.

Lee, J. (2014a). Telephone interview with first author. January 17.

Lee, J. (2014b). Email correspondence with first author. February 4.

Loeffler, K. (2014). Face-to-face interview with first author. January 31.

Morters, M. (2014). Telephone interview with first author. June 10.

Obeyesekere, N. (2014). Telephone interview with first author. January 20.

Plant, M. (2013). Telephone interview with first author. December, 23.

Rowan, A. (2013). Telephone interview with first author. December 27.

Savvides, N. (2014). Telephone interview with author. June 5.

Serpell, J. (2014). Telephone interview with first author. April 16.

Spicer, P. (2014). Telephone interview with first author. April 14.

Subasinghe, D. (2014). Telephone interview with first author. January 20.

Section III
Animal Cruelty—Antecedents and Future Behavior

Chapter 12

Animal Cruelty and Delinquency, Criminality, and Youth Violence

Nik Taylor and Tania Signal

Nearly five decades ago, Margaret Mead (1964, p. 21) stated, "The worst thing that can happen to a child is for him [sic] to harm an animal and get away with it. Animal cruelty kills respect for life." In the intervening years, the concept of the "Link" (i.e., that engagement in deliberate harm of animals is related in some manner to propensity for violence more generally) has been explored from a number of perspectives including (but not limited to) criminology, psychology, sociology, and social work (see HSUS, 2007). Cruelty to animals (CTA) is recognized across these disciplines as being of major concern not only for the health and welfare of the animal victim (Benetato, Reisman, & McCobb, 2011; Taylor & Signal, 2008), but also for the psychological, physical and social well-being of the perpetrator (e.g., Currie, 2006), and for society generally (Hensley, Tallichet, & Dutkiewicz, 2009; McPhedran, 2009). Throughout this chapter, we bear all three groups in mind as we present an overview of the main research in the area of animal cruelty and its links to other delinquency and criminality.

Four Main Areas of Animal-Human Research

In 2004, Becker and French (p. 401) argued that there were four main areas of research into human-animal violence links, namely:

(1) Animal abuse as part of the continuum of abuse within the family (see Chapter 13 in the current volume for a thorough review);

(2) Animal abuse as an indicator of child abuse;

(3) The therapeutic potential of animals in child development and within post-abuse work; and

(4) Animal abuse perpetrated by children who show later aggressive and deviant behaviour.

Animal Abuse as Part of the Continuum of Abuse within the Family and Animal Abuse as an Indicator of Child Abuse

The argument here is that the established continuum of violence within familial relationships needs to be extended to include abuse of animal members of the family. This includes emotional, physical, and sexual abuse. This is supported by evidence which demonstrates that there is a link between interpersonal, familial human-directed violence, and deliberate animal cruelty. For example, Ascione, Weber, and Wood (1997) surveyed 38 women in the U.S. who were entering a refuge to escape violence. They found that of the 74% who had pets, 71% had experienced their partner either threatening to harm or actually harming their pet. A decade later, Volant, Johnson, Gullone, and Coleman (2008) reported very similar percentages within an Australian cohort of women. They surveyed 102 women with a history of family violence and a demographically-matched sample of 102 women without such a history. They found that 53% of the women who reported family violence experience also reported that their pets had been harmed and 17% of these reported that their pets had been killed. This contrasted with only 6% of the matched sample reporting (accidental) harm of animals and no pet deaths. More recently still, Febres et al. (2014) investigated animal abuse among 307 men arrested for domestic violence. They reported that 41% (n=125) had indicated committing at least one act of animal abuse since the age of 18. For these men, physical abuse of an animal occurred with the highest frequency (80%, n=100), followed by threats (71.2%, n=89), followed by neglect (12%, n=15).

Animal harm within a violent/abusive family dynamic may also be indicative of the level of danger presented by the abuser, as can be seen above with its closer linkage to physical violence as opposed to threatening behavior and/or neglect. Simmons and Lehmann (2007) interviewed 1,283 women seeking refuge from domestic violence in Texas (between 1998 and 2002). They concluded that abusers who were violent to their partners, and who also abused the family pet, utilized a greater range, and severity, of aggressive violence including emotional and sexual violence and stalking. They also reported that the men who abused animals as well as their partners engaged in more controlling behavior than did men who did not abuse animals. The tactics utilized by domestic violence perpetrators were even more pronounced among abusers who killed the pet.

A further example of the family violence dynamic can be found in the work of DeViney, Dickert, and Lockwood (1983) who investigated 57 families where physical child abuse had occurred. They found that 50 of these families had incidents whereby at least one family member had also abused the family pet. In the majority of cases, this animal abuse was performed by the abusive parent, but sometimes the abuse was committed by the child. In a retrospective study, utilizing psychiatric intake assessments where a single check box of 'cruelty to animals' had been ticked, Boat et al. (2011) compared frequency of aggressive behavior with abuse history for 55 children. They found that the cruelty group was 2.45 times more likely to have experienced problems with peers, 5.37 times more likely to have perpetrated bullying, and 2.81 times more likely to have experienced sexual abuse, when compared to a control group. The correlation between childhood cruelty to animals and family violence witnessed or experienced, and/or child maltreatment, is noted throughout the literature (e.g., Currie, 2006; DeGue & DiLillo, 2009; Duncan, Thomas & Miller, 2005; McEwan, Moffitt & Arseneault, 2014).

Adams (1995, p. 64), in her analysis of the "woman-animal abuse connections," argued that the pets of abused children were often used to maintain their silence. She also pointed out that child victims of sexual abuse often harmed animals themselves and, thus, child harm of animals should be taken as an indicator of some kind of family dysfunction. In a similar vein, Becker and French (2004) cite the findings from an analysis of case histories drawn from a national, UK-based, specialist service working with children who sexually abused other children and who committed other violent offenses. This analysis demonstrated that approximately one-fifth of the children had a history of sexually abusing animals.

Ascione and Arkow (1999) argued that children in dysfunctional families often have their trauma compounded by witnessing displays of animal abuse. Witnessing these displays alongside the abuse of their mothers may increase the children's later propensity for interpersonal violence as well as increasing the likelihood of their subsequent abuse of animals. This is substantiated by, for example, the findings of Volant et al. (2008) who reported that children were witness to the abuse within the family (both human- and animal-directed) in 29% of the cases. Ascione and Arkow (1999) suggest that domestic violence, animal abuse, and child maltreatment form interlocking circles of abuse. A recent study where children's engagement in animal cruelty (singular and persistent) was assessed bi-annually from age 5 to age 12 along with family risk factors (particularly adult domestic violence and physical maltreatment of the child) found that CTA was more common in children who had been maltreated. However, the strength of the predictive relationship was greater when other risk factors such as an impoverished environment and domestic violence were present (McEwan et al., 2014). (See Chapter 13 for more on animal cruelty and domestic violence.)

The Therapeutic Potential of Animals in Child Development and within Post-Abuse Work

As Becker and French (2004) highlight, the roles that animals can play within therapy are numerous, including sources of comfort and support, the promotion of childhood resilience, the rebuilding of trusting relationships, and the promotion of healing following trauma. It is within this framework that Animal-Assisted Therapy is often used (e.g., Lockwood & Ascione, 1998), building on the pioneering work of Levinson and his dog Jingles with children diagnosed with autism (Levinson, 1978).

In a modern context, a distinction is drawn between Animal-Assisted Therapy (i.e., therapies which involve both the presence of, and interaction with, an animal) and Humane-Education (i.e., curriculum-based presentations regarding animal well-being), although the two may well overlap in practice. Despite superficial differences, both forms of "intervention" are predicated upon the idea that empathy may well be a mediating factor within human-animal violence links (e.g., Hastings, Zahn-Waxler, Robinson, Usher, & Bridges, 2000; Warden & Mackinnon, 2003), thus, Humane Education has been posited as one particularly effective mechanism whereby a lack of human-directed empathy may be remedied by teaching animal-welfare-appropriate attitudes (Ascione, 1992; Ascione & Weber, 1996; Barker, Best, Fredrickson, & Hunter, 2000). Based on similar principles, Animal-Assisted Therapy has been used successfully with a number of groups including incarcerated and institutionalized individuals, the elderly, and victims of trauma (see Beck & Katcher, 1996). Recently Animal-Assisted Therapy has been shown to be effective in not only addressing maladaptive (psychological) correlates of childhood abuse, but to also reduce the prevalence of animal harm by abused children (Taylor, Fraser, Signal & Prentice, 2014).

The final area that Becker and French (2004, p. 401) highlight as being one where particular (research and popular) attention has been paid to human-animal violence links is "animal abuse perpetrated by children who show later aggressive and deviant behaviour." It is to this that the remainder of the chapter now turns.

Animal Abuse Perpetrated by Children Who Show Later Aggressive and Deviant Behavior

The majority of studies in this area involve retrospective accounts of animal cruelty by males incarcerated at the time of the research for violent crimes. For example, Schiff, Louw, and Ascione (1999) documented the animal abuse histories of 117 males in a South African prison. They reported that of the 58 men who had committed aggressive crimes, 63.3 percent also documented cruelty to animals. This was in comparison to 10.5% of the non-aggressive inmates reporting instances of animal cruelty. O'Grady, Kinlock, and Hanlon (2007) examined the relationship of a range of developmental factors (e.g., drug abuse, family history, socio-economic status, engagement in animal abuse, etc.) with history of violent criminal activity in an incarcerated (drug-using) sample. Over 30% of the total sample reported engaging in deliberate animal harm. O'Grady et al. also reported that a history of torturing animals was strongly predictive of the most violent incarcerated individuals (murder or attempted murder).

Engaging in deliberate animal harm at a young age seems to be particularly predictive of a violent or anti-social trajectory. For example, Fleming, Jory, and Burton (2002), following an examination of the family characteristics, victimization histories, and number of offenses committed by young offenders, reported that 96% of those who had engaged in sexual activity with non-human animals had also committed sex offenses against humans. Those who had engaged in sexual activity with non-human animals also reported higher levels of emotional and physical abuse within their families of origin. Age of onset (see later for a discussion of this in relation to psychological diagnoses) has been found to be related to both the frequency of abuse and the type of animal targeted. For example, Tallichet, Hensley, O'Bryan, and Hassel (2005) reported that an earlier onset of cruel acts towards animals was predictive of engaging in multiple acts of animal cruelty within a sample of 261 incarcerated men. Of the men surveyed, 43% disclosed engaging in deliberate animal cruelty. Potentially of significant importance (at least for profilers and researchers) is the fact that those inmates who were younger (i.e., under 12 years of age) when first committing CTA tended to target cats almost exclusively.

Following increased interest in the animal abuse histories of serial killers, researchers have also linked a history of animal cruelty to killings and general violence perpetrated by school-age children (Ascione, 2001). For example, Khan and Cooke (2008) reported that engaging in animal abuse was predictive of serious violence directed at a sibling utilizing a weapon. CTA was also found to relate to "less serious" (i.e., without a weapon) sibling violence, but not as strongly. Other commonalities between bullying and animal abuse have been identified, in particular, an association with delinquency and other anti-social behaviors (e.g., Baldry & Farrington, 2000; Henry, 2004; Sanders et al, 2013, 2014). Looking outside the family, Henry and Sanders (2007) investigated reported experience of animal abuse (witnessing and committing) and bullying (both as a victim and as a perpetrator) as a child within a cohort of 185 male university students. They reported two main findings, firstly that there was a distinct difference between those who were involved in a single episode of animal abuse and those who had multiple experiences of animal abuse. Specifically one-time "abusers" were not statistically different on measures of bullying (victimization or perpetration) from non-abusers. Secondly, they reported a strong interaction between high levels of bullying (again experienced as a victim and/or the perpetrator) and high tolerance of animal cruelty—for those individuals who reported experiencing multiple instances of animal abuse. Henry and Sanders suggest that their findings (in tandem with similar findings from studies such as Baldry, 2003) support the "desensitization" hypothesis—that is, that acts of violence against animals (either witnessed or perpetrated) desensitize an individual to the effects of violence, potentially also reinforcing the use of violence as a means of social control. We return to a discussion of the desensitization hypothesis later in the chapter.

In a later study (Sanders et al., 2013), with 250 male students (enrolled on an Introductory Psychology course at a US institution) confirmed the association between animal abuser and the perpetration of bullying as well as a significant, positive relation between animal abuse and being a victim of bullying. Extending analyses beyond investigations of relations between bullying and animal abuse, Sanders et al, also investigated links with socio-emotional functioning using the Strengths and Difficulties Questionnaire. Bullies, victims and animal abuses all scored highly on the conduct problems and hyperactivity subscales, with hyperactivity being specifically linked to animal abuse perpetration. Animal abuse was more likely to correlate with conduct problems among victims, rather than perpetrators, of bullying and the authors note that despite complex patterns their research suggests that bullying, animal abuse and victimization tend to co-occur. They argue that "a clear picture is beginning to emerge, in which the maltreatment of animals is consistently associated with being both a perpetrator and a victim of bullying" (p. 234).

One of the limitations of Henry and Sanders' (2007) study, however, was the age of the participants (young adults) and the inherent retrospective nature of the data collected. In contrast, Gullone and Robertson (2008) assessed concurrent engagement in bullying behaviors and animal abuse within a sample of 249 adolescents (average age approximately 14 years) attending three secondary schools in Melbourne, Australia. Over 20% of the sample admitted to having engaged in animal abuse, with boys being significantly more likely than girls to engage in such behaviors. Thirty-seven percent of the sample reported witnessing animal abuse, which was most frequently paternally-perpetrated. Consistent with large-scale studies of childhood bullying in Australia, the authors report that nearly 18% of the children had engaged in bullying behaviors in the past year and nearly 30% had been the target of bullying, either on their own or as part of a group. Witnessing animal abuse was found to be a predictor for both engaging in, and being the victim of, bullying. Engagement in animal abuse was predicted by family of origin factors (e.g., violence/conflict). The authors concluded that their study provides further empirical evidence for the co-occurrence of aggressive and anti-social behaviors towards humans and non-humans.

In a more recent study, Knight et al. (2014) utilized data from a national, longitudinal, and multi-generational sample (n=1614; data collected between 1990 and 2004) to investigate both inter- and intra-generational links between domestic violence (DV) and animal abuse. They found that (1) parental history of animal abuse was predictive of the parents' own later involvement in both the perpetration of, and being the victim of, DV; (2) a child's history of animal abuse could be predicted by their parents' perpetration of DV; and, (3) evidence for intergenerational continuity of animal abuse was lacking. Echoing conclusions by Henry and Sanders (2007) and Sanders et al. (2013), outlined above, Knight et al. (2014) argue that "the implications of these findings are that early animal abuse is not only a risk factor for later involvement in violent DV perpetration but also violent victimization" (p. 3027) and also call for further research into animal abuse and victimization, as well as perpetration.

From a psychological viewpoint, the *Diagnostic and Statistical Manual of Psychological Disorders* V contains deliberate animal abuse only as an indicator of Conduct Disorder (CD), with this disorder being posited as a preliminary to later adulthood antisocial behavior (e.g., Cohen & Strayer, 1996). Authors have suggested that approximately 25% of children meeting the criteria for CD engage in deliberate animal harm, and this behavior has been suggested as one of the earliest, observable, symptoms of anti-social behavior (Miller, 2001). Indeed, persistent behavioral (conduct) problems with an early onset are considered a marker of an increased likelihood of developing serious socio-emotional problems later in life (Luk, Staiger, Wong, & Mathai, 1999). For example, Luk et al. (1999) compared a sample of children referred to a mental health service for persistent behavioral issues (meeting at least one criteria other than CTA for Conduct Disorder, n=141) to a community sample all aged between 5 and 12 years of age. Just under a third (28%) of the clinic-referred sample were reported by parents/caregivers to be "cruel to animals." In contrast only one of the non-referred children (n=36) was reported to engage in CTA. Comparing the CTA to non-CTA referred children Luk et al. (1999), noted that the former group tended to be characterized by more severe conduct symptoms and poorer family functioning. Unexpectedly, older CTA children were found to have significantly elevated self-perception, with Luk et al. suggesting that this might be related to the "callous and unemotional" subtype of Conduct Disorder proposed by some researchers as a potential marker for childhood psychopathy and potentially serious adulthood psychopathology/criminality. (See Chapter 16 for further discussion of psychological theories.)

Simons, Wurtele, and Durham (2008) examined the differential, developmental, experiences of 269 convicted sexual offenders. Splitting the offenders into "Rapists" and "Child Abusers" (as defined by more than 80% of their disclosed victims being either an adult or a child), Simons et al. assessed a range of childhood experiences including frequency, severity and type of animal abuse (i.e., physical and sexual). The authors further investigated disclosures of animal abuse by animal type (domestic vs. stray) and ascertained motivations for the disclosed CTA although this was not reported within the publication. Child abusers (n=132) were found to be significantly more likely to have engaged in bestiality as a child (38% vs. 11%), and at a younger age than rapists. In contrast, rapists were significantly more likely to have engaged in non-sexual acts of CTA (68% vs. 44%), with a higher frequency and younger age of onset than child abusers. Importantly, despite the difference in the typologies of animal cruelty and typology of sexual offending, CTA was found to precede human-directed sexual abuse by an average of two years for child abusers and six years for rapists. It must be acknowledged here that there were a number of other significant, differential, developmental experiences between the two "classes" of sexual offender, such as physical abuse and domestic violence in family of origin for rapists, sexual abuse, and early exposure to pornography for child abusers. However, there is a clear need for further research into the links between CTA and sexual offending. Importantly, Simons et al. note that these results and the conclusions drawn from them can't be generalized to female perpetrators as their developmental paths and experiences have not been well-explored.

Gendered Experiences of CTA

As can be seen by the studies summarized above, the majority of the extant literature in this area examines the "Link" within male populations only. Research addressing female-perpetrated CTA remains comparatively rare. Felthous and Yudowitz (1977) compared the histories of 31 female offenders with those of 19 male offenders, finding a significant relation between cruelty to animals and violent criminal activity for female as well as male offenders. The first part of the study involved the comparison of the female offenders with the male offenders and results showed that while the men had a greater tendency to *kill* animals, the prevalence of *torturing* of animals was nearly equal in the two samples. The second part of the study consisted of a comparison between assaultive and non-assaultive female offenders and the results showed that cruelty to animals was the only childhood behavior that differentiated the two groups with statistical significance. Felthous and Yudowitz concluded that experience of deliberate animal harm was as significant for females as for males with equal frequency of perpetration across genders (however, male-perpetrated cruelty more often involved the death of the animal in question).

There has been an apparent increase in scholarly interest in women's experience of CTA, with an emphasis on assessing their direct engagement in CTA rather than as passive or unwilling witnesses to CTA. For example, Connelly (2007) compared the histories of 100 female inmates (41 characterized as aggressive and 59 as non-aggressive) to those of 104 male inmates (59 characterized as aggressive and 45 as non-aggressive). Connelly reported that female inmates were just as likely to have abused animals as male inmates. Interestingly, aggressive female inmates disclosed more overall instances of animal cruelty (particularly in adolescence) and substantially higher rates of sexually abusing animals (including into adulthood) than male inmates. Febres et al. (2012) examined both the prevalence of adulthood animal abuse and its links with interpersonal violence perpetration in a sample of women arrested for domestic violence and referred to batterer intervention programs in the US. They found animal abuse to be over-represented in the sample with 17% of the 87 women reporting at least one instance of animal abuse since the age of 18, compared to a 0.28% prevalence rate among women in the general public. In contrast to assumptions about the gendered nature of neglect (see below) the majority of acts reported were of physical CTA with only one case of neglect mentioned. Importantly most of the women reported multiple acts of CTA (average 8–9) rather than singular experiences with the most commonly endorsed item on the Aggression Toward Animals Scale that concerning threatening behavior toward nonhuman animals (i.e., 'Did you threaten, scare, intimidate, or bully an animal on purpose?') followed by physically aggressive acts (i.e., 'Did you hit an animal with an object that could hurt?'). However, adulthood animal abuse proved to correlate only with severe physical, but not psychological, abuse (of humans). While researchers have shown that a history of specific types of CTA seem to relate to 'styles' of interpersonal violence in male perpetrators (e.g., Merz-Perez et al., 2001) the small sample size precludes similar analyses here. Sanders and Henry (2014) recently extended their examination of links between CTA and psychological variables to a retrospective study of 500 female undergraduates. They concluded that similar patterns of behavioral difficulties were present in female animal abusers as had previously been found with males. Given these two recent studies there is clearly a need to address the gendered nature of violence within larger, community-relevant, samples.

Indeed, despite these studies, there remains a focus on male acts of cruelty to animals within the literature, which reflects a gendered bias within criminology more broadly (e.g., Heidensohn, 2010). This is often reflected within the argument that men abuse whereas women neglect. This is itself a reflection of gendered ideology in that it is an extension of the belief that females are more passive and nurturing than males. Within the human-animal violence literature, women are then taken to task for neglect as opposed to deliberate violence. Similarly, the assumption that males are violent, whereas females are not, is one which pervades criminology (e.g., Heidensohn, 2010) and human-animal scholars need to guard against reproducing these entrenched beliefs through the very design of their studies. There is, similarly, a heteronormative bias in extant literature regarding animal abuse and future research needs to investigate animal abuse perpetration, particularly within the context of domestic violence, within same sex and Lesbian, Gay, Bisexual, Transgender, Queer/Questioning, and Intersex (LGBTQI) relationships.

CTA and Generalized Deviance

Underpinning all ideas of the "Link" are two separate, but related, theses: the graduation thesis and the desensitization (sometimes called "generalization of deviance") thesis. The graduation thesis is based on the idea that those who deliberately harm animals will graduate to the deliberate harm of humans while the desensitization thesis is more concerned with the general levels of callous behavior which permeate modern life. This is seen to manifest itself in certain personality traits such as deliberate animal harm which can then be seen as a risk factor for the development of further anti-social behaviors directed at humans (Beirne, 2004).

Arguably, much of the early research in the area of human-animal violence links prioritized the idea of graduation over desensitization. Following three plus decades of concerted research in the area, however, this is starting to change. In part due to the methodological problems inherent to studies which seek to determine causality between human- and animal-directed violence, more attention is now being paid to the idea of human-animal violence links with generalized deviant behavior (e.g., Arluke, Levin, Luke, & Ascione, 1999). The proposition here is that cruelty to animals is seen as one aspect of a range of maladaptive (antisocial) behaviors that heighten the risk for adulthood antisocial behavior (Dadds, Turner, & McAloon, 2002). For example, when Arluke et al. (1999) examined the criminal records of 153 individuals prosecuted for acts of animal cruelty and a matched sample of non-abusers (who also had criminal records), they found that those who had abused animals were significantly more likely to be involved in other criminal activity (including violent interpersonal behavior). Interestingly, instances of animal cruelty were found to be no more likely to precede, than follow, other criminal activity for this cohort. In a review of studies with incarcerated individuals, Ascione (2001) concluded that deliberate animal abuse may be typical of the developmental histories of between 25% and 66% of violent criminals. Recent research also suggests that simply witnessing animal abuse significantly increases both the likelihood of engaging in such abuse (Thomson & Gullone, 2006) and is a strong predictor for engaging in bullying behaviors (Gullone & Robertson, 2008).

In one of the few studies involving non-incarcerated participants, Henry (2004) asked students (Introductory Psychology, n=169) to recall their past history of either witnessing or engaging in deliberate CTA, their general attitudes towards the treatment of animals, and instances of "delinquent" (i.e., antisocial) behavior. Overall, those who reported either witnessing (51%, n=86) or engaging in animal cruelty (18%, n=30) were more likely to report engaging in a variety of antisocial behaviors. The results of this study are particularly important for the desensitization hypothesis as it illustrates that CTA exists within a "matrix of antisocial behaviors" within a non-incarcerated population. Henry also comments on the interplay between gender and the effect of witnessing CTA (insufficient women reporting engaging in CTA to allow analyses), with women showing heightened sensitivity towards animals and men reduced sensitivity following such exposure. While noting that this pattern warrants further examination, Henry suggests that an individual's response to observing CTA may depend on the context within which the cruelty occurs, particularly whether the individual was a willing observer or coerced. Gender may be correlated strongly with this, with Henry suggesting that the observed, heightened sensitivity towards animal suffering may reflect the fact that women may be non-willing witnesses of animal cruelty

It must be acknowledged, however, that although a number of other studies have found similar patterns of increased criminality and/or elevated propensity for violence linked to experiences of animal abuse (e.g., Kellert & Felthous, 1985), other research has found less support for the link. Miller and Knutson (1997) for example, reported that types of violent criminals could not be differentiated simply by self-reported engagement in animal abuse.

There does exist, however, considerable disagreement regarding the specifics of both these theses, not to mention a lack of (uncontested) empirical data. For example, Tallichet and Hensley (2005) point out that those who harm "convenient" animals (i.e., their own or neighborhood companion animals) may be less at risk of developing serious anti-social behaviors than those who deliberately seek out a range of animals to harm, thus suggesting that even the desensitization thesis may be dependent upon a range of other factors. Other research has failed to find predictive utility in the graduation thesis at all (e.g., Dadds et al., 2006). For example, Taylor and Signal (2004), in an Australian community-based sample, found that links between aggression and animal attitude measures only existed on a correlational level, failing to reach predictive significance.

Despite such problems, there is no lack of public interest in, and awareness of, "The Link." For example, in a study of approximately 1,200 Australians, Taylor and Signal (2006) found that 63% thought there was a link between family violence and deliberate animal harm. Animal protection agencies also utilize "The Link" in their various campaigns, for example, First Strike in Scotland and New Zealand and the Humane Society of the United States. A number of innovative projects have also been established, in response to recognition of human-animal violence links, to foster the companion animals of women entering refuges fleeing violence (e.g., DVConnect's Pets in Crisis, Queensland, Australia),[1] and, increasingly, there is a recognition of the need to provide services for those in violent situations who live with companion animals (see, e.g., Kreinert, Walsh, Matthews & McConkey, 2012). Furthermore, such ideas are now permeating the legal system with, for example, states in the U.S. such as California and Illinois recently enacting legislation that allows judicial discretion to include pets in domestic violence protection orders (see The National Link Coalition for more information, http://www.nationallinkcoalition.org/).

One problem with this, however, is that such campaigns often blur the boundaries between correlational concepts (i.e., that conceptually there is a link between the two forms of aggression) and causality (i.e., that children who are cruel to animals will necessarily go on to become serial killers or other harmers of humans). It remains the case that the empirical evidence for causality is, to date, ambiguous at best.

---

1. For a review of the first six months of this project, see Taylor, Signal, and Stark (2006).

Despite the lack of clear causative evidence, deliberate CTA committed by children and young people has been (and remains) the focus of numerous research endeavours, both theoretical and empirical, all of which indicate the serious implications and/or correlates of this aberrant behavior (Becker & French, 2004). While acknowledged as a behavior that is challenging to define, isolate, explain, and rationalize (Ascione, 2001; Benetato et al., 2011; Gleyzer, Felthous & Holzer, 2002; Hensley et al., 2009), it is also seen as a behavioral anomaly that requires urgent recognition, prevention, and intervention (Arluke & Lockwood, 1997; Flynn, 2000; Lockwood & Hodge, 1986; Merz-Perez, Heide, & Silverman, 2001).

Indeed, Merz-Perez and Heide (2003) suggest that it is more important to understand the motivations behind acts of animal cruelty than the behaviors themselves. Arluke and Sanders (2009) support this, explaining that better knowledge of the motives behind animal cruelty will hopefully result in better prevention (and treatment for abusers), while acknowledging that research in the field has become somewhat preoccupied with the consequences of animal cruelty rather than what underlies it. In (arguably) one of the first studies to try and delineate the motives behind animal cruelty, Kellert and Felthous (1985) derived nine theoretical motivations for adult-perpetrated animal abuse, namely:

1. "Control" of the animal (often under the guise of "training");
2. Retaliation against an animal;
3. Prejudice against a certain species (e.g., cats);
4. Express aggression via animal (e.g., possession of a dog trained to fight);
5. Enhance own aggression (e.g., using an animal as target practice);
6. To shock others (for self-amusement);
7. Retaliate against another person (e.g., kill the neighbor's dog, girlfriend's rabbit);
8. Displaced hostility (abuse animal as harming person is too risky); and
9. Nonspecific sadism (i.e., enjoy the suffering in and of itself).

CTA: Social and Community Considerations

As Ascione (2001) points out, the role of family, social, and community factors should not be overlooked. Two particularly important animal-abuse-related factors which have been gaining a lot of research attention are maladaptive family environment/abusive parental practices (e.g., Ascione, 2001; Hastings, Zahn-Waxler, Usher, Robinson & Bridges, 2000) and empathy (e.g., Taylor & Signal, 2005).

Many researchers have noted that not all children who abuse animals become juvenile offenders or adult criminals, and sometimes these children do not come from dysfunctional, violent families, and indeed appear to be "normal" or "typical" (e.g., Flynn, 2000; Flynn, 2001; Miller & Knutson, 1997; Randour, 2007). According to Dadds et al. (2002), certain features of childhood CTA have been suggested to be more meaningful when assessing the predictive utility of animal abuse, namely: direct involvement, impulsivity, lack of remorse, variety of cruel acts, the species targeted, and the motivations behind the cruelty. Ascione, Thompson, and Black (1997) derived 13 developmentally-related CTA motivations from case reports and interviews with children engaging in animal abuse. These motivations included curiosity/exploration, mood enhancement (i.e., relief of boredom), peer pressure, sexual gratification, abuse (and displaced hostility resulting from same), post-traumatic play, imitation, self-injury, and rehearsal for interpersonal violence. Based on these and experiences of animal protection professionals, Ascione (2001) proposed three general taxonomies for childhood animal abusers:

1. Exploratory/curious animal abuse
2. Pathological animal abuse
3. Delinquent animal abuse

Children in the exploratory/curious animal abuse category are generally very young (i.e., pre-school) and are typified by having little understanding of animal needs and being poorly supervised. It must be noted, however, that age alone is not sufficient for membership in this category as animal cruelty is often one of the first Conduct Disorder (CD) symptoms to be observed. Norris and Wilson (2003) mention a median reporting age (of onset of animal cruelty) of about 6.5 years—earlier than the median age for first report of bullying, cruelty to humans, vandalism or arson. Those with developmental delays may also fall within this exploratory/curious typology despite being older in age (Ascione, 2001). Ascione (2001) suggests that Humane Education interventions would be one way to reduce the prevalence of animal abuse perpetrated by children within this group.

In the second category (pathological), children are generally older (although see the caveats regarding age above) and CTA is indicative of some form of psychological disturbance (e.g., CD, empathy deficit). Researchers have suggested that CTA may be a marker for particularly severe CD with heightened risk for future violence, (e.g., Frick et al., 1993; Luk et al., 1999). In a review of the literature, McPhedran (2009) suggested that the presence of childhood CTA was a marker for a poorer prognosis particularly with a younger age of onset. Importantly, the CTA may also be a result of abuse; specifically, researchers report that children who abuse animals are often victims of sexual or physical abuse themselves (Adams & Donovan, 1995; Currie, 2006). It is with respect to this that childhood CTA should also be taken as a "red flag" warranting further attention/investigation if disclosed regardless of the any other presenting behaviors/indicators (e.g., DeGue & DiLillo, 2009; Lockwood & Hodge, 1986). Ascione (2001) suggests that professional, clinical intervention is needed to reduce animal abuse by those falling within this group.

Individuals in the third, delinquent, group are generally adolescent in age with animal abuse likely to be one of a range of antisocial behaviors they are engaging in (Ascione, 2001). Often animal abuse is carried out with peers and may form part of initiation rituals. Membership of this group is highly correlated with the risk for adulthood criminality (due to engaging in a range of anti-social behaviors not solely due to animal abuse) and interpersonal violence. Ascione (2001) suggests that judicial and clinical intervention is required in order to reduce animal abuse within this cohort. (See Chapters 15 and 16 in the current volume for a more detailed consideration of the motivational factors underlying animal abuse.)

A number of studies have been conducted in an effort to isolate circumstances that precede CTA. The earliest recorded study (Tapia, 1971) and follow-up study (Rigdon & Tapia, 1977) focused on investigating causative variables associated with episodes of childhood CTA. The researchers examined the case histories of 18 male children who were placed in psychiatric care (the average age of the sample was 9½ years), all of whom had presented with a history of CTA. The results indicated that the majority of the children had been raised in a less than ideal environment that included episodes of parental neglect, hostility, violence, and rejection. A follow-up study conducted six years later concluded that in order to reduce the CTA, the best course of action was to remove the child from the chaotic home environment or through treatment practices aimed at altering and improving familial relationships (Rigdon & Tapia, 1977).

Subsequent studies have isolated specific domestic features that present as precursors to childhood CTA. For example, Wax and Haddox (1974) established a positive relationship between childhood CTA and a disorganized household and irregular parental practices while DeViney et al. (1983) (as cited in Flynn, 2000), noted that the presence of child abuse and other practices of violence within the family may be a forerunner for childhood CTA. Ascione (1998) concluded from his research that episodes of domestic violence may increase the likelihood of childhood CTA and may therefore foster psychological instability in the witnessing children. This is likely to be particularly the case where children witness CTA within the violent relationship environment (e.g., Baldry, 2003; Flynn, 1999). Interestingly, in a large, epidemiologic study in the US (with over 30,000 participants) Vaughn et al., (2011) found that experience of childhood sexual, but not physical, abuse significantly increased the odds of individuals engaging in CTA.

Lockwood and Hodge (1986) conclude that evidence of childhood CTA is a positive indication that there is something in the child's life that requires an immediate response. However, identifying CTA as an observer can be very challenging (McPhedran, 2009) for a number of reasons including the often solitary nature of CTA and embarrassment/shame of behalf of the witnessing parent/caregiver. Awareness and acknowledgement of childhood CTA, first and foremost, is the responsibility of those people in close proximity to the child (e.g., parents, neighbors, teachers) (Dadds et al., 2002). However, once the behavior has been recognized, the child needs to be referred to professional practitioners (Dadds et al., 2002).

Methodological Issues

In an attempt to explain the discrepancies in the literature with regard to the link, Felthous and Kellert (1987) have suggested that methodological differences such as the way in which animal abuse histories are derived (interviews vs. chart reviews), and whether researchers examine repeated patterns or single instances of violence, are important. Specifically, they suggest that those studies that have failed to find an association tend to rely on chart reviews rather than interviews and often examine single instances of abuse/violence rather than repeated patterns of violent or cruel behavior.

Research in this area is often marred by methodological issues. For instance, no clear agreement exists on the definition of animal abuse (e.g., Ascione, 2001, Becker & French, 2004, Beirne, 2004) or on whether deliberate neglect should be taken into account (Ascione, 2001). The majority of research utilizes either parental reports of children's animal abuse and/or child self-reports of abuse which often differ drastically in terms of estimated prevalence (Ascione, 2001; Miller, 2001). Additional methodological problems are to be found in the fact that much research rests upon retrospective reports drawn from (male) incarcerated offenders.

This signals a clear need to develop more specific and responsive instruments. For example, much of the work in this area involves the use of generalized instruments such as the Attitude towards the Treatment of Animals Scale (Herzog, Betchart, & Pitman, 1991; Taylor & Signal, 2006). While a robust and useful measure of general attitudes towards the treatment of animals, it may be that it is not specific enough for use within clinical populations where the aim is to test human-animal abuse theses for their predictive ability (nor should it be expected to be given that this was not its purpose by design). Evidence available to date seems to suggest that it is the deliberate cruel treatment of animals — as opposed to generalized attitudes towards them — which is important in predicting human-directed aggression, certainly within clinical/aggressive populations. Similarly, it may be that aggression across species, or animal category (e.g., "wild" animal vs. domesticated animal or vice versa), plays a more important part than general attitude towards animals in predicting those who will graduate from animal-directed to human-directed violence (e.g., Tallichet & Hensley, 2005). Research into human-animal abuse theses has tended to concentrate on, and prioritize, companion animal abuse, although more recent work in the field is beginning to analyze the importance of variables such as cross-species animal abuse and cross-animal category abuse (that is, abusing animals deemed as "pets" or "pests" for example, Merz-Perez et al., 2001).

Conclusion: Condoned Animal Harm

Traditionally, animal cruelty has been defined as " … *socially unacceptable* behavior that intentionally causes unnecessary pain, suffering, or distress to and/or death of an animal" (Ascione, 1993, p. 228). Cazaux (1999, p. 120) points out that research in this area has focused on individual instances of cruelty and abuse against individual (usually companion) animals — at the expense of any other forms of animal cruelty and abuse. She refers to this inattention as selective indignation and posits that one explanation for this may be that such individual instances of animal cruelty are more readily amenable to control and thus more "susceptible to correction and enforcement" and therefore more easily taken up by the criminological community. While discussing criminological approaches to human-animal abuse in particular, Cazaux' point can be generalized to other disciplines; much of the extant research focuses on cruelty considered to be socially unacceptable. As a consequence, much institutionalized and/or *condoned* abuse and cruelty remains under-investigated and under-theorized. Cazaux argues that individual instances of animal abuse are tied to those animals that are deemed subjects (such as "pets") while the vast majority of animal abuse takes place with animals deemed as objects (such as farm animals). In a similar vein, Agnew (1998, p. 179) argues for a broad definition of animal abuse which does encompass these taken-for-granted forms of animal abuse and points out that a further advantage of such a broad perspective is that it would not be "tied to prevailing beliefs about animals … [which] … vary by time and place."

Following similar lines of argument, Beirne (1999a, p. 125) points out that when animals do enter criminological discourse, they "tend to be cast as creatures of anthropocentrism and anthropomorphism, as unproblematic objects that are only coincidentally present in some undesirable aspect of the complex web of human relationships." He further points out that certain existing criminological theories may have potential in extending the boundary of criminology to include animals. For example, Sutherland's argument (1949) that criminologists should study anything defined as socially harmful by any branch of law seems to offer one way forward, as do other forms of non-mainstream criminology, such as postmodern and critical criminologies. However, Beirne (1999a, p. 129) cautions us that we cannot adopt such theories wholesale as they all too often begin from a point of "human exceptionalism and speciesism." He points out that "animals …

remain without standing in a sort of legal and moral wilderness" (Beirne, 1999b, p. 10) and argues that this needs re-addressing in light of new ideas concerning the importance of animal abuse as a legitimate area of study.

The advantages of taking a broader view of animal cruelty and abuse can be seen in the following example which is of particular relevance to this chapter. A small, but growing, body of research points to problems endemic to communities where slaughterhouses and meatworks are located. In 2008, Dillard called for legal redress for "slaughterhouse workers" due to the psychological trauma caused by their daily experience of "large-scale violence and death" (p. 391) within an institutional culture that does little to reduce animal or human suffering. Authors have been quick to point out that the repetitive nature of slaughterhouse work coupled with a modern cultural sensibility which dictates a need to "render invisible what used to be a bloody spectacle" (Vialles, 2002, p. 66) leads to a "lack of identification with one's job" which elsewhere is often experienced as a distressing feature of production line work, yet in the slaughterhouse constitutes "a prerequisite for 'getting used to it'" (Vialles, 2002, p. 51).

Some have argued that it is not surprising, then, that this kind of human suffering gives rise to animal suffering. Indeed, Porcher (2011) argues that animals *and* humans share in physical and mental suffering as a result of modern intensive farming practices which include, but are not limited to, the slaughterhouse. Both Dillard (2008) and Grandin (1998) assert that abuse of animals at meat processing plants occurs frequently. For example, when Grandin (1998) undertook surveys of meat processing plant employees in the United States, she found that approximately 4% of employees directly involved with livestock had committed acts of deliberate animal cruelty in the course of their work. She further added that it appeared that these individuals took pleasure in observing the animals' suffering. Dillard (2008) suggests that employment within the animal production industry (specifically farmers and meatworkers) tends to lower " … employees' ability to empathize and identify with the pain suffered by the animals whose lives (and deaths) they are controlling" (p. 399). Dillard further explains that this type of distancing and compromised/poor attitude towards animals affects the way that workers treat the animals they interact with, specifically that this "disconnect" increases the likelihood of deliberate cruelty. She also suggests that this emotional distancing potentially affects male employees more strongly than female employees (based on findings from Porcher, Cousson-Gélie, & Dantzer, 2004).

While many of these issues obviously need to be addressed from the animal welfare perspective, research into the human-animal violence "Link" would suggest that this needs to be addressed from a human-welfare perspective, too. That is, as detailed above, research indicates that correlations exist between an individual's treatment of animals and his or her treatment of humans. Given that a reduction in empathy towards animals is a prerequisite for slaughterhouse work, and the increasing number of reported instances of cruelty that occurs within the job, as well as evidence that the mere presence of a slaughterhouse in a given community is indicative of higher levels of criminal and antisocial behavior, this is clearly an area in need of further research (e.g., Fitzgerald, 2010; Fitzgerald, Kalof, & Dietz, 2007).

Anecdotal evidence suggests that there may be higher incidences of familial violence as well as other crimes and social problems amongst populations of meatworkers (e.g., Artz, Orazem, & Otto, 2007; Dillard, 2008). For example, the establishment and/or presence of a (large) meat processing plant in a number of rural American towns has been reported to be connected to increases in homelessness, crime, familial violence, and child abuse within the community. Fitzgerald, Kalof, and Dietz (2007) summarized the existing literature (both popular and academic) on this issue, suggesting that three factors are often linked with the observed increase in criminal behavior. These are: (1) pressure on existing social infrastructures resulting in social disorganization, (2) the demographic characteristics of the workforce (e.g., young, male, and often immigrant), and (3) increased unemployment rates (due to high turnover of staff). However, as noted by Fitzgerald et al., none of these have been empirically tested. Indeed when Fitzgerald et al. examined arrest rates across a number of communities comparing situations where either a large animal-processing facility was present or a large-scale manufacturing plant (with similar sized workforce and demographic factors), they reported that the three factors did not, on their own or in combination, account for the increase in total arrest rates. Increases in arrests for violent crime, including rape and other sex offenses, were only observed in communities surrounding meat works. Fitzgerald et al., conclude that there is sufficient evidence to support the existence of the "Sinclair Effect" (i.e., that the unique and violent nature of the work involved has a deleterious effect on employees) (Fitzgerald et al., 2007) which in turn has deleterious effects on the surrounding neighborhoods. In a recent, questionnaire-based, study of the impact of occupation type (i.e., meatworkers and farmers benchmarked against a large community sample) on attitude towards animals and overall propensity for violence, Richards, Signal, and Taylor (2012) reported that meatworkers, but not farmers, showed significantly elevated levels of aggression compared to a community sample. Meatworkers' aggression scores were found to be similar to those reported in some incarcerated samples (e.g., Williams, Boyd, Cascardi, & Poythress, 1996). Richards et al. (2012) suggest that this provides support for assertions by Dillard (2008) regarding the psychological damage done to employees within meat processing plants. That is, that due to constant exposure to violence and the type of institutional climate present at slaughterhouses, workers are vulnerable psychologically. These conclusions also substantiate Fitzgerald et al.'s (2007) findings of a differential effect on violent crime rates by employment within a meat processing facility.

With its focus on individual instances of harm to individual animals deemed "worthy," criminology is currently at risk of ignoring this area as a focus of research. Perhaps because it is easier to research and police, there has been a general focus on interpersonal violence and companion animal abuse. However, this leaves a large area of social and public life unexplored by criminologists and other social scientists when it is actually the case that criminology has a great deal to contribute to this issue (see Taylor, 2011).

What is clear from the foregoing review and discussion of the literature is that this is an area of ongoing import and interest. There is clearly a need for further research into the factors that lead to CTA (e.g., family dynamics, underlying pathology, and gender) and the variables that link CTA with other antisocial, delinquent, and violent behavior. It would seem, from the review, that research attention is turning away from the "triad" (nocturnal enuresis, fire setting, and CTA) and the graduation thesis, with more and more studies depicting CTA as part of a general environment of violence and antisocial behavior (see Chapter 14). The evidence regarding the utility of the "desensitization" approach for predicting and controlling the negative sequelae of CTA at a young age is slowly accruing. For example, studies that show that CTA predates other forms of delinquency and sexual violence (e.g., Simons et al., 2008), in conjunction with those that illustrate the "red flag" nature of CTA for bullying propensity (e.g., Henry, 2004), make CTA a significant behavioral anomaly that warrants close attention. It is an unfortunate truth that the implied risk for future harm of other humans, rather than the harm to the animals themselves, is more likely to produce policy (e.g., cross-reporting; see e.g., Girardi & Pozzulo, 2012) and service provision (e.g., pet fostering for families entering domestic violence refuges) changes. However, we can hope that at least the increased attention, and concomitant earlier detection of CTA, will reduce the number of animals that suffer at the hands of children and adults, abusers and bullies.

References

Adams, C. (1995). Woman battering and harm to animals, in C. Adams & J. Donovan (Eds.) *Animals and women: Feminist theoretical explanations.* Durham and London: Duke University Press.

Adams, C., & Donovan, J. (1995). *Animals and women: Feminist theoretical explanations.* Durham and London: Duke University Press.

Agnew, R. (1998). The causes of animal abuse: A social-psychological analysis, *Theoretical Criminology, 2*(2), 177–209.

Arluke, A., Levin, J., Luke, C., & Ascione, F. (1999). The relationship of animal abuse to violence and other forms of antisocial behavior, *Journal of Interpersonal Violence, 14*(9), 963–975.

Arluke, A., & Lockwood, R. (1997). Guest editors' introduction: Understanding cruelty to animals. *Society & Animals, 5*(3), 183–193.

Artz, G., Orazem, P., & Otto, D. (2007). Measuring the impact of meat packing and processing facilities in nonmetropolitan counties: A difference-in-differences approach, *American Journal of Agricultural Economics, 89,* 557–570.

Ascione, F. (1992). Enhancing children's attitudes about the humane treatment of animals: Generalisation to human-directed empathy, *Anthrozoös, 5*(3), 76–191.

Ascione, F. (1998). Battered women's reports of their partners and their children's cruelty to animals, *Journal of Emotional Abuse, 1,* 119–133.

Ascione, F. (2001). Animal abuse and youth violence, *OJJDP: Juvenile Justice Bulletin,* September, 1–15.

Ascione, F., & Arkow, P. (Eds.) (1999). *Child abuse, domestic violence, and animal abuse: Linking the circles of compassion for prevention and intervention.* Lafayette: Purdue University Press.

Ascione, F., & Weber, C. (1996). Children's attitudes about the humane treatment of animals and empathy: One-year follow-up of a school-based intervention, *Anthrozoos, 9,* 188–195.

Ascione, F., Weber, C., & Wood, D. (1997). The abuse of animals and domestic violence: A national survey of shelters for women who are battered, *Society & Animals, 5*(3), 205–218.

Ascione, F., Thompson, T., & Black, T. (1997). Childhood cruelty to animals: Assessing cruelty dimensions and motivations, *Anthrozoös, 10*(4), 170–182.

Baldry, A. (2003). Animal abuse and exposure to interparental violence in Italian youth. *Journal of Interpersonal Violence, 18,* 258–281.

Baldry, A. C., & Farrington, D. P. (2000). Bullies and delinquents: Personal characteristics and parental styles, *Journal of Community and Applied Social Psychology, 10*(1), 17–31.

Barker, S. B., Best, A. M., Fredrickson, M., & Hunter, G. (2000). Constraints in assessing the impact of animals in education, *Anthrozoös 13*(2): 74–79.

Beck, A., & Katcher, A. (1996). *Between pets and people: The importance of animal companionship.* Indiana: Purdue University Press.

Becker, F., & French, L. (2004). Making the links: Child abuse, animal cruelty and domestic violence, *Child Abuse Review, 13*, 399–414.

Beirne, P. (1999a). For a nonspeciesist criminology: Animal abuse as an object of study, *Criminology, 37*(1), 117–147.

Beirne, P. (1999b). *Confronting Animal Abuse: Law, Criminology and Human-Animal Relationships.* Maryland: Rowman and Littlefield.

Beirne, P. (2004). From animal abuse to interhuman violence? A critical review of the Progression Thesis, *Society & Animals, 1*(1), 39–65.

Benetato, M., Reisman, R., & McCobb, E. (2011). The veterinarian's role in animal cruelty cases. *Journal of the American Veterinary Medical Association, 238*, 31–34.

Boat, B., Pearl, E., Barned, J., Richet, L., Crouch, D., Barzman, D., & Putnam, F. (2011). Childhood cruelty to animals: Psychiatric and demographic correlates, *Journal of Aggression, Maltreatment & Trauma, 20*(7), 812–819.

Cazaux, G. (1999). Beauty and the beast: Animal abuse from a non-speciesist criminological perspective, *Crime, Law & Social Change, 31*(2), 105–126.

Cohen, D., & Strayer, J. (1996). Empathy in conduct-disordered and comparison youth, *Developmental Psychology, 32*(6), 988–998.

Connelly, H. J. (2007). *Animal abuse as an early predictor of violent crime later in life: A comparison of male and female inmates* (Unpublished doctoral dissertation), Alliant International University, California.

Currie, C. L. (2006). Animal cruelty by children exposed to domestic violence. *Child Abuse & Neglect, 30*, 425–435.

Dadds, M. R., Turner, C., & McAloon, J. (2002). Developmental links between cruelty to animals and human violence. *Australian and New Zealand Journal of Criminology, 35*, 363–382.

DeGue, S., & DiLillo, D. (2009). Is animal cruelty a "red flag" for family violence? Investigating co-occurring violence towards children, partners, and pets. *Journal of Interpersonal Violence, 24*, 1036–1056.

DeViney, E., Dickert, J., & Lockwood, R. (1983). The care of pets within child abusing families, *International Journal for the Study of Animal Problems, 4*, 321–329.

Dillard, J. (2008). Slaughterhouse nightmare: Psychological harm suffered by slaughterhouse employees and the possibility of redress through legal reform. *Georgetown Journal on Poverty Law and Policy, 15*(2), 391–408.

Duncan, A., Thomas, J., & Miller, C. (2005). Significance of family risk factors in development of childhood animal cruelty in adolescent boys with conduct problems, *Journal of Family Violence, 20*, 235–239.

Febres J., Shorey, R., Brasfield, H., Zucosky, H., Ninnemann, A., Elmquist, J.,..., & Stuart, G. (2012). Adulthood animal abuse among women court-referred to batterer intervention programs, *Journal of Interpersonal Violence, 27*(15), 3115–3126.

Febres, J., Brasfield, H., Shorey, R., Elmquist, J., Ninnemann, A., Schonbrun, Y.,..., & Strart, G. (2014). Adulthood animal abuse among men arrested for domestic violence, *Violence Against Women, 20*(9), 1059–1077.

Felthous, A. R., & Yudowitz, B. (1977). Approaching a comparative typology of assaultive female offenders. *Psychiatry, 40*(6), 270–276.

Fitzgerald, A. (2010). A social history of the slaughterhouse: From inception to contemporary implications. *Human Ecology Review, 17*(1), 58–69.

Fitzgerald, A. J., Kalof, L., & Dietz, T. (2007). Slaughterhouses and increased crime rates: An empirical analysis of the spillover from "The Jungle" into the surrounding community. *Organization & Environment, 22*(2), 158–184.

Fleming, W. M., Jory, B., & Burton, D. (2002). Characteristics of juvenile offenders admitting to sexual activity with nonhuman animals. *Society & Animals, 10*(1), 31–46.

Flynn, C. (2000). Battered women and their animal companions: Symbolic interaction between human and non-human animals, *Society & Animals, 8*(2), 99–127.

Flynn, C. (2001). Acknowledging the "zoological connection": A sociological analysis of animal cruelty, *Society & Animals, 9*, 71–87.

Flynn, C. P. (1999). Exploring the link between corporal punishment and children's cruelty to animals. *Journal of Marriage & the Family, 61*(4), 971–981.

Frick, P. J., Lahey, B. B., Loeber, R., Tannenbaum, L., Van Horn, Y., Christ, M. A. G,..., & Hanson, K. (1993). Oppositional defiant disorder and conduct disorder: A meta-analytic review of factor analyses and cross-validation in a clinic sample. *Clinical Psychology Review, 13*, 319–340.

Girardi, A., & Pozzulo, J. (2012). The significance of animal cruelty in child protection investigations, *Social Work Research, 36*(1), 53–60.

Gleyzer, R., Felthous, A. R., & Holzer, C. E. (2002). Animal cruelty and psychiatric disorders, *Journal of the American Academy of Psychiatry and Law, 30*, 257–265.

Grandin, T. (1998). Fast food chains audit animal handling practices. *Meat & Poultry*, December, 57.

Gullone, E., & Robertson, N. (2008). The relationship between bullying and animal abuse behaviors in adolescents: The importance of witnessing animal abuse. *Journal of Applied Developmental Psychology, 29*, 371–379.

Hastings, P. D., Zahn-Waxler, C., Robinson, J., Usher, B., & Bridges, D. (2000). The development of concern for others in children with behavior problems. *Developmental Psychology, 36*, 531–546.

Heidensohn, F. (2010). On Writing "The deviance of women": Observations and analysis, *The British Journal of Sociology, 61*, 127–132.

Henry, B. (2004). The relationship between animal cruelty, delinquency, and attitudes toward the treatment of animals. *Society & Animals, 12*(3), 185–207.

Henry, B., & Sanders, C. E. (2007). Bullying and animal abuse: Is there a connection? *Society & Animals, 15*, 107–126.

Hensley, C., Tallichet, S. E., & Dutkiewicz, E. L. (2009). Recurrent childhood animal cruelty: Is there a relationship to adult recurrent interpersonal violence? *Criminal Justice Review, 34*, 248–257.

Herzog, H., Betchart, N., & Pittman, R. (1991). Sex role identity and attitudes toward animals, *Anthrozoös, 4*(3), 184–192.

HSUS. (2007). *American Humane: Protecting children and animals*, Retrieved from: http://www.americanhumane.org/site/PageServer?pagename=lk_home&JServSessionIdr007=a2n8v9wra1.app25a.

Khan, R., & Cooke, D. J. (2008). Risk factors for severe inter-sibling violence: A preliminary study of a youth forensic sample. *Journal of Interpersonal Violence, 23*, 1513–1530.

Kellert, S. R., & Felthous, A. R. (1985). Childhood cruelty toward animals among criminals and non-criminals, *Human Relations, 38*, 1113–1129.

Knight, K., Ellis, C., & Simmons, S. (2014). Parental predictors of children's animal abuse: Findings from a national and intergenerational sample, *Journal of Interpersonal Violence, 29*(16), 3014–3034.

Kreinert, J., Walsh, J., Matthews, K., & McConkey, K. (2012). Examining the nexus between domestic violence and animal abuse in a national sample of service providers, *Violence and Victims, 27*(2), 280–295.

Levinson, B. (1978). Pets and personality development, *Psychological Reports, 42*, 1031–1038.

Lockwood, R., & Ascione, F. (Eds.). (1998). *Cruelty to animals and interpersonal violence.* Indiana: Purdue University Press.

Lockwood, R., & Hodge, G. (1986) The tangled web of animal abuse: the links between cruelty to animals and human violence, *Humane Society News*, Summer, 1–6.

Luk, E. S., Staiger, P. K., Wong, L., & Mathai, J. (1999). Children who are cruel to animals: A revisit. *Australia and New Zealand Journal of Psychiatry, 33*(1), 29–36.

McEwan, F., Moffitt, T., & Arseneault, L. (2014). Is childhood cruelty to animals a marker for physical maltreatment in a prospective cohort study of children? *Child Abuse & Neglect, 38*, 533–543.

McPhedran, S. (2009). Animal abuse, family violence, and child wellbeing. *Journal of Family Violence, 24*, 41–52.

Mead, M. (1964) Cultural factors in the cause of pathological homicide, *Bulletin of the Menninger Clinic, 2*, 11–22.

Merz-Perez, L., & Heide, K. M. (2003). *Animal cruelty: Pathway to violence against people.* Lanham, MD: Rowman & Littlefield.

Merz-Perez, L., Heide, K., & Silverman, I. J. (2001). Childhood cruelty to animals and subsequent violence against humans, *International Journal of Offender Therapy and Comparative Criminology, 45*(5), 556–573.

Miller, C. (2001). Childhood animal cruelty and interpersonal violence, *Clinical Psychology Review, 21*(5), 755–749.

Miller, K. S., & Knutson, J. F. (1997). Reports of severe physical punishment and exposure to animal cruelty by inmates convicted of felonies and by university students, *Child Abuse & Neglect 21*(1), 59–82.

Norris, G., & Wilson, P. (2003). Relationship of criminal behaviour and mental illness in young adults: Conduct Disorder, cruelty to animals and young adult serious violence. *Psychiatry, Psychology and the Law, 10*(1), 239–243.

O'Grady, K. E., Kinlock, T. W., & Hanlon, T. E. (2007). Prediction of violence history in substance-abusing inmates, *The Prison Journal, 87*, 416–433.

Porcher, J. (2011). The relationship between workers and animals in the pork industry: A shared suffering, *Journal of Agricultural and Environmental Ethics, 24*(1), 3–17.

Porcher, J., Cousson-Gélie, F., & Dantzer, R. (2004). Affective components of the human-animal relationship in animal husbandry: Development and validation of a questionnaire, *Psychological Reports, 95*, 275–290.

Randour, M. L. (2007). Integrating animals into the family violence paradigm: Implications for policy and professional standards. *Journal of Emotional Abuse, 7*(3), 97–116.

Richards, E., Signal, T. D., & Taylor, N. (in press). A different cut? Occupation, attitude to animals and propensity for aggression. *Society & Animals*.

Rigdon, J. D., & Tapia, F. (1977). Children who are cruel to animals: A follow-up study. *Journal of Operational Psychiatry, 8*(1), 27–36.

Sanders, C. E., & Henry, B. C. (2014). Nonhuman animal cruelty, bullying and behavioral difficulties among women. *Society & Animals, Advance online*, doi: 10.1163/15685306-12341355.12341355.

Sanders, C., Henry, B., Giuliani, C., & Dimmer, L. (2013). Bullies, victims, and animal abusers: Do they exhibit similar behavioral difficulties? *Society & Animals, 21*, 225–239.

Schiff, K., Louw, D., & Ascione F. (1999). Animal relations in childhood and later violent behaviour against humans, *Acta Criminologica, 12*, 77–86.

Signal, T., & Taylor, N. (2006). Attitudes to animals: Demographics within a Community sample, *Society & Animals, 14*(2), 147–158.

Simmons, C. A., & Lehmann, P. (2007). Exploring the link between pet abuse and controlling behaviors in violent relationships. *Journal of Interpersonal Violence, 22*(9), 1211–1222.

Simons, D. A., Wurtele, S. K., & Durham, R. L. (2008). Developmental experiences of child sexual abusers and rapists. *Child Abuse & Neglect, 32*, 549–560.

Sutherland, E. (1949). *White collar crime*, New York: Holt, Rinehart & Winston.

Tallichet, S. E., & Hensley, C. (2005). Rural and urban differences in the commission of animal cruelty, *International Journal of Offender Therapy and Comparative Criminology, 49*(6), 711–726.

Tallichet, S. E., Hensley, C., O'Bryan, A., & Hassel, H. (2005). Targets for cruelty: Demographic and situational factors affecting the type of animal abused, *Criminal Justice Studies: A Critical Journal of Crime, Law & Society, 18*(2), 173–182.

Tapia, F. (1971). Children who are cruel to animals. *Child Psychiatry & Human Development, 2*(2), 70–77.

Taylor, N. (2011). Criminology and human-animal violence research: The contribution and the challenge, *Critical Criminology, 19*, 251–263.

Taylor, N., Fraser, H., Signal, T., & Prentice, K. (2014). Social Work, Animal Assisted Therapies and Ethical Considerations: A Case Example from Central Queensland. British Journal of Social Work, online first doi: 10.1093/bjsw/bcu115.

Taylor, N., & Signal, T. (2004). Attitudes to animals: An indicator of interpersonal violence? *Journal of the Home Economics Institute of Australia, Inc., 11*(3), 9–12.

Taylor, N., & Signal, T. (2005). Empathy and attitudes towards animals. *Anthrozoos, 18*(1), 18–27.

Taylor, N., & Signal, T. (2006). Community demographics and the propensity to report animal cruelty, *Journal of Applied Animal Welfare Science, 9*(3), 14–20.

Taylor, N., & Signal, T. (2008). Throwing the baby out with the bathwater: Towards a sociology of the human-animal abuse 'link.' *Sociological Research Online, 13*(1/2).

Taylor, N., Signal, T., & Stark, T. (2006). Domestic violence, child abuse and companion animal harm: Service provider perspectives. *Journal of the Home Economics Institute of Australia, 13*(1), 2–5.

Thompson, K., & Gullone, E. (2003). Promotion of empathy and prosocial behaviour in children, *Australian Psychologist, 38*(3), 175–182.

Thompson, K., & Gullone, E. (2006). An investigation into the association between the witnessing of animal abuse and adolescents' behavior toward animals. *Society & Animals, 14*, 223–243.

Vaughn, M. G., Fu, Q., Beaver, K. M., DeLisi, M., Perron, B. E. & Howard, M. O. (2011). Effects of childhood adversity on bullying and cruelty to animals in the United States: Findings from a national sample. Journal of Interpersonal Violence, 26(11), 3509–3525.

Vialles, N. (2002). *Animals to edible*. Cambridge: Cambridge University Press.

Volant, A. M., Johnson, J. A., Gullone, E., & Coleman, G. J. (2008). The relationship between domestic violence and animal abuse: An Australian study, *Journal of Interpersonal Violence, 23*(9), 1277–1295.

Warden, D., & Mackinnon, S. (2003). Prosocial children, bullies and victims: An investigation of their sociometric status, empathy and social problem-solving strategies, *British Journal of Developmental Psychology 21*, 367–385.

Wax, D. E., & Haddox, V. G. (1974). Enuresis, fire setting, and animal cruelty: A useful danger signal in predicting vulnerability of adolescent males to assaultive behavior, *Child Psychiatry and Human Development, 4,* 151–156.

Williams, T. Y., Boyd, J. C., Cascardi, M. A., & Poythress, N. (1996). Factor structure and convergent validity of the aggression questionnaire in an offender population. *Psychological Assessment, 8*(4), 398–403.

Chapter 13

Family Violence and Animal Cruelty

Eleonora Gullone

In recent years, there has been increasing attention given to the importance of companion and other animals in the lives of humans (Amiot & Bastian, 2015). The majority of this attention has been focused on the positive outcomes accrued to humans as a consequence of their interactions with non-human animals. For example, epidemiological studies have shown that people with companion animals were more likely to be alive one year after discharge from a coronary care unit as compared to non-owners, and that dog owners were approximately 8.6 times more likely to be alive after one year as compared to non-dog owners (Friedmann, Katcher, Lynch, & Thomas, 1980; Friedmann & Thomas, 1995; McConnell, Brown, Shoda, Stayton, & Martin, 2011).

Even the mere observation of animals has been shown to result in reduced physiological responses to stressors and increased positive moods (e.g., Rossbach & Wilson, 1992). In their attempts to highlight the salient aspects of the human-animal bond, studies have found that, when asked about the benefits that their companion animals provide, people typically describe their relationships as being characterized by feelings of companionship, security, and being loved (e.g., Siegel, 1990).

As companion animals have increasingly become part of our lives, they have also increasingly assumed an important role within the family system. Not surprisingly, research has painted a picture of human-animal relationships that in many respects is mirroring those between humans and, unfortunately, as is true of relationships between human family members, human-animal relationships are not always positive.

The aim of this chapter is to review the research that has examined relationships between domestic and family violence, and animal cruelty. In the first section of this chapter, child and partner abuse research are reviewed. This is followed by a review of investigations into the relationship between human- and animal-directed violence within the family. The chapter concludes with recommendations based upon current understandings.

Family Violence and Human Aggression Defined

Family violence includes abusive behavior by one family member toward another, including child and elder abuse, and has many forms (Wallace, 2004). It refers to violence that occurs in relationships of intimacy, kinship, dependency or trust (Straka & Montminy, 2008). These forms of violence include actual physical aggression as well as threats of aggression. Sexual, emotional, and psychological abuse including intimidation, stalking and covert abuse such as neglect, are also included (Kazdin, 2011; Shipway, 2004). As will be discussed in more detail later, the witnessing of abuse has also been classified as a form of abuse (Schumacher et al., 2001).

If one considers the conceptualization of aggression, it can be clearly seen that the abuse that occurs within intimate relationships and is otherwise referred to as domestic or family violence, can be argued to be specific forms of aggression. Anderson (2002) defined aggression as behavior performed by a person (the aggressor) with the immediate intention of harming another person (the victim). The perpetrator (aggressor) must believe that the behavior will harm the victim and that the victim is motivated to avoid that intended harm. While Gendreau and Archer (2005) have argued that *harm and injury* to others are the strongest indicators that an aggressive act has occurred, it is noteworthy that, in his definition, Anderson (2002) states that *actual* harm is not a requirement. Also, although research has predominantly focused on physical harm, mental or psychological harm are included as consequences of aggression. Further, Anderson's definition includes "harm" that can be either or both physical harm (e.g., physical abuse) and psychological harm (e.g., verbal abuse).

Gendreau and Archer (2005) cited an important dichotomy in aggression based on the work of Feshbach (1964) which distinguishes between behaviors that have the primary goal of causing injury to the victim and pleasure or satisfaction to the aggressor compared to behaviors that do not have injury as the main goal. In the latter case, the behavior is motivated by the primary goal of obtaining a reward. This type of aggression has been referred to as *instrumental* aggression. Given arguments that family or domestic violence are predominantly motivated by the desire to control the victim of the abuse (Flynn, 2009; Straka & Montminy, 2008), it can be argued that domestic or family violence can be most accurately classified as forms of instrumental aggression.

Family Violence between Humans

Each year, thousands of children and millions of women are abused (Black, Heyman, & Smith Slep, 2001; Kazdin, 2011; Schumacher et al., 2001; Tolan, Gorman-Smith, & Henry, 2006; Wallace, 2004). The outcomes of abuse are significantly damaging, and include medical, behavioral, and emotional problems. For example, research has shown that women who are abused report higher rates of Major Depressive Disorder and Posttraumatic Stress (Cascardi, O'Leary, Lawrence, & Schlee, 1995). Although the majority of research into child abuse remains separate from that examining partner abuse (Heyman & Smith Slep, 2001), available information regarding the comorbidity of the two forms of abuse highlights the significant overlap. For example, in a national survey of over 6,000 U.S. families, 50% of men who frequently assaulted their wives also frequently abused their children (Straus & Gelles, 1990). As with the abuse of adults, that involving children is significantly damaging.

Child Abuse

The experience of parental abuse can be devastating for children, and there is considerable empirical evidence showing that it is one of the most important parenting variables for predicting the development of internalizing and externalizing problems including antisocial behavior (Buka, Stichick, Birdthistle, & Earls, 2001). Indeed, child abuse and child neglect are now commonly accepted to be factors that place abused or neglected children at increased risk of themselves becoming abusing or neglecting parents (Black, et al., 2001; Eron, 1987; Peterson, Gable, Doyle, and Ewugman, 1998; Widom, 1989). According to figures cited by Kaufman and Zigler (1987), approximately 30% of individuals who have experienced abuse (physical, sexual, or severe neglect) as children will abuse their own children compared to 5% in the general population. Other long-term adverse outcomes of direct and indirect abuse include being at greater risk of arrest for violent crime and for earlier and more chronic engagement in criminal behavior.

On the basis of available evidence, it appears that physical abuse has a more consistent link with aggression than do neglect or emotional abuse (Margolin & Gordis, 2000). Increased risk of aggression and externalizing behavior has also been reported in relation to sexual abuse. Though not as consistent as the link with physical abuse, sexual abuse has been linked with aggressive behavior, delinquency, and other externalizing behaviors (Margolin & Gordis, 2000).

In one 20-year follow-up study, Luntz and Widom (1994) found that abused children had twice the likelihood of being diagnosed as having an Antisocial Personality Disorder compared to a matched (on age, race, sex, and family socio-economic status) control sample. Other research has found that the long-term effects of abuse include school suspensions in late adolescence and physical violence (Dodge, Bates, Pettit, 1990; Lansford et al., 2002). In an attempt to control for possible child-related genetic effects, Jaffee, Caspi, Moffitt, and Taylor (2004) studied a large sample of twin pairs in Great Britain. They found that physical maltreatment is strongly causative of children's antisocial behavior development, but found no support for child genetic effects on maltreatment.

As summarized by Maughan and Cicchetti (2002), negative familial experiences including exposure to interpersonal violence and displays of negative affect, interfere with children's developing ability to process and to manage their emotions. The effects of direct maltreatment and exposure to interadult violence include deviations from normality in emotion expression, recognition, understanding, and communication. For example, Fergusson and Horwood (1998) reported strong relationships between children's observing of domestic violence and antisocial behavior at a later time.

Research with 3-month-old maltreated infants has shown that such infants display higher rates of fearfulness, anger, and sadness during interactions with their mothers when compared to non-abused children (Gaensbauer, Mrazek, & Harmon, 1981). The maltreated infants were also found to express a truncated range of emotions, and to display negative emotions for higher durations when compared to their normative peers. For older maltreated children, when compared to non-maltreated peers, researchers have found higher rates of aggression (Shields & Cicchetti, 1998), withdrawn behavior (Haskett & Kistner, 1991), and vigilance in response to aggressive stimuli (Rieder & Cicchetti, 1989).

In their study, Maughan and Cicchetti (2002) compared the socioemotional adjustment of 88 maltreated and 51 non-maltreated children who were otherwise demographically comparable. The children were aged between 4 and 6 years. Consistent with previous research, the mothers of the maltreated children in their sample reported more incidents of interadult verbal aggression and physical violence compared to their non-maltreated sample. Also, the mothers of the maltreated children reported more child behavior problems compared to the non-maltreated children. Physical abuse and neglect independently predicted higher levels of socially problematic behaviors including delinquent and withdrawn behavior. Moreover, physical abuse when compared to non-maltreatment was associated with child aggression.

There is some evidence to indicate that the outcomes of abuse are moderated by other environmental factors, including socio-economic status, leading to the conclusion that other types of disadvantage also play a part in the development of externalizing outcomes. For example, in their 1983 study, Wolfe and Mosk compared abused children with non-abused children from non-disadvantaged or distressed families and with children from generally distressed families. They found that the abused children expressed more externalizing behaviors compared to the non-abused children from non-distressed environments, but there was no difference between children who were abused and children who were not abused but were from distressed family environments. Similar findings were reported by Toth, Manly, and Cicchetti (1992). This is consistent with the findings of Repetti and colleagues that a common pathway to child dysfunction or pathology appears to be distress or dysfunction in the family system (see e.g., Repetti, Taylor, & Seeman, 2002).

There is also evidence regarding the adverse outcomes associated with interadult violence exposure. Although some studies have failed to find a relationship between parental violence and child externalizing behaviors including aggression (e.g., Jouriles, Barling, & O'Leary, 1987), a significant number of studies have found such a link (see Margolin & Gordis, 2000).

Indeed, exposure has been associated with higher rates of both internalizing and externalizing symptomatology (Dutton, 2000; Howell, 2011; Katz & Gottman, 1993). Estimates indicate that children who witness domestic violence are at between 40% to 60% greater risk of developing psychological problems as compared to children from non-violent homes (Graham-Bermann & Hughes, 1998). Studies have reported increased levels of child fear, distress, and concern in addition to anger and aggression in response to witnessed inter-adult anger (e.g., Cummings, 1987; Davies, Myers, Cummings, & Heindel, 1999). Some have also argued that the witnessing of violence by children places them at higher risk of developing post-traumatic stress disorder (Cunningham & Baker, 2004; Graham-Bermann & Levendosky, 1998).

Compellingly, Straus and colleagues (1980) reported that boys who witness paternal violence are at a 1,000% increased risk for assaulting their own partners as adults. A child's exposure to his/her father abusing their mother has been reported to be the strongest predictor for the intergenerational transmission of violent behavior (American Psychological Association, 1996). Importantly, both direct and indirect exposure to violence have been shown to constitute significant risk factors (Baldry, 2003; Fergusson, & Horwood, 1998; Lyons-Ruth, 1996).

Partner Abuse

With regard to partner violence, Schumacher and colleagues (2001) concluded that demographic variables such as socio-economic status, perpetrator age, and education level appear to be only weakly related. In contrast, all forms of family of origin violence factors have been found to moderately to strongly correlate with partner physical abuse. These include history of child sexual victimization and exposure to parental physical and/ or verbal aggression, and violent adult models in childhood, as well as non-family aggression by the parent.

Studies investigating perpetrator personality and personality disorder-related traits have reported elevated levels of aggression, anger, hostility, and impulsivity to be significant predictors of male to female physical abuse (e.g., Hamberger & Hastings, 1991; Hastings & Hamberger, 1994; Murphy, Meyer, & O'Leary, 1993). Not surprisingly, several of the reported risk factors for child and partner abuse overlap with those for juvenile or adult criminality, and with externalizing disorder symptomatology. Among many identified risk factors are those within the family.

The meta-analysis published by Repetti and colleagues (2002) constitutes a comprehensive examination of family-related factors that are important for the mental and physical health outcomes of offspring. These investigators examined the characteristics of what they referred to as "risky families" and found strong support for the important role played by the family environment in the development of antisocial behaviors. According to Repetti et al. (2002), the characteristics that appear most prominently as family "risk" factors include overt family conflict, particularly recurrent episodes of anger and aggression. Deficient nurturing or low warmth particularly characterized by cold, unsupportive, or neglectful parenting was found to be another quality of a risky family. Families with such characteristics are risky because they leave children vulnerable to a range of disorders, both physical and mental.

On the basis of their analysis, Repetti and colleagues developed a model including the pathways of risk through which health in childhood is compromised and through which physical and mental health in later periods of development, including adolescence and adulthood, may be influenced. Emphasizing the importance of interactive processes between nature and nurture, they proposed a "cascade of risk" model. Certain vulnerabilities may be created by risky families and genetically-based vulnerabilities may be exacerbated rather than attenuated as would occur within a healthy or protective family environment. A main proposal put forth by the authors is that risky families create deficits in children's control and expression of their emotions and also in their social competence. They also argued that risky families lead to other disturbances (e.g., physiologic and neuroendocrine system regulation), and that such disturbances can have cumulative and long-term adverse effects.

Consistent with Repetti et al.'s conclusions, among the more prominent variables implicated in the development of externalizing or antisocial behaviors are parental negativity, and inadequate monitoring of children's behavior. Other variables include particular parental disciplinary practices including power-assertive strategies, and parenting that is harsh, inconsistent, or permissive (Burt, McGue, Krueger, & Iacono, 2005; Larsson, Viding, Rijsdijk, & Plomin, 2008; Loeber & Dishion, 1983; O'Connor, 2002; Peterson, Hawkins, Abbott, & Catalano, 1994; Tolan et al., 2006).

Indeed, a relationship between harsh and ineffective parental discipline and child aggressive behavior problems has been reported in children as young as 2 to 3 years of age. Other important variables are insecure attachment relationships—particularly disorganized attachment, direct and indirect exposure to abuse or violence, and conflictive parent-child relationships (Lyons-Ruth, 1996; Simons, Paternite, & Shore, 2001).

Reinforcing the overlap between family violence and antisocial behavior patterns, family violence has been found to be a significant predictor of criminality (Pelcovitz, Kaplan, DeRosa, Mandel, & Salzinger, 2000). Thus, it is clear that for many children at risk of developing conduct problems in childhood and subsequent antisocial problems in adulthood, a risky family environment is a significant predictive factor (e.g., Baldry & Farrington, 2000; Bank & Burraston, 2001; McCloskey, Figueredo, & Koss, 1995; Repetti et al., 2002; Sternberg et al., 1993).

Other important predictive variables for the development of both antisocial and aggressive behaviors include predispositional tendencies such as a low levels of impulse control and empathy, as well as high levels of callousness (Gullone, 2012). In the most severe of situations including domestic violence and child abuse, the behavior problems of youth have been documented to be of an intergenerational nature (Black et al., 2001; Serbin & Karp, 2004).

Research has also shown that the presence of one type of violence or antisocial behavior predicts an increased likelihood of another type (see Chapter 12). Pelcovitz et al. (2000) have noted that as the frequency of marital violence in the family increases, the likelihood that child abuse will also be present increases dramatically. The statistics they provide indicate that one incident of marital violence predicts a 5% probability of child abuse while 50 or more such incidents predict almost certainly that child abuse will occur. However, despite the knowledge that different types of aggression and antisocial behavior co-occur, animal cruelty as a form of violence remains relatively neglected in the mainstream antisocial and aggression literature (Gullone, 2012). Similarly, research outcomes indicating relationships between animal cruelty and human aggression remain largely un-cited in the mainstream literature. Consequently, as will be discussed in a subsequent section of this chapter, intervention and prevention efforts for both human violence and animal cruelty are not as efficacious as they otherwise could be. It is to the animal cruelty research that this chapter will now turn.

Animal Cruelty Defined

Felthous and Kellert (1986) defined cruelty to animals as a behavior pattern that deliberately, repeatedly, and unnecessarily causes harm to vertebrate animals in such a way that is likely to cause them serious injury (see Chapter 1). Brown (1988) defined cruelty as "unnecessary suffering knowingly inflicted on a sentient being (animal or human)" (p. 3). Brown made clear in his definition that the suffering may be of a physical type as in causing the sensation of pain or it may be suffering that causes distress or psychological hurt such as would be the case with maternal deprivation. Brown also argued that cruelty to animals can be either positive or negative such that committing an act against the animal would constitute a positive form of cruelty whereas failing to act as in neglecting to feed an animal or to care for it appropriately would constitute a negative form of cruelty.

Following detailed consideration of a number of definitions of animal cruelty, Dadds, Turner, and McAloon (2002) noted that most definitions comprise a number of features. These include a behavioral dimension that can be in the form of acts of omission (e.g., neglect) or acts of commission (e.g., beating). Another key characteristic is indication that the behavior occurred purposely, that is, with deliberateness and without ignorance. An additional definitional criterion is that the behavior can bring about physical and/or psychological harm. Incorporating these definitional criteria, Dadds (2008) defined animal cruelty as a repetitive and proactive behavior (or pattern of behavior) intended to cause harm to sentient creatures.

Gullone (2012) elaborated further upon Dadds' definition. According to Gullone, animal cruelty can be defined as behavior performed repetitively and proactively by an individual with the deliberate intention of causing harm (i.e., pain, suffering, distress and/or death) to an animal with the understanding that the animal is motivated to avoid that harm. Included in this definition are both physical harm and psychological harm.

Family and Parenting Experiences

In the earliest published investigation of the aetiology of animal cruelty by children, Tapia (1971) reported an analysis of 18 child cases of cruelty to animals selected from the clinical files of the Child Psychiatry Section of the University of Missouri's School of Medicine. In all selected cases, cruelty to animals was either the chief complaint or one of the referring complaints. Among the cases, there was a high male prevalence. The children were of normal intelligence and young in age, spanning from 5 to 15 years, with half of the cases being between 8 and 10 years. A chaotic home environment with aggressive parental models was the most common factor across the cases. On the basis of the case analysis, Tapia concluded that cruelty to animals occurs in conjunction with other hostile behavior including bullying and fighting, lying, stealing, and destructiveness, and that a chaotic home environment, together with aggressive parent models, are common factors.

A follow-up study was conducted in 1977 by Rigdon and Tapia to determine whether the presence of cruelty to animals as a significant clinical feature provides information that is of prognostic value. The original data reported in 1971 were collected between 2 and 9 years earlier. Five of the original 18 children were not able to be located for this follow-up study. The detailed case-by-case analysis revealed that, of the 13 cases followed up, 8 were still cruel to animals as many as 9 years later. The authors concluded that "[m]ost of these children [were] the products of a chaotic home situation with aggressive parents who administered harsh corporal punishment" and that "[t]he most effective form of therapy seemed to be removal from or a significant change in the chaotic home environment" (p. 36).

One of the earliest studies to investigate the relationship between family environment and animal cruelty was the U.K. study by Hutton (1983) who reported Royal Society for the Prevention of Cruelty to Animals (RSPCA) cruelty data for a community in England. The data showed that out of 23 families with a history of animal cruelty, 82% had also been identified by human social services as having children who were at risk of abuse or neglect. Around a decade later in the United States, Arkow (1994) reported a study in which 24% of 122 women seeking refuge from domestic violence and 11% of 1,175 women seeking restraining orders or support services reported observing animal cruelty by the perpetrator.

In other research, Deviney, Dickert, and Lockwood (1983) studied 53 families who had companion animals in their homes and who met New Jersey legal criteria for child abuse and neglect. They found that compared to the general population, there were higher rates of animal cruelty in families where there was substantiated child abuse or neglect. Observations during home interviews revealed that companion animals were abused or neglected in 60% of these families. When the sample was classified according to type of abuse (physical abuse—40%; sexual abuse—10%; neglect—58%), for an alarming 88% of families displaying physical child abuse, cruelty to animals was also present. Two-thirds of the companion animals in these homes were abused by the fathers in the family and one-third by children.

In their work comparing criminal (aggressive versus non-aggressive) and non-criminal retrospective reports of childhood experiences and abuse behaviors, Kellert and Felthous found that domestic violence and particularly paternal abuse and alcoholism, were common factors among those aggressive criminals who had a history of childhood animal cruelty (Felthous, 1980; Felthous & Kellert, 1986; Kellert & Felthous, 1985). According to Kellert and Felthous (1985), the family and childhood experiences of many of the aggressive criminals were particularly violent. The domestic violence in the families of the aggressive criminals was most strongly characterized by paternal violence. Of note, three quarters of the aggressive criminals reported repeated and excessive child abuse compared to 31% of the non-aggressive criminals and 10% of the non-criminals. Among the non-aggressive criminals and non-criminals who were cruel to animals, reports of being physically abused as children were common. As many as 75% of non-criminals who reported experiences of parental abuse also reported being cruel to animals.

In a study by Ressler, Burgess, Hartman, Douglas, and McCormack (1986), 36 convicted sexually-oriented killers were interviewed about their childhood histories. The offenders who were sexually abused in childhood or adolescence were significantly more likely than those who were not abused to report a number of aggressive behaviors including cruelty to animals, cruelty to other children, and assaultive behavior toward adults.

In research examining the relationships between childhood experiences and animal cruelty, Miller and Knutson (1997) compared the self-reports of 314 inmates with those of a group of undergraduate university students. They found modest associations between animal cruelty and punitive and acrimonious childhood histories. On this basis, the authors concluded that there is an association between punitive childhood histories and antisocial behavior.

Also based on retrospective self-reports, Flynn's (1999b) study involved 267 undergraduate students. The results showed a relationship between corporal punishment by parents and the perpetration of animal cruelty. Those who had perpetrated animal cruelty were physically punished more frequently before the teenage years than those who had never been cruel to an animal. Also, more than half of male teenagers who were hit by their fathers reported perpetrating animal cruelty.

Ascione, Friedrich, Heath, and Hayashi (2003) also examined the associations between children's cruelty to animals and physical abuse. In addition, they looked at the relationship between animal cruelty and parental physical fighting. Three groups of children (1. sexually abused group; 2. psychiatric sample with no sexual abuse; 3. control group) aged between 6 and 12 years were involved in the study. Cruelty to animals was associated with a history of abuse, and the association was stronger for children who had been physically abused and those who had witnessed domestic violence.

A study by Duncan, Thomas, and Miller (2005) yielded converging findings through the assessment of charts of boys (aged 8 to 17 years) with conduct problems. The children's histories were also examined to identify the occurrence of physical child abuse, sexual child abuse, paternal alcoholism, paternal unavailability, and domestic violence. Children were grouped according to whether they had or had not been cruel to animals. It was found that children who were cruel to animals were twice as likely to have been physically and/or sexually abused or to have been exposed to domestic violence compared to children who were not cruel to animals.

A more recent study by DeGue and DeLillo (2009) which involved 860 university students from three U.S. universities showed that around about 60% of participants who witnessed or perpetrated animal cruelty as a child also retrospectively reported experiences of child maltreatment or domestic violence. The study results also showed that those who had been sexually or physically abused or neglected as children were those most likely to report that they had been cruel to animals as children.

These findings of research examining the relationships between childhood animal cruelty and parenting and family experiences are consistent with those from the larger literature relating to the development of aggressive and antisocial behavior. Such research, for example, has shown that within homes where there is greater family instability, more conflict, and problematic parenting strategies (i.e., physical punishment), children are more likely to develop along the trajectory of childhood-onset antisocial behavior. In addition to examining the parenting and family factors that are associated with children's animal cruelty, a number of explanations have been espoused to promote better understanding of children's animal cruelty. These are discussed below.

Understanding Children's Cruelty toward Animals

According to Robin and ten Bensel (1985), for some abused or disturbed children, companion animals may represent someone that they can gain power and control over. Thus, cruelty to animals can be conceptualized as a displacement of aggression from humans to animals. This can be explained through the psychological mechanism of identifying with the aggressor. That is, when children are victimized and, as consequence, feel powerless, helpless, and frightened, they may seek to overcome these feelings by exercising control over someone less powerful than themselves. This can be a companion animal, a younger sibling, or even a peer. Exerting such control, and thereby identifying with their abuser, may help children to restore their sense of self-efficacy, albeit in a dysfunctional way (Ascione, 2001). There are indications that other explanations also apply. For example, according to Ascione (1999), some children in abusive situations are forced to abuse animals by the adult perpetrators.

Interestingly, in their survey of 238 abused adolescents aged between 13 and 18 years who were living in juvenile institutions, and 269 control group youth living in the community, Robin and ten Bensel (1985) found that 91% of the abused group said that they had a special companion animal. Moreover, 99% of these youth said that they loved or liked their companion animal very much. Among the comparison group, 90% said that they had a special companion animal and 97% said that they loved or liked the companion animal very much. These findings suggest that companion animals have a prominent place in the emotional lives of children from non-abused as well as abused backgrounds. However, Robin and ten Bensel's study also revealed that the companion animals of the institutionalized group of adolescents suffered more abuse and these adolescents also experienced more violent companion animal loss compared to the control group. Importantly, the abuser was usually someone other than the child. For example, there were several instances of companion animals being hurt or killed as a way of punishing the child. Others (e.g., Muraski, 1992 cited in Arkow, 1996; Summit, 1983) have reported that threatening to harm/kill, or actually harming/killing, a child's companion animals is a common technique used by child abusers to obtain the child's acquiescence or to keep the child quiet about the abuse. Because children are often deeply attached to their companion animals, observing them being violently abused or even killed is emotionally devastating for the child, but is an effective control mechanism for the perpetrator (Ascione, 2001).

There is also the proposal that a central common factor in explaining animal cruelty may be an underdeveloped or compromised level of empathy (e.g., Westbury & Neumann, 2008; see also Chapter 16). As argued by Ascione (1999), abusing animals may represent the perpetrator's reduced capacity to empathize with a potential victim (human or animal). Such a claim is supported by the demonstrated inverse relationship between *callousness* and empathy (Lahey, Waldman, & McBurnett, 1999). Further support for such a claim comes from the literature on childhood externalizing syndromes. Such syndromes, including Conduct Disorder (CD), are characterized by hyperactive, aggressive, and oppositional behaviors as well as the more serious rule violations that can bring the child in contact with the juvenile justice system (American Psychiatric Association, 1994). CD in childhood has been shown to be characterized by low levels of empathy (Hastings, Zahn-Waxler. Robinson, Usher, & Bridges, 2000) and is predictive of other psychological disorders including delinquency, drug abuse, school dropout, suicide, and criminality in adolescence or adulthood (Conduct Problems Prevention Research Group, 1992).

Research by Frick and colleagues has shown that a particular sub-type of early onset CD is differentiated by the presence of callous-unemotional (CU) traits, characteristics also referred to as psychopathy. Subsequent research has indicated that CU traits designate a particularly severe group of antisocial youth characterized by a lack of fearful inhibitions and other emotional deficits including impaired development of empathy and guilt, and an unemotional interpersonal style. A preference for thrill and adventure-seeking activities as well as a greater sensitivity to rewards than to punishments has also been reported (Frick, 1998; Frick, O'Brien, Wootton, & McBurnett, 1994). It is noteworthy that, in extreme forms, this dimension may include finding enjoyment in dominating, intimidating, embarrassing, and hurting others (Lahey et al., 1999).

Of further relevance, the American Psychiatric Association's (American Psychological Association, 2000) Diagnostic and Statistical Manual—IV Text Revised (DSM-IV TR) includes several diagnostic criteria for CD, related to the category of "aggression to people and animals," and including "has been physically cruel to people" and "has been physically cruel to animals" (p.99). Related to this, it is significant that hurting animals is considered to be one of the earliest emerging symptoms, appearing at a mean age of six years. As noted by Ascione (2001), since this behavior emerges earlier than other markers of CD including bullying, cruelty to people, vandalism, and causing fires, the presence of animal cruelty could serve as an important early marker for preventative interventions. Reinforcing Frick's conclusions about the importance of CU traits in predicting a particularly severe trajectory of CD, in a recent investigation, it was found that children who were cruel to animals displayed more severe conduct symptoms in general when compared to children who were not (Luk, Staiger, Wong, & Mathai, 1998). On the basis of their findings, Luk et al., (1998) concluded that cruelty to animals may be a marker of more serious conduct problems. Of relevance, predictors of the development of antisocial, aggressive, or violent behavior in childhood include family and parenting experiences, as well as individual differences in personality and temperament.

Despite the methodological limitations that characterize many of the investigations into children's animal cruelty, the consistent finding of a significant relationship between the experiencing of abuse in childhood and engagement in animal cruelty has emerged (Baldry, 2003; Boat et al., 2011; Currie, 2006; DeGue & DiLillo, 2009, Duncan et al., 2005; McPhedran, 2009). This is of particular note given methodological and sampling differences across studies including different assessment methodologies such as retrospective reporting, self-reports, and other-reports.

Other factors placing children at risk of developing aggressive and antisocial behaviors, of which animal cruelty is one, are those that characterize *risky families* (Repetti et al, 2002). These include overt family conflict, expressions of negative affect, and low nurturance and warmth. Risky parents are cold, unsupportive, or neglectful.

However, although risky parenting and risky family environments leave children vulnerable to the development of psychological and physical disorders, it is important to emphasize the role played by biology, often in interaction with environmental factors such as family environment. Research outcomes converge on the conclusion that certain biologically-based characteristics, such as temperament, are predictive of development along an antisocial behavior trajectory. However, the prediction of such an outcome is stronger if their biologically-based vulnerabilities are reinforced with environmental experiences that place children at risk of developing antisocial and aggressive behaviors such as abusive parenting.

While generally seen as dysfunctional, children's aggressive behavior can also be argued to be adaptive. Thus, children whose aggression increases as they develop, rather than following the normative decreasing pathway, may also be expressing a learned behavior that has survival value in their particular circumstance. That is, as victims of abuse, children experience a sense of powerlessness that, at a very basic level is likely to be experienced as a threat to survival. Identifying with their abuser enables a transformation from a sense of powerlessness to one of being in control. For a child, those who are more vulnerable than oneself are likely to be small animals, thus those animals are the vulnerable others to whom aggression can be displaced.

In addition to research showing significant associations between risky family environments and children's cruelty toward animals, there is a significant body of research showing significant relationships between domestic violence and animal cruelty. Included within many of the studies in this latter area, is further support for the relationship between a dysfunctional family environment, particularly a violent family, and children's cruelty toward animals. The research examining the link between domestic violence and animal cruelty will be reviewed below.

The Relationship between Domestic Violence and Animal Cruelty

Case study accounts of the relationship between domestic and animal cruelty, such as the one that follows, are powerful indicators of a conceptually explicable association that, until recently, had remained largely unexplored and/or undocumented by both researchers and practitioners.

> Mary, J. shot her husband as he entered their trailer, in fact blew the top of his head off. Why? Not because he hit her. He did. Not because he was mean to the children. He was. Not because he had isolated her from her family and friends in a small trailer miles from anything. He had. No, she killed him because he told her he was going to bring home another puppy for her to hold down while he had intercourse with the animal. (Quinslick, 1999; p. 171).

One of the most consistently replicated findings in the animal cruelty literature is a significant co-occurrence between domestic violence and animal cruelty. This research has found that more than 50% of all abused women have companion animals, and in as many as 50% of cases, the animals are abused by the perpetrators of the domestic violence. Motivations for the abuse include hurting and/or controlling the women or their children. The research has also consistently found that concern for the safety of their companion animals keeps many women (and their children) from leaving or staying separated from their abusers. It can be argued that animal cruelty when it occurs within the family home, is a symptom of a deeply dysfunctional family (Lockwood & Hodge, 1986).

In 1997, Ascione and others published a study reporting the findings of a U.S. national survey of shelters. One shelter from nearly every U.S. state was selected for participation. Shelter staff were surveyed about the coexistence of animal cruelty and domestic violence and children's cruelty toward animals. They found that as many as 85% of staff who were interviewed reported that they were aware of incidents of companion animal cruelty. A total of 63% of the staff also reported hearing children talk about animal cruelty. Eighty-three percent of workers answered 'yes' to the question "... have you observed the coexistence of domestic violence and pet abuse?"

In a subsequent study, 38 women who sought shelter for domestic violence were directly interviewed (Ascione, 1998). The author reported that 74% owned a companion animal (and 68% owned more than one companion animal). Of these women, 71% reported that threats of harming, actual harm, or killing of companion animals by the perpetrators had occurred. Also, approximately 30% of children exposed to violence were themselves reported to be cruel toward animals. Ascione also found that a significant proportion (18%) of women delayed seeking shelter for themselves and their children, for fear of their companion animal being harmed.

Quinslick (1999) reported the findings of another survey conducted as part of the Domestic Violence Intervention Project. The study involved 72 female victims of domestic violence of whom 58 had companion animals. Of these women, 68% reported violence directed toward their companion animals. In other cases, women reported experiencing threats to kill or to give away their companion animal(s). In 88% of cases, the cruelty was committed in their presence and in 76% of cases, children had been witness to the cruelty. They found that 54% of child witnesses copied the behaviors they had observed. Of particular note is the fact that Quinslick (1999) reported almost identical results for an additional survey involving 32 women.

A later study by Daniell (2001) reported the findings of a survey conducted by the Ontario Society for the Prevention of Cruelty to Animals (Ontario SPCA). More than 100 women's shelters throughout Ontario were contacted and a total of 21 agreed to participate. This resulted in 130 women being surveyed, 80 of whom owned companion animals at the time of entering the women's refuge and a further 31 who had owned a companion animal in the past 12 months. The results were largely consistent with past studies. Of the 111 women owning companion animals, 44% stated that their partner had previously been cruel or killed one or more of their companions, and 42% stated that their partner had threatened to hurt or kill one of their animals. Finally, as many as 43% of respondents indicated that concern about their companion animal's welfare had caused them remain in their abusive situation longer.

Flynn's (2000) study attempted to replicate and extend upon previous research examining the human-animal violence link. In his study, the participants were asked four questions. These related to the nature and extent of companion animal cruelty suffered by physically abused women, the importance of the companion animals as sources of emotional support for the women, whether they worried about their companion animal's welfare after seeking shelter, and finally whether their concern for the companion animal's welfare delayed their seeking refuge. One hundred and seven women from a South Carolina shelter were involved in the study; 43 of the women had companion animals. Of the companion animal owners, 47% reported that they had experienced threats of harm or actual harm to their animal(s) by the perpetrator of the domestic violence. In contrast to previous research, only two instances of companion animal cruelty by children were reported. Regarding emotional importance, almost half (46%) of the women reported their companion animal to be a very important source of emotional support. Not surprisingly, almost as many (40%) reported being worried about their animal's safety and 19% of the women reported delaying seeking shelter.

Of note, studies examining the associations between animal cruelty and domestic violence have been conducted across several countries including the United States, Canada, and Australia (e.g., Ascione, 1998; Ascione, et al., 2007; Daniell, 2001; Faver & Cavazos,

2007; Flynn, 2000; Quinlisk, 1999; Volant, Johnson, Coleman, & Gullone, 2008). The findings are remarkably consistent across the studies despite their differences in parameters including the country in which the study was conducted, sample size, and the methodology used. However, a limitation of these studies is that, with few exceptions (i.e., Ascione, et al., 2007; Volant et al, 2008), they have not included a comparison group of women who were not in a violent family situation.

In their comparison group study, Ascione, et al. (2007) interviewed 101 women who were recruited through domestic violence shelters as well as a comparison community sample of 60 women who had not experienced family violence. The researchers found that the shelter women were more likely to report that their partners had threatened to hurt their companion animals (52%) and that their partners had actually hurt or killed their companion animals (54%). This compared with 16.7% and 3.5%, respectively in the community sample of women. For the shelter women, their reports included multiple incidents of killing or hurting companion animals in contrast to the community sample for whom incidents were typically isolated and were more likely to occur within the context of disciplining the animal for bad behavior (e.g., biting).

In contrast to the reports obtained from the community sample women, shelter women could not give a reason for the animal cruelty. When women in the shelter group were asked whether concern for the welfare of their companion animal had kept them from seeking refuge sooner, nearly one fourth said "yes." This percentage was markedly higher for those women whose companion animals had already been hurt (35%).

Ascione et al. (2007) also assessed the experiences and behaviors of children. In this regard, over 50% of the shelter women reported that their children had witnessed the companion animal cruelty. This contrasted with less than 4% for the community sample. A total of 39 shelter group children were also directly interviewed. Two-thirds of these children (66.7%) reported that they had witnessed companion animal cruelty incidents as perpetrated (in 46.4% of cases) by their father, stepfather, or women's boyfriend. Of these children, 13.2% admitted that they had hurt companion animals and 7.9% reported hurting or killing the animals. However, more than 50% of the children said that they had protected their companion animal(s) by directly intervening.

In their Australian comparison group investigation, Volant, et al. (2008) surveyed 102 women recruited through 24 domestic violence refuge or outreach services and a non-domestic violence comparison community sample of 102 women. The findings were highly comparable to those of past similar studies and included that 46% of women in the domestic violence sample reported that their partner had *threatened to* hurt or kill their companion animal compared with 6% of women in the community sample. Similarly, a markedly larger percentage of domestic violence group women (56%) reported that their partner had hurt or killed their companion animal compared to 0% of women in the community sample. Of those women recruited through refuge (as opposed to outreach) services (n = 34), 35% reported delaying seeking refuge out of concern for the welfare of their companion animal. Delay periods ranged between one (3%) and eight weeks (24%). A number of the 34 women reported not delaying because they were able to take their companion animals with them.

Also, consistent with past similar studies, Volant et al. (2008) asked the women in the domestic violence sample about their children's experiences. In 29% of cases, children were reported to witness threats of cruelty and the same percentage was reported to witness actual cruelty. A total of 19% of the women reported that their child had been cruel to their companion animal.

In a recent study, researchers took a different approach from the thus far typical one of interviewing female victims of family violence. Febres and colleagues (2014) assessed self-reported adulthood animal abuse, antisocial behavior traits, and alcohol use in a sample of men arrested for family violence. In a sample of 307 men, they examined the prevalence and frequency of adulthood animal abuse, antisocial personality traits, and alcohol use as well as interpersonal violence. As many as 41% of the men reported committing at least one act of animal abuse since the age of 18 years. Individuals who perpetrated animal abuse were found to have several characteristics in common with those who perpetrated interpersonal violence including Antisocial Personality Disorder traits, problems with impulsivity, low empathy, and involvement in other illegal behaviours. The authors concluded that their findings show male perpetrators to also perpetrate a substantial amount of general aggression including aggression toward children.

In summary, the focus of studies examining the relationship between family violence and companion animal cruelty has predominantly been on determining (1) the prevalence of companion animal cruelty within physically violent relationships and (2) the prevalence of women who delay leaving their violent relationship for fear of harm befalling their companion animals in their absence, as well as the length of the delay. In addition, studies have reported the percentages of children exposed to the violence and the percentage of children who are also cruel to animals. The findings have demonstrated that between 11.8% and 39.4% of women report that the perpetrator *threatened to* hurt or kill their companion animals. Further, between 25.6% (Flynn, 2000) and 79.3% (Quinklish, 1999) of women report that the perpetrator has *actually* hurt or killed their companion animal(s). Many of the studies examining animal cruelty within abusive families have also reported that between 18% (Ascione, 1998) and 48% (Carlisle-Frank, Frank, & Nielson, 2004) of women have delayed leaving their violent situation out of fear that their companion animal(s) would be harmed or killed if they were to leave.

The consistent finding in the above studies that children who have witnessed human and animal-directed cruelty are at risk of themselves engaging in abusive behaviors was systematically investigated in a recent investigation by Baldry (2003). Baldry's (2003) investigation involved 1,396 youth aged between 9 and 17 years. Participants were asked about their exposure to animal cruelty and to domestic violence. They were also asked about their own treatment of animals. It was found that almost half of participants reported exposure to at least one form of violence (verbal, physical, or threatening) and a similar proportion reported father-directed violence toward the mother, while more than a third reported mother-directed violence against the father. One fifth of the respondents reported severe violent episodes between their parents.

With regard to animals, it was found that just under half of the youth reported having committed at least one act of animal cruelty with boys being two to three times more likely than girls to have done so. Severe incidents of animal cruelty were reported by a lower 19.4% of youth. Of most relevance, of all participants who reported having engaged in an act of animal cruelty, almost all reported a higher level of exposure to domestic and animal violence. Based on the study outcomes, Baldry concluded that the role of modelling appears to be very important in predicting animal cruelty clearly indicating that violence against animals is likely to be learned from peers or parents. In addition to modelling of cruelty, Reber (1996) has argued that children's cruelty toward animals may be an important marker of attachment disturbances wherein the animal becomes the recipient of a child's uncontrolled rage. Thus, animal cruelty becomes part of the cycle of dysfunction and violence.

Some (although fewer) studies, have investigated the motivations for companion animal abuse with violent families. Consistent with theoretical proposals about underlying motivations, on the whole, the predominant motivation appears to be one of control. According to anecdotal and empirical accounts, animals are killed or harmed in an effort to intimidate, frighten, or control others including battered women or abused children (Arkow, 1996; Ascione, 2001; Ascione & Arkow, 1999; Boat, 1995; Faver & Strand, 2003). For example, in his qualitative study involving 10 women seeking refuge from domestic violence, Flynn (2000) found that batterers use animal cruelty to intimidate, to hurt, or to control their partners.

However, not all batterers are cruel to animals. To determine whether batterers who are cruel to their companion animals differ from those who are not, Simmons and Lehmann (2007) investigated the reports of 1,283 female companion animal owners who were seeking refuge from partner abuse. They found that batterers who were cruel to animals (not all battered animals were companion animals) used more forms of violence compared to those who were not. Specifically, batterers who were cruel to companion animals had higher rates of sexual violence, marital rape, emotional violence, and stalking. They also used more controlling behaviors including isolation, male privilege, blaming, intimidation, threats, and economic abuse. The differences were even greater for those who killed a companion animal compared to those who were not cruel to animals.

The findings reported by Simmons and Lehmann (2007) reinforce the finding from the general aggression literature that individuals whose antisocial acts are more heterogeneous, in this case involving different forms of human and animal abuse, tend to fall at the more severe end of the antisocial spectrum (Dishion, French, & Patterson, 1995; Farrington, 1991; Lynam, 1996). This finding as well as others that have been found within the animal cruelty research, parallel findings from the general aggression literature. This consistency of findings reinforces the argument that animal cruelty is one behavioral manifestation of the aggressive and/or antisocial individual. Some have argued that there is a link between human violence and animal cruelty. Gullone (2012) has argued that in fact, there is more than a link.

More than a Link

As discussed in other chapters in this text, an extensive body of research exists that has examined the aetiology of aggressive behaviors and, more recently, the characteristics and developmental histories of the individuals who engage in such behaviors (Hartup, 2005). Documented risk factors include particular biological predispositions, personality traits, and cognitive structures such as schemas and scripts. Risk factors also include the individual's social environment such as socio-economic status and exposure to violence (Reebye, 2005). Within a developmental framework, others (e.g., Greenberg, Speltz, & DeKlyen, 1993) have identified the importance of contextual factors such as family stressors, parenting, discipline, and attachment. Thus, as with all complex behaviors, causal factors are many. Of particular importance, they include complex interactions amongst the identified aetiological factors.

Supporting the argument that there is more than a link between aggressive and violent behaviors towards humans and animal cruelty behaviors, through comprehensive reviews of existing research and theory, Gullone (2012) demonstrated that animal cruelty behaviors predominantly appear alongside human aggression and violence, as well as other crimes including non-violent crimes. Almost without exception, the perpetrators of animal cruelty crimes are the same individuals who engage in other aggressive or antisocial behavior including partner and child abuse, and bullying. Thus, the co-occurrence that has been consistently reported between animal cruelty and partner as well as child abuse is of little surprise. The same pattern has been found when examining criminal behavior more generally, but particularly violent crimes against the person such as rape (Arluke, Levin, Luke, & Ascione, 1999; Gullone & Clarke, 2008), and bullying (e.g., Gullone & Robertson, 2008). Animal cruelty is currently listed as a diagnostic criterion for CD (i.e. DSM-IV-Test Revised version) (American Psychiatric Association, 2000) and has been since 1987 when it first appeared in the third edition of the Diagnostic and Statistical Manual for Mental Disorders (DSM-III) (American Psychiatric Association, 1987). Moreover, in their meta-analysis, Frick et al. (1993) reported a median age of 6.5 years for the occurrence of the first incident of animal cruelty along with other aggressive behaviors (i.e., fighting, bullying, assaulting others), thus indicating that animal cruelty appears as one of the earliest indicators of CD. Further, as many as 25% of children diagnosed with CD display cruelty to animals. Cruelty to animals was one of several items that discriminated between the children's destructive/non-destructive dichotomy with animal cruelty falling within the destructive category (Frick et al., 1993).

There is also evidence that CU traits and psychopathy may be particularly predictive of animal cruelty behaviors. According to Lynam (1996), psychopathy is characterized by more crimes than is true for the average criminal offender and also by more types of crimes. Such findings are reflective of the criminal behavior profiles of people who are cruel to animals. Such a profile is also reflective of particularly severe and violent antisocial adults (Blair, Peschardt, Budhani, Mitchell, & Pine, 2006).

In a controlled study aimed at identifying risk factors for abuse and interpersonal violence among an urban population, Walton-Moss, Manganello, Frye, and Campbell (2005) compared 845 women who had experienced abuse in the past two years with a control group of non-abused women from the same metropolitan area. Risk factors for the perpetration of interpersonal violence included being a high school drop-out, being in fair or poor mental health, having a problem with drugs or alcohol, and companion animal cruelty.

In the more recent investigation by Vaughn and colleagues (2009), the correlates of lifetime animal cruelty including CD and other disorders, as well as socio-demographic variables were examined. The 2001–2002 data set comprised data from a nationally representative sample of 43,093 non-institutionalized U.S. residents aged 18 years or older. Data were collected via interview by trained interviewers using a validated interview schedule (Grant, Harford, Dawson, & Pickering, 1995).

Among the socio-demographic variables assessed, being male predicted a higher prevalence of animal cruelty as did being younger and from a lower socio-economic background. The findings showed that the prevalence of antisocial behaviors was higher among those with a lifetime history of animal cruelty compared to those without such a history. The most prevalent antisocial behaviors among those who were cruel to animals were crimes including the robbing or mugging of another person. Supporting the role played by developmental family experiences, animal cruelty was associated with a family history of antisocial behavior.

Proposed Strategies for Change

Despite the substantial evidence that an individual's animal cruelty can validly be taken as a warning sign that they are engaging in other criminal, antisocial, or aggressive behaviors, the argument still meets substantial resistance, particularly by many scientists involved in research into aggressive and violent behavior and those within the legal system. This state of affairs is likely related to the fact that the general position held by society and its members is that animals' suffering, when compared to that of humans, is less worthy of both scientific and moral consideration. Since public opinion is related to the law of the land and likewise the law of the land reflects public opinion, this attitude toward animal suffering has become stuck in a vicious cycle of discrimination.

A number of authors (e.g., Clawson, 2009; Lockwood, 2008; Schaffner, 2009) have put forth possible strategies for the promotion of the cultural change needed to enable animal cruelty to be appropriately regarded as the antisocial and aggressive behavior that it is. These strategies include increasing public awareness of animal cruelty and related issues, as well as strengthening animal cruelty legislation. While law often reflects public perceptions, it is also true that law is a major factor in bringing about a change in public perceptions. There is a reciprocal relationship between the two. In this instance, as has happened with child and partner abuse, changes in the law and legal proceedings are required to bring about changes in public perceptions.

First, at the most basic level, the status of animals needs to change in the eyes of the law so that animals are perceived as more than mere property. Additionally, legislative bodies need to enact cruelty laws that appropriately reflect the severity of the offense (Clawson, 2009; Lockwood, 2008; Schaffner, 2009). As argued by Schaffner (2009), "the law should punish violent criminals according to the acts that they perpetrate. Whether the victim is a human being or an animal, a violent crime is a crime against its intended victim, as well a crime against society and its morals" (p. 199).

It goes without saying that the general perception of animal cruelty as relatively unimportant when compared to crimes against humans, is having a negative impact on animals. However, as research has clearly highlighted, the same perception is having a negative impact on humans since many crimes against humans may well have been prevented had any animal cruelty incidents that preceded them been taken more seriously. As cogently stated by Schleuter (2008):

> Most agencies consider crimes against animals complaints to be low-priority calls, regardless of whether they are in-progress crimes, and no matter how violent.... If one pays attention to such crimes occurring particularly in a dysfunctional intra-familial setting or in conjunction with other destructive behaviors, future animal abuse or neglect, as well as similar crimes against vulnerable members of the household, may become potentially preventable if proper interventions are put in place. (p. 378).

Related to acknowledgement of the link between animal cruelty and human-directed aggression or violence is a particularly important strategy that has been proposed by several authors. The strategy is the facilitation of cross-reporting of suspected animal cruelty. Such cross-reporting would involve reporting suspected animal cruelty not only to animal welfare organizations, but also to the police force and human service agencies such as child protective services and adult protective services.

In his chapter specifically addressing the role of laws and policy to address the link of family violence, Schaffner (2009) acknowledges that although social scientists have provided data to support the link, the law has been slow to respond. Current laws independently address crimes depending upon the victim. Thus, there are separate laws for animal cruelty, family or domestic violence, child abuse, and elder abuse. Despite the relationships among these different crimes of abuse, there is no existing single law that covers these relationships.

In providing justification for the proposed need for a law that recognizes the link between different types of abuse, among other reasons, Schaffner (2009) argues that one act of abuse often involves multiple forms of violence such that the abuse of a companion animal also psychologically harms other members of the family. According to Schaffner, if properly implemented, law and policy would be better armed to: (i) prevent human abuse, (ii) detect abuse earlier than is presently the case, (iii) protect family violence victims by providing protective orders and safe havens, (iv) facilitate prosecution of the abuser or perpetrator, and (v) avoid further abuses through provision of appropriate sanctions.

Thus, by enacting adequate laws including animal cruelty laws that properly indicate the seriousness of the animal cruelty crime committed, future violence toward both human and animal victims can be prevented. To properly reflect the seriousness of the offense, the law should impose a minimum sentence (Schaffner, 2009). If the severity of animal cruelty crimes is adequately signaled by law and sanctions, the perceptions of prosecutors will change so that they begin to reflect current scientific understanding in their decisions as opposed to falling prey to existing biases that animals are less worthy of moral consideration. It is ultimately the responsibility of prosecutors to enforce animal cruelty laws by prosecuting animal cruelty cases to the fullest extent of the law.

In conclusion, it is time for law and policymakers to act upon the existing body of research. Laws need to be developed that acknowledge the relationship and similarities between different types of abuse and violence, including animal cruelty. Consistent with this recognition, laws need to be implemented fully and fairly across different abusive behaviors. Based on the empirical information available, there exists no possible justification for relegating animal cruelty offenses to the "less important" category. Consequently, there is no justification for punishing violent criminals significantly more leniently or, as often happens, not at all, if the victim of their violent crime is an animal as opposed to a human being. Indeed, there is a high statistical probability that the victims of the violent or antisocial individual are both animal and human. This strengthens the argument that laws should punish criminals according to the severity of the acts they perpetrate without discrimination or favor based on the target species of the particular crime.

References

American Psychiatric Association (1994). *Diagnostic and statistical manual of mental disorders, 4th Ed. (DSM-IV)*. Washington DC: American Psychiatric Association.

American Psychiatric Association (2000). *Diagnostic and statistical manual of mental disorders 4th ed. Text Revised*. Washington, DC: Author.

American Psychological Association (1996). *Violence in the family: A report of the American Psychological Association*. Washington, DC: Presidential Task Force on Violence and the Family.

Amiot, C. E., & Bastian, B. (2015). Toward a psychology of human-animal relations. *Psychological Bulletin, 141*, 6–47.

Anderson, C. A. (2002). Aggression. (pp. 68–78). In E. Borgatta & R. Montgomery (Eds). *The encyclopedia of sociology*. (2nd Ed.), New York: MacMillan.

Arkow, (1994). Animal abuse and domestic violence: Intake statistics tell a sad story. *Latham Letter, XV*(2), 17.

Arkow, P. (1996). The relationships between animal abuse and other forms of family violence. *Family Violence and Sexual Assault Bulletin, 12,* 29–34.

Arluke, A. (2001). Children who supernurture animals: A call for sociological (and other) study. *Anthrozoos, 14,* 66–71.

Arluke, A., Levin, J., Luke, C., & Ascione, F. (1999). The relationship of animal abuse to violence and other forms of antisocial behavior. *Journal of Interpersonal Violence, 14,* 963–975.

Ascione, F. R. (1998). Battered women's reports of their partners' and their children's cruelty to animals. *Journal of Emotional Abuse, 1,* 119–133.

Ascione, F. R. (1999). The abuse of animals and human interpersonal violence: Making the connection. In Ascione, F.R., & Arkow, P. (1999). (Eds), *Child abuse, domestic violence, and animal abuse: Linking the circles of compassion for prevention and intervention.* (pp. 50–61), West Layfette, IN: Purdue University Press.

Ascione, F. R. (2001). Animal abuse and youth violence. *Juvenile Justice Bulletin, September.*

Ascione, F. R., & Arkow, P. (1999). Preface in F. R. Ascione & P. Arkow (Eds). *Child abuse, domestic violence, and animal abuse.* (pp. xv–xx). West Lafayette, IN: Purdue University Press.

Ascione, F. R., Friedrich, W. N., Heath, J., & Hayashi, K. (2003). Cruelty to animals in normative, sexually abused, and outpatient psychiatric samples of 6- to 12-year-old children: Relations to maltreatment and exposure to domestic violence. *Anthrozoos, 16,* 194–212.

Ascione, F. R., Weber, C. V., & Wood, D. S. (1997). The abuse of animals and domestic violence: A national survey of shelters for women who are battered. *Society & Animals: Journal of Human-Animal Studies, 5,* 205–218.

Ascione, F. R., Weber, C. V., Thompson, T. M., Heath, J., Maruyama, M., & Hayashi, K. (2007). Battered pets and domestic violence: Animal abuse reported by women experiencing intimate violence and by nonabused women. *Violence against Women, 13,* 354–373.

Baldry, A. C. (2003). Animal abuse and exposure to interparental violence in Italian youth. *Journal of Interpersonal Violence, 18,* 258–281.

Baldry, A. C., & Farrington, D. P. (2000). Bullies and delinquents: Personal characteristics and parental styles. *Journal of Community & Applied Social Psychology, 10,* 17–31.

Bank, L., & Burraston, B. (2001). Abusive home environments as predictors of poor adjustment during adolescence and early adulthood. *Journal of Community Psychology, 29,* 195–217.

Black, D. A., Heyman, R. E., & Smith Slep, A. M. (2001). Risk factors for child physical abuse. *Aggression and Violent Behavior, 6,* 121–188.

Blair, R. J. R., Peschardt, K.S., Budhani, S., Mitchell, D. G. V., & Pine, D. S. (2006). The development of psychopathy. *Journal of Child Psychology and Psychiatry. 47,* 262–275.

Boat, B. W. (1995). The relationship between violence to children and violence to animals: An ignored link? *Journal of Interpersonal Violence, 10,* 228–235.

Boat,B. W., Pear., E., Barnes, J. E., Richey, L., Crouch, D., Barzman, D., & Putman, F. W. (2011)._Childhood_cruelty_to_animals: Psychiatric and demographic correlates. *Journal of Aggression, Maltreatment & Trauma, 20,* 812–819.

Burt, S. A., McGue, M., Krueger, R. F., & Iacono. W. G. (2005). How are parent-child conflict and childhood externalizing symptoms related over time? Results from a genetically cross-lagged study. *Development and Psychopathology, 17,* 145–165.

Brown, L. (1988).*Cruelty to animals: The moral debt.* London: Macmillan.

Buka, S. L., Stichick, T. L., Birdthistle, I., & Earls, F. J. (2001). Youth exposure to violence: Prevalence, risks, and consequences. *American Journal of Orthopsychiatry, 71,* 298–310.

Carlisle-Frank, P., Frank, J. M., & Nielsen, L. (2004). Selective battering of the family pet. *Anthrozoos, 17,* 26–42.

Cascardi, M., O'Leary, K. D., Lawrence, E. E., & Schlee, K. (1995). Characteristics of women physically abused by their spouses and who seek treatment regarding marital conflict. *Journal of Clinical and Consulting Psychology, 63,* 616–623.

Clawson, E. (2009). The new canaries in the mine: The priority of human welfare in animal abuse prosecution. In A. Lindzey (Ed.), *The link between animal abuse and human violence* (pp. 190–200). Sussex: Academic Press.

Conduct Problems Prevention Research Group. (1992). A developmental and clinical model for the prevention of conduct disorder: The FAST Track Program. *Development and Psychopathology, 4,* 509–527.

Cummings, E. M. (1987). Coping with background anger in early childhood. *Child Development, 58,* 976–984.

Cunningham, A., & Baker, L. (2004). *What about me! Seeking to understand a child's view of violence in the family.* London: Centre for Children & Families in the Justice System.

Currie, C. L. (2006). Animal cruelty by children exposed to domestic violence. *Child Abuse & Neglect, 30,* 425–435.

Dadds, M. R. (2008). Conduct problems and cruelty to animals in children: What is the link? In F. R. Ascione (ed). *The International Handbook of Animal Abuse and Cruelty: Theory, Research, and Application* (pp. 111–131). West Lafayette, IN: Purdue University Press.

Dadds, M. R., Turner, C. M., & McAloon, J. (2002). Developmental links between cruelty to animals and human violence. *Australian & New Zealand Journal of Counselling, 35,* 363–382.

Daniell, C. (2001). Ontario SPCA's women's shelter survey shows staggering results. *The Latham Letter, Spring,* 16–17.

Davies, P. T., Myers, R. L., Cummings, E. M., & Heindel, S. (1999). Adult conflict history and children's subsequent responses to conflict: An experimental test. *Journal of Family Psychology, 13,* 610–628.

DeGue, S., & DiLillo, D. (2009). Is animal cruelty a "red flag" for family violence?: Investigating co-occurring violence toward children, partners, and pets. *Journal of Interpersonal Violence, 24,* 1036–1056.

Deviney, E., Dickert, J., & Lockwood, R. (1983). The care of pets within child abusing families. *International Journal for the Study of Animal Problems, 4,* 321–329.

Dishion, T. J., French, D. C., & Patterson, G. R. (1995). The development and ecology of antisocial behavior. In D. Cicchetti & D. J. Cohen (Eds.), *Developmental psychopathology, Vol 2: Risk, disorder, and adaptation* (pp. 421–471). Oxford, England: John Wiley & Sons.

Dodge, K. A., Bates, J. E., & Pettit, G. S. (1990). Mechanisms in the cycle of violence. *Science, 250,* 1678–1683.

Duncan, A., Thomas, J. C., & Miller, C. (2005). Significance of family risk factors in development of childhood animal cruelty in adolescent boys with conduct problems. *Journal of Family Violence, 20,* 235–239.

Dutton, D. G. (2000). Witnessing parental violence as a traumatic experience shaping the abusive personality. *Journal of Aggression, Maltreatment and Trauma, 3,* 59–67.

Eron, L. D. (1987). The development of aggressive behaviour from the perspective of a developing behaviorist. *American Psychologist, 42,* 435–442.

Farrington, D. P. (1991). Childhood aggression and adult violence: Early precursors and later life outcomes. In D. J. Peplar & H. K. Rubin (Eds.), *The development and treatment of childhood aggression* (pp. 5–29). Hillsdale, N.J.: Erlbaum.

Faver, C. A., & Cavazos, A. M. (2007). Animal abuse and domestic violence: A view from the border. *Journal of Emotional Abuse, 7,* 59–81.

Faver, C. A., & Strand, E. B. (2003). Domestic violence and animal cruelty: Untangling the web of abuse. *Journal of Social Work Education, 39,* 237–253.

Febres, J., Brasfield, H., Shorey, R. C., Elmquist, J., Ninnemann, A., Schonbrun, Y.C.,..., & Stuart, G.L. (2014). Adulthood animal abuse among men arrested for domestic violence. *Violence Against Women, 20,* 1059–1077.

Felthous, A. R. (1980). Aggression against cats, dogs and people. *Child Psychiatry & Human Development, 10,* 169–177.

Felthous, A. R., & Kellert, S. R. (1986). Violence against animals and people: Is aggression against living creatures generalised? *Bulletin of the American Academy of Psychiatry and Law, 14,* 55–69.

Felthous, A. R., & Kellert, S. R. (1987). Childhood cruelty to animals and later aggression against people: A review. *American Journal of Psychiatry, 144,* 710–717.

Fergusson, D. M., & Horwood, L. J. (1998). Exposure to interparental violence in childhood and psychosocial adjustment in young adulthood. *Child Abuse and Neglect, 22,* 339–357.

Feshbach, S. (1964). The function of aggression and the regulation of aggressive drive. *Psychological Review, 71,* 257–272.

Flynn, C. P. (1999b). Exploring the link between corporal punishment and children's cruelty to animals. *Journal of Marriage & the Family, 61,* 971–981.

Flynn, C. P. (2000). Why family professionals can no longer ignore violence toward animals. *Family Relations: Interdisciplinary Journal of Applied Family Studies, 49,* 87–95.

Flynn, C. P. (2009). Women-battering, pet abuse, and human-animal relationships. In A. Lindzey (Ed.), *The link between animal abuse and human violence* (pp. 116–125). Sussex: Academic Press.

Frick, P. J. (1998). *Conduct disorders and severe antisocial behaviour.* New York: Plenum.

Frick, P. J., Lahey, B. B., Loeber, R., Tannenbaum, L., Van Horn, Y., Christ, M. A. G., ... Hanson, K. (1993). Oppositional defiant disorder and conduct disorder: A meta-analytic review of factor analyses and cross-validation in a clinic sample. *Clinical Psychology Review, 13*(4), 319–340. doi: 10.1016/j.bbr.2011.03.031.

Frick, P. J., O'Brien, B. S., Wootton, J. M., & McBurnett, K. (1994). Psychopathy and conduct problems in children. *Journal of Abnormal Psychology, 103,* 700–707.

Friedmann, E., Katcher, A. H., Lynch, J. J., & Thomas, S. A. (1980). Animal companions and one-year survival of patients after discharge from a coronary unit. *Public Health Reports, 95,* 307–312.

Friedmann, E., & Thomas, S. A. (1995). Pet ownership, social support, and one-year survival after acute myocardial infarction in the Cardiac Arrythmia Suppression Trial (CAST). *American Journal of Cardiology, 76,* 1213–1217.

Gaensbauer, T. J., Mrazek, D., & Harmon, R. J. (1981). Emotional expression in abused and/or neglected infants. In N. Frude (Ed.), *Psychological approaches to child abuse* (pp. 120–135). Totowa, N.J.: Rowan and Littlefield.

Gendreau, P. L., & Archer, J. (2005). Subtypes of aggression in humans and animals. In R. E. Tremblay, W. W. Hartup, & J. Archer (Eds.), *Developmental Origins of Aggression* (pp. 25–45). Guilford Press: New York.

Graham-Bermann, S. A., & Hughes, H. M. (1998). The impact of domestic violence and emotional abuse on children: The intersection of research, theory, and clinical intervention. *Journal of Emotional Abuse, 1,* 1–21.

Graham-Bermann, S. A., & Levendosky, A. A. (1998). Traumatic stress symptoms in children of battered women. *Journal of Interpersonal Violence, 13,* 111–128.

Greenberg, M. T., Speltz, M. L., & DeKlyen, M. (1993). The role of attachment in the early development of disruptive behaviour problems. *Development and Psychopathology, 5,* 191–213.

Gullone, E. (in press). *Animal cruelty, antisocial behaviour, and aggression: More than a link!* United Kingdom: Palgrave-MacMillan.

Gullone, E., & Clarke, J. (2008). Human-animal interactions: The Australian perspective. In F. Ascione (Ed.). *The International Handbook of Theory and Research on Animal Abuse and Cruelty* (pp. 305–335). West Lafayette, IN: Purdue University Press.

Gullone, E., & Robertson, N. (2008). The relationship between bullying and animal abuse in adolescents: The importance of witnessing animal abuse. *Journal of Applied Developmental Psychology, 29,* 371–379.

Hamberger, L. K., & Hastings, J. E. (1991). Personality correlates of men who batter and non-violent men: Some continuities and discontinuities. *Journal of Family Violence, 6,* 131–147.

Hartup, W. W. (2005). The development of aggression. In R. E. Tremblay, W. W. Hartup, & J. Archer (Eds.), *Developmental origins of aggression* (pp. 3–22). Guilford Press: New York.

Hastings, J. E., & Hamberger, L.K. (1994). Psychosocial modifiers of psychopathology for domestically violent and non-violent men. *Psychological Reports, 74,* 112–114.

Hastings, P. D., Zahn-Waxler, C., Robinson, J., Usher, B., & Bridges, D. (2000). The development of concern for others in children with behavior problems. *Developmental Psychology, 36,* 531–546.

Haskett, M. E., & Kistner, J. A. (1991). Social interactions and peer perceptions of young physically abused children. *Child Development, 62,* 979–990.

Heyman, R. E., & Smith Slep, A. M. (2001). Risk factors for family violence: Introduction to the special series. *Aggression and Violent Behavior, 6,* 115–119.

Howell, K. H. (2011). Resilience and psychopathology in children exposed to family violence. *Aggression and Violent Behavior, 16,* 562–569.

Hutton, J. S. (1983). Animal abuse as a diagnostic approach in social work: A pilot study (reprinted). In R. Lockwood & F. R. Ascione (Eds.) (1998). *Cruelty to animals and interpersonal violence: Readings in research and application* (pp. 415–420). West Lafayette, IN: Purdue University Press.

Jaffee, S. R., Caspi, A., Moffitt, T. E., & Taylor, A. (2004). Physical maltreatment victim to antisocial child. Evidence of an environmentally mediated process. *Journal of Abnormal Psychology, 113,* 44–55.

Jouriles, E. N., Barling, J., & O'Leary, K. D. (1987). Predicting child behavior problems in maritally violent families. *Journal of Abnormal Child Psychology, 15,* 165–173.

Katz, L. F., & Gottman, J. (1993). Patterns of marital conflict predict children's internalizing and externalizing disorders. *Developmental Psychology, 29,* 940–950.

Kaufman, J., & Zigler, E. (1987). Do abused children become abusive parents? *American Journal of Orthopsychiatry, 57,* 186–192.

Kazdin, A. E. (2011). Conceptualizing the challenge of reducing interpersonal violence. *Psychology of Violence, 1,* 166–187.

Kellert, S. R., & Felthous, A. R. (1985). Childhood cruelty toward animals among criminals and non-criminals. *Human Relations, 38,* 1113–1129.

Lahey, B. B., Waldman, I. D., & McBurnett, K. (1999). Annotation: The development of antisocial behavior: An integrative causal model. *Journal of Child Psychology and Psychiatry,40,* 669–682.

Lansford, J. A., Dodge, K. A., Pettit, G. S., Bates, J. E., Crozier, J., & Kaplow, J. (2002). A 12-year prospective study of the long-term effects of early child physical maltreatment on psychological, behavioral, and academic problems in adolescence. *Archives of Pediatrics and Adolescent Medicine, 156,* 824–830.

Larsson, H., Viding, E., Rijsdijk, F. V., & Plomin, R. (2008). Relationships between parental negativity and childhood antisocial behavior over time: A bidirectional effects model in a longitudinal genetically informative design. *Journal of Abnormal Child Psychology, 36,* 633–645.

Lockwood, R. (2008). Counting cruelty: Challenges and opportunities in assessing animal abuse and neglect in America. In F.R. Ascione (Ed.). *The international handbook of animal abuse and cruelty: Theory, research, and application* (pp. 87–109*).* West Lafayette, IN: Purdue University.

Lockwood, R., & Hodge, G. R. (1986; 1998). The tangled web of animal abuse: The links between cruelty to animals and human violence. In R. Lockwood & F. R. Ascione (Eds.) *Cruelty to animals and interpersonal violence: Readings in research and application.* (pp. 77–82). West Lafayette, IN: Purdue University Press.

Loeber, R., & Dishion, T. (1983). Early predictors of male delinquency: A review. *Psychological Bulletin, 93,* 68–99.

Loeber, R., & Hay, D. (1997). Key issues in the development of aggression and violence from childhood to early adulthood. *Annual Review of Psychology, 48,* 371–410.

Luk, E. S. L., Staiger, P. K., Wong, L., & Mathai, J. (1998). Children who are cruel to animals: A revisit. *Australian and New Zealand Journal of Psychiatry, 33,* 29–36.

Luntz, B. K. & Widom, C. S. (1994). Antisocial Personality Disorder in abused and neglected children grown up. *The American Journal of Psychiatry, 151,* 670–674.

Lynam, D. R. (1996). Early identification of chronic offenders: Who is the fledgling psychopath? *Psychological Bulletin, 120,* 209–234.

Lyons-Ruth, K. (1996). Attachment relationships among children with aggressive behavior problems: The role of disorganized early attachment patterns. *Journal of Consulting and Clinical Psychology, 64,* 64–73.

McCloskey, L. A., Figueredo, A. J., & Koss, M. P. (1995). The effects of systemic family violence on children's mental health. *Child Development, 66,* 1239–1261.

McConnell, A. R., Brown, C. M., Shoda, A. R., Stayton, L. E., & Martin, C. E. (2011). Friends with benefits: On the positive consequences of pet ownership. *Journal of Personality and Social Psychology, 101,* 1239–1252.

Margolin, G., & Gordis, E. B. (2000). The effects of family and community violence on children. *Annual Review of Psychology, 51,* 445–479.

Maughan, A., & Cicchetti, D. (2002). Impact of child maltreatment and interadult violence on children's emotion regulation abilities and socioemotional adjustment. *Child Development, 73,* 1525–1542.

McPhedran, S. (2009). Animal abuse, family violence and child wellbeing: A review. *Journal of Animal Violence, 24,* 41–52.

Miller, K. S., & Knutson, J. F. (1997). Reports of severe physical punishment and exposure to animal cruelty by inmates convicted of felonies and by university students. *Child Abuse and Neglect, 21,* 59–82.

Murphy, C. M., Meyer, S. L., & O'Leary, K. D. (1993). Family of origin violence and MCMI-II psychopathology among partner assaultive men. *Violence Victims, 8,* 165–176.

O'Connor, T. G. (2002). Annotation: The "effects" of parenting reconsidered: Findings, challenges, and applications. *Journal of Child Psychology and Psychiatry, 43,* 555–572.

Pelcovitz, D., Kaplan, S. J., DeRosa, R. R., Mandel, F. S., & Salzinger, S. (2000). Psychiatric disorders in adolescents exposed to domestic violence and physical abuse. *American Journal of Orthopsychiatry, 70,* 360–369.

Peterson, L., Gable, S., Doyle, C., & Ewugman, B. (1998). Beyond parenting skills: Battling barriers and building bonds to prevent child abuse and neglect. *Cognitive and Behavioral Practice, 4,* 53–74.

Peterson, P. L., Hawkins, J. D., Abbott, R. D., & Catalano, R. F. (1994). Disentangling the effects of parental drinking, family management, and parental alcohol norms on current drinking by black and white adolescents. *Journal of Research on Adolescence, 4,* 203–227.

Quinslick, J. A. (1999). Animal abuse and family violence. In F. R. Ascione & P. Arkow (Eds), *Child abuse, domestic violence, and animal abuse: Linking the circles of compassion for prevention and intervention.* (pp. 168–175). West Lafayette, IN: Purdue University Press.

Reebye, P. (2005). Aggression during early years—Infancy and preschool. *Canadian Child and Adolescent Psychiatry Review, 14,* 16–20.

Repetti, R. L., Taylor, S. E., & Seeman, T. E. (2002). Risky families: Family social environments and the mental and physical health of offspring. *Psychological Bulletin, 128,* 330–366.

Ressler, R. K., Burgess, A. W., Hartman, C. R., Douglas, J. E., & McCormack, A. (1986). Murderers who rape and mutilate. *Journal of Interpersonal Violence, 1,* 273–287.

Rieder, C., & Cicchetti, D. (1989). Organizational perspective on cognitive control functioning and cognitive affective balance in maltreated children. *Developmental Psychology, 25,* 382–393.

Rigdon, J. D., & Tapia, F. (1977). Children who are cruel to animals: A follow-up study. *Journal of Operational Psychiatry, 8,* 27–36.

Robin, M., & ten Bensel, R. T. (1985). Pets and the socialisation of children. *Marriage and Family Review, 8,* 63–78.

Rossbach, K. A., & Wilson, J. P. (1992). Does a dog's presence make a person appear more likeable? *Anthrozoos, 4,* 40–51.

Schaffner, J. E. (2009). Laws and policy to address the link of family violence. In A. Lindzey (Ed.), *The Link between Animal Abuse and Human Violence* (pp. 228–237). Sussex: Academic Press.

Schlueter, S. (2008). Law enforcement perspectives and obligations related to animal abuse. In F. Ascione (Ed.), *The international handbook of theory and research on animal abuse and cruelty* (pp. 375–391). West Lafayette, IN: Purdue University Press.

Serbin, L. A., & Karp, J. (2004). The intergenerational transfer of psychosocial risk: Mediators of vulnerability and resilience. *Annual Review of Psychology, 55,* 333–363.

Shields, A., & Cicchetti, D. (1998). Reactive aggression among maltreated children: The contributions of attention and emotion dysregulation. *Journal of Clinical Child Psychology, 27,* 381–395.

Schumacher, J. A., Feldbau-Kohn, S., Smith Slep, A. M., & Heyman, R. E. (2001). Risk factors for male-to-female partner physical abuse. *Aggression and Violent Behavior, 6,* 281–352.

Siegel, J. M. (1990). Stressful life events and use of physician services among the elderly: The moderating role of pet ownership. *Journal of Personality and Social Psychology, 58,* 1081–1086.

Serbin, L. A., & Karp, J. (2004). The intergenerational transfer of psychosocial risk: Mediators of vulnerability and resilience. *Annual Review of Psychology, 55,* 333–363.

Shipway, L. (2004). *Domestic violence: A handbook for health professionals.* New York: Routledge.

Simmons, C. A., & Lehmann, P. (2007). Exploring the link between pet abuse and controlling behaviors in violent relationships. *Journal of Interpersonal Violence, 22,* 1211–1222.

Simons, K. J., Paternite, C. E., & Shore, C. (2001). Quality of parent/adolescent attachment and aggression in young adolescents. *Journal of Early Adolescence, 21,* 182–203.

Sternberg, K. J., Lamb, M. E., Greenbaum, C., Cicchetti, D. D., Dawud, S., Cortes, R. M., Krispin, O., & Lorey, R. (1993). Effects of domestic violence on children's behavior problems and depression. *Developmental Psychology, 29,* 44–52.

Straka, S. M., & Montminy, L. (2008). Family violence: Through the lens of power and control. *Journal of Emotional Abuse, 8,* 255–279.

Straus, M. A., & Gelles, R. J. (Eds.). (1990). *Physical violence in American families Risk factors and adaptations to violence in 8,145 families.* New Brunswick, N.J.: Transaction Publishers.

Straus, M. A., Gelles, R .J., & Steinmetz, S. K. (1980). *Behind closed doors: Violence in the American family.* Garden City, NY: Anchor Books.

Summit, R. (1983). The child sexual abuse accommodation syndrome. *Child Abuse and Neglect, 7,* 181.

Tapia, F. (1971). Children who are cruel to animals. *Child Psychiatry & Human Development, 2,* 70–77.

Tolan, P., Gorman-Smith, D., & Henry, D. (2006). Family violence. *Annual Review of Psychology, 57,* 557–583.

Toth, S. L., Manly, J. T., & Cicchetti, D. (1992). Child maltreatment and vulnerability to depression. *Developmental Psychopathology, 4,* 97–112.

Vaughn, M. G., Fu, Q., DeLisi, M., Beaver, K. M., Perron, B. E., Terrell, K., & Howard, M. O..(2009). Correlates of cruelty to animals in the United States: Results from the National Epidemiologic Survey on Alcohol and Related Conditions. *Journal of Psychiatric Research, 43*(15), 1213–1218.

Volant, A. M., Johnson, J. A., Gullone, E., & Coleman, G. J. (2008). The relationship between domestic violence and animal abuse: An Australian study. *Journal of Interpersonal Violence, 23,* 1277–1295.

Wallace, H. (2004). *Family Violence: Legal, Medical, and Social Perspectives.* Allyn & Bacon.

Walton-Moss, B. J., Manganello, J., Frye, V., & Campbell, J. C. (2005). Risk Factors for Intimate Partner Violence and Associated Injury Among Urban Women. *Journal of Community Health: The Publication for Health Promotion and Disease Prevention, 30,* 377–389.

Westbury, H. R., & Newmann, D. L. (2008). Empathy-related responses to moving film stimuli depicting human and non-human animal targets in negative circumstances, *Biological Psychology, 78,* 66–74.

Widom, C. S. (1989). Does violence beget violence? A critical examination of the literature. *Psychological Bulletin, 106,* 3–28.

Wolfe, D. A., & Mosk, M. D. (1983). Behavioral comparisons of children from abusive and distressed families. *Journal of Consulting and Clinical Psychology, 51,* 702–708.

Chapter 14

Animal Cruelty, Firesetting, and Homicide

Lindsey S. Davis and Louis B. Schlesinger

The search for predictors of homicide has been ongoing since the initial descriptive studies of offenders by the early alienists. For example, Goring (1913), Krafft-Ebing (1886), Kretchmer (1925), and Lombroso (1876/1911) all attempted to describe and understand the psychosocial backgrounds of individuals who committed murder and how these factors contributed to their criminal conduct. In the first half of the 20th century, the study of homicide was essentially limited to case studies. But by the second half of the century, attention was being given to homicide as an area of serious scientific inquiry, with some empirical support for clinical observations.

MacDonald (1963), for instance, studied 100 inpatients who had been admitted to a psychiatric hospital for evaluation because they had made homicidal threats. Only one patient committed an intentional homicide during the 15-month follow-up period. Thus, the probability of homicidal acting out would seem to be low, but the time period during which a future homicide may occur might be much longer than this follow-up period. MacDonald did find, however, that "in the very sadistic patients, the triad of childhood cruelty to animals, firesetting, and enuresis [bedwetting] was often encountered" (pp. 126–127). Thus, MacDonald believed this triad could be useful in predicting a particular type of offense—the sadistic homicide.

Hellman and Blackman (1966) conducted a study that lent additional statistical support to MacDonald's belief that the childhood triad was correlated with violent behavior at a later age. Hellman and Blackman found that about three-fourths of those charged with violent crimes (not necessarily homicide) revealed a complete or partial triad, whereas only 28% of nonviolent subjects reported a history of these target behaviors. Felthous and Bernard (1979) pointed out methodological weaknesses in Hellman and Blackman's study, but their research did offer some corroboration for MacDonald's early observations. Its simplicity, as well as some empirical support, contributed greatly to "the MacDonald triad" becoming commonly considered a robust and accepted predictor of homicide (Justice, Justice, & Kraft, 1974; Schechter & Everitt, 1996). However, this opinion was never really MacDonald's; as he clearly stated, his findings do not support the notion that "childhood firesetting, cruelty to animals, and enuresis to the age of five or beyond, is significantly higher in persons who have committed criminal homicide than in persons who have made homicidal threats" (MacDonald, 1968, p. 61).

A close look at the clinical and research literature since the 1960s reveals a complex relationship between MacDonald's triad and adult violent crime, particularly murder. The research has addressed the usefulness of (a) the complete triad, (b) a partial triad of animal cruelty and/or firesetting, and (c) other risk factors as being predictive of aggressive and homicidal behavior. But it is often forgotten, or not emphasized, that MacDonald's (1963) observations of the significance of the triad—if there is any significance—related only to "very sadistic" (p. 126) individuals. Therefore, the triad may be useful for examining particular types of violence, specifically, sadistic sexual aggression and sadistic sexual homicide.

Animal Cruelty and Firesetting: Research Findings

Animal Cruelty

The literature is highly inconsistent with respect to the relationship between a history of childhood animal cruelty and the commission of homicide. In fact, most studies (e.g., Hellman & Blackman, 1966) have been overly inclusive, examining the relationship of animal cruelty to adult violent crime, rather than to homicide. For instance, Langevin, Paitich, Orchard, Hardy, and Russon (1983) conducted the only study of MacDonald's triad and its relationship specifically to homicide, and these researchers found little predictive value or significance for the triad. Wax and Haddox (1974) did find significance for the triad in a small number of violent (but not homicidal) male adolescents; they believe this finding confirms the usefulness of the triad to some extent. In 1978, Felthous and Keller reviewed the literature with respect to animal cruelty and aggression (but not homicide). They found the results of various studies to be inconsistent and contradictory, with several methodological problems.

Since then, Merz-Perez, Heide, and Silverman (2001) have found a possible significant relationship between childhood cruelty to animals and later violence against humans. However, Gleyzer, Felthous, and Holzer (2002) reached a different conclusion. These researchers found that a history of substantial animal cruelty is associated with antisocial personality disorder, antisocial personality traits, and substance abuse. Their findings could not determine that a history of animal abuse is predictive of adult violent crime, because many offenders who committed adult violent crimes did not have such a history. This conclusion was echoed by Patterson-Kane and Piper (2009), who also found that animal abuse is not uncommon among violent offenders, but that the majority of violent offenders do not report a history of such abusive behavior.

Haden and Scarpa (2005) found that animal cruelty is not uncommon among children in general and may be associated with some adult criminal behavior, but this relationship is not strong. Similarly, in Levin and Arluke's (2009) sample of undergraduate students, 28% admitted to having abused an animal, a rate far higher than the likelihood of committing a homicide. One of the few studies to look more closely at method, severity, and frequency of animal abuse as possible predictors (Tallichet, Hensley, & Singer, 2005) found no link between childhood animal abuse and violence against humans in a sample of adult offenders. Also demonstrating the continuing inconsistency of the research is a study by Overton, Hensley, and Tallichet (2011), who found that only recurrent *animal cruelty was statistically significantly predictive of adult violence toward humans.*

A graduation hypothesis has been posited, which suggests that the abuse of animals constitutes a lower rung on the ladder that leads to physical aggression against humans.

A meta-analysis by Walters (2013) indicates that this hypothesis is supported in studies which compare violent and non-violent offenders, but only because of other confounding variables; in short, these offenders differ in many ways beyond their animal abuse histories. After adjusting the meta-analysis, Walters (2013) concluded that animal cruelty only predicts later violence towards humans in female subjects; in males, animal cruelty is not predictive of later violent offenses.

A small study (Verlinden, Hersen, & Thomas, 2000) of eight school shootings reported that half of school shooters had committed prior acts of animal cruelty. In a slightly larger study of 23 school shootings (Arluke & Madfis, 2013), 43% of offenders had committed prior acts of animal cruelty. Of those who had committed prior acts of cruelty, 90% committed cruelty in a hands-on manner and 70% abused cats or dogs. Arluke and Madfis (2013) have suggested that it is this type of "up-close and personal method of abuse" that is most predictive of later acts of extreme violence (p. 12). Meanwhile, Dadds, Turner, and McAloon (2002) have suggested that it is not the act of animal abuse, but the malice—or absence of malice—motivating the act that is predictive of later violent behavior.

It is clear that studying only the relationship between animal cruelty and adult violent behavior is much too broad and leads to inconsistent results depending on the sample, methodology, and operational definitions of all variables. Moreover, most violent behavior by adults is not even reported and rarely results in arrest, and a history of animal cruelty is often determined by retrospective self-report, which may or may not be accurate.

Firesetting

Nonserious firesetting is fairly common behavior for children and adolescents, particularly boys (Grolnick, Cole, Laurenitis, & Schwartzman, 1990; Kafry, 1980; Lewis & Yarnell, 1951), but, in some individuals, firesetting becomes pathological. Pathological firesetting is psychologically driven, not motivated by material gain, and typically connotes repetitive or intentionally destructive behavior, as opposed to *fire play*, which is likely to reflect developmentally appropriate curiosity. *Pyromania*—which is rare in both children and adults—literally means "fire madness" and is classified as an impulse-control disorder in the *Diagnostic and Statistical Manual of Mental Disorders IV-TR* (American Psychiatric Association [APA], 2000, p. 669):

> The essential feature of Pyromania is the presence of multiple episodes of deliberate and purposeful fire setting (Criterion A). Individuals with this disorder experience tension or affective arousal before setting a fire (Criterion B). There is a fascination with, interest in, curiosity about, or attraction to fire and its situational contexts (e.g., paraphernalia, uses, consequences) (Criterion C).... Individuals with this disorder experience pleasure, gratification, or a release of tensions when setting the fire, witnessing its effects, or participating in its aftermath (Criterion D). The fire setting is not done for monetary gain, as an expression of sociopolitical ideology, to conceal criminal activity, to express anger or vengeance, to improve one's living circumstances, or in response to a delusion or hallucination (Criterion E). The fire setting does not result from impaired judgment (e.g., in dementia or Mental Retardation). The diagnosis is not made if the fire setting is better accounted for by Conduct Disorder, a Manic Episode, or Antisocial Personality Disorder (Criterion F).

The fifth edition of the *Diagnostic and Statistical Manual of Mental Disorders* ([DSM-5]; APA, 2013) reports that this is a statistically rare condition, even among incarcerated individuals with histories of repeated firesetting.

Although there are logical motives for setting a fire (such as to collect insurance money on the destroyed property or to cover up another crime), the pathological firesetter sets fires irrationally—to express aggression or hostility, avenge a real or perceived wrong, gain attention or recognition, build self-worth, obtain sensual or sexual satisfaction, or respond to a delusional hallucination (Rider, 1980). Compulsive firesetting is not driven by a rational decision-making process but by an irresistible impulse (or compulsion) to set fires; the pyromaniacs studied by Lewis and Yarnell (1951), for example, "said they set their fires for no practical reason and received no material profit from the act, their only motive being to obtain some sort of sensual satisfaction" (p. 86).

Further, setting fires provides a means of expressing anger and frustration and creating destruction while avoiding a direct confrontation with the source of those unpleasant emotions. Children who set fires commonly cite revenge and retaliation as their primary motives (Mavromatis, 2000); however, children and adolescents may be unable to identify and verbalize the underlying dynamics that guide their behavior. For example, Swaffer and Hollin (1995) interviewed 17 juvenile firesetters regarding the motives for their crimes. The most commonly reported motive—endorsed by 29.4% of the sample—was revenge, followed by peer pressure (17.6%), concealment of another crime (17.6%), self-harm (17.6%; all female), and fascination with fire (5.9%). Three of the juveniles denied having intentionally set the fires.

Lewis and Yarnell (1951, p. 398) stated, "A persistently recurring motive given by these firesetters is that they were impelled to set a fire because they wanted to see a fire: logical but tautological, and it would seem that this 'motive' comes close to approximating pure instinctual impulse." Many researchers have concluded that this "irresistible impulse," coupled with the presence of mounting tension before and relief after the firesetting, indicates an underlying sexual element to these crimes. "They describe mounting tension, the restlessness, the urge for motion, the conversion symptoms such as headaches, palpitations, ringing in the ears, and the gradual merging of their identity into a state of unreality; then the fires are set" (Lewis & Yarnell, 1951, p. 87). As one 15-year-old boy explained: "When I light a fire, it's like eating. It's an urge and I get rid of it. After the urge is done with, I'm satisfied for a while" (as cited in Sakheim & Osborn, 1994, p. 27). An adult male in Lewis and Yarnell's (1951) study related, "After the firesetting, it was a common practice for me to go home and to go to sleep; this argues a relief of tension. If tension was present when I went to bed, it would scarcely be possible for me to go to sleep" (p. 164).

Deviant sexual fantasy gets redirected into acting out in a variety of ways; in some individuals, urges are satiated through firesetting behavior. Most repetitive firesetting involves less obvious sexual dynamics; therefore, the sexual element in these crimes is often missed by law enforcement (Banay, 1969; Schlesinger & Revitch, 1997). In fact, the sexual motivation may not be elicited during a brief interview process but may rather be revealed only through an extensive therapeutic relationship. Based on his review of the literature, Fras (1983, p. 200) concluded that "the sexually-motivated fire setter's goals are to achieve both instinctual gratification of the sexual need and the magic resolution of the interpsychic conflict—all of this in an individual who has started out with feelings of sexual inferiority and recently suffered social setbacks." Like other types of compulsive-repetitive offenders, this type of firesetter typically repeats the behavior until apprehended.

Some disagreement remains, however, about the sexual nature of firesetting. For example, Quinsey, Chaplin, and Upfold (1989) observed no sexual arousal to fire stimuli in their sample of firesetters and interpreted their results as a lack of support for a sexual theory. Fras (1983, p. 198) argued:

> [In juvenile firesetters, sexuality] seems to play no greater a part than any other aspect of their mental apparatus.... Most of these children and adolescents are psychosexually delayed and, in the case of the adolescents, sexually most disinterested. There is no indication that fire setting is a substitution for sexuality; rather, their lack of sexual interest and activity is one of the facets of severe maturational delay.

Setting fires has been theorized by some to be a displacement of anger toward a rejecting or neglectful parent (Sakheim, Vigdor, Gordon, & Helprin, 1985; Yarnell, 1940), and firesetters may be likely to have a history of sexual abuse (Martin, Bergen, Richardson, Roeger, & Allison, 2004). In a study of 205 juvenile firesetters referred for assessment and treatment (Root, MacKay, Henderson, Del Bove, & Warling, 2008), 48% of the sample had experienced maltreatment. Maltreated children more frequently than children who were not maltreated reported setting fires out of anger and more frequently described setting fires immediately after a family-related stressor. Maltreated children were also more likely to engage in repeated firesetting, both in the number of fires and in the duration of firesetting behavior. It is believed that firesetting can provide a sense of agency that might otherwise be unavailable in the environments of these juveniles.

It is not surprising that firesetters display a wide range of psychopathology. For example, Moore, Thompson-Pope, and Whited (1996) found those with a history of firesetting had more pathological MMPI-A profiles; Leong (1992) found most (70.3%) of a sample of firesetters had prior psychiatric hospitalizations, and more than half (51.7%) were psychotic at the time of their offense. Many firesetters appear to have learning delays or disabilities and/or deficits in executive functioning (Sakheim et al., 1985). Similarly, many in Yarnell's (1940) study exhibited learning disabilities, and Lewis and Yarnell (1951) described a group of "mental defective" firesetters who set fires predominantly to see a fire or to see fire engines. One such 21-year-old had set a fire in a factory and adjacent sheds with the hope of asphyxiating the townspeople and destroying the town. "Fire thrilled him more than anything else and he was mad at everybody, because all the children teased him. In early childhood, he had burned a rooster, and set a fire in the home when he was angry with his sister" (p. 131). Sakheim et al. (1985) characterized child firesetters as "emotionally complex youngsters whose capacity for deliberation, self-control, and direct verbal expression of inner impulses and feelings is quite limited. They are troubled children who resort to primitive behavioral mechanisms for the expression of confused inner needs, at times wreaking havoc and creating tragedy" (p. 468). Further research has found that depression, Oppositional Defiant Disorder (ODD), and Attention Deficit Hyperactivity Disorder (ADHD) are all risk factors for firesetting (Becker et al., 2004).

In addition to various forms of psychopathology, firesetters also display a constellation of antisocial behaviors and violence. Firesetting juveniles have been reported to exhibit significantly more lying, stealing, destructive behavior, running away, sexual misbehavior, and other antisocial conduct than do children who do not set fires (Jacobson, 1985; Martin et al., 2004). "Firesetting with the intention of causing serious damage" is listed among the diagnostic criteria for Conduct Disorder, a childhood behavior disorder characterized by persistent violation of age-appropriate norms and the rights of others (APA, 2000, p. 99), and research has consistently shown a relationship between firesetting and diagnoses of Conduct Disorder (e.g., Heath, Hardesty, Goldfine, & Walker, 1985; Sakheim et al., 1985).

Thus, both Kolko, Kazdin, and Meyer (1985) and Stickle and Blechman (2002) found that firesetting juveniles engage in more aggressive behavior than their peers. In a sample of nonclinical, outpatient, and inpatient children (Kolko & Kazdin, 1991), those who had engaged in firesetting in the previous 12 months showed higher levels of behavioral dysfunction, antisocial behavior, hostility, emotionality, and impulsivity than those who had not engaged in firesetting. Unsurprisingly, in Becker, Stuewig, Herrera, and McCloskey's (2004) longitudinal study of children who had set fires prior to the first interview in 1990, 40.6% had been referred to juvenile court for violent offenses by 2000, as compared with just 12% of the non-firesetting children.

More recently, a ten-year longitudinal study of youth referred to the New Zealand Fire Awareness and Intervention Program (Lambie, Ioane, Randell, & Seymour, 2013) indicated that more than half of the program participants referred for firesetting behavior went on to commit criminal offenses within the ten-year window. The crimes committed by these 108 offenders included violent and non-violent crimes of varying severity; however, not one of the offenders in the sample went on to commit a murder during the follow-up period. Among those with a firesetting history, it appears that being male and having been exposed to abuse were risk factors for later criminal offending. On the other hand, living in an intact household with both parents was a protective factor, associated with a lower likelihood of future offending.

It is clear that firesetting and other dysfunctional behavioral patterns that begin during childhood and adolescence often become increasingly serious throughout the individual's lifetime, particularly if appropriate disciplinary measures are not taken to address the behavior early on and when additional stressors are present in the home environment. Wax and Haddox (1974, p. 155), for example, cautioned that "in adolescents a lack of mastery over [enuresis, animal cruelty, and especially firesetting] must represent a clear failure in the development of various controls and therefore must be viewed as a warning signaling vulnerability to explosive impulse expression." In a study of psychiatric inpatients aged 15 to 30 (Felthous & Bernard, 1979), the presence of two or more elements of the predictive triad was extremely rare but was associated with the presence of two or more aggressive behaviors (i.e., homicidal threats, carrying a deadly weapon, physical assault). In a second study of 450 U.S. naval servicemen (Felthous & Bernard, 1979), those subjects exhibiting two-thirds of the triad were among the most aggressive in the sample. In a sample of 45,915 arson cases (Soothill, Francis, & Liu, 2008), a survival analysis technique estimated that approximately one out of every 160 arsonists was convicted of a homicide offense within the 20-year follow-up period, indicating a significantly elevated risk.

In offender samples, the rates of firesetting histories tend to be quite high. For example, in one study of adult offenders (Langevin, Ben-Aron, Wright, Marchese, & Hardy, 1988), 50% of murderers and 18% of sex offenders had a history of firesetting. Meanwhile, in Leong's (1992) sample of adult arsonists, 31% had prior arrests for violent offenses.

Conclusion

The empirical research with respect to animal cruelty, firesetting, and their relationship specifically to homicide is inconsistent and insufficient. But to conclude that MacDonald's (1963) early observation of the triad has no importance is incorrect. Instead of asking a general question about the predictive significance of animal cruelty, firesetting, or both to homicide or interpersonal violence, a more specific question should be framed, keeping in mind that MacDonald's observations related not to all criminal offenders, but only to the "very sadistic" ones.

Motivational Spectrum in the Classification of Homicide

All murder is not alike. Revitch (1977), Revitch and Schlesinger (1981), and Schlesinger (2004a) have argued that homicide must be classified in a rational manner in order to understand its psychopathology, psychodynamics, and prognostic factors. Thus, behavior such as animal cruelty or firesetting may have different predictive significance for different types of homicide. And, in keeping with MacDonald's observations, it would seem that sadistic murder is the type of homicide in which animal cruelty and firesetting are most relevant.

In search of a common denominator to be used as a basis for classification—and from which predictions could be derived—Revitch and Schlesinger (1978, 1981) and Schlesinger (2004a) developed the concept of the motivational spectrum of homicide, which comes from an analysis of the dynamics of the antisocial act itself. These motivational stimuli are spectrally distributed with purely external (sociogenic) factors on one end of the continuum and purely internal (psychogenic) factors on the other end. From the external to the internal range of the continuum, five separate categories of homicide have been differentiated: (1) sociogenic or environmental, (2) situational, (3) impulsive, (4) catathymic, and (5) compulsive. In compulsive offenses, external factors play a minimal role, while internal (psychogenic) pressures are paramount. The reverse is true for the environmental/socially-stimulated offenses. The other categories of offenses have a mixture of external and internal factors, depending on their position on the continuum.

Separate from the motivational spectrum are homicides that are a direct outgrowth of a primary psychiatric disorder such as a psychosis, an organic condition, or a toxic state. In such cases, an individual responds to psychotic symptoms, the disinhibiting effects of various substances, or perhaps the weakening of controls caused by various organic disorders. An example is the case of a 29-year-old male who became overtly psychotic and believed his pet dog was communicating telepathically, making faces at him, and threatening him. He disemboweled the dog with a steak knife and buried her in the woods. This individual had no prior acts of aggression and no prior psychotic episodes.

Environmental/Sociogenic Homicides

Many crimes throughout history have been a result of external or social influences rather than psychological forces within the individual. Contract killing and terroristic murder are two examples of homicide derived from social-environmental factors, specifically cultural influences in the case of contract murder and religious/political influences in the case of terroristic murder. A history of animal cruelty would probably have little relevance in this type of homicide. And firesetting can occur during riots or wartime, for example, as a form of revenge (Revitch, 1977).

Situational Homicides

Situational homicides are essentially reactions to stressful circumstances (Schlesinger, 2004a). They may be committed by individuals with little or minimal psychopathology; however, all types of personalities may be involved. The biblical Cain-Abel murder is the prototype of a situationally stimulated homicide: the murder occurred suddenly, as a result of an argument between family members, stemming in part from jealousy and anger. According to the Federal Bureau of Investigation's (FBI) Uniform Crime Reports (U.S. Department of Justice, 2010), about 60% of all homicides would fall in the situational category; they include domestic murders, felony murders, murders within romantic triangles, and the like. There may be some relevance of animal cruelty and firesetting to this type of homicide because these background behaviors indicate a predisposition to violent and aggressive reactions. For example, the research (e.g., Merz-Perez et al., 2001; Overton et al., 2011; Wax & Haddox, 1974) seems to suggest that animal cruelty has some relationship to or indicates a predisposition toward violence, as does firesetting (Mavromatis, 2000).

Impulsive Homicides

Impulsive individuals typically react to situations in a diffuse stimulus-response manner, with little ability to modulate emotion. Such individuals tend to drift in and out of behavioral difficulties, with a life pattern characterized by unpredictability and lack of direction. An illustrative case is that of a 25-year-old male who impulsively strangled a woman after intercourse in response to her threat of accusing him of rape. A history of minor antisocial acts, low average intelligence, and lack of direction were found in his background. In impulsive homicides, animal cruelty or firesetting may have some predictive relevance because they can serve as a marker for a general expression of hostility and anger (Revitch & Schlesinger, 1981).

Catathymic Homicides

The concept of catathymia was originally introduced in the field of criminal behavior by Wertham (1937) as an explanation for unprovoked, isolated episodes of severe violence without an organic basis. Wertham's original definition of catathymic crisis was "a transformation of the stream of thought, as the result of certain complexes of ideas, that are charged with a strong affect, usually a wish, a fear, or an ambivalent striving" (p. 975). Revitch and Schlesinger (1981) and Schlesinger (2004b) updated the concept of catathymia; they considered it to be not a diagnostic entity (as did Wertham) but rather a psychodynamic or motivational process. Revitch (1977), Revitch and Schlesinger (1981), and Schlesinger (2004b, 2007) differentiated two types of catathymic homicides, acute and chronic. The acute process is essentially a sudden, unprovoked murder or severe assault triggered by the eruption of an overwhelming emotion attached to internal ideas or conflicts—typically inadequacy extending to the sexual arena. An example of an acute catathymic homicide is that of an 18-year-old high school senior who strangled a woman to death after he was unable to effect an erection following her seductive advances and ridiculing remarks. The subject was able to recall the event, but initially believed it was a dream (Revitch & Schlesinger, 1978).

In the chronic catathymic process, depressed mood and obsessive rumination precede the violent act for weeks or many months. Here, the subject develops a fixed idea that the only way to free himself from the source of threat to his psychic stability and inner tension is through violence. The aggressive act itself seems ego-alien, with a dreamlike quality. The typical victim of a chronic catathymic homicide is usually a romantic partner, a no-longer-loved one, or sometimes a relative stranger with whom the subject has become obsessed and whom the subject has often stalked (Meloy, 1992). In some cases, the anger is turned inward and suicide or murder-suicide results.

Catathymic homicides of both acute and chronic types derive from a breakthrough of underlying sexual conflicts, typically deep feelings of sexual inadequacy with which the offender has been secretly struggling. Because catathymic homicides are a form of sexual homicide, both animal cruelty and firesetting in the offender's background have relevance. An account of a chronic catathymic arson was graphically described by Yukio Mishima (1956) in his novel *The Temple of the Golden Pavilion*. Mishima's main character sets fire to an iconic building and he has distinct sexual emotions and a feeling of relief while watching the structure burn.

Compulsive Homicides

Compulsive homicides are on the extreme end of the motivational spectrum and stem from internal psychogenic forces with little or no environmental influence. These offenses may be committed in a specific, repetitive-ritualistic manner (Meloy, 2000), or they may be of a diffuse nature. Fantasies usually precede the homicide by many years. Compulsive murders are also sexual murders, but they do not stem from underlying sexual conflicts as do catathymic homicides. Instead, killing the victim is itself sexually arousing and part of the offender's sexual-arousal pattern (Schlesinger, 2004b, 2007, 2008). And the offender's behavior at the crime scene almost always involves ritualistic conduct—which is sexually gratifying—such as leaving the victim in a degrading position or with insertions of foreign objects (Schlesinger, Kassen, Mesa, & Pinizzotto, 2010).

Once a murderer begins, the killing may be repeated frequently—in serial fashion—or at intervals with years in between. The murder is repeated because it is so sexually stimulating and gratifying. Numerous accounts in the literature tell of individuals who committed a homicide and served a lengthy prison term, only to repeat a similar homicide when released on parole (Guttmacher, 1963; Revitch, 1977). Compulsive-repetitive murder is the most relevant type for understanding the predictive significance of both animal cruelty and firesetting in the future offender's background (Schlesinger, 2001). In fact, a review of the research literature with respect to animal cruelty and firesetting shows that these behaviors are most significant in sexually-motivated cases. For example, Ressler, Burgess, Hartman, and Douglas (1986) found that zoophilia and general cruelty to animals were prominent in the childhood histories of murderers who committed rape and mutilated their victims.

Petersen and Farrington (2007) also reported case histories of serial sexual killers and mass murderers who were cruel to animals during their childhoods. Hensley and Tallichet (2008) found that children who abuse an animal out of fun are significantly more likely to engage in interpersonal violence as an adult than are those who do not abuse animals. Hensley and Tallichet (2009) also concluded that drowning an animal and having sex with an animal were both predictive of adult interpersonal violence. And Ascione, Friedrich, Heath, and Hayashi (2003) found that animal cruelty and sexual contact with animals were positively associated with a history of sexual abuse. In addition, Hensley, Tallichet, and Dutkiewicz (2010) found that childhood bestiality was a significant positive predictor of adult interpersonal violence.

Animal Cruelty, Firesetting, and Sexual Homicide

Animal Cruelty

The earliest descriptions of sexual murderers regularly noted a history of animal cruelty in their childhoods. For example, Krafft-Ebing (1886) discussed the case of Vincenz Verzeni, who was a sexual murderer and had a background of animal cruelty. "When he was twelve years old, he experienced a peculiar feeling of pleasure while wringing the necks of chickens. After this he often killed great numbers of them" (p. 67). Krafft-Ebing also reported the case of Sergeant Bertrand, who fantasized about having sex with dead animals, later engaged in such activities, and then progressed to disinterring human bodies and having sex with corpses. Krafft-Ebing reported many other cases of animal cruelty in the backgrounds of sexual murderers. He theorized that, as youngsters, such individuals are afraid of committing a criminal act with a human, but engage in torture of animals "to stimulate or excite their lust" (p. 84).

In the 20th century, Peter Kurten (Wilson & Pitman, 1962), who, in his adolescent years, became involved with bestiality, progressed to serial sexual murder as an adult. Kurten befriended a dog catcher who taught him how to torture and masturbate animals. From ages 13 through 15, Kurten engaged in numerous sexual acts with pigs, sheep, and goats, sometimes stabbing the animals to death while having intercourse with them.

Guttmacher (1960) also found that sexual murderers frequently had a background of animal cruelty. He offered his theory for their conduct, which differed in some ways from Krafft-Ebing's view (1886, p. 100):

> [Offenders] give vent to their hostile impulses through cruelty to animals. Their real hatred is not against animals but, of course, against their fellow man. Animals are mere substitutes, they serve as scapegoats. Furthermore, dumb brutes cannot file complaints with the police and in some quarters a certain degree of cruelty to animals is accepted as a sublimation of sadistic impulses. Certainly, this is true of hunting.

Perhaps one of the most well-known contemporary cases illustrating the connection between animal cruelty and serial sexual murder is that of Jeffrey Dahmer (Schwartz, 1992). As a child, Dahmer was fascinated with road-kill, butchered and dissected small animals, nailed cats and frogs to trees behind his house, and once put a dog's head on a stick. Dahmer killed 17 men, most of whom he picked up in gay bars. He engaged in cannibalism and necrophilic rape and also attempted to make his victims zombies by injecting muriatic acid into their brains with a turkey baster. Eventually arrested, he pled guilty and was later killed in prison by a fellow inmate.

A number of studies have also demonstrated the ominous significance of animal cruelty in the backgrounds of sexual murderers and potential sex murderers. Johnson and Becker (1997) found that 34% of their adolescent subjects who wanted to commit serial sexual murder reported severe animal cruelty. One child shot, drowned, stabbed, or set on fire numerous animals, sometimes injuring or killing 10 animals a day. Another of their adolescent subjects felt sexual arousal after dissecting animals once he killed them; he kept many of their skulls in his bedroom as trophies. Another subject killed dogs by snapping their necks while they were alive, and yet another killed snakes and rabbits and often searched for road-kill, cutting them open and examining their insides. Myers, Burgess, and Nelson (1998) similarly found that 28% of their sample of adolescents who had already committed one sexual murder also had a history of animal cruelty.

Positive associations between psychopathy—a condition characterized by lack of remorse, impulsivity, and callousness—and the killing and torture of animals (e.g., Kavanagh, Signal, & Taylor, 2013) and between psychopathy and sexual sadism (e.g., Holt, Meloy, & Strack, 1999) suggest that psychopathic tendencies may underlie the connection between animal cruelty and sadistic violence. As Meloy (2000, p.7) stated, "virtually all" known perpetrators of sexual homicide present with psychopathic features. Furthermore, a recent study (Mesa, 2012) indicated that serial sexual homicide offenders were more likely than non-serial homicide offenders to have histories of animal cruelty.

The Significance of Cats

Revitch (1978), Revitch and Schlesinger (1981, 1989), and Schlesinger and Revitch (1997) noted that cruelty to cats, in particular, was found in the childhood backgrounds of individuals who went on to commit serial sexual homicides. Perhaps this pattern is found because cats are generally considered a female symbol, more than other animals such as dogs (Revitch, 1978). Cats arouse anger in the potential sex murderer, who almost always is a male fantasizing about killing a female. Felthous (1980) concluded that "cats more than dogs seem to induce a child's sadistic projections and cruel behavior. [A number of subjects in the study] who had tortured cats admitted an intense dislike of this animal, in particular, but disclosed no insight into the animosity" (p. 175). Revitch (1978) reported the case of an adolescent who set cats on fire and experienced a euphoric feeling while watching them burn. This offender compared cats to women, noting similarities in their looks and behavior. Tapia (1971) similarly found that out of 18 subjects with a history of severe violence, only one had not previously hurt a cat.

Ressler and Schachtman (1992) described two serial sexual murderers who had tortured cats when they were children. One individual attached cherry bombs to cats' legs and made "many cats in his neighborhood three-legged" (p. 96). In fact, Albert DeSalvo, commonly known as the Boston Strangler, tortured cats during his childhood and described his behavior:

> I don't like cats.... I used to shoot cats with a bow-and-arrow, put it right through their belly and sometimes they ran with the arrow right through them yowling, and I don't recall being too upset by that.... Sometimes when I would see them, before the shoot, I'd get such a feeling of anger that I think I could tear those cats apart with my bare hands. I don't understand this, but just that I hated them and they had done nothing to me [as cited in Rae, 1967, p. 61].

In Ressler, Burgess, and Douglas' (1988) study, carried out under the auspices of the Federal Bureau of Investigation (FBI), a nonrandom national sample of 36 incarcerated sexual murderers was extensively studied. These investigators found repetitive examples of childhood sadistic behavior toward animals, particularly cats. One of their subjects said: "I killed a cat once. I can't tell you why. I was just mad and the cat came at the wrong time and I strangled this cat" (p. 38). Another subject also described killing cats (p. 38):

> One time I found a kitten and it was raining. The kitten was shivering and I brought it home. About two weeks later the house was full of fleas. From there I just started hating cats.... I don't know what happened. My father thought I did something to it, and I thought my father did something to it because I came

home from school one day and the cat just wasn't there.... That's when I got to tying cherry bombs to cats' leg, light it, and watch the cat run down the street.... Made a lot of one-legged cats.

The following two cases assessed by the author (Schlesinger) are additional examples of cat-killing in the backgrounds of serial sexual murderers.

Case Study 1

A 32-year-old male was arrested after he brutally attacked and almost killed a woman who came to his assistance after his car broke down on a highway. He smashed her in the nose and eyes multiple times, shoved his fingers up her rectum while strangling her and, at the same time, bit her on the chin and then bit her on her left breast. After the assault, the offender threw the victim out of his moving car and assumed that she had died. She miraculously lived, and the offender was arrested.

The distinct placement of the bite marks resulted in his being linked to a similar ritualistic sexual murder in a different state. In this murder, he met a woman who was walking home from a store on a busy highway. The offender grabbed her, dragged her inside a construction area, shoved his fingers up her rectum while strangling her, and bit her on the chin and her left breast. He said he wanted to look at the victim's eyes while killing her and watching her die slowly at his hands.

This offender's history included chronic behavior problems, school expulsion, and an allegation of being sexually abused. Interestingly, his friends had nicknamed him "Catman" because, as an adolescent, he was known to have killed many cats after engaging in some type of sexual activity with them.

Case Study 2

A 30-year-old male was convicted of the murder of a 26-year-old woman and her two young children. He also murdered two other women ages 62 and 40. The offender killed all the victims by manual strangulation after hogtying them, raping them anally and vaginally, and making small knife cuts all over their bodies to cause pain and suffering. All the crime scenes had an absence of physical evidence because the offender shaved his entire body of hair and entered the homes naked, except for sneakers with several socks pulled over them. He poured alcohol in the vaginas and rectums of his victims because he believed alcohol would remove any trace of DNA. This offender said he got the idea of using alcohol from the well-known film *Presumed Innocent*, whose plot involved the use of a spermicide to eliminate semen. However, he did not know that alcohol does not eliminate DNA, but rather preserves it, which led to his arrest, conviction, and execution.

As a child, the future offender tortured and killed cats. In fact, his mother found a number of strangled cats hanging from her clothesline when he was 8 or 9 years old. He was sent for an evaluation, but there was never any follow-up.

Firesetting

Just as there are many notorious sexual murderers with a history of animal cruelty, there is no shortage of sexual murderers with a history of firesetting. Prolific serial murderer

Peter Kurten not only abused animals but was also a serial arsonist as an adolescent (Wilson & Pitman, 1962). He derived pleasure from setting and watching fires and continued setting fires into adulthood, even setting on fire the body of one of his many victims. Jane Toppan, the psychopathic nurse who poisoned an unknown number of patients in the late 1800s, was also a pyromaniac who derived erotic pleasure from watching fires. After an entire household under her care turned up dead, Toppan was arrested and admitted that she had an irresistible sexual impulse to kill (Schechter, 2003). Thomas Piper, who raped and bludgeoned to death four victims, had a history of firesetting (Schechter & Everitt, 1996), as did Arthur Shawcross, who killed numerous prostitutes.

Case Study 3

Arthur Shawcross exhibited all three prongs of MacDonald's triad. As a child, he had frequent nightmares that caused him to wet the bed (Olsen, 1993). By adolescence, he had begun torturing animals and setting fires. Shawcross enjoyed burning barrels of trash and once set a brushfire that had to be extinguished by firefighters.

With his small stature and bizarre affectations, he was a natural target for bullies at school. His classmates called him "Oddie" and tormented him relentlessly (Berry-Dee, 2003). At home, he felt that he could never please his domineering mother (Olsen, 1993). From an early age, it was apparent that Shawcross escaped into a rich fantasy world, speaking aloud to imaginary friends, daydreaming often, and fantasizing about his sister, Jean. He claims to have engaged in sexual activity with her and also to have been molested by an adult man (Olsen, 1993). He was held back in school and eventually dropped out.

After a stint serving in the Vietnam War, Shawcross returned to setting fires, destroying a barn, a milk-bottling plant, and the paper factory where he was employed (Berry-Dee, 2003). He was apprehended while attempting to rob a gas station and sentenced to a 5-year prison term, of which he served only 22 months. After his release, Shawcross's criminal behavior escalated dramatically. He raped a 16-year-old girl. Then, he raped, killed, and mutilated a 10-year-old boy. Soon thereafter, he raped and strangled a 7-year-old girl, stuffing grass into her orifices and leaving her body in a sewage pipe. He was again imprisoned for these crimes and again conned his way into early parole.

Upon release, Shawcross began a string of murders. He seized upon vulnerable women, mainly drug addicts and prostitutes, strangling or beating them to death and leaving their bodies exposed to the elements to deteriorate (Berry-Dee, 2003). Shawcross' fantasies were expressed in his ritualistic treatment of the bodies; most bodies had vegetation inserted into their orifices, many showed signs of cannibalism (to which Shawcross has admitted), and the genitals were frequently mutilated or excised. Shawcross claims to have taken 53 lives in total (Berry-Dee, 2003).

Ressler et al. (1988) found that in their sample of 36 sexual murderers, 56% had set fires during childhood, 52% set had fires during adolescence, and 28% had set fires during adulthood. Langevin and his colleagues (1988) found a somewhat lower rate (33%) in their sample of sexual killers. In a sample of adolescent sexual murderers (Myers et al., 1998), 36% had a history of firesetting, often in conjunction with animal cruelty and fighting. One young man attempted to burn down his mother's home, set a van on fire, and set his aunt's bed on fire as a child, stating that he "wanted to see someone burn" (p.

324). He and a peer were responsible for raping and bludgeoning to death an adult woman in her home, allegedly to avenge an outstanding drug debt.

A social-learning theory of serial murder (Hale, 1993) suggests that such offenders endure humiliating experiences in youth and internalize them. Never able to retaliate directly, perhaps because the humiliator is a parent, the child cannot release his frustration and later vents his rage against a symbolic victim. Consistent with this theory, the childhoods of sexual murderers, like the childhoods of firesetters, often include parental alienation and unstable family life (Marshall, 1989; Ressler et al., 1988). Two-thirds of the serial killers reviewed by Stone (2001) indicated emotional abuse during youth in the form of parental humiliation, often in the context of sexuality.

Singer and Hensley (2004) investigated the histories of three notorious sexual murderers—Carl Panzram, Ottis Toole, and David Berkowitz—in order to test this social-learning theory of serial killing. The authors believe that early attempts to vent frustration through firesetting may be insufficient, leading to increasingly aggressive forms of expression, ultimately culminating in homicide. All three of these individuals experienced rejection and humiliation at the hands of a parent or parents, against whom they could not retaliate. A single fire was insufficient to alleviate the tension, leading to the setting of multiple fires. Eventually, this behavior escalated to murder.

Panzram, beaten and neglected by his parents, began setting fires in adolescence and killed random victims as an adult. Toole's father abandoned the family, and, during childhood, Toole's mother dressed him as a girl. He often burned vacant buildings and continued setting fires in response to stress throughout his adult life. And Berkowitz developed a generalized hatred for women—possibly as a result of an unresolved conflict surrounding his being abandoned by his biological mother—and was known as a loner. He recorded 1,488 fires in his diary before and during the time he committed a series of murders of female strangers. Ressler and Schachtman (1992) believe that Berkowitz's firesetting was an extension of his desire for control over others: "These fires were all a prelude to his moving into the arena in which he could exercise the ultimate control, homicide" (p. 80). The following case of Joseph "The Shoemaker" Kallinger illustrates the connection between sexual murder and a background of firesetting as an important factor in understanding the offender's conduct (Schreiber, 1983):

Case Study 4

Joseph Kallinger, born in 1936, was abandoned as an infant and was adopted by a couple who subjected him to severe physical and emotional abuse. The couple showed him no affection, hit him with a hammer, held his hand over a flame, told him that his penis was defective, and regularly threatened to send him back to the orphanage. As a child, he was molested at knifepoint by a group of older boys. He began engaging in antisocial behavior out of rage and frustration and heard voices instructing him to cut someone. By adolescence, Kallinger had developed sadistic fantasies, masturbating while stabbing at pornographic images with a knife.

At the age of 15, after the voice of God told Kallinger that it was his mission to heal people through their feet, he became ardently invested in shoemaking. In 1958, at age 22, a figure appeared to him, commanding that he burn down his house. Although this fire was set as a result of a hallucination and resulted in material gain from an insurance claim, a sexual element was quite clear. As he related to author Flora Schreiber (1983), having an orgasm as he spoke, "It was thrilling and the flames brought me a lot of joy. Fire gave me the same kind of sexual feeling I had from holding a knife in my left hand" (p. 118). He later set fire to his next home four times, and he once set fire to his place of work, a shoemaker's shop.

Kallinger was married twice and had six children. Three of Kallinger's children filed abuse charges against him in 1972; he was convicted, but served only a few months of his sentence. Soon thereafter, an invisible floating head named "Charlie" commanded him to castrate and murder young boys.

In 1974, Kallinger and his 13-year-old son, Michael, lured a 10-year-old boy into an abandoned factory, tortured him, sliced off his penis, and killed him. Three weeks later, Kallinger drowned his 12-year-old son, Joey, while Michael watched. In November 1974, Kallinger and his son began invading homes, holding the residents captive, sexually assaulting the women, and stealing their valuables. Their spree ended in January 1975, when Kallinger slit the throat of one of his eight captives in a home in New Jersey. Two weeks later, Kallinger and his son were arrested. Kallinger was sentenced to life in prison, where he died of a seizure in 1996, at the age of 59.

Discussion

Substantial evidence shows that animal cruelty and firesetting are behaviors indicative of severe emotional disturbance, but this disturbance may manifest itself in various ways and does not necessarily predict homicide. Although animal cruelty and firesetting appear to be more common in homicidal populations than in nonoffender samples, there is insufficient evidence that MacDonald's triad is a valid predictor of homicidal behavior, a conclusion at which MacDonald himself also arrived. Far more people exhibit the complete or partial triad than actually commit homicide, and the triad fails to reliably discriminate homicidal offenders from other types of offenders; however, the triad behaviors appear to be better predictors when they co-occur rather than appear independently.

As we observe in many of the reported cases, the triad typically appears amidst a wide array of maladaptive behaviors and traumatic or invalidating experiences. For instance, a child who has sexual encounters with relatives, is constantly bullied, performs poorly in school, and feels unable to please his parents might have significant behavioral troubles, even in the absence of animal cruelty, firesetting, or enuresis. But when significant acting out, such as hurting animals and setting fires, occurs, the likelihood of a good adjustment in adulthood is remote. The more severe the acting out in childhood is, the poorer the prognosis.

Unfortunately, the research is limited in quantity and suffers a variety of methodological problems. Much of the literature relies on case studies, and the available empirical studies often lack control groups (Sakheim et al., 1985). Even in the empirical studies, the data are often based solely on self-report, which renders their reliability questionable. Furthermore, because of the rarity of youth firesetting and animal cruelty—as well as the social stigma associated with being identified as a child who engages in these behaviors—most studies suffer from small sample sizes, which severely limit the statistical conclusions and generalizability of the findings. Stone's (2001) review of killers' biographies highlights the fact that information about childhood firesetting, animal cruelty, and enuresis is often not available; when looking into an offender's background, if information on these features is not available, we can conclude neither their presence nor their absence.

Lack of agreed-on operational definitions, particularly around firesetting behaviors, adds to the methodological problems. For example, terms such as *firesetting, fire play, pyromania, arson,* and *pyrophilia* are often used; however, each has a nuanced definition, and not all refer to a type of pathological firesetting that may have predictive value. In addition, many fires do not meet the legal definition of arson (Grant & Kim, 2007); therefore, any study of arsonists will systematically exclude a large portion of pathological firesetters, and effects observed in these samples may be diluted by the more logical profit-motivated and crime-concealment firesetters. Similarly, *animal cruelty* encompasses a wide range of behaviors, some of which may be predictive while others may not.

Sampling bias is another considerable source of error in this area of research, as arson studies sample only those who have been identified and apprehended. Essentially, we are studying only unsuccessful pathological firesetters (i.e., those who get caught), as we know little about those who have not been identified. The same dilemma plagues research on sexual homicide, in which the field of knowledge is confined to those killers who have been apprehended; at-large killers are necessarily beyond the purview of study. In both cases, one might expect some systematic differences between the type of offender who gets caught and the type of offender who does not.

Despite Hellman and Blackman's (1966) conclusion that the triad should be used as a prognostic indicator of aggressive behavior in adulthood, it seems that MacDonald's initial view that the triad is most relevant to sadistic criminal behavior is more valid. Intuitively, it would seem that a child who takes joy in drowning a kitten or electrocuting a dog might later get aroused by exacting cruelty on humans. Whereas most acts of homicide are committed in the context of a conflict between the offender and the victim, sexual homicide most often reflects the offender's enjoyment of dominating another human being in a sadistic manner. Future research on sadistic and sexually-motivated homicide offenders—using larger samples, appropriate case controls, and strict operational definitions of firesetting and animal cruelty—would be a logical next step toward supporting the usefulness of MacDonald's proposed triad.

References

American Psychiatric Association (2000). *Diagnostic and statistical manual of mental disorders* (4th ed., text rev.). Washington, DC: Author.

Arluke, A., & Madfis, E. (2013). Animal abuse as a warning sign of school massacres: A critique and refinement. *Homicide studies,* doi:1088767913511459.

Ascione, F. R., Friedrich, W. N., Heath, J., & Hayashi, K. (2003). Cruelty to animals in normative, sexually abused, and outpatient psychiatric samples of six to twelve year old children: Relations to maltreatment and exposure to domestic violence. *Anthrozoos, 16,* 194–212.

Banay, R. S. (1969). Unconscious sexual motivation in crime. *Medical Aspects of Human Sexuality, 3,* 91–102.

Becker, K. D., Stuewig, J., Herrera, V. M., & McCloskey, L. A. (2004). A study of firesetting and animal cruelty in children: Family influences and adolescent outcomes. *Journal of the American Academy of Child and Adolescent Psychiatry, 43*(7), 905–912.

Berry-Dee, C. (2003). *Talking with serial killers: The most evil people in the world tell their own stories.* London: Blake.

Dadds, M. R., Turner, C. M., & McAloon, J. (2002). Developmental links between cruelty to animals and human violence. The Australian & New Zealand Journal of Criminology, 35, 363–382.

Felthous, A. R. (1980). Aggression against cats, dogs, and people. *Clinical Psychiatry in Human Development, 10,* 169–177.

Felthous, A. R., & Bernard, H. (1979). Enuresis, firesetting, and cruelty to animals: The significance of two thirds of this triad. *Journal of Forensic Sciences, 24*(1), 240–246.

Felthous, A. R., & Keller, S. R. (1987). Childhood cruelty to animals and later aggression against people: A review. *American Journal of Psychiatry, 144,* 710–717.

Fras, I. (1983). Fire setting (pyromania) and its relationship to sexuality. In L. B. Schlesinger & E. Revitch (Eds.), *Sexual dynamics of antisocial behavior* (pp. 192–205). Springfield, IL: Thomas.

Gleyzer, R., Felthous, A. R., & Holzer, C. E. (2002). Animal cruelty and psychiatric disorders. *Journal of the American Academy of Psychiatry and Law, 30,* 257–265.

Goring, C. (1913). *The English convict.* London: Her Majesty's Stationary Office.

Grant, J. E., & Kim, S. W. (2007). Clinical characteristics and psychiatric comorbidity of pyromania. *Journal of Clinical Psychiatry, 68*(11), 1717–1722.

Grolnick, W. S., Cole, R. E., Laurenitis, L., & Schwartzman, P. (1990). Playing with fire: A developmental assessment of children's fire understanding and experience. *Journal of Clinical Child Psychology, 19*(2), 128–135.

Guttmacher, M. S. (1960). *The mind of the murderer.* New York: Farrar, Straus, and Cudahy.

Guttmacher, M. S. (1963). Dangerous offenders. *Crime and Delinquency, 9,* 381–390.

Haden, S. C., & Scarpa, A. (2005). Childhood animal cruelty: A review of research, assessment, and therapeutic issues. *Forensic Examiner, 14,* 23–32.

Hale, R. L. (1993). The application of learning theory to serial murder or "You too can learn to be a serial killer." *American Journal of Criminal Justice, 17*(2), 37–45.

Heath, G. A., Hardesty, V. A., Goldfine, P. E., & Walker, A. M. (1985). Diagnosis and childhood fire-setting. *Journal of Clinical Psychology, 41*(4), 571–575.

Hellman, D. D., & Blackman, N. (1966). Enuresis, firesetting, and cruelty to animals: A triad predictive of adult crime. *American Journal of Psychiatry, 122,* 1431–1435.

Hensley, C., & Tallichet, S. E. (2008). The effects of inmate self-reported childhood and adolescent animal cruelty: Motivations and the number of convictions for adult violent interpersonal crimes. *International Journal of Offender Therapy and Comparative Criminology, 52,* 175–184.

Hensley, C., & Tallichet, S. E. (2009). Childhood and adolescent animal cruelty methods and their possible link to adult violent crimes. *Journal of Interpersonal Violence, 24,* 147–158.

Hensley, C., Tallichet, S. E., & Dutkiewicz, E. L. (2010). Childhood bestiality: A potential precursor to adult interpersonal violence. *Journal of Interpersonal Violence, 25,* 557–567.

Holt, S. E., Meloy, J. R. & Strack, S. (1999). Sadism and psychopathy in violent and sexually violent offenders. *Journal of the American Academy of Psychiatry and the Law, 27*(1), 23–32.

Jacobson, R. R. (1985). Child firesetters: A clinical investigation. *Journal of Child Psychology and Psychiatry, 26*(5), 759–768.

Johnson, B. R., & Becker, J. V. (1997). Natural born killers? The development of the sexually sadistic serial killer. *Journal of the American Academy of Psychiatry and Law, 25*, 335–348.

Justice, B., Justice, R., & Kraft, I. (1974). Early-warning signs of violence: Is a triad enough? *American Journal of Psychiatry, 131*, 457–459.

Kafry, D. (1980). Playing with matches: Children and fire. In D. Canter (Ed.), *Fires and human behavior* (pp. 47–61). New York: Wiley.

Kavanagh, P. S., Signal, T. D., & Taylor, N. (2013). The Dark Triad and animal cruelty: Dark personalities, dark attitudes, and dark behaviors. *Personality and Individual Differences, 55*(6), 666–670.

Kolko, D. J., & Kazdin, A. E. (1991). Aggression and psychopathology in matchplaying and firesetting children: A replication and extension. *Journal of Clinical Child Psychology, 20*(2), 191–201.

Kolko, D. J., & Kazdin, A. E. (1991). Motives of childhood firesetters: Firesetting characteristics and psychological correlates. *Journal of Child Psychology and Psychiatry, 32*(3), 535–550.

Kolko, D. J., Kazdin, A. E., & Meyer, E. C. (1985). Aggression and psychopathology in childhood firesetters: Parent and child reports. *Journal of Consulting and Clinical Psychology, 53*(3), 377–385.

Krafft-Ebing, R. von (1886). *Psychopathia sexualis* (C. G. Chaddock, Trans.). Philadelphia: Davis.

Kretchmer, E. (1925). *Physique and character.* London: Kegan Paul.

Lambie, I., Ioane, J., Randell, I., & Seymour, F. (2013). Offending behaviours of child and adolescent firesetters over a 10-year follow-up. *Journal of Child Psychology and Psychiatry, 54*(12), 1295–1307.

Langevin, R., Ben-Aron, M. H., Wright, P., Marchese, V., & Handy, L. (1988). The sex killer. *Annals of Sex Research, 1*(2), 263–302.

Langevin, R., Paitich, D., Orchard, B., Hardy, L., & Russon, A. (1983). Childhood and family background of killers, seen for psychiatric assessment: A controlled study. *Bulletin of the American Academy of Psychiatry and Law, 11*, 331–341.

Leong, G. B. (1992). A psychiatric study of persons charged with arson. *Journal of Forensic Sciences, 37*(5), 1319–1326.

Lewis, N. D. C., & Yarnell, H. (1951). Pathological firesetting (Pyromania). In *Nervous and mental disease monograph no. 82*, New York: Coolidge Foundation.

Lombroso, C. (1911). *Crime: Its causes and remedies* (H. P. Horton, Trans.). Boston: Little, Brown. (Original work published 1876.)

MacDonald, J. M. (1963). The threat to kill. *American Journal of Psychiatry, 121*, 125–130.

MacDonald, J. M. (1968). *Homicidal threats.* Springfield, IL: Thomas.

Marshall, W. L. (1989). Intimacy, loneliness, and sexual offenders. Behavioral *Research and Therapy, 27*, 491–503.

Martin, G., Bergen, H. A., Richardson, A. S., Roeger, L., & Allison, S. (2004). Correlates of firesetting in a community sample of young adolescents. *Australian and New Zealand Journal of Psychiatry, 38*(3), 148–154.

Mavromatis, M. (2000). Serial arson: Repetitive firesetting and pyromania. In L.B. Schlesinger (Ed.), *Serial offenders* (pp. 67–102). Boca Raton, FL: CRC Press.

Meloy, J. R. (1992). *Violent attachments.* Northvale, NJ: Aronson.

Meloy, J. R. (2000). The nature and dynamics of sexual homicide: An integrative review. *Aggression and Violent Behavior, 5,* 1–22.

Merz-Perez, L., Heide, K. M., & Silverman, I. J. (2001). Childhood cruelty to animals and subsequent violence against humans. *International Journal of Offender Therapy and Comparative Criminology, 45,* 556–573.

Mesa, V. B. (2012). *Criminal, antisocial, and temporal patterns in the histories of serial and non-serial sexual murderers.* City University of New York.

Mishima, Y. (1956). *The Temple of the Golden Pavilion* (I. Morris, Trans.). New York: Berkley.

Moore, J. M., Jr., Thompson-Pope, S. K., & Whited, R. M. (1996). MMPI-A profiles of adolescent boys with a history of firesetting. *Journal of Personality Assessment, 67*(1), 116–126.

Myers, W. C., Burgess, A., & Nelson, J. A. (1998). Criminal and behavioral aspects of juvenile sexual homicide. *Journal of Forensic Sciences, 43,* 321–328.

Olsen, J. (1993). *The misbegotten son: A serial killer and his victims.* New York: Delacorte.

Overton, J. C., Hensley, C., & Tallichet, S. E. (2011). Examining the relationship between childhood animal cruelty motives and recurrent adult violent crimes towards humans. *Journal of Interpersonal Violence, 20,* 1–17.

Patterson-Kane, E. G., & Piper, H. (2009). Animal abuse as a sentinel for human violence: A critique. *Journal of Social Issues, 65,* 589–614.

Petersen, M. L., & Farrington, D. P. (2007). Cruelty to animals and violence to people. *Victims and Offenders, 2,* 21–43.

Quinsey, V. L., Chaplin, T. C., & Upfold, D. (1989). Arsonists and sexual arousal to fire setting: Correlation unsupported. *Journal of Behavior Therapy and Experimental Psychiatry, 20*(3), 203–209.

Rae, G. W. (1967). *Confessions of the Boston Strangler.* New York: Pyramid Press.

Ressler, R. K., Burgess, A. W., & Douglas, J. E. (1988). *Sexual homicide: Patterns and motives.* New York: Free Press.

Ressler, R. K., Burgess, A. W., Hartman, C. R., & Douglas, J. E. (1986). Murderers who rape and mutilate. *Journal of Interpersonal Violence, 1,* 273–287.

Ressler, R. K., & Schachtman, T. (1992). *Whoever fights monsters.* New York: St. Martin's Press.

Revitch, E. (1977). Classification of offenders for prognostic and dispositional evaluation. *Bulletin of the American Academy of Psychiatry and Law, 5,* 41–50.

Revitch, E. (1978). Sexually motivated burglaries. *Bulletin of the American Academy of Psychiatry and Law, 6,* 277–283.

Revitch, E., & Schlesinger, L. B. (1978). Murder: Evaluation, classification, and predicting. In I. L. Kutash, S. B. Kutash, & L. B. Schlesinger (Eds.), *Violence: Perspectives on murder and aggression* (pp. 138–164). San Francisco: Jossey-Bass.

Revitch, E., & Schlesinger, L. B. (1981). *Psychopathology of homicide.* Springfield, IL: Thomas.

Revitch, E., & Schlesinger, L. B. (1989). *Sex murder and sex aggression.* Springfield, IL: Thomas.

Rider, A. O. (1980). The firesetter: A psychological profile, Part II. *FBI Law Enforcement Bulletin, 49*(7), 7–17.

Root, C., MacKay, S., Henderson, J., Del Bove, G., & Warling, D. (2008). The link between maltreatment and juvenile firesetting: Correlates and underlying mechanisms. *Child Abuse & Neglect, 32,* 161–176.

Sakheim, G. A., & Osborn, E. (1994). *Firesetting children: Risk assessment and treatment.* Washington, DC: Child League of America.

Sakheim, G. A., Vigdor, M. G., Gordon, M., & Helprin, L. M. (1985). A psychological profile of juvenile firesetters in residential treatment. *Child Welfare, 64*(5), 453–476.

Schechter, H. (2003). *The serial killer files: The who, what, where, how, and why of the world's most terrifying murderers.* New York: Ballantine.

Schechter, H., & Everitt, D. (1996). *The A–Z encyclopedia of serial killers.* New York: Pocket Books.

Schlesinger, L. B. (2001). The potential sex murderer: Ominous signs, risk assessment. *Journal of Threat Assessment, 1,* 47–72.

Schlesinger, L. B. (2004a). Classification of antisocial behavior for prognostic purposes: Study the motivation, not the crime. *Journal of Psychiatry and Law, 32,* 191–219.

Schlesinger, L. B. (2004b). *Sexual murder: Catathymic and compulsive homicides.* Boca Raton, FL: CRC Press.

Schlesinger, L. B. (2007). Sexual homicide: Differentiating catathymic and compulsive murders. *Aggression and Violent Behavior, 12,* 242–256.

Schlesinger, L. B. (2008). Compulsive-repetitive offenders: Behavioral patterns, motivational dynamics. In R. N. Kocsis (Ed.), *Serial murder and the psychology of violent crimes* (pp. 15–33). Totowa, NJ: Humana Press.

Schlesinger, L. B., Kassen. M., Mesa, V. B., & Pinizzotto, A. J. (2010). Ritual and signature in serial sexual homicide. *Journal of the American Academy of Psychiatry and Law, 38,* 239–246.

Schlesinger, L. B., & Revitch, E. (1997). Sexual dynamics in homicide and assault. In L. B. Schlesinger & E. Revitch (Eds.), *Sexual dynamics of antisocial behavior* (2nd ed.) (pp. 203–223). Springfield, IL: Thomas.

Schreiber, F. R. (1983). *The Shoemaker: The anatomy of a psychotic.* New York: Signet.

Schwartz, A. D. (1992). *The man who could not kill enough.* Secaucus, NJ: Carol.

Singer, S. D., & Hensley, C. (2004). Applying social learning theory to childhood and adolescent firesetting: Can it lead to serial murder? *International Journal of Offender Therapy and Comparative Criminology, 48*(4), 461–476.

Soothill, K., Francis, B., & Liu, J. (2008). Does serious offending lead to homicide? Exploring the interrelationships and sequencing of serious crime. *British Journal of Criminology, 48,* 522–537.

Stickle, T. R., & Blechman, E. A. (2002). Aggression and fire: Antisocial behavior in firesetting and nonfiresetting juvenile offenders. *Journal of Psychopathology and Behavioral Assessment, 24*(3), 177–193.

Stone, M. H. (2001). Serial sexual homicide: Biological, psychological, and sociological aspects. *Journal of Personality Disorders, 15*, 1–18.

Swaffer, T., & Hollin, C. R. (1995). Adolescent firesetting: Why do they say they do it? *Journal of Adolescence, 18*, 619–623.

Tallichet, S. E., Hensley, C., & Singer, S. D. (2005). Unraveling the methods of childhood and adolescent cruelty to nonhuman animals. *Society & Animals, 13*(2), 91–108.

Tapia, F. (1971). Children who are cruel to animals. *Child Psychiatry and Human Development, 2*, 70–77.

U.S. Department of Justice (2010). *Crime in the United States: FBI's uniform crime reports.* Washington, DC: U.S. Government Printing Office.

Verlinden, S., Hersen, M., & Thomas, J. (2000). Risk factors in school shootings. *Clinical Psychology Review, 20*(1), 3–56.

Walters, G. D. (2013). Testing the specificity postulate of the violence graduation hypothesis: Meta-analyses of the animal cruelty–offending relationship. *Aggression and Violent Behavior, 18*(6), 797–802.

Wax, D. E., & Haddox, V. G. (1974). Enuresis, fire setting, and animal cruelty: A useful danger signal in predicting vulnerability of adolescent males to assaultive behavior. *Child Psychiatry and Human Development, 4*(3), 151–156.

Wertham, F. (1937). The catathymic crisis: A clinical entity. *Archives of Neurology and Psychiatry, 37*, 974–977.

Wilson, C., & Pitman, P. (1962). *Encyclopedia of murder.* New York: Putnam.

Yarnell, H. (1940). Fire setting in children. *American Journal of Orthopsychiatry, 10*, 272–286.

Section IV
Theoretical Perspectives

Chapter 15

Examining Animal Abuse through a Sociological Lens: Theoretical and Empirical Developments

Amy J. Fitzgerald, Rochelle Stevenson, and Antonio R. Verbora

Introduction

The purpose of this chapter is to provide a survey of sociological theorizing of animal abuse and the studies that have begun to test these theories. The amount of theorizing and empirical research in this area has increased dramatically in the past two decades. Here, we isolate and discuss nine theories that employ sociological (and often other disciplinary) insights to better understand animal abuse.

Sociology has a long history of questioning boundaries and taken-for-granted assumptions, and this *modus operandi* can be usefully extended to examining animal abuse. Theoretical and empirical examinations of animal abuse have thus far tended to focus on intentional actions defined as illegal and unnecessary, primarily against companion animals (for critiques of this focus see Agnew, 1998; Beirne, 1999; Cazaux, 1999). Limiting the discussion in this way, however, renders invisible most of the harms animals are subjected to in our culture: harm through neglect, harm defined as legal, harm against species other than companion animals, and harms deemed necessary. We agree with Beirne's (2002, p. 385) position that we have "no legitimate warrant arbitrarily to restrict ... inquiries into animal abuse to a notion of harm defined as such either by state authorities or by fickle public opinion," and therefore extend our analysis in this chapter beyond the boundaries of what has been socially and legally recognized as harmful.

In order to include harms against animals that are socially authorized in our analysis, we must employ a broad and encompassing definition of animal abuse. Consequently, we employ Agnew's (1998) definition of animal abuse herein. He defines animal abuse

> as any act that contributes to the pain or death of an animal or that otherwise threatens the welfare of an animal. Such abuse may be physical (including sexual) or mental, may involve active maltreatment or passive neglect, may be direct or indirect, intentional or unintentional, socially approved or condemned, and/or necessary or unnecessary (however defined) (p. 179).

We also adopt Beirne's (2014) use of the term theriocide to refer to the killing of animals by people. He recommends the use of this term as a parallel to the use of the term homicide to refer to the killing of one human by another, notably because

> if the killing of animals by humans is as harmful to them as homicides are to humans, then the proper naming of such deaths offers a respectful remedy, however small, to the extensive privileging of human lives over those of animals. (p. 62)

If there is a drawback to such encompassing definitions of harming and killing animals, it is that theorizing can become somewhat more complicated. However, we consider this difficulty more desirable than somewhat arbitrarily truncating the scope of the discussion.

Our discussion of the theories we focus on here flows from the micro to the macro level of analysis, and moves roughly from a focus on the etiology of socially disapproved harms against animals and theriocide, to analyses of the connections between the lethal and sub-lethal harms perpetrated against animals and those perpetrated against people (both socially approved and disapproved of). In each case, we provide an overview of the central tenets of the theory and explore how each one has been applied through empirical research. Due to the scope of this chapter and space limitations, we cannot provide an exhaustive overview of all sociological theories that might be brought to bear on the subject of animal abuse and theriocide, all of the research associated with each theory, or all of the potential limitations of each theory. We therefore focus our discussion here on the most commonly used applications of sociological theories to understand animal abuse (social learning, frustration and strain, differential coercion, violence graduation, generalization of deviance, feminist, masculinities, (eco)Marxist, and cultural spillover), a sample of the empirical applications of each, and the most significant limitations of each theory.

Social Learning Theory

The fundamental assumption of social learning theory is that we learn our behavior from important others (such as peers, family members, or even respected celebrities) and then repeat the behavior through imitation or modelling. In the literature on animal abuse, there are three primary ways that social learning is thought to occur: (1) witnessing animal abuse leads to the modelling of the behavior directly; (2) the experience of victimization leads to enacting the behavior against animals; and (3) the observation of violence against humans leads to modelling the behavior against animals.

The power of direct modeling in explaining animal abuse has been demonstrated empirically. For instance, Baldry (2003) surveyed Italian youth about their exposure to and commission of various kinds of violence, including animal abuse. About half of the 1,396 youth aged 9 to 17 who participated reported having committed animal abuse, with boys more likely than girls to have abused animals. The strongest predictor for committing acts of animal abuse was being exposed to animal abuse committed by peers, followed by exposure to parental abuse of an animal (Baldry, 2003). In short, seeing peers abuse animals, especially given the adolescent desire to fit in and be accepted, can lead to imitating the behavior. In situations of exposure to parental violence against animals, the reasons for imitating the behavior could be as simple as wanting to model the behavior of a respected parent, or as complex as needing to feel the power and control that the parent is perceived to hold. The behavior could also be imitated due to more general communication of attitudes about the appropriate treatment of animals, that "such behavior is acceptable or perhaps even admirable" (Henry, 2004a, p. 291).

Henry (2004a, 2004b) also explored the role that exposure to animal abuse had in relation to engaging in abusing animals but did not differentiate or limit the relationships of the individuals involved. Using questionnaires distributed to 206 undergraduate students, Henry (2004a) found that students who reported they had observed animal abuse prior to age 13 (i.e., prior to adolescence) were over three times more likely to report that they had subsequently engaged in animal abuse than those who had not observed any animal abuse. Again, using undergraduate students, Henry (2004b) found that the strength of the correlation between observation and commission of animal abuse increased with the frequency of observation. Students who had observed more than one act of animal cruelty were significantly more likely to engage in animal abuse than students who had never observed or only once observed animal abuse. Henry's (2004a, 2004b) results suggest that age of exposure to animal abuse, along with the frequency of exposure, have a fairly strong impact on the likelihood of the individual engaging in acts of animal cruelty, supporting a social learning theory of animal abuse.

Hensley and Tallichet (2005) examined both the observation of and participation in acts of animal cruelty in their sample of incarcerated male offenders. Witnessing a family member or a friend hurt or kill an animal was positively correlated with the number of times the respondents hurt or killed an animal. However, witnessing a neighbor commit animal cruelty was not correlated with the respondent's own acts of animal abuse. These findings provide a potentially important qualification of social learning theory for explaining animal abuse: the behavior of those who are not part of one's close social sphere may not be as consequential.

In addition to those studies demonstrating the role of social learning in the perpetration of animal abuse and theriocide, research on bystander behavior also indicates that social learning can contribute to non-engagement by bystanders. In an evaluation of bystander behavior, Arluke (2012) conducted interviews with undergraduate students who had witnessed abuse of animals, but who had not participated in the abuse themselves. He found that the degree of acceptance of the animal abuse by bystanders was rooted in peer relationships: the bystanders had learned the social group's definition of the animal's reaction to the abuse as amusing and that the abuse was to be kept from adults and those in authority in order to preserve the friendships.

Though Baldry (2003), Henry (2004a, 2004b), and Hensley and Tallichet (2005) focused on direct modeling of animal abuse (and Arluke's 2012 study explored the modeling of nonintervention), social learning can also occur through the observation of violence against people or through the experience of being a victim of violence. The intergenerational transmission (IGT) hypothesis focuses more specifically on intra-familial relationships, and applied to animal abuse, the IGT hypothesis illuminates the possibility of modeling through observation of violence against humans and animals, as well as experiences of victimization. There are two basic forms of modelling in this context: (1) specific modelling, where the specific behavior of the parent or important figure is imitated, often in a gendered or role-based way, and (2) general modelling, where the general patterns of violence and aggression observed or experienced are carried forward into relationships with others, including animals.

A recent study has found mixed evidence regarding the IGT hypothesis. Knight, Ellis, and Simmons (2014) found a positive correlation between parents' commission of intimate partner violence (IPV) and animal abuse by their children, but the parents' victimization had no significant bearing on subsequent animal abuse by the children. The study also looked at the potential of intergenerational continuity of animal abuse, meaning that animal abuse by the parent would be continued by the child, and found no support for the IGT in this regard.

Other research has found a relationship between physical punishment by a parent and the perpetration of animal abuse by the subject of the punishment. For instance, in a sample of 256 undergraduate students, Flynn (1999) documents a significant positive relationship between the frequency of physical punishment and the commission of animal abuse, but this relationship differed based on gender. While there was no significant relationship for female students, almost 60 percent of male students who had been physically punished had engaged in animal cruelty versus a 23 percent commission rate by male students who had not been corporally punished. Further, Flynn (1999) found that this relationship was only significant when the physical punishment came from the male parent. This suggests a blend of general and specific modelling in connection to animal abuse. The physical punishment was modelled in the generalized aggression against animal others, while the specific gendered role of dominance and aggression was modelled using animals as targets. Flynn (1999) proposes that this can be understood via social learning as "the socialization experience for male children emphasizes dominance and aggression [and] cruelty to animals may provide some males with the opportunity to rehearse these skills" (p. 978). This research points to a specific way that the intergenerational transmission of violence can occur.

A significant proportion of the research looking at the IGT of animal abuse focuses on exposure to domestic violence more broadly and tends to support the general modelling context of IGT. The connection between children's exposure to domestic violence and their subsequent commission of animal abuse is well-documented. In an early study, Kellert and Felthous (1985) found that incarcerated men who reported experiencing domestic violence in childhood were more likely to report committing acts of animal cruelty. Nearly every youth in Baldry's (2003) study who engaged in animal abuse also reported that they had witnessed violence between their parents. In Ascione's (1998) research, women who attended a domestic violence shelter with their children were questioned about animal abuse. Based on maternal reports, 32 percent of children engaged in cruelty against the family pet (Ascione, 1998). Other studies (e.g., Ascione & Arkow, 1999; Ascione, Weber, & Wood, 1997; DeGue & DeLillo, 2009; Gullone, 2014; Quinlisk, 1999; Stevenson, 2009; Zilney, 2007) document similar patterns connecting exposure to violence in the family and abuse against animals.

Subsequent studies using control groups also offer strong support for the IGT hypothesis. Ascione et al. (2007), Currie (2006), and Volant, Johnson, Gullone, & Coleman (2008) all used samples drawn from domestic violence shelters, as well as control groups that had not experienced domestic violence, in order to explore the prevalence of animal abuse in families with violence. In her Canadian study, Currie (2006) found that children who had been exposed to domestic violence were nearly three times more likely to be cruel to animals than children who had not experienced violence in the home. In Australia, Volant et al. (2008) found that 29 percent of children in the domestic violence group had been exposed to animal abuse in the home versus none of the children in the control group. Additionally, and importantly for the IGT hypothesis, children who had experienced domestic violence and witnessed animal abuse were significantly more likely than children with no exposure to have engaged in animal abuse themselves. Ascione et al. (2007) discovered that the women in their sample drawn from a shelter for abused women who reported that their partners had committed animal abuse also reported that the children had witnessed the abuse of the pet. Further, between maternal reports and the children's self-disclosure, nearly 40 percent of children had engaged in abuse against the family pet. This would indicate support for the IGT of animal cruelty for a sizable proportion of the children. Perhaps the most interesting result of Ascione et al.'s (2007) study, however, was the revelation that nearly half of the children had actively placed themselves in harm's way to protect their pet from the abuse perpetrated against them. This would contradict social learning and IGT more specifically in that those children evidence the opposite attitude and behavior than what is being modelled in the home. This highlights one of the critiques of social learning theory and the related IGT hypothesis: there is difficulty explaining why only certain individuals, and not every person who witnesses violence in the home or against animals, model the behavior in the form of animal abuse. Further research is needed to better understand the trajectory of perpetrating animal abuse and to tease apart the significance of the three social learning routes to perpetration.

Frustration and Strain

A somewhat related explanation of animal abuse theorizes that it occurs as the result of frustration or strain. According to this perspective, individuals might engage in animal abuse because they have learned that it is a suitable vehicle for reducing stress and strain, and abusive behavior may occur as more expressive aggression in response to frustration and strain. The frustration and strain theories were developed to explain aggression more generally, and both point to blocked goals as important precursors (Dollard, Doob, Miller, Mowrer, & Sears, 1939; Einstadter & Henry, 2010). According to the frustration theory, "aggression, rather than occurring spontaneously for no reason, is the response to the frustration of some goal-directed behavior by an outside source" (Linsely, 2006, p. 18). The general strain theory builds upon and goes beyond frustration related to blocked goal-directed behavior. According to early formulations of strain theory, criminality is the result of the failure to achieve conventional goals (Tibbetts & Hemmens, 2009). The revised, or more general strain theory, theorizes that criminal activity can also result from the removal of positive stimuli and from negative affective states, such as anger and frustration (Agnew, 2010, p. 202).

Agnew (1998) developed a specific theoretical model to explain animal abuse. His model integrates insights from several theories, including social learning, strain theory, and control theory to help explain why individuals abuse animals. Agnew's theory focuses on three factors related to the likelihood that an individual will harm animals. He argues that animal abuse will likely occur when individuals (1) are unaware of the consequences of their abusive actions; (2) believe the abuse is justified; and (3) perceive that the benefits of their actions outweigh the costs. Agnew (1998) further identifies five other factors that can interact with the three main factors: (1) individual traits (e.g., empathy); (2) socialization; (3) strain or stress; (4) degree of social control; and (5) the characteristics of the animal involved. Finally, all of these factors can be impacted by structural or demographic variables, such as gender, race/ethnicity, age, education, occupation, urban/rural location, and region. To summarize, according to his thorough model of animal abuse, individuals who experience frustration or strain (which can take many forms) may engage in animal abuse to manage their associated negative emotions (Agnew, 1998). However, this strain does not occur in a vacuum—it is related to other individual traits (e.g., socialization, social control) and structural variables—and the actions occur within the context of specific knowledge, beliefs, and attitudes related to animals, as well as in relation to the perceived costs and benefits of the action (Agnew, 1998).

Consistent with the theoretical work, empirical research has uncovered a wide variety of motivations for animal abuse among those who admit to being perpetrators, and this research indicates that stress and frustration can indeed play a role. For instance, in their research on men with histories of animal abuse, Kellert and Felthous (1985) identify nine reported motives. As listed previously in Chapter 12, the motivations include the following:

1. To control an animal.
2. To express aggression and frustration through an animal.
3. To retaliate against another person.
4. To retaliate against the animal.
5. To satisfy a prejudice against a species or breed.
6. To express one's own aggressiveness.
7. To shock people for amusement.
8. Displacement of hostility from a person to an animal.
9. Non-specific sadism.

Strain or frustration are most evident in the motivations they describe as expressing aggression and frustration through an animal (#2) and displacement of hostility from a person to an animal (#8), although they may be implicit in some of the other motivations, as animal abuse is often multidimensional and not caused by one single motivating factor (Gullone, 2009).

A more recent study found that strain and frustration can play an important role in animal abuse amongst adolescents. Using data from the 2006 Swiss National Self-Reported Delinquency Survey, Lucia and Killias (2011) explored cruelty toward animals among 3,600 pupils in 7th, 8th, and 9th grades (ages 13 to 16). Taking into account personal background, personality characteristics, and social context, their findings indicate that adolescents may engage in animal cruelty to avoid dealing with painful or aversive situations. For instance, an adolescent compelled to remain in a particular environment that is painful or aversive (e.g., family household or school) or enduring traumatic events (e.g., divorce or death) may experience strain and frustration as a result, which can contribute to delinquency, including animal abuse. In short, the incapacity to cope with strain, frustration, and anger can push an individual toward animal maltreatment. Research points to the same abusive trajectory amongst adults. For instance, through analysis of case studies of animal abuse, Howells, Watt, Hall, and Baldwin (1997) point to the contributory role of stress and frustration caused by breakdowns of several valued relationships, the deterioration of relationships with family, and problems at work. They also identify poor self-control and poor anger control as fundamental underlying problems (see also Lucia & Killias, 2011). The likelihood that stress and frustration exacerbated by poor self-control will result in animal abuse amongst adolescents and adults could be mitigated by empathy, as illustrated in Agnew's (1998) model. In the absence of empathy, however, animal abuse becomes more likely (Ascione, 1993).

Despite some limitations of the aforementioned studies (e.g., lack of adequate control or comparison groups), they do provide at least partial support for the stress and frustration theories. Support is found across various respondent groups (e.g., school-based youth and incarcerated adults) and data collection methods (e.g., self-reporting, third-party reports, and analysis of criminal records). However, additional research is necessary to determine the potential of strain and frustration in explaining animal abuse and theriocide across disparate contexts along the continuum of socially approved/disapproved harm. Agnew (1998) himself cautions that his theoretical model is based on limited empirical research. As Flynn (2010) points out, the applicability of each of the factors in Agnew's theory of animal abuse will likely vary depending upon the level of social permissibility of the action. Further, although Agnew (1998) points to some important structural and demographic variables that can be related to animal abuse (e.g., gender and age), there is a need to look at cultural forces even more broadly (examined later in this chapter). In particular, Flynn (2010) suggests examining the ways in which various social institutions, such as the economy and religion, facilitate animal abuse. Doing so will be necessary to develop a comprehensive understanding of animal harm and theriocide.

Differential Coercion

Not only can contexts of strain and frustration be conducive to animal abuse, so can contexts of coercion. The connection between coercion and crime was first made in the context of delinquency and the family dynamic (see Brown, Esbensen, & Geis, 2012). Subsequent research explored the coercive control patterns in workplaces, schools, and among peers and their connection to serious, chronic delinquency (Colvin, 2000). Borrowing insights from Lonnie Athens, John D. Hewitt, Robert Agnew, Travis Hirschi, and Michael R. Gottfredson, Mark Colvin (2000) developed an integrated theory of chronic criminality, which he termed "differential coercion." His theory ties together several distinct patterns of coercion and connects them to social-psychological states which are conducive to criminality. In terms of exploring the etiology of criminal activity, Colvin (2000) argues that

> Criminals are made, not born. They emerge from a developmental process that is punctuated by recurring erratic episodes of coercion. They become both the recipients and the perpetrators of coercion, entrapped in a dynamic that propels them along a pathway toward chronic criminality (p. 1).

This theory foregrounds the differential levels and forms of coercion to which people are exposed and points to two different sources of coercion: interpersonal and impersonal. Interpersonal coercion is direct; that is, it involves the use or threat of force as well as the intimidation from significant others (e.g., parents and peers). Impersonal coercion, on the other hand, is indirect. This type of coercion involves pressures beyond individual control (e.g., social and economic pressure), which can be directly linked to poverty and unemployment. In sum, according to this theory, being exposed to high levels of interpersonal and/or impersonal coercion likely triggers the development of social-psychological deficits (Colvin, 2000). These deficits increase the likelihood of engaging in criminal activity, such as animal abuse.

Recent research has addressed how aspects of differential coercion theory could be used to explain the behavior of those who mistreat animals. Animal abuse may be related to coercion in at least two ways: individuals subjected to a coercive environment may perpetrate animal abuse and the threat of perpetration of animal abuse may be used to coerce an individual into doing something against their will. In the context of the former pathway to animal abuse, Ascione (1993) argues that children raised by parents who rely on punitive or aversive control (e.g., harming a child's pet to foster compliance) may learn to generalize aversive control techniques to their companion animals. Loring and Bolden-Hines (2004) have explored the latter possibility, focusing specifically on how coercion in the form of threats to harm pets can play a role in the commission of other crimes. The authors studied a group of emotionally and physically abused women at a shelter for abused women. Participants reported several forms of coercion used by their abusive partners, such as threats or actual harm to their pets or children, to coerce them into committing illegal acts (e.g., fraud, robbery, and drug trafficking). One-third of Loring and Bolden-Hines' (2004) sample of women who had committed at least one illegal act and had a pet reported they had engaged in illegal act(s) to spare their pet from abuse.

Coercion can also be used to induce victims of IPV into engaging in animal abuse: A number of cases have been identified where abused women have been coerced into assisting their abuser in perpetrating animal cruelty in order to keep themselves and their children out of harm's way (Roguski, 2012; Tiplady, 2013). Hicks (2012) describes a specific case where a man coerced his girlfriend into holding their puppy so he could drill into their puppy's head. Police reportedly found 29 dog carcasses on the property, illegal guns, blood and hair covered tools, and a beagle dog's pelt and eyes in a jar. There are also instances where women may even end their pet's life so as to avoid further animal cruelty at the hands of their abusive partner (see Tiplady, 2013; Walker, 1984). One example involved a domestic violence victim who drowned her kittens, rather than allowing her husband to "take pot shots at them with his rifle" (Hunter, 2006, p. 188). Victims of IPV can also be coerced into performing sexually abusive acts with their companion animal(s) (Tiplady, 2013; see also Abrahams, 2007; Adams, 2004; and Flynn, 2010 on the role that coercion can play in animal abuse in the context of IPV).

More research is needed to uncover additional ways in which coercion may play a role in the perpetration of animal abuse and to provide insight into how much animal abuse and theriocide overall can actually be attributed to coercion. The focus of the application of this theory to animal abuse to date has exclusively been on individual, interpersonal coercion. It may be worth expanding the application of this theory by addressing the second source of coercion—impersonal coercion—and the role it may play in animal abuse. Doing so would necessitate unpacking and examining the forms of cultural coercion that can impact (and help to rationalize) the actions of individuals and groups.

Violence Graduation Hypothesis

The theories discussed up to this point have focused on the etiology of animal abuse. The subsequent theories we discuss shift the focus from pure etiology to also explore how animal abuse is related to the perpetration of harm against people. The violence graduation hypothesis (VGH), also called the progression thesis (Beirne, 2004), is likely the most well-known of these types of theories. Commonly referred to in reference to spree killers and serial murderers, the VGH states that perpetrators begin with violence against animals and then "graduate" or "progress" to violence against humans (Ressler, Burgess, Hartman, Douglas, & McCormack, 1986; Wright & Hensley, 2003). There are two key elements of this theory: a temporal element where the animal abuse must precede the human-directed violence and a correlational element in which individuals who commit animal abuse are more likely than those who do not to engage in violence against humans.

The VGH is also one of the oldest theories about animal abuse. The British philosopher, John Locke, argued that youth should be watched for cruelty against animals as this could lead to further cruelty against others (Unti, 2008). The theory also appeared in art, the most famous being William Hogarth's 1750/1 release of *The Four Stages of Cruelty*, which graphically depicted the progression from animal cruelty in childhood to violence against humans in adulthood. Concern about the connection between animal abuse and subsequent violence against people continued into the twentieth century. The Macdonald Triad of firesetting, enuresis (bedwetting), and animal cruelty, developed in 1961 was considered to be a predictor of later violence against humans (see Chapter 14); children were said to graduate from these unacceptable and destructive behaviors to violent behaviors in adulthood, including harming other people (Hellman & Blackman, 1966; Wax & Haddox, 1973). Anthropologist Margaret Mead (1964) asserted that animal abuse was a warning sign for future delinquency and violence, and therefore needed to be addressed with punishment to discourage the behavior.

Studies analyzing the childhood and adolescent behavior of serial and spree murderers offered some support for the VGH. Wright and Hensley (2003) examined the histories of five serial murders, including Jeffrey Dahmer and Henry Lee Lucas, all of whom had first engaged in or experimented with abuse or killing of animals before "graduating" to violence against humans. In some cases, the methods used to abuse the animals were the same methods utilized in the later brutalization of their human victims. As noted in Chapter 14, Arluke and Madfis (2014) examined cases of school shooters to determine the value of using animal abuse as a predictor for future episodes of violence against humans. While they did find evidence of animal abuse in the histories of 43 percent of school shooters, Arluke and Madfis (2014) question the strength of the connection and the widely held belief in the veracity of the VGH. Case studies, while powerful examples, offer limited utility for supporting the VGH as they tend to be limited in number and restricted to rare incidents of extreme violence.

The most common method used in violence graduation research has been to identify convicted violent offenders in adulthood and then use retrospective reports of animal cruelty in childhood or adolescence to search for violence progression. For instance, Tallichet and Hensley (2004) used the number of convictions for murder, attempted murder, rape, attempted rape, and aggravated assault to measure interpersonal violence in an incarcerated sample of men. Previous acts of animal cruelty were measured by the question "how many times have you hurt or killed animals, other than for hunting?" (Tallichet & Hensley, 2004, p. 310). In their sample, committing animal cruelty was the most powerful predictor of committing repeated acts of interpersonal violence in adulthood, stronger than even race, age, or educational attainment. The respondents who had engaged in animal cruelty in childhood or adolescence had an average of 1.33 convictions for violent offenses in adulthood compared to the average of 0.56 violent offenses among those who had not committed animal abuse (Tallichet & Hensley, 2004). Hensley, Tallichet, and Dutkiewicz (2009) replicated Tallichet and Hensley's (2004) study with a different sample of incarcerated men and added simple assault and robbery to the list of violent offenses with nearly identical results. Participants who had a higher number of convictions for violent offenses were more likely to have committed animal cruelty in childhood or adolescence (Hensley, Tallichet, & Dutkiewicz, 2009). Other researchers, such as Kellert and Felthous (1985), Merz-Perez, Heide, and Silverman (2001), and Merz-Perez and Heide (2004), have come to the same conclusion as Hensley, Tallichet, and colleagues (2009): aggressive or violent offenders are more likely to report committing animal cruelty in childhood.

A recent study used a sample of the general population drawn from the National Youth Survey Family Study (NYSFS) in the Unites States to examine the VGH. Using this longitudinal and multigenerational data, Knight, Ellis, and Simmons (2014) tested both intra- and intergenerational aspects of animal abuse. On an intragenerational level, respondents who reported engaging in animal abuse in childhood were over three times more likely to have committed IPV in adulthood, results which show strong support for the VGH.

These studies testing the VGH have important limitations worth noting (for a detailed overview see Beirne, 2009). First, retrospective reports can be limited, particularly in attempting to recall the temporal order of events (i.e., did animal abuse precede violence against humans). The research by Knight et al. (2014) does partly address this, although the limitation of recall was still present in this study. Questions about animal abuse were only added in much later waves of the survey, meaning that adults were questioned about their commission of animal abuse during childhood and adolescence. Although the children (mean age 17.56) of the adults in the study were also questioned about their animal abuse, the issue of recall was still present as the youth were asked if they had ever committed animal abuse, as well as the age at which the act was committed. This allowed Knight et al. (2014) to calculate that the average recall range for the incident for the youth was 7 years. Longitudinal research with waves beginning in childhood and with questions about animal abuse would help to mitigate the issues with memory and recall prevalent in the existing literature testing the VGH, as recommended by Petersen and Farrington (2007), as well as Flynn (2011). Second, there is a flaw in using incarcerated male populations to test the VGH, which compose the majority of participants in VGH research. According to the principles of the VGH, the focus of the aggression shifts from or graduates to violence against humans, which implies a desistance from violence against animals in favor of violence against humans in adulthood. When the participants are incarcerated, in some cases serving life sentences, they do not have the ability to offend against humans or animals, and the presence or absence of animal abuse in adulthood cannot necessarily be measured.

Generalization of Deviance Hypothesis

The generalization of deviance hypothesis is typically presented as an alternative to the violence graduation hypothesis. This theory holds that animal abuse is part of a spectrum of antisocial and criminal behavior, and not specifically connected to violence against other humans. The generality of deviance hypothesis also does not have a temporal element, but treats animal abuse as one of many possible deviant behaviors that individuals of any age can engage in.

One of the few studies to specifically examine the generality thesis was conducted by Arluke, Levin, Luke, and Ascione (1999). Matching official records of the Massachusetts Society for the Prevention of Cruelty to Animals with the police records of offenders, the authors assessed the generality versus the specificity of the non-animal-related offenses. Arluke et al. (1999) also used a control group of individuals selected from the same neighborhood and of the same age and gender as the abusive group. The results support the hypothesis: the abusive group was over three times more likely to have a criminal record, including violent, drug, and property related offenses than the control group. Arluke et al. (1999) acknowledge the possibility of graduation in forms of deviance, but propose that the graduation may not be simply temporal and there are other dimensions to consider. It could be that individuals may graduate from abusing more remote targets (stray animals or strangers) to more intimate targets (friends, partners, or pets).

A subsequent study conducted by the Chicago Police Department found similar results in that 86 percent of those who had been arrested for animal cruelty had convictions for a variety of other offences as well (Flynn, 2011). Like the study by Arluke et al. (1999), the Chicago Police Department evaluated criminal records. A focus on adult records does present a limitation, as juvenile offences are not likely to be noted in the records of adult offenders, so any potential graduation of violence is unknown to the researchers. This limitation could result in confirmation bias for the generalization of deviance hypothesis, rather than a true test of the theory.

Other researchers have focused on the potential generalization of aggression more specifically. Henry and Sanders (2007), for instance, looked at the concurrence of incidents of animal abuse and bullying behavior in both the victimization and perpetration spheres. They recruited male undergraduate students from a first-year psychology class and assessed the victimization and perpetration rates of both physical and verbal bullying as well as reported incidents of animal abuse. Most of the reported animal abuse took place in two age groups, 6 to 12 and 13 to 18, and the majority of bullying occurred during elementary and high school (matching the age groups for animal abuse). Henry and Sanders (2007) found that multiple acts of animal abuse were significantly associated with relatively high rates (33 percent of participants) of physical bullying, but not verbal bullying. Given the concurrent time frames, these data suggest some degree of generalized aggression when it comes to bullying behavior.

Gullone and Robertson (2008) also examined the relationship between bullying and animal abuse, but they surveyed a younger population: secondary school students between the ages of 12 and 16. Examining the age group with the highest incidence of perpetrating animal abuse minimized the limitation of retrospective accounts and memory recall. They found that witnessing animal abuse was a significant predictor of bullying perpetration as well as committing animal abuse. Further, Gullone and Robertson (2008) state that given the number of respondents who reported engaging in animal abuse "sometimes" (20 percent) and bulling behaviors in the past year (18 percent), both behaviors are relatively common during adolescence. This offers additional support for the generality of aggression premise.

Further research, ideally studies using a longitudinal design and multiple sources of data, and control groups, is needed to examine the multifaceted relationship between various forms of animal abuse and forms of deviance, including aggression. The bulk of the research conducted has thus far focused primarily on socially disapproved of harms against animals and the relationship to deviance and aggression (Flynn, 2002 is a noteworthy exception). There is little information available about the potential connection between socially approved forms of animal harm and deviance.

Feminist Theories

Feminist theorists have illuminated the cultural normalization of violence, particularly against women. They argue that this violence is symptomatic of a patriarchal culture that privileges masculinity while devaluing femininity, and that patriarchy legitimizes the use of violence to achieve power and control with the goal of maintaining the sexist status quo. Such theorizing shifts the level of analysis from the individual to the larger structures that facilitate violence. Feminist examinations of animal abuse have extended this analysis and argue that patriarchy and speciesism (the privileging of one's own species above others) are mutually reinforcing and both facilitate violence. Much of this theorizing has taken place under the banner of ecofeminism. It should be noted that some ecofeminist theorizing relies on simplistic, essentialized conceptions of gender differences, and theorizes a biological basis for the "caring nature" of women (Dejmanee, 2013). Providing a detailed account of the problems associated with such a perspective is well beyond the scope of this chapter. Instead, we focus on more social constructionist-oriented threads of ecofeminism that do not necessarily share these limitations.

To explain why sexism and the exploitation of animals are related, social ecofeminists point to the similar ways in which women and animals have been constructed as the Other to privileged masculinity. These classes of Other have been relegated to the devalued side of many normative dualisms in patriarchal culture, including culture/nature, public/private, and mind/body (see Adams, 1990; Kheel, 1995; King, 1991; Noske, 1989). Noske (1989) explores the culture/nature dualism in detail and explains that, as a result of this particular dualism, humans consider themselves unique and vastly different from animals, and nature more generally. Humans are believed to belong to an entirely different order, the realm of culture, whereas other beings are regarded simply as nature. However, membership in the realm of the cultural has not been equally afforded to humans: hegemonic conceptions of masculinity (discussed in the next section) have been associated with culture, whereas women and subordinated masculinities have been largely identified with nature. As a result, nature, and those associated with it, have been constructed as the Other and of lesser value than those associated with culture.

Similarities in the mechanisms through which women and animals have been oppressed, the ways in which this oppression is obfuscated, how it is rationalized, and the language used to denigrate both groups are illustrative of how interconnected these forms of oppression actually are. Two examples from the literature are useful in illustrating this interconnection. The first is the argument that animals and women have been treated like natural resources. More specifically, the productive and reproductive capacities of women and animals are expropriated, and their contributions are simultaneously undervalued (Salleh, 1995). For women, this manifests itself in, among other things, attacks against their reproductive rights and the devaluation of their reproductive labor. There are countless examples of how animals are treated like natural resources. For instance, female "livestock" animals are bred to create more livestock animals. The products of their reproductive labor are taken from them and commodified (e.g., their offspring, milk, and eggs). This connection is also evidenced by similar trajectories of trafficking of women, children, and animals, through which the victims are commodified as resources (Sollund, 2013).

Another thread within the literature examines how animals and women have been constructed in such similar ways that a structure of absent referents exists whereby one group can stand in for the other. Adams (1990) has been at the forefront of this theorizing. She explains,

> Sexual violence and meat eating, which appear to be discrete forms of violence, find a point of intersection in the absent referent. Cultural images of sexual violence, and actual sexual violence, often rely on our knowledge of how animals are butchered and eaten (p. 68).

In her work, Adams elucidates the numerous ways in which actual animals have been obfuscated in the process of people consuming their flesh (e.g., through packaging and advertising). They are similarly bracketed out, or used as the absent referent, in the use of meat as a metaphor for women's oppression (e.g., references to women as pieces of meat).

Adams (1990) and Salleh (1995) therefore argue that not only are there similarities in the oppression of women and animals, but importantly these forms of oppression become mutually reinforcing. In addition to the conceptual connections between the oppression and abuse of women and animals, feminist theorists and researchers have also identified some more manifest relationships between these forms of oppression.

Patriarchal/speciesist culture goes beyond just devaluing nature and those associated with it. Adams (1994) argues that this culture is also characterized by a reverence for and promotion of dominance and control. The abuse of animals may be one mechanism through which one can accomplish this culturally prescribed pursuit of dominance and control. In fact, research indicates that the desire for control is a common motivator of animal abuse, particularly among serial animal abusers. A study of 112 inmates found that those who admitted to multiple acts of animal abuse were three times more likely to report being motivated by a desire to control the animal than those who admitted to few acts of animal abuse (Hensley & Tallichet, 2005). Research also indicates that animal abuse can be a vehicle for establishing dominance and control over people. This dynamic has been prominent in the research on IPV.

A recent study using a national, longitudinal dataset finds that controlling for other predictive variables, an earlier history of engaging in animal abuse significantly predicts subsequent perpetration of violent IPV, such that an individual who was engaged in animal abuse when younger has a 3.61 greater likelihood of perpetrating violent IPV than those without histories of animal abuse perpetration (Knight et al., 2014). This relationship between animal abuse and IPV has also been documented through accounts of abused women. Studies in Canada and the U.S. have found that anywhere from 25 percent (Simmons & Lehmann, 2007) to 86 percent (Strand & Faver, 2005) of abused women with pets report that their pets were also mistreated by their abusers. Recent studies in other countries, including Ireland (Allen, Gallagher, & Jones, 2006), Australia (Volant et al., 2008), and the Bahamas (Fielding, 2010) have found similar rates of coexistence between animal abuse and IPV. In addition to finding significant overlap between these forms of abuse, the research indicates that animal abuse is most likely to be present in the more severe cases of IPV (e.g., Ascione et al., 2007; DeGue & DiLillo, 2008; Simmons & Lehmann, 2007) and that batterers who abuse pets tend to use more forms of violence and exhibit more controlling behaviors (Simmons & Lehmann, 2007).

Interview-based research with abused women indicates that the women believe that the abuse of their pets by their abusive partners did not originate from their partners' loss of control and uncontrollable aggression as many might assume; instead, they report the mistreatment of their pets was used as a tool to further abuse them and their children. Animal abuse can be a particularly useful tool because many of these women and children form very close relationships with their pets (Fitzgerald, 2005; Flynn, 2000). These relationships can be so close that some abused women refer to their pets as part of their "strategies for survival," and describe how their pets assisted them with depression and feelings of despair, to the point that, for some abused women, their pets are the one thing that keeps them from killing themselves (Fitzgerald, 2007). This research has corroborated Adams' (1995) earlier theorizing that the abuse of animals can be instrumentalized by batterers to achieve power and control over their partners and/or the children.

Feminist analyses of animal abuse, therefore, highlight both the conceptual and lived connections between the oppression of women and animals. This foregrounding of the ways in which forms of human oppression are connected with the oppression and abuse of animals is a notable strength of feminist analyses of animal abuse (Taylor, 2010). At the same time, however, we must guard against anthropocentric evaluations of animal abuse which problematize it solely on the grounds that it is connected conceptually and sometimes practically to the oppression and abuse of people (Beirne, 1999). Some feminist scholars have gone beyond simply using the connections between the oppression of women and animals as the basis for arguing against the (ab)use of animals, and additionally assert that women have a positive moral duty to care for animals, or to promote nonharm through carefulness (see Aristarkhova, 2012; Donovan & Adams, 2007). However, we must also be careful not to make women solely responsible for challenging harm to animals and for bearing the burden of their care (Dejmanee, 2013).

To summarize, according to feminist theorizing, women and animals have been relegated to the devalued, nature side of the culture/nature binary. This devaluation, along with the valorization of control and dominance within patriarchal culture, puts animals at risk of abuse. This combination places animals at risk of socially approved violence (e.g., being used as natural resources) and socially disapproved violence, where they can be abused to satisfy someone's desire to exert control and dominance over them or as a vehicle to establish control and dominance over a human victim. This pursuit of dominance and control is an important part of the hegemonic masculinity concept, a topic we turn to next.

Masculinities

Examinations problematizing the construction of masculinity emerged from feminist theorizing of gender. At the forefront of this endeavor, Connell (1987) explains that masculinity is not only socially constructed, but it "is always constructed in relation to various subordinated masculinities as well as in relation to women" (p. 183). A hegemonic form of masculinity emerges from these constructions. Simply put, this is the cultural ideal of masculinity. This ideal is connected to heteronormativity, economic success, dominance, and control, among other things (for a review of the concept and response to critiques see Connell & Messerschmidt, 2005). This form of masculinity is not static: it varies across space and time.

Messerschmidt (2004) has made an important contribution by applying this concept to understand crime. He describes how men who do not meet the lofty characteristics of the hegemonic ideal (e.g., wealthy, white, strong, aggressive, dominant, and heterosexual) can use crime to accomplish masculinity. In other words, crime is structured action; "men construct masculinities in accord with their position in social structures and, therefore, their access to power and resources" (Messerschmidt, 2004, p. 3). Critical examinations of masculinity are particularly important in the context of understanding crime because the vast majority of perpetrators are men. For instance, men are responsible for approximately 90 percent of violent crimes (Chesney-Lind & Faith, 2001).

Such analyses can be usefully extended to analyzing animal abuse. As with violent crime in general, the majority of perpetrators of animal abuse are male. Data from a nationally representative sample in the U.S. indicate that 83.78 percent of those who report committing animal abuse are men (Vaughn et al., 2009). One of the strongest and most consistent predictors of perpetrating animal abuse and supporting animal exploitation is being male (Baldry, 2003; Herzog, 2007; Luke, 2007). A recent study using hypothetical animal abuse scenarios found that 20 percent of female versus 40 percent of male participants endorsed the harmful behavior taking place in the scenario (Alleyne, Tilston, Parfitt, &

Butcher, 2015). This relationship between gender and animal abuse is strong across age categories (Gullone, 2014). Whereas men engage in more animal abuse, the reverse is true for women in the aggregate: they exhibit less aggressive, more positive, and less dominionistic attitudes towards animals (Herzog, 2007; Matthews & Herzog, 1997; Signal & Taylor, 2006). In general, the size of the influence of gender on attitudes towards animals has ranged rather dramatically in research, but it generally meets the threshold to be considered a moderate effect (Herzog, 2007; Kavanagh, Signal, & Taylor, 2013).

Some theorists (e.g., Agnew, 1998; Beirne, 1995) have noted that animal abuse might be a particularly useful mechanism for accomplishing masculinity. Agnew (1998) explains that animal abuse could be particularly useful for accomplishing masculinity because the direct abuse of an animal displays aggression and dominance and simultaneously requires emotional detachment, all qualities of hegemonic masculinity. Research has provided some indirect evidence for this proposition. In their early research on animal abuse (as mentioned earlier), Kellert and Felthous (1985) identified nine main motivations reported by their (all male) participants (listed earlier). What is interesting is that the majority of motivations they identified could be connected to accomplishing masculinity. Animal abuse could be used as a resource for accomplishing masculinity by exerting and demonstrating control (motivation #1), to retaliate against perceived wrongs and perhaps more specific challenges to masculinity (motivations #2 and #7), to demonstrate and enhance aggression (motivations #4 and #5), and shocking the sensibilities of others (motivation #6).

Research on wildlife crime has drawn a more explicit link between masculinity and animal abuse. As a result of this research, a typology of wildlife regulation violators has been developed, and one of the four categories identified encompasses offenders who are "primarily motivated by power and notions of masculinity" (Nurse, 2013, p. 135). These types of offenders are most likely to engage in their harmful behavior with others, and these offenders are likely to derive pleasure from their actions. Further, these offenders are likely to argue that their actions are justified based on tradition and/or that the animals involved do not feel pain (Nurse, 2013).

Cross-cultural research on "blood sports" also highlights the role that masculinity plays in motivating participation (of mainly men). Ethnographic research, in particular, has documented how men construct their own masculine identities through blood sports, such as dog, cock, and bull fighting (see Evans et al., 1998; Geertz, 1973; and Marvin, 1988). In a review of such studies, Iliopoulou and Rosenbaum (2013, pp. 134–135) conclude that

> violence, power, control, and aggression are common themes associated with masculinity for all three contexts [dog, cock, and bull fighting] and might explain why animal cruelty associated with blood sport becomes 'legitimized' or 'normal' in an effort to achieve manhood.

This normalization of animal abuse, particularly in the context of "doing masculinity," can contribute to a great deal of abuse being dismissed as simply "boys being boys." Arluke (2002) found in his research on histories of animal abuse among undergraduate students that a significant proportion of animal abuse is currently constructed as normative. He suggests that some forms of animal abuse are defined as a form of what Fine (1986) refers to as "dirty play." Building on Hughes' (1962) concept of "dirty work," Fine (1986) asserts that "dirty play" is part of the process of socializing boys into men. He reasons that actions by boys, such as aggressive pranks, use of sexualized language, and use of racist language should be conceptualized as dirty play because they generally take place in the presence of friends, which he considers quite different from the perpetration of such actions while alone, which would be indicative of a "destructive impulse." There is research evidence indicating that a sizable proportion of young men do engage in animal abuse in the presence of others. For instance, 48 percent of abusers in a Massachusetts sample abused animals in the presence of others (Arluke & Luke, 1997) and 47 percent of a Swiss sample reported they engaged in animal abuse in the presence of others (Lucia & Killias, 2011). Further, a survey of 112 inmates, who admitted to animal abuse, found that 38 percent reported the abuse was perpetrated for fun (Hensley & Tallichet, 2005). Hensley, Tallichet, and Dutkiewicz (2012) found in their sample of inmates in a Southern state in the U.S. that only one type of animal abuse was consistently concealed: sexual animal abuse. These findings would appear to be conceptually consistent with motivation #6 delineated by Kellert and Felthous (1985): to shock people for amusement. In making sense of the seemingly normative character of some forms of animal abuse, Arluke (2002, p. 406) explains that "abusers may gain things from their acts that the larger society supports and defines as essential." Pagani and colleagues (2010) propose that what is gained from animal abuse is aggression, competition, and diminished empathy—all characteristics associated with hegemonic masculinity.

Boys and young men who lack power and resources as a result of their social positioning, particularly due to their age, may find animal abuse powerful as a vehicle for accomplishing masculinity, and they may also by extension become apathetic bystanders in the face of abuse. This argument is put forward by Evans, Gauthier, and Forsyth (1998) to explain the attraction of dog fighting for working class men in the Southern U.S. This animal abuse is not only perpetrated in response to larger social structures, it can also serve to reinforce these structures. This way of "doing gender" perpetuates some of the most problematic aspects of masculinity, such as lack of empathy and aggression as well as the speciesism that has normalized the instrumentalization of animals to serve humans ends. In more recent research on actions of bystanders in the presence of animal abuse, such as dog fighting, Arluke (2012) finds that one of the barriers to bystander intervention is the definition of much animal abuse as "dirty play," instead of as morally problematic or criminal.

Masculinity is also linked to animal harm in less direct ways. Adams (1990) argues there is a connection between masculinity and meat consumption in our culture. She describes how in historic times of crisis, the consumption of meat by men has been privileged. It was believed to provide them with the strength and aggressiveness required of masculinity. Today, meat and masculinity remain closely connected, and men who refrain from the consumption of meat risk having their masculinity questioned. A recent study by Rothgerber (2012) of undergraduate students empirically tests this connection between meat consumption and masculinity, and finds that not only do levels of meat consumption vary by gender, but justifications of meat consumption are also gendered. The male students in the study were significantly more likely to justify their meat consumption by denying that the animals suffer, asserting that animals are lower than humans in the hierarchy of beings, utilizing religious or health justifications, and espousing the belief that humans are destined to consume animals. The female student participants, on the other hand, were more likely to use indirect methods to justify meat consumption, such as avoiding thinking about their consumption of animals and trying to dissociate the meat they consume from the animal it once was. Rothgerber (2012) also used a scale to measure masculinity among the participants and found that it was positively related to all of the justifications used most commonly by the male participants to justify meat consumption, and additionally, high levels of meat consumption were positively associated with the masculinity scale.

This connection between masculinity and the consumption of animals is illustrated in contemporary advertisements. Rogers (2008) documents numerous examples of companies using the perceived "crisis in masculinity" to sell their product by framing said products as a way to restore the "natural" gender balance. For instance, men whose masculinity has been "challenged" (e.g., by successful women) are viewed in advertisements for fast food restaurants restoring the balance by purchasing and consuming hamburgers. Thus, the use and exploitation of animals can be used as an indirect mechanism for accomplishing masculinity.

As discussed above, the abuse and exploitation of animals may be a particularly useful mechanism for accomplishing masculinity because it requires the suppression of empathy and emotion, implicit or explicit aggression, and the expression of dominance and control. Luke (2007) further suggests that men may be more inclined to harm animals because they have fewer opportunities to create and sustain life, and many forms of animal exploitation are framed as generativity (e.g., hunting and animal agriculture creates food, vivisection creates scientific discoveries and saves lives). He reasons that women are less likely to support the institutions of animal exploitation because they do not gain a sense of purpose from them as men do. Luke (2007) suggests that this is not only important for understanding the perpetuation of harm against animals, but also for those who seek to understand the successes of and challenges facing the animal rights movement. The two main areas of success in the movement have been the substantial reduction in the testing of cosmetics on animals and sustained campaigns against the purchase of fur products, yet these are not necessarily more harmful quantitatively and qualitatively than other uses of animals. Luke (2007) clarifies this point:

> Trapping, ranching, testing on animals—these are not inherently more pernicious than other forms of animal exploitation. But since their products are thought to result from women's demands, we are able to approach a societal consensus that they represent unacceptable levels of cruelty to animals. Killing animals for sport, for science, for a steak dinner, or a leather jacket—that is not excessive violence, that is men's violence (p.18).

The feminist and masculinities perspectives point to the larger structure of patriarchy as influencing who harms animals, and these perspectives partially address the question of why. In order to more fully address this question, however, we must also attend to the larger political economic structure. The vast majority of harm to which animals are exposed (e.g., through agriculture and entertainment) is at least partially related to commodification and the pursuit of profits and is largely institutionalized.

(Eco)Marxism

As discussed earlier, in his theoretical model of animal abuse, Agnew (1998) identifies the "perceived benefits of abuse outweigh[ing] the costs" as one of three factors that directly increases the likelihood of animal abuse. In many forms of harms against animals, the benefit is an economic one (see Benton, 1993; Boggs, 2007). To illustrate this point, Agnew (1998) quotes Alex Pacheco, co-director of the largest animal rights organization in the world, as saying "'the whole problem is a business problem. The reason animals are in the predicament they are in today is that it's a good business proposition'" (p. 190). And the costs of animal exploitation, particularly in the form of regulatory and legal sanctions, are notoriously low.

Legally defined as property, animals are used as instruments in the production of capital (see Fitzgerald, 2015; Gunderson, 2011; Nibert, 2002; Torres, 2007). The animal agriculture industry is a good illustration of how this process works. "Livestock animals," a term which is demonstrative of their commodification, are kept alive using a calculation to maximize production. Inputs of protein-dense food make them bulk up quickly and medications are used to reduce "product loss" through disease and death. Costs are kept to a minimum by housing as many animals in as little space as possible. Once they reach a plateau in their production (meat animals have bulked up as much as possible, dairy cows' production of milk begins to taper, egg production among chickens begins to drop off) they are slaughtered (for a more detailed description of this process see Fitzgerald, 2015; Foer, 2010; Mason & Finelli, 2006). Even the slaughtering process is designed to reduce costs. There is a highly specialized division of labor and the speed of the (dis)assembly line has been increased to maximize production to the point that worker injuries are common, as are improperly stunned animals (see Eisnitz, 1997; Fitzgerald, 2010; Schlosser, 2005). Although diagnoses of the problems associated with modern animal agriculture often point to technology and its intervention in animal lives, the root of the problem is capital's drive for profit maximization (Gunderson, 2011). Thus, the profit motive works against the best interests of the animals, and the animal welfare laws that are in place to prevent "abuses" of animals are based on the premise that some harm is necessary. It is the harms deemed economically unnecessary that are considered abusive.

Although some minor changes are afoot (such as increases in cage sizes for chickens and pigs in some jurisdictions), the size of the industry globally, and the number of animals subjected to harm within it, is expected to increase. Novek (2003) frames the increase in industrial animal agriculture in North America as part of an international treadmill of production (on the topic of expanding the conceptualization of the treadmill of production, see also Lynch, Long, Barrett, & Stretsky, 2013). In the pursuit of profits, the industry has to continually increase production and stimulate demand. The international demand for meat is growing, and the transition to a meat-based diet, especially in Asia, is expected to increase demand even further. Using the expansion of the hog industry in Manitoba as an example, Novek (2003) points to some of the outcomes of this treadmill of production:

> The expansion of the hog industry in Manitoba presents a useful case study of the global treadmill of production in agriculture. It has been characterized by the ascendancy of large-scale, specialized producers allied with meat processors, suppliers and other corporate interests. Smaller hog producers and more traditional mixed farmers have found themselves at a disadvantage compared to factory farms (p. 19).

Thus, the "factory farm" or Confined Animal Feeding Operation (CAFO) becomes hegemonic. This will subject greater numbers of animals to harm in the name of productivity and profit.

Just as some of the earlier theories discussed posit a relationship between the perpetration of harm against animals and that against people, those coming from an (eco)Marxist perspective also envision a connection between these forms of harm grounded in the capitalist economic system. Nibert (2002, 2007) argues that the exploitation of animals and human groups have similar historic origins and that these forms of oppression remain mutually reinforcing. In recognition of the similar historic trajectories of oppression, some have suggested looking to successful fights for human rights to develop strategies for institutionalizing more humane treatment of animals. Anderson (2011) recommends looking at the history of child labor law reform for strategies to agitate for improved living and dying conditions for animals. The speciesism that makes the commodification of animals possible, however, must also be addressed.

Boggs (2007) argues that the only way to overturn the economically-grounded exploitation of animals, which he refers to as "institutionalized barbarism," is "subversion of those hegemonic beliefs and attitudes which maintain speciesism in its multiple forms." He acknowledges that this is difficult to do in the face of the immense power wielded by corporations, which does not show signs of weakening any time soon. The power of these corporations vis-à-vis animal exploitation has recently been evidenced by their successful lobbying in some states (e.g., Iowa, Missouri, Utah) to get laws passed to criminalize taking pictures or videos inside animal agriculture facilities and misrepresenting one's intentions in gaining employment in such a facility (known colloquially as "ag-gag" laws), essentially outlawing what has been a rather successful form of whistleblowing and repressing freedom of expression (Frye, 2014; Liebmann, 2014; Pitts, 2012).

Economic factors not only contribute to the harm experienced by animals used as food, they also influence the use of animals as entertainment. For instance, many blood sports (e.g., dog fighting, cock fighting, bull fighting, and fox hunting) originated with the affluent classes. It is suggested that these sports gained popularity historically because they offer an "even playing field" between the classes, whereby lower status classes can use these practices as a means for attaining status otherwise not afforded to them. Even when privileged classes abandon a specific blood sport, it may nonetheless live on among the less affluent (Iliopoulou & Rosenbaum, 2013).

An industry has even been built around our culture's most beloved animals: companion or "pet" animals. This industry commodifies animals, modifies their physiology to suit human tastes in some cases, and profits by selling these sentient "products" to consumers (Sollund, 2011). Although they are the most beloved group of animals, they are also vulnerable to economic forces. For instance, the economic recession that began in 2007, and the accompanying foreclosure crisis resulted in a dramatic increase in the number of animals surrendered at shelters and "economic euthanasia" among those who could no longer afford to care for their pets (Nowicki, 2011). This is yet another example of the way that the suffering of human groups and animals can be intertwined, and a recent study by Morris (2013) shows that this is even apparent at the national level. His examination of the relationship between animal welfare, income, and income inequality across countries finds that nations with greater income equality tend to have higher levels of animal welfare (as measured by consumption of animal products, regulation of the most egregious abuses of farm animals, and the use of animals in experiments). Morris (2013) finds that nations characterized by greater income equality consume less meat and have more stringent regulations governing the most harmful forms of intensive animal agriculture. He concludes that it is

> quite possible that the relationship between better welfare and income equality is not causal but is related to some factor (like curtailment of corporate power) that improves both welfare and income inequality. Societies that promote income distribution may also generally be fairer societies that also promote better treatment of animals. (Morris, 2013, p. 291)

The consequences of the economic factors described above are twofold. The first consequence is the most obvious: a growing number of animals are being subjected to harmful living (not to mention dying) conditions in the pursuit of profits. The second consequence is cultural. The endorsement of the use of animals as a means to an end, as property to be used to extract profit, by the political economic system sends a more general cultural message that the (ab)use of animals is acceptable, and even encouraged in certain contexts (see Verbora, 2015). This sentiment can spill over into our other relations with animals, and perhaps even to our relations with other people. The (eco)Marxist perspective is not well-equipped to address this latter consequence. To do so, we turn to an emerging area of theorizing being applied to animal (ab)use: cultural spillover.

Cultural Spillover

This perspective is somewhat similar to the violence graduation hypothesis and the deviance generalization hypothesis discussed earlier. Whereas those hypotheses focus on disapproved forms of animal harm, the cultural spillover hypothesis proposes that socially approved violence can also be associated with unapproved of forms of violence and/or aggression. Beirne (2004) begins to articulate this possibility in relation to the human-animal relationship by suggesting that "[w]henever human-animal relationships are marked by authority and power, and thus by institutionalized social distance, there is an aggravated possibility of extra-institutional violence" (p. 54). Although in this context the focus is on human-animal relationships, this proposition parallels studies of other contexts where socially approved harm against people is said to spill over into unapproved harm against people, such as studies documenting extra-institutional violence among military personnel (e.g., Allen, 2000; Marshall, Panuzio, & Taft, 2005; Marshall & McShane, 2000; Mercier, 2000; Rosen, Kaminski, Parmley, Knudson, & Fancher, 2003) and prison guards (Black, 1982; Kauffman, 1988; Stack & Tsoudis, 1997).

There are a number of scenarios that are possible when applying this hypothesis to human-animal relationships. First, it is possible that socially approved of violence against people (such as in the contexts of the military or prisons) could spill over into disapproved of violence against animals (e.g., cruelty against companion animals). This would not be particularly surprising, given the above cited research indicating that socially approved violence against people can spill over into disapproved of violence against people; research into this possibility is necessary.

Second, it is possible that authorized violence against animals could spill over into unauthorized violence against animals. Flynn (2001, p. 79) presents this possibility as follows: "The more we harm animals in ways that society deems acceptable, the more likely individuals may be to engage in animal cruelty and the less likely individuals and social institutions may be to seriously sanction it." There is anecdotal evidence of animal abuse by some slaughterhouse workers. In 2008, for instance, two workers at a slaughterhouse in California were captured on undercover video kicking, shocking, and dragging "downed" (i.e., injured or disabled) cattle. The president of the company that owned the facility attempted to assuage the public by depicting the abuse as the actions of two rogue individuals (Associated Press, 2008), implying that it was an individual-level and not a systemic problem. However, there is reason to think that this goes beyond the problematic actions of a couple of individuals.

Gullone (2014, p. 74) warns more specifically that "given the pivotal roles for aggression learning played by witnessing cruelty, exposure to aggressive models, and media violence, concern is warranted also with regard to legalized aggressive behaviors such as hunting, attending rodeos, and fishing." For instance, research indicates that those who work in primary industries (such as animal agriculture) have more negative or utilitarian/dominionistic attitudes towards animals (Signal & Taylor, 2006). It is possible that such attitudes could spill over into harmful actions towards animals that are not socially approved. That is, being immersed in an environment where animals are used as instruments for socially approved ends might extend to using animals as instruments for socially disapproved of ends. Of course, that does not suggest that all people who use animals instrumentally would eventually engage in what is legally defined as animal abuse; however, it is possible that such an environment would facilitate such a boundary transgression, more than one in which animals are viewed as individual, sentient beings with inviolable interests and even rights. Research is needed to examine the likelihood and mechanisms behind such boundary transgressions.

Third, and finally, it is possible that socially-approved violence against animals could spill over into aggression and violence against people. Research in this area is also just beginning. A study by Fitzgerald, Kalof, and Dietz (2009) was designed specifically to examine the potential spill over from the industrialized slaughter of animals used as food to violence against people in the broader community. This study was prompted by a number of community studies that found that crime rates increased dramatically in areas where large slaughterhouse facilities had opened (see, for instance, Stull & Broadway, 2004). The study by Fitzgerald and colleagues (2009) set out to examine whether crime rates and slaughterhouse employment levels were related across 581 counties in the U.S. Even when controlling for factors commonly associated with crime (e.g., population density, number of young men in the population, and income levels), they found that slaughterhouse employment levels are related at the county level to total arrest rates, arrests for violent crimes, rape, and other sex offenses. They also found that this relationship does not exist among other industries (in fact, several had negative relationships with these crime variables). These findings are corroborated by another study that, although not devised to specifically examine the potential of a spillover effect, found that counties with expansion in meatpacking or slaughterhouses experience faster growth in violent crime (Artz, Orazem, & Otto, 2007).

A more recent study conducted in Turkey provides some exploratory data on the psychological effects of slaughterhouse work in particular. The study compared the psychological well-being of forty-three butchers working in slaughterhouses and thirty-nine butchers working in supermarkets with a control group of office workers. Among their samples, the butchers report statistically greater experiences of somatization, obsessive-compulsiveness, interpersonal sensitivity, depression, anxiety, anger-hostility, phobic anxiety, paranoid ideation, and psychosis than the control group (Emhan, Yildiz, Bez, & Kingir, 2012). Importantly, however, it is unclear if these problems developed in the course of their work or if these problems predated their employment as butchers.

MacNair's (2002) work on perpetration-induced stress among soldiers, executioners, and law enforcement officers can help to theoretically contextualize the findings of these studies. MacNair argues that even the perpetration of socially approved violence can have significant negative psychological consequences for the perpetrators, even when they were just following orders in perpetrating the violence. Although slaughterhouse workers are not one of the groups MacNair studied, she suggests that they be examined for perpetration-induced traumatic stress. She asks the following worthwhile questions:

> Does the fact that these are merely animals prevent the psychological consequences that would accrue if people were to be treated in this way? Does the fact that this kind of violence is done in massive numbers make it more of a psychological problem than violence to one or a few animals would? (MacNair, 2002, p. 88).

Research examining the actions of those who witness animal abuse (i.e., bystanders) indicates that one of the barriers to action most commonly identified is that the abuse took place within a larger social context of normalized violence. In other words, the bystanders see the violence "as part of a broader pattern of inevitable, albeit unfortunate, everyday violence toward humans and animals" (Arluke, 2013, p. 11). Thus, socially approved violence may not only spill over into harmful behavior against animals, it may also spill over and create a more general environment of apathy, where those who witness even extreme forms of abusive behavior are disinclined to intervene.

Although the studies described in this section cannot conclude that there is a causal spillover effect, through their use of time-series design, statistical controls, and use of comparison industries, they provide suggestive evidence. Further research is needed to examine this and other contexts where socially authorized animal harm may spill over into the unauthorized harming of animals and people. In his thorough review of the literature on the relationship between animal abuse and interpersonal violence, Flynn (2011) also recommends the pursuit of further research in this area, in particular.

Conclusion

Several conclusions can be drawn from this overview of current sociological theorizing of animal abuse. First, although we have discussed each of the nine theories addressed in this chapter separately, it should be clear from our review that there are some important points of convergence between many of the theories. For instance, gender recurs in several theories. It is most explicit in the feminist and masculinities perspectives, but also appears more subtly and intersects with the more micro-level theories discussed (particularly social learning). Such commonalities between these theories present particularly fertile ground for further development and potential theoretical integration.

Second, it should be apparent from our discussions here that there is a great deal of research that still needs to be done to better understand the explanatory potential of the sociological theories presented in this chapter. The testing of these theories through additional empirical research will no doubt lead to theoretical refinements and a greater understanding of places where theoretical integration may be useful.

Finally, we have argued throughout this chapter that theoretical and empirical attention should be paid to both harms to animals legally defined as abusive as well as harms to animals currently not prohibited and even socially accepted. Doing so will require some theoretical dexterity. However, if we truly wish to understand the harmful treatment of animals in our culture, we must be willing to explore the spectrum of harmful treatment—from the socially prohibited, through the socially discouraged, to the socially accepted. The gradations along this spectrum will continue to shift over time, but the speciesism that grounds the entire continuum must be confronted.

References

Abrahams, H. (2007). *Supporting women after domestic violence: Loss, trauma and recovery.* London: Jessica Kingsley Publishers.

Adams, C. J. (1990). *The sexual politics of meat: A feminist-vegetarian critical theory.* New York: Continuum.

Adams, C. J. (1994). Bringing peace home: A Feminist philosophical perspective on the abuse of women, children, and pet animals. *Hypatia: A Journal of Feminist Philosophy,* 9(2), 63–84.

Adams, C. J. (1995). Woman-battering and harm to animals. In C. J. Adams & J. Donovan (Eds.), *Animals & women: Feminist theoretical explorations* (pp. 55–84). Duke University Press.

Agnew, R. (1998). The causes of animal abuse: A social-psychological analysis. *Theoretical Criminology, 2*(2), 177–209.

Agnew, R. (2010). Pressured into crime: General strain theory. In F. Cullen & R. Agnew (Eds.), *Criminological theory: Past to present (Essential readings)* (pp. 201–209). Los Angeles: Roxbury Publishing.

Allen, L. C. (2000). The influence of military training and combat experience on domestic violence. In P. Mercier & J. Mercier (Eds.) *Battle cries on the homefront* (pp. 81–103). Springfield: Charles C. Thomas.

Allen, M., Gallagher, B., & Jones, B. (2006) Domestic violence and the abuse of pets: Researching the link and its implications in Ireland. *Practice, 18*(3), 167–181.

Alleyne, E., Tilston, L., Parfitt, C., & Butcher, R. (2015). Adult-perpetrated animal abuse: Development of a proclivity scale. *Psychology, Crime & Law, 21*(6), 570–588.

Anderson, J. L. (2011). Protection for the powerless: Political economy history lessons for the animal welfare movement. *Stanford Journal of Animal Law and Policy*, 4, 1–63.

Aristarkhova, I. (2012). Thou shall not harm all living beings: Feminism, Jainism, and animals. *Hypatia, 27*(3), 636–650.

Arluke, A. (2002). Animal abuse as dirty play. *Symbolic Interactionism, 25*(4), 405–430.

Arluke, A. (2012). Interpersonal barriers to stopping animal abuse: Exploring the role of adolescent friendship norms and breeches. *Journal of Interpersonal Violence, 27*(15), 2939–2958.

Arluke, A., Levin, J., Luke, C., & Ascione, F. R. (1999). The relationship of animal abuse to violence and other forms of antisocial behavior. *Journal of Interpersonal Violence, 14*(9), 963–975.

Arluke. A., & Luke, C. (1997). Physical cruelty toward animals in Massachusetts, 1975–1996. *Society & Animals*, 5(3), 195–204.

Arluke, A., & Madfis, E. (2014). Animal abuse as a warning sign of school massacres: A critique and refinement. *Homicide Studies, 18*(1), 7–22.

Artz, G.M., Orazem, P. F., and Otto, D. M. (2007). Measuring the impact of meat packing and processing facilities in nonmetropolitan counties: A difference-in-differences approach. *American Journal of Agricultural Economics, 89*, 557–570.

Ascione, F. R. (1993). Children who are cruel to animals: A review of research and implications for developmental psychology. *Anthrozoos, 6*(4), 226–247.

Ascione, F. R. (1998). Battered women's reports of their partners' and their children's cruelty to animals. *Journal of Emotional Abuse, 1*(1), 119–133.

Ascione, F. R., & Arkow, P. (Eds.). (1999). *Child abuse, domestic violence, and animal abuse: Linking the circles of compassion for prevention and intervention*. West Lafayette, IN: Purdue University Press.

Ascione, F. R., Weber, C. V., & Wood, D. S. (1997). The abuse of animals and domestic violence: A national survey of shelters for women who are battered. *Society & Animals, 5*(3), 205–218.

Ascione, F. R., Weber, C. V., Thompson, T. M., Heath, J., Maruyama, M., & Hayashi, K. (2007). Battered pets and domestic violence: Animal abuse reported by women experiencing intimate violence and by nonabused women. *Violence Against Women, 13*(4), 354–373.

Associated Press. (2008, February 17). Two slaughterhouse workers charged with abuse. *USA Today*. Retrieved from http://usatoday30.usatoday.com/money/industries/food/2008-02-15-slaughterhouse-charges_N.htm.

Baldry, A. C. (2003). Animal abuse and exposure to interparental violence in Italian youth. *Journal of Interpersonal Violence, 18*(3), 258–281.

Beirne, P. (1995). The use and abuse of animals in criminology: A brief history and current review. *Social Justice, 22*(1), 5–31.

Beirne, P. (1999). For a nonspeciesist criminology: Animal abuse as an object of study. *Criminology, 37*(1), 117–147.

Beirne, P. (2002). Criminology and animal studies: A sociological view. *Society & Animals, 10*(4), 381–386.

Beirne, P. (2004). From animal abuse to interhuman violence? A critical review of the progression thesis. *Society & Animals, 12*(1), 39–65.

Beirne, P. (2007). Animal rights, animal abuse and green criminology. In P. Beirne, & N. South (Eds.), *Issues in green criminology* (pp. 55–83). Cullompton, Devon: Willan.

Beirne, P. (2009). *Confronting animal abuse: Law, criminology, and human-animal relationships*. Lanham, MD: Rowman & Littlefield.

Beirne, P. (2014). Theriocide: Naming animal killing. *International Journal for Crime, Justice and Social Democracy, 3*(2), 49–66.

Beirne, P., & South, N. (Eds.). (2007). *Issues in green criminology*. Cullompton, Devon: Willan.

Benton, T. (1993). *Natural relations: Ecology, animal rights & social justice*. New York: Verso.

Benton, T. (2003). Marxism and the moral status of animals. *Society & Animals, 11*(1), 73–79.

Black, R. (1982). Stress and the correctional officer. *Police Stress, 5*, 10–16.

Boggs, C. (2007). Corporate power, ecological crisis, and animal rights. *Fast Capitalism 2*(2).

Brown, S. E., Esbensen, F.A., & Geis, G. (2012). *Criminology: Explaining crime and its context*. Waltham, MA: Routledge.

Cazaux, G. (1999). Beauty and the beast: Animal abuse from a non-speciesist criminological perspective. *Crime, Law and Social Change, 31*(2), 105–126.

Chesney-Lind, M., & Faith, K. (2001). What about feminism? Engendering theory-making in criminology. In R. Paternoster & R. Bachman (Eds.), *Explaining crime and criminals* (pp. 287–302). Los Angeles: Roxbury.

Colvin, M. (2000). *Crime and coercion: An integrated theory of chronic criminality*. New York: Palgrave Macmillan.

Connell, R. W. (1987). *Gender and power*. Stanford: Stanford University Press.

Connell, R. W., & Messerschmidt, J. W. (2005). Hegemonic masculinity: Rethinking the concept. *Gender & Society, 19*(6), 829–859.

Currie, C. L. (2006). Animal cruelty by children exposed to domestic violence. *Child Abuse & Neglect, 30*(4), 425–435.

DeGue, S., & DiLillo, D. (2009). Is animal cruelty a "red flag" for family violence? Investigating co-occurring violence toward children, partners, and pets. *Journal of Interpersonal Violence, 24*(6), 1036–1056.

Dejmanee, T. (2013). The burdens of caring: A postfeminist perspective on PETA's animal protection campaigns. *Australian Feminist Studies, 28*(77), 311–322.

Dollard, J., Doob, L., Miller, N., Mowrer, O., & Sears, R. (1939). *Frustration and aggression.* New Haven, CT: Yale University Press.

Donovan, J. & Adams, C. (Eds.) (2007). *The feminist care tradition in animal ethics.* New York: Columbia University Press.

Einstadter, W. J., & Henry, S. (2006). *Criminological theory: An analysis of its underlying assumptions.* Boulder, CO: Rowman and Littlefield.

Emhan, A., Yildiz, A., Bez, Y., and Kingir, S. (2012). Psychological symptom profile of butchers working in slaughterhouse and retail meat packing business: A comparative study. *Kafkas Universitesi Veteriner Fakültesi Dergisi, 18,* 319–22.

Eisnitz, G. (1997). *Slaughterhouse: The shocking story of greed, neglect, and inhumane treatment inside the U.S. meat industry.* New York: Prometheus.

Evans, R., Gauthier, D. K., & Forsyth, C. J. (1998). Dogfighting: Symbolic expression and validation of masculinity. *Sex Roles, 39*(11–12), 825–837.

Fielding, W. (2010). Domestic violence and dog care in New Providence, The Bahamas. *Society & Animals, 18*(2), 183–203.

Fine, G. A. (1986). The dirty play of little boys. *Society, 24*(1), 63–67.

Fitzgerald, A. (2015). *Animals as food: (Re)connecting production, processing, consumption, and impacts.* East Lansing: Michigan State University Press.

Fitzgerald, A. J. (2005). *Animal abuse and family violence: Researching the interrelationships of abusive power.* Lewistown, NY: Edwin Mellen.

Fitzgerald, A. J. (2007). 'They gave me a reason to live': The protective effects of companion animals on the suicidality of abused women. *Humanity & Society, 31,* 355–378.

Fitzgerald, A. J. (2010). A social history of the slaughterhouse: From inception to contemporary implications. *Human Ecology Review, 17*(1), 58–69.

Fitzgerald, A. J., Kalof, L., & Dietz, T. (2009). Slaughterhouses and increased crime rates: An empirical analysis of spillover from "The jungle" into the surrounding community. *Organization & Environment, 22*(2), 158–184.

Flynn, C. P. (1999). Exploring the link between corporal punishment and children's cruelty to animals. *Journal of Marriage and the Family, 61*(4), 971–981.

Flynn, C. P. (2000). Battered women and their animal companions: Symbolic interaction between human and nonhuman animals. *Society & Animals, 8*(2), 99–127.

Flynn, C. P. (2001). Acknowledging the "zoological connection": A sociological analysis of animal cruelty. *Society & Animals, 9*(1), 71–87.

Flynn, C. P. (2002). Hunting and illegal violence against humans and other animals: exploring the relationship. *Society & Animals, 10,* 137–154.

Flynn, C. P. (2010). A sociological analysis of animal abuse. In F. Ascione (Ed.), *The international handbook of animal abuse and cruelty: Theory, research, and application* (pp. 155–174). West Lafayette: Purdue University Press.

Flynn, C. P. (2011). Examining the links between animal abuse and human violence. *Crime, Law, and Social Change, 55*, 453–468.

Foer, J. S. (2010). *Eating animals*. New York: Back Bay Books.

Frye, J. (2014). Big ag gags the freedom of expression. *First Amendment Studies, 48*(1), 27–43.

Geertz, C. (1973). Deep Play: Notes on the Balinese Cockfight. The Interpretation of Cultures, 412–453. New York: Basic Books.

Gullone, E. (2009). A lifespan perspective on human aggression and animal abuse. In A. Linzey (Ed.), *The link between animal abuse and human violence* (pp. 38–60). Brighton/Portland: Sussex Academic Press.

Gullone, E. (2014). Risk factors for the development of animal cruelty. *Journal of Animal Ethics, 4*(2), 61–79.

Gullone, E., & Robertson, N. (2008). The relationship between bullying and animal abuse in adolescents: The importance of witnessing animal abuse. *Journal of Applied Developmental Psychology, 29*, 371–379.

Gunderson, R. (2011). From cattle to capital: Exchange value, animal commodification, and barbarism. *Critical Sociology, 39*(2), 259–275.

Hellman, D. S., & Blackman, N. (1966). Enuresis, firesetting and cruelty to animals: A triad predictive of adult crime. *American Journal of Psychiatry, 122*, 1431–1435.

Henry, B. C. (2004a). Exposure to animal abuse and group context: Two factors affecting participation in animal abuse. *Anthrozoos, 17*(4), 290–305.

Henry, B. C. (2004b). The relationship between animal cruelty, delinquency, and attitudes toward the treatment of animals. *Society & Animals, 12*(4), 185–207.

Henry, B. C., & Sanders, C. E. (2007). Bullying and animal abuse: Is there a connection? *Society & Animals, 15*(2), 107–126.

Hensley, C., & Tallichet, S. E. (2005). Learning to be cruel?: Exploring the onset and frequency of animal cruelty. *International Journal of Offender Therapy and Comparative Criminology, 49*(1), 37–47.

Hensley, C., Tallichet, S. E., & Dutkiewicz, E. L. (2009). Recurrent childhood animal cruelty: Is there a relationship to adult recurrent interpersonal violence? *Criminal Justice Review, 34*(2), 248–257.

Hensely, C., Tallichet, S. E., & Dutkiewicz, E. L. (2012). The predictive value of childhood animal cruelty methods on later adult violence: Examining demographic and situational correlates. *International Journal of Offender Therapy and Comparative Criminology, 56*(2), 281–295.

Herzog, H. (2007). Gender differences in human-animal interactions: A review. *Anthrozoos, 20*(1), 7–21.

Hicks, I. (2012, April 5). Guilty in dog torture case. *The Intelligencer*. Retrieved from http://theintelligencer.net/page/content.detail/id/568137/Guilty-In-Dog-Torture-Case.html.

Howells, K., Watt, B., Hall, G., & Baldwin, S. (1997). Developing programs for violent offenders. *Legal and Criminological Psychology, 2*(1), 117–128.

Hunter, R. (2006). *Point Last Seen*. Sunshine Coast, Australia: Debut Publishing.

Iliopoulou, M. A., & Rosenbaum, R. P. (2013). Understanding blood sports. *Journal of Animal and Natural Resource Law, 9*, 125–140.

Kauffman, K. (1988). *Prison officers and their world.* Cambridge: Harvard University Press.

Kavanagh, P., Signal, T., & Taylor, N. (2013). The Dark Triad and animal cruelty: Dark personalities, dark attitudes, and dark behaviors. *Personality and Individual Differences, 55*, 666–670.

Kellert, S. R., & Felthous, A. R. (1985). Childhood cruelty toward animals among criminals and noncriminals. *Human Relations, 38*(12), 1113–1129.

Kheel, M. (1995). License to kill: An ecofeminist critique of hunters' discourse. In C. J. Adams, & J. Donovan (Eds.), *Animals and women: Feminist theoretical explorations* (pp. 85–125). Durham, NC: Duke University Press.

King, R. J. H. (1991). Environmental ethics and the case for hunting. *Environmental Ethics, 13*, 59–85.

Knight, K. E., Ellis, C., & Simmons, B. (2014). Parental predictors of children's animal abuse: Findings from a national and intergenerational sample. *Journal of Interpersonal Violence, 29*(16), 3014–3034.

Liebmann, L. (2014). Fraud and First Amendment protections of false speech: How United States v. Alvarez impacts constitutional challenges to ag-gag laws. *Pace Environmental Law Review, 31*(2), 566–593.

Linsely, P. (2006). *Violence and aggression in the workplace: A practical guide for all healthcare staff.* Abingdon, UK: Radcliffe Publishing.

Loring, M. T., & Bolden-Hines, T. A. (2004). Pet abuse by batterers as a means of coercing battered women into committing illegal behaviour. *Journal of Emotional Abuse, 4*(1), 27–37.

Lucia, S., & Killias, M. (2011). Is animal cruelty a marker of interpersonal violence and delinquency? Results of a Swiss national self-report study. *Psychology of Violence, 1*(2), 93–105.

Luke, B. (2007). *Brutal: Manhood and the exploitation of animals.* Urbana, Chicago: University of Illinois Press.

Lynch, M. J., Long, M. A., Barrett, K. L., & Stretesky, P. B. (2013). Is it a crime to produce ecological disorganization? Why green criminology and political economy matter in the analysis of global ecological harms. *British Journal of Criminology, 53*, 997–1016.

MacNair, R. (2002). *Perpetration-induced traumatic stress: The psychological consequences of killing.* Westport, London: Praeger.

Marshall, A. D., Panuzio, J., & Taft, C. T. (2005). Intimate partner violence among military veterans and active duty servicemen. *Clinical Psychology Review, 25*, 862–876.

Marshall, D., & McShane, M. (2000). First to fight: Domestic violence and the subculture of the Marine Corps. In P. Mercier & J. Mercier (Eds.), *Battle cries on the homefront: Violence in the military family* (pp. 15–29). Springfield, IL: Charles C. Thomas.

Marvin, G. (1988). *Bullfight.* Oxford: Blackwell.

Mason, J., & Finelli, M. (2006). Brave new farm? In *In defense of animals: The second wave* (pp. 104–122). Edited by Peter Singer. Blackwell Publishing.

Matthews, S. & Herzog, H. (1997). Personality and attitudes toward the treatment of animals. *Society & Animals, 5*(2), 169–175.

Mead, M. (1964). Cultural factors in the cause and prevention of pathological homicide. *Bulletin in the Menninger Clinic, 28*, 11–22.

Mercier, P. J. (2000). Violence in the military family. In P. Mercier & J. Mercier (Eds.), *Battle cries on the homefront: Violence in the military family* (pp. 3–11). Springfield, IL: Charles C. Thomas.

Merz-Perez, L., & Heide, K. M. (2004). *Animal cruelty: Pathway to violence against people.* Lanham: MD: Altamira.

Merz-Perez, L., Heide, K. M., & Silverman, I. J. (2001). Childhood cruelty to animals and subsequent violence against humans. *International Journal of Offender Therapy and Comparative Criminology, 45*(5), 556–573.

Messerschmidt, J. (2004). Varieties of 'real men'. In M. Kimmel & M. Messner (Eds.), *Men's lives* (6th ed.) (pp. 3–20). Toronto: Pearson.

Morris, M. C. (2013). Improved nonhuman animal welfare is related more to income equality than it is to income. *Journal of Applied Animal Welfare Science, 16,* 272–293.

Nibert, D. A. (2002). *Animal rights/human rights: Entanglements of oppression and liberation.* Lanham, MD: Rowman & Littlefield.

Nibert, D. A. (2013). *Animal oppression and human violence: Domesecration, capitalism, and global conflict.* New York: Columbia University Press.

Noske, B. (1989). *Humans and other animals: Beyond the boundaries of anthropology.* London: Pluto Press.

Novek, J. (2003). Intensive hog farming in Manitoba: Transnational treadmills and local conflicts. *The Canadian Review of Sociology and Anthropology, 40*(1), 3–26.

Nowicki, S. A. (2011). Give me shelter: The foreclosure crisis and its effects on America's animals. *Stanford Journal of Animal Law and Policy, 4,* 97–121.

Nurse, A. (2013). Perspectives on criminality in wildlife. In R. Walters, D.S. Westerhuis, & T. Wyatt (Eds.), *Emerging issues in green criminology: Exploring power, justice, and harm* (pp. 127–143). London: Palgrave MacMillan.

Quinlisk, J. A. (1999). Animal abuse and family violence. In F. R. Ascione, & P. Arkow (Eds.), *Child abuse, domestic violence, and animal abuse: Linking the circles of compassion for prevention and intervention* (pp. 168–175). West Lafayette, IN: Purdue University Press.

Pagani, C., Robustelli, F., & Ascione, F. R. (2010). Investigating animal abuse: Some theoretical and methodological issues. *Anthrozoos, 23*(3), 259–276.

Patterson, G. (1982). *An evaluation of parent training programmes as an intervention method for families of children with conduct problems: The Patterson model.* Los Angeles: Wadsworth.

Peterson, M. L., & Farrington, D. P. (2007). Cruelty to animals and violence to people. *Victims & Offenders, 2,* 21–43.

Pitts, J. (2012). 'Ag-gag' legislation and public choice theory: Maintaining a diffuse public by limiting information. *American Journal of Criminal Law, 40,* 95–110.

Ressler, R. K., Burgess, A. W., Hartman, C. R., Douglas, J. E., & McCormack, A. (1986). Murderers who rape and mutilate. *Journal of Interpersonal Violence, 1*(3), 273–287.

Rogers, R. (2008). Beasts, burgers and Hummers: The crisis of masculinity in contemporary television. *Environmental Communication, 2*(3), 281–301.

Roguski, M. (2012). *Pets as Pawns: The Co-existence of Animal Cruelty and Family Violence.* Royal New Zealand Society for the Prevention of Cruelty to Animals and The National Collective of Independent Women's Refuges, Auckland, New Zealand.

Rosen, L. N., Kaminski, R. J., Parmley, A. M., Knudson, K. H., & Fancher, P. (2003). The effects of peer group climate on intimate partner violence among married male U.S. army soldiers. *Violence against Women, 9*, 1045–1071.

Rothgerber, H. (2012). Real men don't eat (vegetable) quiche: Masculinity and the justification of meat consumption. *Psychology of Men and Masculinity, 14*(4), 363–375.

Salleh, A. (1995). Nature, woman, labor, capital: Living the deepest contradiction. *Capitalism, Nature, Socialism, 6*(1), 106–124.

Schlosser, E. (2005). *Fast food nation: The dark side of the all-American meal.* New York: Houghton Mifflin.

Signal, T. D., & Taylor, N. (2006). Attitudes to animals: Demographics within a community sample. *Society & Animals, 14*(2), 147–157.

Simmons, C. A., & Lehmann, P. (2007). Exploring the link between pet abuse and controlling behaviors in violent relationships. *Journal of Interpersonal Violence, 22*(9), 1211–1222.

Sollund, R. (2011). Expressions of speciesism: The effects of keeping companion animals on animal abuse, animal trafficking and species decline. *Crime, Law, and Social Change, 55*, 437–451.

Sollund, R. (2011). The victimization of women, children, and non-human species through trafficking and trade: Crimes understood through an ecofeminist perspective. In N. South & A. Brisman (Eds.), *Routledge international handbook of green criminology* (pp. 317–330). London: Routledge.

South, N., & Beirne, P. (2006). Introduction. In N. South & P. Beirne (Eds.), *Green criminology* (pp. xiiv–xxvii). Burlington, VT: Ashgate.

Stack, S. J., & Tsoudis, O. (1997). Suicide risk among correctional officers: A logistic regression analysis. *Archives of Suicide Research, 3*, 183–186.

Stevenson, R. (2009). *Violence affects all members of the family: Safe pet programs in western Canada.* (Unpublished BA (Honors)). Simon Fraser University, Burnaby, BC.

Strand, E. B., & Faver, C. A. (2005). Battered women's concern for their pets: A closer look. *Journal of Family Social Work, 9*(4), 39–58.

Stull, D., & Broadway, M. (2004). *Slaughterhouse blues: The meat and poultry industry in North America.* Toronto: Wadsworth.

Tallichet, S. E., & Hensley, C. (2004). Exploring the link between recurrent acts of childhood and adolescent animal cruelty and subsequent violent crime. *Criminal Justice Review, 29*(2), 304–316.

Taylor, N. (2011). Criminology and human-animal violence research: The contribution and the challenge. *Critical Criminology, 19*(3), 251–263.

Torres, B. (2007). *Making a killing: The political economy of animal rights.* Oakland, CA: AK Press.

Tibbetts, S. G., & Hemmens, C. (2010). *Criminological Theory: A Text/Reader.* Thousand Oaks, CA: SAGE Publications, Inc.

Tiplady, C. (2013). *Animal Abuse: Helping Animals and People.* Wallingford, Oxfordshire, UK: CABI Publishing.

Unti, B. (2008). Cruelty indivisible: Historical perspectives on the link between cruelty to animals and interpersonal violence. In F. R. Ascione (Ed.), *The international handbook of animal abuse and cruelty: Theory, research, and application* (pp. 7–30). West Lafayette, IN: Purdue University Press.

Vaughn, M. G., Fu, Q., DeLisi, M., Beaver, K. M., Perron, B. E., Terrell, K., & Howard, M. O. (2009). Correlates of cruelty to animals in the United States: Results from the national epidemiologic survey on alcohol and related conditions. *Journal of Psychiatric Research, 43*(15), 1213–1218.

Verbora, A. (2015). The political landscape surrounding anti-cruelty legislation in Canada. *Society and Animals, 23*(1), 45–67.

Volant, A. M., Johnson, J. A., Gullone, E., & Coleman, G. J. (2008). The relationship between domestic violence and animal abuse: An Australian study. *Journal of Interpersonal Violence, 23*(9), 1277–1295.

Walker, L. E. (1984). *The Battered Woman Syndrome*. New York: Springer Publishing.

Walters, G. D. (2014). Testing the direct, indirect, and moderated effects of childhood animal cruelty on future aggressive and non-aggressive offending. *Aggressive Behaviour, 40*(1), 238–249.

Wax, D. E., & Haddox, V. G. (1973). Sexual aberrance in male adolescents manifesting a behavioral triad considered predictive of extreme violence: Some clinical observations. *Journal of Forensic Sciences, 19*(1), 102–108.

Wright, J., & Hensley, C. (2003). From animal cruelty to serial murder: Applying the graduation hypothesis. *International Journal of Offender Therapy and Comparative Criminology, 47*(1), 71–88.

Zilney, L. A. (2007). *Linking animal cruelty and family violence*. Youngstown, NY: Cambria Press.

Chapter 16

Psychological Theories of Animal Cruelty

Mary Lou Randour and Maya Gupta

Introduction

The purpose of this chapter is to offer an approach to understanding the psychological theories underlying cruelty to animals. Just as there could be no one psychological theory for *all* forms of human-directed harm and violence, the same is true for animal-directed violence. Both forms of violence encompass many different types of behaviors, attitudes, and practices. For example, animal-directed violence may refer to mild to serious neglect, intentionally inflicting harm or death, hoarding, animal fighting, or bestiality and other sexual disorders. (See Chapters 1, 5, 8, 9, and 10.) In addition, some might argue that there are practices that—although legal and falling within societal and professional norms—are cruel toward animals, such as factory farming (see Chapters 4 and 8) and laboratory animal research. The viewpoint that some socially acceptable practices also amount to cruelty toward animals is worthy of more discussion and debate than it usually receives.

For the purposes of this discussion, we will be guided by two definitions of animal cruelty. The first is proposed by Ascione and Shapiro (2009, p. 570): "non-accidental, socially unacceptable behavior that causes pain, suffering or distress to and/or the death of an animal." The second definition, which is comparable to the one proposed by Ascione, was developed by the Uniform Crime Reporting Program of the Federal Bureau of Investigation when it added the category of animal cruelty to the National Incident Based Reporting System (NIBRS) in September, 2014. In NIBRS animal cruelty is defined as:

> Intentionally, knowingly, or recklessly taking an action that mistreats or kills any animal without just cause, such as torturing, tormenting, mutilation, maiming, poisoning, or abandonment. Included are instances of failure of duty to provide care, e.g., shelter, food, water, care if sick or injured; transporting or confining an animal in a manner likely to cause injury or death; causing an animal to fight with another; inflicting excessive or repeated unnecessary pain or suffering (e.g., uses objects to beat or injure an animal).

This definition does not include proper maintenance of animals for show or sport; use of animals for food, lawful hunting, fishing or trapping.

In brief, our exploration into the psychologies of animal cruelty will discuss how a particular psychological theory or conceptual framework may be used to better understand one aspect or type of animal cruelty versus another. Our intention is to illustrate that animal cruelty is a heterogeneous behavior and that examining its etiology and function on a case-by-case basis may offer greater insights into prevention and intervention than simply painting all animal cruelty with a single brush.

Before reviewing the psychological theories and frameworks that may be applicable to animal cruelty, it is helpful to lay out the empirical basis with the following short review of the existing literature on the causes and correlates of animal cruelty.

Causes and Correlates of Animal Cruelty

The accumulating and convincing research that concurrently links animal cruelty behavior to other forms of violence, as well as to the development of antisocial and aggressive behavior, motivates the desire among researchers, policymakers, and program developers to better understand the psychologies of animal cruelty as well as the underlying biological, social, and emotional mechanisms that influence behavior and attitudes toward animals. Other writers in this volume have offered a detailed and comprehensive discussion of the empirical evidence for the association between animal cruelty and other types of crime. For example, researchers have found a strong association between animal cruelty and other crimes, including interpersonal violence, illegal possession of drugs and guns, and property destruction (Ascione, 2001; Ascione et al., 2007; Vaughn, Fu, DeLisi, Beaver, & Perron, 2009). Moreover, participation in animal cruelty in childhood is a significant marker for the development of aggressive and antisocial behavior (Merz-Perez, Heide & Silverman, 2001; R. Loeber, personal communication, June 24, 2004); in particular, recurrent acts of animal cruelty during childhood are predictive of later recurring violent aggression against humans (Hensley, Tallichet, & Dutkiewcki, 2008). Animal cruelty is also related to engaging in domestic violence (Febres et al., 2014), and is one factor that predicts which individuals will engage in domestic violence (Walton-Moss, Manganello, Frye, & Campbell, 2005), as well as manifesting controlling behavior in the context of domestic violence (Simmons & Lehmann, 2007).

In a replication of an earlier study, Henderson, Hensley, and Tallichet (2011) examined the relationship between methods of animal cruelty (drowned, hit, shot, kicked, choked, burned, and sexual cruelty) and interpersonal violence against humans among a population of 180 inmates at medium- and maximum-security prisons. Four out of five inmates reported having hit animals, while one in five acknowledged having had sex with an animal. The authors report that "[r]egression analyses revealed that the age at which offenders began committing animal cruelty and having sex with animals were predictive of adult interpersonal violence" (Henderson et al., 2011, p. 2211).

In 1987, the mental health profession acknowledged the significance of animal cruelty with its inclusion of "Physical aggression to people and animals" as a criterion for a diagnosis of conduct disorder in the revised third edition of the *Diagnostic and Statistical Manual of Mental Disorders* by the American Psychiatric Association. Supporting and reinforcing the inclusion of animal cruelty for a diagnosis of conduct disorder also comes from meta-analytic review of the symptoms of conduct disorder (Frick et al, 1993). Cruelty to animals was considered to be one of the earliest reported symptoms, appearing at 6.75 years of age. In addition, children who are cruel to animals exhibit more severe conduct disorder problems than other children (Luk, Staiger, Wong, & Mathai, 1999). In another study of a sample of normative, sexually abused, and outpatient psychiatric children, ages 10–12, the researchers found that cruelty to animals was significantly associated with cruelty to humans for all three groups (Ascione, Friedrich, Heath, & Hayashi, 2003).

The question of whether children who have themselves been mistreated are more likely to abuse animals has somewhat mixed findings. On the one hand, there are studies which have found that children who were cruel to animals were more likely to have been maltreated as children (McEwen, Moffitt, & Arsenault, 2014) and that a parent's involvement in interpersonal violence was "predictive of their children's history of animal cruelty..." (Knight, Ellis, & Simmons, 2014, p. 1). Another study that examined the effects of childhood adversity on bullying and cruelty to animals, however, concluded that "[t]he final models indicated that the cumulative burden of childhood adversities had strong effects on the increased likelihood of bullying but not cruelty to animals" (Vaughn et al., 2011, p. 3509). One possible explanation for the disparity in these findings is that the study by Vaughn et al. used a national sample, but only asked one question about animal cruelty. The study by McEwen et al. (2014) was longitudinal so mothers were asked at four different points if their children were cruel to animals (ages 5, 7, 10 and 12). The data are richer if there are multiple times that information can be obtained about a studied variable, such as animal cruelty. (Any data set would also be more robust if data were collected from a number of different sources about a studied variable, as was the case in the studies by Loeber and his colleagues, which were both longitudinal and used multiple sources.)

Although research into the causes and correlates of animal cruelty has seen a substantial increase in the last twenty-five years, it also the case that a number of these studies have been limited by relying on retrospection, the use of convenience samples, and a lack of experimental controls or other methods to enhance the scientific rigor of the research. At the same time, while any one study may have limitations, the body of evidence supports two propositions: 1) the co-occurrence of animal cruelty and the commission of other violent offenses, in particular domestic violence, and 2) the potential significance of childhood animal cruelty for later development.

Psychological Theories for Understanding Animal Cruelty

The theories and approaches considered here to understand cruelty toward animals include the following: instinct and drive theories, theories of social learning, conceptual frameworks of bimodal types of aggression, and neurobiological influences. Additionally, the literature on cognitive models of explication, the developmental pathways of antisocial behavior, and theories of attachment and empathy development will be reviewed for their relevance in understanding animal cruelty.

Instinct and Drive Theories

Instinct theory, as represented by Freud and Lorenz, proposed that human beings were animated by an aggressive energy that requires expression, which is biological in nature. The popular notion that anger is an emotion that is stored inside and needs to be "released" in order to prevent an uncontrolled explosion is derived from this theoretical approach. Research demonstrates that this is not the case. For more than 40 years, studies have revealed that encouraging the expression of anger directly toward another person or indirectly (such as toward an object) actually increases aggression. The discharge of "excess energy" toward safe targets will not decrease aggression. In fact, it will increase it (Thomas, 2003; Travis, 1982). Drive theories, also mentioned by Pepler and Slaby (1994), focus not on instincts but on internal drives that are vulnerable to external stimuli. The frustration-aggression theory (Dollard, Doob, Miller, Mowrer, & Sears, 1939), proposes that the existence of frustration would inevitably lead to aggression. Frustration, however, is only one of many potential instigators of aggressive behavior. Moreover, rather than frustration, Berkowitz (1993) found that the aversive experiences themselves led to aggression. Simple reliance on either instinct or drive theory may not be useful for trying to understand the particular type of aggression of animal cruelty. Later thinking by scholars in the field of ethology suggests that most learning is based on general processes; however, it also is "customized through the operation of natural selection in context- and species-specific ways to solve particular problems" (Gould, 2002, p. 1).

Social Learning Theory

Social learning theory is considered both a sociological and psychological theory (see Chapter 15). Bandura (1973) posited that individuals can learn behaviors not only through experiencing the consequences of their own actions, but also through observing the actions of others and their consequences. In the "Bobo doll" experiments (Bandura, Ross, & Ross, 1961), children who observed an adult behaving violently toward a doll subsequently behaved more aggressively when given the opportunity to play with the doll and other toys. Although these studies are not without criticisms, Bandura's model provides a useful framework for examining the potential for observational learning of animal cruelty. Can observing someone harming an animal teach someone to engage in animal cruelty?

Agnew (1998) draws upon social learning theory in his integrated theory of the causes of animal cruelty, considering both socially unacceptable and socially accepted forms of harm to animals. In Agnew's integrated theory, social learning underlies the view that animal cruelty is likely when an individual perceives that the benefits of the cruelty outweigh the costs, and that animal cruelty is further driven by general socialization. Agnew notes that if children observe parents mistreating animals, they may imitate the cruelty; similarly, parents who demonstrate kindness toward animals may serve as models for appropriate interactions. Traditional behavior theory suggests that children's imitative behavior may then be reinforced by their parents' response: directly rewarding the act (e.g., praising the child), rewarding the child through attention (whether positive or negative), or tolerating the behavior and failing to correct or punish the child. Social learning theory adds that the child may experience intrinsic reinforcement for the behavior, such as satisfaction.

Several studies have documented a connection between witnessing violence toward animals and engaging in animal cruelty. Baldry (2003) found that witnessing animal cruelty by peers and/or by mothers was the strongest predictor (beyond gender) for children perpetrating animal cruelty themselves. Thompson and Gullone (2006) also noted an association between witnessing and perpetrating animal cruelty, with higher frequency of witnessing and greater closeness of relationship to the abuser (stranger vs. family member/friend) playing a particular role. DeGue and DiLillo (2009) found that individuals who had witnessed animal cruelty were eight times more likely than those who had not witnessed animal cruelty to perpetrate animal cruelty themselves. Together, these studies are broadly consistent with a social learning model.

Can individuals learn to abuse animals if they are either the victims of violence or have witnessed violence against people? Ascione (1993) has suggested such a generalization, as well as Flynn (1999) who observed an association between corporal punishment and perpetrating animal cruelty. Corroborating this finding is a study by McEwen et al. (2014) that children who are cruel to animals were more likely to have been mistreated than other children.

There are other studies, however, that do not support the idea that being abused or witnessing family violence puts an individual at greater risk for abusing an animal. In a study (Baldry, 2003) that examined, among other factors, the association between interparental violence and engaging in animal cruelty, no association was found. There was, however, a finding that, for children who had both witnessed domestic violence and been cruel themselves, maternal violence against the father was also a significant predictor of children's cruelty toward animals. Unlike findings from some of the authors noted above (Flynn, 1999; McEwen et al, 2014), the work of Dadds, Whiting, and Hawes (2006) demonstrated no relationship between abusive or high conflict family environments and children's perpetration of animal cruelty. In the absence of this association, the authors offered support for a dispositional model of animal cruelty based on callous-unemotional personality traits (described later in this chapter). Another study found that only exposure to animal cruelty predicted later animal cruelty, and not exposure to family violence or family conflict (DeGue & DeLillo, 2009). Juxtaposed to this finding is another study by Gullone and Robertson (2008) which found that both family conflict and witnessing animal cruelty predicted animal cruelty perpetration in adolescents. Bullying victimization did not.

Dadds et al. (2006) suggest that one possible reason for these mixed findings on the presence or absence of a relationship between witnessing or being the victim of family violence and perpetrating animal cruelty may be sampling differences: the association may be stronger in clinical samples where family violence tends to be more severe. Similarly, work by Currie (2005) indicating that children exposed to domestic violence were more likely to abuse animals employed a sample screened in for male-to-female domestic violence, in which the females had received counseling concerning the violence. That study also suggested that differences in age of participants across studies may be salient, particularly in combination with exposure to violence: children exposed to domestic violence who become cruel to animals may be reflecting the influence of that exposure over time ("pathological animal cruelty" in Ascione's [2001] typology), as distinct from children not exposed to domestic violence who abuse animals for other reasons and who may thus be younger as a whole.

With respect to bullying as a potential social learning model for the development of animal cruelty, gender may explain mixed findings: Baldry (2005) found that bullying victimization was predictive of animal cruelty only among boys, whereas Gullone and Robertson (2008) saw no association between bullying victimization and animal cruelty but did not conduct separate analyses by gender. Frequency of animal cruelty may also be significant. For example, Henry and Sanders (2007) found that neither a history of bullying victimization nor bullying perpetration differentiated college males who reported engaging in no animal cruelty from those who reported abusing animals only once. Bullying victimization and perpetration were uniquely associated with those who engaged in multiple acts of animal cruelty as opposed to one or no acts. As noted earlier in the section on the causes and correlates of animal cruelty, studies that have collected information at multiple points and/or from multiple sources may provide stronger findings. For both bullying and family violence, ongoing work to disentangle witnessing from victimization may be warranted, as well as sex differences.

Future research on the applicability of social learning theory to animal cruelty may shed light on some of these finer-grained aspects. For example, since social learning theory holds that witnessing the consequences of a behavior observed in others can also influence whether the behavior is learned and imitated, it would be worthwhile to investigate whether children whose peer or adult models were punished for abusing animals are less likely to engage in animal cruelty themselves than those whose models were reinforced for the behavior (for example, receiving approval from others) or who simply got away with it. Further, social learning based on direct observation may be less readily apparent as an explanation for situations where a child is cruel toward animals despite family members and peers consistently modeling positive interactions with animals. In some of these cases, there may simply be an unknown external person modeling animal cruelty for the child. However, it is also possible that other forms of social learning may be operating in such situations: verbal instruction (hearing a description of a behavior and how to engage in it, rather than directly observing it) or symbolic learning (e.g., reading about a real or fictional character engaging in the behavior). These forms of learning may be relevant to "copycat" crimes of animal cruelty, particularly in our media-saturated age.

Bimodal Theories of Aggression

Both the literature on children's aggression and that on adult aggression have broadly converged on a bimodal classification, using such terms as predatory/proactive/ premeditated/instrumental to describe one general mode of aggression and affective/ reactive/impulsive/expressive to describe the other (Berkowitz, 1993; Campbell, Muncer, McManus, & Woodhouse, 1999; Crick & Dodge, 1996; Meloy, 1988; Weinshenker & Siegel, 2002). Babcock, Tharp, Sharp, Heppner, and Stanford (2014) caution that the two primary terminology schemes, impulsive/premeditated and reactive/proactive aggression, may not be as interchangeable as previously thought and may actually measure somewhat separate constructs. For the purpose of this discussion, however, we use the terms "reactive" and "proactive" to denote a general distinction between the two major modes of aggression.

Reactive aggression typically occurs in response to a perceived threat or provocation. Meloy (1988, 2002) sees this as "garden variety" violence that typically is preceded by an intense autonomic arousal and a subjective experience of conscious emotion, typically anger or fear. A threat is perceived, it is time limited, and the goal of the violence is to "return to normal." This contrasts with predatory, or proactive, aggression in which minimal emotion is present and, when present, tends to be positive due to a sense of exhilaration and enhanced self-esteem.

Raine et al. (1998) hypothesized that affectively (reactively) violent offenders would have lower prefrontal activity, higher subcortical activity, and reduced prefrontal/subcortical ratios relative to controls, while predatory violent offenders would show relatively normal brain functioning. They studied 15 predatory murderers and nine affective murderers in the left and right hemisphere prefrontal (medial and lateral) and subcortical (amygdala, midbrain, hippocampus, and thalamus) regions, comparing them to 41 "normal" controls. Glucose metabolism was assessed using positron emission tomography in 41 comparison subjects and the 24 violent offender subjects. The authors suggested that unplanned and impulsive acts of murder were the result of participants having less ability to regulate and control aggressive impulses due to deficient prefrontal regulation. Raine et al. hypothesized that affective aggression is associated with the development of a lack of control mechanisms identified with prefrontal functioning in the brain, while predatory murderers do not lack this ability.

Other research on reactive violence that may be relevant for understanding the psychology of animal cruelty offenders includes that of Tweed and Dutton (1998), who noted that individuals who exhibit affective or reactive styles may be more likely to engage in interpersonal violence because of a loss of self-control, or because they lack any other coping strategies. The work of Downey & Feldman (1996) on rejection sensitivity may also be useful: individuals who are highly rejection-sensitive tend to defensively expect, readily perceive, and overreact to perceived rejection by others. In combination with high investment in dating relationships, rejection sensitivity predicts dating violence in college men (Downey, Feldman, & Ayduk, 2000).

Seeking to apply previous work on reactive and proactive violence to the study of animal cruelty, Gupta (2008) examined college students' self-reports of animal cruelty and intimate partner violence. She found strong associations between rejection sensitivity and expressive (reactive) representations of aggression, and between callousness and instrumental (proactive) representations of aggression. For males, callousness directly predicted both intimate partner violence (IPV) and animal cruelty. For females, the pattern appeared more complex. Similar to males, callousness was strongly associated with instrumental, but not expressive representations, and rejection sensitivity was associated with expressive but not instrumental representations. However, unlike with males, for females instrumental representations were associated with animal cruelty, but not with intimate partner violence.

More recently, Walters and Noon (2015) also attempted to examine reactive vs. proactive aggression in its potential link to animal cruelty. Their results suggested that animal cruelty is associated primarily with tendencies toward proactive behavior and "and earns its reputation as a predictor of future criminality by virtue of its association with behaviors that center on instrumental criminality and premeditated violence" (p. 1381). Direct comparison between this finding and those of Gupta (2008) is difficult, however, due to differences in the populations studied: Walters and Noon's sample was predominantly male, and consisted of delinquent youth rather than college students.

To the extent that callousness may be linked to proactive aggression, several studies that have examined associations between callousness and animal cruelty warrant mention here. A connection between callousness and violent and/or generally antisocial behavior is already fairly well established: Frick, Stickle, Dandreaux, Farrell and Kimonis (2005) found that the presence of callous-unemotional (CU) traits in antisocial youth may designate an especially severe, aggressive, and chronic type of psychopathic disturbance. Directly relating callousness to animal cruelty, Dadds et al. (2006) studied the associations among cruelty to animals, family conflict, and psychopathic traits in childhood. They found that for both genders, callous-unemotional (CU) traits were associated strongly with animal cruelty. The authors conclude:

> These results suggest that cruelty to animals may be an early manifestation of the subgroup of children developing conduct problems associated with traits of low empathy and callous disregard rather than the more common pathway of externalizing problems and parenting problems. (p. 411)

Similarly, Vaughn et al. (2011) conclude that "individuals who are cruel to animals are more likely to possess a liability toward callous, unemotional traits that are highly inheritable and less likely to be modified by the environmental input than are bullying behaviors" (p.3509). Supporting this conclusion, in their prison study cited earlier, Hensley and

Tallichet (2008) found that abusing animals "for fun" was closely linked to committing interpersonal violence as an adult. While callousness was not measured directly, participants' indication that they engaged in animal cruelty for amusement points to a strong possibility of callousness among these individuals.

Further study of reactive and proactive styles of aggression, and their relative associations with such traits as rejection sensitivity and callousness, could hold promise for validating a typology of animal abuse motivations that provides stronger models for prevention, prediction, and intervention. For example, Cavell (2000) notes that treatments that teach self-control could benefit the reactive aggressive child more than the proactively aggressive child. Walters, Frederick, and Schlauch (2007) also suggest that different therapy approaches, both cognitive and psychotropic, may be warranted for adults who engage in either proactive or reactive violence. In the treatment of animal cruelty, it could be similarly helpful to know the chosen aggression modality of a perpetrator of animal cruelty because of the potential to develop tailored treatments for both children and adults.

Neurobiological Theories

Understanding the role that genetics and biology might play in the development of aggressive and antisocial behavior and, in particular, intentional cruelty toward animals could be a fruitful line of investigation. Any such discussion should acknowledge that genetic and biological factors are not solely determinative of behavior but have a complex influence on it. Biology is not destiny; however, biological and genetic factors may make individuals more or less vulnerable to other factors such as family dysfunction, early trauma, poor nutrition, and inadequate education. Numerous factors contribute to the development of childhood aggression, including animal cruelty; however, they can be classified into two major factors: biological and psychosocial (Jianghong, 2004). Moreover, because research suggests that intentional animal cruelty begins at an early age (Loeber, Farrington, & Petechuck, 2003; Patterson, Forgatch, Yoeger, & Stoolmiller, 1998), it is reasonable to speculate that some forms of early onset animal cruelty may be influenced by neurobiological events.

> In general, the line of research that examines biological underpinnings suggests that ... hyperaggressive youngsters appear to live in a state of chronic central nervous system underarousal.... (I)t is possible that low arousal might indicate an impaired sense of fear or anxiety, which in turn might make it more difficult for the hyper-aggressive youth to learn from punishment. (Moeller, 2001, p. 91)

A selected and targeted review of the neuroimaging literature on psychopathic tendencies and antisocial behavior sought to explore the extent to which this literature supports recent cognitive neuro-scientific models of psychopathy and antisocial behavior. Neuroimaging research reveals that individuals who present with a tendency for reactive, but not instrumental aggression show increased amygdala response to emotionally evocative stimuli. In contrast, individuals with psychopathic tendencies exhibit decreased amygdala and orbitofrontal cortex responses to emotionally provocative stimuli or during emotional learning paradigms (Blair, 2010). Neurobiological weaknesses, as demonstrated by the decreased amygdala response, do not mean that these individuals only have a reduced ability to understand the emotion of others. Instead, evidence suggests that an individual who shows little arousal to the distress of others also will exhibit decreased physiological arousal to her or his own distress (Shirtcliff et al., 2009).

Individuals who commit intentional acts of animal cruelty may exhibit different degrees of biological influences. Those individuals who act because they lack control mechanisms in their brain would need a different type of intervention and would have a different prognosis. For example, a 24-year-old man convicted by a Texas court of aggravated animal cruelty displayed signs of predatory aggression. He was convicted of the torture and death of a cat, whom he had taken from her front porch. Over a period of several hours and in several locations, he tortured her in various ways until the animal died. This is contrasted with other criminal conviction of a young man from Maryland who was convicted of the death of an animal. Enraged at his pit bull puppy, he beat him to death and discarded his body on the street. His act appeared to be impulsive and not planned.

Neurobiological approaches also can be useful for understanding hoarding, another form of animal cruelty. Dementia and other types of cognitive decline and impairment, including deficits in the areas of attention, memory, decision-making, and categorization have been associated with hoarding in general (Grisham, Brown, Savage, Steketee, & Barlow, 2007; Grisham, Norberg, William, Certoma, & Kadib, 2010). In Chapter 9 of this book, "Animal Hoarding," the authors detail the characteristics, causes, and interventions for animal hoarding. Noting the similarities between hoarding and animal hoarding, they note that a survey of health officers revealed that approximately one-third of hoarding cases were animal hoarding and that "the primary difference between the two is that animal hoarding is likely to be more severe" (Arluke & Patronek, 2013, p. 200). Animal hoarding behaviors that have a neurophysiological substrate might indicate a different intervention approach, including use of psychotropic medication.

Cognitive Theories

There has been considerable research on the relationship between intelligence and other forms of aggressive behavior. The research on the effect of measured IQ on subsequent antisocial behavior coalesces around the following findings: antisocial youth score 8 to 10 points below the mean on IQ; the non-verbal intelligence of antisocial youth is lower that "normal" youth; neuropsychological measures indicate that aggressive children also display verbal deficits; and differences in IQ are not explained by socioeconomic status or racial difference, or a greater likelihood in being arrested. Low IQ is both linked to youthful antisocial behavior and later antisocial behavior (Farrington, 2005; Moeller, 2001).

In general, cognitive impairment, or low intelligence, is defined as having low-level verbal intelligence as well as difficulty in manipulating non-verbal concepts and poor reasoning skills (Farrington, 2005). In discussing these cognitive factors, Prior and Paris (2005, p. 17) note, "All of these factors are seen as significant in terms of the development and consolidation of cognitive impairment …" Determining the cognitive ability of a child, youth, or adult who engages in any form of animal cruelty would be an important factor to consider in designing an intervention. However, as Moeller notes, the research findings are correlative and not causal; "low IQ alone does not seem responsible for children's aggression, and low IQ might only characterize a certain portion of hyper-aggressive children" (2001, p. 188).

Contrasted to level of intelligence are theories of cognitive development, such as that of Piaget. The focus is on stages of development in the thinking process, not on general intelligence. In this construction, there are four stages of cognitive development: the sensorimotor; preoperational, concrete operational and formal operational. Each individual must acquire the skills in one stage before he or she can enter the next stage of development. In the sensorimotor stage, one of the major accomplishments is object permanence (i.e., an object continues to exist when out of sight). At the pre-operational stage, it is difficult for the child to take another person's viewpoint. By the concrete operational stage, thinking becomes more logical and less egocentric, but only in the formal operational stage is it possible to entertain multiple potential solutions to problems. When advancing through stages, it is not simply that the child has more information about the world, but that the child fundamentally has a different approach to how the world is understood (Evans, 1973).

Some forms of animal cruelty, especially the neglect of an animal, can be partly explained by the possibility that the individual has not progressed beyond a concrete operational stage of thinking to a formal operational style. Especially in the early stages of concrete thinking, it is difficult to understand another's viewpoint. In this situation, an individual's assessment of an animal on a chain without proper nutrition may not be the same as an individual who had gained a higher degree of cognitive development. The remediation in this case would be an educational approach that focused on the person's ability to take another's perspective or feeling state.

Relevant to the development of aggression is the concept of hostile attributional bias. Aggressive children tend to do two things: attribute hostile attentions to others and view these others as enemies who require a forceful response. Cognitive-behavior based treatment is clearly one of the treatments of choice for conduct disordered children (Kazdin, 1994) and is the basis for the AniCare approach to the treatment of animal cruelty in children and adults (Shapiro, Randour, Krinsk, & Wolf, 2014). For example, a child with tendencies toward hostile attributional bias may be more likely to assume that the reason his dog upset his water bowl was to "get even" with him for not taking him for a walk. He could respond by beating the dog, who in turn becomes more wary of the child, leading the child to assume that the dog is punishing him.

In addition to the specific case of attributional bias as a cognitive miscue that can lead to poor decision-making, other cognitive factors include models of problem solving, notions of information processing, formulations of social skills, and concepts of social scripts (Pepler & Slaby, 1994).

The implication of applying cognitive theories to any form of animal cruelty, whether neglect or intentional, animal fighting or animal hoarding, is that there is an assumption that cognitions can be altered. For example, the ways in which children use social information processing skills influences their choice of behavior. Reactive-aggressive children demonstrate a hostile bias, leading to reactive anger. Other aggressive children evaluate aggression and its consequences as relatively useful in achieving desired outcomes and some social information processing leads children to select instrumental goals in a situation rather than relational goals (Crick & Dodge, 1996). Interventions would target these cognitions, challenge them, and offer alternatives that produce more desirable outcomes.

Developmental Pathways of Aggression

The literature on developmental pathways, rather than seeking to create typologies of violent behavior such as predatory and affective, focuses more on trying to understand how this behavior develops and maintains itself, or is extinguished, over a lifetime. Some of the literature on developmental pathways focuses on trying to identify "onset" and then tracking which factors are associated with the continuation of antisocial behavior into adolescence and adulthood, as well as those that may "protect" an individual from such a trajectory. There is consistent agreement in the field of developmental pathways of aggression that early aggression is "a behavioral problem that is a major risk factor for later juvenile delinquency, adult crime, and violence" (Farrington, 1995; Moffitt, Caspi, Dickson, Silva & Stanton, 1996). Underscoring the importance of early onset, DeLisi et al. (2013, p. 12) somewhat ironically noted, "The broader significance of early onset delinquency is never trite."

In the following section, we will examine the literature on developmental pathways of aggressive behavior in general and then look at research which provides evidence for the notion that the appearance of animal cruelty is a significant indicator in the developmental pathways of aggressive behavior.

Models for aggression in general. Reviewing the research on child delinquency, Loeber et al. (2003) make the following points:

- Years of criminology research strongly support the notion that the best predictor of future behavior is past behavior.
- The antisocial careers of male juvenile offenders start, on average, at age 7.
- The preschool years are critical times to identify, and intervene, to prevent disruptive behavior.

The authors also list the factors that could have the most influence on the development of anti- and pro-social behavior during preschool and beyond: language, temperamental characteristics (which would include neurobiological factors), and low attachment to caregivers. We discuss the influences of neurobiological factors and ability to attach in other sections of this chapter.

Key findings from longitudinal data analyzed by Tremblay, Vitaro, Nagin, Pagini, and Seguin (2003) support some of the points made by Loeber and his associates (Loeber, Slot, & Stouthamer-Loeber, 2006). These findings include: 1) that kindergarten disruptive behavior predicts delinquency during the transition from childhood to early adolescence, and 2) kindergarten personality predicts delinquency during the transition from childhood in adolescence. Regarding personality, high impulsive and low anxious low reward dependent subjects were the most at risk for antisocial behavior.

Considering the early onset of aggressive behaviors, Tremblay et al. (2003) wondered, "When does it begin?" The question is significant because if animal cruelty is one of the manifestations of deviant behavior then it is critical to identify and understand it, and develop appropriate responses to it.

One of the problems for understanding the development of animal cruelty has been that very few studies on the development of aggression have included questions about animal cruelty. However, one significant longitudinal study, "the Pittsburgh study," did so. The researchers (Loeber et al., 2006) use a model that stresses the interaction among risk and protective factors which influence a tendency to engage in antisocial acts and to commit offenses. They assume that individual development occurs in the context of different influences on the child. In addition to looking at predictors and trajectories of the development of antisocial, aggressive behavior, factors associated with persistence, and desistence, in antisocial behavior were examined.

Of interest to the purposes here, one of the four factors associated with persistence in antisocial, aggressive behavior from early childhood to adulthood was physical aggression toward people and animals. (R. Loeber, personal communication, June 24, 2004).

Appearance of animal cruelty and developmental pathways of aggression. Offering support to the proposal that early onset and persistent animal cruelty is an important factor in the development of aggressive behaviors, Hensley and Tallichet (2008) examined the relationship of inmates' self-reported childhood and adolescent and animal cruelty on the number of convictions for adult violent interpersonal crimes. From their sample of 261 inmates at medium and maximum-security prisons, they found that subjects who abused animals at an earlier age and those who did so out of anger or for fun were more likely to repeat the offense.

As mentioned earlier, many of the studies on the causes and correlates of animal cruelty have been limited by their design (e.g., use of convenience samples, lack of a control group). A prospective study avoids some of those limitations. For example, Becker, Stuweig, Herrera, and McCloskey (2004) conducted a 10-year prospective study that provided information about family risk factors and childhood problem behavior. Subjects were interviewed and their court records were reviewed. Animal cruelty was related to self-reported violent crime and the authors conclude that "These findings indicate that family variables increase the likelihood of childhood fire setting and animal cruelty and that these behaviors are related to adolescent delinquency" (Becker et al., 2004, p. 905).

Integrating the literature on the developmental pathways of aggression with the literature that has a focus on the etiology of animal cruelty could be a productive effort. The research findings from the extensive research on developmental pathways are robust and can support and explicate the research that has focused on the significance of animal cruelty as an early marker of deviant behavior.

Trying to understand the etiology and maintenance of aggression, including animal cruelty as one type of aggressive behavior, is a complicated endeavor. Few would contend that there is *one* individual representation of aggression or antisocial behavior that would offer a direct causal link to later aggression, whether it is animal cruelty, low verbal skills, or an impulsive temperament. Human behavior is complex and there are multiple influences on behavior. And yet there has been a discussion by some (Arluke, Luke, & Ascione, 1999; Piper, 2003) of a "violence graduation hypothesis" that "posit(s) a direct causal link between animal cruelty and subsequent violent offending" (Walters, 2013, p. 797).

Research that has found a relationship between early, recurrent animal cruelty and later antisocial behavior has not asserted that there is some sort of "inevitability" involved, or a simple "graduation" from animal abuse to violent offender, as it has been characterized by some. No direct causal link has been claimed in the body of research literature. Rather research—whether looking at aggression in general or animal cruelty in particular—points to the significance of animal cruelty as one of the complex set of psychosocial factors to consider in the developmental pathways of aggression.

Attachment

The "father" of attachment theory was John Bowlby, who established the core of attachment theory with his three volumes, Attachment (1969), Separation (1973) and Loss (1980). Drawing upon concepts from ethology, cybernetics, information processing, developmental psychology, and psychoanalysis, the basic premise of attachment theory is that there is a primary attachment between a child and her or his caregiver which is "hard wired" for evolutionary purposes and that anxiety is experienced when that attachment is threatened. Additionally, grief is experienced when there is a loss. If Bowlby was the "father" of attachment theory, then Mary Ainsworth was the "mother," or perhaps the "big sister," by expanding and validating his theory with the innovative methodology referred to as the "Strange Situation." This paradigm tested types of attachment children had to their caregivers. In this test situation, an infant and his or her caregiver would be brought into a room with an adult stranger, and the mother would leave. The reaction of the infant when the caregiver left and then returned was noted. Since Bowlby and

Ainsworth there have been scores of researchers examining various facets of attachment and its importance to development, well-being, and its relationship to violent behavior.

Ainsworth (1978) and her colleagues discovered three styles of attachment, two of which were pathological. Secure attachment was characterized by infants who competently expressed their needs and accepted maternal care. The other two were pathological: avoidant, represented by infants who appeared minimally distressed when the caregiver left and avoided her when she returned, and the ambivalent/resistant types who had great difficulty with separating and also could not find comfort from the caregiver when she returned.

More recently, Bartholomew (1990, 1994, 1997) has expanded on the Bowlby/Ainsworth work to develop models of adult attachment. In the adult model, three pathological types of attachment are considered: 1) preoccupied individuals who have a negative perception of self and a positive perception of others and are very dependent on the other's approval and acceptance; 2) fearful individuals who have a negative perception of self and others and avoid close contact, fearing rejection; 3) dismissing individuals who have a positive perception of self and a negative perception of others. Meloy (2002) notes that "there has been substantial research on both concurrent and predictive validity of her model" (p. 514). A fourth type of adult attachment pathology not included in the Bartholomew model is the disorganized individual, which has limited research but appears associated with severely disturbed individuals (Fonagy, 1996).

Meloy (2002) examined the pathologies of attachment, violence, and criminality and concluded: "Research on attachment and violence during the past decade has largely focused on intimate partner, or domestic violence. There has been limited research on attachment and violent criminality. The discoveries are new and very promising" (p. 514).

Dadds, Jambrak, Pasalich, Hawes, and Brennan, (2011) studied males with conduct problems who were assessed to demonstrate high levels of CU traits. Researchers used the methodology of measuring eye contact between attachment figures and high CU boys to ascertain the relationship between high callousness and difficulties with attachment. Males with high CU traits showed consistent impairments in eye contact toward their parents.

Another view of the relationship between attachment and psychopathy is proposed by Khetrapal (2009). He notes that individuals showing psychopathology also exhibit a form of disorganized attachment. He continues, "The erratic style of attachment not only negatively affects psychosocial adjustment but also has a negative influence on the neurobiological systems ... that are responsible for functions like emotional processing and social adjustment" (p. 9).

It also appears that forensic patients have significantly higher presence of unsafe attachment representations (dismissed and disorganized/unresolved attachment styles) than those in control groups. Van den Berg and Oei (2009) explain,

> Dismissed and disorganized/unresolved attachment representations can fairly easily be identified in PCL-R items; factors 1 and 2: the interpersonal and affective factors, provide insights into how psychopathic patients avoid reciprocal relationships; factor 4, the antisocial lifestyle factor, corresponds to disorganized attachment representations, recognizable by impulsive and irresponsible behavior (p. 49).

Other studies of attachment representations of juvenile and incarcerated adult offenders support the idea that psychopathy, in part, is influenced by impairments in attachment, and is a developmental process (Frodi, Dernevik, Sepa, Philipson, & Bragesjo, 2001; Saltaris, 2002). In a Swedish study, 24 adult psychopathic criminal offenders incarcerated in either a psychiatric hospital or a medium security prison were assessed with Hare's PCL-R, and then interviewed with an the Adult Attachment Interview, and completed a self-report questionnaire about parent rearing techniques. There was an extensive over-representation of individuals who were dismissive of attachment and attachment-related experiences. Also, there was an association between a higher psychopathy score and family constellation of a rejecting father and an emotionally very warm, idealized mother (Frodi et al., 2001).

Attachment style as an explanatory system for different types of animal cruelty forms one of the bases for the AniCare approach to the treatment of animal cruelty in both children and adults (Jory & Randour, 1999; Shapiro, Randour, Krinsk, & Wolf, 2014), emphasizing the importance of assessing the abuser's attachment to the animal (presence or absence of attachment, as well as style of attachment). Attachment also has been proposed as an important factor in the psychology of hoarding (Patronek & Nathanson, 2009; see Chapter 9). It is proposed that avoidance and insecure attachment are central to many of animal hoarding cases, and suggest that the compulsive caregiving and self-reparative relationships described in the literature on disordered attachment styles may lend themselves to the accumulation of animals perceived to be in need. While this chapter separates hoarding from other forms of cruelty, it appears that attachment and attachment problems may form a useful framework for examining the full spectrum of animal cruelty to the extent that we conceptualize cruelty as "the human-animal bond gone awry."

As Meloy (2002) notes, studies have found that antisocial personality disorder or conduct disorder in adolescence seems to be associated with dismissing or disorganized attachment pathology. Additionally, although less developed, the research into attachment and criminality has found the following:

- Insecure attachment is a risk factor for violent criminality.
- Secure attachment is likely a protective factor, particularly when the child is raised in a deprived environment.
- The capacity to reflect, or take another's perspective, may be an important mediating variable for affective violence.
- Dismissing pathologies of attachment may be associated with constitutional, or temperamental, characteristics and disorganized attachment may be associated with trauma.

In general, the interesting research findings from the field of attachment and violence provide strong support for the careful examination of how attachment styles may influence the etiology and typologies of animal cruelty offenders and how interventions should be tailored to take this into account.

Empathy Development

Up to this point, we have focused on the rich data that link callousness to the etiology and manifestation of violent behavior, including animal cruelty. However, as Shirtcliff et al. (2009) note, there is a "counterpart" to callousness and many researchers have suggested that the counterpart is the trait of empathy. Some have suggested that callousness is a disorder of empathy (Soderstrom, 2003). Callousness is a key trait in psychopathy, and psychopathy has been termed a disorder of empathy (Soderstrom, 2003).

Numerous studies have documented that empathy plays a central role in moral reasoning, motivates prosocial behaviors, and inhibits aggression toward others (Decety & Lamm, 2006). Empathy involves neural processes and social learning. Decety and Lamm conclude that empathy relies "both on bottom-up information processing (shared neural systems between first-hand emotional experiences and the perception or imagination of the other's experience) as well as top-down information processing that allows modulation and self-regulation" (p. 1160). Some of the latest research on how to understand empathy and its development also focuses on mapping neural pathways (Interlandi, 2015). The interest in finding neural pathways to the development of empathy in no way implies that this learning is fixed. Rather, the development and alternation of neural pathways, to some extent, can be influenced by behavioral and social interventions.

While acknowledging the interplay of brain structure, hormonal processing, and social and psychological learning in the development of empathy, Randour (2005) reviewed the research on the development and teaching of empathy and proposed that empathy is a skill that can be taught and learned. Noting that empathy plays an important role in children's success at school and in their social and personal lives, she linked empathy development to the role that animals play in its creation and development.

Recognizing the development of empathy may be especially appropriate for treating certain types of offenders who exhibit little concern for others (i.e., callousness). Burke (2001) identified the development of empathy as a part of the treatment for adolescent sex offenders. Another study employed the use of rescued shelter animals to teach a message of anti-violence and to convey principles of prosocial behavior to children in elementary and middle school (Sprinkle, 2008). Using student self-report, disciplinary, and teacher observational data to measure violent and aggressive behaviors, beliefs about aggression, and level of empathy, the study found the programs significantly altered students' normative beliefs about aggression, levels of empathy, and the students participating also showed a decrease in aggressive behaviors.

Conclusion

The idea that there are many different psychological theories that can aid our understanding of the psychology of animal cruelty was proposed in this chapter. As cruelty to animals may occur in many different ways—simple neglect, intentional cruelty, hoarding, animal fighting, and bestiality—it follows that one theory would be insufficient to address so many different forms of behavior and pathology. Moreover, there is more than one theory that can address any one form of animal cruelty. For example, in the case of animal hoarding, knowledge from psychological theories of attachment as well as information about the underlying biological and psychological factors related to compulsive behavior could provide insights. Further, within a single form of animal cruelty, and even between two apparently similar acts (for example, two ten-year-old children, each referred to a psychologist after kicking the family dog), individual presentations and motivations may differ greatly, requiring different theories to explain each case.

In brief, our exploration into the psychologies of animal cruelty discussed how a particular psychological theory or conceptual framework may be used to better understand one aspect or type of animal cruelty. This chapter addressed several psychological theories or approaches: instinct and drive theories, theories of social learning, conceptual frameworks of bimodal types of aggression, neurobiological influences, cognitive models of explication, developmental pathways of antisocial behavior, and theories of attachment and empathy. As we posited in introducing this discussion, no one theory can totally explain one or another form of animal cruelty (e.g., intentional cruelty or animal fighting). Taken both individually and together, each theory deepens our understanding of aggression toward, and neglect of, animals.

References

Agnew, R. (1998). The causes of animal abuse: A social-psychological analysis. *Theoretical Criminology, 22*, 177–209.

Ainsworth, M. D. S., Blehar, M. C., Waters, E., & Wall, S. (1978). *Patterns of attachment: A psychological study of the strange situation.* Hillsdale, NJ: Lawrence Erlbaum Associates.

American Psychiatric Publishing. (2013). Diagnostic and Statistical Manual of Mental Disorders (DSM-5R). (5th Ed.). Arlington, VA.

Arluke, A., Levin, J., Luke, C. & Ascione, F. (1999). The relationship of animal abuse to violence and other forms of antisocial behavior. *Journal of Interpersonal Violence, 14*, 963–975.

Ascione, F. R. (1993). Children who are cruel to animals: A review of research and implications for developmental psychopathology. *Anthrozoös, 6*, 226–247.

Ascione, F. R. (2001). Animal abuse and youth violence. *Juvenile Justice Bulletin.* Washington, D.C.: U.S. Department of Justice.

Ascione, F. R., & Shapiro, K. (2009). People and animals, kindness and cruelty: Research directions and policy implications. *Journal of Social Issues, 65(3)*, 569–587.

Ascione, F. R., Friedrich, W. N., Heath, J, & Hayashi, K. (2003). Cruelty to animals in normative, sexually abused, and outpatient psychiatric samples of 6- to 12-year-old children: Relations to maltreatment and exposure to domestic violence. *Anthrozoös, 16*, 194–210.

Ascione, F. R., Weber, C. V., Thompson, T. M., Heath, J., Maruyama, M., & Hayashi, K. (2007). Battered pets and domestic violence: Animal abuse reported by women experiencing intimate violence and by non-abused women. *Violence Against Women, 13*, 354–373.

Babcock, J. C., Tharp, A. L. T., Sharp, C., Heppner, W., & Stanford, M. S. (2014). Similarities and differences in impulsive/premeditated and reactive/proactive bimodal classifications of aggression. *Aggression and Violent Behavior, 19*, 251–262.

Baldry, A. C. (2003). Animal abuse and exposure to interparental violence in Italian youth. *Journal of Interpersonal Violence, 18*, 258–281.

Baldry, A. C. (2005). Animal abuse among preadolescents directly and indirectly victimized at school and at home. *Criminal Behavior and Mental Health, 15*, 97–110.

Bandura, A., Ross, D. & Ross, S. A. (1961). Transmission of aggression through imitation of aggressive models. *Journal of Abnormal and Social Psychology, 63*, 575–82.

Bandura, A. (1973). *Aggression: A social learning analysis.* Englewood Cliffs, NJ: Prentice Hall.

Bartholomew, K. (1990). Avoidance of intimacy: An attachment perspective. *Journal of Social and Personal Relationships, 7*, 147–178.

Bartholomew, K. (1994). The assessment of individual differences in adult attachment. *Psychological Inquiry, 5*, 23–17.

Bartholomew, K. (1997). Adult attachment processes: Individual and couple perspectives. British *Journal of Medical Psychology, 70*, 249–263.

Becker, K. K., Stuwig, J., Herrera, V. M., & McCloskey, L. A. (2004). A study of firesettting and animal cruelty in children: Family influences and adolescent outcomes. *Journal of the American Academy of Child & Adolescent Psychiatry, 43*, 905–912.

Berkowitz, L. (1993). *Aggression: Its causes, consequences, and control.* New York: McGraw-Hill.

Blair, R. J. (2010). Neuroimaging of psychopathy and antisocial behavior: A targeted review. *Current Psychiatry Reports, 12*, 76–82.

Bowlby, J. (1969*). Attachment & loss: Vol. 1: Attachment* (2nd ed.). New York: Basic Books.

Bowlby, J. (1973). *Attachment and loss: Vol. 2. Separation.* New York: Basic Books.

Bowlby, J. (1980). *Attachment & loss. Vol. 3. Loss, sadness, and depression.* New York: Basic Books.

Burke, D. M. (2001). Empathy in sexually offending and non-offending adolescent males. *Journal of Interpersonal Violence, 16*, 222–233.

Campbell, A., Muncer, S., McManus, I. C., & Woodhouse, D. (1999). Instrumental and expressive representations of aggression: One scale or two? *Aggressive Behavior, 25*, 435–444.

Cavell, T. A. (2000*). Working with parents of aggressive children: A practitioner's guide.* Washington, D.C.: American Psychological Association.

Crick, N. R. & Dodge, K. A. (1996). Social information processing mechanisms in reactive and proactive aggression. *Child Development, 67*, 993–1002.

Currie, C. L. (2006). Animal cruelty by children exposed to domestic violence. *Child Cruelty & Neglect, 30*, 425–435.

Dadds, M. R., Whiting, C., & Hawes, D. J. (2006). Associations among cruelty to animals, family conflict, and psychopathic traits in childhood. *Journal of Interpersonal Violence, 3*, 411–429.

Dadds, M. R. Jambrak, J., Pasalich, D., Hawes, D. J., & Brennan, J. (2011) Impaired attention to the eyes of attachment figures and the developmental origins of psychopathy. *Journal of Child Psychology and Psychiatry, 52*, 238–245.

Decety, J., & Lamm, C. (2006), Human empathy through the lens of social neuroscience. *The Scientific Journal, 6*, 1146–1163.

DeGue, S., & DiLillo, D. (2009). Is animal cruelty a "red flag" for family violence? Investigating co-occurring violence toward children, partners, and pets. *Journal of Interpersonal Violence, 24*, 1036–1056.

DeLisi, M., Neppl, T. K., Lohman, B. J., Vaughn, M. G., & Shook, J. J. (2013). Early starters: Which type of criminal onset matters most for delinquent careers? *Journal of Criminal Justice, 41*, 12–17.

Dollard, J., Doob, L. W., Miller, N. E., Mowrer, O. H., & Sears, R. R. (1939). *Frustration and aggression.* New Haven, CT: Yale University Press.

Downey, G., & Feldman, S. I. (1996). Implications of rejection sensitivity for intimate relationships. *Journal of Personality and Social Psychology.* 70, 1327–1343.

Downey, G., Feldman, S. & Ayduk, O. (2000) Rejection sensitivity and male violence in romantic relationships. *Personal Relationships, 7,* 45–61.

Evans, R. (1973). *Jean Piaget: The Man and His Ideas.* New York: E. P. Dutton & Co., Inc.

Farrington, D. P. (1995). The development of offending and anti-social behavior from childhood: *Child Psychology and Psychiatry, 36,* 929–964.

Farrington, D. P. (2005). Childhood origins of antisocial behavior. Special issue. *Forensic Psychology, 12,* 177–190.

Febres, J., Brasfield, H., Shorey, R. C., Elmquist, J., Ninnemann, A., Schonrum, Y. C. Stuart, G. (2014). Adulthood animal abuse among men arrested for domestic violence. *Violence Against Women, 20,* 1059–1077.

Flynn, C. P. (1999). Animal abuse in childhood and later support for interpersonal violence in families. *Society & Animals, 8,* 99–127.

Fonagy, P. (1996). Male perpetrators of violence against women: An attachment theory perspective. *Journal of Applied Psychoanalytic Studies, 1,* 7–27.

Frick, P. J., Lahey, B. B., Loeber, R., Tannenbaum, L., Van Horn, Y., Christ, M. A. G., & Hanson, K. (1993). Oppositional defiant disorder and conduct disorder: A meta-analytic review of factor analyses and cross-validation in a clinic sample. *Clinical Psychology Review, 13*(4), 319–340.

Frick, P. J., Stickle, T. R., Dandreaux, D. M., Farrell, J. J., & Kimonis, E. R. (2005). Traits in predicting the severity and stability of conduct disorder and delinquency. *Journal of Abnormal Psychology, 33,* 471–487.

Frodi, A., Dernevik, M., Sepa, A., Philipson, J., & Bragesjo, M. (2001). Current attachment representations of incarcerated offenders varying in degree of psychopathy. *Attachment and Human Development, 3*(2), 269–283.

Gould, J. L. 2002. Learning instincts. In C. R. Gallistel (Ed.), *Stevens' handbook of experimental psychology* (3rd ed.) (pp. 239–257). New York: John Wiley and Sons.

Grisham, J. R., Brown, T. A., Savage, C. R., Steketee, G., & Barlow, D. H. (2007). Neuropsychological impairment associated with compulsive hoarding. *Behavioral Research Therapy, 45,* 1471–1483.

Grisham, J. R., Norberg, M. M., Williams, A. D., Certoma, S. P. & Kadib, R. (2010). Categorization and cognitive deficits in compulsive hoarding. *Behavior Research Therapy. 48,* 866–872.

Gullone, E., & Robertson, N. (2008). The relationship between bullying and animal abuse behaviors in adolescents: The importance of witnessing animal abuse. *Journal of Applied Developmental Psychology, 29,* 371–379.

Gupta, M. (2008). Functional links between intimate partner violence and animal abuse: Personality features and representations of aggression. *Society & Animals, 16,* 223–242.

Hensley, C., & Tallichet, S. E. (2008). The effect of inmates' self-reported childhood and adolescent animal cruelty: Motivations on the number of convictions for adult violent interpersonal crimes. *International Journal of Offender Therapy and Comparative Criminology, 52,* 175–184.

Henderson, B. B., Hensley, C., & Tallichet, S. E. (2011). Childhood animal cruelty methods and their link to adult interpersonal violence. *Journal of Interpersonal Violence, 26*, 2211–2227.

Henry, B. C., & Sanders, C. E. (2007). Bullying and animal abuse: Is there a connection? *Society & Animals, 15*, 107–126.

Hensley, C. & Tallichet, S. E. (2008). The effect of inmates' self-reported childhood and adolescent animal cruelty motivations on the number of convictions for adult violent interpersonal crimes. *Journal of Offender Therapy and Comparative Criminology, 52*, 175–184.

Hensley, C., Tallichet, S. & Dutkiewicz, E. (2008). Recurrent animal cruelty: Is there a relationship to adult recurrent interpersonal violence? *Criminal Justice Review, 34*, 248–257.

Interlandi, J. (2015, March 22). The empathy gap. *The New York Times Magazine*, 50.

Jianghong, L. (2004). Childhood externalizing behavior: theory and implications. *Journal of Child and Adolescent Psychiatric Nursing, 17*, 93–103.

Jory, B., & Randour, M. L. (1999). *The AniCare model of treatment for animal abuse.* Washington Grove, MD: Society & Animals Forum.

Kazdin, A. E. (1994). Intervention for aggressive and antisocial children. In L. D.Eron, J. H, Gentry & P. Schegel (Eds.), *Reason to hope: A psychosocial perspective on violence & youth* (pp. 341–382). Washington, D.C.: American Psychological Association.

Khetrapal, N. (2009). The early attachment experiences are the roots of psychopathy. *Interpersona: An International Journal of Personal Relationships, 3*, 1–13.

Knight, K. E., Ellis, C. & Simmons, S. B. (2014). Parental predictors of children's animal abuse: Findings from a national and intergenerational sample. *Journal of Interpersonal Violence*, 1–21.

Loeber, R., Farrington, D. P., Petechuck, D. (2003). Child delinquency: Early intervention and prevention. *Bulletin*. Washington, DC: U.S. Department of Justice, Office of Juvenile Justice and Delinquency Prevention.

Loeber, R., Slot, N. W. & Stouthamer-Loeber, M. (2006). A three-dimensional, cumulative developmental model of serious delinquency. In P. O. H. Wilstrom & R. Sampson (Eds.), *The explanation of crime: Contexts and mechanisms* (pp.153–194). Cambridge, England: Cambridge University Press.

Luk, E. S. L., Staiger, P. K., Wong, L. & Mathai, J. (1999). Children who are cruel to animals: A revisit. *Australian and New Zealand Journal of Psychiatry, 33*, 29–36.

McEwen, F. S., Moffitt, T. E., Arseneault, L. (2014). Is childhood cruelty to animals a marker for physical maltreatment in a prospective cohort study of children? *Child Cruelty & Neglect, 28*, 533–543.

Meloy, R. J. (1988). *The psychopathic mind: Origins, dynamics, and treatment.* Lanhan, MD: Jason Aronson.

Meloy, R. J. (2002). Pathologies of attachment, violence, and criminality. In A. Goldstein (Ed.), *Handbook of psychology, 11*, 509–526. New York: Wiley.

Merz-Perez, L., Heide, K. J., & Silverman, I. J. (2001) Childhood cruelty to animals and subsequent violence against animals. *International Journal of Offender Therapy and Comparative Criminology, 45*, 556–573.

Moeller, T. G. (2001). *Youth aggression and violence: A psychological approach*. Mahwah, NJ: Lawrence Erlbaum Associates.

Moffitt, T. E., Caspi, A., Dickson, N., Silva, P., & Stanton, W. (1996). Childhood-onset versus adolescent-onset antisocial conduct problems in males: Natural history from ages 3 to 18 years. *Development and Psychopathology, 1*, 104–118.

Patronek, G. J., & Nathanson, J. N. (2009). A theoretical perspective to inform assessment and treatment strategies for animal hoarders. *Clinical Psychology Review, 29*, 274–281.

Pepler, D. J. & Slaby, R. G. (1994. Theoretical and developmental perspectives on youth and violence. In L. D. Eron, J. H. Gentry & P. Schegel (Eds.), *Reason to hope: A psychosocial perspective on violence & youth*. Washington, D.C.: American Psychological Association.

Patterson, G. R., Forgatch, M. S., Yoerger, K. L., & Stoolmiller, M. (1998). Variables that initiate and maintain an early-onset trajectory for juvenile offending. *Development and Psychopathology, 10*, 531–547.

Piper, H. (2003). The linkage of animal abuse with interpersonal violence: A sheep in wolf's clothing? *Journal of Social Work, 3*, 161–177.

Prior, D. & Paris, A. (2005). Preventing children's involvement in crime and anti-social behavior: A literature review. National Evaluation of the Children's Fund. Research Report. No. 623. University of Birmingham.

Raine, A., Meloy, J. R., Bihrle, S. Stoddard, J., Lacasse, L. & Buchsbaum, M. S. (1998). Reduced prefrontal and increased subcortical brain functioning assessed using positron emission tomography to predatory and affective murderers. *Behavioral Science & the Law, 16*, 319–332.

Randour, M. L. (2005). *The empathy connection*. Washington, D.C.: Doris Day Animal Foundation.

Saltaris, C. (2002). Psychopathy in juvenile offenders: Can temperament and attachment be considered as robust developmental precursors? *Clinical Psychology Review, 22*, 729–752.

Shapiro, K., Randour, M. L., Krinsk, S., & Wolf, J. (2014). *The assessment and treatment of children who abuse animals: The AniCare Child approach*. New York: Springer.

Shirtcliff, E. A., Vitacco, M. J., Graf, S. R., Gostisha, A. J., Merz, J. L., & Zahn-Waxler, C. (2009) Neurobiology of empathy and callousness: implications for the development of antisocial behavior. *Behavioral Science & Law, 27*(2), 137–71.

Simmons, C. A. & Lehmann, P. (2007). Exploring the link between pet abuse and controlling behaviors in violent relationships. *Journal of Interpersonal Violence, 22*, 1211–1222.

Soderstrom, H. (2003). Psychopathy as a disorder of empathy. *European Child & Adolescent Psychiatry, 12*, 249–252.

Sprinkle, J. E. (2008). Animals, empathy, and violence: Can animals be used to convey principles of prosocial behavior to children? *Youth Violence and Juvenile Justice, 6*, 47–58.

Thomas, S. P. (2003). Anger: The mismanaged emotion. *Dermatology Nursing, 15*, 351–357.

Thompson, K. L., & Gullone, E. (2006). An investigation into the association between the witnessing of animal abuse and adolescents' behavior toward animals. *Society & Animals, 14*, 221–243.

Tavris, C. (1982). *Anger: The misunderstood emotion.* New York: Simon & Schuster.

Tremblay, R. E., Vitaro, F., Nagin, D., Pagani, L. & Seguin, J. R. (2003). The Montreal longitudinal and experimental study: Rediscovering the power of descriptions. In T. P. Thornberry & M. D. Krohn (Eds.), *Taking stock of delinquency: An overview of findings from contemporary longitudinal studies* (pp. 205–254). New York: Kluwer Academic.

Tweed, R. G. & Dutton, D. G. (1998). A comparison of impulsive and instrumental subgroups of batterers. *Violence and Victims, 13,* 217–230.

Van den Berg, A. & Oei, T. L. (2009). Attachment and psychopathy in forensic patients. *Mental Health Review Journal, 14,* 40–51.

Vaughn, M. G., Fu, W., DeLisi, M., Beaver, K. M., Perron, B. E. (2009). Correlates of cruelty to animals in the United States: Results from the National Epidemiologic Survey on Alcohol and Related Conditions. *Journal of Psychiatric Research, 43,* 1213–1218.

Vaughn, M. G., Fu, Q., Beaver, K. M., DeLisi, M., Perron, B. E., & Howard, M. O. (2011). Effects of childhood adversity on bullying and cruelty to animals in the United States: Findings from a national sample. *Journal of Interpersonal Violence, 26,* 3509–3525.

Walters, G. D. (2013). Testing the specificity postulate of the violence graduation hypothesis: Meta-analyses of the animal cruelty-offending relationship. *Aggression and Violent Behavior, 18,* 797–802.

Walters, G. D., Frederick, A. A., & Schlauch, C. (2007). Postdicting arrests for proactive and reactive aggression with the PICTS Proactive and Reactive Composite Scales. *Journal of Interpersonal Violence, 22,* 1415–1430.

Walters, G. D. & Noon, A. (2015). Family context and externalizing correlates of childhood animal cruelty in adjudicated delinquents. *Journal of Interpersonal Violence, 30,* 1369–1386.

Walton-Moss, B. J., Manganello, J., Frye, V., & Campbell, J. D. (2005). Risk factors for intimate partner violence and associated injury among urban women. *Journal of Community Health, 30,* 377–389.

Weinshenker, N. J., & Siegel, A. (2002). Bimodal classification of aggression: Affective defense and predatory attack. *Aggression and Violent Behavior, 7,* 237–250.

Section V
Current and Controversial Topics

Chapter 17

Animal Cruelty and Reality Television: A Critical Review

Claire Molloy

Introduction

Popular media is central to the framing of public debates about animal cruelty (Molloy, 2011). Coverage of individual cruelty cases as well as commentary on animal advocacy, legislation, and policy indicate that news media continue to play a key role in shaping the public discourse on animal cruelty and abuse. Across other media channels, advocacy groups, welfare organizations, and campaigners make use of social media technologies which have facilitated the sharing of information about animal abuse, often including video material and other visual imagery. While campaigns against animal cruelty may benefit from social media sharing, at the same time, images and video of animal cruelty are also constructed for the purposes of entertainment and, in the case of "crush" films, even sexual pleasure for some viewers. Welfare campaigns and fetishistic sexual practices occupy polarized positions and illustrate extremes of difference in the use of depictions of animal cruelty. At the same time, the representation of animal cruelty in both of these cases relies on the authenticity of the depiction in the sense that both welfare campaign videos and crush movies, depict "real" rather than simulated or fictional animal cruelty. In the first case, animal cruelty is recorded for the purposes of documenting an incident or action, in what can be described as an evidential mode and the animal cruelty is not perpetrated for the purposes of the filming. In the case of "crush" films, the opposite is true and cruelty is intentionally inflicted for the purposes of being recorded, commodified, and distributed as fetishistic entertainment. These two examples can be located within existing common sense moral boundaries; one is disturbing but, arguably, necessary as evidence or information, while the other is alarming, deviant, and indefensible. For the purposes of this chapter, these examples mark out two points on a continuum of representations of animal cruelty. Somewhere along this continuum, mainstream television shows that depict animal cruelty for the purposes of general entertainment are also located and it is these programs which form the focus here.

This chapter examines syndicated television programs which depict animal cruelty. It locates their development in the reality television formats of the 1990s that grew out of the deregulation of the U.K. and U.S. television sector. Offering an overview of a history of reality-based animal programs, this chapter discusses their increasing popularity throughout the late 1990s and 2000s and examines the mixing of hospital and crime drama genre conventions with those of the documentary genre and investigative journalism. From these hybrid shows, a group of programs emerged which focus specifically on animal cruelty and the professionals involved in its investigation. Although there is a wide range of reality TV programs that depict aspects of animal cruelty, this chapter distinguishes a particular subset of these which demonstrate common structures, genre elements, narratives, and ideologies. Referred to as "animal cop shows" here, the discussion in this chapter examines how genre elements are combined in these programs. It analyzes their structure and seeks to explain how the organization of elements supports particular ideologies and moral boundaries. In doing so, this chapter examines the functions of animals and their suffering within reality television narratives. It concludes with a discussion of the questions raised by these programs, particularly in relation to the viewing pleasures they seek to engender.

Institutional Context

The 1980s and 1990s witnessed a proliferation of reality television shows devoted to animals, wildlife, and animal welfare. In the U.S., this type of programming emerged from a changing broadcasting industry, brought about by deregulation policies under the Reagan administration. The sector experienced major transformations with the launch of four new television networks, beginning with Fox in 1986 and followed by The WB, UPN, and PAX during the 1990s, as well as an increase in the take-up of cable and satellite television subscriptions. With the rapid increase in the number of networks in the 1990s, the television sector underwent fragmentation which manifested through the development of niche channels aimed at smaller, but more targeted, audience demographics. One impact of these changes was that competition for advertising revenue increased as it dispersed across the sector and advertisers took advantage of the new niche channels which gave them access to a more focused demographic. Cuts in advertising revenue forced cable and broadcasting to look for less costly forms of programming and so began the development of nonfiction reality formats with animal-based themes and content.

In the U.K., where animal television experienced growth in parallel with that of the U.S., deregulation of the broadcasting sector in the 1990s opened up the market and increased competition between public sector and commercial broadcasters. This led to pressure on the public service broadcaster from the then Conservative government to deliver more popular programming. The response from the BBC was similar to that of U.S. networks: the development of inexpensive factual programming and in particular reality formats which proved popular with audiences. From these formats, those that became known as "pet programmes" attracted significant viewing figures which peaked between 1995 and 1999 with, for instance, individual series such as *Animal Police* and *Animal Hospital* claiming audience shares of 24 and 43 percent, respectively (Hill, 2005, p. 149).

In 1996, a joint venture between Discovery and the BBC led to the launch of Animal Planet, a channel devoted to animal programming. The roots of this endeavor went back to the mid-1980s and the launch of the Discovery Channel in 1985 which had focused on science, natural history, and nature, programming that other networks considered unprofitable. Through deals with multisystem operators, Tele-Communications Inc. (TCI), Newhouse Broadcasting Corporation, Cox Cable Communications, and United Television Cable Corporation, Discovery was able to grow its U.S. subscriptions to 60.5

million by 1994 and was ranked, the same year, with CNN, ESPN, USA Network, TBS, and TNT, as one of the six most fully distributed networks in the country (Chris, 2006, p. 85). Discovery's focus on wildlife and nature programming proved profitable and led to expansion into global territories across Europe, Latin America, and Asia. The next stage of development involved product differentiation, central to which was the launch of Animal Planet, the channel created through the alliance with the BBC that gave the latter organization a twenty-percent share in the U.S. version of the network and a 50-percent interest in other markets (Chris, 2006, p. 91).

In 2006, the BBC sold back its interests in Animal Planet U.S. and, although it maintained a co-production agreement to produce programming until 2014, four years later, in 2010, also sold its 50-percent interest in non-U.S. markets to Discovery (BBC, 2010). During this time, Animal Planet's brand identity changed. Initially targeted at a broad family audience with what was regarded as "softer" animal programming than Discovery, in 2008, following disappointing ratings, Animal Planet was rebranded with a new identity and programming aimed at adults which featured fewer host-driven formats and an increase in "predation" programming. The rebranding of the channel was described in the company's press release as being expressed through "new graphics, a new feel and new sounds that bring out the raw, visceral emotion in the animal kingdom" (Animal Planet, 2008).

Cultural Context

Inasmuch as changes to broadcasting in the U.S. and U.K. created the industrial conditions which gave rise to the animal television boom of the 1990s, other changes, particularly the rapid growth of companion animal-keeping, provided subject matter for the early pet-related shows as well as the cultural context for their public reception. In the U.K., the dog population exceeded six million in 1984. It continued to show an increase year after year jumping from 6.3 million in 1985 to 6.9 million in 1986 and then to 7.2 million in 1987 (Pet Food Manufacturers' Association, 2004). Between 1988 and 1990, the number of dogs in the U.K. reached its peak at 7.4 million, showing a slight but steady decrease in the following five years, falling from 7.3 million in 1991 to 6.6 million in 1996 (Pet Food Manufacturers' Association, 2004). In 1998, numbers again increased to 6.9 million, but then continued to fall to 6.1 million in 2002 (Pet Food Manufacturers' Association, 2004). This change in the dog population did not signal an overall reduction in companion animal ownership however. In the same period of time, the U.K. cat population increased steadily from 5.9 million in 1984 to 7.2 million in 1994, exceeding, for the first time since records had been available, the dog population by 300,000 (Pet Food Manufacturers' Association, 2004). The numbers of cats continued to grow to eight million in 1998 and following three years when the population fluctuated, decreasing at one point to 7.5 million, numbers showed a dramatic rise to 9.2 million in 2003 and 9.6 million in 2004 (Pet Food Manufacturers' Association, 2004).

Despite fluctuations in the dog population, the U.K. pet food market has not reflected these trends, showing a year-on-year increase in value. For instance, in the period from 1990 to 2000, the value of the U.K. pet food market increased from £630.2 million to £808.4 million, with the most significant growth in value being in the "treats" market which grew from £68.6 million to £118.7 million (Pet Food Manufacturers' Association, 2008). This particular segment of the market showed even stronger growth in the next seven years increasing in value to £183 million in 2007 (Pet Food Manufacturers' Association,

2008). Not only are owners spending more money on their companion animals, they spend increasingly greater amounts on non-essential items. Unsurprisingly, given the increase in population, the market for cat food and cat treats also demonstrated similar rapidity of growth.

In the U.S., the dog population increased from 50 million (Hill, 2005) to 70 million (American Veterinary Medical Association, 2012) between 1981 and 2011 and the number of cats rocketed from 44 million to 74.1 million in the same time period. The American Pet Products Association (APPA) (American Pet Products Association, 2015) reports that over a twenty-year period from 1988, the percentage of U.S. households with companion animals increased from 56 percent to 65 percent, equating to 79.7 million American homes with a pet by 2015. This growth in the number of companion animals has been reflected in the value of the U.S. pet industry which has shown a year on year increase from $17 billion in 1994 to $60.59 (estimated) billion in 2015 (American Pet Products Association, 2015). The costs of pet ownership are reflected in the breakdown of basic annual expenses reported by the APPA National Pet Owners Survey which identifies that, on average, costs associated with maintaining the basic general welfare of a pet (veterinary visits and food) amounted to $1,055 for dogs and $840 for cats annually (2015–2016) (American Pet Products Association, 2015). Owners surveyed spent an additional $108 per year on dog treats and toys and $79 on the same types of items for cats. Other expenses included vitamins for dogs and cats with costs of $62 and $33 respectively per year and grooming costing a further $83 and $43 in annual expenditure (American Pet Products Association, 2015).

The growth in the pet industry suggests that we are willing to make greater financial investments in our relationships with companion animals and this may also indicate an increased emotional investment. Indeed, it is now widely acknowledged that companion animals "confer many social, physical, and psychological benefits" providing love, affection, security, and protection, and pet ownership is "associated with better overall physical health" (Hunt, Al-Awadi, & Johnson, 2008, p. 110). Yet Annette Hill points out that there is a paradox in the changing attitudes towards companion animals. She writes: "Alongside changes in social attitudes to pets from playthings to companions, there has also been an increase in animal rescue organizations in Western society" (Hill, 2005, p. 141). For Hill, this growth in rescue organizations signals an inconsistency in the treatment of pets which are receiving ever-greater financial investment but at the same time remain "throwaway objects to be discarded when they become inconvenient or cease to give pleasure" (Garner as cited in Hill, 2005, p. 142). It is precisely this ambiguity in the human–companion-animal bond which reality animal programming exploits. Through various techniques which will be discussed within this chapter, the paradoxical conditions of companion animal ownership are reorganized through binaries of good and bad, victim and abuser, innocence and guilt.

Reality Television

As this chapter locates the depiction of animal cruelty within what is broadly termed "reality television," it is useful to first examine what this general category of programming encompasses. In describing its range and scope, Annette Hill explains: "There are a variety of styles and techniques associated with reality TV, such as non-professional actors, unscripted dialogue, surveillance footage, hand-held cameras, seeing events unfold as they were happening in front of the camera" (Hill, 2005, p. 41). Hill's explanation attends to the apparently factual basis of reality television which draws on the aesthetics and techniques of documentary filmmaking to construct a sense of immediacy and, supposedly, offer unmediated depictions of reality. However, the idea that reality television can capture or even attempt to depict "reality" is open to challenge. As Richard Kilborn and John Izod suggest, "all the conventions that separate documentary from fiction (including those governing viewers' expectations) come under pressure in reality programming, which depends for some of its impact on blurring the boundaries" (Kilborn & Izod, 1997, p. 134). Although writing at a comparatively early point in the history of reality television, Kilborn and Izod's point remains important in that they draw attention to the merging of documentary and fiction conventions in ways that lead to questions about the extent to which this type of programming can reveal "real life." To complicate matters further, reality TV is not a straightforward hybrid of documentary and fiction. Indeed, it draws from an expansive range of genre conventions. John Corner (2000), for instance, argues that reality TV formats have been influenced by soap operas, talk shows, and game shows, while other scholars examine the subgenres within reality TV to find that they borrow from tabloid news, investigative journalism, and advice programs. This highly complex and wide-ranging set of influences leads Hill (2005) to suggest, quite rightly, that "[s]cholars of popular factual television can be in danger of genre overload when defining the reality genre" (p. 49). She concludes that:

> There is no one definition of reality programming, but many, competing definitions of what has come to be called the reality genre. This is because the reality genre is made of a number of distinctive and historically based television genres, such as lifestyle, or documentary. (Hill, 2005, p. 55)

Although there is no single overarching definition which scholars can agree upon, there are attempts to identify the common characteristics that tie together various iterations of the genre. In trying to define the boundaries of what constitutes reality television, Anita Biressi and Heather Nunn (2005) propose that "as a broad category reality genres […] may be said to include video diaries, game shows […], talent shows, talk shows, observational documentaries, dramatic reconstructions and CCTV and camcorder-based programming such as law and order and emergency services programming" (p. 10). The common aspects of this variety of programming they note are that it revolves around "an emphasis on the representation of ordinary people and allegedly unscripted or spontaneous moments that supposedly reveal unmediated reality" (pp. 10–11). Rather than classify programs as either fact or fiction, Hill (2005, pp. 55–56) suggests that it is more appropriate to think of reality television as existing on a continuum which is judged, in terms of its "reality" by the audience. Hill (2005, pp. 61–62) argues:

> For television audiences, the criteria applied to documentary are closely connected with expectations about the accuracy and impartiality of television news. When viewers come to watch reality television these expectations do not disappear. Viewers are most likely to trust the evidential power of reality TV when the factual footage is closest to footage viewers associate with news, or investigative journalism.

The question of audience trust is an interesting one. Given that audiences are increasingly aware of how shows are produced and that there is a detectable cynicism toward factual media, arguably due to reality TV "fatigue," it is salient to this discussion to consider the findings of audience studies carried out in 2010. When respondents were asked to comment on the perceived accuracy of nature and wildlife programs, 91 percent regarded such programs as accurate "always or most of the time" (The Office of Communications as cited in Molloy, 2011, p. 75). Of those, 40 percent considered nature programs to be "always" accurate, a figure which can be usefully compared with only 24 percent of respondents who believed that the same could be said for news programs (Molloy, 2011,

p. 75). These figures are important as they suggest that factual television programs which depict animals have greater levels of perceived truth. In answering why this should be the case, it is possible to speculate that viewers believe that humans, being aware of cameras, will be more inclined to regulate their behavior accordingly; animals, on the other hand, have no such sense and therefore their actions are judged to be "real" and their depiction in television shows perceived to have greater accuracy. This would explain why audiences react so vehemently when wildlife films and natural history documentaries are revealed to have "faked" scenes (Molloy, 2011). Such revelations undercut the sense of access to the unmediated reality of animals' lives which factual programming works so hard to construct. Yet, while this type of programming relies on documentary techniques to enhance the levels of perceived truth for viewers, wildlife television programs have, since the 1990s, blurred genre boundaries by, for instance, mixing the conventions of soap opera formats with those of natural history documentaries to produce new types of programming, such as *Big Cat Diary* and *Meerkat Manor*, as a way to address declining audience numbers (Molloy, 2011). It is thus possible to discern, across animal programming, a move since the 1980s towards genre hybridity and a continual reworking of the boundaries between fact and entertainment (Molloy, 2011). Into this wider mix of hybrid animal programs are animals cop shows, a group of popular animal programs distinguished by their focus on investigating and finding evidence of animal cruelty and their use of techniques associated with investigative journalism. This potent combination of rescue narrative and investigation presented in an evidentiary mode substantially enhances the "reality" of animal cop shows. Moreover, because the evidence is most often an animal or an animal's body which is located within a discourse of welfare, this further emphasizes the "real" dimension of the program. In this sense, the visual documenting of animal suffering is suffused with an immediacy and sense of stark realism that is unlikely to be fabricated. As has been argued elsewhere, "authenticity [is] framed by the expectations that genre inheres within the audience" (Molloy, 2011, p. 82). It is thus important to identify the extent to which the genre hybridity of animal cop shows frames viewer understanding of animal cruelty, and how this is managed through associations with other television genres.

Genre Hybrids

Animal programming exists as various reality television formats, although the depiction of animal suffering tends to be clustered within magazine-format shows based around crime and health stories which mix the conventions of documentary and investigative journalism with those of hospital and police dramas. In the case of animal reality television, programs that deal with issues of animal health, cruelty, and abuse focus primarily on the work of vets, animal welfare organizations, police, enforcement agents, and, to a lesser extent, other emergency services. These programs share characteristics with crime, rescue, and law and order shows that have been popular in both the U.S. and the U.K., early forms of which attracted large audiences and included *America's Most Wanted* (Fox, 1988–2011), *Rescue 911* (CBS, 1989–1996), and *Cops* (Fox 1991–present) (Biressi & Nunn, 2005). In the U.K., similar police and emergency service programs included *Emergency 999* (BBC, 1992–2003) and *Police, Camera, Action* (ITC, 1994–2002). Richard Kilborn (2003) refers to this type of format as the "Accident and Emergency strand" of reality television and he notes that its development has been driven by the need to capture the attention of channel-hopping audiences. He proposes: "There is evidence to suggest that broadcasters are seeking ever more sensational events or occurrences to capture the attention of the action-hungry viewer" (Kilborn, 2003, p. 57). Biressi and Nunn (2005, p.120) also comment on the spectacular qualities of the crime entertainment genre noting that since the 1990s:

> They constitute a new spectacle of criminality in which it is not the punishment but the scene [...] of the crime itself which is present and made highly visible in the public sphere. Criminality, which we would expect to be hidden from view, is made visible and frequently seen to be dramatic, apparently random and unprovoked.

Police and emergency service formats thus tend towards action-oriented spectacle which foregrounds a crime or accident, often in graphic detail. In addressing a popular audience, however, the format must find a reassuring resolution to what are presented as unpredictable, risky events and activities. As Kilborn (2003, p. 56) writes:

> This is achieved either by getting the avuncular anchorperson to voice words of reassurance following the mayhem which the viewers have witnessed or it may involve focusing on the competence and efficiency displayed by the emergency services in restoring, however briefly, order to a seemingly chaotic world.

Kilborn's description reflects the conventions of emergency service and animal rescue programs in the U.K. where a presenter is on location with the vet or animal welfare officer. Programs within this category would include *Animal 24:7* and the U.K. program which first demonstrated the huge popular appeal of such formats, *Animal Hospital*. In the case of U.S. reality formats, particularly those that deal with animal cruelty investigations, a voiceover commentary replaces the presenter and thus provides the reassurance to which Kilborn refers. In addition to a voiceover, emergency service formats utilize personnel to provide expert statements to guide the viewers' understanding of the events. A program such as *Wild Rescues* (1997—2002), for example, reconstructs dramatic rescue narratives which include animals, either as victims or rescuers, using news footage, reconstructions of events, eyewitness accounts, expert interviews, and a voiceover. The range of experts in *Wild Rescues* is broad and incorporates vets, zoo workers, police, and other emergency services personnel. While stories of animal cruelty are included in a program such as this, it is the drama of the rescue which is central to the narrative and not the cruelty itself. For example, an episode from 2001 reconstructs the story of a dog shot with a BB gun, hit by a car, and then thrown from a bridge, beginning from the point when she is discovered by rescue workers. The storyline makes use of news footage of the rescue, interviews with an animal control officer, a vet, and the woman who later adopts the dog, and a reconstruction of the emergency call being received at the Los Angeles Animal Control Center. The narrative focuses mainly on the dramatic rescue, concluding the storyline with the subsequent successful adoption of the still partly-paralyzed dog. In this storyline, there is no investigation of the cruelty and, although there is an interview with an animal control officer, the account he gives is in relation to the rescue, how it was achieved, and the difficulties involved in getting the dog out of a flood control channel beneath a bridge. The account of the abuse inflicted on the dog is given by a vet who refers to x-rays to point out where BB gun pellets had been lodged in the dog's body. Each episode of *Wild Rescues* has multiple stories and, in this case, the second concerns the rescue of animals from a pet shop fire, a narrative which has nothing to do with animal cruelty, and the third covers the story of two koalas stolen from the San Francisco Zoo. Thus, it is not the purpose of these shows to investigate cruelty and for these reasons, they borrow more from accident and emergency reconstruction shows and less from the genre elements associated with, for example, investigative journalism.

According to Richard Kilborn, the reconstruction of events exemplifies the extent to which reality television blurs the boundaries between fact and fiction, and he notes that this technique lends itself to criticisms that such shows are "dramatically entertaining rather than factually enlightening" (Kilborn, 2003, p. 72). He proposes that

> [t]he dramatic reconstruction of incidents and events certainly leaves the way open for various kinds of fictional embellishment, and it is this which has led to expressions of disquiet that the boundaries between factual and fictional genres will become progressively more blurred. (Kilborn, 2003, p. 72)

A program such as *Wild Rescues* thus deals with themes of endangerment, heroism, and rescue by re-constructing the events in such a way as to emphasize the drama, action, and a "race against time." In this sense, the rescue narrative is always time-sensitive and derives much of its drama from constant reminders that a failure to rescue within a particular time period will result in tragedy.

The reconstruction of events in *Wild Rescues* is somewhat different from the approach taken in "animal cop" shows, examples of which premiered on Animal Planet and include: *Animal Precinct* (US, 2001–2008), *Animal Cops: Houston* (US, 2003–present), *Animal Cops: Detroit* (US, 2002–2008), *Animal Cops: Philadelphia* (US, 2009–present), *Animal Cops: San Francisco* (US, 2005), *Animal Cops: South Africa* (US, 2008), *Animal Cops: Phoenix* (US, 2008), *Animal Cops: Miami* (US, 2010–present) and *Miami Animal Police* (US, 2004–2010). Also within this genre is *Philly Undercover* (US, 2012), which premiered on the cable/satellite channel Nat Geo WILD and features five of the law enforcement agents who also appear in *Animal Cops: Philadelphia*. This group of programs follows animal cruelty investigators, animal services personnel, and law enforcement officers, who act as the expert witnesses at the scene and are a crucial aspect of the genre.

Animal Cop Shows: Voiceovers

Animal cop shows borrow techniques from investigative journalism, most notably in the use of footage that is shot as events occur and which Kilborn refers to as "actuality footage," noting that it is "the most highly prized asset" for reality TV producers (Kilborn, 2003, p.71). The viewer accompanies the officer as the events unfold, experiencing the same disturbing incidents as the professionals, the experience framed by voiceover narration and expert on-location interview material. After an event, an officer will often provide a straight-to-camera interview where the details of the cruelty are explained and he or she may speculate about the eventual outcomes for the animal and for the human responsible for the cruel action.

Each of the programs uses a voiceover, a documentary technique which reality television borrows "to persuade the viewer that this is an authoritative, credible account of events" (Kilborn, 2003, p. 117). Kilborn notes that:

> In as far as it usually seeks to communicate a single perspective on events, the commentary has an ideological significance in that it frequently presents an account which reflects a particular value system or set of beliefs. Viewers are thus guided or nudged into putting a particular interpretation on the account that is rendered.
>
> (Kilborn, 2003, p. 117)

The authoritative voiceover used in animal cop shows is always male, maintaining a gendered ideology within which masculinity is associated with seriousness and rational judgment. Gender operates through binaries in which, by contrast, femininity is more often associated with emotion and these dualisms are particularly evident when related to discussions about animals and animal treatment. As Carol J. Adams writes:

> Rationality became associated with being male and human and white. Linked with women, people of color, animals and nature, feelings became suspect. One reason "sympathy" has faced a difficult time being recognized as an ethical position is its association with the body and women. (Adams, 2004, p. 40)

The animal cop show voiceover maintains the narrative flow, giving the audience clear cues about the time of day and location, names the officers (and other personnel) involved, offers context for the scene or event the viewer is about to witness, gives details about the human abuser, explicates particular points of law, and gives a summary of events when returning to an earlier storyline or after an advertising break. The male voiceover commentary thus performs a central ideological function through a range of techniques. Yet animal cop shows are constructed in such a way as to elicit emotional responses from the audience, albeit ones of horror, disgust, or shock, as well as sympathy for the animals. The male voiceover is thus one of the ways in which the program balances the drama of the events and maintains its links to "serious" documentary as well as cultural associations which naturalize the entanglement of masculinity with law enforcement. In this sense, Adams' comments about male/female dualisms are still pertinent and the male voiceover is used as an authoritative rational director which cues the audience response in ways that reinforce particular moral and therefore ideological boundaries.

Animal Cop Shows: Titles

The title sequences of these series borrow elements from police and crime dramas to situate the viewers' understanding of the show within the first few moments. By providing genre cues, titles perform an important function in that they organize the expectations of an audience and, in the case of reality formats, they often signal that risk and danger are part of everyday life and contemporary society. For instance, during the titles for *Philly Undercover* a voiceover informs the viewer that "every day these men and women lay their lives on the line" while the viewer is confronted with images of dogs in the city, on the streets, in apartments, and chained up in yards. The urban imagery that accompanies the voiceover thus reinforces the sense of the "everyday" which pervades these programs. The presenter of the U.K. program *Animal 24:7* who introduces each episode from a different outside location also emphasizes that animal cruelty and danger is ever-present saying:

> Britain's animals are under threat. All too often our wildlife and domestic pets are the victims of cruelty, persecution, and neglect. Fighting to save them is a dedicated band of people trying to protect and care for them right around the clock. This is Animal 24:7.

Title sequences for animal cop programs convey the idea that the observing camera will capture evidence of crime, deviancy, abuse, and cruelty, and that viewers will witness aspects of life that would otherwise remain hidden from them, seen only by professionals in the course of their official duties. This may suggest one appeal for audiences in that these programs promise viewers something which they should not ordinarily witness. *Animal Precinct* reinforces this notion, beginning with the caution "due to the graphic nature of this program, viewer discretion is advised," the words "graphic nature" and "viewer discretion" being twice the size of the other text. Behind the words, angular blue graphic shapes flash across the screen, simulating the flashing lightbars of a police vehicle, as the program title flashes across different segments of the screen in a military stencil font, signifying the tough, hard-hitting tone and content of the program. The title music, in a minor key, is electronic with a low pulsating beat that communicates a sense of urgency. An image of a law enforcement pursuit vehicle leaving a garage with sirens blaring is accompanied by the introductory voiceover saying "coming up on Animal Precinct" followed by a teaser segment comprised of one or two action shots from each of the storylines included in that episode. This is followed by the full title sequence in which a blue colorized shot of the city skyline is accompanied by a voiceover and simultaneous onscreen text which say: "New York City; eight million people; five million pets; fifteen animal cruelty agents with full police powers. Welcome to the Animal Precinct." The remainder of the title sequence is comprised of shots of iconic New York landmarks, images of the agents, pursuit vehicles, and the program title in the military stencil font.

Utilizing the same visual signifiers as *Animal Precinct*, *Animal Cops: Philadelphia* also has an on-screen warning in the opening title sequence which states, "Due to the graphic nature of this program viewer discretion is advised." A Humane Society Police badge is superimposed over the cityscape which dissolves into red flashing siren lights and then into a close-up of the badge. A low-frequency bass note combined with a high-pitched strings sound accompanies the warning and the male voiceover which says: "coming up on Animal Cops, Philadelphia." A short teaser segment offers a few shots of the animal cruelty cases which will be featured in the show. This is followed by the remainder of the title sequence which uses red colorized city images, the red flashing siren lights, images of individual enforcement agents, shots of individual animals whose stories are featured in the series, images of laboratory equipment and x-rays, and superimposed text taken from warrants and official reports. The sequence ends with a shot of the agents walking, in a group, towards the camera, the wings of a bird and the show's title in which the "o" of Cops has been replaced by the Humane Society Police badge.

By way of a comparison, *Miami Animal Police* is somewhat different in tone due primarily to its setting in Miami. For this reason, while *Animal Cops: Philadelphia* and *Animal Precinct* use primary colors (red and blue) against a dark background to recall the conventions of crime drama and the notion that crime happens in the metaphoric shadowy underbelly of society, *Miami Animal Police*, by contrast, communicates its sense of place by having titles which are bright and bold, signifying a warmer sunnier climate. Nonetheless, the titles remain strongly tied to the conventions of other cop shows using iconic law enforcement imagery; *Miami Animal Police* also opens with the image of police badge, the series title in gold and blue with a male voiceover which says, "On this edition of Miami animal police," followed by the preview of the storylines to be featured, although in this case, an accompanying voiceover provides a headline-style summary for each. A wide shot pulls out to reveal the Miami waterfront followed by images of a young woman in shorts walking away from the camera, a surfer, the Miami Beach welcome sign, a young man doing pull-ups, a young woman in a white thong bikini, a young man skating, angled shots of beachfront hotels, and images of people sunbathing and playing volleyball on the beach. The sense of place is, again, clearly signaled by this imagery which, to this point, has not included a single image of a nonhuman animal. Instead the title sequence depicts beautiful people in a beautiful setting, genre elements which are associated, for instance, with the police drama series *Miami Vice* (1984–1990). A voiceover identifies the show's location and the scale of the region (i.e., "2,000 square miles") covered by the officers. The title sequence then continues with a montage of images of animals many of which (a monkey, an iguana, a giant tortoise, a panther, a puma, an alligator, and a snake) can be described as exotic when compared with the dogs, cats, horses, and cockerels which feature in the title sequences of other animal cop shows. Exterior shots of the Miami-Dade Police Department Animal Services building come after the animal images and the voiceover explains that there are "millions of creatures, from panthers to pythons, but just one police animal services unit dedicated to animal emergencies." As in other series, the commentary places emphasis on the immense volume of work the officers deal with, explaining that "just twenty animal control officers respond to more than 150 calls each day, from dogs on the loose to gators on the highway […]" The show's theme music has a distinct calypso feel to it and features the same instrumentation as the title music for *Miami Vice*.

As this analysis of three different titles sequences illustrates, when it comes to constructing audience expectations, genre elements borrowed from successful police drama shows are woven throughout the title sequences of animal cop reality shows. The law enforcement vehicle leaving the garage in the *Animal Precinct* titles is a reference to the same iconic shot at the beginning of *Hill Street Blues* (1981–1987) and the superimposed text from official documents and siren flashes in *Animal Cops: Philadelphia* bears strong similarities with the graphics that feature in the *CSI: New York* (2004–present) titles. For the U.K. program *Animal 24:7*, the title sequence uses digital style numerals which pulse across the screen combined with high energy title music, elements in common with the title sequence for the series *24* (2001–2010).

These animal cop show titles are significant in that they signal to viewers how they should engage with the program content. The title sequences leave the viewer with little doubt about the moral boundaries and socially acceptable behavior which will frame the narrative. In drawing on the well-established conventions of police dramas, the show thus marks out a clear delineation between good and bad, innocence and guilt, and establishes the agent or officer as "a personal representative of legality, against whom the otherness of crime and its perpetrators are measured" (Bignell, 2004, p. 118). By borrowing signifiers of police crime drama, particularly the images of police badges as well as the intertextual references to other well established drama series, the genre conventions used in animal cop titles close down the range of possible interpretations available to the viewer from the outset. In other words, as Helen Fulton proposes, "there are ideological effects of television genre, to the extent that genre conventions naturalize or normalize particular ways of seeing the world and provide limits to the interpretive context available to the audience" (Fulton, 2005, p. 133).

Animal Cop Shows: Structure and Binaries

In the case of police crime drama, the central characters must have an "innate sense of justice" (Bignell, 2005, p. 132). Jonathan Bignell (2005, p. 132) writes that, "success in catching criminals and doing the right thing is proof of their efficiency and the appropriateness of the ideologies that underlie their actions." By adopting genre elements of crime drama series, animal cop shows naturalize the position of the investigator as representing authority and justice but, like many other reality police programs, the shows do not tend to follow a storyline through to a conviction, a convention that is signaled by disclaimers in the end credits of, for instance, *Animal Cops: Philadelphia* which state: "Individuals seen under investigation or arrest in the program [...] are presumed innocent until proven otherwise in a court of law and may be cleared of any and all charges." In this sense, the programs depict the discovery of cruelty or neglect and the viewer bears witness to the outcome of that cruelty which is evident in the situation or condition of the animal. With little or no opportunity for an investigation into the human behavior or context that has led to the animal's situation, the human owners are already classified as guilty through the binaries which structure the narratives. Writing about police reality shows, Bignell notes a similar structuring binary in which those who are depicted in the storylines are "already categorized as potentially deviant" leading to "a danger of a rush to judgement [sic] in this television form" (Bignell, 2005, p. 133). The points that Bignell makes in relation to police reality shows are thus similarly applicable to animal cop shows and he writes: "Explanation, justification, background and context are all factors which in a court of law might either excuse or at least explain such action, but in reality TV the moment of seeing is simultaneously a moment of judging" (Bignell, 2005, p. 133).

The immediacy of judgment on the part of the viewer is aided by the absence of an accused person which, in animal cop shows, is particularly prevalent in cases of animal abandonment. Where a perpetrator is filmed, his or her presence is managed by particular televisual codes which include: obscuring their faces; only broadcasting one side of a conversation, interview, or phone call between an investigator and a person accused of cruelty; and, using the voiceover commentary to summarize the reasons given by an accused person for his or her actions. For example, an abandonment storyline in an episode of *Animal Cops: Houston* includes scenes in which a man accused of leaving his three parrots without adequate care, food, or water is filmed appearing at the hearing to determine who will take custody of the birds, the judge having to make a decision as to whether the birds should be returned to the original owner or given to the Society for the Prevention of Cruelty to Animals (SPCA). The voiceover introduces the scene as a case of abandonment, leaving the viewer in no doubt as to the man's guilt, even before the judge has made his ruling. The man's face is obscured throughout the hearing and his voice is only audible when confronted with a picture of an African Grey who has plucked out her own feathers. At this point, the owner states that the feather-plucking condition is common. The voiceover then summarizes the man's defense of his actions saying "the owner strongly denies neglect, ... he *says* he'd been working out of town but made arrangements for the birds to be fed in his absence." The scene in the courthouse ends with the judge awarding the birds to the SPCA and the investigators outside the courthouse being interviewed, pleased with the result. The point here is that the program is structured in such a way as to exclude ambiguity. The viewer does not hear or see the owner make his defense and therefore cannot make any judgment based on the believability of the man's tone, gesture, or explanation. The owner is present but because his face is obscured and his statements summarized by the voiceover, his presence is marked by televisual codes which construct him through forms of absence, that is, an absence of gesture and voice, elements which could be used by viewers to reach their own conclusions about the owner's innocence or guilt. The voices which predominate throughout the scene are those of the judge, the investigators, the Assistant County Attorney (on behalf of the SPCA), and the voiceover. In this way, while depicting the exercise of justice, the program leaves no room for the viewer to question decisions that have been made nor the ideology which underpins them.

The programs are structured, through the generic conventions of the police drama, in such a way as to suggest that the viewer's judgment is straightforward. Biressi and Nunn (2005) summarize the criticisms of reality crime shows when they write:

As a form of "tabloid television" they represent all that is generally condemned in popular culture; tending towards the reactionary and the retributive, exciting, exploitative, voyeuristic and entertaining. […] And the informational content, such as it is, is expressed within "common sense" discourses about justice and law and order that produce a knowledge about victimhood and criminality which is usually retributive and highly conservative. (p. 121)

There are some cases which are do not appear to be dealt with in this way, however, and it is worthwhile considering how these are structured and ideologically managed. These are the cases in which the investigating officer makes the decision not to cite owners for cruelty on the basis that they lack education or are living in extreme poverty. Although seldom, such incidences have their part to play in animal cop show narratives. For instance, in an episode of *Animal Cops: Philadelphia*, a dog is found to be living under a house. The first shot of the dog reveals that she is severely underweight, and has patches of missing hair and bleeding sores. The voiceover confirms that she has a skin condition and that her only shelter is a "hole in the wall." A discussion between the Pennsylvania Society for the Prevention of Cruelty to Animals (PSPCA) officer and the owner confirms that the owner cannot afford to take the dog, named Butter, to a vet for treatment. The voiceover explains that the owner loves his dog, but cannot afford her care. The owner agrees to surrender his dog into the care of the PSPCA, accompanied by a shot of him stroking the dog who looks upwards with her tail wagging, a visual confirmation for the viewer that a bond exists between owner and dog. In an interview at the location, the officer explains that the owner "just doesn't know" and rather than fine him, he will educate the owner. A shot of the outside of the house confirms the officer's claim that the owner is so poor that he has plastic where the windows should be. The education takes the form of an explanation by the officer that a dog "is a living thing that has to be taken to the vet," which is accompanied by close-ups of the dog's face looking bewildered. The voiceover informs the viewer that, although Butter's condition is such that the owner *could* be cited for cruelty, "in a case like this, owners need education not punishment," and as the door of the PSPCA van is closed on Butter, concludes: "Officers for humane law enforcement have to make difficult decisions every day. In this case, Smith is confident he made the right call." Throughout the segment, although the face of the owner is obscured, conversations between him and the officer are shown. A shot of the owner petting the dog and saying, on camera, that he loves her are combined with imagery of a dilapidated house and area. While the voiceover is clear that the dog's condition warrants the charge of cruelty, the officer, representing the benevolent face of humane law enforcement, makes, what is suggested by the voiceover to be, a difficult decision. In this case, the context for the cruelty is easily communicated to the viewer. By presenting the viewer with what seems to be a moral dilemma, the sequence is constructed in such a way as to delineate between "poor people" who love their dogs and people who abuse animals without reason. The audience is not given any additional information about the owners' circumstances and, from what has been depicted, can only assign them with the identity of poor and uneducated. In much the same way that the case of the owner of the abandoned parrots was structured through binaries of guilt and innocence by limiting the amount of information available to the audience, in the case of Butter the emaciated dog, the viewer has only minimal context on which to base a judgment about the owner. Because of the way in which cases are presented as self-evident, this style of animal cop programming is thus open to similar criticisms as other tabloid media, in that it lacks complexity, it structures storylines through easily understood binary oppositions of guilt and innocence, and it mixes dramatic and documentary elements to maximize popular appeal and spectacle.

Visual Evidence

Animal cop shows use a magazine format which deals with multiple storylines throughout the course of each episode. *Animal Cops: Houston* is typical in this regard. Each episode follows a similar structure that begins with the title sequence and a male voice commentary which states the location (Houston), gives the human population figures, introduces the Houston SPCA, and the number of cruelty cases reported each year (around 9,500). With the context set, the first storyline and the investigating officer involved are introduced. Onscreen graphics confirm the investigator's name and he or she gives a short interview to provide details about the first case. The first storyline will reach a mini-cliffhanger, for instance, at the point in the narrative where the officer has brought an injured animal to a vet or an investigator has to leave and return to a location on another day. The narrator may reinforce the dramatic tension by making some reference to the need to return to the storyline later to discover the outcome for the animal.

Changes in music and location signal the start of additional storylines which are constructed as if they are unfolding in parallel. In much the same way as the first storyline, the investigators will give their impressions of the situation to an unseen interviewer providing an expert commentary at the location. This narrative line is then suspended at a point designed to encourage the viewer to continue watching as the program alternates between different cases. Each storyline appears to run in parallel and even though incidents may not have actually occurred on the same day, the program is structured in such a way as to organize the narrative flow around a logical chronology. Thus, the narrator links between segments by using phrases such as "back at the [location]...," "just across town...," or "in another part of the city..." to relate the events to each other in terms of time and space. A single program will thus be comprised of four or five different storylines, each of which is suspended and returned to during the show, although one story, usually the most dramatic, will have more screen time than the others with multiple mini-cliffhangers to increase the tension. A positive resolution to at least one story usually concludes the program prior to the end credits.

Storylines involving dogs are the most common across animal cop shows, although *Animal Cops: Miami* is distinguished from other programs by the number of storylines involving alligators, a characteristic of the show which is signaled in the opening titles. The types of cruelty cases depicted vary across series with a notably high frequency of stories which deal with abandonment, neglect, animal hoarding, and animal fighting. In addition to the voiceover, investigators also play a pivotal role in discriminating between innocence and guilt and in guiding viewers' understanding of what constitutes criminality and animal cruelty. The gathering of evidence is central to this and is one further convention shared between animal cop shows and crime drama. In dogfighting cases, the narrative often relies on the investigator as a central character to give order and meaning to the imagery set before the viewer. It may not be immediately apparent to the viewer that the dogs depicted in a storyline about dogfighting are the victims of cruelty, particularly if they seem in apparent good condition and wagging their tails.

A case in point is included in an episode of *Animal Cops: Houston*, in which the program follows humane society officers and police as they raid a pit-bull training camp. The electronic music which accompanies the officers' briefing is slow and ominous. Officers' faces are obscured and the camera shots frame them in such a way as to show their bodies and not their faces, reinforcing the need for their identities to remain secret, emphasizing the danger and risk they are about to face, and increasing the narrative tension. The camerawork is loose and handheld, the zooms and pans are uneven, and shots are not fully focused. These are all technical signifiers of the documenting of events as they unfold and connote actuality footage and a sense of immediacy. The voiceover quantifies the danger of the operation, explaining that the owners of the property to be raided have firearms and are also involved in dealing crack cocaine. An interview with an investigator at the scene picks up the storyline and explains the procedures being followed. A police officer is interviewed and his comments are matched by visual evidence of shotguns being removed from the property, as well as syringes and different sized bottles of fluid which are explained as being "used for the dogs." A wide shot of the property shows multiple wooden dog houses, large basins of water, and dogs tethered to the kennels on chains. This cuts to a close up of a dog on top of a wooden table, a dog in a kennel, and a dog straining of the end of a chain. The voiceover identifies the type of dog being depicted, confirming that "there are pit-bulls chained up everywhere." Up to this point, the images of the dogs do not indicate that any mistreatment has taken place, however, the sequence is edited in such a way that—when the voiceover says "the discovery comes as a shock even to experienced officers […]"—on the word "shock," the shot cuts to an image of a chained dog whose front legs appear to be severely deformed. An officer then explains that one of the dog's legs is broken and that the dog is unable to walk properly. As he describes the dog's condition, the camera cuts back to a wide shot of the dog to reinforce the description and provide visual verification of the injuries. This is followed by a close-up of the dog's broken leg, which pans to his head before cutting back to the shocked officer saying "look at him, look at him." In this way, the viewer appears to be invited to look, although the structure of the program and the number of close-ups effectively give audiences no choice but to look. There is thus a blurring of the line between providing the viewer with evidence to support the moral ideology of the show and the construction of suffering as a spectacle.

If evidence is associated with forms of objective observation, then it is also the case that spectacle is aligned with voyeuristic processes of looking. There are then distinctions to be made between the different types of "looking" in which these programs encourage a viewer to engage. The depiction of animal suffering is one, if not the most important, element of the program. Indeed, animal suffering is a generic element in the sense that it distinguishes animal cop shows from other police or emergency services programs. Within these shows, the animals thus have a number of functions: they are the "evidence" of cruelty; they are a visual spectacle of suffering; and, they can be main characters in the narrative. Because suffering is so central to these programs, aspects of health-based reality shows also inform animal program formats. The shows thus add to the mix elements of medical dramas to tell stories which focus on trauma, tragedy, and transformation (Hill, 2005). In noting that this type of programming often has a moral agenda, Annette Hill (2005, p. 151) writes:

> The dramatic formula of health-based reality programmes—definition, prevention and treatment of illness—would suggest that the transformative characteristics of such programmes primarily relate to an ethics of care. In pet programmes, the transformation is provided within the narrative arc, so that critical illness leads to recovery and recovery affirms a community of care, in the particular instance a community of animals, vets, and their owners, but in the wider sense a community of carers and dependents.

Many animal cop shows utilize a similar narrative arc wherein animal victims are depicted as suffering, are rescued, and receive veterinary care, and the decision is then made to either rehome or euthanize them. In cases where animals are rehomed, their bodily transformation is central to the narrative arc which utilizes the "before and after" convention of makeover shows to more fully illustrate the difference between a suffering abused animal and a healthy well-cared-for animal. Those humans involved in that transformation—investigators, vets, and adoptive owners—are thus established by the narrative as the community of carers, a community the intended viewer can identify with. These programs thus function to reassure viewers that their own practices and human-animal relationships are aligned with those of a just and caring community. At the same time, this identification reinforces shared ideological positions and moral boundaries.

Conclusion

Viewers are not offered complex moral dilemmas in these shows. On the contrary, as far as possible, any moral ambiguity is removed and the narrative is tightly structured through binaries such as good and bad, guilt and innocence, to leave little space for alternative readings of any of the situations. Animals are the subjects of these stories and thus the narration and expert commentary become especially important in that they frame the representations, providing important information about each animal's condition and an assessment of how the animal feel. In this way, while images may depict the severity of an animal's state of health, using close-ups of wounds, emaciated bodies, broken limbs, sores, and scars, humans speak on its behalf, guiding the viewer as to the appropriate level of concern and serving to heighten tension at particular moments in the narrative. Suffering as a visual spectacle is managed through this framing to elicit an affective response. Such framing is especially important if the intention is to trigger compassion on the part of the viewer. As Keith Tester writes, "compassion requires that individual actors orient themselves towards others and, in particular, towards what others appear to be experiencing" (Tester, 2001, pp. 64–65). Tester proposes that compassion is a moral sensibility that "means an orientation towards others to work out what ought to be done, and if those others provide no clues or no incitement then it is possible to believe that nothing needs to be done" (Tester, 2001, p. 65). Although Tester writes specifically about media depictions of human suffering, his point can be applied to animal suffering and particularly to the case of wild animals whose condition or pain may not be immediately apparent. It is common in animal programs for a vet to offer an expert commentary and point out that, for reasons of self-preservation, a wild animal will often not signal its suffering, an action which would alert potential predators. In this way, the viewer is invited to reorient his or her response to the visual depiction of the animal whose suffering may be hidden and only made "visible" through the description offered by the narration and expert comment. As Tester suggests, compassion "emphasizes attending to others and implies that the individual need feel no ethical or moral concerns all the time that others are not seen to be suffering or miserable" (Tester, 2011, p. 65).

Through their adherence to particular genre conventions, codes, and narrative structures, animal cop shows raise questions about the ethics of depicting animal abuse, neglect, and cruelty as a television spectacle. It is in the context of television entertainment that viewers are able to observe animal suffering at close quarters where the abused animal is the object of the viewers' gaze, its suffering depicted through the use of lengthy shots and close-ups. The narrative arcs of these shows follow the trauma to transformation format of other reality TV programs such as diet and makeover shows. The construction of the trauma that precedes the transformation in all of these cases, whether human or animal, is reliant on the depiction of broken suffering bodies. In this type of programming, animal suffering is always morally unambiguous and indefensible in the sense that animals are always innocent victims, their suffering is authentic and therefore the reality of the show itself is seldom brought into question. Yet it remains salient to ask, "At what point should the camera look away?" Animal shows have, since the 1990s, been an inexpensive form of programming, an area ripe for exploitation by tabloid, sensationalistic television. These shows offer viewers reassurance that animal cruelty is not tolerated in society and that it does not go unpunished. Viewers can also identify with a community of professional carers and satisfy themselves that they share particular values and moral boundaries. At the same time, these programs engender voyeuristic patterns of looking that revolve around the construction of animal suffering as a television spectacle and necessarily close-down alternative interpretations of events, eliminating any ambiguity or the possibility that the viewer might identify with anyone other than the investigator and the ideologies which underpin the officer's actions. Animal cop shows thus raise important and complex questions about the circulation of images of animal suffering as entertainment, their uses, and the modes of looking that they engender.

References

Adams, C. (2004). *The pornography of meat.* New York & London: Continuum.

American Pet Products Association (2012) *Industry statistics and trends.* Retrieved January 12, 2012, from http://www.americanpetproducts.org/press_industrytrends.asp.

American Pet Products Association (2015) *Industry statistics and trends.* Retrieved June 17, 2015, from http://www.americanpetproducts.org/press_industrytrends.asp.

American Veterinary Medical Association. (2001). Market research statistics—U.S. pet ownership 2001. Retrieved on August 30, 2012, from https://www.avma.org/KB/Resources/Statistics/.

American Veterinary Medical Association. (2012). Market research statistics—U.S. pet ownership 2001. Retrieved June 17, 2015, from https://www.avma.org/KB/Resources/Statistics/.

Animal Planet. (2008). *Animal Planet reveals a new species of entertainment for 2008.* Retrieved January 12, 2012, from http://www.reuters.com/article/2008/01/14/idUS156303+14-Jan-2008+PRN20080114.

BBC Worldwide/ Discovery. (2010). *BBC and Discovery Communications announce new partnership and BBC Worldwide sells its interest in joint venture to Discovery.* Retrieved January 12, 2012, from http://www.bbc.co.uk/pressoffice/bbcworldwide/ worldwidestories/pressreleases/2010/11_november/discovery_bbc.shtml.

Bignell, J. (2005). *An introduction to television studies.* London: Routledge.

Biressi, A., & Nunn, H. (2005). *Reality TV: Realism and revelation.* New York: Wallflower Press.

Chris, C. (2006). *Watching wildlife.* Minneapolis: University of Minnesota Press.

Corner, J. (2000). What can we say about "documentary"? *Media, Culture & Society, 22*, 681–688.

Fulton, H. (2005). *Narrative and media*. New York: Cambridge University Press.

Hill, A. (2005). *Reality TV: Audiences and popular factual television*. New York: Routledge.

Hunt, M., Al-Awadi, H., & Johnson, M. (2008). Psychological sequelae of pet loss following Hurricane Katrina, *Anthrozoös, 21*(2), 109–121.

Kilborn, R. (2003). *Staging the real: Factual TV programming in the age of Big Brother*. Manchester: Manchester University Press.

Kilborn, R., & Izod, J. (1997). *An introduction to television documentary: Confronting reality*. Manchester: Manchester University Press.

Molloy, C. (2011). *Popular media and animals*. London: Palgrave Macmillan.

Pet Food Manufacturers' Association. (2004). *Historical pet ownership 1965–2004*. Retrieved on January 12, 2012, from http://www.pfma.org.uk/_assets/images/general/file/Historical%20pet%20population%20data(1).pdf.

Pet Food Manufacturers' Association. (2008). UK pet food market 1987–2007. Retrieved January 12, 2012, from http://www.pfma.org.uk/_assets/images/general/file/UK%20Pet%20Food %20Market%201987-2007%20_%C2%A6%C2%A3million_(1).pdf.

Tester, K (2001) *Compassion, morality and the media*. Philadelphia: Open University Press.

Chapter 18

Emerging Issues and Future Directions in the Area of Animal Cruelty

Mary P. Brewster and Shannon T. Grugan

Introduction

Earlier chapters in this text have addressed the past and current status of anti-cruelty legislation, public perceptions of cruelty, media portrayal of animal cruelty, the prevalence and incidence of cruelty, types of animal cruelty, links between animal cruelty and other criminality, and theoretical approaches to understanding the phenomenon. In this chapter, we will explore emerging issues related to animal cruelty and discuss future directions in the nature, legislation, and study and documentation of this behavior.

Advocacy and Activism

Journalist Will Potter (2009, p. 671) recently wrote that as "going green has gone mainstream in the United States, ... there has been growing public concern for animal-welfare issues." This concern has resulted in ever-increasing levels of advocacy and activism. Advocacy is defined as "the act or process of ... supporting a cause or proposal" (Merriam-Webster, 2015). The Humane Society of the United States (2009) reports that there are over "17,000 U.S. nonprofit organizations that seek to protect, provide services to or advocate for animals." Activism, on the other hand, is defined as "a doctrine or practice that emphasizes direct vigorous action especially in support of or opposition to one side of a controversial issue" (Merriam-Webster, 2015). Some animal rights organizations that are typically considered to be activist groups include People for the Ethical Treatment of Animals (PETA) and the Animal Liberation Front (ALF). Members of these organizations have been known to take extreme and sometimes violent action to get their message across. Because of this, there is often a misconception that activist groups are not interested in effecting change through more peaceful efforts.

While the distinction between the terms *advocacy* and *activism* may appear to be slight, some advocates do not want to be "confused" with activists due to the widespread view of activists as violent extremists. In fact, the recent passage of a federal eco-terrorism law and the framing by the media of activism/activists as violent terrorism/terrorists have further added to this perception held by the general public and by many advocates themselves. One study of volunteers in the purebred rescue movement illustrated advocates' concerns regarding being labeled as activists. Qualitative interviews with 26 rescue workers, most of whom had either a college degree or graduate degree, overwhelmingly viewed themselves as advocates, rather than activists, due to the nature of their work not involving "picketing, protesting, being political, [or] being 'in-your-face'" (Greenebaum, 2009, p. 295). Moreover, the rescue workers were concerned that they might be "associated with activism ... and the radical and extreme" PETA. According to Greenebaum, the rescuers had more of an "animal welfare perspective" than an "animal rights stance;" that is, they thought that animals had "intrinsic value," but only "*limited* rights" such as the right to a quality life (p. 297).

The stereotypical view of animal activists is that of people who commit threatening and violent acts. Included in these activities would be such incidents as that of the assassination of Dutch politician Pim Fortuyn in 2002 by vegan animal rights activist Volkert van der Graaf. The murder presumably occurred because van der Graaf was angered by Fortuyn's supportive stance regarding intensive farming and fur farming (Munro, 2005). Another example of extreme activist violence was the Animal Liberation Front's bombing of two meat-transport trucks in Switzerland in 2007 (Flükiger, 2008). Media coverage of the Dutch and Swiss cases and other extreme actions taken by self-proclaimed activists in the U.S., U.K., and Australia has helped to create and perpetuate the image of activists as irrational and violent. Sensationalistic coverage by the news media of these types of relatively infrequent, though extreme and destructive, incidents may undermine the efforts of nonviolent activists as they seek change in the treatment of animals.

The public view of animal rights activists is often colored by media coverage of violent forms of protest. Legislative reactions to these types of incidents have included the passage of the Serious and Organized Crime and Police Act in the U.K. in 2005 and the 2008 Animal Enterprise Terrorism Act in the U.S. The U.K. Act "allow[s] stiff sentences to be imposed on those who intimidate companies and individuals that contract with animal-testing labs" and the U.S. Act is intended "to combat property damage and threats that produce 'a reasonable fear' of death and injury for researchers or their relatives" (Cressey, 2011, p. 452). While the U.K law has resulted in convictions of violent activists, the application of the U.S. law "has been challenged in the courts" (Cressey, 2011, p. 452). Rather than prosecuting violent "ecoterrorists," the U.S. law has targeted animal advocates who have engaged in nonviolent protests. There has been some evidence that the criminalization of conventional and nonviolent protest activity is spreading to other countries (e.g., Yates, 2011).

Violent animal activism is the exception, not the rule, despite the media coverage that often suggests the contrary. In fact, most modern-day activist groups are likely to use a wide array of nonviolent strategies, and believe that "violence is ... counterproductive to the movement's goal in promoting the compassionate treatment of nonhuman animals" (Doherty, 2002, p. 90). Some of the nonviolent tactics used by activists include demonstrations, lobbying, pamphleteering, and pursuing animal protection litigation (Tauber, 2010). Use of alternatives to violence gives "protestors a moral advantage" (Munro, 2005, p. 80). Additionally, modern-day access to the mass media enhances the ability of activists to spread the word about their protests and the mistreatment of animals (Munro, 2005).

Research on Animal Advocates and Activists

Within the realm of study related to animal cruelty, most research focusing on humans has involved studying the perpetrators of the abuse (e.g., hoarders, those committing intentional harm to animals, etc.). While not a new area of research, another important body of literature focuses on animal advocates and animal activists. It is likely to be this group that influences public perceptions of the issue of animal cruelty, and with that, effects cultural and legislative change.

The research on animal activism thus far suggests that, whether the result of biology, social learning, or "identif[ication] with the oppressed status of animals" (Gaarder, 2011), the majority of animal activists are women (see e.g., Carmona, 2012), and women are stronger proponents of animal rights than are men (Kruse, 1999). Initial involvement in activism may be due to any number of reasons. For example, a survey of vegan animal activists in Spain revealed that exposure to information about animal cruelty was a common reason provided for the conversion to veganism and animal rights activism (Carmona, 2012). Education through the school system and mass media, then, may be key to increasing public awareness and concern for animals, and the public's involvement as advocates and activists in anti-cruelty efforts. This increased awareness among the general public, as well as among law enforcement officers, social service providers, and mental health professionals, may help to mitigate the impact of animal cruelty.

In Chapter 17 of this text, Molloy highlights some aspects of the media's (albeit, at times, exploitative) role in disseminating information related to cruelty. Coverage of certain high profile cases in the mainstream *news* media may even more effectively serve to heighten public awareness about animal cruelty, as occurred in the Michael Vick dogfighting case (more fully discussed in Chapters 7 and 8). In addition to the news media as influential in reaching potential activists, the dissemination of information about animal protection can also take place in the school setting. Thomas and Beirne (2002) argue for the inclusion of humane education in character education among youth for the "cultivation of empathy" (p. 190). They claim that there is an absence of humane education at the middle and high school levels, and that teenagers "are ripe for activism" (Thomas & Beirne, 2002, p. 195).

Effectiveness of Activism

Animal activism appears to have been effective in several cases throughout the world. For example, beginning in the late nineteenth century, a group of biologists became active in an attempt to fend off the extinction of the American alligator. Eventually (in the middle of the 20th century), they joined forces with others wildlife advocates and with policymakers in the creation of the American Alligator Council (Barrow, 2009). The results of their work included both research on the species as well as the passage of local, state, and federal laws to protect the American alligator. In 1987, the U.S. Fish and Wildlife Service removed the American alligator from its endangered species list due to a "complete recovery of the species" (National Parks Conservation Association, n.d.). Another example of effective activism is the significant role played by the Humane Society of the United States (HSUS) in the creation and passage of felony anti-cruelty laws (Allen, 2005, p. 443). Legislation will be discussed in greater detail below, but as a result of the push for felony legislation, currently all 50 U.S. states have felony anti-cruelty statutes (Berry, 2014).

Dillard (2002) argues that activists can be persuasive when using civil disobedience that is "nonviolent/non-threatening … and when participants demonstrate not only a willingness to suffer for their beliefs but also an interest in communicating that suffering to onlookers" (p. 47). This was illustrated by the protests organized by The Fund for Animals against the annual Fred Coleman Memorial Shoot. The event, which was colloquially known as the Hegins pigeon shoot, was the largest event of its kind in the United States. Event organizers purchased over 5,000 pigeons from breeders and caged them for days or weeks leading up to the Labor Day event. Up to 250 shooters participated in taking aim at the pigeons that were released one at a time from their cages. Fewer than one-third of the birds were estimated to have died instantly from gunshot wounds. Often, the birds were merely wounded and dropped to the field. Young "trapper boys" were assigned the task of retrieving the injured birds from the field and decapitating them "over the rim of a barrel or with their bare hands" (Dillard, 2002, p. 50). The dead birds were later disposed of as trash.

Early protests at the event were disorganized and tense, and did not garner the public support desired by the protestors. In 1996, the Fund for Animals sent only a small contingent of protestors whose sole purpose was to help the pigeons without engaging in name calling, insults, threats, shoving, etc. A dozen protestors engaged in civil disobedience by lying on the killing field and delaying the start of the event by two hours. The remaining activists later assisted in rescuing injured pigeons from the field. Interviews with event observers revealed that the impact of the activists was much more positive and emphasized the suffering of the pigeons rather than the conflict between the activists and pigeon shoot participants. The result was more positive press coverage and perceptions by observers (Dillard, 2002). Following the event in 1998, the Hegins Township Labor Day Committee decided to end the 65-year-old fundraising tradition allegedly because they were "exhausted from 12 years of battling animal rights activists who relentlessly sued them" (Latty, 2000). Live pigeon shoots are still legal in Pennsylvania and have continued to take place at private gun clubs. A bill (H.B. 1750) sponsored by Rep. John Maher (R-Allegheny) to ban these shoots in the state of Pennsylvania , which has been pending for many years was finally passed in the Pennsylvania Senate in 2014, however, the House of Representatives failed to vote on the bill before the end of the 2014 session (Worden, 2014). Some have argued that the National Rifle Association's political clout is preventing the passage of the bill (Humane Society Legislative Fund, 2012).

Continued research on advocacy and activism may help to further efforts in animal protection. Specifically, research focused on gaining a better understanding of how activists are "created," public perceptions of and responses to activism, and the impact of activism on legislative change, may help to encourage more effective strategies in anti-cruelty efforts. Research on violent activism and resultant legislation that restricts activities of activists might also further our understanding of the legislative process.

Public Awareness and Mass Media

The actions of both animal advocates and activists have played a part in increasing public awareness of cruelty to animals, but a more popular source of information has, not surprisingly, been the media. As mentioned previously, extreme cases of animal abuse that have been picked up by the media can bring to the public's attention the problem of animal cruelty. For example, beginning in the early 1990s in southern England, a series of horse assaults ("maimings") occurred and media coverage of the events led to a moral panic—one of the first moral panics (if not *the* first moral panic) involving victims that were nonhuman animals (Yates, Powell, & Beirne, 2001). Interestingly, though, there has been relatively little press coverage of the cruelty inflicted upon over 200 racehorses annually in Britain (Yates et al., 2001). Without media coverage, little public pressure for change exists. Once "picked up" by the media, however, news of animal cruelty spreads quickly.

The impact of the news media on animal cruelty cannot be overstated. Mass media coverage of animal cruelty has been found to impact meat demand (Tonsor & Olynk, 2011) and support altering farming and research practices (Bayvel, 2005). Dissemination of information has shown the potential for garnering public support for banning inhumane practices in farming (Tuyttens et al., 2011). A number of "activist documentaries" such as *"The Cove, Mine,* and *Food, INC.* each use the documentary genre to advocate for change, whether in regards to mass wild animal kills, companion animals in natural disasters, or the modern food industry" (Woodson, 2011, p. 200). Similarly, shocking footage of animal cruelty that has been posted online and/or circulated by means of social media can have an impact on public views of animals and their treatment. For example, in 2008, PETA posted online video recordings of severe abuses against pigs at a factory farm (PETA, n.d.). This case of "shock advocacy" appeared to effectively raise the public's consciousness (Scutter & Mills, 2009), and led to charges being filed against, and the subsequent convictions of, the perpetrators of the cruelty (PETA, 2009).

As the media increase coverage of animal cruelty as sport, it is likely that public outrage will increase to the point at which citizens will pressure legislators to pass new laws to prohibit or at least control the conditions surrounding these activities. Long-standing cultural and institutionalized cruelty towards animals in "sport" will likely become increasingly scrutinized as has been seen in the case of bull-fighting (e.g., Beilin, 2012) and whip use during Thoroughbred racing (e.g., Evans & McGreevy, 2011). For example, Evans and McGreevy (2011) analyzed the usefulness of whip use during horse racing and found that there was no statistical association between frequency of whip use and velocity, deeming this cruel behavior unnecessary and ineffective in accomplishing its intended purpose. Increasing public awareness of cruel practices in animal-related "sports" can alter public perception and ultimately lead to changes in practice. For example, in Barcelona, one former 20,000-seat bullring has been repurposed and transformed into a thriving "retail and entertainment complex" with a multiplex movie theater, a gym, and museum, and retail stores (Brown, 2012). The bullring transformation was not purely due to a change in morals. In fact, as is often the case, the decision was largely a financial one; with greater public concern for animal protection came a loss of interest in attending bullfights and thus reduced profits. One might expect similar changes to occur in Thoroughbred horse and greyhound racing, as well as in rodeos.

Mass media has proven to be a double-edged sword. While it has provided important information to the public about the abuses of animals in various industries throughout the world, it has also sometimes created moral panic. Such was the case in the U.K. following a 1990 fatal attack on an 11-year-old boy by two Rottweilers and two 1991 nonfatal attacks by pit bulls. Very soon after the dog attacks, the *Dangerous Dogs Act* (1991) was passed in the U.K., which criminalized the owning, breeding, and sale of pit bulls as well as three other dog breeds. Within five years of the passage of the Act, over 1,000 dogs deemed "weapon dogs" or "dangerous dogs" were seized from their owners and subsequently killed (Hallsworth, 2011). As mass media continues to expand, so too will its potential to both help and harm animals.

Other examples of the mass media's ability to undermine efforts to protect animals include the proliferation of online puppy mills, web-based trade of exotic animals, and the availability of crush videos on the internet. The nature of the electronic dissemination of information and constitutional protections in the United States make legislation of the industries particularly challenging. (See Chapter 8). In 1999, federal legislation (18 U.S.C. § 48) was passed to prevent "crush videos," but was deemed unconstitutional (due to overbreadth) by the U.S. Supreme Court ruled in 2010 (United States v. Stevens, 2010). The law was written in such a way that it would subject to "up to five years in prison, anyone who 'knowingly creates, sells, or possesses a depiction of animal cruelty with the intention of placing that depiction in interstate or foreign commerce for commercial gain'" (Zimmerman, 2010, p. 17). Despite its presence on the books for over a decade, the law was never actually used to prosecute creators or distributors of crush videos. It was, however, applied to a few cases of the distribution of images of animal fighting. Immediately after the Supreme Court's decision to strike the law, a new federal bill was introduced and passed into law—H.R. 5566, the Animal Crush Video Prohibition Act of 2010. This law had bipartisan support and is worded more specifically to prohibit "videos where an animal is 'tortured, maimed, or mutilated,' and also specifically does not apply to depictions of hunting" (Zimmerman, 2010, p. 18). Following the first prosecution of two Texas individuals under this leglislation, the law was deemed unconstitutional by a district court. However, the United States Court of Appeals for the Fifth Circuit reversed the district court's judgment and upheld the constitutionality of the Act, holding that "on its face § 48 is limited to unprotected obscenity and therefore facially constitutional" (United States v. Ashley Nicole Richards; Brent Justice, 2014).

Changing Views of Animals and of Cruelty

A survey of 1,031 U.S. households conducted by Edge Research in 2004 revealed that animal protection was important to respondents. When asked "How important is it to you that animals are protected from cruelty and abuse?" two-thirds of respondents reported that it was "very important" (Lockwood, 2006, p. 9). The treatment of nonhuman animals has focused on "[t]he level of sentience and consciousness in other species" (Burghardt, 2009, p. 499) or "level of awareness or consciousness of ill treatment" (p. 499). Many have suggested that anthropomorphism is a key element in determining views of animals (e.g., Herzog & Galvin, 1997; Hills, 1995). That is, the greater the attribution of human (emotional and intellectual) characteristics to an animal, the greater one's concern for a given species' welfare. However, humans may not portray all species of animals equally. The idea of the phylogenetic continuum was first introduced by Aristotle; the higher an animal on the phylogenetic scale, the more complex the animal and the greater the number of humanlike attributes possessed by the animal. Species, then, can be viewed along a continuum; people would presumably be less anthropomorphic in their perceptions of a frog or a fish than of a dog or a chimpanzee (see e.g., Knight, Vrij, Bard, & Brandon, 2009).[1] In a study of punishment

---

1. Burghardt (2009) points out that extant research literature provides information regarding "the similarities and differences between human and non-human animals and their relevance for decisions about our treatment of other species" (p. 515), but that this anthropocentric approach is not necessarily that useful. Burghardt questions whether "consciousness and sentience [are] overvalued as markers on the ethical ruler" and suggests that perhaps "our moral philosophy" should be balanced by "an ecological vision" (p. 516) and a new ethics of "environmental survival" (p. 517).

recommendations for animal abusers, Allen and colleagues (2002) found that the greater the perceived similarity between abused animals and humans, the more harshly the research subjects believed the perpetrators should be punished.

Considering the results of the Edge Survey, it is somewhat surprising that humans are able to behave in ways that may contribute to cruelty towards nonhuman animals. For example, the vast majority of people eat the meat of animals bred on factory farms and use products tested on animals or made from animal parts. These same people may be opposed to the use of cats, dogs, and chimpanzees in scientific research. How is it, then, that people hold seemingly contradictory views of animals? It may be due, in part, to ignorance regarding the ways in which animals are treated in factory farm and scientific lab settings. It may also "be due to the belief in the mentality of different species, as well as … affection for particular kinds of animals" (Knight, Vrij, Bard, & Brandon, 2009, p 467).

Research on the varying human attitudes towards nonhuman animal use and abuse has been relatively scant. One study examined the attitudes and beliefs of scientists, animal welfarists, and laypeople towards the use of animals for medical research, dissection in biology class, entertainment (i.e., hunting and "keeping animals in zoos"), and personal decoration ("clothing made from animal products, cosmetics testing") (Knight et al., 2009, 476). Other variables included on the survey included perceptions of choice (i.e., "the existence of alternatives to using animals"), views of humans as superior to animals, and "belief in animal mind" (p. 467). While the attitudes of animal welfarists were largely consistent across types of animals and the purpose of animal use, scientists' attitudes were "multidimensional;" they "did not support the use of animals for dissection, personal decoration, and entertainment," although they were proponents of the use of animals in research (Knight et al., 2009, p. 476). The polarized views of scientists and animal welfarists towards the use of animals in scientific research could be explained by their conflicting views of the availability of alternatives; scientists typically justified their support of animal use in research by arguing that there were no suitable alternatives.

The more educated that people become about factory farming, the use of animals for testing purposes in laboratories, etc., the greater the cognitive dissonance and resultant discomfort and anxiety that people experience. When there is a disconnect between one's actions and moral standards, social and psychological processes can help to mitigate the anxiety caused by one's behavior. Those who are aware of their actions may use various techniques of neutralization (as discussed in Chapter 8) to downplay the harm to the animal victims (Sykes & Matza, 1957). Similarly, Bandura created the concept of moral disengagement to explain how a person can act in an inhumane way despite contradictions with one's standards (Bandura, 1999). Both techniques of neutralization and mechanisms of moral disengagement involve cognitively reframing the nature of one's actions in order to make them appear justifiable. This can be accomplished through the marginalization of one's victims, the denial of harm to victims, and other minimizations of one's harm to animals. There has been some evidence to support the validity of both techniques of neutralization and moral disengagement among deer poachers (Eliason & Dodder, 1999), bloodsport participants (see Chapter 8), and hunters (Presser & Taylor, 2011). Some have even noted the applicability of moral disengagement in terms of people's unwillingness to punish perpetrators of animal cruelty (Vollum, Buffington-Vollum, & Longmire, 2004). Inconsistency between morals and behavior is not limited to laypersons; in one study, 40% of animal activists were reportedly meat eaters (Herzog & Golden, 2009).

Current Application and Future Trends in Anti-Cruelty Legislation

Legislative evolution often reflects (or is the result of) the evolution of social consciousness. As humans become aware of animal cruelty, through mass media and other means, resultant change in cultural norms, values, and politically important public opinion, become reflected in legislation. While the shifts in awareness of animal cruelty and perceptions of animals have facilitated improvement in the protections outlined in current anti-cruelty legislation in the United States, there are still many issues and obstacles to overcome in establishing consistency in defining animals, prohibited behaviors, and appropriate sanctions.

Although every state currently has laws that prohibit some form of animal cruelty, legislators across the United States are continuing to grapple with specification of the actions that constitute improper treatment of animals (including how to handle the issue of intent), the types animals that should be included under protective laws, the penalties for engaging in prohibited behavior, and the best ways to regulate cruelty going forward. Similarly, the legal status of animals as property is just beginning to be challenged in the court system. However, as it will be discussed below, defining the status of animals is as contentious, and at times contradictory, as defining cruelty. Recently enacted pieces of state legislation, pending state and federal legislation, and recent court decisions are good examples of this disjointed patchwork and indicate that lawmakers and judicial representatives are far from achieving consensus on many issues pertaining to animal cruelty. While the specific topical issues may change, it is likely that legislators will continue to produce these mismatched and contradictory laws that add to the existing assortment of animal cruelty legislation the United States for the foreseeable future.

Recent Laws, Judicial Action, and Pending Legislation

For every state that passes a law expanding definitions of certain types of cruelty, increasing the power of regulatory agencies, or increasing penalties, there is another that vetoes similar legislation or passes laws that limit the definition of cruelty, associated penalties, or requirements. According to the Animal Law Coalition (2012a), since 2010 nearly every state has passed laws or has legislation pending focused on animal cruelty and related protective rights. During 2014 alone, the HSUS reported that 137 new laws were passed at the state and local level that enhanced the protection of a variety of different animals (Pacelle, 2015). With so many, they cannot all be discussed at length. Some representative examples of recently enacted legislation that have expanded provisions related to cruelty at the state level include:

- All 50 states currently identify some form of animal cruelty as a felony level offense. South Dakota was the last state to enact a felony level provision for acts of cruelty in 2014 (Berry, 2014).
- Also in 2014, New York and New Jersey became the first states to ban the sale of ivory (Animal Welfare Institute, 2014) Seventeen other states currently have pending legislation regarding a ban on the sale of ivory (Elephants DC, 2015).
- A Massachusetts law passed in 2010 banned the questionable veterinary practice of "devocalization" unless it was medically necessary. Devocalization involves

removal of tissue from the vocal chords for the purpose of permanently minimizing the volume of cat meowing or dog barking (Keiper, 2010). As of 2015, this procedure remains legal in a majority of states; however, Maryland, New Jersey and Ohio have also recently outlawed this procedure (American Veterinary Medical Association, 2014).

- A Maryland law passed in 2014 prohibited other unnecessary and inhumane veterinary practices including ear cropping, tail docking, and declawing of dogs (Animal Legal and Historical Center, 2015).

While the above laws indicate promising expansions of animal cruelty protections, there have also been a number of recently enacted laws that do just the opposite. In many instances, the rollback of provisions and penalties for animal-based regulation is due to intense lobbying by those with legitimate financial interests as stake, such as commercial breeders, pet store owners, and livestock farmers. Breeders and puppy mill owners have put intense pressure on regulation of breeding that has resulted in laws being modified or outright repealed. For example, in 2011 Missouri repealed a proposition that was voted into law by the Missouri public earlier that year requiring commercial breeders to limit the number of breeding dogs to 50 and provide rest periods for breeding females between breeding cycles (Animal Law Coalition, 2012a; Associated Press, 2011). Similarly, McNutt (2012) reports that a law passed in Oklahoma in 2012 relaxed existing regulation of commercial pet breeding and transferred inspection and oversight of breeding from an independent board to the state's Department of Agriculture. Many believe that the transfer of oversight to the existing agency will decrease the standard of care provided by commercial breeders (Animal Law Coalition, 2012b; McNutt, 2012). More recently, in 2015 lawmakers in Alabama have refused to review a piece of legislation calling for increased standards of care for breeders with 10 or more breeding dogs (Edgemon, 2015) Additionally, according to the Animal Law Coalition, horse slaughter has become a particularly active arena for animal legislation—for both opposition and support of slaughter—due largely to the lifting of the federal ban on the practice in late 2011 and its subsequent reinstatement in 2014. Even before the ban was lifted in 2011, many states had laws banning slaughter of horses for meat for a very long time. New Jersey led the charge to keep the transportation/slaughter of horses for meat illegal in the wake of the federal ban, while a number of states, including Idaho, Wyoming, North Dakota, Nebraska, and Montana, had enacted laws allowing horse slaughter and the sale of horse meat (Animal Law Coalition, 2012). In terms of lobbying, many of the state laws allowing horse slaughter or transportation for slaughter were symbolic gestures that were actually passed prior to the lift of the federal ban to show support for the practice. According to Massey (2014), by 2013, plans were in place to open active horse slaughterhouses in New Mexico, Missouri, and Iowa. However, none of these plants was ever opened due to potential violations of environmental and food production laws unrelated to cruelty (Massey, 2014). With the reinstatement of the ban, slaughter or horses for meat on U.S. soil has been stopped for the time being; however, transportation of horses from the U.S. to places like Mexico and Canada for slaughter remains a legal, though contentious issue.

In terms of the courts, state judiciaries do not make direct changes to policy in regard to animal cruelty but in recent cases, the status of animals as property has been questioned in the courtroom. Recent court decisions, while perhaps precedent setting, have also been contradictory. Many court cases addressing issues of cruelty have grappled with the rights of animals, or lack thereof. For example, in 2012, the New Jersey State Supreme Court effectively reinforced the long-held notion that animals are property when it ruled that a dog owner was entitled to damages, but not payment, for emotional stress for a killed pet (Newcomer, 2012). Within days of the ruling in New Jersey, the Oregon State Supreme Court ruled that animals are not just property, arguing that animals can be considered victims of a crime when cruelty occurs. According to the court, their "primary concern was to protect individual animals as sentient beings, rather than to vindicate a more generalized public interest in their welfare" (Wright, 2012). As of this writing, there is a similar case pending in New York in which the court is to determine whether or not *habeas corpus*[2] applies to two chimpanzees held in a university's research laboratory (Volokh, 2015). The outcome of this case is likely to impact views of animals and their rights in the courts going forward.

While recently enacted state legislation and court decisions are indicative of a contradictory patchwork of current regulatory practices, pending federal legislation and state legislation paint a slightly more consistent picture of potential enhancement of enumerated protections for animals. However, since the below are pending, it is possible that many will never come to pass. Some notable pending legislation includes:

- Animal Fighting Spectator Act of 2013, a federal act that would impose a fine and up to a year in prison for willful spectators of animal fights and up to three years in prison for anyone who causes a minor to attend an animal fight (H.R. 366 2013).
- Preventing Cruelty and Torture Act of 2015, a federal act that would allow the Federal Bureau of Investigation and U.S. Attorneys to investigate and prosecute interstate and international acts of cruelty (H.R. 2293 2015).
- Pet and Women's Safety Act of 2015, a federal act that would prohibit threats or acts of violence against an individual's pet animal by someone stalking them and/or violating a protection from abuse order (H.R. 1258, 2015).
- Proposed state legislation in Pennsylvania banning the possession of animal fighting paraphernalia such as treadmills, breaking sticks, and other equipment used in both dog and bird fighting (PA H.B. 164, 2015).

Recent and pending legislation like that above indicate that, at the very least, lawmakers are taking animal cruelty issues seriously and are devoting an ever-increasing amount of attention to the phenomenon. However, even with an upward trend in regulations that are intended to afford additional protections, the creation of laws regarding animal abuse remain piecemeal and inconsistent. Additionally, some of these laws can be ineffective and difficult to successfully prosecute. This is especially the case when looking at interstate transport activities where certain actions may be prohibited in one state but not another. The distant future may include resolution to these problems in the form of more action and oversight from the federal government.

Centralized Federal Regulation: The Way Forward?

Some have likened the trajectory of animal cruelty and protective laws in the United States to that of environmental protection in the late 1960s and early 1970s (Senatori &

---

2. A writ of *habeas corpus* is filed by individuals who claim that their detention is illegal or that they have been wrongly imprisoned.

Frasch, 2010). Early environmental protection began with disjointed state laws and lack of public understanding and support. Over time, the environmental protection movement began building momentum, gaining the attention of the federal government, and increasing the public's level of understanding and support until a number of important federal laws were passed and the Environmental Protection Agency (EPA) was created to provide oversight and enforcement support. Senatori and Frasch (2010) argue that just like environmental regulation in the 1970s, animal cruelty regulation could ultimately be centralized, with oversight given to a federal agency that they theoretically dub the "Animal Protection Agency," or APA. Of course, federal oversight will not be a panacea that eradicates or even appropriately deals with acts of animal cruelty. In fact, if extending the analogy between environmental protection and animal welfare, the creation of the EPA has not been a cure-all for the environmental ills that plague the environment, simply because, like many of the social problems that have demanded centralized regulation under the federal government, there is no feasible way of eradicating the sources of the problems. What centralized agency regulation can do is just that—regulate the problem at hand so that it is manageable and handled in a consistent uniform manner throughout the country. Additionally, given the current world economic climate and increasing international political tensions, it is likely that policymakers at a federal level would argue that there are more pressing anthropocentric concerns on the federal agenda than a newly formed agency for animals that would cost time, money, and manpower. However, from an animal rights perspective, the argument can be made that centralized federal oversight could transform what is currently a mess of disjointed, jumbled, and disorganized state level laws into a streamlined and comprehensive scheme of centralized federal regulation.

Important Emerging Legislative Issues

Horsemeat production and puppy mills are not the only hot button issues to be handled by lawmakers in recent sessions. Other issues of animal cruelty currently in the forefront of new legislative acts that are currently being developed at both the state and federal levels include shark-finning and the use of hidden cameras at factory farming facilities. According to the Humane Society International (2012), shark-finning is a form of wildlife cruelty that involves capture of sharks for the purpose of removing their fins, which are sought after for the purpose of making soup. The sharks are then released back into the sea finless, leaving them incapable of swimming properly. The sharks will usually die shortly after being released as a result of blood loss, suffocation, or attack from other predators. Millions of sharks are killed as a result of finning each year (Humane Society International, 2012). While boats and vessels registered to the U.S. have been prohibited by federal law from engaging in shark-finning since passage of the Shark Finning Protection Act of 2000, shark hunting (i.e., killing the shark and taking the entire carcass) and possession of shark fins currently remain legal at the federal level (H.R. 5461, 2000). While federal government regulation has been lax, state legislators are beginning to address the issues of shark hunting and shark-finning by targeting the shark fin market For example, the Humane Society of the United States (HSUS) reports that in 2011, Hawaii became the first state to ban the sale and distribution of shark fin products, including shark fin soup (HSUS, 2011). Illinois, California, Hawaii, Oregon, and Washington, Maryland, Delaware, and New York have passed laws joining Hawaii in this ban (HSUS, 2012d; Shark Stewards, 2015).

While shark-finning legislation continues to build momentum, another emerging trend in anti-cruelty legislation may be a step backwards. Legislation criminalizing the use of hidden cameras by investigative journalists, activists, and whistleblowing employees and/or requiring pre-screening of potential employees of factory farms to ensure they are not affiliated with a news organization, humane organization, or activist group—so called, "ag-gag" laws—are controversial and seen by many as a troubling development in humane legislation (HSUS, 2012a). Proponents of the ag-gag laws (most of whom are industry insiders) argue, weakly, that prohibiting hidden cameras "protect[s] the nation's food supply" (Rasmussen, 2012, p. 4). Opponents of the legislation argue that hidden camera footage has been an important source for investigative journalists providing information on factory farming to the public and has served as compelling evidence in investigations when recorded by whistleblowers and undercover activists (HSUS 2012a; Rasmussen, 2012). Since 2012, 24 states have attempted to pass some form of ag-gag legislation, but passage has only been successful in 6 states, including Iowa, Utah, Kansas, Missouri, Montana, and North Dakota. However, since Kansas has had the law in place since 1990, many are more concerned about the precedent sent by the 2012 passage of the first recent ag-gag statute in Iowa and the subsequent passage in the additional states listed here (Animal Law Coalition, 2012; American Society for the Prevention of Cruelty to Animals, 2015; Rasmussen, 2012;). Animal advocates view the passage of ag-gag laws as problematic, not only because it could set the stage for other states to follow suit, but also because states like Iowa for instance are top producers of agricultural food products in the United States, meaning that numerous hens, pigs, cattle, and other livestock animals may be in danger of experiencing cruel farming practices that will go undocumented due to these laws (Carlson, 2012). Ag-gag laws also create potential problems for human health. According to the Humane Society Veterinary Medical Association (2012), there is growing concern that without the ability to document and investigate practices at factory farms, these farms will continue to engage in subpar practices that leave their food products tainted with dangerous and potentially deadly bacteria, pathogens, and other harmful substances. Two additional states—Wyoming and North Carolina—have ag-gag legislation pending, indicating that the push to eliminate video evidence and infiltration by journalists and activists, while defeated in many place, remains a very active area of cruelty legislation (American Society for the Prevention of Cruelty to Animals, 2015).

The Future of Anti-Cruelty Legislation

While the United States has made notable strides in provisions for animal welfare and the prevention of cruelty over the last 150 years, legislation is far from perfect and there is still much work to be done. There is a pressing need to standardize definitions of cruelty, the legal status of animals, and the proper way of handling offenders. It is unlikely that national consensus on these issues will come in the form of state-based legislation but the future of federal oversight, while a novel idea, is only hypothetical at the current time. For the time being, it appears that most forms of animal protection will primarily be state issues and that these concerns will in turn have to be addressed at the state level.

Any legislative body in the United States, state or federal, would benefit from looking to the European Union (EU) as an example. According to the European Commission on Health and Consumers, the EU has formally recognized in the Treaty of Lisbon, which was entered in 2009, that "animals are sentient beings" capable of suffering and feeling pain, with various EU laws reflecting this view ("The EU and animal welfare," n.d.). While there are movements to reinforce the rights that are inherent in sentience, the United States generally still holds a 19th-century view of animals as property. This has impeded expansion of appropriate legal protections. The bottom line is that animal cruelty legislation in the United States, while uneven and lacking in uniformity on a national scale, is moving in the right direction in regards to some types of cruelty and may be moving in the wrong direction in others. Hopefully, someday, animals may be afforded legal uniform protections appropriate to their status at both the state and federal level.

Improvement in the Investigation and Prosecution of Animal Cruelty Cases

Due to increases in legislative provisions, education and training of investigative professionals and prosecutors, and public awareness, there have been numerous improvements made in the handling of animal cruelty cases as criminal events in recent years. These improvements span the entire enforcement life cycle, with many resources available for training and a move towards cooperation, information-sharing, and knowledge-sharing between animal cruelty investigators, police, prosecutors, and other law enforcement agencies. These improvements are ongoing and new to many jurisdictions, but as these improvements continue to develop, it is likely that enforcement of anti-cruelty laws in the United States, in the form of efficient investigations and prosecutions, will continue to improve as well.

Numerous training programs and instructional tools have been developed in recent times to assist police officers, animal cruelty investigators, and other law enforcement personnel with issues related to proper investigation of animal cruelty. A number of schools and educational vendors have begun to provide certification and training for animal cruelty investigators and police officers. For example, the University of Missouri Law Enforcement Training Institute houses the National Animal Cruelty Investigations School, which provides training on animal law, proper levels of care for various species, recognition of cruelty and dangers in the field, and other issues relevant to police and veterinary personnel throughout the United States (National Animal Cruelty Investigations School, n.d.). In addition to training courses, many organizations have created standalone training materials and guidance documentation that provide information on how to determine if cruelty is occurring or has occurred. For example, the Humane Society of the United States (HSUS) has made available a "Q and A" packet entitled "Making the Connection: What Law Enforcers Need to Know" that contains information regarding the definition of animal abuse and tips for enforcement. The packet describes how both humane investigators and police officers are responsible for the enforcement of anti-cruelty laws (HSUS, n.d.). There are similar texts at the state level, for example, the New York State Humane Society has a guidance document entitled "How to Investigate Animal Cruelty in New York State—A Manual of Procedures." This document includes step-by-step instructions on preparations that should be made prior to even receiving animal cruelty complaints or tips as well as procedures to follow during investigations and prosecution. This manual has been lauded by judges, police officers, other emergency responders, and even the HSUS as a comprehensive guide to investigating animal cruelty for New York and beyond (New York State Humane Association, n.d.).

In addition to the focus on better training for field investigators, there have also recent advances in the use of veterinary forensics and as a result, development of better training for veterinarians involved in animal cruelty investigations. Collection, identification, and analysis of evidence by forensic veterinarians have begun to strengthen investigations and resulting enforcement actions levied against animal cruelty perpetrators. For example, in 2011, a case of animal cruelty involving two cats that were tortured and killed was the first case successfully resolved based upon analyses of animals' DNA. One cat's DNA evidence was found on the couch on which he was set on fire, and the other's DNA was found on part of an umbrella used to beat and kill her (Baldwin, 2011; Newman, 2011). In recognition of the fact that forensic analysis can be useful in cases of animal cruelty, there has been a surge in creation of tools and a movement towards better training for forensics-based veterinary medicine. In terms of forensic tools, the American Society for the Prevention of Cruelty to Animals (ASPCA) has created its own mobile crime scene unit which provides equipment for forensic evaluation as well as on-site medical response for wounded animals. This vehicle "includes a fully equipped surgical suite, medical supplies, a digital microscope, exhumation apparatus, an entomology kit, blood-testing equipment, and evidence collection supplies" and was paid for by an anonymous donor so that forensic veterinarian Dr. Melinda Merck could further her work (which included assistance in the Michael Vick dogfighting case) in gathering evidence to help prosecute people involved in dogfighting, puppy mills, and extreme cases of hoarding ("ASPCA unleashes animal CSI unit," 2008). In terms of education and training, the ASPCA and the University of Florida partnered to begin the ASPCA Veterinary Forensic Science program in 2009. This program provides general forensics-based training courses for both law enforcement personnel and veterinarians as well as a graduate certificate program in forensic science for veterinarians (University of Florida, n.d.). Well-trained investigators and the emergence of forensic evidence as an important investigative tool are likely to improve the overall quality of animal cruelty investigations and may result in an increase in the number of successful prosecutions in the future (see also Chapter 5 of this text).

With the above in mind, successful prosecution of animal cruelty rests upon three related elements: (1) improvements in investigation and the scientific advances discussed above, (2) procedures, definitions, and prohibited actions specified in anti-cruelty legislation discussed previously in this chapter and throughout the text, and (3) the prosecutor's knowledge of animal law and animal cruelty. In regard to this third element, Lockwood (2006) argues that the "successful prosecution of crimes against animals requires specialized knowledge of not only relevant laws, but also of veterinary medicine, veterinary forensics, animal care, and the practices used in organized crimes against animals, such as dog and cockfighting" (p. 3). Training, guidance documents, and tools similar to those for investigators exist to provide understanding of these issues to prosecutors. For example, the National District Attorneys Association, in partnership with the ASPCA and the Animal Legal Defense League (ALDF), has created the National Center for Prosecution of Animal Abuse (NCPAA) with the mission of educating prosecutors and others with roles that are important to the outcome of cases (like veterinarians and investigators) on effective ways of handling cruelty cases (National District Attorneys Association, n.d.).

All of the above improvements in enforcement point to the practices of cooperation, information sharing, and collaboration among investigators, medical professionals, and prosecuting attorneys. While these practices are fundamental to increasing effectiveness of any enforcement endeavor, this is especially true of animal cruelty crimes because historically, these have not been the typical day to day crimes encountered by police or prosecutors. In this regard, Hughes and Lawson (2011) argue that there is a plurality in the policing of animal cruelty, because the responsibility of investigating animal cruelty "from initial inquiry to prosecution and back again to prevention" falls to both private humane organizations (such as local SPCAs and other organizations that provide humane law enforcement) as well as government-run police departments and prosecutor's offices (p. 378). Therefore, sharing of information and strategies between agencies is of particular importance for prevention of cruelty, as well as identification and ultimately, the appropriate disposition of cruelty cases. In fact, the HSUS suggests in its aforementioned training materials for police officers that police should "get to know local humane investigators who may be aware of potentially violent situations that have not come to the attention of the police" (HSUS, n.d.). Additionally, the ASPCA has been instrumental in leading the charge for better sharing of best practices by partnering with law enforcement agencies to create resources for the various stakeholders in animal cruelty enforcement cases. For example, the U.S. Department of Justice, Office of Community Oriented Policing Services (COPS), and the ASPCA collaborated to create the Dogfighting Toolkit for Law Enforcement—a manual to help police, other investigators, prosecutors and veterinarians who encounter dog fighting rings or signs of dog fighting (ASPCAPro, n.d.a.) The ASPCA also has a repository of templates for the various forms and legal documentation that are likely to be required in cruelty cases, including forms for voluntary surrender of animals and a number of forms related to the cataloging of evidence and tracking of forensic information. The documents in this repository are available for public use by any law enforcement agency or veterinarian (ASPCAPro, n.d.b.).

Beyond sharing information and practices, actual cooperation within investigations has started to appear in the form of state and local animal cruelty task forces. The makeup of these task forces varies from place to place but they generally include police officers, humane law officers/animal control officers, and representatives from local prosecutors' offices. For example, according to the Los Angeles Animal Services Office (n.d.), the city's Animal Cruelty Task Force (ACTF) includes two animal control officers and five police officers from the Los Angeles Police Department (LAPD), including two detectives and three patrol officers, who work collaboratively with veterinarians as well as a group of prosecutors specifically trained to handle animal cruelty crimes. In 2006, the year in which the task force was established, the ACTF successfully investigated 290 complaints, resulting in numerous citations and removal of many animals from dangerous conditions as well as 51 arrests and 15 felony prosecutions (L.A. Animal Services Office, n.d.). According to Zilney and Zilney (2005), in a slightly different example of agency investigatory cooperation in Canada, Ontario's Family and Child Services (FCS) and the Ontario Humane Society engaged in a yearlong pilot program of referrals for suspected cases of animal and domestic abuse, respectively. This reciprocation resulted in FCS referring 20% of their home visits to the Humane Society for concerns about animal welfare and likewise, the Humane Society referred almost 5% of its cases to FCS for potential family abuse situations that would likely have gone undiscovered otherwise (Zilney & Zilney, 2005). This indicates that agency cooperation can result in better investigations of animal cruelty crimes as well as other types of co-occurring crimes. Another example of collaboration occurs during hearings or trial, with investigators providing testimony and specific details of their evidence and veterinarians and forensic scientists serving as expert witnesses. According to Lockwood (2006), veterinarians are crucial to a prosecution's case in provision of information including the physical condition of all animals involved and their response to treatment, the actions that could have prevented the injuries, illness, death, or other harm done to the animals, and the time and cause of death for animals that are killed as a result of the cruelty.

The way forward for investigation and prosecution of animal crimes is one of increasing education, training, and collaboration. Emergence of these elements can already be seen to have increased the efficacy of animal cruelty cases in the examples discussed above. As these investigators, veterinarians, prosecutors, and other professionals involved in animal cruelty enforcement initiatives continue to increase their knowledge, skills, and levels of cooperation with one another, it is likely that enforcement of anti-cruelty laws in the

United States will continue on to improve in regard to efficient identification and proper investigation and prosecution of cruelty cases.

Increased Legitimacy as a Social Phenomenon

The study of animal cruelty has sometimes been considered a pseudo-intellectual endeavor; the topic has historically been on the fringes of the mainstream social sciences. As illustrated throughout earlier chapters of this book, there is, cumulatively, a broad body of literature from a variety of disciplines including law, philosophy, ethics, veterinary sciences, biology, sociology, psychology, and criminology. Despite this, the study of animal abuse and animal rights has traditionally been viewed as a less-than-credible niche rather than a legitimate topic of rigorous and legitimate research and theoretical endeavors. This has especially been the case within the social sciences. Although Bryant (1979) called for the sociological study of "zoological crime" more than three decades ago, relatively little empirical response ensued (Flynn, 2001). It was a bit of a breakthrough, then, when in 1998 Nigel South and Piers Beirne edited a special issue of the journal, *Theoretical Criminology*, that focused on "a green criminology" and included essays related to the moral and legal standing of animals (Benton, 1998) and the need for expansion of the definition of animal abuse (Agnew, 1998). Over a decade later, Beirne coedited a special issue of *Crime, Law and Social Change* that focused specifically on animal abuse. Beirne described the volume as "the first issue in any criminology journal to be devoted entirely to the study of animal abuse" (Beirne, 2011, p. 355). In his introduction to the volume, Beirne (2011) described a symposium that he attended in Wales a year earlier, entitled "Situating Animal Abuse in Criminology." The meeting was attended by "20 or so criminologists and scholar activists ... in order to encourage the study of animal abuse in criminology" (Beirne, 2011, p. 549). While the conference was not as well-attended as the more mainstream gatherings in the field of criminology, the international group of scholars from England, Wales, Ireland, Norway, and the United States shared ideas in the form of discussion and formal paper presentations.

> What has criminology to say about human-animal relationships and about animal abuse, in particular? From a discipline much of whose focus is provided by concepts of harm, pain, suffering, inequality, social exclusion and identity fractures, the brief answer to this question is: very little indeed. (Beirne, 2011, p. 353)

This is surprising considering that

> the study of animal abuse lies squarely within criminology's moral and intellectual compass.... [A]t this moment, the prospects for a pro-animal research programme in the sociology and criminology of animal abuse are quite bright [and there have been] many scholarly studies of animal abuse ... published in the last two or three years. (Beirne, 2011, p. 353)

Several arguments have been made to support the legitimacy and importance of studying animal abuse (Beirne, 1999; Calley, 2011). Many of these have been supported, at least to some extent, by content within this text. First, as described in Chapters 12 and 13 in this volume, there is some evidence to suggest that animal abuse is linked to other aggression, delinquency, and criminality. While additional research is needed, the mere possibility of this link calls for attention to animal cruelty. As described in Chapters 2, 3, and 4, a body of legislation exists prohibiting various acts of cruelty to animals. Beirne (1999) points out Edwin Sutherland's suggestion "that criminologists ... study anything defined as *socially harmful* by any branch of law" (p. 129), as well as Jeremy Bentham's argument for the humane treatment of animals in his utilitarian calculus (see Chapters 1 and 2). One of the strongest arguments for the legitimacy and importance of studying animal abuse is that animal abuse is a violation of the animals' rights as "moral patients"; that is, animals have "the right not to be harmed" (Beirne, 1999, p.134). "[A]s an act of violence against innocent nonhuman victims," animal abuse is ripe for further "empirical investigation, theory development, and the practical application of research findings to social policy" (Flynn, 2011, p. 466). Finally, as described in Chapter 15, animal abuse is "one of several forms of oppression identified by feminists as an interconnected whole" (Beirne, 1999, p. 140).

The Status of Empirical Study of Animal Violence

Because of the long-standing view of animal cruelty as something either outside of the realm of the social sciences or as niche topic, there is still much work to be done in assessing animal cruelty from a criminological perspective. There has been very little theory development and even less empirical testing. Animal cruelty is a somewhat unusual topic of study in criminology due to the fact that the victims in these crimes are non-human and criminology is generally considered to be anthropocentric and concerned with human interactions, human criminal behavior, and human victims (Beirne, 1999). Although willfully causing harm to animals is generally thought of as deviant behavior and many forms of cruelty have been formally criminalized in the eyes of the law, scholarly study of animal abuse as a crime phenomenon in its own right has been very limited. In a statement that mirrors the legal treatment of animals in the United States as property, Taylor (2011) acknowledges that "animals only enter the realm of criminology currently as 'objects' and never as 'subjects'" (p. 252). And indeed, as described elsewhere in this text, existing animal cruelty research is dominated by identification of correlations between an individual's violent acts towards animals and violent acts towards humans, such as animal violence as a component of the psychopathic triad or as a correlate of domestic violence (e.g., Arluke, Levin, Luke, & Ascione, 1999; DeGue & Dilillo, 2009; Flynn, 2011).

There is a need to clarify the relationship between animal cruelty and other forms of violence but the future of this research is discussed at length elsewhere in this book in Chapters 12 and 13. Less attention has been paid to animal cruelty as a topic of criminological study in its own right. There are many questions to be answered including: What causes a person to engage in animal violence? Is violence towards animals different from violence towards humans? Is violence towards animals always indicative of violence towards humans? What is the impact of this violence on the whole of society?

"Sui generis" study of animal cruelty

There has been an initiative over the last decade to view animal abuse as an object of criminological study under the broader guise of human-animal interaction and not solely as a signifier of additional criminality perpetrated against human victims. This came out as part of the realization there is much to be gained from examining animal abuse "sui generis," meaning that it can stand alone as a legitimate and important topic of theory development and study in the field, separate from solely focusing on implications for human criminality and/or human victimization (Beirne, 1999, p 117). Beirne (1999) has been the most prolific proponent of this initiative and justifies the importance of criminological research of animal violence based on:

> the status of animal abuse as (1) a signifier of actual or potential interhuman conflict [as outlined in detail in the studies discussed within other chapters of this book], (2) an existing object of criminal law, (3) an item in the utilitarian calculus on the avoidance of pain and suffering,[3] (4) a violation of rights, and (5) [as previously mentioned] one of several oppressions identified by feminism as an interconnected whole. (p. 117)

So far, this expansion of animal abuse has been comprised of scant literature that is more philosophical and theoretical than it is empirical. This is likely because animal abuse study for the sake of animals goes against the grain of the more mainstream anthropocentric paradigm of criminology. It has even been argued that criminology is currently ill-equipped to engage in study of animal violence and that new and innovative methodological frameworks need to first be developed before "sui generis" study of animal crime can begin (Taylor, 2011).

Agnew's (1998) Integrative Model of Animal Violence

Agnew (1998) has developed one of the only proposed theoretical frameworks for causation of animal violence. In it, he applies aspects of social control, social learning, and general strain theory, arguing that animal violence generally occurs when various aspects of these theories[4] coincide or manifest within individuals who are "unaware of the abusive consequences of their behavior for animals..., do not think their abusive behavior is wrong, and ... believe they benefit from their abusive behavior" (Agnew, 1998, p. 182). Perceptions of animals are an important implied piece of Agnew's framework. The general idea is that background characteristics, traits, and experiences can together or separately shape an individual's attitudes and beliefs about animals. In cases where an individual's beliefs are negative, they may be more likely to abuse or neglect a pet or could be more easily triggered to do so due to frustration or strains that trigger abusive outbursts. There have been many studies of people's perception of animals. However, since criminology has consistently ignored animal violence, these studies have occurred outside the realm of criminology. The general finding of existing studies is that while most people believe that there is a moral obligation to do no harm to animals, there are those who take the amoral approach, seeing animals as non-feeling or inferior, or as nothing more than objects or property to do with as they please (Kellert, 1988). Research outside of criminology has shown that characteristics like age, gender, race, and level of education can directly affect attitudes and beliefs about animals (Kellert, 1988; Pifer, 1996).

Likewise, early socialization and certain personality traits may also influence an individual's perception of animals. In terms of socialization, Gottfredson and Hirschi (1990) argue that while level of self-control remains essentially stable over the life-course, it is not a set trait in an individual until about eight years of age. So in this case, experiences in early childhood can impact the level of self-control one will have later in life. When

---

3. Beirne (1999) expounds on this later by saying "animals are sentient beings who can suffer and feel pain ... they have an interest in avoiding pain ... [therefore] humans are obliged not to inflict it on them" (p. 131).

4. For example, preexisting weak attachments to peers and family (social control), having previously witnessed animal violence (social learning), or experiencing some type of stress then coping by engaging in violence towards animals (general strain theory).

looking at the direct influence of socialization on attitudes about animals, it has previously been discussed in this text that experiencing and observing abuse—of humans or animals—as a child is correlated with later abuse of animals. When looking at resulting personality traits, low self-control and lack of empathy are specifically mentioned in Agnew's (1998) theoretical construct. According to Agnew (1998), in regard to those with low self-control, as specified by Gottfredson and Hirschi (1990, p. 194),

> it seems reasonable to suppose that such an individual would be less aware of the abusive consequence of their actions for the animal, less willing to grant animals moral consideration and less aware and concerned about the negative personal consequences of their actions.

While Agnew has developed an elegant and comprehensive framework that would appear to make intuitive sense, his integration of seminal theories of crime has yet to be empirically evaluated in light of causes of animal violence. Even more puzzling is the fact that none of the component theories has been tested individually in regard to animal violence either. There may be issues with measurement specification and operationalization of certain concepts, but the more likely reason for this lack of empirical study is the human-centric view held by the field of criminology.

From a criminological standpoint, animal cruelty and animal violence are much more complex than it would initially appear. There is more to animal violence as crime than merely the relationships of animal violence and psychopathy or animal violence and domestic violence. From a less anthropocentric orientation, criminological research could and should contribute a great deal to the understanding of human-animal interaction and in turn, will enhance the field's overall understanding of the nature of crime. As issues of animal cruelty become more prominent in the realm of criminal justice, the hope is that criminologists will follow Agnew's (1998) example and will begin to see violence perpetrated against animals as legitimate crimes and that these actions should be probed, investigated, and analyzed in the same way as other criminal behaviors. A reorientation of the perceptions of crime, violence, and victimization, and the framework for studying them, appears to be taking shape and will be necessary for animal violence to take its rightful place in the study of crime and crime causation.

The Future of Animal Cruelty Research

There is evidence that animal cruelty is emerging as a recognized and legitimate area of study. As an area of study becomes deemed worthwhile and legitimate, there is often a corresponding surge in the proliferation of related educational programs, scholarly publications, and organizations. We are beginning to see this occur in the area of human-animal studies. According to the Animals and Society Institute, there are currently more than three dozen university-level programs in human-animal studies in the U.S., Canada, U.K., Germany, Switzerland, Israel, and Netherlands, in addition to nine such programs in veterinary schools in the U.S. and Canada and six U.S. animal law programs (Animals and Society Institute, 2011).

National professional organizations in the fields of psychology and sociology have created special sections on humans and animals; the American Psychological Association has a section on animal-human interaction (American Psychological Association, 2012), and the American Sociological Association began a section on animals and society (American Sociological Association, 2012). The American Bar Association has formed an Animal Committee "to address all issues concerning the intersection of animals and the law to create a paradigm shift resulting in a just world for all" (American Bar Association, n.d.). About 40 organizations and research institutes related to animals and society and at least 15 scholarly journals devoted to this subject matter (Animals and Society Institute, 2011). Animal cruelty, ethical treatment of animals, and animal welfare are emphasized by these programs, organizations, and journals.

One university program related to animal protection and animal cruelty is notable due its being offered through the Humane Society of the United States (HSUS). In the fall of 2009, the HSUS became "the first animal welfare organization to receive [the] authority and distinction of receiv[ing] a license as a higher education degree-granting institution by the District of Columbia Education Licensure Commission" (Humane Society of the United States, 2009). The University offers baccalaureate degrees and graduate certificates in animal policy and advocacy, and humane leadership. Additionally, according to the Animals and Society Institute (n.d.), there are currently 50 colleges and universities in the United States and abroad that offer degrees and certifications in animal advocacy, humane education, animal protection, and related topics.

Data Collection, Maintenance, and Dissemination

As phenomena become legitimate areas for attention and scientific inquiry, the government typically subsidizes the collection of data to measure the prevalence and incidence of said phenomena. Such has been the case with population rates, immigration rates, unemployment rates, and crime rates. Unfortunately, this has not historically been the case with animal cruelty; the government has not previously sponsored the maintenance of rates of crimes against animals. However, as mentioned earlier in this text, in 2014, the Federal Bureau of Investigation announced that beginning in 2016, cases of animal cruelty will for the first time specifically be counted and identified as animal cruelty in the FBI's Uniform Crime Report, annual reporting of crime in the U.S (Manning, 2014). This government-sponsored collection of animal cruelty incidence and prevalence data will further legitimize the study of animal cruelty and, perhaps more importantly, the moral standing of animals.

Conclusion/Future Directions

The overarching theme of this text has been the recognition of animal cruelty as a problem as reflected in legislation, research, and theoretical development. Among the topics related to animal cruelty that are truly emerging and likely to be predictive of future directions are growth in the involvement in and impact of animal advocacy and nonviolent animal rights activism; increased public awareness of the nature and extent of various types of animal cruelty, largely due to the expansion of the role of the media in covering some of the most extreme cases; the continued evolution of animal protection and anti-cruelty legislation; the further growth of degree-granting programs and animal welfare curricula in institutions of higher learning; a slow, but steady, increase in animal cruelty research; and increased legitimacy of the study of animal cruelty (victims and perpetrators) in its own right. If the recent past is any indication of the future, we can, unfortunately, also expect to see the continuation and growth of some less desirable trends and activities (e.g., crush films, online puppy mills, etc.).

References

Agnew, R. (1998). The causes of animal abuse: A social-psychological analysis. *Theoretical Criminology. 2*(2), 177–209.

Allen, M. D. (2005). Laying down the law? Interest group influences on state adoption of animal cruelty felony laws. *Policy Studies Journal, 33*(3), 443–457.

Allen, M. W., Hunstone, M., Waerstad, J., Foy, E., Hobbins, T., Wikner, B., & Wirrel, J. (2002). Human-to-animal similarity and participant mood influence punishment recommendations for animal abusers. *Society & Animals, 10*(3), 267–284.

American Bar Association. (n.d.) Animal law. Retrieved from http://apps.americanbar.org/dch/committee.cfm?com=IL201050.

American Psychological Association. (2012). *Human-animal interaction.* Retrieved August 9, 2012, from http://www.apa.org/divisions/div17/sections/sec13/Home.html.

American Sociological Association (2012). *Animals and society.* Retrieved August 9, 2012, from http://www2.asanet.org/sectionanimals/.

American Society for the Prevention of Cruelty to Animals. (2015). Ag-gag bills at the state level. Retrieved May 21, 2015, from https://www.aspca.org/fight-cruelty/advocacy-center/ag-gag-whistleblower-suppression-legislation/ag-gag-bills-state-level.

American Veterinary Medical Association. (2014). State laws governing elective surgery procedures. Retrieved May 21, 2015, from https://www.avma.org/Advocacy/StateAndLocal/Pages/sr-elective-procedures.aspx.

Animal Law Coalition. (2012a). *Pending animal bills.* Retrieved August 1, 2012, from http://www.animallawcoalition.com/bills.

Animal Law Coalition (2012b). *Gov signs weakened ok breeder bill into law.* Retrieved August 1, 2012, from http://www.animallawcoalition.com/companion-animal-breeding/article/1207.

Animal Legal and Historical Center. (2015). Table of state law amendments from 2014. Retrieved May 20, 2015, from https://www.animallaw.info/topic/table-2014-amendments-state laws.

Animals and Society Institute. (2011). *Human-Animal Studies.* Retrieved August 9, 2012, from http://www.animalsandsociety.org/pages/human-animal-studies.

Animals and Society Institute. (n.d.). *HAS certificate and degree programs.* Retrieved September 5, 2012, from http://www.animalsandsociety.org/degreeprograms.

Animal Welfare Institute (2014). New Jersey, New York pass laws to ban trade in ivory and rhino horns. Retrieved May 20, 2015, from https://awionline.org/awi-quarterly/2014-fall/new-jersey-new-york-pass-laws-ban-trade-ivory-and-rhino-horns.

Arluke, A., Levin, J., Luke, C., & Ascione, F. (1999). The relationship of animal abuse to violence and other forms of antisocial behavior. *Journal of Interpersonal Violence, 14*(9): 963–975.

ASPCAPro. (n.d.a). *Training: Dogfighting toolkit for law enforcement.* Retrieved August 14, 2012, from http://www.aspcapro.org/dogfighting-toolkit-for-law-enforcement.php.

ASPCAPro. (n.d.b). *Sample forms: Legal forms & veterinary forms.* Retrieved August 14, 2012, from http://www.aspcapro.org/sample-forms.php.

ASPCA unleashes animal CSI unit. (2008). *Law Enforcement Technology*, July, 80.

Associated Press. (2011). Missouri legislators undo puppy mill law. *The Washington Times Online*. Retrieved August 4, 2012, from http://www.washingtontimes.com/news/2011/apr/14/missouri-legislators-undo-puppy-mill-law/.

Bandura, A. (1999). Moral disengagement in the perpetration of inhumanities. *Personality and Social Psychology Review, 3*(3), 193–209.

Baldwin, C. (2011). Animal abusers put in jail thanks to DNA evidence. *Metro New York Online*. Retrieved August 16, 2012, from http://www.metro.us/newyork/local/article/811736--animal-abusers-put-in-jail-thanks-to-dna-evidence.

Barrow, M. (2009). Dragon in distress: Naturalists as bioactivists in the campaign to save the American alligator. *Journal of the History of Biology, 42*(2), 267–288.

Bayvel, A. C. D. (2005). Animals in science and agriculture—A global perspective. *Animal Welfare, 52*(6), 339–344.

Beilin, K. O. (2012). Bullfighting and the War on Terror: Debates on culture and torture in Spain, 2004–11. *International Journal of Iberian Studies, 25*(1), 61–72.

Beirne, P. (2011). Animal abuse and criminology: Introduction to a special issue. *Crime, Law and Social Change, 55*, 349–357.

Beirne, P. (1999). For a nonspeciest criminology: Animal abuse as an object of study. *Criminology, 27*(1), 117–147.

Benton, T. (1998). Rights and justice on a shared planet: More rights or new relations, *Theoretical Criminology, 2*(2), 149–175.

Berry, C. (2014). All 50 states now have felony animal cruelty provisions. Animal Legal Defense Fund. Retrieved May 20, 2015, from http://aldf.org/blog/50-states-now-have-felony-animal-cruelty-provisions/.

Brown, J. L. (2012). Bull market. *Civil Engineering, 81*(1), 62–69.

Bryant, C. (1979). The zoological connection: Animal-related human behavior. *Social Forces, 58*, 399–421.

Burghardt, G. M. (2009). Ethics and animal consciousness: How rubber the ethical ruler? *Journal of Social Issues, 65*(3), 499–521.

Calley, D. (2011). Developing a common law of animal welfare: Offences against animals and offences against persons compared. *Crime, Law and Social Change, 55*(5), 513–525.

Carlson, C. (2012) The ag gag laws: Hiding factory farm abuses from public scrutiny. *The Atlantic* Online. Retrieved August 17, 2012, from http://www.theatlantic.com/health/archive/2012/03/the-ag-gag-laws-hiding-factory-farm-abuses-from-public-scrutiny/254674/.

Carmona, E. D. (2012). Perfil del vegano/a de liberación animal en España. Revista Española de Investigaciones Sociológicas, *139*, 175–188.

Cressey, D. (2011). Battle scars. *Nature, 470*(February 24), 452–453.

DeGue, S., & DiLillo, D. (2009). Is animal cruelty a "red flag" for family violence? *Journal of Interpersonal Violence, 24*(6), 1036–1056.

Dillard, C. L. (2002). Civil disobedience: A case study in factors of effectiveness. *Society and Animals, 10*(1), 47–62.

Doherty, B. (2002). *Ideas and actions in the Green Movement.* New York: Routledge.

The EU and animal welfare: policy objectives (n.d.). *Animal Welfare and Health.* Retrieved August 4, 2012, from http://ec.europa.eu/food/animal/welfare/policy/index_en.htm.

Edgemon, E. (2015). Alabama lawmaker blocks legislation restricting puppy mills. AL.com. Retrieved May 20, 2015, from http://www.al.com/news/index.ssf/2015/05/alabama_lawmaker_refuses_to_le.html.

ElephantsDC (2015). Why ban ivory sales? The facts. Retrieved May 20, 2015, from http://www.elephantsdc.org/the-facts2.html.

Eliason, S. L., & Dodder, R. A. (1999). Techniques of neutralization used by deer poachers in the western United States: A research note. *Deviant Behavior: An Interdisciplinary Journal, 20*, 233–252.

Evans, D., & McGreevy, P. (2011). An investigation of racing performances and whip use by jockeys in Thoroughbred races. *PLoS ONE, 6*(1), 1–5.

Flynn, C. (2011). Examining the links between animal abuse and human violence. *Crime, Law and Social Change, 55*, 453–468.

Flynn, C. P. (2001). Acknowledging the "zoological connection": A sociological analysis of animal cruelty. *Society & Animals, 9*(1), 71–87.

Flükiger, J. (2008). An appraisal of the Radical Animal Liberation Movement in Switzerland: 2003 to March 2007. *Studies in Conflict and Terrorism, 31*, 145–157.

Gaarder, E. (2011). Where the boys aren't: The predominance of women in animal rights activism. *Feminist Formations, 23*(2), 54–76.

Gottfredson, M., & Hirschi, T. (1990). *A general theory of crime.* Palo Alto, CA: Stanford University Press.

Greenebaum, J. (2009). "I'm not an activist!": Animal rights vs. animal welfare in the purebred dog rescue movement. *Society & Animals, 17*, 289–304.

Hallsworth, S. (2011). Then they came for the dogs! *Crime, Law, and Social Change, 55*, 391–403.

Herzog, H. A., & Galvin, S. (1997). Common sense and the mental lives of animals. An empirical approach. In R.W. Mitchell (Ed.), *Anthropomorphism, anecdotes and animals* (pp. 237–253), Albany: State University of New York Press.

Herzog, H. A., & Golden, L. L. (2009). Moral emotions and social activism: The case of animal rights. *Journal of Social Issues, 65*(3), 485–498.

Hills, A. M. (1995). Empathy and belief in the mental experiences of animals. Reviews and Research Reports. *Anthrozoös, 8*, 132–142.

H.R. 5461—106th Congress: Shark Finning Prohibition Act. (2000). In GovTrack.us. Retrieved August 17, 2012, from http://www.govtrack.us/congress/bills/106/hr5.

H.R. 366 — 113th Congress: Animal Fighting Spectator Act of 2013. (2013). Retrieved May 20, 2015, from https://www.congress.gov/bill/113th-congress/house-bill/366.

H.R. 1258—114th Congress: Pet and Women Safety Act of 2015. (2015). In GovTrack.us. Retrieved May 20, 2015, from https://www.govtrack.us/congress/bills/114/hr1258/summary.

H.R. 2293—114th Congress: Preventing Animal Cruelty Torture Act (2015). Retrieved May 20, 2015, from https://www.congress.gov/bill/114th-congress/house-bill/2293/amendments.

Hughes, G., & Lawson, C. (2011). RSPCA and the criminology of social control. *Crime, Law and Social Changes, 55*, 375–389.

Humane Society International. (2012). *Shark Finning in Focus: What HSI is doing to save sharks from a brutal practice.* Retrieved August 17, 2012, from http://www.hsi.org/news/news/2012/06/shark_finning_in_focus_061512.html.

Humane Society Legislative Fund. (2012). Ayes and nays. *Humane Activist,* March/April, 8.

Humane Society of the United States. (2009). *Humane Society University to offer college degrees in animal protection studies.* Retrieved on August 1, 2012, from http://www.humanesociety.org/news/press_releases/2009/06/humane_society_university_degrees_animal_protection_studies_061809.html.

Humane Society of the United States. (2011). *Hawaii's shark fin product ban takes effect July 1.* Retrieved August 17, 2012, from http://www.humanesociety.org/news/press_releases/2011/06/hawaii_shark_fin_ban_062811.html.

Humane Society of the United States. (2012a). *Ag-gag bills and whistleblower suppression.* Retrieved August 17, 2012, from http://www.humanesociety.org/issues/campaigns/factory_farming/fact-sheets/ag_gag.html.

Humane Society of the United States. (2012c). *The HSUS urges Pennsylvania lawmakers to protect sharks from the fin trade.* Retrieved August 17, 2012, from http://www.humanesociety.org/news/press_releases/2012/08/pennsylvania_shark_finning_081712.html.

Humane Society of the United States. (2012d). *Illinois becomes fifth state to ban shark fin trade.* Retrieved August 17, 2012, http://www.humanesociety.org/news/press_releases/2012/07/ illinois_bans_shark_fin_trade_070112.html.

Humane Society Veterinary Medical Association. (2012). HSVMA opposes "ag-gag" laws in order to preserve public scrutiny of food safety, animal health and handling on industrial farms. Retrieved May 20, 2015, from http://www.hsvma.org/ag-gag_law_opposition_041112#.VV5i4flViko.

Humane Society of the United States. (n.d.). *Making the connection: What law enforcers need to know.* Brochure.

Keiper, L. (2010). Dogs and cats have a voice under new Massachusetts law. *Reuters Online.* Retrieved August 1, 2012, from http://www.reuters.com/article/2010/07/20/us-usa-pets-devocalization-idUSTRE66J3Z220100720.

Kellert, S. R. (1988). Human-animal interactions: A review of American attitudes to wild and domestic animals in the twentieth century, in A. N. Rowan (Ed.) *Animals and People Sharing the World,* (pp. 137–175). Hanover, NH: University Press of New England.

Knight, S., Vrij, A., Bard, K., & Brandon, D. (2009). Science versus human welfare? Understanding attitudes towards animal use. *Journal of Social Work Issues,* 65(3), 463–483.

Kruse, C. R. (1999). Gender, views of nature, and support for animal rights. *Society and Animals,* 7(3), 179–198.

Latty, Y. (2000). Hegins, Pa. ends annual pigeon shoot. Daily News, Feb. 1, 2000. Retrieved August 30, 2012, from http://articles.philly.com/2000-02-01/news/25575515_1_robert-tobashlabor-day-committee-hegins-park.

Lockwood, R. (2006). *Animal cruelty prosecution. Opportunities for early response to crime and interpersonal violence.* Alexandria: APRI.

Los Angeles Animal Service Office. (n.d.). *Animal Cruelty Task Force.* Retrieved August 12, 2012, from http://www.laanimalservices.com/about_us/ACTF.htm.

Manning, S. (2014). FBI makes animal cruelty a top-tier felony to help track abuse. *Huffington Post,* online. Retrieved May 20, 2015, from http://www.huffingtonpost.com/2014/10/01/fbi-animal-cruelty-felony_n_5913364.html.

Massey, B. (2014). Horse slaughter blocked by federal law. *USA Today.* Retrieved May 21, 2015, from http://www.usatoday.com/story/money/business/2014/01/17/horse-slaughter-blocked-by-federal-law/4604929/.

McNutt, M. (2012). Oklahoma pet breeders board not fighting legislation that could eliminate it. NewsOK, March 28. Retrieved from http://newsok.com/oklahoma-pet-breeders-board-not-fighting-legislation-that-could-eliminate-it/article/3661423.

Merriam-Webster Dictionary. (2015). Retrieved June 18, 2015, from http://www.merriam-webster.com/dictionary/advocacy.

Munro, L. (2005). Strategies, action repertoires and DIY activism in the animal rights movement. *Social Movement Studies, 4*(1), 75–94.

National Animal Cruelty Investigations School. (n.d.). *University of Missouri Law Enforcement Training Institute.* Retrieved August 14, 2012, from http://leti.missouri.edu/animal-cruelty.aspx.

National District Attorneys Association. (n.d.). National Center for Prosecution of Animal Abuse. Retrieved August 14, 2012, from http://www.ndaa.org/animal_abuse_home.html.

National Parks Conservation Association. (n.d.). American alligator. Retrieved June 15, 2015, from http://www.npca.org/protecting-our-parks/wildlife_facts/alligator.html.

Newcomer, E. (2012). New Jersey's highest court bars distress claims in death of pets. *New York Times Online.* Retrieved June 15, 2015, from http://www.nytimes.com/2012/08/02/nyregion/new-jersey-supreme-court-bars-claims-of-distress-in-pet-deaths.html.

Newman, A. (2011, March 23). Animals' DNA is used to win convictions of abusers. *New York Times*, p. 24.

New York State Humane Society (n.d.). *How to investigate animal cruelty in NY State—A manual of procedures.* Retrieved August 12, 2012, from http://www.nyshumane.org/manual/manual.htm.

Pacelle, W. (2015). States make strides in passing animal protection laws. A humane nation. Retrieved May 20, 2015, from http://blog.humanesociety.org/wayne/2015/01/state-legislative-rankings.html.

PA H.B. 164—2015 Session. Retrieved May 21, 2015, from http://www.legis.state.pa.us/CFDOCS/Legis/PN/Public/btCheck.cfm?txtType=HTM&sessYr=2015&sessInd=0&billBody=H&billTyp=B&billNbr=0164&pn=0664.

PETA. (n.d.). Mother pigs and piglets abused by Hormel supplier. Retrieved June 15, 2015, from https://secure.peta.org/site/Advocacy?cmd=display&page=UserAction&id=1131.

PETA. (2009, June 24). Four more Iowa pig factory farm workers admit guilt! Retrieved June 15, 2015, from http://www.peta.org/b/thepetafiles/archive/2009/06/24/four-more-former-iowa-pig-factory-farm-workers-admit-guilt.aspx.

Pifer, L. (1996). Exploring the gender gap in young adults' attitudes about animal research. *Society & Animals, 4,* 37–52.

Potter, W. (2009). The green scare. *Vermont Law Review, 36*, 671–687.

Presser, L., & Taylor, W. V. (2011). An autoethnography of hunting. *Crime, Law and Social Change, 55*, 483–494.

Rasmussen, K. (2012). Efforts to restrict recordings of animal abuse could impede news-gathering. *News Media & the Law.* Spring, 4–8.

Scutter, J. N., & Mills, C. B. (2009). The credibility of shock advocacy: Animal rights attack messages. *Public Relations Review, 35*(2), 162–164.

Senatori, M., & Frasch, P. (2010). The future of animal law: Moving beyond preaching to the choir. *Journal of Legal Education, 60*(2), 209–236.

Shark Stewards (2015). U.S. states with shark fin trade regulations and penalties. Retrieved May 20, 2015, from http://sharkstewards.org/fin-free-tool/us-states-with-shark-fin-trade-regulations-penalties/.

South, N., & Beirne, P. (Eds.). (1998). *Theoretical Criminology. Special Issue: For a Green Criminology, 2*(2), 147–278.

Sykes, G. M., & Matza, D. (1957). Techniques of neutralization: A theory of delinquency. *American Sociological Review, 22*, 664–670.

Tauber, S. (2010). The influence of animal advocacy groups in state courts of last resort. *Society & Animals, 18*, 58–74.

Taylor, N. (2011). Criminology and human-animal violence research: The contribution and the challenge. *Critical Criminology, 19*: 251–263.

Thomas, S. C., & Beirne, P. (2002). Humane education and humanistic philosophy: Toward a new curriculum. *Journal of Humanistic Counseling, Education and Development, 41*(Fall), 190–199.

Tonsor, G. T., & Olynk, N. J. (2011). Impacts of animal well-being and welfare media on meat demand. *Journal of Agricultural Economics, 62*(1), 59–72.

Tuyttens, F. A. M., Vanhonacker, F., Langendries, K., Aluwe, M, Millet, S. Bekaert, K, & Verbeke, W. (2011). Effect of information provisioning on attitude toward surgical castration of male piglets and alternative strategies for avoiding boar taint. *Research in Veterinary Science, 91*(2), 327–332.

United States v. Ashley Nicole Richards; Brent Justice, No. 13-20265 5th Cir. (2014).

United States v. Stevens, 130 S.Ct. L. Ed., 15777 (2010).

University of Florida (n.d.). *About: The ASPCA Veterinary Forensic Sciences Program.*Retrieved August 14, 2012 from http://forensics.med.ufl.edu/about/.

Vollum, S., Buffington-Vollum, J., & Longmire, D. R. (2004). Moral disengagement and attitudes about violence towards animals. *Society & Animals, 12*(3), 209–235.

Volokh, E. (2015). Chimpanzee almost gets *habeas corpus*—and in any event the Nonhuman Rights Project gets a court hearing. *The Washington Post Online.* Retrieved May 20, 2015 from http://www.washingtonpost.com/news/volokh-conspiracy/wp/2015/04/22/chimpanzee-almost-gets-habeas-corpus-and-in-any-event-the-nonhuman-rights-project-gets-a-court-hearing/.

Woodson, M. B. (2011). Three cases of advocacy: The Cove, Mine, and Food, INC. *Society & Animals, 18*, 200–204.

Worden, A. (2014). NRA claims 11th hour victory in battle over live pigeon shoots. *Philadelphia Inquirer* Retrieved May 20, 2015, from http://www.philly.com/philly/blogs/pets/House-battle-over-live-pigeon-shoots-goes-down-to-the-wire-NRA-prevails.html?c=r.

Wright, P. (2012). Ore. court rules animals aren't just property. *San Francisco Chronicle Online*. Retrieved on August 2, 2012, from http://www.sfgate.com/news/article/Ore-court-rules-animals-aren-t-just-property-3757952.php.

Yates, R. (2011). Criminalizing protests about animal abuse. Recent Irish experience in global context. *Crime, Law and Social Change, 55*, 469–482.

Yates, R., Powell, C., & Beirne, P. (2001). Horse maiming in the English countryside: Moral panic, human deviance, and the social construction of victimhood. *Society & Animals, 9*(1), 1–23.

Zilney, L., & Zilney, M. (2005). Reunification of child and animal welfare agencies: Cross-reporting of abuse in Wellington County, Ontario. *Child Welfare, 84*(1), 47–66.

Zimmerman, M. (2010). Justices toss law banning videos of animal cruelty. *News Media and the Law, 34*(2), 17–18.

Section VI
Appendix

Animal Protection Agencies and Organizations

The following is a compilation of animal protection agencies and organizations. Below each agency/organization name and Website Uniform Resource Locator (URL) is a quote describing the agency/organization in its own words. Please note that this list merely provides a sample of agencies and is by no means exhaustive, nor does it imply that organizations omitted from the list have not made substantial contributions to the area of animal protection.

Alley Cat Allies

http://www.alleycat.org/

"Alley Cat Allies is the only national advocacy organization dedicated to the protection and humane treatment of cats. An engine for social change, Alley Cat Allies was the first organization to introduce and advocate for humane methods of feral cat care, particularly Trap-Neuter-Return, in the American animal protection community. By establishing and promoting standards of care, our organization has brought humane treatment of cats into the national spotlight, now embraced by major cities and animal protection organizations coast to coast. In 20 short years, we've changed America to better understand and respect the lives of cats.

"Today, more than 260,000 supporters look to Alley Cat Allies for leadership in the movement to protect cats' lives. We promote progressive policies for cats in communities all over America and we work towards a world that values the lives of all animals. Our two decades of experience in grassroots organizing, hands-on activism, and education has empowered policymakers, veterinarians, nonprofit and volunteer groups, activists, and caregivers nationwide with the tools and knowledge to practice, teach, and advocate for humane care for cats in their own communities. From a headquarters in Bethesda, Maryland, Alley Cat Allies' staff of nearly 30 people provides the national voice for cats and the millions of Americans that value cats' lives."

American Anti-Vivisection Society

http://www.aavs.org/site/c.bkLTKfOSLhK6E/b.6353579/k.2B2E/ Working_to_end_the_use_of_animals_in_science.htm

"The mission of AAVS is to unequivocally oppose and work to end experimentation on animals and oppose all forms of cruelty to animals.

"Founded in 1883, the American Anti-Vivisection Society (AAVS) is the first non-profit animal advocacy and educational organization in the United States dedicated to ending experimentation on animals in research, testing, and education. AAVS also opposes and works to end other forms of cruelty to animals. We work with students, grassroots groups, individuals, teachers, the media, other national organizations, government officials, members of the scientific community, and advocates in other countries to legally and effectively end the use of animals in science through education, advocacy, and the development of alternative methods to animal use."

American Humane Association

http://www.americanhumane.org/

"Since 1877 the historic American Humane Association has been at the forefront of every major advancement in protecting children, pets and farm animals from abuse and neglect. Today we're also leading the way in understanding human-animal interaction and its role in society.

"As the nation's voice for the protection of children and animals, American Humane Association reaches millions of people every day through groundbreaking research, education, training and services that span a wide network of organizations, agencies and businesses."

American Society for the Prevention of Cruelty to Animals (ASPCA)

http://www.aspca.org/

"Founded in 1866, the ASPCA was the first humane organization in the Western Hemisphere. Our mission, as stated by founder Henry Bergh, is 'to provide effective means for the prevention of cruelty to animals throughout the United States.' The ASPCA works to rescue animals from abuse, pass humane laws and share resources with shelters nationwide."

Animal Defenders International

http://www.ad-international.org/home/

"Our group of organisations, *Animal Defenders International*, the *National Anti-Vivisection Society*, and the *Lord Dowding Fund for Humane Research*, work together globally for the protection of animals."

Animal Farm Foundation, Inc.

http://www.animalfarmfoundation.org/

"Animal Farm Foundation, Inc., a not-for-profit corporation, has been rescuing and re-homing animals, as well as making grants to other humane organizations, since the mid-1980s. We are located in Dutchess County, NY.

"We currently dedicate our resources to securing equal treatment and opportunity for 'pit bull' dogs. Whether the dog is called a 'pit bull' because of a documented pedigree, or merely on the basis of physical appearance, recognizing that these dogs are individuals for whom we are responsible is an integral step toward a compassionate future for all dogs."

Animal Legal Defense Fund

http://www.aldf.org/

"For more than three decades, the Animal Legal Defense Fund has been fighting to protect the lives and advance the interests of animals through the legal system. Founded in 1979 by attorneys active in shaping the emerging field of animal law, ALDF has blazed the trail for stronger enforcement of anti-cruelty laws and more humane treatment of animals in every corner of American life. Today, ALDF's groundbreaking efforts to push the U.S. legal system to end the suffering of abused animals are supported by thousands of dedicated attorneys and more than 100,000 members."

Animal Protection Institute (Born Free USA)

http://www.bornfreeusa.org/

"Born Free USA is a national animal advocacy nonprofit 501(c)(3) organization, contributions to which are tax-deductible. Our mission is to end the suffering of wild animals in captivity, rescue individual animals in need, protect wildlife—including highly endangered species—in their natural habitats, and encourage compassionate conservation globally."

Animal Protection and Rescue League

http://www.aprl.org/

"The Animal Protection and Rescue League is a grassroots 501(c)(3) nonprofit organization based in San Diego which works to document and expose animal cruelty occurring behind closed doors, educates the public on animals issues through innovative outreach campaigns, and works with policymakers and politicians to implement humane change!

"Since forming in 2003, APRL has garnered the attention of national and international media, influenced animal protection legislation, conducted numerous rescues of abused factory farmed animals, influenced cities to adopt humane solutions to wildlife management, and created a network of grassroots outreach volunteers."

Animal Rescue Corps

http://animalrescuecorps.org/

"The establishing members of Animal Rescue Corps (ARC) have more than 40 years of collective experience in animal protection. Founded by Scotlund Haisley, a 20-year veteran in this field, ARC provides expert animal protection services throughout the US and beyond.

"ARC brings the professional expertise, human resources, tactical equipment, and financial backing necessary for its rescue operations, including investigations and permanent placements. ARC works with communities that don't have the resources to confront the cruelty themselves, especially when large numbers of suffering animals are involved.

"ARC further addresses animal cruelty by generating public awareness, training volunteers, increasing community involvement and other measurable actions. Ultimately, ARC works within the legal system to affect lasting change from the inside out.

"Animal Rescue Corps is unique because of its streamlined internal structure and its well-proven methods of external operations. Efficiency, effectiveness and expertise make ARC a leader in rescuing animals and serving communities."

Animalearn

http://www.animalearn.org/

"At Animalearn, we work to foster an awareness of and a respect for animals used in education. We strive to eliminate the use of animals in education and we are dedicated to assisting educators and students to find the most effective non-animal methods to teach and study science.

"Animalearn has created The Science Bank, our lending program of new and innovative life science software and educational products that enable educators and students to learn anatomy, physiology, and psychology lessons without harming animals, themselves, or the Earth. Our loan program has been offering products to thousands of people for over a decade, and it is continually growing and expanding. Animalearn also provides humane education curricula and materials free of charge for educators and students."

Animals and Society Institute

http://www.animalsandsociety.org/

"The Animals and Society Institute develops *knowledge* in the field of human-animal studies, supports *practice* to address the relation between animal cruelty and other violence and promotes *action* to protect animals through the adoption of ethical, compassionate public policy. An independent research and educational organization, we work to enhance understanding of our complex relationships with other animals, stop the cycle of violence and promote stricter animal protection laws."

Animal Welfare Institute

http://www.awionline.org/

"Since its founding in 1951, AWI has sought to alleviate the suffering inflicted on animals by people. In the organization's early years, our particular emphasis was on the desperate needs of animals used for experimentation. In the decades that followed, we expanded the scope of our work to address many other areas of animal suffering.

"Today, one of our greatest areas of emphasis is cruel animal factories, which raise and slaughter pigs, cows, chickens and other animals. The biggest are in our country, and they are expanding worldwide."

Anti-Fur Society

http://www.antifursociety.org/

"The Anti-Fur Society is a group of dedicated, committed and caring volunteers working around the world to better the lives of fur-bearing animals. The Anti-Fur Society is a project of the Misha Foundation, a 501(c)(4) non-profit organization that operates solely on its founder's donations. Because the Misha Foundation/Anti-Fur Society is a 501(c)(4) organization, it is not restricted in its political involvement. Its members can lobby public officials and campaign for or against candidates for public office."

A Tail to Tell, Inc.

http://atailtotell.com/newwebsite/

"A Tail To Tell, Inc. is a group of men and women in Lancaster County, Pennsylvania dedicated to freeing dogs from the horrors of the puppy mills. We retrieve canine survivors from the Amish and Mennonite mills in our area and from other commercial breeders in the Northeast US. We provide veterinary care and loving foster homes while we work to find the best forever homes possible for our dogs."

Best Friends Animal Society

http://www.bestfriends.org/

"Best Friends Animal Society is guided by a simple philosophy: kindness to animals builds a better world for all of us. In the late 1980s, when Best Friends was in its early days, roughly 17 million dogs and cats were being killed in shelters every year. Despite the commitment of shelter workers to the animal in their care, the conventional belief was that little could be done to lower that terrible number."

Big Cat Rescue

http://bigcatrescue.org/

"Big Cat Rescue is the largest accredited sanctuary in the world dedicated entirely to abused and abandoned big cats. We are home to over 100 lions, tigers, bobcats, cougars and other species most of whom have been abandoned, abused, orphaned, saved from being turned into fur coats, or retired from performing acts. Our dual mission is to provide the best home we can for the cats in our care and educate the public about the plight of these majestic animals, both in captivity and in the wild, to end abuse and avoid extinction."

Chimpanzee Sanctuary Northwest

http://www.chimpsanctuarynw.org/

"Chimpanzee Sanctuary Northwest (CSNW) is located on a 26-acre farm in the Cascade mountains, due east of Seattle. CSNW is one of only nine sanctuaries in the country that cares for chimpanzees.

"CSNW was founded in 2003 to provide sanctuary for chimpanzees discarded from the entertainment and biomedical testing industries."

Chipangali Wildlife Orphanage

http://www.chipangali.com/

"Chipangali is a haven for wild animals which have little hope for survival in the wild—creatures which have been orphaned, abandoned, injured, born in captivity or brought up unsuccessfully as pets. It is often the last refuge for those brought in sick or injured, and increasingly it is a sanctuary for confiscated animals."

Companion Animal Protection Alliance

http://forourcompanions.com/home.html

"The Companion Animal Protection Alliance (CAPA) is a coalition of individuals brought together by the common desire to protect our companion animals from veterinary malpractice—which we believe has touched all of our lives by either taking the lives of our dear animal friends or injuring them irreparably."

Compassion Over Killing

http://www.cok.net/

"COK is a nonprofit animal advocacy organization headquartered in Washington, D.C. with an additional office in Los Angeles. Working to end animal abuse since 1995, COK focuses on cruelty to animals in agriculture and promotes vegetarian eating as a way to build a kinder world for all of us, both human and nonhuman."

Darwin Animal Doctors

http://darwinanimaldoctors.org/

"Darwin Animal Doctors provides comprehensive veterinary care for the animals of the Galapagos Islands. We're committed to saving animals, and the Galapagos."

Defenders of Wildlife

http://www.defenders.org/

"For more than six decades, Defenders of Wildlife has been a leading force in the protection of wildlife and wild lands. We employ innovative, science-based approaches to protect imperiled wildlife, advocate for wildlife friendly climate and renewable energy policies and conserve and restore native habitat."

Dogs Deserve Better

http://www.dogsdeservebetter.org/

"DOGS DESERVE BETTER is a 501c3 nonprofit organization dedicated to freeing the chained dog, and bringing our best friend into the home and family. Our mission is to free them through education, rescue and rehabilitation [sic], grassroots legislation, and fencing programs."

Doris Day Animal League

http://www.ddal.org/

"The Doris Day Animal League's overriding mission is to reduce the pain and suffering of non-human animals through legislative initiatives, education, and programs to enforce statutes and regulations which have already been enacted protecting animals. We strongly encourage the spaying and neutering of companion animals."

Farm Sanctuary

http://www.farmsanctuary.org/

"Our Mission: To protect farm animals from cruelty, inspire change in the way society views and treats farm animals, and promote compassionate vegan living.

Factory Farming

"In an ideal world, there would be no need for Farm Sanctuary as it exists today. There would be no factory farms or stockyards. Cows, pigs, chickens, turkeys, and sheep would be free to roam in their pastures, sleep in the sun, scratch at the earth, and enjoy life. Animals in today's industrialized farms are treated like commodities. They are crowded into warehouses, confined so tightly that they cannot easily walk or even turn around. They are de-beaked, de-toed, and their tails are docked without anesthetic. Their bones break because their bodies have been manipulated to grow so fast that they can't support their own weight. Factory farm animals are denied fresh air, sun, wholesome food, room to move, and the freedom to exhibit their natural behaviors. This rampant abuse of millions of animals every day is largely invisible to the public.

Farm Sanctuary

"Farm Sanctuary was founded in 1986 to combat the abuses of factory farming and encourage a new awareness and understanding about farm animals. Today, Farm Sanctuary is the nation's largest and most effective farm animal rescue and protection organization. We have rescued thousands of animals and cared for them at our sanctuaries in Watkins Glen, New York; Northern California (Orland); and the Los Angeles area. At Farm Sanctuary, these animals are our friends, not our food. We educate millions of people about their plight and the effects of factory farming on our health and environment. We advocate for laws and policies to prevent suffering and promote compassion, and we reach out to legislators and businesses to bring about institutional reforms."

Fixit Foundation

http://fixit-foundation.org/

"FiXiT Foundation, a 501(c)(3) tax exempt nonprofit based in Norfolk, VA, was formed in response to the death of millions of cats and dogs every year in U.S. shelters. Current low cost spay/neuter efforts have placed us on a plateau with minimal change in the rate of euthanasia over the past 10 years. We knew that a new strategy was needed to stop this needless loss of life, one that was informed by strategic research and one that responds to the different perspectives of pet owners across the country."

Friends of Animals

http://www.friendsofanimals.org/

"Friends of Animals is a non-profit, international animal advocacy organization, incorporated in the state of New York since 1957. Friends of Animals works to cultivate a respectful view of nonhuman animals, free-living and domestic. Our goal is to free animals from cruelty and institutionalized exploitation around the world."

Global Federation of Animal Sanctuaries

http://www.sanctuaryfederation.org/gfas/home/

"Animal protection leaders from a number of organizations came together in 2007 to found the Global Federation of Animal Sanctuaries (GFAS). This was in response to:
- virtually unchecked and hidden animal exploitation of inhumanely kept wildlife
- the wildlife trade itself
- the flood of horses, captive wild parrots and abandoned "pet" reptiles suddenly without homes
- the growing demand for sanctuary for farmed animals and animals used in labs
- the plight of animals left in need by natural disasters and wars
- the need for the public to be able to differentiate exploitative operations from legitimate sanctuaries
- the need for global animal specific standards and operational standards for sanctuaries, based on the fine work of the former The Association of Sanctuaries, the former Captive Wild Animal Protection Coalition, and others.

"The GFAS mission is to promote excellence in sanctuary management and in humane care of animals through international accreditation, collaboration, mentoring, and greater recognition and resources for sanctuaries, while seeking to eliminate the causes of displaced animals."

The Humane League

http://www.thehumaneleague.com/

"The Humane League is a 501(c)3 animal advocacy organization that works to protect all animals through public education, campaigns and rescue. We have staffed offices serving the greater metro regions of Philadelphia, Boston, Maryland and New York City, and our work for animals extends nationwide. Funding comes from our over 6,000 members and supporters.

"Since our founding in 2005, our mission has been to save the lives of as many animals as possible and to reduce as much animal cruelty as we can. We want a world where people, companies and legislators are making choices that help and not hurt animals, a world in which all animals are treated with the same respect and compassion that we show to our beloved family dog or cat. We invest our time, money and energy where they will do the most good for the greatest number of animals. As a result, our primary focus is on farmed animal issues. Farmed animals represent over 98% of the animals used and killed in the United States, and because they are excluded from state anti-cruelty laws they suffer intensely on today's 'factory farms.'"

The Humane Society of the United States (HSUS)

http://www.humanesociety.org/

"Established in 1954, The HSUS seeks a humane and sustainable world for all animals—a world that will also benefit people. We are America's mainstream force against cruelty, exploitation and neglect, as well as the most trusted voice extolling the human-animal bond."

Humane Society International

http://www.hsi.org/

"Humane Society International is one of the only international animal protection organizations in the world working to protect all animals—including animals in laboratories, farm animals, companion animals, and wildlife—and our record of achievement demonstrates our dedication and effectiveness."

Humane Society Veterinary Medical Association

http://www.hsvma.org/

"The Humane Society Veterinary Medical Association (HSVMA) was formed as a home for veterinary professionals who want to engage in direct care programs for animals in need and educate the public and others in the profession about animal welfare issues.

"HSVMA Rural Area Veterinary Services (HSVMA-RAVS), is our primary direct care program. We are also actively involved in advocating for better public policies for animals and advancing humane alternatives in veterinary education."

Institute for Humane Education

http://www.humaneeducation.org/

"The Institute for Humane Education (IHE) is a non-profit, 501(c)(3) educational organization dedicated to creating a humane world through humane education."

International Fund for Animal Welfare

http://www.ifaw.org/united-states/

"Founded in 1969, the International Fund for Animal Welfare saves individual animals, animal populations and habitats all over the world. With projects in more than 40 countries, IFAW provides hands-on assistance to animals in need, whether it's dogs and cats, wildlife and livestock, or rescuing animals in the wake of disasters. We also advocate saving populations from cruelty and depletion, such as our campaign to end commercial whaling and seal hunts."

International Primate Protection League

http://www.ippl.org/gibbon/

"IPPL is a grassroots nonprofit organization dedicated to protecting the world's remaining primates, great and small.

"Since 1973, we have worked to expose primate abuse and battled international traffickers. We also operate a sanctuary for gibbons (the smallest of the apes) in South Carolina and support primate rescue efforts worldwide, especially in countries where primates are native."

The Latham Foundation

http://www.latham.org/

"Founded in 1918, Latham is a clearinghouse for information about:
- Human issues and activities
- The human-companion animal bond (HCAB)
- Animal-assisted therapy
- The connections between child and animal abuse and other forms of violence

League Against Cruel Sports

http://www.league.org.uk/

"The League is a charity that brings together people who want to stop cruelty to animals in the name of sport.

"Established in 1924, we successfully use lawful investigations, campaigning and lobbying to make a difference in the UK and around the world."

Leaping Bunny Program

http://www.leapingbunny.org/indexcus.php

"The Coalition for Consumer Information on Cosmetics' (CCIC) Leaping Bunny Program administers a cruelty-free standard and the internationally recognized Leaping Bunny Logo for companies producing cosmetic, personal care, and household products. The Leaping Bunny Program provides the best assurance that no new animal testing is used in any phase of product development by the company, its laboratories, or suppliers."

Marine Mammal Stranding Center

http://www.marinemammalstrandingcenter.org/home.html

"The Marine Mammal Stranding Center, a private, non-profit organization, started in 1978 with a handful of volunteers and a C.E.T.A. grant, was founded, and is still directed by Robert Schoelkopf. He and his wife, Sheila Dean, along with a small paid staff and volunteers with a wide variety of talents and professional backgrounds, continue to work with the animals. Originally based in Gardner's Basin in the inlet section of Atlantic City, the Center is now located on the barrier island of Brigantine, which borders coastal New Jersey's largest wildlife refuge."

Mercy for Animals

http://www.mercyforanimals.org/

"MFA works to create a society where all animals are treated with the compassion and respect they so rightfully deserve.

"We serve as a voice for animals through proactive consumer education initiatives, cruelty investigations, corporate outreach, and legal advocacy."

National Canine Research Council

http://nationalcanineresearchcouncil.com/

"The National Canine Research Council is committed to preserving the human-canine bond. We publish, underwrite, and reprint accurate, documented, reliable research to promote a better understanding of our relationship with dogs.

"We make grants to universities, independent research organizations and independent scholars. We also conduct our own research on contemporary issues that impact the human-canine bond, including the dynamics of popular attitudes toward dogs and canine aggression; public health reporting on dog bites; public policy concerning companion animals; and media reporting on dogs."

Nonhuman Rights Project

http://www.nonhumanrightsproject.org/

"The Nonhuman Rights Project is the only organization working toward actual LEGAL rights for members of species other than our own. Our mission is to change the common law status of at least some nonhuman animals from mere 'things,' which lack the capacity to possess any legal right, to 'persons,' who possess such fundamental rights as bodily integrity and bodily liberty, and those other legal rights to which evolving standards of morality, scientific discovery, and human experience entitle them. Our first cases are being prepared for filing in 2013."

Pennsylvania Society for the Prevention of Cruelty to Animals

http://www.pspca.org/

"In 1867, Colonel M. Richards Mucklé, a Philadelphia businessman, was disheartened by the violence he witnessed against animals. Horses pulling over-laden carts and streetcars were often beaten unmercifully or worked to death. Many, if not most of the city's work horses were lame, sore and weak from carrying heavy cargo and passenger loads across cobbled streets during icy winters and sweltering summers....

"With the reduction of the use of horses in daily life, the society continued to shift its focus. Investigations and prosecutions of the abusers of dogs and cats curtailed the violence in the lives of these innocent animals. Shelters were erected to house, feed and care for homeless or unwanted animals. Over the years, the Society launched programs focusing on humane care such low-cost veterinary care for companion animals, adoption of homeless animals from shelters and spay & neuter to prevent unwanted births; programs that exist to this very day.

"Humane issues concerning animals have continued to shift throughout the history of the organization. The demand for our work is as overwhelming today as it was when Colonel Mucklé founded the Society. We must constantly struggle to replace ignorance and callousness with knowledge and kindness. With your help, the Pennsylvania SPCA will continue to make a difference in our world through education, compassion and consideration."

People for the Ethical Treatment of Animals

http://www.peta.org/

"People for the Ethical Treatment of Animals (PETA) is the largest animal rights organization in the world, with more than 3 million members and supporters.

"PETA focuses its attention on the four areas in which the largest numbers of animals suffer the most intensely for the longest periods of time: on factory farms, in the clothing trade, in laboratories, and in the entertainment industry. We also work on a variety of other issues, including the cruel killing of beavers, birds, and other 'pests' as well as cruelty to domesticated animals.

"PETA works through public education, cruelty investigations, research, animal rescue, legislation, special events, celebrity involvement, and protest campaigns."

Pet-Abuse.com

http://www.pet-abuse.com/

"Pet-Abuse.Com is a national animal protection organization that researches and tracks incidents of criminal animal cruelty. We offer a wide range of service and tools for animal advocates, humane law enforcement, researchers and prosecutors."

Presidential Pits

http://www.presidentialpits.org/

"Presidential Pits is a 501(c)(3) organization that is staffed entirely by volunteers. Our mission is to provide rescue, education, and community outreach for the promotion and protection of pit bull-type dogs in the District of Columbia and surrounding areas."

Progressive Animal Welfare Society

http://www.paws.org/

"PAWS is people helping animals. We are the kind of people who delight in the company of an animal friend, who are awed by a majestic eagle in flight. Like you, we understand that animals enrich our lives. We also know they cannot speak for themselves and need protection. That is why PAWS brings together people like you to ensure animals are respected, safe and have a voice."

RabbitWise

http://www.rabbitwise.org/

"RABBITWISE is an all volunteer, non-profit 501c3 public charities organization whose primary client is the domestic rabbit. Our mission is: to PREVENT irresponsible acquisition and care of companion rabbits; to improve RETENTION rates of rabbits already living in homes in order to avoid them being relinquished or abandoned; to EDUCATE persons who live with, shelter, and/or treat rabbits to give them the best care possible; and to ADVOCATE for the broader welfare of rabbits in general."

Showing Animals Respect and Kindness

http://www.sharkonline.org/

"SHARK is a non-profit organization with supporters around the US and beyond. SHARK receives no government funding and completely relies on donations and grants to work on issues ranging in scope from local to worldwide.

"With a small core of volunteers, and a staff of three (two are part-time), SHARK battles tirelessly against bullfighting, pigeon shoots, turkey shoots, canned hunts (and all hunting), rodeos, circuses, zoos, and marine parks … any issue that involves violation of the innate rights of living creatures."

South Florida Wildlife Center

http://www.humanesociety.org/animal_community/shelters/wildlife_care_center/

"At the South Florida Wildlife Center, our mission is to rescue and rehabilitate wildlife and treat other animals in need in South Florida and help the community celebrate our wild neighbors and find solutions to any challenges they pose."

Tigers in America

http://www.tigersinamerica.org/

"Tigers in America is committed to rescuing unwanted or neglected tigers from inadequate or failed facilities."

United Poultry Concerns

http://upc-online.org/

"'Founded in 1990 by Karen Davis, United Poultry Concerns is the world's foremost non-profit organization dedicated to promoting the respectful treatment of domestic fowl. UPC runs a haven for chickens in Virginia, and also teaches people about the egg and chicken meat industries, the natural lives of free chickens, pleasures and benefits of human-chicken companionship, and alternatives to chicken farming and the use of chickens in education and scientific experimentation.' — Dr. Annie Potts, *Chicken*, 2012"

Wildlife Alliance

http://www.wildlifealliance.org/wildlife

"Wildlife Alliance is the leader in direct protection to forests and wildlife in the Southeast Asian tropical belt. Our mission is to combat deforestation, wildlife extinction, climate change, and poverty by partnering with local communities and governments."

World Society for the Protection of Animals

http://www.wspa-international.org/

"Our vision: a world where animal welfare matters and animal cruelty has ended. The World Society for the Protection of Animals exists to tackle animal cruelty across the globe. We work directly with animals and the people and organisations that can ensure animals are treated with respect and compassion.

"With your support, we campaign effectively to combat the world's most intense and large-scale animal welfare issues. We bring about lasting change by:

- helping people understand the critical importance of good animal welfare
- encouraging nations to commit to animal-friendly practices
- building the scientific case for the better treatment of animals."

World Wildlife Fund (Federation)

http://www.wwf.org/

"WWF's mission is to stop the degradation of the planet's natural environment and to build a future in which humans live in harmony with nature, by:

- conserving the world's biological diversity
- ensuring that the use of renewable natural resources is sustainable
- promoting the reduction of pollution and wasteful consumption."

Author Biographies

Phil Arkow is a coordinator of the National Link Coalition and a consultant for the American Society for the Prevention of Cruelty to Animals. He chairs the Latham Foundation's Animal Abuse and Family Violence Prevention Project. He co-founded the National Link Coalition, the National Animal Control Association, the Animal Welfare Federation of New Jersey, and the Colorado Federation of Animal Welfare Agencies. He trains internationally on a variety of human-animal bond and anti-cruelty topics. He is an adjunct faculty member at Harcum College and Camden County College where he teaches Certificate courses in Animal-Assisted Therapy, and at the University of Florida where he co-wrote the course on Animal Abuse and Interpersonal Violence. A former newspaper reporter and foundation communications officer, Arkow is a prolific writer. He has also served with the American Veterinary Medical Association, the Delta Society, the American Humane Association, the Academy on Violence and Abuse, the National Coalition on Violence Against Animals, and the American Association of Human-Animal Bond Veterinarians.

Arnie Arluke, Ph.D., is a Professor of Sociology and Anthropology at Northeastern University, Vice President and Director of Research at Forensic Veterinary Investigations, and a Visiting Scholar at the International Fund for Animal Welfare. His research examines conflicts and contradictions in human-animal relationships. He has published over 100 articles and twelve books, including *Regarding Animals*, *Brute Force*, *Just a Dog*, *The Sacrifice*, *Between the Species*, *The Photographed Cat*, and *Beauty and the Beast*. His research has received awards from the American Sociological Association, the Society for the Study of Symbolic Interaction, the International Association for Human-Animal Interaction Organizations, and the Massachusetts Society for the Prevention of Cruelty to Animals. He also co-edits the Animals, Culture, and Society series for Temple University Press.

Kate Nattrass Atema, M.S., is Director of the Global Companion Animal Programme at the International Fund for Animal Welfare (IFAW) overseeing community-based dog and cat welfare projects in 12 countries on 5 continents, and Chairperson of the International Companion Animal Management Coalition (ICAM). Kate began her career in research at the Social Science Research Center of Berlin (WZB) in Germany, and holds a degree Animals and Public Policy from Tufts University, where she subsequently served as adjunct faculty and enjoys mentoring students in global animal welfare policy and research. Kate has published numerous articles in scientific and popular literature on topics ranging from assistance dogs to Animal Law, and has presented her work at numerous symposiums internationally with emphasis on the impacts of animal welfare on communities. Her work at IFAW focuses on the development and implementation of participatory processes for empowering communities to sustainably address both human and animal welfare development challenges.

Mary P. Brewster, Ph.D., is a Professor and Chair of Criminal Justice at West Chester University of Pennsylvania. Her research interests include victimology and domestic violence, and she was principal investigator of a National Institute of Justice-sponsored project on former intimate stalking. She has published numerous articles and book chapters on various topics including the media and the Michael Vick dogfighting case, bystander behavior, stalking, domestic violence, specialized courts, crime victims, and sex offender registries. Dr. Brewster was editor of previous books (*Stalking: Psychology, Risk Factors, Interventions, and Law; Pennsylvania Criminal Justice System*), Contributing Editor of *Criminal Justice Research Reports*, and Associate Editor of the forthcoming *Encyclopedia of Criminology & Criminal Justice*.

Lindsey S. Davis, M.A., is a doctoral student in Clinical Forensic Psychology at John Jay College of Criminal Justice in New York, NY. She received her B.A. in Psychological and Brain Sciences from Dartmouth College in 2005 and her M.A. in Forensic Psychology from John Jay College in 2011. Lindsey conducts research on sexual homicide and other extraordinary crimes under the advisement of Dr. Louis Schlesinger in conjunction with the FBI's Behavioral Science Unit.

Yolanda Eisenstein, J.D., is an attorney with an animal law practice in Dallas, Texas. She is an adjunct professor in animal law at Southern Methodist University (SMU) Dedman School of Law. She is past chair of the American Bar Association Tort Trial and Insurance Practice Section Animal Law Committee and former chair of the State Bar of Texas Animal Law Section. She speaks regularly on animal law and animal protection issues and is the author of *Careers in Animal Law* and *The American Bar Association Legal Guide for Dog Owners*. Eisenstein graduated with honors from SMU Dedman School of Law and is licensed to practice in Texas and New Mexico.

David Favre, J.D., is a professor of law at Michigan State University College of Law. Over the past twenty years Professor Favre has written several articles and books dealing with animal issues including such topics as animal cruelty, wildlife law, the use of animals for scientific research, and international control of animal trade. His books include the case book *Animal Law: Welfare, Interest, and Rights (2nd ed.)*, as well as, *Animal Law and Dog Behavior* and *International Trade in Endangered Species*. He also has presented to international audiences on these topics. He created and is editor-in-chief of the largest animal legal web resource, www.animallaw.info. Now residing on a farm in lower Michigan, Professor Favre shares his space with sheep, chickens and the usual assortment of dogs and cats.

Amy J. Fitzgerald is an Associate Professor in the Department of Sociology, Anthropology and Criminology at the University of Windsor in Ontario, Canada. Her areas of interest and specialization include critical animal studies, green criminology, gender studies, and environmental sociology. More specifically, her research focuses on the perpetration of harms (criminal and otherwise) by humans against the environment and non-human animals. She has published articles and books on the coexistence of animal abuse and intimate partner violence, sport hunting culture, and harms produced by the human and "pet" food industries.

Egan K. Green, Ph.D., grew up in the mountains of western North Carolina where he was indoctrinated into rural lifestyles and norms. He carried this background into his studies as he completed his Bachelor of Science degree at Appalachian State University before completing his Master of Arts in Criminology at East Tennessee State University and his Ph.D. in Criminology at Indiana University of Pennsylvania. His master's thesis as well as his doctoral dissertation addresses wildlife crime and law enforcement issues. He has presented papers at national and regional conferences on rural criminal justice issues including conservation crime and law enforcement as well as illicit alcohol production, use and distribution. He has also published journal articles and book chapters on natural resource crimes as well as criminal justice ethics issues. Dr. Green recently co-authored a text on police management.

Shannon Grugan earned her Ph.D. in Criminal Justice from Rutgers University and is currently an Assistant Professor at West Chester University. Her research interests include environmental crime, animal cruelty, crime and justice on college campuses, and situational analysis and prevention of crime events.

Eleonora Gullone, Ph.D., is Associate Professor (Adjunct) in the School of Psychological Sciences at Monash University, Australia. She is an academic and developmental psychologist with an excess of 100 refereed publications plus several chapters and books. In the past 20 or so years, she has focused her research on human-animal interactions and has carried out several empirical works in this area including the first Australian study to examine the relationship between family violence and animal abuse. Her work examining the more general relationship between human aggression and animal cruelty has culminated in a book published in 2012 (*Animal Cruelty, Antisocial Behaviour and Aggression: More than a link*). More recently she has turned her attention to politics and is now actively involved in the Australian Animal Justice Party—a national political party aimed at improving the lives of our non-human brethren.

Maya Gupta, Ph.D., earned her BA from Columbia University and both her master's degree and PhD in clinical psychology from the University of Georgia, where her research focused on the connections between animal cruelty and domestic violence. She is Executive Director of the Animals and Society Institute, which promotes more positive relationships between humans and animals by providing information and evidence-based resources to scholars, professionals, and advocates. Dr. Gupta was previously Executive Director of Ahimsa House, a Georgia-based nonprofit organization dedicated to helping human and animal victims of domestic violence across the state reach safety together. She currently serves on the Steering Committee of the National Link Coalition, on the Animal Cruelty Advisory Council of the Association of Prosecuting Attorneys, as Training Director of the Section on Human-Animal Interaction in the American Psychological Association, as adjunct faculty in the Anthrozoology program at Canisius College, and as assistant instructor in the Veterinary Forensic Sciences program at the University of Florida.

Christopher Hensley, Ph.D, is a full professor of criminal justice in the Department of Criminal Justice at the University of Tennessee at Chattanooga. He received his doctorate in sociology from Mississippi State University. His most recent publications appear in the *International Journal of Offender Therapy and Comparative Criminology* and the *Journal of Interpersonal Violence*. His research interests include the link between childhood animal cruelty and later violence toward humans, prison sexuality, and attitudes toward correctional issues.

Randall Lockwood, Ph.D., is Senior Vice President for Forensic Sciences and Anti-Cruelty Projects with the ASPCA. For over thirty years Dr. Lockwood has worked with law-enforcement agencies serving as an expert on the interactions between people and animals. He has testified in dozens of trials involving cruelty to animals or the treatment of animals in the context of other crimes, including dogfighting, child abuse, domestic violence and homicide. His efforts to increase awareness of the connection between animal abuse and other forms of violence were profiled in an award-winning 1999 Arts & Entertainment Network documentary entitled "*The Cruelty Connection*", and in 2008 he received a Public Service Award from the United States' Attorney's Office for his assistance in the Michael Vick dogfighting case.

Dr. Lockwood is a member of the American Academy of Forensic Sciences, a founding member of the International Veterinary Forensic Sciences Association, and a member of the Advisory Board of the National Center for the Prosecution of Animal Abuse and the

Association of Prosecuting Attorneys. He is a Fellow of the Oxford Center for Animal Ethics and the Denver University Center for Human-Animal Interaction and Affiliate Assistant Professor, Small Animal Clinical Sciences, at the University of Florida College of Veterinary Medicine.

Claire Molloy, Ph.D., is a professor and holds the Chair in Film, Television and Digital Media at Edge Hill University. She is the author of *Memento* (2010) and *Popular Media and Animals* (2011) and co-editor of *Beyond Human: From Animality to Transhumanism* (2012), *American Independent Cinema: Indie, indiewood and beyond* (2012) and The Routledge Companion to Film and Politics (2016). Claire is Co-Director of the Centre for Human Animal Studies.

John C. Navarro is a doctoral student at University of Louisville, Louisville Kentucky in the Criminal Justice department. He graduated with a Bachelor of Arts in Psychology with a minor in Criminal Justice Sciences from Illinois State University in 2011, and subsequently a Master's of Science in Criminal Justice Sciences in 2014. Navarro was the recipient of the Fisher Award for Outstanding Thesis for the College of Applied Sciences and Technology in 2015. His current research interests include sexual deviance, identity theft, crime mapping, and mental illness.

Gary Patronek, V.M.D., Ph.D, is a veterinary epidemiologist and Adjunct Assistant Professor at the Cummings School of Veterinary Medicine at Tufts University. His interest in animal hoarding stems from his experience as a first responder to many animal hoarding cases while working in animal welfare administration. He founded the Hoarding of Animals Research Consortium (HARC) in 1997, whose research was instrumental in the mention of animal hoarding under the new [object] hoarding disorder listed in DSM-5. He has published numerous papers and textbook chapters on the subject of animal hoarding, and has just completed work on an edited volume about the psychological evaluation of animal maltreatment offenders. He currently works as an independent consultant.

Bethanie A. Poe, LMSW, is a PhD candidate in social work at the University of Tennessee College of Social Work. She is a certified Veterinary Social Worker specializing in the area violence towards people and animals. For the past several years she has worked in mental health education and suicide prevention, and has previous experience working in the fields of domestic violence and child protection. Her current research focuses on what animal related professionals experience regarding human welfare issues while at work.

Mary Lou Randour, Ph.D., a psychologist, is Senior Advisor, Animal Cruelty Programs and Training for the Animal Welfare Institute. In that role, she identifies programs, policy, and research projects—and builds coalitions to support them—on the topic of animal abuse and human violence. She was a practicing clinician for 17 years, received postgraduate training at the Cambridge Hospital at Harvard Medical School and the Washington Psychoanalytic Institute and holds the position of adjunct assistant professor of psychiatry at the Uniformed Services University of the Health Services. She is the organizer and past chair of the Section on Human Animal Interaction, Society of Counseling Psychology, American Psychological Association. Dr. Randour initiated an effort over twelve years ago to have the Federal Bureau of Investigation include animal cruelty crimes in the agency's national database of crime statistics. This effort successfully concluded with the FBI's addition of animal cruelty to Group A of the National Incident Based Reporting System (NIBRS), and classifying it as a Crime Against Society in September of 2014 … Dr. Randour also serves on the Animal Cruelty Advisory Council of the Association of Prosecuting Attorneys. She is the author of handbooks such as: *A Common Bond: Child Maltreatment and Animals in the Family*, *AniCare Child*, *The AniCare Model of Treatment* *for Animal Abuse,* various professional publications, and is the editor of one book and author of two; her latest is *Animal Grace.*

Cassandra L. Reyes, Ph.D., is an Associate Professor of Criminal Justice at West Chester University of Pennsylvania. She received her doctorate in criminology at Indiana University of Pennsylvania and her dissertation was entitled, "Of fists and fangs: An exploration of the degree to which the Graduation Hypothesis predicts future adolescent delinquency and aggression" that was published as a book by VDM Verlag Dr. Müller in 2009. She has presented numerous papers on animal cruelty at national criminology, criminal justice, and sociology conferences. In addition, she recently wrote an encyclopedia entry entitled, "Animal Victims" in the *Encyclopedia of Criminology & Criminal Justice.* She has also provided regional and national trainings on the link between animal cruelty and the criminal justice system for probation and parole officers. Her main teaching and research area of interest is on the relationship between animal cruelty and other forms of delinquency and criminality, and created an animal cruelty and criminal justice course at West Chester University in the spring 2010 semester, which she teaches nearly every semester. In addition, she is a certified veterinary assistant and has previously worked as a kennel nurse for a short time at a veterinary hospital in southern New Jersey. She currently resides with her four cats, whom she considers her "furry kids."

Christina Risley-Curtiss, Ph.D., an Associate Professor of Social Work at Arizona State University has 40+ years of practice/teaching and research experience in public health, child welfare, and animal-human relations. Her areas of research and current publications are in animal-human relationships. She developed, implemented and directs the only assessment and intervention program of its kind in the country for children who are abusing animals. She is a Fellow at the Oxford Centre on Animal Ethics, a member of the National Link Coalition steering committee and the Arizona Professional Animal Cruelty Task Force. She presents at numerous conferences internationally/nationally on the positive role of animals in our lives; the co-occurrence of animal and human violence and intervening with children who are abusing animals. She does hands-on rescue work including having volunteered to help animals during the Katrina rescue and currently lives in a trans-species cultural home with a number of cats and chickens, and a horse.

Joan E. Schaffner, J.D., Associate Professor of Law, George Washington University Law School, B.S mechanical engineering and J.D., University of Southern California, M.S. mechanical engineering, Massachusetts Institute of Technology. Professor Schaffner teaches Civil Procedure, Remedies, and Sexuality and the Law, and directs the GW Animal Law Program. She has authored *Introduction to Animals and the Law* and the chapters, "Valuing Nature in Environmental Law: Lessons for Animal Law and the Valuation of Animals" in *What Can Animal Law Learn from Environmental Law?* and "Laws and Policy to Address the Link of Family Violence" in *The Link Between Animal Abuse and Humane Violence.* She is a co-author and editor of *A Lawyer's Guide to Dangerous Dog Issues* and *Litigating Animal Law Disputes: A Complete Guide for Lawyers*, Professor Schaffner is Past Chair and Newsletter Editor, ABA TIPS Animal Law Committee; Founding Chair and 2015 Chair, AALS Section on Animal Law; and Fellow, Oxford Centre for Animal Ethics.

Louis B. Schlesinger, Ph.D., is a Professor of Forensic Psychology, John Jay College of Criminal Justice, Diplomate in Forensic Psychology of the American Board of Professional Psychology, and Distinguished Practitioner in the National Academies of Practice. He is co-principal investigator of a major research project on extraordinary crime with the FBI Behavioral Science Unit and a regular lecturer at the FBI Behavioral Analysis Unit in Quantico. Past President of the New Jersey Psychological Association, Dr. Schlesinger was also a recipient of the American Psychological Association's Karl F. Heiser Presidential Award.

Jacqueline L. Schneider, Ph.D., is the Chair and Professor in the Department of Criminal Justice Sciences at Illinois State University, Normal, IL. She earned her doctorate from the University of Cincinnati and a master's degree in public administration from The Ohio State University. She taught and conducted research in England where her work on stolen goods has been put forward as best practice and has attracted interest by policy makers in Chilé. In addition to her many other grants, Schneider was the first recipient of the Home Office's Innovative Research Challenge Grant (UK), and she received an outstanding teaching award in the United States. Her published works include several academic papers and chapters in book. Her main research areas include stolen goods markets and the illegal trade in endangered species. Her book, *Sold into Extinction: The Global Trade in Endangered Species* was named the American Society of Criminology, Division of International Criminology's Distinguished Book Award, 2012.

Tania Signal, Ph.D., is an Associate Professor-Senior Lecturer in Psychology at Central Queensland University, Rockhampton. She is originally from New Zealand and received her PhD from the University of Waikato in 2002. Her interest in the psychological underpinning of the human-animal dynamic has resulted in over 30 peer-reviewed journal articles, several book chapters and a co-edited book (with Associate Professor Taylor). She is part of the editorial panel for a number of human-animal studies journals such as Society & Animals and Human-Animal Interaction Bulletin and regularly reviews for a number of other journals. She is also an Animals and Society Institute Charter Scholar Member and part of the Animal Ethics Education Reference Group in Queensland.

Rochelle Stevenson is completing her Ph.D. in Sociology at the University of Windsor. Coming from an academic background in criminology (BA (Hons) Simon Fraser University, MA University of Ottawa), the majority of her research has been focused on cruelty to animals, ranging from legislative reform attempts to its connection with intimate partner violence. Her PhD research is looking at the inclusion of companion animals in violent intimate relationships through the perspective of the male abusive partner.

Elizabeth B. Strand, Ph.D., is a Clinical Associate Professor and the Founding Director of Veterinary Social Work (VSW) at the University of Tennessee College of Veterinary Medicine and College of Social Work. She is a licensed clinical social worker, experienced family therapist, Grief Recovery Specialist, and a Mindfulness-Based Stress Reduction Teacher. She also is trained as a Rule 31 Mediator, Anicare animal abuse treatment counselor and trainer, a Compassion Fatigue Specialist and holds a Doctor of Philosophy in Social Work. She is also an ordained Interfaith Minister. Her interest-areas include the link between human and animal violence, animals in family systems, communication skills, conflict resolution and stress management in animal welfare environments, and the scholarly and practice development of veterinary social work. Her personal and professional mission is to encourage the humane treatment of both people and animals.

Suzanne E. Tallichet is a professor of sociology in the Department of Sociology, Social Work, and Criminology at Morehead State University. She received her doctorate in rural sociology from Pennsylvania State University in 1991. Her most recent publications appear in the *International Journal of Offender Therapy and Comparative Criminology* and the *Journal of Interpersonal Violence*. Her research interests include animals and society, environmental sociology, and regional studies.

Nik Taylor, Associate Professor, is a sociologist who has been researching human-animal relations for over 15 years. She has published 4 books and over 40 journal articles and book chapters on the human-pet bond; treatment of animals and animal welfare; links between human aggression and animal cruelty; slaughterhouses; meat-eating, and, animal shelter work. Her most recent books include *The Rise of Critical Animal Studies* (ed., with Richard Twine, Routledge, 2014), *Humans, Animals and Society* (Lantern Books, 2013) and *Animals at Work* (with Lindsay Hamilton, Brill Academic, 2013). She is the Managing Editor of *Society & Animals*; a charter scholar of the Animals and Society Institute and member of the ASI's Human-Animal Studies Executive Committee and sits on the Board of the International Society for Anthrozoology.

Rachel Touroo, DVM, joined the ASPCA in March 2012 as the director of its Veterinary Forensics program. In this role, Dr. Touroo assists law enforcement with animal cruelty cases throughout the United States, develops and carries out novel research in the area of veterinary forensics, and teaches Veterinary Forensic Medicine at the University of Florida, College of Veterinary Medicine. Prior to joining the ASPCA, Dr. Touroo worked as the Staff Veterinarian for Animal Care with the Virginia Department of Agriculture and Consumer Services in Richmond, Va. During her time there she provided training, resources and assistance to law enforcement throughout the state in handling animal cruelty investigations.

Dr. Touroo started her career in animal welfare in 2001 as a research assistant at the Animal Behavior and Welfare group at Michigan State University. From 2007 to 2008, she was employed as an associate veterinarian in a small animal practice in Bethesda, Md. Dr. Touroo graduated from Michigan State University with a Bachelor of Science degree in animal science. She received her Doctorate of Veterinary Medicine from the Michigan State University College of Veterinary Medicine. Currently Dr. Touroo is based at the University Of Florida College Of Veterinary Medicine, where she holds a courtesy faculty appointment.

Caleb Trentham received his B.S. in Criminal Justice from the University of Tennessee at Chattanooga (UTC). He is currently working on his M.S.C.J. at UTC. He served in the U.S. Marine Corps.

Antonio R. Verbora is a criminology doctoral student at the University of Ottawa. He completed his Master's Degree in criminology at the University of Windsor. His MA Thesis examined the politics of animal anti-cruelty legislation in Canada. Using official transcripts of Canadian parliamentary debates, the study analyzed fifteen Bills introduced to the House and Senate from 1999 to 2012. Among other things, the findings indicate that while there has been modest progress in the form of numerous attempts to improve the legal protections afforded to animals in Canada, political resistance from the Conservative Party and animal-use industries has been, and will likely continue to be, significant enough to circumvent real legal changes to the status of animals in Canada. The goal of this research was to contribute to the literature on critical animal studies and green criminology, as well as broadening the literature on social justice and public policy.

Index

Page numbers followed by an "f" indicate a figure; those by a "t," a table.

A
abandonment, animal
   gender differences in, 56
   in NY anti-cruelty law, 30, 44
   on reality TV, 390
abuse
   crimes of, 291
   organized, 102
   ritualized, 102–103
   sexual, 103
   witnessing of, 276
   See also animal abuse; child abuse
abuse behaviors, childhood experiences and, 281–282
abusers
   in accumulated animal cruelty cases, 143–144
   broad spectrum of, 56
   caregivers as, 144
   criminal records of, 334, 335
   See also offenders
Acione, F. R., 331–332
activism
   vs. advocacy, 397–398
   effectiveness of, 399–400
activism, animal
   of animal rights organizations, 397
   violent, 398
activists, animal, 8
   civil disobedience of, 399–400
   and public view of animal rights, 398
   research on, 399
   stereotypical view of, 398
   undercover, 408
activists, nonviolent tactics used by, 398
"actuality footage," 386
Adams, Carol J., 255, 336, 337, 340, 387

adaptive approach behaviors, in biophilia hypothesis, 114
addiction, compared with animal hoarding, 203
   See also substance abuse
Addington, Lynn, 141, 142
adolescence
   animal abuse and bullying behaviors in, 335
   firesetting behavior during, 306
adolescents, animal abuse among, 330
adult attachment, 367
Adult Attachment Interview, 368
advertising revenue, and reality TV, 380
   See also profits
advocacy
   vs. activism, 397–398
   defined, 397
   shock, 401
advocacy, animal, in higher education, 416
advocates, animal
   censoring of, 77
   rescue workers as, 398
   research on, 399
African Americans
   cockfighting supported by, 174
   companion animal ownership of, 127
"Age Graph for Animal Abusers," 154
agency cooperation, 410–411
age ranges, of offenders, 144
   in animal fighting, 148
   in animal theft, 153
   and beating of animals, 145–146
   in burning offenses, 146–147
   in choking, strangulation, or suffocation, 147
   in drowning, 147–148
   for hanging offense, 148

for hoarding, 152–153
for kicking offenses, 149
for mutilation offenses, 149
in neglect or abandonment, 152
for poisoning offenses, 149
in shooting offenses, 150
for stabbing offense, 150
in throwing offense, 150–151
in unlawful trade, 153
for unlawful trapping or hunting, 151
for vehicular offenses, 151
"ag-gag" laws, 77–78, 343, 408
Aggrawal, A., 219
aggression
   and animal cruelty, 280, 289–290, 412–413
   bimodal theories of, 360–362
   childhood, 362
   and CTA, 265
     defined, 276
     developmental pathways of, 364–366
     etiology and maintenance of, 366
     frustration and strain theories of, 329
     instrumental, 276
     and partner abuse, 278
     potential generalization of, 335
     predatory, 363
     proactive, 360, 361
     reactive, 360
     in violation graduation hypothesis, 334
     See also bullying; violence
aggression, physical, in family violence, 276
Aggression Toward Animals scale, 259
aggressive behaviors
   and abuse history, 254
   and childhood animal cruelty, 356
   children's, 285
   and ineffective parental discipline, 279
   legalized, 344
   predictors of, 279, 284
   risk factors for, 289
Agnew, Robert, 265, 325, 329, 330, 331, 339, 341, 358, 414–415
agricultural fairs, 67
agricultural workers, exemptions for, 48
agriculture, animal, 19, 121
   industrial, 162, 342

   See also factory farms; farms; livestock
Agriculture, New Jersey Dept. of, 77
Agriculture, U.S. Dept. of (USDA), 177
   APHIS of, 66
   AWA standards enforced by, 181
   captured orca whales licensed by, 70
Ainsworth, Mary, 116, 117, 366–367
Alabama
   animal cruelty statutes in, 13, 19
   bestiality statutes in, 229
   hog-dogging in, 179
   reporting of animal cruelty in, 92
   standards of care for breeders in, 405
Alaska
   animal cruelty statutes in, 10, 11, 18
   bestiality statutes in, 229
alcohol abuse, of offenders, 144
alcoholism, and childhood animal cruelty, 281
Allen, 241
Alley Cat Allies, 427
alligator, American, 399
Alys, L., 225
Alzheimer's patients, 115
American Academy of Forensic Sciences, 90
American Alligator Council, 399
American Anti-Vivisection Society, 428
American Bar Association, 415–416
American Humane Association, 428
American Pet Products Association (APPA), 382
American Pet Products Manufacturers Association, AHB survey of, 128
American Psychological Association, 415
American Psychological Association (APA), 202, 284, 356
American Society for Prevention of Cruelty to Animals (ASPCA), 31, 89, 145, 160, 428
   disaster-type responses coordinated by, 208
   early cases of, 31–32
   mobile crime scene unit of, 410
   National Animal Poison Control Center of, 101
   New York's, 29–30
   partnering with law enforcement agencies of, 411
American Sociological Association, 415

Americans with Disabilities Act (ADA) (1990), 123
American Veterinary Medical Association (AVMA), 89
   AHB survey of, 128
   euthanasia guidelines of, 105
   forensic guidelines from, 94
Amsterdam, Treaty of, 162
amusement parks, 186–188
Anderson, C. A., 276
Anderson, J. L., 342
anger, and partner abuse, 278
   See also aggression; domestic violence
AniCare approach, 368
AniCare Model for Adults and Children, 130
animal abuse, 4, 15
   vs. animal cruelty, 7
   bestiality as, 220, 225, 226
   and bullying, 335
   bystander behavior in, 327
   childhood attempt to protect pet in, 329
   classification of, 144
   consistently concealed, 340
   in cultural festivals, 159
   defining, 10, 126, 264, 325–326, 412
   and deviance, 334–335
   diagnosing, 92
   effective response to, 20
   explaining, 327
   exposure to, 327
   and family violence, 128–129
   feminist analyses of, 337–338
   forms of, 10–12
   IGT hypothesis of, 327–328
   as indicator of child abuse, 254–255
   and IPV, 327–328, 337
   motivations for, 17, 330
   normalization of, 339–340
   physical, 11
   predictors of, 326, 327, 329
   and punishment by parent, 328
   recognizing, 5
   of serial murderers, 333
   sexual, 11, 92, 103
   sociological theorizing of, 325
   study of, 412–413
   typology of, 16t
   in veterinary forensic science, 91–92
animal abuse, intentional
   blunt force trauma, 99–100
   forensic documentation of, 99
   projectile injuries, 100
   sharp force trauma, 100
animal abuse, theories of
   cultural spillover, 344–346
   differential coercion, 331–332
   (eco)Marxism, 341–344
   feminist theory, 335–338
   frustration and strain theories, 329–331
   generalization of deviance hypothesis, 334–335
   masculinities in, 338–341
   social learning theory, 326–329
   sociological, 346
   violence graduation hypothesis, 332–334
animal abuse by children
   bullying and, 256–257
   parental history in, 257–258
   at young age, 256–258
   See also childhood animal cruelty
"Animal Abuse Crime Database," 154
Animal Abuse Registry Database Administration System (AARDAS), 154
   anonymous sources reporting to, 143
   classifications provided by, 142
animal agriculture facilities, taking pictures or videos in, 343
   See also factory farms; slaughterhouses
Animal and Plant Health Inspection Service (APHIS), of USDA, 66, 67
animal-assisted activity (AAA) animals, 122–123
animal-assisted intervention (AAI), 122–123
   in criminal justice, 131–133
   research on, 129
animal-assisted therapy (AAT), 122–123, 255
animal attachment scale, racial/ethnic differences in, 127
animal control fines, 241
animal control officers, 125
   investigations carried on by, 57
   as victims, 54
Animal Cops: Houston (TV show), 390, 392–393
Animal Cops: Miami (TV show), 392

Animal Cops: Philadelphia (TV show), 388, 389, 390, 391
animal cop shows, 380, 386
    as action-oriented spectacle, 385
    criticism of, 391–392
    exploitation of, 395
    genre hybridity of, 384
    magazine format of, 392
    narrative of, 392, 394
    shared ideological positions on, 394
    structure and binaries of, 389–392
    titles in, 387–389
    visual evidence in, 392–394
    voiceovers in, 386–387
    See also reality TV
animal cruelty
    bestiality as, 225
    causes and correlates of, 356–357, 366
    changing views of, 402–403
    childhood experiences and, 282
    classification systems for, 15, 16t
    and corporal punishment by parents, 282
    data on, 141–142
    defining, 3, 4–6, 6–7, 7, 10, 265, 280, 355
    and domestic violence, 285–289, 332
    and emotional disturbance, 315
    and exposure to violence as child, 288
    forms of, 91
    international problems with, 7
    investigating, 57–58
    and IPV, 333–334
    laws addressing, 3
    limits to information about, 315–316
    local recognition of, 5
    mass, 235
    motives behind, 17–18, 262
    multiple violations, 54
    need for more research in, 229–230
    new category of aggravated, 13
    passive, 211
    predictive for homicide, 307
    predictive significance of, 309
    prevalence of, 141
    psychologies of, 355
    public awareness of, 416
    on reality TV, 385
    recognition of, 5, 92–95, 416
    reporting, 57–58
    research in, 253, 413
    responding to, 92–95
    role of veterinarian in, 92–93
    and serial sexual murder, 310
    sexual abuse, 92, 103, 229
    of sexual murderers, 310–312
    and significance of cats, 311–313
    smuggling, 153–154
    socio-demographic variables associated with, 290
    theft, 153
    unlawful trade, 153–154
    and violence, 285–289
    See also bestiality; children's cruelty toward animals; cruelty to animals
animal cruelty, active, 145
    beating, 145–147
    bestiality, 146
    burning with caustic substances, 146
    burning with fire or fireworks, 146–147
    choking, strangulation, or suffocation, 147
    drowning, 147–148
    fighting, 148
    hanging, 148
    kicking or stomping, 148–149
    mutilation, 149
    poisoning, 149
    shooting, 150
    stabbing, 150
    throwing, 150–151
    torture, 149
    unlawful hunting, 151
    unlawful trapping, 151
    vehicular, 151
animal cruelty, emerging issues in, 409
    advocacy and activism, 397–402
    changing views of, 402–403
    legislative trends, 404
    mass media, 400–402
    public awareness, 400–402
animal cruelty, passive, 151–152
    hoarding, 152–153
    neglect or abandonment, 152
animal cruelty, predictors of
    being male, 338
    callousness, 361
    childhood exposure to, 359
    parental IPV, 357
    witnessing violence, 358, 359

animal cruelty, study of, 413
    Agnew's integrative model of animal violence in, 414–415
    data collection in, 416
    recognition of, 416
    research in, 415
    "*Sui generis*", 413–414
animal cruelty cases
    investigation and prosecution of, 409–412
    on reality TV, 388
animal cruelty in United States, 141
    national assessment of, 128
    Pet-Abuse.com, 142–145
animal cruelty investigators, 409
animal cruelty laws
    enforcement of, 58–59
    ethical debates in, 9
    need for appropriate, 291–292
    in U.S., 130
animal cruelty protections, expansions of, 405
animal cruelty statutes
    and animal hoarding, 209
    ill-defined, 13
    violations of, 210–211
animal cruelty task forces, 411
Animal Crush Video Prohibition Act, U.S. (2010), 227, 402
Animal Defenders International, 429
Animalearn, 430
Animal Enterprise Terrorism Act (2008), 398
Animal Farm Foundation, Inc., 429
animal fighting, 38, 126
    prevalence of, 148
    punishments for, 102
    See also blood sports
Animal Fighting Prohibition Enforcement Act (2007), 176
Animal Fighting Spectator Act (2013), 406
Animal Hospital (TV show), 385
animal-human bond (AHB), 113, 133
    assessment and response to, 129–130
    cultural influences in, 126–129
    grief in, 121
    in laboratory settings, 125
    measuring, 117
    negative, 126
    positive, 122

    recognition of, 113
    research on, 129
    violence and, 126
animal-human bond (AHB), and criminal justice, 129
    animal-assisted interventions, 131–133
    assessment and response to, 129–130
    preventing and treating violence towards animals, 130–131
animal-human bond (AHB), kinds of, 119–121
    for animal-related professionals, 122–123
    assistance animals, 122–123
    companion animals, 119–121
    farm animals, 121–122
    wildlife, 124
animal-human bond (AHB), theories of, 114
    anthropomorphic-integrated-chattel orientation continuum, 115–116
    attachment theory, 116–117
    biophilia hypothesis, 114–115
    social support theory, 118–119
animal-human relationships, study of, 114
animal husbandry, 121, 160
    See also agriculture, animal
Animal Law Coalition, 404, 405
Animal Legal Defense Fund (ALDF), 20, 212, 410, 429
Animal Liberation, 8
Animal Liberation Front (ALF), 397, 398
Animal Machines (Harrison), 7
animal maltreatment
    active *vs.* passive, 16t
    clinical diagnoses of, 14
    as felony, 20
    motivation for, 17
    types of, 10
Animal Planet (TV show), 199
    brand identity of, 381
    launch of, 380–381
Animal Precinct (TV show), 387–388, 389
animal production, large-scale industrial, 235
    See also factory farming
animal protection, 8
    inconsistencies in, 14
    objectivity *vs.* subjectivity in, 14–15, 16t

animal protection agencies, 427
"Animal Protection Agency" (APA), 407
Animal Protection and Rescue League (Born Free USA), 429, 430
animal protection laws
    and human concerns, 47
    societal readiness for, 32, 33
    See also specific law
animal protection lawyers, 77
animal protection movement, international, 61–62
animal protection societies, 32
    See also specific societies
animal-related human experience (ARHE) perspective, in biophilia hypothesis, 114
animal relationships, working, 113
    See also animal-human bond
Animal Rescue Corps., 430
animal rights
    consideration of, 39–42
    Five Freedoms, 7–8, 209–210, 210f
    and public opinion, 8
Animal Rights Action Network (ARAN), 180
animals
    as absent referent, 336
    anthropomorphized view of, 115
    changing views of, 402–403
    defining, 18–19, 106
    as distinct from other property, 54
    ethical status of, 41
    female, 336
    legal status of, 42, 291
    oppression of, 336
    in production of capital, 341–342
    as property, 4, 9, 25–26, 41, 47, 341
    as sentient beings, 86
    Virginia's definition of, 38
    See also companion animals
animal sacrifice, 103
Animal Safe House Program (MASH), Maricopa County Sheriff's Office's, 125
Animals and Society Institute, 431
Animals Defenders International (ADI), 183
animal sexual assault, 92, 103
Animal 24:7 (TV show), 385, 387, 389
animal use
    in Britain, 27
    motivation associated with, 16t

See also food, animals used for
Animal Use and Animal Exploitation, 8
animal violence
    Agnew's integrative model of, 414–415
    study of, 413
animal welfare
    concept of, 33–34
    defined, 66n4
    OIE definition of, 66
    terminology and, 34–37
Animal Welfare Act (AWA), U.S. (1971), 37, 66, 160, 181
    enforcement of, 69
    exemptions in, 67
    and internet sellers of animals, 67
    provisions of, 66–67
    retail pet store in, 67–69
Animal Welfare and Animal Control, 8
animal-welfare-appropriate attitudes, teaching, 255
Animal Welfare Institute, 431
animal welfare laws, 9
    animal rights in, 40
    development of, 38
    inconsistency of, 85
    modern, 37–39
    private enforcement of, 81–85
    under-enforcement of, 81–82
animal welfare organizations
    in investigation of animal cruelty, 58
    and prosecution of abusers, 59
ankuses, as training tools, 181
anthropomorphism, 402
anti-cruelty laws
    differing by state, 48, 48n2
    enforcement of, 409–412
    permitted conduct in, 65–66
    prohibited conduct in, 47–48
anti-cruelty laws, history of, 25
    animals as property, 25–26
    Bergh Era, 29–31
    in Britain, 26–28
    concept of animal welfare in, 33–34
    enforcement in NYC, 31–32
    legal status denied, 25, 26
    New York law of 1829, 28–29
anti-cruelty statutes, state, 5
    language of, 12–14
    problems in enforcing, 17
    scope and content of, 49

Anti-Fur Society, 431
anti-parasite methods, topical, 242–243
antisocial behavior
    of abused child, 314
    and childhood animal cruelty, 356
    childhood-onset, 282
    and CTA, 260
    development of, 365
    within families, 279
    and history of animal cruelty, 290
    physical maltreatment causative of, 277
    prediction of, 284, 365
    and punitive childhood histories, 282
    See also aggression; bullying
Antisocial Personality Disorder, 277
Antonacopoulos, Duvall, 119
anxiety, in attachment theory, 366
Archer, J., 276
Arizona
    animal cruelty statutes in, 11, 19
    bestiality statutes in, 228
    fines for animal cruelty in, 60
    puppy lemon law of, 161
    reporting of animal cruelty in, 92, 152
    roaming dogs in, 239
Arkansas
    animal cruelty reported in, 152
    animal cruelty statutes in, 10, 18
    bestiality statutes in, 229
Arkow, Phil, 15, 255, 281, 443
Arlington, TX, cruelty seizure of animals in, 59, 59n26
Arluke, Arnold, 206, 207, 209, 212, 225, 262, 302, 333, 334, 335, 339, 340, 443
arrests, in NY anti-cruelty law, 44
Ascione, Frank R., 7, 103, 220, 225, 254, 255, 256, 260, 262, 263, 264, 282, 283, 284, 285, 286, 287, 309, 328, 329, 334, 355, 359
Asian Americans, companion animal ownership of, 127
Asian elephants, 83
Asian medicines, 168
Asians, cockfighting supported by, 174
assessment, at crime scene, 96
assistance animals, defined, 122–123
assistance dog, loss of, 123
Association of Prosecuting Attorneys, 212
Association of Shelter Veterinarians, *Guidelines* of, 14

Atema, Kate Nattrass, 443
Athens, Lonnie, 331
attachment
    adult, 367
    pathological, 367
    problems, 203
    styles of, 367
attachment theory, 116–117, 366–368
attention deficit hyperactivity disorder (ADHD), and firesetting, 305
attitudes
    about animals, 414
    diversity of, 8
    towards proper treatment of animals, 210
Attitude towards the Treatment of Animals Scale, 264
Attorney General, U.S., 177
Australia
    animal cruelty and domestic violence in, 286–287, 328–329
    cane toads in, 236
    domestic violence with animal abuse in, 328–329
    primate research in, 68
    roaming dogs in, 237, 239, 241, 243, 244
Austria
    circus animals banned in, 183
    primate research in, 68
autism
    child-dog interactions in, 123
    children with, 255
avoidance behaviors, 114–115

B

Babcock, J. C., 360
Bachelor of Veterinary Science (BVS), 89
Bad Newz Kennels, 147
Bahamas, roaming dogs in, 236, 237, 238, 240, 241, 243
baiting, 38
baiting sports, 176
balanced and restorative justice (BARJ) model, 4
Baldry, A. C., 257, 288, 326, 327, 328, 358, 359
Baldwin, S., 330
Bali, roaming dogs in, 239
Bandura, A., 358, 403

Bangkok, Thailand, roaming dogs in, 239
"barbarism, institutionalized," 343
Barnum & Bailey Circus, 182, 183
Bartholomew, K., 123, 367
"battered pet" syndrome, 14
batterers, animals cruelty used by, 289
battery cages, 165
bear baiting, 81
bear gall bladders, illegal trade in, 168
beast, use of term, 26
beasts of burden, 36
beating of animals, statistics for, 145–147
Beck, A. M., 115, 203
Beck Depression Inventory (BDI), 132
Becker, F., 255, 256
Becker, J. V., 310
Becker, K. D., 306
Becker, K. K., 366
Beetz, A. M., 221, 225
behavioral problems, and animal hoarding, 206–207
Beirne, Piers, 103, 220, 221, 226, 265, 325, 326, 344, 399, 412, 413, 414n3
Belgium, primate research in, 68
beliefs, about animals, 414
Bell, Silvia, 116
beluga whales
    for public display, 80, 80n110
    transporting, 81
Bennett, James Gordon, 32
Bentham, Jeremy, 4, 8, 27, 413
Berget, B., 132
Bergh, Henry, 29, 31–32, 32, 36, 49, 89, 90
Berkowitz, David, 314
Berkowitz, L., 358
Bernard, H., 301
Best Friends Animal Society, 432
Best Friends magazine, 129
bestialics
    demographics for, 224–225
    education of, 224–225
    fantasies of, 223
    and violence, 223–224
bestiality, 103, 126
    of child abusers, 258
    childhood, 309
    cruelty of, 7
    crush videos, 226–227
    defined, 146

    dynamics associated with, 221–224
    as form of animal abuse, 220
    and interpersonal violence, 224–225, 226
    perpetrators of, 221
    research on, 220, 221–224
    of sexual murder, 310
    statistics on, 146, 221
    theorizing about, 225
    and zoophilia, 219–220
bestiality laws, 228
    felony state statutes of, 228
    misdemeanor state statutes, 229
Bhutan, roaming dogs in, 244
Big Cat Diary (film), 384
Big Cat Rescue, 432
Bignell, Jonathan, 389–392, 390
binding, in animal abuse cases, 144–145
biophilia hypothesis, 114–115
bird feeding, 124
birds
    hoarding of, 200
    as victims, 142, 147, 149, 150, 151, 152
Biressi, A., 385, 390–391
bites, dog, 238, 243
bite wounds, 100
Bjerke, T., 124
Black, T., 262
Blackfish (film), 187
Blackman, N., 301, 316
black market, trophy-sized animals in, 169
Black's Law Dictionary (2012), 6
bleaching of fur, 99
Blechman, E. A., 306
Blood, D. C., 6
bloodsport participants, moral disengagement of, 403
blood sports, 102, 159, 169, 172, 178–179
    bullfighting, 178
    and class status, 343
    cockfighting, 172–175
    constructing masculine identities through, 339
    cross-cultural research on, 339
    dogfighting, 175–177
blunt force trauma, 99–100
Boat, B., 254
Bobby Roberts Super Circus, 181, 183
"Bobo doll" experiments, 358
Boggs, C., 343

Bojicic, 240
Bolden-Hines, T. A., 332
Bolivia, circus animals banned in, 183
bond, use of term, 113–114
    See also animal-human bond
Boone and Crockett Club, 170–171
Born Free USA, 429
Bosnia
    circus animals banned in, 183
    roaming dogs in, 236, 240
Bowe, J. E., 170
bowhunting, 81
Bowlby, John, 116, 366–367
Braastad, B. O., 132
Brambell, Roger, 7
Brambell Commission, 7
breeders
    breeder-hoarders, 201
    irresponsible, 56
    laws regulating, 50–51
    puppy mills run by, 50–51
breeding, 159, 160
    in factory farming, 163–164
    irresponsible, 205
    and law, 160–161
    regulation of, 405
    selective, 121
    See also puppy mills
breeding, selective
    costs of, 163
    defined, 163
Brennan, J., 367
Brewster, Mary P., 443
Britain, anti-cruelty laws in, 26–28
    See also United Kingdom
British Broadcasting Corp. (BBC), 380
British Columbia, animal tourism in, 186
brood bitches, abuse of, 160
Brown, C. M., 118
Brown, L., 280
Brown, S. E., 127, 128
Bryant, C., 412
bull baiting
    in NY anti-cruelty law, 42–43
    12th century practice of, 175–176
bull dogs, non-pit
    theft of, 153
    as victims, 142, 146–153, 155
    See also pit bull dogs
bullfighting, 169, 172
    masculinity associated with, 339
    media coverage of, 401
    origins of, 178
    supporters of, 178
bull hooks, 85, 183
    as training tools, 181
    used with elephants, 82, 84
bulls
    running with, 180–181
    "taming," 180
    training of, 178
bullying
    and animal abuse, 256–257, 335
    and animal cruelty, 290
    and CTA, 267
    in development of animal cruelty, 359
    in history of sex murderers, 313
    and violence to animals, 126, 131
    See also Aggression
Burgess, A. W., 282, 309, 311
Burghardt, G. M., 402n1
Burke, D. M., 369
burning offenses
    forensic analysis of, 101
    statistics on, 146–147
Burton, D. L., 222, 256
butchers, psychological effects of work on, 345
    See also slaughterhouse workers
Butterball turkey farm, 166
bystanders
    actions of, 345
    in animal abuse, 327
    apathetic, 340

C
cage layer osteoporosis, 165
Cain-Abel murder, biblical, 308
Cajun Rules (1950s), 177
California
    animal protection law in, 33
    bestiality statutes in, 229
    Proposition 2 (2008) in, 74
    puppy mills in, 51
    reporting of animal cruelty in, 92, 148, 149, 150, 151
    running of bulls in, 181
    shark fin products banned in, 407
callousness
    and aggression, 361

as disorder of empathy, 368
callous-unemotional (CU) traits, 284, 290, 367
　and animal cruelty, 361–362
　in antisocial youth, 361
calves, intensive confinement of, 76–77
Cambodia, roaming dogs in, 238
camels, 183
Campbell, J. C., 290
Canada
　animal cruelty and domestic violence in, 286–287
　domestic violence with animal abuse in, 328–329
　horses transported for slaughter to, 72
　roaming dogs in, 236–237, 237, 239
Canada, First Nations people of
　attitudes toward dogs of, 240
　veterinarian intervention sought by, 344
Canary Islands, bullfighting banned in, 178
canine-human connections, secure base in, 117
canine officers, 125
cannibalism
　in factory farms, 165
　in hoarding environments, 99
Capps, Rep. Lois, 161
captivity, orca whales in, 69–70
caregivers
　as abusers, 144
　overwhelmed, 201
care-giving, adult compulsive, 203–204
Caribbean, swimming with dolphins in, 187
Carmack, B. J., 121
case law, 51–52
　crush videos in, 51
　19th-century legal precedent in, 51
Caspi, A., 277
Cassidy, J., 116
castration, 75
Catalonia, bullfighting banned in, 178
"cat ladies," 199, 205
cat massacre, great French, 235
cats
　abused by children, 256
　assessment of care for, 14
　hoarding of, 200
　numbers for, 381, 382
　significance of, 311–313
　theft of, 153
　as victims, 142, 146, 147, 148, 149, 150, 151, 152, 153
cattle, transportation of, 182
　See also cows
Cavazos, A. M., 128
Cavell, T. A., 362
Cazaux, G., 265
chain of custody, preservation of, 95
chains, used with elephants, 82, 84
Chaplin, T. C., 304
chart reviews, in animal abuse research, 264
chattel, animals as, 115–116
Chicago Police Dept., 335
chickens
　backyard, 122
　cage ban for, 165–166
　consumer costs of, 165
　in factory farms, 165–166
　selective breeding of, 163–164
　as victims, 142, 148
child abuse
　and aggressive behaviors, 282
　animal abuse as indicator of, 254–255
　and animal cruelty, 284–285, 290
　long-term adverse outcomes of, 277
　maltreated infants, 277
　outcomes of, 278
　and presence of meat processing plant, 266
　and therapeutic potential of animals, 255–256
child conduct disorder problems, and animal cruelty, 356–357
child delinquency, 365
child-dog interactions, of service dogs, 123
childhood
　aggression, 362
　externalizing syndromes of, 283
　firesetting behavior during, 306
childhood animal abusers, general taxonomics for, 263
childhood animal cruelty
　and domestic violence, 328–329
　and homicide, 302
　and later development, 357357
childhood triad, 301
　See also MacDonald triad

child maltreatment, and animal cruelty, 357
child neglect, long-term adverse outcomes of, 277
children
    aggressive, 364
    animal cruelty of, 255
    companion animal cruelty witnessed by, 287
    exposure to violence of, 288
    and parental abuse, 276–277
    reactive-aggressive, 364
Children and Animals Together (CAT) Assessment and Diversion Program (CAT), 130
children's cruelty toward animals, 255
    family environment and, 281
    origins of, 280–281
    and physical abuse, 282
    research in, 262
    understanding, 283–285
Chile, roaming dogs in, 238
chimpanzees
    at NIH, 89
    in research laboratories, 406
Chimpanzee Sanctuary Northwest (CSNW), 432
Chimp Haven in Louisiana, 69
China, animal protection law in, 61
Chinese medicine, 168
Chipangali Wildlife Orphanage, 433
choking offense, statistics for, 147
Chur-Hansen, A., 116
Cicchetti, D., 277, 278
circuses, 181–183
    bans against animals in, 183
    confinement and traveling in, 182
    employees and training, 182–183
    regulation of, 181
    transient nature of, 181
civil disobedience, of animal activists, 399–400
Civil Rights Act (1871), 57
Clarke, J., 225
Coalition for Consumer Information on Cosmetics (CCIC), 438
Cobb, Sidney, 118
cockers, 173, 174
cockfighting, 14, 97, 102, 169, 172
    associated with masculinity, 339
    banned in U.S., 175
    code of conduct during, 173
    criminalization of, 173
    gambling in, 174, 175
    history of social acceptance of, 172, 173
    in modern times, 173–174
    and NY anti-cruelty law, 42–43
    policing of, 174–175
    tacit support, 174–175
cockfighting circles, membership in, 175
coercion
    and crime, 331–332
    impersonal, 331
    interpersonal, 331
    theory of differential, 331–332
cognitive development, 363–364
cognitive theories, of animal cruelty, 363–366
Coleman, G. J., 254, 328
Coleman, Sydney, 32
collaboration
    in animal cruelty crimes, 410–411
    for investigation and prosecution, 411–412
collectors, 11
color, people of, companion animal ownership of, 129
Colorado
    animal cruelty statutes in, 11, 18
    bestiality statutes in, 229
    definition of companion animal in, 53
    reporting of animal cruelty in, 92, 147, 166
    shelter requirements in, 213
Colorado Veterinary Medical Association, guidelines from, 93–94
Colvin, Mark, 331
Commerce Clause, of U.S. Constitution, 65
Commercial Dog and Cat Breeders Act, Texas (2011), 51
commodification, and animal harm, 341
common law
    judicial system, 51
    vs. statutory law, 49
Commonwealth v. Brown, 37
community
    animal hoarding cases in, 206–207
    ordinances limiting pets in, 213

community health, animal hoarding in, 201–202
community service
 in animal cruelty convictions, 60
 programs, 132
companion animal ownership, racial/ethnic differences in, 127
Companion Animal Protection Alliance, 433
Companion Animal Protection Society, 160
companion animals, 53, 62
 abuse of, 16t, 265, 292
 and domestic violence, 285–287
 in emotional lives of children, 283
 family abuse of, 281
 with fins, 53
 growth in number of, 382
 human–companion-animal bond, 119–120
 industry built around, 343
 legal rights for, 38–39
 over-population of, 125
 owners' cost for, 382
 people highly attached to, 119
 positive outcomes with, 275
 poverty and, 391
 and prohibited conduct, 49
 and reality TV, 381
 social support offered by, 118–119
"compassion fatigue," of animal-related professionals, 125
Compassion Over Killing (COK), 433
conduct disorder (CD)
 and animal abuse by children, 258
 animal cruelty in, 356
 animal cruelty symptoms of, 263
 in childhood, 283
 defined, 305
conduct disordered children, cognitive-behavior based treatment for, 364
Confined Animal Feeding Operation (CAFO), hegemony of, 342
confinement
 in animal abuse cases, 144–145
 in NY anti-cruelty law, 43
 See also factory farms
Connecticut
 animal cruelty reported in, 146, 149, 150, 152

animal cruelty statutes in, 9–10, 18
bestiality statutes in, 229
definition of companion animal in, 53
unlawful trapping or hunting in, 151
Connell, R. W., 338
Connelly, H. J., 259
Constitution, U.S., animals not mentioned in, 85
consumer disclosures, for dog sales, 50
Continuing bonds (CB) theory, 121
"contract comfort," 116
contract killing, 307
controlling behavior, and animal abuse, 254
Convention on International Trade in Endangered Species of Wild Fauna and Flora (CITES), 78–79
Cooke, D. J., 256
cooperation in enforcement, in animal cruelty crimes, 410–411
coprophilia, 218
"copycat" crimes, of animal cruelty, 360
Cornell University, 89
Corner, John, 383
corporal punishment, and animal cruelty, 359
corporations, vis-a-vis animal exploitation, 343
 See also factory farms; profits
correctional facilities, animal-related intervention programs in, 131
 See also prison-based animal programs
counseling
 in animal cruelty convictions, 60
 for animal hoarders, 213
 for animal workers, 55
court documents, data collected from, 142
court opinions, 34
courts
 animal welfare cases in, 34–37
 definitions provided by, 35–37
 role of veterinarian in, 104
 terminology used in, 34–37
Cousson-Gélie, F., 122
The Cove (film), 186, 187, 401
cows
 in factory farms, 164
 tail-docking of, 167
 transportation of, 182
 as victims, 142, 150, 152

crime
  and animal cruelty, 58–59, 356
  "broken windows approach" to, 212
  and coercion theory, 331–332
  and early aggression, 364–365
  and masculinity, 338
  and presence of meat processing plant, 266
  wildlife, 339
crime rates, and slaughterhouse employment, 73
crime scene, forensic veterinarian at
  assessment, 96
  evidence handling, 96
  necropsy, 96–97
  triage, 95–96
criminality
  and animal cruelty, 412–413
  family violence as predictor of, 279
criminal justice authorities, interventions by, 214
criminal justice system
  and AHB, 125, 126
  defining animal cruelty in, 3
criminal records, of animal abusers, 334, 335
criminals
  animal abuse of, 260, 261
  at dogfighting matches, 177
  See also offenders
criminology, animal cruelty as topic of study in, 267
critical triage, 95
Croatia, circus animals banned in, 183
cross-reporting
  laws, 130
  of suspected animal cruelty, 291
cruel acts
  committed knowingly, 55
  willful, 55–56
cruelty
  absence of universal standard of, 13–14, 15
  categorizing, 235
  courts' definition of, 35–36
  defining, 5
  in NY anti-cruelty law, 42
  and violence against humans, 73
  See also animal cruelty
cruelty laws, need for appropriate, 291
  See also animal cruelty laws
cruelty statutes, 36
cruelty to animals (CTA), 253
  childhood, 262, 264
  in childhood histories of murderers, 309
  circumstances preceding, 263
  factors leading to, 267
  gendered experiences of, 259
  and generalized deviance, 260–262
  methodological issues in research on, 264–265
  reducing, 264
  social and community considerations, 262–264
  See also animal cruelty
crush videos, 51, 226–227, 229, 379
  court rulings on, 227
  on Internet, 402
cultural change, needed for animal cruelty understanding, 291
cultural festivals, 179–183
  circuses, 181–183
  Jallikattu, 180
  Palio horse race, 179
  running with bulls, 180–181
cultural norms, 3
cultural spillover, of animal abuse theories, 344–346
culture
  and AHB, 126–129
  normative dualisms in patriarchal, 336
Culver, Gov. Chester, 160–161
Currie, C. L., 328, 359
Custance, D., 117

D
Dadds, M. R., 262, 280, 303, 359, 361, 367
Dahmer, Jeffrey, 310
Dallas Animal Cruelty Unit, 58
Dandreaux, D. M., 361
Dangerous Dogs Act, U.K. (1991), 401
dangerous dog statutes, 37
Daniell, C., 286
Dantzer, R., 122
Darden, D. K., 175
Darnell, Kenny, 183
Darwin Animal Doctors, 433

data, animal cruelty
    AARDAS database, 154
    "dark figure of crime" in, 154
    state-level collection of, 141–142
data collection, 416
Daugaard, Gov. Dennis, 141
Davis, Lindsey S., 444
dealers, animal
    and AWA requirements, 68
    defined, 66
Dean, Sheila, 438
death
    and animal hoarding, 206–207
    in necropsy report, 97
debeaking, 75, 165
Decety, J., 369
decoration, personal, attitudes toward animals, 403
deer, as victims, 151
deer poachers, moral disengagement of, 403
Defenders of Wildlife, 433
defense, in animal cruelty statutes, 48
defenses, used in animal cruelty cases
    accident, 104
    another person, 104
    hospice provider claim, 105
    mercy killing, 104–105
    picky eater, 105
    recently rescued in bad condition, 105
    self-defense, 105
    and veterinary forensics, 104
definitions, based on medical evaluations, 18
    See also terminology
DeGue, S., 282
dehorning, 75, 75n72
Delaware
    animal cruelty statutes in, 18
    bestiality statutes in, 228
    shark fin products banned in, 407
DeLillo, D., 282
delinquency
    and animal cruelty, 412–413
    and CTA, 267
    prediction of, 365
DeLisi, M., 364–365
demographic variables, in theories of animal abuse, 329–330

depression
    and attachment to companion animals, 119
    and firesetting, 305
Derango, R., 161, 165
DeSalvo, Albert, 311
desensitization thesis, of CTA, 260, 261
developmental pathways of aggression, 364–366
development delays, 263
deviance, and animal abuse, 334–335
    See also sexual deviance
deviance generalization hypothesis, 344
DeViney, E., 254, 264, 281
devocalization, 404–405
Diagnostic and Statistical Manual of Mental Disorders (DSM) (APA), 214, 217, 218, 219, 303, 356
    animal abuse as indicator of conduct disorder in, 258
    animal cruelty in, 290
    animal hoarding in, 202
    diagnostic criteria for CD in, 284
    pyromania in, 303
Dickert, J., 254, 281
Dick Martin's Act (1822), 27–28, 27n10
Dietz, T., 345
differential coercion theory, of animal abuse, 331–332
Dillard, C. L., 399
Dillard, J., 266, 267
discipline, pain associated with, 36
Discovery Channel
    coverage of hoarding on, 199
    U.S. subscriptions of, 380–381
disease
    and animal hoarding, 201, 206–207
    and captive hunting, 172
DNA, analyses of animals', 410
Doberman pinscher, docking ears of, 14
Doctor of Veterinary Medicine (DVM), 89
documentaries
    "activist," 401
    vs. "reality TV," 383
dog attacks, media coverage of, 401
dog bites
    public's fear of, 243
    with roaming dogs, 238
dog-breeding operations, large-scale commercial, 50

See also puppy mills
dogcatchers, 236
dogfighting, 60, 97, 102, 169, 172, 175–177
    attraction of, 340
    baiting in, 175–176
    bystanders in presence of, 340
    crimes accompanying, 177
    of gang members, 177
    historical accounts of, 175–176
    masculinity associated with, 339
    in modern times, 176
    networks and events, 176–177
    in NY anti-cruelty law, 42–43
    social acceptance of, 176
    in U.S., 176
dogfighting rings, 176
Dogfighting Toolkit for Law Enforcement (manual), 411
"dog lady," 205
dogs
    on animal cop shows, 392
    assessment of care for, 14
    AWA provisions for, 68
    breeding, 159–160
    in community service programs, 132
    determining value of, 52
    eating, 14
    hoarding of, 200
    legal status denied, 25, 26
    numbers for, 381, 382
    police shootings of, 56–57
dogs, roaming, 235, 238
    abusing and neglecting, 236–238
    attitudes toward, 236
    bounties for, 237
    changing perception of, 245
    cruelty toward, 236, 237
    as danger, 238–239
    educational interventions for, 244
    and indifference or neglect, 237–238
    passive acceptance of, 238
    physical appearance of, 235
    reversing cruelty toward, 242–244
    self-fulfilling prophecy for, 240–241
    social conflict over, 237
    support for harming, 237
    veterinary interventions for, 242–244
dogs, roaming, explaining cruelty toward
    dogs as dangers, 238–239

    dogs as homeless, 241–242
    dogs as nuisances, 239–241
dogs before vehicles, in NY anti-cruelty law, 43
Dogs Deserve Better, 434
dog sledding, 186
dolphinaria, banned in India, 85
domestic animals
    in forensic analysis, 102
    legal rights of, 40–41
    as personal property, 39–40, 41
    relations with humans of, 41
    See also companion animals; livestock
domestic violence, 116
    and AHB, 129–130
    and animal abuse, 254–255
    and animal cruelty, 285–289, 328–329, 332, 356
    and childhood CTA, 264, 281, 282, 328–329, 359
    children's exposure to, 277, 328
    as instrumental aggression, 276
    role of pets in, 337
    witnessed by children, 278
Domestic Violence Intervention Project, 286
dominance and control
    culturally prescribed, 337
    of masculinity, 338
Dominica, roaming dogs in, 241
Donathy, M. L., 222
donkey owners
donkey taxis, 185
Doris Day Animal League, 434
Douglas, J. E., 282, 309, 311
Downey, G., 361
draft horses, welfare of, 9
drive theories, 358
drowning offense
    forensic analysis of, 101
    prevalence of, 147–148
drug abuse, of offenders, 144
drug trafficking operations, guard dogs for, 177
Duffield, G., 222
Duncan, A., 282
"dunghill roosters," 174
Durbin, Sen. Richard, 161
Durham, R. L., 258
Dutkiewicz, E. L., 309, 333, 340

Dutton, D. G., 361

E

Eastern European countries, roaming dogs in, 236
(eco)Marxism, 341–344
economic success, of masculinity, 338
the economy
    and animal abuse, 331
    animals as entertainment in, 331
eco-terrorism law, federal, 397
"ecoterrorists," 398
eco-tourism, 184
Edge Research, 2004 survey of, 402, 403
educational interventions
    for investigation and prosecution, 411–412
    for roaming dogs, 244
Edwards, N. E., 115
eggs, free range, 166
Egypt, donkey taxis in, 185
Eisenstein, Yolanda, 444
electric prods, 181, 183
elephants
    abusive treatment of, 83, 181, 183, 185
    Asian, 83
    under AWA, 82–85
    domesticated, 185
    illegal operations with, 185
    illicit trade in, 168
    leading cause of death in captive, 182, 183
    training of, 183
    transportation of, 182
    tuberculosis among, 182, 183
Ellis, C., 327, 334
emetophilia, 218
emotional abuse, 11–12
emotional dependency, 115
empathy
    development of, 368–369
    research on, 369
endangered species
    and animal tourism, 184
    at hunting ranches, 171
    illegal markets in, 167
    illicit trade in, 168
    trading in, 168–169
    See also wildlife

Endangered Species Act (ESA) (1973), 78–79, 182
enforcement
    of animal cruelty laws, 58–59
    cooperation in, 410–411
    of humane husbandry practices, 77
    private, 81–85
    of Twenty-Eight-Hour Law, 73
entertainment
    animal cruelty in, 159
    animals used for, 62, 188
    attitudes toward animals in, 403
    economics of animals as, 343
    fetishistic, 379
    See also blood sports; cultural festivals
enuresis, limits to information about, 315–316
    See also MacDonald's Triad
Environmental Protection Agency (EPA), 407
environmental protection movement, 407
equine welfare, standardized assessment tools in, 14
Erickson hoarding case, 200n1, 202–203, 204, 205, 206, 209
    charges in, 212
    community handling in, 206–207
    condition of dogs in, 211
    neighbors complaints in, 207
    recidivism in, 214
    seizing animals in, 208, 209
Erskine, Lord, 27
ethics
    of captive hunting, 171
    of depicting animal abuse, 394–395
ethology, 116
European Convention for the Protection of Pet Animals (2012), 6161
European Union (EU)
    animal crates banned by, 164
    cage ban in, 165–166
    Lisbon Treaty of, 86
    transporters regulated in, 73, 73n58
    Treaty of Lisbon recognized by, 408
European Union (EU) treaty, 61
euthanasia
    AVMA guidelines for, 105
    choosing, 56
    economic, 343
    in open-admission shelters, 205

rationale for, 97
Evans, R., 340
Everett, Rep. Terry, 161
evidence, forensic, 410
evidence handling, at crime scene, 96
examinations, veterinary, in animal sexual assault, 103
exceptionalism, human, 265
exhibitors
    and AWA requirements, 68
    defined, 66–67
exotic animals
    cruelty seizure of, 59
    media coverage of, 401–402
    on reality TV, 389
    restrictions on, 37
    in traveling circuses, 82
    web-based trade of, 401–402
    See also endangered species; wildlife
expert opinion, 58
expert witness
    testimony of, 14
    veterinarian as, 92
exploitation, commercial, 16t
    See also profits

F
factory farming, 162, 355
    justification of, 163
    problems in, 162–163
    selective breeding in, 163–164
factory farming facilities, hidden cameras at, 407
factory farms
    confinement in, 163
    for fowl, 165–166
    hegemony of, 342
    hidden cameras in, 408
    ignorance of conditions in, 403
    mutilations in, 166–167
    overcrowding of, 163
    subpar practices of, 408
    swine in, 164
    welfare problems of, 163
    workers in, 73
False Claims Act, 77
families
    deeply dysfunctional, 85, 255
    risky, 279, 284

Family and Child Services (FCS), Ontario's, 411
family dynamics, for bestialics, 223
Family Research Council, 228
family system, companion animals in, 275
family violence, 39, 116
    and animal abuse, 60, 128–129, 254
    and animal cruelty, 275–292
    child abuse in, 276–278
    defined, 275–276
    and deliberate animal harm, 261
    between humans, 276
    as instrumental aggression, 276
    among meatworkers, 266–267
    men arrested for, 288
    partner abuse, 278–280
fantasies, of bestialics, 223
farm animals
    AHB with, 121–122
    laws governing, 74–78
Farm Animal Welfare Advisory Committee, 7
Farm Animal Welfare Council, 7, 8
farmers
    affective relationships with animals of, 122
    and animal welfare, 162
farmers markets, 166
farming, mass media coverage of, 401
    See also agriculture; factory farms; livestock
Farm Sanctuary, 434–435
Farnsworth, C. L., 167
Farr, Rep. Sam, 161
Farrell, J. J., 361
Farrington, D. P., 309, 334
Faver, C. A., 128
Favre, David, 444
feather-plucking condition, 390
Febres, J., 254, 259, 288
Federal Bureau of Investigation (FBI), 106, 142
    dogfighting raid of, 177
    Uniform Crime Reporting Program of, 106–107, 142, 308, 355, 416
Federal Meat Inspection Act (FMIA) (1906), 71
Feld Entertainment, 82, 84, 182
Feldman, S., 361
felony, 9, 28n13

animal cruelty as, 48, 60
  in animal welfare law, 38–39
  classification of, 60
  compared with misdemeanor, 13, 55
Felthous, A. R., 6, 259, 262, 280, 281–282, 301, 302, 311, 328, 330, 333, 339, 340
feminist theory
  absent referent in, 336–337
  animal abuse in, 335–338
  devaluation of women and animals in, 338
  dominance and control in, 337
  normative dualism in, 336
  violence in, 335–336
Fergusson, D. M., 277
Feshbach, S., 276
fetishistic entertainment, 379
Field, N. P., 121
fighting animals
  breeding, 126
  law protecting, 30
financial harm, 40
Fine, G. A., 339
fines, for animal abuse convictions, 60
fire play, 303
firesetters
  childhoods of, 314
  psychopathology of, 305
firesetting
  case studies, 313, 314–315
  and emotional disturbance, 315
  limits to information about, 315–316
  motivation for, 304
  operational definitions for, 316
  pathological, 303, 304
  predictive for homicide, 307
  predictive significance of, 309
  repetitive, 304
  sexual element to, 304–305
  of sexual murderers, 312–315, 313
First Strike in Scotland and New Zealand, 261
Fish and Wildlife Service (FWS), U.S.
  Forensic Laboratory of, 106
  on illegal animal trade, 167
fishing
  for recreation, 124
  in U.S., 169
Fishing, Hunting, and Wildlife-Associated Recreation, National Survey of, 124

Fitzgerald, Amy J., 267, 345, 444
Five Freedoms
  and animal hoarding, 209–210, 210f
  codification of, 7–8
Fixit Foundation, 435
fleas, with roaming dogs, 242
Fleming, W. M., 222, 256
flora, illegal harvesting of, 170
Flores, P., 203
Florida
  animal cruelty reported in, 146, 147, 148, 150, 151, 152, 153
  bestiality statutes in, 229
  hog-dogging in, 179
  running of bulls in, 181
  torture defined in, 18
Florida, University of
  School of Veterinary Medicine in, 208
  veterinary curricula at, 107
  Veterinary Forensic Sciences program at, 90
Flynn, C. P., 221, 226, 282, 286, 328, 331, 344, 346, 359
food, animals used for, 62, 65
  humane methods of slaughter, 70–73
  laws governing farm animals, 74–78
  and Twenty-Eight-Hour Law, 73
  wildlife, 78–81
Food, INC. (film), 401
Food Safety and Inspection Service (FSIS), of USDA, 71, 72–73
forced feeding, in factory farms, 165
forensic medicine, clinical, 90
forensic sciences, veterinary
  animal cruelty reporting in, 107
  defined, 90–91
  future needs in, 106
  history of, 89–90
  improved tracking of cases, 106–107
  improvement in, 409–410
  in interventions, 208
  methods and techniques in, 95
  necessary diagnostics in, 94
  role of veterinarian in, 92–93
  specialty laboratories in, 106
  terminology in, 7
  trends in, 106
  wildlife, 106
forensics in animal cruelty, 97
  animal hoarding, 98–99

animal sexual assault, 92, 103
   in blunt force trauma, 99–100
   in burning, 101
   drowning, 101
   institutional neglect, 97–98
   intentional abuse, 99–102
   neglect, 97–98
   organized abuse, 102
   poisoning, 101–102
   projectile injuries, 100
   ritualized abuse, 102–103
   severe neglect, 98
   sharp force trauma, 100
   strangulation, 101
Forsyth, C. J., 340
Fortuyn, Pim, 398
Foss, C. M., 222
The Four Stages of Cruelty (Hogarth), 333
Fourth Amendment, 57
Fras, I., 304, 305
Frasch, P., 407
Frederick, A. A., 362
free-range, definition of, 165
free-range species, protection of, 172
Free Willy (film trilogy), 188
French, L., 255, 256
Freud, Sigmund, 357
Frick, P. J., 284, 361
Friedrich, W. N., 282, 309
Friends of Animals, 435
Frumkin, H., 114
frustration-aggression theory, 358
frustration theory
   aggression in, 329
   animal abuse in, 329–331
   animal abuse to reduce, 329–331
Frye, V., 290
Fulton, Helen, 389
The Fund for Animals, against the annual Fred Coleman Memorial Shoot, 400

G

Galapagos Islands, 184, 433
gambling
   in cockfighting, 174, 175
   with dogfighting, 176, 177
Garcia, Michael, 53
Garrity, T. F., 127
Gauthier, D. K., 340

gender
   and attitudes towards wild animals, 124
   and fighting animals, 126
gender differences
   in animal abuse, 56, 326, 328, 339, 346
   on animal cop shows, 387
   in animal cruelty and firesetting, 303
   in animal fighting, 148
   in animal theft, 153
   in bestiality, 221, 222
   in bullying in development of animal cruelty, 359
   in children's animal abuse, 257
   in exploitation of animals, 341
   for hoarding, 152–153
   in neglect or abandonment, 152
   in reported animal cruelty cases, 144
   in representations of aggression, 361
   with roaming dogs, 241–242
gender differences, in active animal cruelty, 155, 259–260
   in beating of animals, 145–146
   with burning offenses, 146–147
   in choking, strangulation, or suffocation, 147
   drowning offenses, 147–148
   hanging offenses, 148
   for kicking offenses, 149
   for mutilations, 149
   for poisoning offenses, 149
   in shooting offenses, 150
   for stabbing offenses, 150
   in throwing offense, 150–151
   in unlawful trade, 153
   for unlawful trapping or hunting, 151
   for vehicular offenses, 151
Gendreau, P. L., 276
generalized deviance hypothesis, 225, 260, 334–335
Generalized Self-Efficacy Scale, 132
genetic engineering, in selective breeding, 163
genetics, in selective breeding, 163
genre hybrids, 384–386
Geographic Expeditions, 184n1
Georgia
   animal cruelty reported in, 147, 149, 150, 152, 153
   animal cruelty statutes in, 18, 19
   bestiality statutes in, 228

Gerbasi, K. C., 142
Gerlach, Rep. Jim, 161
Germany, animal welfare law in, 86
gestation crates, 163
    justification for, 165
    for pigs, 164
gibbon, white-handed, 188
Gibson, H., 177
Gleyzer, R., 302
Global Assessment of Functioning (GAF) scores, for animal owners, 120
Global Federation of Animal Sanctuaries, 435
goat owners, 122
goats, as victims, 142, 149, 152
gorillas, Bwindi, 184
Goring, C., 301
Gottfredson, M., 414, 415
Gottfredson, Michael R., 331
government panels, animal cruelty interpreted by, 7–8
graduation thesis, of CTA, 260, 302–303
Grandin, T., 266
Great Apes, used in research, 68
Great Bull Run, 180
Greece
    captured bears in, 185
    circus animals banned in, 183
Green, C., 120, 121
Green, Egan K., 444
green-coded animals, at forensic crime scene, 95
"green criminology," 412
Greenebaum, J., 398
greyhounds, fostering of, 131
grief
    animal-related, 121
    in attachment theory, 366
    of leaving companion animal behind, 130
Grise v. State, 35
group counseling, in prisons, 132–133
Grugan, Shannon, 445
Guatemala, roaming dogs in, 238
Guelph, University of, Ontario, Canada, 103
Gullone, Eleonora, 114, 115, 254, 257, 280, 289, 328, 335, 344, 358, 359, 445
Gupta, Maya, 361, 445
Guttmacher, M. S., 310

H

habeas corpus, writ of, 406, 406n2
habitat loss, for wildlife animals, 188
Haddox, V. G., 264, 302, 306
Haden, S. C., 302
Hall, G., 330
Ham, S. H., 124
hanging offenses
    forensic analysis of, 101
    statistics on, 148
Hanlon, T. E., 256
Hannah, 236
hard crush, 226–227
Hardy, L., 302
Hare's PCL-R, 368
Harlow, Harry, 116
harm
    financial, 40
    mental, 276
    physical, 280
    psychological, 276, 280
harm, animal, 10
    in capitalist economic system, 342
    with commodification, 341
    condoned, 265–268
    masculinity linked to, 340
    necessary, 342
    socially authorized, 325, 346
Hartman, C. R., 282, 309
Hassel, H., 256
Hassiotis, A., 222
Hawaii
    animal cruelty defined in, 6
    shark fin products banned in, 407
Hawes, D. J., 367
Hawley, F., 174, 175
Hayashi, K., 282, 309
Hays, K., 130
Healing Species program, 131
Heath, J., 282, 309
Hegins Township Labor Day Committee, 400
Heide, K. M., 224, 226, 262, 302, 333
Heiligmann v. Rose, 52
Hellman, D. D., 301, 316
Hells Angels, 57
Hemingway, Ernest, 180
Henderson, B. B., 356
Hennessy, M. B., 132

Henry, B. C., 257, 259, 260–261, 327, 335, 359
hens, laws governing egg-laying, 74
    See also chickens
Hensley, Christopher, 224, 225, 256, 261, 302, 309, 314, 327, 333, 340, 356, 361, 365, 445
Heppner, W., 360
Herrera, V. M., 306, 366
Herzog, H., 125
heteronormativity, of masculinity, 338
Hewitt, John D., 331
Hicks, I., 332
Hill, Annette, 382, 383, 393
Hinde, Robert, 116
Hirschi, Travis, 331, 414, 415
Hispanics
    cockfighting supported by, 174
    companion animal ownership of, 127
hoarders, 11, 56
hoarders, animal
    applying labels to, 204–205
    breeder-hoarder, 201
    characteristics of, 200–201
    descriptions of, 207
    diagnosis for, 207
    psychological characteristics of, 203–204, 204f
    psychological counseling for, 212–213
    reaction to seizure of, 209
    recidivism of, 213–214
    supervised probation for, 212
    types of, 201
    See also Erickson hoarding case
hoarding
    prevalence of, 199
    as psychological problem, 60
hoarding, animal, 8, 11, 151–152
    characteristics of, 199–202
    defining, 126, 199
    delusional aspects of, 202
    development of, 203–204, 204f
    forensic documentation of, 98–99
    intervention in, 130–131
    interventions for, 206–207
    medico-legal options in, 209–214, 210f
    mental health issues in, 214
    neurobiological approaches to, 363
    vs. object hoarding, 202
    as pathological altruism, 203
    prevalence of, 152, 199–200
    prosecution of, 211
    in psychology of attachment, 368
    seizing animals, 208–209
    in veterinary forensic science, 91
    victims of, 201
hoarding, causes of animal, 202
    psychological disorder, 202–205, 204f
    social enabling, 205–206
hoarding cases
    aggressive prosecution in, 212
    investigation of, 210
    news reports of, 211–212
    results for, 212
    See also Erickson hoarding case
Hoarding of Animals Research Consortium (HARC), 199
Hodge, G., 264
Hodge v. State, 36
Hogarth, William, 333
hog-dog fighting, 178–179
hog industry, in Manitoba, 342
Holley, L. C., 127
Hollin, C. R., 304
Holzer, C. E., 302
homeless
    animals, 125
    dogs as, 241–242
    See also dogs, roaming of
homelessness, and presence of meat processing plant, 266
homicides
    catathymic, 308–309
    classification of, 307
    compulsive, 309
    environmental/sociogenic, 307
    impulsive, 308
    motivational spectrum of, 307–309
    predictors of, 301
    sadistic, 301
    sexual, 310
    situational, 308
    study of, 301
horse abuse, 14
horse assaults, media coverage of, 400–401
horse doctors, self-styled, 89
horsemeat production, 407
horses
    in Palio race, 179

slaughter of, 72
theft of, 153
as victims, 142, 147, 149, 150, 151, 152, 153
welfare of working, 89
Horton v. State, 35
Horwood, L. J., 277
hostile attributional bias, 364
hostility, and partner abuse, 278
household pet, defined, 18
  See also companion animals
housing of dogs, standard for outdoor, 17
Houston, roaming dogs in, 239
Howells, K., 330
Hughes, E, C., 339
Hughes, G., 410
human-animal abuse, criminological approaches to, 265
human-animal bond
  companion animals in, 275
  and veterinarian interventions, 243
  See also animal-human bond
human-animal relationships
  and criminology, 412
  and cultural spillover, 344
human-animal studies, university-level programs in, 415
human-animal violence, 253
  and animal-assisted therapy, 255
  causality in, 261
  and child abuse, 254–255
  in child development, 255
  empathy in, 255
  in family continuum, 254–255
  gender differences in, 260
  recognition of, 261
  research in, 260
  in slaughterhouses, 266
humane behavior, categories of, 16t
humane education, 255
Humane Education interventions, for childhood animal abusers, 263
humane education programs, 131
The Humane League, 436
Humane Methods of Slaughter Act (HMSA) (1958), 71
humane societies, in investigation of animal cruelty, 58
Humane Society International, 407, 436

Humane Society of United States (HSUS), 160, 261, 397, 411, 436
  disaster-type responses coordinated by, 208
  felony legislation supported by, 399–400
  as higher education degree-granting institution, 416
  "Q and A" packet of, 409
Humane Society Veterinary Medical Association, 408, 436–437
Humans and Animals Learning Together, 130
hunters
  exemptions in place for, 48
  moral disengagement of, 403
hunting, 19, 124
  canned/captive, 170–172
  vs. cruelty, 36
  cruelty associated with, 310
  illegal, 97, 151
  legal form of, 172
  public support for, 170
  in U.S., 169
hunting preserves, private, 170–171
Hurricane Katrina, impact on animals shelters of, 161–162
husbandry practices, defined as routine, 76
Hutton, J. S., 281

I
Iceland, whale hunting of, 169
Idaho
  "ag gag" laws of, 77–78
  animal cruelty reported in, 150
  animal hoarding case in, 207
  bestiality statutes in, 229
  horse slaughter in, 405
Idaho Humane Society, 207
Iliopoulou, M. A., 339
Illinois
  animal cruelty statutes in, 12, 13
  animal protection law in, 32, 33
  bestiality statutes in, 228
  definition of companion animal in, 53
  Pamplona-like events in, 180
  reporting of animal cruelty in, 92, 146, 147, 149, 150
  running of bulls in, 181
  shark fin products banned in, 407

torture defined in, 18
immigrants, companion animal ownership of, 127–128
impounding, in NY anti-cruelty law, 43
impulse control problems, compared with animal hoarding, 203
impulsivity, and partner abuse, 278
incarcerated adults, AAI for, 131
Incident-Based Reporting Systems, 142
income equality, and meat consumption, 343
India
    dolphinaria banned in, 85
    Jallikattu in, 180
    roaming dogs in, 236, 237, 238, 240, 243, 244
Indiana
    animal cruelty reported in, 150, 152
    animal cruelty statutes in, 11, 13
    torture defined in, 18
indifference, cruelty of, 56
Indigenous people, companion animal ownership of, 127–128
industrial farms, production expectations of, 162
    See also factory farms
information sharing, in animal cruelty crimes, 410–411
inmates, self-reported childhood animal abuse of, 365–366
    See also offenders
instinct theory, of animal cruelty, 357–358
Institute for Animals and Society, AniCare Model for Adults and Children of, 130
Institute for Humane Education, 437
Institutional Animal Care and Use Committee (IACUC), 125
intake triage, 95
intelligence, low, 363
intent, establishing, 17–18
intergenerational transmission (IGT) hypothesis, 327–328, 329
    of animal abuse, 327–328, 328
    critique of, 329
international animal protection movement, 61–62
International Association of Chiefs of Police, 106
International Court of Justice (ICJ), and Japanese whaling program, 169

International Fund for Animal Welfare, 437
International Primate Protection League, 437
International Veterinary Forensic Sciences Association, 90, 208
International Whaling Commission (IWC), 168
Internet
    animals sold on, 67
    crush videos on, 227
    dogfighting on, 176
interpersonal violence (IPV)
    animal abuse as predictor of, 333–334
    and childhood animal cruelty, 356
Interpol, on endangered flora and fauna, 167
interviews, in animal abuse research, 264
intimate partner violence (IPV)
    and animal abuse, 327–328, 337
    and coercion, 332
    dominance and control in, 337
    victims of, 332
investigation, in animal cop shows, 384
Iowa
    "ag gag" laws in, 408
    animal cruelty reported in, 148, 149, 152, 166
    animal cruelty statutes in, 13, 18
    bestiality statutes in, 229
    puppy mills in, 160–161
IQ, and antisocial behavior, 363
Italy, Palio horse race banned in, 179
Izod, John, 383

J
Jaffee, S. R., 27
Jallikattu, 180
Jambrak, J., 367
Japan
    hunting and killing of whales in, 168–169
    primate research in, 68
Johnson, B. R., 310
Johnson, J. A., 254, 328
Johnson, R. A., 128
Johnson, T. P., 127
Jordan, donkey taxis in, 185
Jory, B., 222, 256
journalism, investigative, 386

on reality TV, 385–386
judges, in animal cruelty cases, 20
  See also courts
judgment, immediacy of, on reality TV, 390
juvenile delinquency, and early aggression, 364–365
juveniles
  bestiality among, 222
  firesetting, 305, 306

K
Kageyama, Y., 186
Kallinger, Joseph, 314–315
Kalof, L., 345
Kansas
  "ag gag" laws in, 408
  animal cruelty statutes in, 19
  bestiality statutes in, 229
  definition of companion animal in, 53
  reporting of animal cruelty in, 92, 152
Kant, Immanuel, 3–4
Kaplan, N., 116
Kaufman, J., 277
Kazdin, A. E., 306
Keiko, 188
Kellert, S. R., 6, 262, 280, 281–282, 302, 328, 330, 333, 339, 340
Kentucky
  animal cruelty defined in, 17
  animal cruelty reported in, 152
  animal cruelty statutes in, 18
Kenya, roaming dogs in, 241
Khan, R., 256
Khetrapal, N., 367
kicking or stomping offense, statistics on, 148–149
Killborn, Richard, 383, 384, 385, 386
Killeen, Celeste, 203, 204, 206, 207, 209, 212
Killias, M., 330
killing, vs. cruelty, 35
Kimonis, E. R., 361
Kinlock, T. W., 256
Kinsey, A. C., 221
klismaphilia, 218
Kluger, J., 171
Knight, K. E., 257, 327, 334
Knutson, J. F., 261, 282
Kodiene, S., 127

Kogan, L. R., 127
Kolko, D. J., 306
Kosher slaughter, 12
Krafft-Ebing, Richard von, 301, 310
Kretchmer, E., 301
Krupa, T., 120
Kurten, Peter, 310
Kwong, M., 123

L
laboratory experimentation, with animals, 19, 355
  AHB in, 125
  ignorance of conditions in, 403
  See also research
Lakey, B., 118
lameness, of factory farm cows, 164
Lamm, C., 369
Langevin, R., 302, 313
The Latham Foundation, 437–438
Latin America, swimming with dolphins in, 187
Latina/o groups, companion animal ownership of, 127
Law, James, 89
law enforcement agencies, tracking systems of, 107
law enforcement authorities
  and animal hoarding, 207
  in animal seizures, 208–209
  interventions by, 214
law enforcement personnel, 399, 409
law enforcement training, in animal cruelty investigation, 107
laws
  and breeding, 160–161
  and cultural norms, 3
Lawson, C., 410
League Against Cruel Sports, 438
Leaping Bunny Program, 438
Lee, J., 237
legal personality, of animals, 41
leg-hold traps, 81
legislation, animal welfare, 29
legislation, anti-cruelty, 404
  "ag gag" laws, 408
  centralized federal regulation, 406–407
  in courts, 405–406
  future of, 408–409
  shark finning, 407

state action in, 404–406
Lehmann, P., 254, 289
lemon laws, for puppies, 161
Leong, G. B., 305, 306
Levin, J., 225, 302, 334
Levinson, B., 255
Lewis, N. D. C., 304, 305
Lexington Attachment to Pets Scale, 127
Liautard, Alexandre, 89
Licensing and Regulation, Texas Dept. of (TDLR), 51
Liebel Family Circus, 182
Lim, E., 115
Lincoln, Pres. Abraham, 8, 172
Linden, F., 132
Lisbon, Treaty of, 86, 408
livestock, 165
    defined, 71–72
    demographics for, 121
    See also chickens; cows; elephants; horses
"livestock animals," 342
livestock care programs, 131–132
living beings, animals as, 40
Locke, John, 332–333
Lockwood, Randall, 254, 264, 281, 411, 445–446
Loeber, R., 365
logging industry, use of elephants in, 185
Lolita, at Miami Seaquarium, 69–70
Lombroso, C., 301
Lorenz, Konrad, 116, 357
Loring, M. T., 332
Los Angeles Animal Cruelty Task Force (ACTF), 411
Los Angeles Service Office, 411
loss, of companion animal, 130
Louisiana
    animal cruelty reported in, 146, 150, 153
    animal cruelty statutes in, 18
    bestiality statutes in, 229
    cockfighting in, 173
Louw, D., 256
Lucia, S., 330
Luk, E. S., 258
Luke, C., 225, 334, 341
Luntz, B. K., 277

M
MacDonald, J. M., 301
MacDonald's Triad, 301, 333
    and adult violent crime, 301–302
    case study for, 313
    predictive nature of, 306–307
    as predictor of homicidal behavior, 315, 316
    usefulness of, 316
machismo
    of cockfighting, 174
    and dogfighting, 177
    See also masculinity
MacNair, R., 345
Madfis, E., 333
Maher, Rep. John, 400
mahouts, 185
Main, M., 116
Maine
    animal cruelty statutes in, 11, 12, 13
    bestiality statutes in, 229
    reporting of animal cruelty in, 92, 150
male/female dualisms, 387
    on reality TV, 387
    See also feminist theory; gender differences
malice
    defined, 56
    as predictive of violent behavior, 303
malicious harm, 17
malnutrition, in animal hoarding, 201
maltreated children, firesetting of, 305
maltreatment, legal definitions, 5
Manganello, J., 290
mange, roaming dogs with, 242
Manly, J. T., 278
Marine Mammal Protection Act (MMPA), 79–81, 80
marine mammals
    man's impact upon, 79
    public display of, 80
Marine Mammal Stranding Center, 438
marital violence, and child abuse, 280
    See also domestic violence
Marquis, J., 19
Martin, C. E., 118
Martin, Richard, 27
Martinsen, E. W., 132
Marx, M. B., 127

Maryland
  animal cruelty reported in, 152
  animal cruelty statutes in, 18
  animal protection law in, 33
  bestiality statutes in, 229
  certain veterinary practices banned in, 405
  devocalization law in, 405
  shark fin products banned in, 407
masculinity
  animal abuse to accomplish, 339
  and animal cop shows, 386–387
  and consumption of animals, 340–341
  hegemonic ideal of, 338, 339, 340
  and normalization of animal abuse, 339–340
  social construction of, 338
Massachusetts
  animal cruelty reported in, 146, 147, 150
  animal protection law in, 33
  bestiality statutes in, 229
  cockfighting in, 173
  devocalization law in, 404–405
  early animal protection law in, 32
Massey, B., 405
mass media
  modern-day access to, 398
  and public awareness, 400–402
  See also media
mastitis, diagnosed in factory farms, 164
Maughan, A., 277
Maunula, M., 172, 175
McAloon, J., 280, 303
McCloskey, L. A., 306, 366
McConnell, A. R., 118
McCormack, A., 282
McDonald's (fast food restaurant), 166
McEwen, B. J., 106
McEwen, F. S., 357, 359
McNutt, M., 405
McPhedran, S., 262
Mead, Margaret, 253, 333
Meadows, R. L., 128
meat
  international demand for, 342
  and masculinity, 340
meat consumption
  and income equality, 343
  justification of, 340
  sexual violence and, 336
meat demand, mass media coverage of, 401
meat eating, sexual violence and, 336
meatpacking, and violent crime, 345
meat processing plant employees, 266
  aggression scores of, 267
  familial violence among, 266–267
  See also slaughterhouses; slaughterhouse workers
meatworks, 266
media, 400
  activists framed as violent terrorists by, 397–398
  animal cruelty in, 379
  data collected from, 142
  image of activists in, 398
  impact on animal cruelty of, 401
  and public awareness, 143
medical research, attitudes toward animals in, 403
  See also laboratory experimentation; research
medical teaching facilities, 36
Medlen v. Strickland, 52
Meerkat Manor (film), 384
Meloy, R. J., 311, 360, 367, 368
mens rea, 17, 55
mental health issues
  and AAI, 132
  animal hoarding as, 205
  and pet ownership, 120
  violence to animals as, 130
mental health professionals, 399
Merck, Melinda, 410
Mercy for Animals, 166, 438
mercy killing, as animal cruelty defense, 104–105
  See also Euthanasia
Merz-Perez, L., 224, 226, 262, 302, 333
Messerschmidt, J. W., 338
Mexico
  circus animals banned in, 183
  horses transported for slaughter to, 72
  roaming dogs in, 241, 242
  swimming with dolphins in, 187
Meyer, E. C., 306
Miami Animal Police (TV show), 388–389
Miami Seaquarium, Lolita at, 69–70

Michigan
    animal cruelty reported in, 148, 152
    animal cruelty statutes in, 12
    animal protection law of, 33
    bestiality statutes in, 229
microchips, used at hunting ranches, 171
Milani, Myna, 115, 116, 121
Miletski, H., 221, 222, 223
milk production, of factory farms, 164
Miller, C., 261
Miller, K. S., 282
Miltiades, H., 120
Minatrea, N. B., 132
Mine (film), 401
Minnesota
    animal cruelty statutes in, 11, 13
    anti-cruelty law in, 26
    bestiality statutes in, 229
    reporting of animal cruelty in, 92, 152, 153, 166
    running of bulls in, 181
misdemeanor, 9, 28n13
    animal cruelty as, 28–29
    in animal welfare law, 38–39
    classification of, 60
    compared with felony, 13, 55
    in NY law, 30
Misha Foundation, 431
Mishima, Yukio, 309
Mississippi
    animal cruelty reported in, 148, 152, 153, 154
    animal cruelty statutes in, 18
    animal protection law in, 33
    bestiality statutes in, 229
Missouri
    "ag gag" laws in, 408
    animal cruelty reported in, 152
    animal cruelty statutes in, 12
    bestiality statutes in, 229
    dogfighting raid in, 177
    puppy mills in, 51, 161
Missouri State Highway Patrol, 177
mobility problems, of roaming dogs, 242
Moeller, T. G., 363
Moffitt, T. E., 277
Molloy, Claire, 399, 446
Montana
    "ag gag" laws in, 408
    bestiality statutes in, 229

horse slaughter in, 405
reporting of animal cruelty in, 148
Moore, J. R., 305
moral boundaries, and reality TV, 394
moral disengagement, 403
Moran, Rep. Jim, 84
Morgan, K., 8
Morris, A., 132
Morris, M. C., 343
mortality, in factory farming, 163
Mosk, M. D., 278
Munchausen syndrome by proxy, 115
Munro, H. M. C., 14–15
murder, sadistic, 307
    See also homicides
murderers, prefrontal regulation of, 360–361
Muth, R. M., 170
mutilations, 76
    in factory farms, 166–167
    forensic analysis of, 100
    statistics on, 149
Mutt-i-grees® program, 131

N
Nagin, D., 365
narrative
    of animals cop shows, 394
    on reality television, 380
    of rescue drama, 385
narrator, in animal cop shows, 392
Nathanson, J., 203
National Animal Cruelty Investigations School, at Missouri Law Enforcement Training Institute, 409
National Canine Research Council, 439
National Center for Prosecution of Animal Abuse (NCPAA), 410
National District Attorneys Association, 4, 410
National Education for Assistance Dog Services (NEADS), Canines for Combat Veterans and Trauma Alert Dog Program of, 123
National Incident Based Reporting System (NIBRS), 142, 355
National Institutes of Health (NIH), chimpanzees owned by, 69
National Marine Fisheries Service (NMFS), 80

National Marine Fisheries Service (NMFS) for cetaceans and seals, 79
National Oceanic and Atmospheric Administration (NOAA), and MMPA, 79
National Pet Owners Survey, of APPA, 382
National Rifle Association (NRA), 400
National Sheriffs Association, 106
National Youth Survey Family Study (NYSFS), 333
Native American reservations, roaming dogs on, 239, 240
natural history documentaries, 384
nature programs, 383
Navajo reservation, roaming dogs on, 236
Navarro, John C., 446
Nebraska
   animal cruelty statutes in, 10, 11
   animal protection law in, 33
   bestiality statutes in, 229
   horse slaughter in, 405
   reporting of animal cruelty in, 92, 152
necrophilia, 218
necropsy, forensic, 96–97
neglect, animal, 56, 60
   animal hoarding as, 11, 212 (*see also* hoarding)
   vs. animal hoarding cases, 211
   cognitive theories in, 364
   definitions of, 4–5, 10–11, 13
   effective response to, 20
   forensic documentation of, 97–98
   institutional, 97–98
   motivation for, 17
   recognizing, 5
   severe, 8
   and socially problematic behaviors, 277–278
   typology of, 16t
   of unowned dogs, 243
   in veterinary forensic science, 91
negligence, defined, 55
neighbors
   acts of cruelty committed by, 56
   hoarder complaints of, 207
   as reporting parties, 143
Nepal, animal tourism in, 186
the Netherlands, primate research in, 68
neurobiological theories, of animal cruelty, 362–363
Nevada, animal cruelty statutes in, 11, 13

New Hampshire
   animal cruelty reported in, 154
   animal protection law in, 32, 33
New Jersey
   animal cruelty reported in, 147, 148
   animal cruelty statutes in, 10, 18
   devocalization law in, 405
   early animal protection law in, 32
   horse slaughter banned in, 405
   humane treatment of livestock in, 75–77
   ivory sales banned in, 404
New Jersey Society for the Prevention of Cruelty to Animals (New Jersey SPCA), 75, 76, 77
New Jersey State Supreme Court, 405–406
"A New Leash on Life" program, 131
New Mexico, animal cruelty reported in, 152, 153
New York
   animal cruelty defined in, 17
   animal cruelty reported in, 146, 147, 148, 149, 150, 151, 152, 153
   animal protection law in, 33
   bestiality statutes in, 229
   ivory sales banned in, 404
   shark fin products banned in, 407
New York Anti-Cruelty law (1829), 28–29
New York Anti-Cruelty law (1867), 25, 29–30, 32, 33
   enforcement of, 31
   exemption from, 31
   provisions of, 42–44
   ripple effect of, 32–33
New York City
   Animal Precinct in, 388
   early animal protection law in, 31–32
New York Herald (newspaper), 32
New York Marine Court, animal protection law in, 34
New York State College of Veterinary Medicine, 89
New York State Humane Society, guidance document of, 409
New Zealand
   animal welfare law in, 62
   primate research in, 68
New Zealand Fire Awareness and Intervention Program, 306
Nixon, Gov. Jay, 161

nomenclature, 20
non-accidental injuries (NAIs), 11, 77, 99, 145
  See also animal abuse, intentional
Nonhuman Rights Project, 42, 439
Noon, A., 361
Norris, G., 263
North Carolina
  animal cruelty defined in, 18
  animal cruelty reported in, 148, 152, 166
North Dakota
  "ag gag" laws in, 408
  bestiality statutes in, 229
  horse slaughter in, 405
  reporting of animal cruelty in, 92
Norway, whale hunting of, 169
Noske, B., 336
Novek, J., 342
nuisances, roaming dogs as, 239–241
Nunn, H., 385, 390–391

O
Oaxaca, Mexico, roaming dogs in, 238
Obama, Pres. Barack, 72, 227
Obeyesekere, 244
O'Bryan, A., 256
observational learning, of animal cruelty, 358
Odendaal, J. S. J., 15
Oei, T. L., 367
offenders
  attachment assessment of, 368
  bestiality among, 224
  childhood animal cruelty of, 333
  drug abuse of, 144
  firesetting behavior of, 306
  firesetting histories among, 306
  sexual homicide, 225–226
  See also abusers
offenders, incarcerated
  AAI for, 131
  retrospective reports from, 264
O'Grady, K. E., 256
Ohio
  animal cruelty reported in, 147, 152
  devocalization law in, 405
  farm animal conditions in, 74
  torture defined in, 18
  unlawful trapping or hunting in, 151

Ohio Livestock Care Standards Board, 74
Ohta, M., 124
Oklahoma
  bestiality statutes in, 229
  commercial pet breeding in, 405
  reporting of animal cruelty in, 92, 150, 153
older adults, attachment to companion animals of, 120
omission
  acts of, 151–152
  defined, 55
  proving act of, 17
  unlawful act of, 17
  See also neglect
Ontario Humane Society, 411
Ontario Society for the Prevention of Cruelty to Animals (Ontario SPCA), 286
oosiks, illegal trade in, 168
opossums, as victims, 147
oppositional defiant disorder (ODD), and firesetting, 305
oppression, historic trajectories of, 342
orca whales
  in captivity, 69–70, 79, 80
  commercial exploitation of, 187
  at Sea World, 41
  SRKW Distinct Population Segment of, 70
Orchard, B., 302
Oregon
  animal cruelty defined in, 17
  animal cruelty statutes in, 19
  animal hoarding case in, 207
  animal protection law in, 54
  bestiality statutes in, 229
  mandatory veterinary reporting law of, 93
  reporting of animal cruelty in, 92, 148, 150, 152
  shark fin products banned in, 407
  unlawful trapping or hunting in, 151
Oregon's Malheur County, shelter requirements in, 213
Oregon State Supreme Court, 406
Orehek, E., 118
Ostdahl, T., 124
osteoporosis, cage layer, 165
overcrowding
  of chickens, 165

in factory farms, 163
overdriving
  in animal cruelty statutes, 12
  in NY anti-cruelty law, 42
overloading, in animal cruelty statutes, 12
Overton, J. C., 302
overworking, in animal cruelty statutes, 12
Owen, Keith, 166
owners, of companion animals, 144
  positive duty for, 38–39
  special responsibility of, 56
owners, passive, 240

P

Pacheco, Alex, 341
Packman, W., 121
Pagani, C., 340
Pagini, L., 365
Palio horse race, 179
Palmer, R., 117
Palo Mayombe, ritualized abuse associated with, 102
Pamplona, running of bulls in, 180
Panzram, Carl, 314
paranoia, of hoarders, 202
paraphilias
  continuum for, 217
  history of, 218
  use of term, 217
  zoophilia, 219
paraphilic behaviors, 217
paraphilic disorder
  classification of, 218
  defining, 218
parental reports, in animal abuse research, 264
parental violence against animals, exposure to, 326–327
parents
  abusive, 284
  risky, 284, 285
Paris, A., 363
parrots, wild, 186
partialism, 218
partner abuse
  and animal cruelty, 290
  and childhood health, 279
  See also domestic violence
partner violence, demographic variables in, 278

Pasalich, D., 367
paternal violence, and childhood animal cruelty, 281
patriarchal culture, normative dualisms in, 336
patriarchy
  and animal harm, 341
  and speciesism, 335–336
Patrich, D., 302
Patronek, Gary J., 8, 14, 199, 203, 212, 446
Patterson-Kane, E. G., 302
Paulo's Circus, 183
Peacock, J., 116, 117
Peck, D., 124
Pedersen, I., 132
peer relationships, and animal abuse, 327
peers, coercive control patterns of, 331
Pelcovitz, D., 280
Pennsylvania
  animal fighting paraphernalia in, 406
  bestiality statutes in, 229
  cockfighting in, 173
  early animal protection law in, 32
  pigeon shoots in, 400
  prohibited conduct in, 55
  puppy-mill law in, 161
  reporting of animal cruelty in, 92, 150, 152, 153
  running of bulls in, 181
Pennsylvania Society for Prevention of Cruelty to Animals, 439–440
People for the Ethical Treatment of Animals (PETA), 440
  activism of, 397
  and bestiality laws, 228
  and Jallikattu, 180
People v. Garcia, 53
Pepler, D. J., 358
perception of animals, studies of people's, 414
Peretti, P. O., 222
permitted conduct, 65–66
personality disorders, animal hoarders with, 201
Peru, circus animals banned in, 183
pet
  defined, 61
  use of term, 65n1

Pet-Abuse.com, 440
   animal cruelty case trend seen on, 143
   data detected by, 142–145
   general perpetrator characteristics, 143–144
   goals of, 154
   reporting parties for, 143
pet adoption programs, 132
Pet and Women's Safety Act (2015), 406
"Pet Attachment Questionnaire" (PAQ), 117117
Petersen, M. L., 309, 334
pet food market, in UK, 381–382
pet industry, growth in, 382
Pet Industry Joint Advisory Council (PIJAC), 160
pet marine mammals, as victims, 149
pet ownership
   beneficial aspects of, 120
   in China, 61
   and SPMI, 120–121
pet programs
   popularity of, 380
   on reality TV, 393
pet protection laws, 54
pets
   backyard chickens as, 122
   bringing nature closer, 115
   See also companion animals
pet stores, retail
   defined, 50
   puppies sold at, 160
   redefining, 67–69
petty offenses, 9
Philippines, roaming dogs in, 244
Phillips, C., 124
Philly Undercover (TV show), 386, 387
photographic documentation, at crime scene, 96
photography
   in animal cruelty report, 94
   forensic, 94–95
phylogenetic continuum, 402
physical abuse
   and aggressive behavior, 277
   and socially problematic behaviors, 277–278
   See also abuse
physical findings, in animal cruelty report, 94

Piaget, Jean, 363
Pickett, H., 165
pigeon shoots, in PA, 400
pigs
   in factory farms, 165
   intensive confinement of, 76–77
   laws governing pregnant, 74
   tails cut off of, 166
   as victims, 148
   See also swine
Piper, H., 302
Piper, Thomas, 313
pit bull dogs
   theft of, 153
   as victims, 142, 147, 148, 149, 150, 151, 152
pit bull terriers
   American, 176
   in hog-dog fighting, 178
pitchforks, as training tools, 181
"the Pittsburgh study," 365
plea bargains, 60
poachers, non-commercial, 170
poaching
   definitions for, 170
   in U.S. national parks, 169
Poe, Bethanie A., 446
poisoning, 101
   forensic analysis of, 101–102
   prevalence of, 149
police crime drama, and animal cop shows, 389
police immunity, limit to, 57
police officers, 409
   dogs killed by, 56–57
   working with dogs, 125
police records, data collected from, 142
politics. and anti-cruelty laws, 50
Porcher, J., 122, 266
posttraumatic stress disorder, in children witnessing violence, 278
Potter, Will, 397
poultry, excluded from HMSA protection, 71
   See also chickens
power relationships, with farm animals, 122
preschool years, 365
Presidential Pits, 440

Preventing Cruelty and Torture Act (2015), 406
primates
  AWA provisions for, 68
  used in research, 68
Primatt, Rev. Humphry, 4, 26–27
Prior, D., 363
prison-based animal programs (PAPs), 113, 123
  livestock programs, 132
  national survey of adult, 131
  participation in, 132
probation system, 213
"production animals," 121
professionals, animals used by, 124–125
profits
  animal cruelty for, 159
  and animal harm, 341
  animals for, 188
  and breeding, 160
  and factory farming, 162
  maximization of, 342
  and public concern for, 401
progression thesis, 332
Progressive Animal Welfare Society (PAWS), 440–441
prohibited conduct, 48
  in case law, 51–52
  with companion animals, 49, 53
  in Constitution, 51
  puppy mills, 50–51
  in statutory law, 49–51
  terms used to define, 55
  19th-century legal precedent for, 51
  victims of, 54–55
projectile injuries, forensic analysis of, 100
Project Pooch, 131
Project Second Chance, 131
property, animals as, 4, 9, 25–26, 341
  classification of, 47
  and legal rights, 41
  and study of animal cruelty, 413
prosecution of animal cruelty cases, 20, 58–59
  dogfighting, 102
  successful, 410
"prosecutorial discretion," 59
prosecutors, in animal cruelty cases, 20
protest activity, criminalization of, 398

proximity maintenance, in attachment theory, 116
psychiatrists, 214
psychological disorder, animal hoarding as, 202–205, 204f
psychological disturbance, CTA as, 263
psychological theories of animal cruelty, 357–358, 369–370
  attachment theory, 366–368
  bimodal theories of aggression, 360–362
  cognitive theories, 363–366
  empathy development, 368–369
  instinct and drive theories, 357–358
  neurobiological theories, 362–363
  social learning theory, 358–360
psychological well-being, with presence of animals, 117
psychologists, forensic, 214
psychopathic behaviors, 15
psychopathy, 290
  attachment and, 367
  cognitive neuro-scientific models of, 362
  and killing and torture of animals, 311
psychosexual disorders, paraphilias as, 218
public, as victim of animal cruelty, 54
public attitudes, regarding animal cruelty, 54
public awareness of animal cruelty
  of animal cruelty, 416
  and mass media, 400–402
  role of AARDAS in, 155
  and role of media, 143, 399
public display
  of beluga whales, 80, 80n110
  of marine mammals, 80
public opinion, 325
  of animal rights activists, 398
  and definitions, 8–9
  influence on, 399
  and puppy mills, 51
  and wildlife management practices, 170
Puerto Rico, animal cruelty statutes in, 11
punishment
  and animal cruelty, 359
  in animal cruelty conviction, 60–61
punishment, parental, and animal abuse, 328

Puppies Behind Bars (PBB) program, 113, 130
Puppy Mill Cruelty Prevention Act (2011), Missouri, 161
puppy mills, 147, 407
    beginnings of, 159
    conditions in, 160
    cruelty in, 50–51
    defined, 160
    and local shelters, 161–162
    media coverage of, 401–402
    raids, 59
puppy-producing facility, requirements for, 160
Puppy Uniform Protection Act (2011), 161
Puppy Uniform Protection and Safety Act (2013–2014), 161
purebred rescue movement, 398
Purina, dog and cat scales of, 14
pyromania, 303
    See also firesetting
Pyshyl, Timothy A., 119

Q
quadrupeds, as livestock, 71–72
"qualified immunity," for police officers, 56–57
quality of life, and Five Freedoms, 209, 210f
quasi-relational support, 118
Quinsey, V. L., 304
Quinslick, J. A., 286

R
rabbits
    as companion animals, 65
    as victims, 142, 150
Rabbit Wise, 441
rabies transmission, fear of, 239
racehorses, cruelty inflicted upon, 401
    See also horses
racial/ethnic differences, in companion animal ownership, 127
radiography, in diagnosis of blunt trauma, 100
Raine, A., 360–361
Randour, Mary Lou, 141, 142, 369, 446–447
"rape kit," 103
Reagan administration, deregulation policies of, 380

reality crime, criticisms of, 390–391
reality programming, definition of, 383
reality shows, 387
    See also animal cop shows
reality TV
    animal, 380
    animal cruelty in, 379
    audience trust in, 383–384
    and boundaries between fact and fiction, 386
    fact *vs.* entertainment in, 384
    formats of, 383
    genre hybrids, 384–386
    pet-related shows, 381
    "predation" programming on, 381
    range and scope of, 382–384
    spectacle in, 393
    technical signifiers in, 393
    visual evidence on, 392–394
reality TV formats, 379
Reber, K., 288
record keeping, 95
The Records of North American Big Game, 171
recreation, wildlife associated, 124
red-coded animals, at forensic crime scene, 95
reimbursement, in animal cruelty conviction, 60
relational support, 118
religion, and animal abuse, 12, 331
Repetti, R. L., 278, 279
reptiles
    hoarding of, 200
    as victims, 151, 153
rescue, of hoarded animals, 208
rescue drama
    in animal cop shows, 384
    narrative of, 385
rescue volunteers, as victims, 54
rescue workers, as advocates, 398
research
    animals used for, 65
    caregivers of animals used for, 125
    mass media coverage of, 401
researchers
    animal cruelty defined by, 6–7
    exemptions in place for, 48
research facilities
    AWA provisions for, 68

definition of, 67
research protocol, 68
Ressler, R. K., 224, 282, 309, 311, 313, 314
restoration and stress recovery, in biophilia theory, 114, 115
retaliation
　against animal's bad behavior, 144
　and shooting offenses, 150
retrospection, reliance of, 357
Revitch, E., 307, 308, 311
Reyes, Cassandra L., 447
rhinoceroses, illicit trade in, 168
Rhode Island
　animal cruelty reported in, 149, 152
　bestiality statutes in, 229
Richards, E., 267
Rider, Thomas, 82–83, 83, 84
Rigdon, J. D., 281
Ring, D., 178
Ringling Brothers Circus, 82, 83, 84, 85, 182, 183
　elephants retired from, 183
　fines issued against, 182
ringworm, roaming dogs with, 242
risk factors, for abuse and neglect, 14–15
Risley-Curtiss, Christina, 127, 130, 447
ritualistic sacrifice, 97
Robertson, N., 257, 335, 359
Robin, M., 283
rodeos, 67
Rogers, R., 340–341
Romania
　eradication program of, 237
　roaming dogs in, 237, 242
Ronen, R., 121
Rosenbaum, R. P., 339
Rothgerber, H., 340
Rowan, A. N., 15
Rowan, M., 222
Royal Society for Prevention of Cruelty to Animals (RSPCA), 281
Royal Society for the Protection of Animals, 28
running with bulls, 180–181
Russon, A., 302

S

sadomasochistic sexual practices, 223
Saedi, G., 120, 121

Safeguard American Food Exports (SAFE) Act, 72
safe haven
　in attachment theory, 116
　in human-service dog attachment, 123
safety, sense of, with roaming dogs, 243
Sakagami, T., 124
Sakheim, G. A., 305
Salleh, A., 337
Samoa, roaming dogs in, 237, 239, 240, 241–242
sampling bias, 316
sanctions, against animal cruelty crimes, 292
Sanders, C. E., 257, 259, 262, 335, 359
Sandnabba, N. K., 223
San Jose Charter of Hells Angels v. City of San Jose (2003), 57
Santeria, ritualized abuse associated with, 102
Santorini (Greek Island), 185
Santorum, Sen. Rick, 161
Scarpa, A., 302
Schachtman, T., 311, 314
Schaefer, K., 130
Schaffner, J. E., 291, 292
Schaffner, Joan E., 447
Schiff, K., 256
Schlauch, C., 362
Schlesinger, Louis B., 307, 308, 311, 447
Schleuter, S., 291
Schneider, Jacqueline L., 167, 448
Schoelkopf, Robert, 438
Schoenfeld-Tacher, R., 127
schools
　behavioral troubles in, 315
　coercive control patterns in, 331
　humane education programs in, 131
　information about animal protection in, 399
school shooters, 333
school shootings, 303
Schreiber, Flora, 314
Schumacher, J. A., 278
scientific experiments, in NY anti-cruelty law, 44
scientific research
　animals used for, 62
　attitudes toward animals in, 403
　See also research

Sealand, 187
sea turtles, 30, 32
Sea World
    orca whales at, 41
    trainer killed at, 79, 80
SeaWorld Orlando, 187
Second Chance Shelter, 207
secure base
    in attachment theory, 116, 117
    in human-service dog attachment, 123
Seguin, J. R., 365
seizing animals, 208–209
seizures, 58
selective breeding, 121
self defense, claimed in court, 105
self-reports
    reliability of, 315
    retrospective, 282, 303
Senatori, M., 407
separation distress, in attachment theory, 116
serial killers, 309
    animal abuse histories of, 256, 333
    animals hoarders as, 211
serial murder, social-learning theory of, 314
Serious and Organized Crime and Police Act, U.K. (2005), 398
seriously and persistently mentally ill (SPMI), 120
service animals
    civil rights protection for, 123
    compared with companion animals, 123
    people who benefit from, 123
    trained by prison inmates, 113
service animal socialization programs, 132
service dogs, training of, 123
sexism, and exploitation of animals, 336
sex offenders, youthful interspecies, 222
sexual abuse
    and aggressive behavior, 277
    of animals, 103, 340
    child victims, 255
sexual deviance, 217
    bestiality as, 220
    classification of, 218
    See also paraphilia
sexual fantasies, and paraphilia, 217
sexual homicide, 316

sexual homicide offenders, 225–226
sexuality, infantile, 226
sexual murderers, 313
    case studies, 312
    childhoods of, 314
    with history of firesetting, 312–315
    incarcerated, 311–312
    and significance of cats, 311
sexual murders
    childhood animal cruelty of, 310–312
    and firesetting background, 314–315
sexual offenders
    crossover behavior of, 224
    developmental experiences of, 258
sexual sadism, psychopathy of, 311
sexual violence
    and CTA, 267
    and meat eating, 336
Shapiro, K., 7, 355
shark dives, 184
shark finning, 407
Shark Finning Protection Act (2000), 407
Sharp, C., 360
sharp force injuries, 100
Shawcross, Arthur, 313
Shearer, J., 120
shelter animals, rescued, 369
shelter dogs, in prison-based socialization program, 132
shelters, and puppy mill seizures, 161
shelter workers, as victims, 54
Shirtcliff, E. A., 368
"shock advocacy," 401
Shoda, T. M., 118
shooting offenses, prevalence of, 150
Showing Animals Respect and Kindness (SHARK), 441
Signal, Tania, 261, 267, 448
signalment, in animal cruelty report, 94
Silverman, I. J., 333
Simmons, B., 327, 334
Simmons, C. A., 254, 289
Simons, D. A., 258
"Sinclair Effect," 267
Singer, S. D., 314
Situating Animal Abuse in Criminology (symposium), 412
Slaby, R. G., 358
slaughter
    of dolphins and porpoises, 186

humane methods of, 70–73
slaughterhouses
  communities with, 266
  crime rates and, 345
  transport to, 31
  videos in, 344
slaughterhouse workers, 73, 266
  animal abuse by, 344
  psychological effects of work on, 345
slaughtering, in (eco) Marxism, 342
Slayton, L. E., 118
Smith, L. D. G., 124
smuggling, unlawful, 153–154
snake charmers, 186
Sochi, Russia, roaming dogs in, 240
social contract, for animal well-being, 39
social learning theory, 326–329, 329, 358–360
social media
  animal cruelty posted online, 401
  technologies, 379
social norms, 3
social phenomenon, increased legitimacy as, 412–413
social service providers, 399
social supports, animals as, 119
social support theory, 117, 118–119
Societies for Prevention of Cruelty to Animals (SPCAs)
  state, 33
  of Texas, 59
  See also American Society for Prevention of Cruelty to Animals
socioemotional adjustment, of maltreated children, 277
sociology
  of animal abuse, 325
  applications of, 326
sociopaths, animal hoarders as, 201
Solomon, O., 123
the South
  cockfighting in, 172–173
  dogfighting in, 176
  hog-dog fighting in, 178
South, Nigel, 412
South Carolina
  animal cruelty reported in, 147, 148, 150, 152, 153
  animal cruelty statutes in, 19
  bestiality statutes in, 228–229
  hog-dogging in, 179
South Dakota
  animal cruelty law in, 141
  anti-cruelty law in, 404
  bestiality statutes in, 228
  unlawful trapping or hunting in, 151
Southern Resident Killer Whale (SRKW), 70
South Florida Wildlife Center, 441
sow stalls, 164
Sparboe Egg Farms, 166
sparrow war, American, 235
speciesism, 343
  and commodification of animals, 342
  confronting, 345
  human, 365
  patriarchy and, 335–336
sport
  animal cruelty for, 159
  animals for, 188
  dogfighting as, 175
  media coverage of animal cruelty as, 401
  See also blood sports
sporting activities, 169
  canned/captive hunting, 170–172
  hunting and fishing in U.S., 169–170
Sri Lanka, roaming dogs in, 239, 243, 244
Srinivasan, K., 240
stabbing offenses, prevalence of, 150
Stallones, L., 127
standing
  doctrine of, 82
  prudential, 82, 83
Stanford, M. S., 360
starvation, with animal hoarding, 206–207
state decisis, legal doctrine of, 51
state law, wildlife protection in, 81
  See also specific states
state of mind, establishing, 17–18
State of Oregon v. Nix, 54
states, anti-cruelty law in, 404–406
state statutes
  antiquated anti-cruelty language of, 9
  bestiality, 228
  cruelty defined in, 17
  defenses and exemptions in, 19
  definitional limitations of, 20
State-Trait Anxiety Inventory-State Subscale, 132

State v. Allison, 37
State v. Avery, 36
State v. Bruner, 35
statutory law, 49–51
    vs. common law, 49
    language of, 34–35
Steiner, R., 130
Steketee, G., 126
Stephens v. State of Mississippi, 24n39, 33–34
sterilization
    appearance affected by, 242
    and dog behavior, 243
Stevens, Robert J., 51
Stevenson, Rochelle, 448
Stickle, T. R., 306, 361
Stone, M. H., 315
strain theory
    aggression in, 329
    animal abuse in, 329–331
Strand, Elizabeth B., 448
"Strange Situation," 366
    See also attachment theory
"Strange Situation" test, Ainsworth's, 116, 117
strangulation
    forensic analysis of, 101
    statistics on, 147
Straus, M. A., 278
Strengths and Difficulties Questionnaire, 257
stress, animal abuse to reduce, 329–331
Studdert, V. P., 6
Stuewig, J., 306, 366
substance abuse
    and AAI, 132
    compared with animal hoarding, 203
    of offenders, 144
sudden-death syndrome, in factory farms, 165
suffering
    unnecessary, 13
    as visual spectacle, 394
suffering, animal, 4
    as entertainment, 395
    on reality TV, 384, 393
suffocation offense, prevalence of, 147
Sugawara, A., 120
Supreme Court, U.S., on crush videos, 402

survival behaviors, in biophilia theory, 114, 115
Sutherland, Edwin, 265, 413
Swaffer, T., 304
Sweden, primate research in, 68
swimming with dolphins, 184, 187
swine
    in factory farms, 165
    transportation of, 182
    See also pigs
Swiss National Self-Reported Delinquency Survey, 330
Switzerland
    animal welfare law in, 85–86
    free range in, 166

T
tail docking, 75
    in factory farms, 167
    in routine husbandry practice, 76
A Tail to Tell, Inc., 432
Taiwan
    anti-cruelty laws in, 61
    roaming dogs in, 238
the "take"
    defined, 78
    standards for, 80–81
Tallichet, Suzanne E., 256, 261, 302, 309, 327, 333, 340, 356, 362, 365, 448
Tapia, F., 280–281, 311
task forces, animal cruelty, 20
Taylor, A., 277
Taylor, Nik, 261, 267, 448–449
telephone scatologia, 218
television
    animal reality, 384
    deregulation of, 379
    See also reality TV
ten Bensel, R. T., 283
Tennessee
    animal cruelty defined in, 17
    animal cruelty reported in, 148
    animal cruelty statutes in, 10, 11
    bestiality statutes in, 228
terminology
    challenges to definitions in, 12–15, 16t, 17–19
    definitions, 5–6
    perceptions shaped by, 65n1
    and scope of animal welfare, 34–37

vague objectifying with, 15
terroristic murder, 307
Tester, Keith, 394
tethering, in animal abuse cases, 144–145
Texas
   animal cruelty reported in, 152
   animal cruelty statutes in, 13, 19
   animal protection law in, 51
   cruelty seizure of animals in, 59, 59n26
   puppy mills in, 51
   running of bulls in, 181
Thailand
   elephants in, 185
   roaming dogs in, 240
Tharp, A. L. T., 360
theft, as form of animal cruelty, 153
theriocide, 331
   use of term, 326
Thomas, J. C., 282
Thomas, S. C., 399
St. Thomas Aquinas, 3
Thompson, K. L., 262, 358
Thompson-Pope, S. K., 305
throwing offense, statistics on, 150
Thrusfield, M. V., 14–15
tiger bones, illegal trade in, 168
tigers, 183
   transportation of, 182
   at zoo, 124
Tigers in America, 441
Tilikum, 187
Toman, P., 225
Toole, Ottis, 314
Toppan, Jane, 313
torment, defined in court, 37
torture, 17
   vs. cruelty, 36
   defined in court, 37
   statistics on, 149
Toth, S. L., 278
tourism, and roaming dogs, 238, 240
tourism, animal, 184
   amusement parks, 186–188
   destination trips, 184–186
Touroo, Rachel, 449
trade, illegal
   as animal cruelty, 153–154
   in endangered species, 167

trafficking, illegal
   and demand, 168
   in endangered species, 167
training
   for field investigators, 409
   for forensics-based veterinary medicine, 410
   for investigation and prosecution, 411–412
   pain associated with, 36
transponders, used at hunting ranches, 171
transportation of animals
   in Europe, 73, 73n58
   in NY law, 30, 43
transporters, 67
transvestic fetishism, 218
trappers, exemptions in place for, 48
trapping
   as cruelty, 36
   prevalence of unlawful, 151
treadmill of production, 342
Tremblay, R. E., 365
Trentham, Caleb, 449
triage, at crime scene, 95–96
trial, animal cruelty, 60
"trunking," 177
trusts for animals, 41
tuberculosis, among elephants, 182, 183
Tufts Animal Care and Condition scales, 14
Turkey
   captured bears in, 185
   slaughterhouse work in, 345
Turner, C. M., 280, 303
Tweed, R. G., 361
Twenty-Eight-Hour Law (1906), 73

U

Unform Code of Military Justice (UCM), 228
Uniform Crime Reports (UCR), FBI's, 106–107, 142, 308, 355, 416
United Kingdom (U.K.)
   animal reality TV in, 384–385
   debeaking banned in, 165
   dogfighting in, 176
   Five Freedoms in, 8, 209
   forced feeding banned in, 165
   free range in, 166

gestation crates banned in, 164
horse assaults in, 400–401
number of cats in, 381
number of dogs in, 381
pet food market in, 381–382
primate research in, 68
reality TV in, 380
wild animals in traveling circuses in, 84–85
United Poultry Concerns, 442
United States Marshalls, 177
United States (U.S.)
animal cruelty and domestic violence in, 286–287
animal reality TV in, 384–385
dogfighting in, 176
dog population in, 382
hunting and fishing in, 169–170
number of cats in, 382
running of bulls in, 180–181
swimming with dolphins in, 187
universal standard of cruelty, 13–14, 15
University of Tennessee, Veterinary Social Work Program of, 121
unnecessary pain and suffering, 13, 25
Upfold, D., 304
upper respiratory ailments, 99
urban dogfights, 177
urban societies, 121
urine scalds, 99
urophilia, 218
U.S. v. Stevens (2010), 52
Utah
"ag gag" laws in, 77–78, 408
bestiality statutes in, 229

V

Van den Berg, A., 367
van der Graaf, Volkert, 398
Vaughn, M. G., 128, 264, 290, 357, 361
veal calves
in factory farms, 164
laws governing, 74
veal crates, 164
veganism, conversion to, 399
vehicular offense, defined, 151
verbal account, in animal cruelty report, 94
Verbora, Antonio R., 449
Vermuelen, H., 15

Verzeni, Vincenz, 310
veterans, paired with service dogs, 123
veterinarians
abuse awareness of, 15
in animal cruelty cases, 20
exemptions in place for, 48
lack of standards for, 89
role of, 92–93
veterinarians, forensic
common cases seen by, 91–92
in court, 104
at crime scene, 95
role of, 90, 91
skills and experience of, 90–91
veterinary interventions, for roaming dogs, 242–244
veterinary medicine, and animal protection efforts, 89
veterinary procedures, conventional *vs.* forensic, 93
veterinary sciences, pioneering publications in, 90
Vick, Michael, 147, 148, 175, 176, 399, 410
victims
of animal cruelty, 54–55
definition for, 54
of IPV, 332
video documentation, at crime scene, 96
Vietnam, animal tourism in, 185
violence
activist, 398
and AHB, 119, 126
and animal cruelty, 285–290, 289–290
animal-directed, 355
and bestialics, 223–224
bestiality linked to, 229–260
cultural normalization of, 335
dating, 361
and early aggression, 364–365
exposure of child to, 278
extra-institutional, 344
gendered nature of, 259
institutionalized cruelty, 73
reactive, 361
socially approved, 344, 346
See also domestic violence; family violence; human-animal violence
violence, human
animal abuse and, 58

and animal cruelty, 289
violence, interpersonal
  and AHB, 119
  and animal abuse, 99–100
  animal cruelty and, 92
  and animal sexual assault, 103
  and bestiality, 220, 224–225, 226
  and childhood cruelty to animals, 309
  risk factors for, 290
  and specific types of CTA, 259
violence graduation hypothesis (VGH), 332–334, 334, 344, 366
violence toward animals
  learned from peers or parents, 288
  preventing and treating, 130–131
  among school-aged children, 131
violent behavior
  and childhood triad, 301
  intergenerational transmission of, 278
  predictors of, 284
violent offenders, childhood animal cruelty of, 302
Virginia
  animal cruelty reported in, 150, 152
  animal welfare law in, 37–38
  bestiality statutes in, 228
  running of bulls in, 180–181
Virgin Island, US, animal cruelty defined in, 17
Vitaro, F., 365
Vitter, Sen. David, 161
Vizard, E., 222
vocational programs, animals in
voiceovers, on animal cop shows, 386–387
Volant, A. M., 254, 255, 287, 328
Voodoo, ritualized abuse associated with, 102

W

Walrus penis bones, illegal trade in, 168
Walters, G. D., 303, 361, 362
Walton-Moss, B. J., 290
warrants, 58
Washington State
  animal cruelty reported in, 149, 150, 152
  animal cruelty statutes in, 12
  bestiality statutes in, 228
  shark fin products banned in, 407
waste disease, chronic, 172
Wathes, C., 8
Watson, J. C., 132
Watt, B., 330
Wax, D. E., 264, 302, 306
Weber, C., 254
Weiler, B. V., 124
Weiss, K. J., 8
welfare campaign video, 379
well-being, and presence of companions animals, 117
Wertham, F., 308
Wesley, M. C., 132
West Virginia
  animal cruelty statutes in, 18
  reporting of animal cruelty in, 92, 152
whales, Japan's hunting and killing of, 168–169
whale sharks, dives with, 184–185
whale watching, 187
whip use, media coverage of, 401
whistleblowers, 408
whistleblowing, 343
Whited, R. M., 305
Whites
  cockfighting supported by, 174
  companion animal ownership of, 127
Widom, C. S., 277
Wilcox, D. T., 222, 224
wild animals
  animal rights of, 40
  in circuses, 181
  domestic animals compared with, 121
  and legality of hunting in U.S., 169
  as property of "common," 47
wildlife
  Endangered Species Act, 78–79
  interacting with, 124
  and Marine Mammal Protection Act, 79–81
  as tourist attractions, 188
  as victims, 151
  See also endangered species
Wildlife Alliance, 442
wildlife crime, 339
wildlife films, 384
wildlife forensics, 106
wildlife management agencies, and hunting ranches, 171
wildlife management practices, success of, 170

wildlife protection, at state level, 81
wildlife rehabilitation programs, 131
wildlife watching, 124
Wild Rescues (TV show), 385, 386
Williams, T., 171
Wilson, E. O., 114
Wilson, J. C., 225
Wilson, P., 263
Winefield, H. R., 116
Wisconsin
    animal cruelty statutes in, 10, 18
    bestiality statutes in, 229
    reporting of animal cruelty in, 92, 154
    unlawful trapping or hunting in, 151
Wisdom, J., 120, 121
witnessing violence, and animal cruelty, 358
Wolf, S., 127
Wolfe, D. A., 278
women
    as absent referent, 336
    as animal activists, 399
    in crush videos, 226–227
    Major Depressive Disorder of, 276
    oppression of, 336
        See also domestic violence; feminist theory
Wood, D., 254
Woods lamp, 10
Woolf, B. N., 160
Worden, S. K., 175
workers
    poultry slaughterhouse, 71
    shelter, 54
    slaughterhouse, 73, 266, 344, 345
workplaces, coercive control patterns in, 331
World Association of Zoos and Aquariums, Conference Proceeding for, 124
World Organisation for Animal Health (OIE), 66
World Society for the Protection of Animals, 442
World Wildlife Fund (Federation), 442
worms, roaming dogs with, 242
Worth, C., 203
Wright, J., 333
Wright, M. L., 127
Wurtele, S. K., 258
Wyoming
    animal cruelty statutes in, 18, 19
    horse slaughter in, 405
    prohibited conduct in, 55
    torture defined in, 18

Y

Yarnell, H., 304, 305
yellow-coded animals, at forensic crime scene, 95
youth, bestiality among, 222–223
Yudowitz, B., 259

Z

Zasloff, L., 122
Zigler, E., 277
Zilcha-Mano, S., 117
Zilney, L., 411
Zilney, M., 411
Zimolag, U., 120
zoo, visits to, 124
zookeepers, 124
zookeeper-tiger bonds, 124
zoonotic diseases, 98
zoophiles (zoos), 219
    classes of, 219–220
    justification of, 220
zoophilia, 126, 218, 219–220
    in childhood histories of murderers, 309
zoosexuals, 219–220